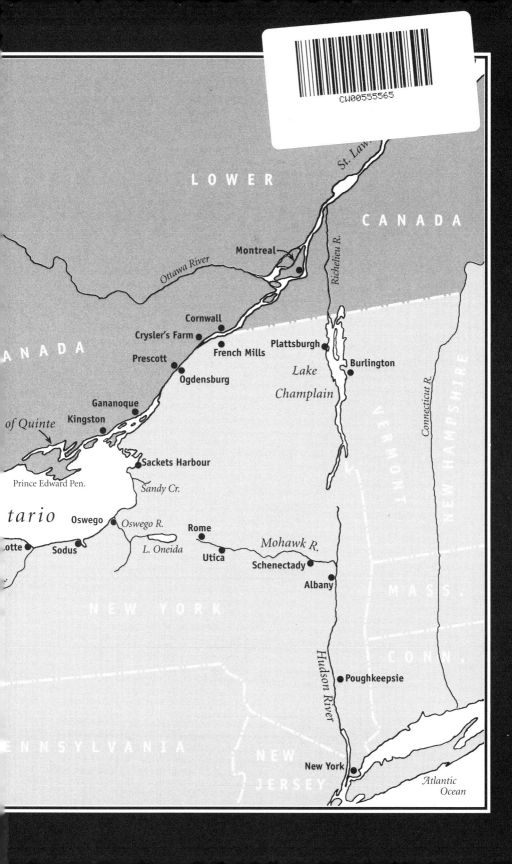

LOWER

CANADA

St. Law.

Montreal

Richelieu R.

Ottawa River

Cornwall

Crysler's Farm

Prescott

French Mills

Plattsburgh

Burlington

ANADA

Ogdensburg

Lake

Champlain

Gananoque

Kingston

of Quinte

Sackets Harbour

VERMONT

Connecticut R.

NEW HAMPSHIRE

Prince Edward Pen.

Sandy Cr.

tario

Oswego

Oswego R.

Rome

Mohawk R.

L. Oneida

Utica

Schenectady

Albany

MASS.

otte

Sodus

NEW   YORK

CONN.

Hudson River

Poughkeepsie

ENNSYLVANIA

NEW

JERSEY

New York

Atlantic Ocean

Lords of the Lake

Lightning strikes HMS *St. Lawrence*, 1814. Sudden death was always close at hand during the naval war on Lake Ontario. On 19 October 1814, lightning almost destroyed HMS *St. Lawrence*, the largest sailing warship that ever cruised Lake Ontario. (Oil painting by Peter Rindlisbacher, courtesy of the artist)

LORDS
of the
LAKE

THE NAVAL WAR

ON LAKE ONTARIO,

1812–1814

~

ROBERT MALCOMSON

~

Foreword by

DONALD E. GRAVES

CHATHAM PUBLISHING

LONDON

Published 1998 by Robin Brass Studio
10 Blantyre Avenue, Toronto, Ontario M1N 2R4, Canada
Fax: (416) 698-2120 / e-mail: rbrass@total.net

Published in the UK 1999 by Chatham Publishing
61 Frith Street, London W1V 5TA

Chatham Publishing is an imprint of Gerald Duckworth & Co. Ltd.

British Library Cataloguing in Publication Data
A catalogue record for this book is available from the British Library.

ISBN 1 86176 112 0

Printed and bound in Canada

For
Janet Catherine Malcomson
Meae amicae carissimae

Contents

PART VI ~ **THE CURTAIN FALLS**

APPENDICES

MAPS AND CHARTS

Foreword

BY DONALD E. GRAVES

I am pleased to contribute a foreword to Robert Malcomson's *Lords of the Lake*. I have known the author and his work for a number of years and I can think of few historians, in Canada or the United States, better equipped to tackle the subject of naval operations during the War of 1812, particularly on Lake Ontario.

His is not an easy subject but it is an important one. There were no climactic naval battles, no dramatic victories or defeats, on Ontario during the war, a fact that has led historians to pay polite but scant reference to naval matters on that body of water. The attention paid to these operations, however, is in inverse proportion to their significance because the opposing naval commanders in the northern theatre, Commodores Isaac Chauncey, USN, and Sir James Lucas Yeo, RN, established their headquarters on Lake Ontario and their decisions and actions affected their respective satellite squadrons on Lakes Champlain and Erie. In no event is this more clear than in Yeo's refusal to provide his subordinate, Commander Robert Heriot Barclay, with adequate numbers of trained seamen, one of the contributory causes of Barclay's defeat at Put-In-Bay on 10 September 1813 – the result was American domination on Erie and a British withdrawal from the Detroit area. To fully comprehend naval operations on *all* the Great Lakes, at both the strategical and operational level, the historian first has to understand the complexities faced by Chauncey and Yeo on Lake Ontario. Both officers were criticized by their superiors and army counterparts for their seeming reluctance to engage in battle, but it should be remembered – as was said about a later admiral, Lord Jellicoe, in 1914 – that they were men "who could lose the war in an afternoon." A major defeat for either commander on Lake Ontario meant not only losing control of that body of water: it meant losing the ability to carry out major operations on any of the Great Lakes, and without naval support, as the author conclusively demonstrates, land campaigns in the north were doomed to failure.

The United States and Britain devoted great resources and energy to ensuring that control of Lake Ontario was not lost. Malcomson is relentless in his depiction of the cost, in time, money and labour, of the massive construction programs at the main bases of the opposing navies: Sackets Harbour for the United States Navy and Kingston for the Royal Navy. To Britain, with the largest and finest navy in the world, the lake service was always a sideshow, but to the United States Navy the lake service became its major activity as the war progressed. The officers and crews of the superb American frigates and smaller warships stationed in Atlantic ports were successively transferred north to Lake Ontario because they could not challenge the might of the British blockade of the eastern seaboard, and by 1814 the sleepy little upstate New York village of Sackets Harbour had become the largest military and naval station in the United States.

The naval war on Lake Ontario is thus an important subject and Robert Malcomson is not the only historian to tackle it. The first commentators were the Briton William James, whose *Naval History of Great Britain from ... 1793 to the Accession of George IV* appeared shortly after the war ended, and the American novelist James Fenimore Cooper, whose *History of the Navy of the United States* was published in 1839. These early works were marred by bias and incomplete research but the same criticisms cannot be levelled against Theodore Roosevelt, whose 1882 *Naval War of 1812* was, for its time, a well-researched and well-balanced assessment of the two opponents. Roosevelt was followed in 1905 by the outstanding naval strategist of the late 19th and early 20th centuries, Alfred Thayer Mahan, whose magisterial *Seapower in its Relations to the War of 1812* analyzed both land and naval operations – and their interconnection. It is a fascinating matter to speculate just how much of Mahan's well-known "fleet in being" thesis – the premise that any fleet, even if it is not active, still presents such a potential threat that it will virtually immobilize and render impotent an opposing fleet – was derived from the situation on Lake Ontario in 1812-1814.

The author, therefore, is in good company. *Lords of the Lake*, however, stands out because it is the first major study devoted entirely to naval operations on Lake Ontario in 1812-1814 . His predecessors only discussed those operations as part of the larger naval conflict. Malcomson has built on the foundations put in place by Mahan and Roosevelt and has also used to great advantage evidence they did not possess, some of it contained in William Dudley's excellent *Naval War of 1812: A Documentary History.*

Robert Malcomson's book is an impressive and welcome contribution to the naval literature of the War of 1812 and can be read with great profit by professional historians. But *Lords of the Lake* will also appeal to the general reader because, in all his archival research and scholarship, Malcomson has not lost sight of the individual human being. Illuminating his text like flashes of lightning are the experiences of ordinary men, and what a splendid cast of characters they are – gallant professionals such as Captains William Howe Mulcaster of the RN and Arthur Sinclair of the USN; thoroughgoing rascals such as James Leonard and the infamous "Mrs. Leonard" who so dismayed polite society at Sackets Harbour; efficient technicians, the most notable being Henry Eckford, who seemed able to transform woods into warships almost overnight; buffoons like Thomas Plucknett, who nearly derailed British shipbuilding during the spring of 1813; and ordinary mortals like Midshipman David Wingfield, RN, who, with few prospects of promotion, volunteers for the lake service in the hope that it will gain him advancement, and Able Seaman Ned Myers, USN, the archetype of the "jolly jack tar," whose vessel sinks from beneath him during a stormy night in August 1813.

American, British or Canadian – heroes, rascals, buffoons and ordinary men – Robert Malcomson treats them all equally in this extensively-researched and beautifully-illustrated book. There is not the slightest hint of the national bias in *Lords of the Lake* that has marred so many works on the War of 1812, and in fact if I did not know that the author is a Canadian, I would be hard put to discern his nationality from his text so even-handed and fair is his treatment of the opposing forces. This makes very good sense because there was little to choose between the American and British sailors on the lake – they shared a common language, a common heritage, and they struggled not only against each other but against a common enemy, the treacherous elements. There was much hard service and precious little glory on Lake Ontario in 1812-1814 but the officers and men of both nations carried out their duties in the highest traditions of their respective navies.

Donald E. Graves
Almonte, Canada

Preface

On 14 April 1814 crowds of people crossed the Cataraqui River from Kingston, Canada, to the Royal Navy dockyard at Point Frederick to view the spectacle that was about to take place. John Le Couteur, a lieutenant in the British 104th Regiment of Foot, was among the throng that waited through a drizzly afternoon until finally, at 5:30 p.m., the first of the two warships that had been under construction for six months descended the slipway and splashed into the deep water of Navy Bay. "The pretty Frigate *Princess Charlotte*," Le Couteur wrote in his journal, "glided into the smooth fresh water, dashing the white foam before Her in her plunge. The gallant Mulcaster, her Captain, was launched with Her." After the wallowing hull had been brought under control and hauled to shore, the second frigate, the *Prince Regent*, a massive fifty-six-gun vessel, slid down the tallow-greased ways. "He, not *she*," noted the lieutenant, "went off beautifully, plunging into the calm waters then rode in Triumph a real Lord of the Lake."[1]

After two years of war, Britain was demonstrating its continued determination to protect the Canadian provinces from American invasion, in part, with the construction of the largest warships launched to that date on the Great Lakes. Seamen and marines had marched to Kingston during the winter to man the new ships and revitalize the squadron that Commodore Sir James Yeo, RN, had commanded for nearly a year. His arrival at the head of more than 450 Royal Navy officers and men in May 1813 had helped to stymie enemy incursions into Upper Canada, and now, in 1814, Yeo hoped to go on the offensive, employing his greatly strengthened squadron in cooperation with the army under Lieutenant General Gordon Drummond to destroy the American base at Sackets Harbour. Such a feat would not be easily accomplished, for the Americans were also working industriously to prepare for the upcoming campaign. Commodore Isaac Chauncey, USN, was building powerful frigates of his own while men and guns, stores and rigging clogged the roads and waterways from New York City to Sackets. Unchallenged mastery of the all-important waters of Lake Ontario had been within Chauncey's grasp several times during the past two years and he meant to settle the question once and for all by winning the contest in the coming summer. Like Yeo, he longed to prevail, to lead his warships into action, secure victory and be crowned lord of the lake.

Though crucial to a full understanding of the conflict involving the United States and Britain, the naval war on Lake Ontario between 1812 and 1814 has never been the subject of a book-length study. The prolific Canadian historian Ernest A. Cruikshank wrote two papers on the topic early in this century, and authorities from William James to Alfred T. Mahan covered events on the lake in their studies of naval operations, but without the depth and zeal they devoted to more spectacular episodes of the war, such as the famous duel between the USS *Constitution* and HMS *Guerriere* or Oliver Hazard Perry's unprecedented victory on Lake Erie. Theodore Roosevelt did not overstate the situation when he wrote: "It is to be regretted that most of the histories written on the subject ... should be of the 'hurrah' order of literature, with no attempt whatever to get at the truth, but merely to explain away the defeats or immensely exaggerate the victories."[2]

Getting at the truth of the story, finding out what happened and why, and how it influenced events elsewhere, were the main goals that motivated my interest in the naval war on Lake Ontario. They arose in the wake of the book that my brother, Tom, and I wrote about the Battle of Put-in-Bay on 10 September 1813, which aimed to elucidate the British side of that battle, a viewpoint that has been virtually overlooked. The contest on Lake Ontario presented a similar predicament. Two and a half years of uninterrupted activity had gone on in every corner of the lake, but the historians concluded that "little enough" was actually accomplished. Thousands of men had crewed dozens of warships that participated in more than twenty raids, chases, battles and engagements, but one contemporary still saw fit to brand Yeo and Chauncey the "Heroes of defeat."[3] It is hoped that this book will set the record straight, or at least go far enough to provide a firm foundation upon which a better understanding may be gained about how the conflict on Lake Ontario evolved and affected the war in general.

This project began in 1991 and has followed a long and draft-strewn course; I have written a million words and kept about one in ten. The study ran aground more than once, but helping hands always pulled it off the rocks and showed me how to find a safer and wiser way to my destination. To all those people, I extend my sincere gratitude; your advice and tips, your encouragement and criticism made this "happy return" possible.

The only place to begin with recognition of individual contributions is with my brother. This book was going to be our second co-publication, but it grew too unruly to be raised up by separate hands, and so I assumed full parenthood. Tom's touch never left the work though, much to my salvation as I searched for the exact dimension or the perfect quote and found it in an obscure muster roll or paper or chart that he had uncovered in some archive beyond my reach. He continues to point discoveries out to me, and our boyhood fascination with ships endures.

Several years ago Donald E. Graves telephoned me to discuss an article I had written, and the rest, pun fully intended, is history. It is an invaluable asset to have the foremost Canadian authority on the War of 1812 in your corner, and that is where Don has been for me. His wealth of knowledge, his passion for accuracy and, above all, his encouragement to struggle on have been inspirational. He has spent countless hours helping me produce a sound manuscript and all for a glass, or two, of single malt. I am deeply indebted to Don and hope I can pay him back in kind as time passes.

And then there is a long list of other individuals who assisted me; Peter Rindlisbacher loved all the details and created one illuminating image after another; Patrick Wilder reacted with enthusiasm for the topic and shared his knowledge of sources, such as the Sinclair papers; Dan Nelson, the man who discovered the sunken *Hamilton* and *Scourge*, lent a copy of the *Wolfe* log; Kevin Crisman eagerly sent some of the fine diagrams that have appeared in his works; I spent hours in Jim Straiton's workshop deliberating over the intricacies of his ship models; Ross Mackenzie and John Pike opened up one of the treasure rooms at the Royal Military College in Kingston to show me the Spilsbury material; the crew of the US Brig *Niagara* welcomed me aboard for brief voyages and Captain Walter Rybka thoughtfully explained the logistics of sailing and fighting a crowded warship; Chris Magoc of the Erie Maritime Museum helped with illustrations; Sandy Antal provided facts needed from the William Hull memoirs; John Elting and Ozzie Schenk sent pieces of art; two former students helped out – Craig Burtch brought the photographs he had taken in Scotland and Felicia Mings had her grandfather do the Latin translation; and C. S. Forester, Patrick O'Brian and, of course, K.V. provided original inspiration.

Much research was done in the James A. Gibson Library at Brock University, where the inter-library loan department was a great help and John Burtniak and Lynn Prunskus gave me free rein in the special collections room. Of similar significance were the holdings of the National Archives of Canada, with expert assistance provided by Tim Dubé and people in the graphics departments. The following institutions also facilitated my work: the Niagara-on-the-Lake Public Library, the St. Catharines Public Library, the Mills Library at McMaster University, the Archives of Ontario, the Royal Ontario Museum, the Toronto Reference

Library, Huronia Historical Parks at Midland, the Hamilton/Scourge Society, Parks Canada, the United States Naval Historical Center, the National Archives of the United States in Washington, the William L. Clements Library, the Detroit Public Library, the Buffalo and Erie County Historical Society, the Historical Society of Pennsylvania, the Power Corporation and the Town Hall, Langholm, Dumfriesshire, Scotland, where J. Grace Brown, the registrar, graciously arranged for a photo-print to be made of the portrait of Lieutenant Colonel James Malcolm of the Royal Marines.

A host of readers have turned their critical attention to the various drafts over the years, including Ken Macpherson, Carl Benn, Peter Rindlisbacher, Patrick Wilder, Joe Thatcher, Jonathan Moore and the ever-thorough Donald E. Graves. They worked hard to help me perfect this study; if any errors persist in this work, they result from my inattention alone. Scott Belliveau of the Naval Institute Press has encouraged the project through several drafts and his reviewers offered many worthwhile suggestions. Robert Gardiner of Chatham Publishing has been similarly encouraging. I feel fortunate that Robin Brass selected this book as one of the first to appear under his imprint. It has been rewarding to work with someone who is so devoted to the essence of a book.

The most enduring assistance I received anywhere was found right here at home. My mother always asked how the book was coming and let me know that she was proud of the publications I completed along the way, most of which ended up on her coffee table. Carrie and Melanie, who were young teenagers when I began the project, have grown up now, but they still have that unconditional, youthful enthusiasm that makes them claim that their dad is bound for glory. They value this strange passion of mine, and I thank them very much for their loving attention.

There would be no book at all, however, if it were not for my wife, Janet. It is not easy to be married to a writer, but Janet has encouraged me faithfully and has always been eager to hop in the car and go in search of yet another dusty library or a distant shore by some unremarkable-looking stretch of water. She has allowed me the space and time to learn the ropes of writing history and has pulled me back to reality when the broadsides deafened me. As constant as the pole star has she been, and, though it hardly measures up to the contribution Janet has made to this work and to my life, I recognize her influence by dedicating this book to her.

Robert Malcomson

St. Catharines, 21 October 1998, Trafalgar Day

A NOTE ABOUT TIME AND TERMINOLOGY

The subject matter of this book poses a number of problems concerning the interpretation of period records. Time keeping during the War of 1812 is one of these, since no standard had been established and British and American records of specific events differed by as much as an hour and a half. To maintain conformity, the British standard is used throughout this study. The dating of events was uniform from side to side, except in the logbooks kept aboard the US Schooner (later, brig) *Sylph* and the US Brig *Jones*, where 12:00 noon marked the official beginning of a day that was everywhere else shown as commencing at midnight twelve hours later. Adjustments were made to account for this difference when the American logbooks were the sole sources for dating specific incidents, with the traditional calendar prevailing. I looked for this discrepancy in the many reports that Isaac Chauncey wrote, but could find only rare instances where he seemed to be basing his accounts on the twelve-hour discrepancy in the logbooks. British logbooks kept track of each day in the conventional style.

The navies worked in close cooperation with the armies throughout this conflict, which brings a long list of regiments into the story. To avoid confusion, British regiments have been represented by numerals (e.g., 8th Foot), whereas American units have been represented by words (e.g., Twenty-first U.S. Infantry Regiment).

Some places mentioned in despatches bore different names according to who was describing them; people on both sides, for instance, occasionally referred to Wolfe Island as Long Island. Throughout this work modern names are used, with a few exceptions, such as the towns of York (now Toronto) and Niagara (Niagara-on-the-Lake). Modern spellings of place names have served as the standard, except for Sackets Harbour, which I intransigently insist on depicting in the traditional British-Canadian style.

Ordnance presented a number of perplexities. There was a constant shifting of long guns and carronades from ship to ship and from ship to shore, and a persistent shortage of reliable records that clearly identified the ordnance carried aboard each vessel. Explaining the many changes to the reader could lead to narrative-jamming tangles of numbers and calibres, a stumbling block that has been avoided, I hope, by portraying the squadrons in their various formats in the appendices. Every effort has been made to confirm battery strengths or to point out that some aspects of armament have been based on speculation. Broadside weight-of-metal, a measurement often used by historians to compare vessels or squadrons, has also been tabulated in the appendices. As pointed out in a note in Appendix E, Yeo and Chauncey used different and unexplained methods to calculate weight-of-metal, whereas I arrived at these figures by totalling the weight of a single-shotted broadside fired by all guns that could bear on one side. Since the ordnance was often double-shotted and topped with a round of canister, and some weapons might be unserviceable or could not be employed under certain conditions, the usefulness of the weight-of-metal standard is limited, although in this study such comparisons help to clarify the difference in ordnance between the squadrons, an important tactical factor, especially in 1813.

Standard depictions of fleet engagements portray the lines of battle with each vessel shown in position. Here, that is next to impossible to do. Although the participants occasionally mentioned various vessels being in a specific order on certain dates, there is no dependable record of either side having a consistent arrangement. During the first two years, the warships sailed very unevenly, especially the converted lakers in Chauncey's squadron, with the result that the order of battle was rarely maintained. Similarly, it is almost impossible to describe line locations during engagements with any certainty; for example, apart from the main elements shown in the battle diagrams for the Burlington Races, the positions of most of the vessels must be speculated. As noted above, the reader will find such speculations identified in the text and the notes. As a substitute for the customary line-of-battle diagrams, squadron courses are shown in charts based on logbook and despatch information.

A warship under sail was an extremely complex machine, as was the terminology used to name its parts and their functions. Although every effort has been made to explain intricate manoeuvres as clearly as possible in the text, a glossary has been placed after the appendices to define the many different nautical terms, as well as numerous other terms that appear in this study.

The glossary defines the following terms, but some additional comments are necessary. Everyone involved in the war interchanged the words "squadron" and "fleet" in their memoirs, letters and reports without differentiation between the two. Since none of the senior naval officers on the lakes achieved the rank of admiral during the war (the rank did not come into existence in the U. S. Navy until the 1860s), it was deemed appropriate to refer to their commands as squadrons consistently throughout the text. Another fine point concerns the term "sloop," which, apart from identifying a single-masted, fore-and-aft-rigged vessel, was applied to a warship commanded by an officer one step higher in rank than lieutenant: that is, commander (RN), master commandant (USN) or master and commander (Provincial Marine). For that reason, the reader will note that a few of the vessels mentioned here are referred to as schooners or brigs at one point and then as sloops when officers of these ranks take command of them, and then back to their original class when junior officers replace them

PART I

The Curtain Rises

FROM "JONATHAN AT A HALT"

Fair Jonathan would make a dash
  But something intervenes,
What? Only sir the want of cash,
  Of men, and ways and means.

THE QUEBEC MERCURY, 18 NOVEMBER 1811

The *Lord Nelson* sets sail. The *Lord Nelson's* headsails are hauled into place as it leaves the Niagara River. The American Fort Niagara is seen to the left while the British town of Niagara lies behind the schooner with the lighthouse on Mississauga Point almost dead astern. (Oil painting by Peter Rindlisbacher, courtesy of the artist)

CHAPTER 1

"On the Banks of the Lake"[1]

LAKE ONTARIO BEFORE THE WAR

*A*fter eons of gouging and scraping the land, the last of the towering ice sheets withdrew from the central regions of North America 11,000 years ago, leaving behind a chain of lakes unparalleled in the world. The largest reservoir of fresh water on the planet, the Great Lakes drain nearly 295,000 square miles of land in the North Central Basin, ultimately passing that water down the St. Lawrence River to the ocean. The final step in the chain of lakes, 245 feet above sea level, is Lake Ontario. Covering approximately 7,500 square miles, it has the smallest surface area of the lakes, though its depth exceeds 800 feet in its deepest valleys and averages 283, making it the eighth largest body of fresh water on the continent. Between extremes, this lake measures nearly 193 miles long and 53 miles across, and around its shoreline lie a wide range of geologic structures, from the sandy beaches at Burlington to the bluffs that rise 300 feet above the water at Scarborough to the rocky outcroppings around Kingston. Situated in a moderate climate zone, the lake does not freeze over during the winter, though when the season is severe, ice packs accumulate along its edges, jamming the river mouths shut for months. The volatile contrasts in the weather patterns can turn the lake into a mill pond one day and a boisterous maelstrom the next, teaching unwary mariners their final, harsh lesson. Whatever its mood, the lake presents a majestic sight, as one visitor noted when he first viewed it in 1810: "In walking on the banks of the lake, we should have thought ourselves on the shores of the Atlantic."[2]

Native peoples had plied its shores and made risky crossings in fragile bark canoes for centuries before the Europeans arrived in the early 1600s. A Frenchman, Étienne Brûlé, is credited with being the first foreigner to reach the lake during a voyage of exploration in 1615, hearing perhaps the Iroquoian word *Ontario*, meaning "beautiful lake" or "sparkling water," which began appearing on maps of the region by mid-century. It took another century before Europeans brought their wars to Lake Ontario when British and French squadrons battled briefly on its waters during the Seven Years War (1756-1763) Though control of the waterway eventually fell into British hands, it was not until the 1780s that the first major wave of settlers, Loyalist refugees from the American Revolution, made new homes along the northern shores of Lake Ontario. In 1791 the old province of Quebec was split in two by the formation of Lower Canada (modern-day Quebec) and Upper Canada (Ontario) to accommodate the flood of immigrants, and Lieutenant Colonel John Graves Simcoe soon arrived from England to turn the upper province into an organized and productive colony. Townships spread around the northern rim of Lake Ontario, and the seeds of a new British society were sown.

By 1810 the communities around the shores of Lake Ontario had progressed well beyond the level of bare subsistence that had at first characterized the lives of the people who moved into that region. The population of Upper Canada numbered a few more than 70,000, and as many people probably lived in the territory that drained into the lake on the American side. Commerce had developed in which natural resources and farm products of the region were traded for the manufactured conveniences of the outside world. Typical of this interchange was an advertisement that appeared in a November 1807 issue of the *Gazette*, published at York, the capital of Upper Canada. Placed by Quetton de St. George, a merchant who owned stores in several British towns and villages, the advertisement announced that the latest shipment of goods had been received from Montreal, including "Crockery, Glass Ware, Cutlery and Ironmongery ... [and,] from New York a variety of Beaver Bonnets ... [and] a general assortment of Millinery among which are ... the most fashionable Ostrich Feathers."[3] As payment for such luxurious items, St. George was willing to accept from the farmers, millers and tradesmen "Flour, Wheat, Indian Corn, Oats, Pease and Pork ... [the latter being] well cured and packed in sufficient barrels and warranted for twelve months." St. George could not transport such goods and produce over the rudimentary road system, so he dealt mainly with the masters of the merchant vessels that provided the best means of carrying his cargo to and from the key transhipment ports on the lake.

A little more than two dozen vessels serviced the towns and villages around Lake Ontario.[4] They ranged in size from open boats, known as bateaux, that could barely carry 30 tons to the schooner *Governor Simcoe*, which stowed 137 tons of cargo in its hold. The vessels were classed as schooners (two masts) or sloops (one mast) and most were fitted with large fore and aft-rigged sails that could be handled by a minimum number of hands although a few mixed square sails with the fore and aft canvas, giving them the rigs of cutters, snows or brigs.

In 1810 William and James Crooks, who aspired to increase the fortunes they were accumulating through the operation of a mill, a brewery and a distillery, decided to go into the profitable shipping business. They hired an American shipwright to build them a sixty-foot schooner capable of carrying forty-five tons of cargo in its hold. Constructed near the town of Niagara during the winter of 1810, the vessel was launched the following May and named the *Lord Nelson*. The Crooks paid to have the figurehead of a two-armed, vaguely sailor-like fellow shipped from New York so that an effigy of the great British hero could lead their little money-maker around the lake.

For a merchant schooner like the *Lord Nelson*, the most distant ports of call were the British village of Prescott and the American village of Ogdensburg, across from each other almost seventy miles down the St. Lawrence River.[5] Beyond that point the river became shallow and strewn with rapids as it ran down to Montreal, and on that stretch of the river all goods had to be carried by bateaux and portaged around the worst cascades.

Many lakers avoided the trip downstream by unloading their cargoes at Kingston for transhipment to Prescott. In 1811 Kingston was inhabited by about a thousand residents, living and working in nearly two hundred wood and stone buildings arranged on its carefully patterned streets. Situated at the mouth of the Cataraqui River, the town was a busy commercial centre, offering a wide and deep harbour lined with wharves. Shoals dotted the Kingston Channel that lay between the town and Wolfe Island, but even as water levels dropped after the spring run-off, the entrance to the harbour was not blocked by a bar.

There was no fort at Kingston, although troops were housed in barracks at the northern end of town and two batteries had been prepared to the south of the town at Points Mississauga and Murney. Across the harbour was the low-lying peninsula known as Point Frederick, where the Provincial Marine had its headquarters, dockyard and anchorage, Navy Bay. On the other side of the bay rose the gentle slopes of Point Henry, which had yet to be fortified in any way.

Small boat traffic heading upstream from Kingston followed the Bay of Quinte route, the inshore waterway that looped around on the north side of the Prince Edward Peninsula. At the head of the bay goods had to be portaged over an isthmus to Presqu'ile Bay and the village of Newcastle, from where the journey could be continued along the coast in bateau or laker.[6]

York Barracks. Established in the 1790s, Fort York provided accommodations for the army, but little in the way of defences. Shown here in 1804, the fort had not been greatly improved by 1812. Note the canoes and bateaux at the water's edge below the bank upon which the fort was situated. (Watercolour by S. Stretton, courtesy of the National Archives of Canada, C-14905)

The first major port west of Kingston was York (present-day Toronto) where a sprawling peninsula swept around in a gentle, six-mile arc to form a harbour that was serviceable but not as deep or as easy to enter as Kingston's. Since it was farther from the American side, Lieutenant Governor Simcoe had considered York a better location for the province's navy, but no effort had been made before the war to transfer it there. Boasting a population of 600, the town was the provincial capital, the legislature buildings being located near the head of the bay by the Don River and the lieutenant governor's residence on the western edge of town at the bay's mouth. An army detachment occupied a blockhouse by the legislative building, and the blockhouse and huts that formed Fort York were contained within a lightly built palisade at the opening to the harbour. Almost directly across from it was a lighthouse standing on Gibraltar Point, the western tip of the peninsula.

From York the lakeshore angled sharply southwestward for thirty miles, then bent due east to form Burlington Bay and the northern coast of the Niagara Peninsula. Cut off from Burlington Bay by a wide, sandy bar was Little Lake (today's Hamilton Harbour), and at its western extreme a lofty peninsula of land known as Burlington Heights separated Little Lake from another large pond known as Coote's Paradise. Nearby stood the villages of Dundas and Ancaster. Major streams were named for their distance either from York or from the Niagara River. The pilot of a schooner proceeding eastward along the

Niagara Peninsula would mark his progress as he passed Forty Mile Creek, then the Twenty and Twelve and on to the town of Niagara, or Newark, at the mouth of the Niagara River.

Originally the province's capital and site of Simcoe's first legislative session, Niagara consisted of about eighty buildings in 1810 and was one of the most important centres in the province. Behind the town, on the bank above the river, stood Fort George, below which were located storehouses belonging to the Provincial Marine. Entrance to the river was dominated by the more advantageously located ramparts of the American Fort Niagara on the opposite shore, although as war neared both it and Fort George were in a state of great disrepair.

The Niagara River, or the Strait of Niagara as it was sometimes called, was navigable for seven miles. Lakers would work their way south to the village of Lewiston on the American side or farther up to Queenston on the Canadian side, where their cargoes and passengers would be off-loaded. Transportation around the Niagara gorge and the famous cataracts was by the portage roads that led either to the American Fort Schlosser or the British village of Chippawa.

Fort George. As seen from the American side of the Niagara River, Fort George stood atop a rise of ground, overlooking the Provincial Marine buildings and traffic in the river. Though its bastions, palisade and blockhouses looked formidable, the fort was in bad repair at the outbreak of war and, being located a mile upstream, did not control the river's mouth as did Fort Niagara. (Coloured engraving by Edward Walsh, courtesy of the National Archives Canada, C-26)

Along the American shore of the lake some of the streams were named by their distance from the Niagara River, with the closest good anchorage located off Four Mile Creek. Seventy-five miles down the coast the hamlet of Charlotte stood at the mouth of the Genesee River, and thirty miles beyond that point was the village of Sodus. Oswego, 130 miles east of Niagara, was the busiest American lakeport of the period, having a few hundred residents, forty houses, several warehouses and inns, numerous wharves and a small shipyard. Its importance rested on its connection to New York City via the Hudson and

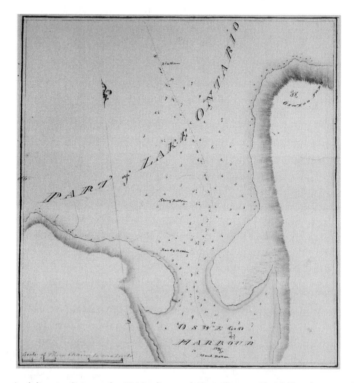

Oswego. A visitor to Oswego in 1810 observed that the mouth of the river was twelve chains (792 feet) wide, which was reduced to about 150 feet because of a bar. He added that a thirty-foot-wide channel curved through the opening, though the water seldom rose above eight and a half feet. Mariners identified the narrow passage by the blackness of the water that flowed through it. (Chart by Joseph Bouchette in the 1790s, courtesy of the Archives of Ontario, F47-5-3-0-1, folder N-1137)

(Facing page) **The eastern end of Lake Ontario.** By water, the distance from Kingston to Sackets Harbour was thirty-five miles. This chart shows the variation in place names typical of the period with Simcoe Island also known at Forrest Island, Wolfe as Grand Isle, Chaumont Bay as Hungry Bay and the Galloo Islands as Isle aux Gallops. (From original chart by W. F. W. Owen, 1815, courtesy of the National Archives of Canada, NMC-19618)

Mohawk rivers and the shallow canals that joined them to creeks feeding Lake Oneida. The Oneida River flowed westward from that lake to Three River Point where it met the Seneca River and combined with it to form the Oswego River. From Three River Point to Oswego, the river ran for twenty-four miles down one set of rapids after another and over a twelve-foot cataract at the hamlet of Fredericksburgh (present-day Fulton), halfway to the lake. Though the route was a long one, and during the dry summers, slow and frustrating, the connection to New York made Oswego a rival to Kingston for transhipment purposes. In addition, it was the key exporting centre for the vast quantities of salt that were produced in the neighbourhood of Salina on the Seneca River. Oswego's prosperity was hampered, however, by the gravelly bar that crossed the mouth of the river, restricting passage to vessels of the shallowest draught.

The next port of call for the lakers was the village of Sackets Harbour. On the southern lip of Black River Bay in the easternmost corner of the lake, Sackets Harbour did not have as direct a water link with New York as Oswego did, so its importance before the war was not great. What led to its rapid expansion was the fact that it possessed the key attribute that Oswego lacked, namely a deep and accessible harbour. Augustus Sacket had purchased the site in 1801. The natural beauty of the region and the fertility of the soil had drawn his attention, but he had been most attracted by the sheltered bay upon which he hung his name. A long limestone cliff, thirty feet high, jutted out into Black River Bay, and at the northeast terminus of this bluff a wide peninsula looped back halfway to the mainland creating a deep basin thirty acres in size. Sackett built a Georgian-style house facing the basin and during the next decade a small village grew up around the foot of the harbour; in 1810 the population of the surrounding township was nearly one thousand. From the protected anchorage, access to the lake and communication with Kingston, just thirty-five miles north by boat, was relatively easy. More arduous was an overland journey to the large centres to the south because the roads that connected Sackets Harbour to the Mohawk River at Rome and Utica were barely better than cart tracks, becoming all but impassable during wet spells.

The profits that could be made by providing quick and efficient transportation by water had enticed James and William Crooks to operate their own schooner. Unfortunately for them, the events of the outside world soon interrupted their plans and turned the freshwater highway into a battlefield. Like a prized piece of real estate, Lake Ontario would become the object of a contentious struggle between the United States and Britain. The Crooks' dreams of commercial expansion would be dashed, and the little *Lord Nelson* would take on a role its builders never imagined.

CHAPTER 2

"Opposing Force to Force"[1]

WAR IS DECLARED: 18 JUNE 1812

*T*he War of 1812 began poorly for the United States. With all the rhetoric of the nation's leaders, especially the loud protests emanating from the members of the Twelfth Congress, some quick accomplishments on the battlefield might have been expected. As was soon discovered by the advocates of war, however, it took more than words alone to answer "the insolence of British cannon, [with] the peals of American thunder."[2]

President James Madison and his colleagues chose war as the means by which to seek retribution for the years of depredations suffered at the hands of the British.[3] After the failure of the Peace of Amiens in 1802 sent Britain and France back to the battlefield in the company of their various allies, American trade opportunities abroad rose significantly. By 1807 foreign business was worth more than $100 million to the United States, but this boom abruptly came to an end. The year before, Napoleon had issued his Berlin Decree by which all British goods entering French ports were seized even if carried by the vessels of neutral nations. The government in London responded with regulations that placed similar restrictions on any trade with France. Although Napoleon countered the British orders-in-council with his Milan Decree, Britain's policies proved to be more effective because its vast navy prowled the European coast in a relentless blockade that was more aggressive than anything the French navy could manage. Neutral nations suffered because of these commercial restraints, and chief among the injured parties was the United States. From 1807 to 1812, close to 900 American vessels were detained in foreign ports and at sea by the belligerents, although Britain was seen by Americans to be the worse offender. Trade profits plummeted.

In an attempt to retaliate against such audacious foreign interference, Congress, at President Thomas Jefferson's request, approved the Embargo Act in January 1807, which prohibited virtually all exporting and importing by Americans. It was soon apparent that this legislation hurt domestic finances more than the intended victims overseas. Trade with neighbours across the border in British North America was now deemed to be smuggling, and when troops were sent to impose the law, shots were fired and the Potash Rebellion flared up.[4] Shortly after James Madison was elected to succeed Jefferson in 1809, the Embargo Act was replaced with less restrictive regulations, which eased the situation.

While the trade conflict raised the ire of American interests, so did the insulting practice of impressment. Constantly short of seamen, Royal Navy captains had continued their longstanding custom of reclaiming so-called British deserters from foreign merchantmen, who could offer no resistance when their best hands were impressed into the British service. More than 6,000 American sailors were estimated to have been seized in this manner between 1803 and 1812 in open violation of their rights as citizens of the United States. The incident

The *Leopard–Chesapeake* incident, 22 June 1807. The determination of the Royal Navy to prevent deserters from escaping its grasp prompted Captain Salusbury Humphreys of HMS *Leopard*, 50, to forcibly detain the USS *Chesapeake*, 38, off Chesapeake Bay on 22 June 1807. Humphrey's boarding party seized four "deserters," and aroused the universal indignation of the American public by demonstrating British disrespect for sailors' rights. (Sketch by F. S. Cozzens, courtesy of the U.S. Naval Historical Center, NH-74526)

President James Madison (1751-1836).
A close friend of Thomas Jefferson,
Madison had been involved in American
politics for thirty-five years before he
succeeded Jefferson as president in 1809.
Small of stature and frail, Madison
worked tirelessly to mediate the
conflicting needs of the federal and state
governments. (Portrait by Gilbert Stuart,
courtesy of the Virginia Historical Society
and the U.S. Naval Historical Center,
NH-48047)

that most startled the American public occurred on 22 June 1807 when the USS
Chesapeake, 38 guns, was fired on by HMS *Leopard*, 50, after refusing to allow
the British captain to send a search party on board. With three men killed and
eighteen wounded from the *Leopard's* broadside, the *Chesapeake* stopped and
suffered the indignity of allowing four suspected deserters to be taken from its
crew. In time, reparations were made for this act, but the event served to epito-
mize Britain's disdain for America's hard-earned liberties.

While unrest fermented that would lead to the birth of the slogan "Free
trade and sailors rights," trouble also brewed in the interior of North America.
As the United States spread westward, pioneers and traders had come into conflict with Indian nations who seemed to be on the verge of forming a confed-
eracy that would offer stiff opposition to expansion. The long history of clashes
between the two parties persisted, with sharp losses suffered on both sides. Repeatedly, the British were accused of arming and provisioning the Indians as a
means of maintaining their territorial claims in the northwest.

By the autumn of 1811 frustrations had reached a boiling point as the Twelfth
Congress convened in Washington. Recent elections had sent sixty-three (out
of 140) new faces to the House of Representatives, among them a vociferous
group of young Republicans labelled the "war hawks" by their Federalist opponents. On 5 November, in his annual message to Congress, President Madison
attacked Britain for its "hostile inflexibility in trampling on rights which no

independent nation can relinquish." He called upon the members of the House and Senate to "feel the duty of putting the United States into an armor and an attitude demanded by the crisis."[5]

The legislators responded enthusiastically, their committee on foreign relations declaring that "the patriotic fire of the Revolution still burns in the american [sic] breast with a holy & unextinguishable flame."[6] By wide margins they quickly passed six resolutions designed to prepare the nation for war, prompting Henry Clay, the influential Speaker of the House and leader of the War Hawks, to comment to a correspondent late in December, "The War preparations are advancing with the support of an immense majority."[7]

Despite the fever, Clay saw signs of trouble ahead: "Our greatest difficulty will be revenue, and I do not well see how we can dispense with internal taxes. This is the delicate and trying topic, and that I fear on which we shall have the greatest desertion."[8] The desertions came when Secretary of the Treasury Albert Gallatin revealed that $50 million would be needed to fight a war and that he intended to raise the funds by borrowing money and imposing taxes. Congressmen and senators balked, and passionate militants jumped ship at the thought of the projected invoices. A naval bill ordering the construction of twelve line-of-battle ships, ten new frigates, a dry dock and stocks of wood and fittings was slashed to allow for only the restoration of three existing frigates and the accumulation of limited building materials. Only half the original amount requested for building coastal defences was approved, and legislation to provide arms for the militia failed. In February 1812 the use of taxation was approved, but only if a war had broken out, which prompted one observer to wonder if "the war [would] float the taxes, or the taxes sink the war."[9]

Political infighting and philosophical debates also dampened the momentum created by martial spirits. Madison's cabinet originally wanted to fill the ranks of the regular army to 10,000 and to enlist a further 10,000 men for a period of three years, but efforts by members of the Federalist party who sought to embarrass the government led to the approval of a virtually unattainable and excessively expensive army, on paper, of 35,000. The president and his advisers had hoped to depend on volunteers and militia for the manpower to wage a land war against the British in North America. Obstructions to this plan were erected by legislation that took control of voluntary officers and units from Washington and gave it to the state governments at the same time as the notion of allowing militiamen to cross the border into Canada was decried as unconstitutional. Even the employment of the nation's sparse naval force was questioned. While some spokesmen advocated commitment to a maritime war alone, others saw no value in challenging Britain for dominion of the waves; as

Adam Seybert, a Republican from Pennsylvania, attested, "Our vessels will only tend to swell the present catalogue of the British navy."[10]

The government of the United States was barely capable of preparing for war, let alone administering it. William Eustis, the Secretary of War, ran a department that employed a chief clerk and several junior clerks, but no staff officers to lend professional advice on how to direct military affairs. Madison's recommendation that two assistant secretaries be assigned to the department was ignored. In April a Commissary-General and a Quartermaster Department were appointed, and in May an Ordnance Department was finally established. Despite all the thousands of soldiers who marched on columns of Congressional paper, in June 1812 the U.S. Army numbered only about 6,700 men, plus 5,000 recent recruits.

Having suffered through the cutbacks of the Jefferson administration, the army lacked youthful senior officers with experience and talent to map out an effective strategy for war. Of the eight generals in the regular army, the youngest, James Wilkinson, was fifty-five years old. Secretary Eustis looked to Major General Henry Dearborn and Brigadier General William Hull, both veterans of the Revolutionary War, for their advice and participation. In April Dearborn proposed that a main thrust be made against Montreal with an army of regulars, while waves of militia units crossed into Canada from Detroit, Fort Niagara and Sackets Harbour. The first movement would cut essential supply lines, and the others would subdue the upper province. William Hull was ordered to lead an army across the Detroit River, and Dearborn was placed in charge of forces directed at the three other targets. The secretary neglected to make this arrangement clear to the latter officer, who was surprised to learn that his responsibilities also included cooperation with Hull. Dearborn had been busy dealing with the failure of Massachusetts and Connecticut to raise militia units, and late in July, when he arrived at his headquarters at Albany, he discovered his army to be weak in numbers, deficient in training and ill-equipped. Furthermore, the forces poised to invade Canada along the Niagara River were commanded by Stephen Van Rensselaer, a major general in the militia who had no military experience.

The Department of the Navy was also weakly staffed. As war became more likely in the spring of 1812, Secretary Paul Hamilton and his staff of four clerks were almost overcome by a flood of paperwork and consultations even though the navy possessed only seventeen vessels. The fact that Hamilton drank to excess and was the subject of much criticism in Washington circles detracted even further from the successful management of the department. Luckily, the energetic commitment to the service of skillful senior officers like Captains John

Paul Hamilton (1762-1816). Hamilton was secretary of the navy from May 1809 until December 1812. A veteran of the Revolutionary War from South Carolina, his term in office began successfully, but his lack of administrative skills eventually led to confusion over accounts, appointments and official instructions. (Portrait by G. B. Matthews, courtesy of the U.S. Naval Historical Center, NH-54757)

Rodgers, Isaac Hull, William Bainbridge and Stephen Decatur would save face for the navy and soon win several brilliant victories on the maritime front where the nation had been belittled for so long.

Whenever a war against Canada was discussed, control of the Great Lakes was seen as essential for success. John Armstrong, another Revolutionary War veteran, and former ambassador to France, had recommended to William Eustis in January 1812 that: "Resting, as the line of Canadian defence does, in its whole extent on navigable lakes and rivers, no time should be lost in getting a naval ascendancy on both for … the belligerent who is the first to obtain this advantage will (miracles excepted) win the game."[11]

The same point had been made by William Hull during meetings with James Madison early in the spring. He called for the construction of vessels on Lake Erie to support his land campaign, and one of the twelve captains in the navy, Charles Stewart, was offered the job. Stewart refused the appointment, and in the wake of Congressional decisions against strengthening the navy, nothing more was done.[12] On Lake Erie only the diminutive brig *Detroit*, a U.S. Army transport, would support Hull, while the sole U.S. Navy vessel on the Great Lakes was the brig *Oneida* on Lake Ontario.

As a final warning to Britain, a ninety-day embargo was enacted early in April 1812. Diplomatic concessions were looked for among the documents delivered to New York from Britain by the USS *Hornet* on 19 May, but they were not to be found. On 1 June Madison delivered a secret message to Congress in which he reviewed British aggressions and concluded that there was "on the side of Great Britain a state of war against the United States, and on the side of the United States a state of peace toward Great Britain."[13] The President's message became the nucleus of a war manifesto, debated in the House and the Senate with motions still being entertained about restricting war to the oceans and declaring hostilities against Britain and France simultaneously. By 17 June a war bill was passed with the approval of only 61 per cent of the legislators, the smallest majority supporting any similar American declaration. James Madison signed the document the next day, and the long-promised war was on.

As orders were transmitted for the land forces to begin their approach toward Canada, the burden of command on the Great Lakes rested on the shoulders of an American naval lieutenant named Melancthon Woolsey.[14] He was a native of New York State, born on 5 June 1780; his father was an army officer in the war against Britain and later the customs official at Plattsburgh. Woolsey began a career in law but gave it up to join the navy as a midshipman in 1800. He served in the West Indies and the Mediterranean and was promoted to the rank of lieutenant in 1807. In August of the next year he was sent to Oswego on Lake Ontario to supervise the building of a vessel meant to be employed in the enforcement of President Jefferson's embargo.

Originally intended to be a gunboat, the dimensions of this vessel were enlarged until it took the form of a formidable brig, measuring a little longer than eighty-five feet on its upper deck.[15] It was to be armed with sixteen 24-pdr. carronades at gunports along the sides and a 32-pdr. long gun on the forecastle. The gun was a heavy piece of ordnance, easily weighing a ton and a half, but its

Master Commandant Melancthon Taylor Woolsey, USN (1780-1838). The son of a revenue collector at Plattsburgh, New York, Woolsey entered the U.S. Navy as a midshipman in 1800 and saw action in the Tripolitan War. He was promoted to lieutenant in 1807 and sent the next year to his home state to establish the navy's presence on the Great Lakes. (Courtesy of the U.S. Naval Historical Center, NRL-11122)

size and length meant that it could hurl an iron shot, weighing thirty-two pounds, about a mile. Mounted on a stoutly-built wooden carriage fixed to a circular track on the deck, it could fire in a wide arc ahead and abeam of the vessel. The carronades were of much lighter construction. The barrel of a typical 24-pdr. weighed about 1,300 pounds, owing to its shorter length and thinner walls, and could be attached to a smaller carriage. The relative lightness of the carronades yielded two advantages for their use on ships: they took up less room and required a smaller gun crew. As compensation, though, carronades lacked range and were best used at distances of less than 500 yards.[16]

Construction of the new brig commenced at Oswego in September 1808 under the direction of Lieutenant Woolsey and continued through the winter. It was launched the following March and rigged and ready for service by early May. Woolsey named the warship *Oneida* and, with affectionate hyperbole, declared it "the handsomest vessel in the Navy."[17] Woolsey's dreams of sailing to confront smugglers were soon ended because by the spring of 1809 Jefferson's embargo had been repealed, terminating the border dispute and eliminating the need for a watchdog with iron teeth no matter how handsome it was. In June Lieutenant Woolsey received orders from the Navy Department to lay up the *Oneida* in Oswego Bay rather than commissioning it.

A year later the decision-makers in Washington changed their minds and, deciding that an active warship on Lake Ontario was a good idea, instructed Woolsey to return to the lake, commission the brig and establish a base of operations. In the meantime the *Oneida* had been pushed ashore by ice, and it took all of September and October for Woolsey and his men to prepare it for duty.[18]

Oswego was in some ways a good location for a naval establishment, situated as it was at the greatest possible distance from the Canadian shore and at the transhipment point for provisions sent from New York via the Hudson, Mohawk and Oswego river systems. At its mouth, the river was nearly 800 feet across, but most of it was blocked by a bar so that the river was usually no deeper than eight and half feet in the spring, and less than that during the rest of the year. Though built with a draught that was shallow for a warship, the *Oneida* drew more than eight and a half feet of water, so basing it at Oswego was impractical. As it was, removing the vessel from the bay proved to be a fatiguing chore. All its ordnance, stores and rigging had to be carried ashore so that the brig would sit as high as possible. Even then, it could not clear the bar in October, so "camels," a pair of sealed, box-like scows, were manoeuvred along its sides and scuttled. Woolsey's men secured the camels tightly to the brig's hull and pumped them dry, thereby lifting their vessel high enough in the water to allow it to sail awkwardly onto the lake.

The US Brig *Oneida*. This view shows the *Oneida* with nearly all of its square- and fore-and-aft sails set on its two masts and a 24-pdr. carronade mounted in each of its starboard gunports. Missing is the 32-pdr. long gun, which Woolsey removed from the forecastle to improve the vessel's sailing qualities. Note the rolled-up hammocks stowed in the hammock rail along the top of the bulwark, providing extra cover for the brig's gun crews. (Drawing by Kevin Crisman, courtesy of the artist)

When Woolsey and his crew, numbering only seven hands, had re-armed, stocked and rigged the *Oneida*, they set sail on the brig's maiden voyage during the second week of November 1810. Since Oswego, or other bar-locked bays like it, would not do as a home port for the navy, Sackets Harbour was the best alternative. Within the protection of its deep basin, vessels could be serviced easily while there was a perfect site for a shipyard on the spacious and gently sloping shore. As protection, construction of a small fortification, which would eventually be named Fort Tompkins, had been begun at the head of the basin on the promontory facing the lake. Though the British forces at Kingston were perilously close (thirty-five miles away by water), there was no better location along the American shore for Woolsey to found his naval establishment. During 1811 he purchased the peninsula that created the harbour and two acres of land adjoining it, erecting a guardroom, a boat house and a large messroom.[19] As news from Washington warned of an impending conflict, Woolsey sought to fill up his crew by enlisting recruits from as far away as Buffalo and even the British side of the Niagara River. He also gathered information about the state of the Provincial Marine, the British naval force based at Kingston, reporting to Washington in July that it consisted of five vessels capable of carrying a total of seventy carronades and long guns. Faced with such opposition, Woolsey identified nine commercial schooners in American ports that could be purchased into the service and armed if the British squadron threatened an attack.

By January 1812 the complement of the *Oneida* stood at ninety-six, two dozen or so men short of its rated strength. Immediately after President Madison endorsed the ninety-day embargo that was supposed to be a final warning to the British, Woolsey finally received the orders he had been waiting for, to seek out and apprehend customs violators. Early in May the *Oneida's* patrols of the coast began, and on 5 June Woolsey detained his first suspect, the British schooner *Lord Nelson*, off the Genesee River. Its master, John Johnson, was unable to show Woolsey the proper clearance certificate from American officials at Cape Vincent at the head of the St. Lawrence, so the lieutenant put a prize crew aboard and the schooner was sailed to Sackets. A second schooner, the *Mary Hatt*, was pursued, but it slipped over the line before the *Oneida* could catch it.[20]

In the weeks leading up to the declaration of war the only assistance that Woolsey received from the Navy Department was a small detachment of marines sent to the lake in May.[21] Although the *Oneida* would have to play a significant role in Dearborn's plan to attack from Sackets Harbour, Secretary of the Navy Paul Hamilton issued no specific instructions to Woolsey even after Madison signed the war bill, apart from those contained in a circular distributed to naval officers on 19 June. Woolsey was an energetic officer, however, and he did not wait for guidance. After a conference with Brigadier General Jacob Brown of the New York militia, he obtained twenty-seven volunteers who agreed to join the brig for one cruise as marines. Woolsey also ordered the conversion of the *Lord Nelson* and a second laker, the *Julia*, for duty as gunboats. He had only four long guns (three 6-pdrs. and the 32-pdr. from the brig) with

(Facing page) **Capture of the schooner *Lord Nelson*, 5 June 1812.** While patrolling in the *Oneida* off the Genesee River on 4 June 1812, Lieutenant Woolsey spotted vessels making for the American shore and decided to inspect them. When they fled, Woolsey pursued them and, the next day, stopped the Crooks brothers' merchantman *Lord Nelson*, aboard which he discovered a mixed cargo, but no customs clearance papers to prove that it was not contraband. Under the strictures of the embargo then in place, Woolsey impounded the schooner and sailed it to Sackets Harbour. (Watercolour by Owen Staples, courtesy of the Toronto Reference Library, T-15223)

which to arm them, so he wrote to Captain Isaac Chauncey, commandant of the Navy Yard at New York City, for a shipment of thirty 6-pdrs. Paying for the conversions, plus the equipment, ammunition and men needed would be a costly matter, and on 4 July Woolsey petitioned Secretary Hamilton for some help: "The whole northern part of this State particularly on the frontier *depend* on Naval protection. For the recruiting Service Sir I shall want *Money* – as much as you will please to remit me."[22]

Woolsey needed more than money, though, given the information he had transmitted to Washington the previous summer about the strength of the British squadron on Lake Ontario. He was in a precarious situation and lived in expectation of seeing the Provincial Marine sail into view at any time and pummel the *Oneida* into submission. Furthermore, if Dearborn's action against Kingston was undertaken, which was still fully intended in the middle of August, Woolsey would only have the brig and a couple of converted lakers to fight his way past several warships as he transported the invaders to their target.[23] Whether Secretary Hamilton, the president and the other members of the cabinet understood the situation on Lake Ontario is doubtful because they allowed two months to slip by before deciding to increase the naval force. Despite hot language about "armor" and "attitude," the decision-makers in Washington were slow in backing words with action.

In the meantime, Hamilton dispatched his first specific order to Woolsey on 2 July, requiring him to transport military provisions meant for General Hull's army from Oswego to Fort Niagara "If in Your opinion, You can, without exposing Yourself to imminent danger from a Superior force."[24] Woolsey never made that trip, for the "superior force" soon appeared off his shore.

PART II

The Importance of
Controlling the Lake

JULY 1812 – APRIL 1813

Ye honest tars of Yankee mould,
Whose gallant actions fame has told!
Permit a brother tar to greet
The flag of our "MUSQUETO FLEET,"
Which ye have taught to triumph o'er
That flag which ruled the waves before!

WAR JOURNAL, 25 JUNE 1813

A figurehead for the *Earl of Moira*, 1805. A rare contemporary view of a Provincial Marine vessel, this drawing shows a figurehead design proposed for the *Earl of Moira*. It probably represented the prominent British general Francis Lord Rawdon, the Second Earl of Moira. At least two other designs were considered, but whether any of them was used is unknown. (Pen and ink, with watercolour, by François Baillarge, courtesy of the National Archives of Canada, C-15227)

CHAPTER 3

"Our Navy ... Is Worse Than Nothing" [1]

THE FAILURE OF THE PROVINCIAL MARINE: JULY–NOVEMBER 1812

*T*he British Provincial Marine squadron on Lake Ontario was superior to Melancthon Woolsey's force in numbers and firepower. In July 1812 it comprised two ships and two schooners armed with nearly fifty carronades. If strength of broadsides was to be the deciding factor in the coming naval contest, then Woolsey's suffering would end quickly. As was shown during the early months of the war, however, and repeatedly through the subsequent conflict, other factors figured more heavily than sheer force in determining who would hold supremacy on the lake.

The Provincial Marine was a product of the Seven Years War, when a Royal Navy detachment operated a number of small vessels against the French on Lake Ontario, Lake Champlain and the St. Lawrence River. During the Revolutionary War a flotilla commanded by a former Royal Navy officer and about 300 British sailors supported military activities and maintained supply routes. Following the war the strength of the flotilla, which gradually became known as the Provincial Marine, diminished, and the Quartermaster General's Department of the British Army assumed command. Naval stations were developed at Quebec, Kingston and Amherstburg, the latter two ports housing the establishments for squadrons on Lake Ontario and Lake Erie respectively. Early in 1812 only nine officers, 101 seamen and five artificers were affiliated with the two lake squadrons. The role of the Marine Department, as the Provincial Marine was also known, was restricted to the transport of provisions and personnel for the army and the provincial government. [2]

On Lake Ontario the oldest Provincial Marine vessel was the derelict *Duke of*

Provincial Marine Schooner *Prince Regent*, **1812.** With a pair of square sails on its foremast, the *Prince Regent* was typical of the topsail schooners of the Provincial Marine at the outbreak of war. It is uncertain whether a long gun was mounted at either end of the vessel as this impression, drawn around 1913, shows. The schooner was renamed the *Lord Beresford* in 1813 and the *Netley* in 1814. (Pencil and watercolour by Owen Staples, courtesy of the Toronto Reference Library, T-15218)

Kent, anchored in retirement in Navy Bay beside the dockyard on Point Frederick, across the Cataraqui River from Kingston. Its sailing days over, the *Kent* served as a hospital and a winter barrack for the seamen.[3] Next in age came the *Earl of Moira*, launched at Point Frederick in 1805. Its main deck measured only seventy feet in length, but it had three masts rigged with a full set of square sails (and was, therefore, classed as a "ship"), which was uncommon for so small a vessel. A proposal made early in 1812 to increase the *Moira's* battery by lengthening its hull was rejected when an inspection of its timbers revealed widespread rot despite the salt that had been packed between the frames as a preservative when it had been built.[4] An extensive repair was conducted instead, and the *Moira* continued to be armed with only ten 18-pdr. carronades. The schooner *Duke of Gloucester* had been launched at Point Frederick in 1807.

Smaller than even the *Moira*, the schooner was considered more useful than its sister ships because its draught was shallow enough to permit entry to most ports in any season. Armed with six 6-pdr. carronades or long guns, it was retained for the exclusive use of the provincial government rather than the army, but despite being barely five years old, the vessel was so riddled by decay by 1812 that a replacement was ordered. This vessel, also a schooner, was laid down at York in the spring of 1812 and made its maiden voyage in July. Named the *Prince Regent*, it measured nearly seventy-two feet on its deck and was equipped with ten 12-pdr. carronades.

The largest warship on Lake Ontario was the *Royal George*, with an upper deck 101 feet long upon which twenty 32-pdr. carronades could be mounted. Rigged as a ship and formally classed as a "corvette," the *Royal George* owed its existence to Melancthon Woolsey's *Oneida*. When news reached British ears during the autumn of 1808 that the U.S. Navy had arrived at Oswego to build a stoutly armed brig, British officials were alarmed at the threat it would pose. Their response was to order the construction of a warship that would match the *Oneida*.[5] Accordingly, the keel to a corvette was laid at Point Frederick in February 1809 under the watchful eye of the Provincial Marine's master shipwright, John Dennis, who had built the other vessels. It was launched the following July, but owing to the repeal of Jefferson's embargo, the *Royal George* remained uncommissioned at Point Frederick through 1811. As the cry for war rose south of the border, the Provincial Marine armed and crewed the ship and put it into service.

The Provincial Marine was only one element of the British armed forces that were hurriedly preparing for war late in 1811. Directing the mobilization was Lieutenant General Sir George Prevost, who had arrived in Canada in October 1811 to assume the role of governor-in-chief of British North America and commander-in-chief of its military and naval forces. Prevost was forty-four years of age when he took over at Quebec. He had joined the army as an ensign in his father's regiment, the 60th Foot, just before his twelfth birthday and had climbed steadily up the ranks until becoming lieutenant colonel of that regiment in 1796. He saw action against the French in the West Indies and after 1800 served as the lieutenant governor of St. Lucia, Dominica and Nova Scotia. From the latter post he was transferred to Lower Canada to replace Sir James Craig as governor-in-chief.[6]

As war approached in the spring of 1812 Prevost commanded about 11,500 men in regular regiments and the Canadian fencible regiments that had been raised in British North America. More than 4,300 of them were stationed at maritime centres in Nova Scotia, New Brunswick and Newfoundland, leaving

Lieutenant General Sir George Prevost, British Army (1767-1816). Prevost's main talent lay in his ability to work as a conciliator among opposing civil factions in the various colonial posts that he held. Though also experienced as a commander in campaigns against the French in the West Indies, his cautious military leadership during the War of 1812 was questioned by subordinates who favoured more aggressive policies. (Courtesy of the National Archives of Canada, C-6152)

Prevost about 7,200 professional troops, backed by more than 70,000 militiamen, to defend Lower and Upper Canada. Since the dependability of the militia was never certain, Sir George was required to divide his serviceable regular regiments among the key locations near the American border. Because he "considered the preservation of Quebec as the first object, and to which all others must be subordinate," Prevost concentrated the bulk of his force (about 5,500 men) in Lower Canada.[7] The remaining 1,700 regulars and fencibles he delegated for deployment in Upper Canada.

Command of the forces in the upper province was held by forty-two-year-old Major General Isaac Brock.[8] Like Prevost, Brock had entered the army at an early age and advanced through the ranks until voyaging to Quebec in 1802 as lieutenant colonel of the 49th Regiment of Foot. Except for a brief visit to England, Brock spent the next ten years in Canada gaining practical knowledge of the settlements and garrisons strung along the extensive boundary with the United States. Promoted to major general in 1811, he took charge of civil affairs in Upper Canada in October of that year when Lieutenant Governor Francis Gore obtained permission to return to England for health reasons.

Brock assumed that the Americans would direct their main thrust against the upper province. Between January and June of 1812 he distributed his force at garrisons on St. Joseph Island (fifteen miles southeast of present-day Sault Ste. Marie) and along the Detroit, Niagara and St. Lawrence rivers. He ordered the construction of batteries, the repair of fortifications and the call for militia to parade under arms. Knowing that his potential enemy was not well equipped to fight a war, Brock was eager to make a pre-emptive strike against the weak American forts that stood across the rivers from his positions, particularly at Detroit, but Prevost forbade any such aggression for fear that it would provide a clear and unifying reason for Congress to vote for war.[9]

Isaac Brock also assessed the condition of the Provincial Marine. Along with Captain Andrew Gray, who had recently taken over the position of assistant deputy quartermaster general with special responsibility for the Marine Department, he made recommendations to Prevost about the changes that were needed to prepare the squadrons for war. They approved the retirement of the senior officer on Lake Ontario, seventy-five-year-old "Commodore" John Steel, replacing him with Hugh Earl, a forty-seven-year-old lieutenant with twenty years in the Marine, who was promoted to master and commander in the *Royal George*.[10] Gray was quick to identify a problem with the officers in the Provincial Marine, remarking to Prevost in January 1812, "The officers serving in this division of the Province are in some instances extremely inefficient, and, in short, totally unfit for the situations they hold."[11] Besides John Steel, however, only one officer was removed from his post, this being Deputy Assistant

Major General Isaac Brock, British Army (1769-1812). The loss of Brock at the Battle of Queenston Heights early on the morning of 13 October 1812 was universally lamented through British North America. Unknown to the fallen general was that his capture of the American army at Detroit in August had been honoured on 9 October by the Prince Regent's order for Brock to be appointed an extra knight of the Order of the Bath. (Courtesy of the National Archives of Canada, C-36181)

20 Dollars Bounty,
will be paid to able SEAMEN,
AND
12 Dollars Bounty
will be given to ordinary SEA-
MEN, on entering for the Marine
Service for Three Years. Apply
to Lieutenant FISH.
Marine Department.
York, May 21, 1812.

Recruitment of seamen at York, 1812. At General Brock's suggestions, Lieutenant William Fish, Provincial Marine, had this advertisement published in the *Upper Canada Gazette* during the spring of 1812 in an effort to raise a crew for the new schooner *Prince Regent*, then under construction at York, and which he commanded upon its launch in July. (Courtesy of the National Archives of Canada, C-107049)

Quartermaster General Major Thomas Fuller, who was transferred from Kingston to York. Nothing was done to replace the half dozen or so men who officered the ships, although there was ample time for an appeal for experienced Royal Navy officers to be sent from Halifax or the naval ships that routinely visited Quebec.

Gray's January 1812 report also addressed the deficiency in the manpower of the Lake Ontario squadron and prompted the enlistment of several young men as midshipmen, the promotion of at least two others to junior lieutenants and the addition of fifty seamen to the squadron in the spring. Brock recommended that 100 seamen be found at Quebec and that two companies of the Royal Newfoundland Fencible Regiment be detached from Lower Canada for service on the lakes; Prevost later approved the deployment of five Newfoundland companies to Upper Canada.[12]

The decision to replace the *Duke of Gloucester* with the new schooner, *Prince Regent*, also resulted from Gray's report to Prevost. Selecting York rather than Kingston as the construction site reflected the view of Brock, Gray and others that the naval establishment at Kingston was too exposed to attack by the Americans and that it should be moved to the provincial capital. Like Kingston, York had a well-protected anchorage, government store houses, and good sites for fortifications and a dockyard, but at greater distance from the foreign shore.

Business in Quebec kept Prevost from travelling to Upper Canada to inspect the frontier himself in the spring of 1812 as he had informed Brock he would. Instead, he gained his information about naval preparations on Lake Ontario and Lake Erie from correspondence with Gray and Brock. Confident that the Provincial Marine was ready to deal with hostilities, Prevost wrote to Lord Liverpool, the British prime minister, on 14 April 1812:

Considering a naval force properly constructed the most efficient and cheapest mode of defence, I have gradually increased the naval force on the lakes, and I have ordered five companies of the Royal Newfoundland Regiment to proceed to Upper Canada as soon as the season will permit, to be employed afloat, being men accustomed to boats and vessels.[13]

During the second week of July 1812 the squadron on Lake Ontario consisted of the *Royal George* under Master Commandant Hugh Earl, the *Earl of Moira*, commanded by Lieutenant Theophilus Sampson, the *Prince Regent*, Lieutenant William Fish, and the *Duke of Gloucester* (still in use by necessity), Lieutenant Francis Gauvreau. Together, the vessels carried forty-six carronades, nearly three times the armament of the US Brig *Oneida*, but two dozen short of the estimate that Lieutenant Woolsey had submitted to the Navy Department in July 1811.[14] A single broadside from the British could potentially hurl 328 pounds of shot at the *Oneida*, which was capable of returning only 192 pounds. With this advantage the squadron would have been a perfect vehicle for launching raids against the weakly prepared American garrisons and ports at Fort Niagara, Oswego, Ogdensburg and Sackets Harbour. Despite the declaration of war, however, Prevost stuck to his policy of non-aggression. Brock argued in favour of attacking, but Prevost overruled him by repeating that such an act would unite the otherwise disparate states, and adding that Brock had too few men to sustain the losses that would be incurred and that there were insufficient funds in the military purse to afford an offensive campaign.[15]

Seen in the context of Prevost's policy of non-aggression, the events that took place at Sackets Harbour on 19 July are bewildering.[16] As dawn broke at the American naval base that day, five vessels appeared in the offing. Woolsey ordered his men into action, and at 6:00 a.m. the *Oneida* sailed out to investigate. Having recognized the four vessels of the Provincial Marine (the fifth was never named), Woolsey had it in mind to separate one or two of them from the rest and do battle. The British drew together and, with a steady wind from the north, cut off the *Oneida's* route to the open lake around 8:00. Woolsey quickly reversed his course and anchored the brig in Black River Bay near the naval yard. He also dropped his stream anchor and, with a second cable attached like a spring between the anchor cable and the capstan, he hauled *Oneida* around so that its larboard guns faced the enemy, three of which (the *George*, *Moira* and *Regent*) were steering for the bay. Woolsey next removed the eight carronades from the starboard side and had them carried ashore for installation in the battery that stood on the head of land above the shipyard. According to Woolsey, the breeze failed and the approach of the British was so slow that he was able to

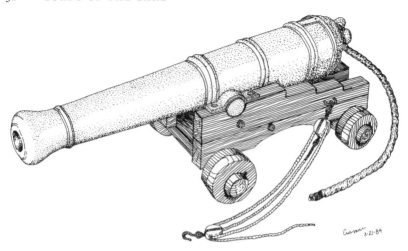

The long gun. The calibre of a long gun was based on the weight of the shot it fired.
On Lake Ontario, warships carried a variety of guns from 4-pdrs. to 32-pdrs. With a
charge of black powder equal to one-third the weight of the shot, a 32-pdr. long gun
had a range of more than 1,000 yards, depending on its elevation. As many as
fourteen men were needed to handle such a gun, which might measure ten feet in
length and weigh 6,500 pounds, its carriage adding another half ton. (Drawing by
Kevin Crisman, courtesy of the artist)

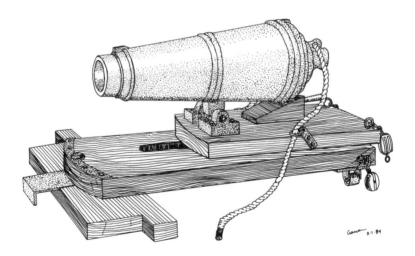

The carronade. Measuring a little over four feet in length and weighing 2,000 pounds,
a typical 32-pdr. carronade, fitted to a slide-carriage weighing several hundred pounds,
required a crew of only seven men. With its normal charge of one-ninth the weight of
the shot and its shorter barrel, a 32-pdr. carronade was most effective at a range of
less than 500 yards. (Drawing by Kevin Crisman, courtesy of the artist)

complete the prodigious task of transferring his carronades and mounting them in the fort before the *George* could get closer than one and half miles from shore.

Leaving Midshipman Henry Wells in command of the *Oneida*, Woolsey assumed command of the land battery, soon to be named Fort Tompkins in honour of New York State's governor, Daniel Tompkins. In addition to eight carronades, he had six long guns mounted in the bastion – three 6-pdrs., two 9-pdrs. and the 32-pdr. long gun that had been intended originally for use on the brig. With this latter weapon he opened fire against the British and claimed to "hull" the *George* several times. One story told after the affair mentioned that at least one 32-pdr. shot from the British carronades was retrieved for use in the American gun, for which adequate ammunition was lacking. Woolsey confirmed this story by noting that a pair of 32-pdr. shot were picked up by his men, so it would seem that the *George* must have sailed within a mile (maximum carronade range) of the shore. The British did not get much closer for they soon broke off the attack and departed.

What was Commander Earl trying to achieve by attacking Sackets Harbour? His report on the incident has not survived, and nothing appeared in the correspondence of Prevost or Brock to explain the actions of the Provincial Marine that day. Anecdotal evidence suggests that Earl captured a boat on his approach and sent its occupants to shore with a warning that the village would be burned if the *Lord Nelson* and the *Oneida* were not surrendered.[17] Such a story hints that Earl might have been attempting to do what Captain Charles Roberts of the 10th Royal Veteran Battalion had managed two days before in the northern reaches of Lake Huron.

On 17 July Roberts had landed at the American post on Mackinac Island with 45 regular soldiers, 180 fur traders and 400 Indians and convinced the Americans to surrender. His actions had been prompted by a series of letters written by Brock in which the general had advised him "to adopt the most prudent measures either of offence or defence which circumstances might point out."[18] Believing that his own fort on St. Joseph Island was about to be raided, and having enough men on hand who seemed willing to fight, Roberts had taken the initiative to seize Mackinac and thereby gain control of the northern bottleneck in the western trading routes. When Prevost received word of the event, he remarked: "Great credit is certainly due to that officer for the zeal and promptitude with which he has performed that service." Prevost was relieved that it had occurred after Brigadier General William Hull crossed the Detroit River into Upper Canada (12 July) because "it would not only have been in violation of Captain Roberts's orders, but have afforded a just ground for the subsequent conduct of the enemy."[19]

Despite Prevost's lukewarm response, the capture of Mackinac was one of the most significant acts in the opening weeks of the war. British possession of the post distracted the American leadership for the rest of the conflict, repeatedly causing them to commit forces to its recapture and away from the main theatre of operations around Lake Ontario. A similar objective might have been behind the attack on Sackets Harbour. Possibly, Brock and Earl discussed the great advantage to be gained by seizing the *Oneida* and reducing the naval station at Sackets, with the general advising Earl "to adopt the most prudent measures...." Some circumstantial evidence supports this notion. One hundred men and several pieces of artillery embarked on the *Royal George* at the town of Niagara on 14 July, according to one American source, while another reported that "the British have sent from Little York every armed ship in pursuit of the brig *Oneida*."[20] Brock also addressed his correspondence from Fort George during the week before the attack, meaning he had opportunities to meet with Earl before 14 July. There the trail of clues ends, however, and the origins of the mission remain uncertain.

More obvious was the inability of Earl's squadron to execute an effective attack. Woolsey's report suggested that a stronger breeze might have helped the British in their endeavour, but he also implied that the squadron was not up to the task. "From the confusion that appeared at one time on board the *Royal George*," Woolsey noted, "I am induced to believe that some serious damage must have been done by our shot."[21] That confusion existed among the British is not surprising for this was the first time since the Revolutionary War that the Provincial Marine had exchanged shots with an enemy. The squadron was commanded by an officer who had spent two decades on Lake Ontario in small Provincial Marine vessels and had never fired a carronade in anger let alone managed a squadron in battle.[22] His subordinates, trained as transport officers, were similarly unsuited for their task, and the ships themselves were undermanned; the enlistment effort at Quebec had netted only a few hands and some of the promised detachments of the Royal Newfoundland Regiment had yet to leave Lower Canada.[23] In short, the steps that Prevost and his officers had taken to "increase the naval forces on the lakes" had proved far from adequate.

Less than two weeks after the Sackets Harbour affair the Provincial Marine again demonstrated its weakness while the Americans revealed audacious self-confidence. After the declaration of war a number of American lakers had taken shelter at Ogdensburg, the port located seventy miles down the St. Lawrence River across from the village of Prescott. Hearing that the *Moira* and the *Gloucester* were headed in that direction, Woolsey became concerned about the safety of the lakers, which he hoped could be converted for war use. He decided to arm the schooner *Julia* with a pair of long sixes and the long 32-pdr. and send it to Ogdensburg "in order if possible to capture, distroy [sic] or cripple the British."[24] Command of the expedition was given to Midshipman Wells, whom Woolsey had promoted to acting lieutenant. With Wells went part of the *Oneida's* crew, a number of local mariners as volunteers and thirty regulars of the U.S. Rifle Regiment.

The *George* was prowling near the confluence of the lake and the St. Lawrence River, but Wells easily evaded it and proceeded down the river on 30 July. The next afternoon the *Julia* was cruising close to the British shore near Elizabethtown when it came upon the *Moira* and the *Gloucester*. The *Moira* fired three carronades, which caused no damage, but musketry from the shore prompted Wells to sail over to the American side, from which he opened fire at a distance of about one and a quarter miles. The British vessels and a shore battery returned fire, their shots falling well short. The range was closed to about three quarters of a mile (a very long shot for the *Moira's* carronades) as small boats hauled the British vessels upstream, and still the *Julia* escaped injury.

With night falling and both sides obscured by smoke, Wells broke off the fight, which had lasted for three hours, and continued down the short distance to Ogdensburg. The next day the *Moira* and *Gloucester* were positioned in the middle of the river within sight of the town and the Americans hurriedly prepared to fend off an attack. None came, and Wells left the *Julia* and, at Woolsey's request, returned by land to Sackets with the *Oneida* men. By the end of August the declaration of a temporary pause in hostilities allowed the blockaded American lakers and the *Julia* to sail unmolested to the lake, where most of them were soon purchased by the U.S. Navy for use as gunboats.[25]

The only successful offensive mission by the Provincial Marine occurred on 1 October 1812 when Earl anchored his flagship off the Genesee River and sent eighty armed men ashore at the village of Charlotte, where they seized a dismantled sixty-ton sloop, the *Lady Murray,* and a revenue cutter and left; they returned the next day to demand the masts and rigging of the sloop. Farther up the river three schooners, which had been in convoy from Fort Niagara, lay concealed and safe from the British raid, apparently because Earl lacked enough men to risk probing inland. Enclosed with a claim for prize money submitted by Earl a year later was a muster roll of the men serving on the *George* on 1 October. Probably the only extant Provincial Marine muster roll from that period, the list reveals that the ship was crewed by fifty officers and seamen, supplemented by sixty-four officers and men from the Royal Newfoundland Regiment. This number was far short of the 155 officers and seamen who would operate the ship the following year when the Royal Navy arrived to take command.[26]

With few opportunities to attack the enemy and no apparent orders being given to that effect during the summer and fall of 1812, Earl's squadron was used primarily in its traditional role as a transport service. From the first days of the war the vessels carried men and munitions from Kingston to York and Fort George and back. After General Hull surrendered his army and his post at Detroit on 16 August, he and nearly 600 men were allowed to rest their feet for a couple of days during their long trek to imprisonment at Quebec as they were ferried by the Provincial Marine from Niagara to Kingston. Two months later, as shock waves of disbelief fanned out across Upper Canada when people heard that Brock had died at Queenston Heights, the same conveyance was provided for the hundreds of Americans captured by the army under Major General Roger Sheaffe.

By October 1812 the situation on Lake Ontario was about to change radically. President Madison and his cabinet had realized the importance of gaining control of the Great Lakes and moved to increase the strength of their naval force there significantly. News of this escalation reached the British side and caused some alarm since it had become obvious that the Provincial Marine, as it existed, would be unable to cope with a naval opponent capable of challenging it for supremacy on the lake. The Reverend John Strachan, one of the leading citizens of the province, reflected public opinion when he commented that "as to our Navy it is worse than nothing – the Officers are the greatest cowards that have ever lived, and would fly from a single Bateau."[27] Seeing no other way to remedy the situation, Prevost appealed for help from the home government through Lord Bathurst, the Secretary for War and the Colonies. On 17 October he wrote to ask "that tried officers of the rank of lieutenants and trusty men from the [Royal N]avy should be ... sent to me as early as possible next spring." Explaining that his attempts at recruiting sailors and his deployment of the Royal Newfoundland Regiment had still left the squadron's crews shorthanded, he added, "the officers are deficient in experience and particularly in that energetic spirit which distinguishes British seamen."[28]

With Prevost's allegations about their lack of spirit, Earl and his colleagues became the first British scapegoats in the naval war. Although they had vessels and ordnance enough to vanquish the *Oneida,* they lacked the proper crews and training, through no fault of their own, to use their ships properly. Their deficiencies had been reported plainly to Prevost ten months before, but little had been done to rectify the situation, and Brock, who had been familiar with the Provincial Marine for a decade, had failed to recognize the need to appoint experienced naval officers before the war began. Though he made preparations in other sectors in his jurisdiction, Brock had not imposed a system of discipline and drill upon the Marine that would have raised its fighting ability nearer to the high level that his own rank and file infantry demonstrated.

The Battle of Queenston Heights, 13 October 1812. Captain James Dennis of the Grenadier company in the 49th Regiment of Foot, a participant in the battle, painted this panorama showing all phases of the action, from the invasion craft crossing the river to the death of Brock and Sheaffe's victory on the Heights late in the afternoon. (Courtesy of the Weir Foundation, Queenston)

The only argument raised in defence of the Provincial Marine came from the pen of James Richardson, second lieutenant on the *Moira*. He had joined that service in 1809 at the age of eighteen, following in the footsteps of his father, James Richardson senior, an old Royal Navy man who had emigrated to Upper Canada and worked as the master of several merchantmen on Lake Ontario. The younger Richardson was promoted to lieutenant during the spring of 1812 as part of the effort to bolster the number of officers. He appears to have been the sole member of the Marine who sailed with Hugh Earl, witnessed the events of 1812 on the lake and left a memoir of his war days. Regarding the July attack on Sackets and the duel with the *Julia*, Richardson recorded nothing, but, stung by the criticisms directed at the Provincial Marine during and after the war, he wrote:

> Our little squadron, though not very much celebrated for exploits in the way of fighting, managed, however, to keep open the communication between the Eastern and Western Divisions of the Army.... The importance of such services in the then uninhabited state of the country, and the lack of land conveyance owing to the badness of the roads must be obvious.[29]

Though the Marine played a useful role as a transport service, its superior firepower was wasted, and its mismanagement robbed the British of early opportunities to gain control of Lake Ontario. The cost of that mismanagement became obvious during the autumn of 1812 when the Americans sent a competent and ambitious naval officer to the northern frontier to gain the naval initiative.

CHAPTER 4

"The Command of Lake Ontario"[1]

CHAUNCEY'S SEASON OF SUCCESS: SEPTEMBER–DECEMBER 1812

President James Madison and his wife departed from Washington on 28 August to spend some time at their home in Montpelier, Virginia. That evening an express rider caught up to them with despatches containing devastating news: Brigadier General William Hull had surrendered his entire army of more than 2,000 men at Detroit twelve days earlier without having made any attempt to withstand an attack from a smaller British force led by Brock. The next day Madison returned to the capital and summoned his cabinet officials to discuss Hull's capitulation and its repercussions on the campaign against Upper Canada.

During the meeting two firm decisions were reached. The first was to order Brigadier General James Winchester to lead an army toward Detroit with assistance from Brigadier General William Henry Harrison; and the second, to create naval squadrons that would gain control of Lakes Ontario and Erie.[2] The most senior captains in the United States Navy, including Isaac Hull, Stephen Decatur and William Bainbridge, were already fully occupied with the command of the navy's few but powerful frigates, so Madison's cabinet continued down the seniority list until they reached the tenth spot. In that place was Isaac Chauncey, commandant of the navy yard at New York, who had developed the expertise during his career that would make him the perfect choice for the difficult task of building a navy on the lakes.

Isaac Chauncey was forty years old in August of 1812.[3] His father, Wolcott Chauncey, had been a successful farmer in Black Rock, Connecticut, and had afforded a good education for his son, who was destined for a career in law until the romance of the sea turned his head. The young Chauncey left home at age twelve to sail before the mast on merchant ships and was so quick in learning the skills of seamanship and command that he advanced to the station of master by the time he was nineteen and soon captained vessels belonging to the financier John Jacob Astor on voyages that took him around the world to the East Indies.

In the spring of 1798 the Department of the Navy officially came into existence, and fifty-nine officers were selected for the handful of ships then in service. Among them was Isaac Chauncey, who received a commission as lieutenant, dated 17 September 1798, and the order to superintend the construction of the forty-four-gun frigate *President* at New York. After its launch in April 1800, Captain Thomas Truxtun took command of the ship with Chauncey as his first lieutenant and made one cruise to the West Indies during the brief period of hostilities between the United States and France that became known as the Quasi-War. When peace came, the government reduced the strength of its army and navy, but Lieutenant Chauncey kept his rank and sailed to the Mediterranean Sea in the USS *President* under Commodore Richard Dale in May 1801.

As Dale's squadron crossed the Atlantic, vessels travelled in the opposite direction bearing news that the Pasha of Tripoli, Yusuf Karamanli, had declared war on the United States. It had become the custom for foreign governments to pay "protection money" to the Tripolitan ruler in order to safeguard their merchant fleets from financial ruin at the hands of the scourge of the Mediterranean Sea, the pirates based in northern Africa. When the government of Thomas Jefferson refused to meet the demands of Karamanli, he opted to declare war, which Jefferson received with aplomb, dispatching the U.S. Navy to protect commerce and uphold national honour. The events of the next four years provided Chauncey and his contemporaries with their first real taste of active service.[4]

Commodore Dale's squadron remained only briefly in the Mediterranean Sea before returning home, but when Commodore Richard Morris led another force there in 1802 Chauncey accompanied him aboard the frigate *Chesapeake*, 36 guns, as flag captain (though still officially a lieutenant). The next year he transferred with Morris into the *New York*, 36, and in that ship almost saw his career go up in flames, literally. During a voyage to Malta in April 1803 an explosion rocked the lower decks of the *New York,* and Chauncey instantly ordered the crew "beat to quarters," which he considered the best way to avoid confusion caused by the smoke that billowed up from below. Morris charged on deck, assessed the situation, and instructed all hands to abandon ship, which prompted some men to launch the ship's boats while others sprinted up the

Commodore Isaac Chauncey, USN (1772-1840). By the time Chauncey was nineteen years old, he had been put in command of a merchant ship by John Jacob Astor. Shortly thereafter he is said to have completed a voyage from Charleston to New York single-handedly when his crew was felled by yellow fever. Chauncey joined the United States Navy as a lieutenant in 1798. He was promoted to master commandant in 1804 and to captain in 1806. (Courtesy of the Toronto Reference Library, T-15206)

rigging and out upon the bowsprit to get as far away from the impending detonation of the ship's magazine as possible. Seeing little value in retreat,
Chauncey gathered a gang of willing hands and hurried below to fight the fire,
reputedly proclaiming, "It is the same to be blown up through three decks as
through one!" A bucket brigade was formed, blankets were soaked to smother
the flames and after a desperate struggle the threat was extinguished, winning
the lieutenant universal praise for his courage and presence of mind. Fourteen
men died in the fire, including the master gunner, whose careless handling of
powder had almost reduced the *New York* to kindling.

Chauncey gained promotion to master commandant on 23 May 1804 and
with it command of the USS *John Adams*, 28. On duty again in Tripoli, this time
under Commodore Edward Preble, Chauncey was witness to some of the hard-
est fighting of the war, but because his ship had been converted into a transport
he missed most of the action. The closest he came to the intense fighting was on
a couple of occasions when he and a portion of his crew volunteered aboard
Preble's flagship, the *Constitution,* 44, as it participated in shelling the enemy
positions ashore. The war ended in June 1805, and Chauncey sailed for New
York, where he was advanced to the rank of captain on 24 April 1806.

The postwar reduction of the navy, and the preference of President Thomas
Jefferson's administration for gunboats rather than frigates, combined to
shrink the service. Although he had been at sea for the better part of six years,
Chauncey looked around for alternate employment and found it in an offer
from his old friend John Jacob Astor. Leaving his wife, Catharine, and young
son, John, behind once more, Captain Chauncey signed on as master of the
merchant ship *Beaver* and set a course for China in 1806. It was in the waters off
the Whampoa River that he encountered the antagonism of the Royal Navy for
the first time in his career. HMS *Lion*, 64, was anchored in the river, and its captain viewed the *Beaver* as an easy source of seasoned hands. He dispatched a
lieutenant to order Chauncey to muster his crew, but Chauncey refused, and his
ship was soon surrounded by boats and armed men, who stormed aboard, lowered the flag and seized control. Ordered to produce the muster books,
Chauncey again refused and was escorted to the *Lion,* where the British captain
declared that he would impress every man aboard the *Beaver*. In response
Chauncey shrugged and admitted that since his ship had been captured he really did not command it anymore and had no more to say about its disposition.
Suddenly aware that he might have overstepped his bounds and was about to
create a sticky international situation, the Briton backpeddled, releasing
Chauncey and his ship to resume the voyage unmolested.

When he returned home in 1807, the Department of the Navy offered

The *President–Little Belt* incident, 16 May 1811. Commodore John Rodgers in the USS *President*, 44, encountered HMS *Little Belt*, 20, off New Jersey during the night of 16 May 1811 and fired his broadsides into the smaller vessel because its conduct through a long chase earlier in the day had been suspicious. Nine British crew members were killed and twenty-three wounded, which incited indignation in Britain and the Canadian provinces. (From a painting by B. R. Robinson, courtesy of the U.S. Naval Historical Center, NH-56739)

Chauncey command of the naval yard at New York, located near present-day Brooklyn. He spent the next five years on that station organizing stores and munitions and overseeing the repairs and refits of various vessels. He also served on the board of officers convened to examine the circumstances that had allowed the USS *Chesapeake* to be treated so ignominiously by HMS *Leopard* in June 1807, which resulted in Commodore James Barron's suspension without pay for five years. As well, Chauncey sat on at least two other committees during this period, one that examined the value of torpedo devices being developed by Robert Fulton and another that looked into the USS *President's* "accidental" attack upon HMS *Little Belt* in May 1811.

Chauncey was at New York when hostilities broke out in June 1812 and was soon occupied in helping prepare the navy's few warships for action. Although he was not offered the independent command of a frigate and missed the glorious opportunity that Isaac Hull demonstrated was attainable when the

Constitution captured HMS *Guerriere* in August 1812, Chauncey's appointment to the Great Lakes station was a significant acknowledgement of the reputation he had earned during his fourteen-year career. Secretary of the Navy Paul Hamilton stated as much when he concluded his orders of 31 August 1812 with the assurance that "in conferring upon you this appointment … you will find evidence of the high confidence placed by your government in your capacity, discretion, valor & vigour."[5]

Madison and his cabinet granted Chauncey "unlimited authority to carry into effect the object of these instructions," authorizing him, as commodore, to buy, lease or build whatever shipping he needed, find officers and crews for the vessels, supply and arm them by using every available resource, and transport men and munitions to the lakes as expeditiously as possible. He was to establish a base on each of the lower lakes, likely at Sackets Harbour and at Buffalo, choosing one as his headquarters and assigning an officer to supervise the other. A supplementary set of instructions emphasized the importance of building up the Lake Erie force as energetically as the squadron on Lake Ontario could be assembled. They also underlined the importance of cooperating with the army by discussing with Major General Henry Dearborn at Albany the strength of the enemy and the steps that should be taken to win control of the lakes.

Chauncey faced a tremendous challenge. Only Lieutenant Melancthon Woolsey and a hundred or so men were stationed on Lake Ontario with the *Oneida* and one converted laker, while there were no armed vessels on Lake Erie. Rather than hesitate to ponder the enormity of Hamilton's instructions, however, Chauncey accepted the assignment with enthusiasm and before the sun set on 3 September, the day his orders arrived, he wrote to the secretary that he accepted "this flattering mark of confidence … with pleasure" and that he had already put the wheels in motion that would carry to the lakes an unprecedented quantity of materiel and enough sailors to man a squadron.[6] Over the next thirty-four months the commodore would dedicate himself to the needs of his freshwater command, and his energy and accomplishments would rarely disappoint his superiors.

In the three weeks following receipt of his orders Chauncey was busy from dawn to dusk with a myriad preparations. One of his first concerns being the need to convert merchant lakers for naval service and to build new vessels, he sent forty shipwrights to Sackets Harbour on 5 September. They were soon followed by 100 others under the supervision of Henry Eckford, the talented architect and efficient constructor from New York whom Chauncey had known for years.[7] Eckford's job was to lay out a shipyard at Sackets Harbour and put his labourers to work cutting timber and altering the merchant craft that Lieutenant Woolsey had purchased at Chauncey's orders. Although his correspondence was businesslike, the commodore was aware that Woolsey might feel slighted at being superseded in the command he had held off and on since 1808, so he took a few sentences to appease the lieutenant. "I have reason to felicitate myself," Chauncey wrote on 3 September, "on being so fortunate as to be so well seconded as I shall be by your advice and assistance."[8] Woolsey was unfazed by the change and expressed to Chauncey the pleasure he had felt upon learning he would work again with "an Officer with whom I have seen much service and for whose person and talents I have a sincere veneration."[9]

Crews for the warships were the next priority. In all, about 600 officers and men embarked in sloops and steamboats for the journey up the Hudson to Albany during September. They were taken from the frigate *John Adams* and from the gunboats stationed at New York, every one of them a volunteer, as the commodore proudly announced to Secretary Hamilton. A detachment of 100 U.S. Marines was also collected from the frigate and the land station, although its departure was postponed until fatigue clothing could be obtained. Captain Richard Smith and Lieutenant Charles Hanna led the marines, while eight sailing masters and four lieutenants supervised the seamen, having been ordered by Chauncey to "be very vigilant and see that none of your men desert or commit any depredation upon persons or property on your route."[10]

Noteworthy among the men going to the lake were Jesse Duncan Elliott and Ned Myers. Elliott was a thirty-year-old lieutenant from Maryland who had entered the service as a midshipman in 1804.[11] The most significant event in his

Henry Eckford (1775-1832). Born in Scotland, Eckford emigrated to Quebec in 1791 and worked for five years in his uncle's shipyard. Having learned the trade, he moved to New York City, where he eventually set up his own shipyard. (Photogravure by W. Sartain, courtesy of the U.S. Naval Historical Center, NH-66615)

Lieutenant Jesse Duncan Elliott, USN (1782-1845). Assigned to the lakes, Elliott was quick to demonstrate his worth by participating in the capture of two British armed vessels, the *Detroit* and *Caledonia*, off Fort Erie on 8 October 1812. The British managed to destroy the former vessel, but Elliott saved the *Caledonia*, which eventually formed part of Perry's Lake Erie squadron. He was later promoted to master commandant and captain, as shown here. (Courtesy, Enoch Pratt Library and the U.S. Naval Institute)

brief career had been his presence aboard the USS *Chesapeake* as a midshipman in 1807 when it was humiliated by HMS *Leopard*. He had demonstrated energy and competence, and Chauncey's faith in his abilities was justified on numerous occasions, the first being when Elliott cut out two British vessels from their anchorage off Fort Erie early in October.[12] Ned Myers was an able seaman who had volunteered for the lake service along with his mates in the gunboats at New York mainly because, as he recollected, "we hated the gunboats and would go anywhere to be quit of them."[13] A grant of twenty-four hours liberty and a little bit of pocket money were also attractive enticements since they allowed for a "run ashore" before boarding the sloops for Albany. Myers stands out from his peers because his recollections of recruitment for the lakes and events that occurred there were recorded in a biography published by James Fenimore Cooper in 1843, providing a rare, lower-deck view of the maritime campaign on the lakes.

Seamen and officers alike would need a vast array of equipment to wage war on Lake Ontario, and arranging for all the various munitions and supplies was probably Chauncey's most complicated task.[14] Crucial to this aspect of the undertaking were John Bullus, the navy agent at the New York naval yard, and Sam Anderson, a naval storekeeper and Chauncey's private secretary, who supervised shipment of goods in transit from Albany to the lake. With their help, Chauncey organized the shipment of more than 100 pieces of ordnance, ranging in calibre from 32-pdr. long guns to 12-pdr. carronades. Along with them

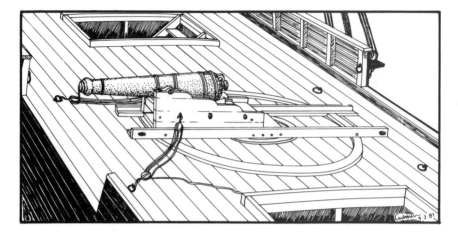

Circle-mounted long gun. To employ heavy-calibre long guns in the lake vessels, some were fastened to circular tracks that allowed them to be fired on both sides of the vessels. Such "circles" were mounted on the forecastle or the quarterdeck or amidship. (Drawing by Kevin Crisman, courtesy of the artist)

went carriages and slides, rammers, sponges, tackle, linstocks, cylinders and priming wires, some of which were taken from the shipping and storehouses at the yard, the balance being quickly fabricated. Thousands of round, grape and canister shot, plus hundreds of barrels of powder were transported. Muskets, pistols, cutlasses, boarding pikes (360 of each) were boxed and dispatched as were clothing, medicines and hospital stores along with sails, rigging, blocks, cables, anchors and cabouses (galley stoves) for the vessels Chauncey intended to build. Luckily, it was not necessary to transport food to the lake as Woolsey and an army agent made arrangements on the frontier to obtain the beef, pork, peas, cheese and biscuit that were the staples of the seaman's diet.

À parade of materiel moved north from the city to Albany. From there it was unloaded and carted for a short distance over the turnpike to Schenectady, where riverboats received the cargo and headed west along the Mohawk River.[15] Navigation of the Mohawk ended at Rome where a canal had been dug to Wood Creek, which in turn was linked to Lake Oneida and eventually the Oswego River. Low water levels impeded progress along this route, as Chauncey would soon discover, making it necessary to cart a large portion of his supplies overland from Utica and Rome.

While overseeing this massive logistical exercise, Chauncey also had to formulate his strategic plans. To obtain their insights and advice, he wrote to Major General Stephen Van Rensselaer, commanding the army on the Niagara

River, General Dearborn, at his headquarters in Albany, and the governor of New York, Daniel Tompkins.[16] Chauncey informed them of his appointment and his intention to establish a base on Lake Ontario where, besides converting lakers, he would build a 300-ton vessel and three gunboats at the same time as he set up a base on Lake Erie where two 300-ton vessels and three gunboats would be constructed. The sailors, marines, ordnance and supplies were to be divided equally between the two places, and while he went to Sackets Harbour, Lieutenant Elliott would begin organizing affairs at Buffalo.

Circumstances on the Niagara frontier soon caused Chauncey to revise his plan of action. Van Rensselaer advised Elliott to convert several schooners that were lying in the Genesee River, prompting the commodore to redirect men, guns and stores originally intended for Buffalo to the Genesee. Shortly thereafter, when he learned that the supply train had bogged down because of low water levels in the Mohawk and the canal and creeks beyond Rome, Chauncey decided to concentrate the energies of his men on getting enough guns and stores to Sackets so that he could have a squadron on the lake by 1 November.[17] As a result, readiness on Lake Ontario became the priority, while only rudimentary steps were taken by Lieutenant Samuel Angus, USN, whom Chauncey ordered to set up a yard at Black Rock, two miles down the Niagara River from Buffalo.[18]

Finally on 26 September 1812, Chauncey bid his wife and family farewell and stepped aboard a steamboat bound for Albany. After conferring with Dearborn at Albany, the commodore continued his journey in company with Governor Tompkins. It is likely that they travelled by stage coach along the turnpike to Utica and then turned north for Sackets Harbour. Chauncey reached his destination on 6 October, having seen first-hand the dreadful condition of the roads and the transportation delays on the Mohawk. While these impediments caused him to despair about being able to meet the enemy before the navigation season ended, Chauncey was pleased with the industry demonstrated at Sackets by Woolsey and Eckford. Barracks for sailors, marines and soldiers were under construction, five schooners lay within the protective arm of Navy Point being transformed into warships, and the keel of a twenty-four-gun corvette was already in place and sprouting frames.

By 12 October the first wagonloads of materiel arrived at Sackets and within a week groups of sailors began marching into the village, but the long guns needed to outfit the converted lakers were delayed.[19] Impatiently, Chauncey embarked in the *Julia* for Oswego on 18 October in the hope of expediting the delivery of the ordnance. There he was delighted to find four more schooners that would meet his needs and he quickly bought them, the bill for all nine former merchantmen, including their refit, rising to $45,499.25.[20] While some of the provisions had already descended the Oswego River, Chauncey had to wait until 24 October before the first of the guns arrived and were loaded aboard one of the newly-purchased schooners for the trip to Sackets. The trickle of provisions and ordnance soon turned into a steady stream, the number of vessels at Sackets Harbour increasing in number and taking on the appearance of men of war.

As the finishing touches were being put to his squadron, Commodore Chauncey encountered his British adversaries for the first time. Sentries on Horse Island, about a mile west of Fort Tompkins, spotted a schooner snooping around Henderson Harbour on 2 November. Fearful that the enemy might snap up one of his heavily burdened craft coasting down from Oswego, Chauncey set sail in the *Oneida* to cut off the intruder. Night fell, bringing with it squalls of rain, and when the sun cleared the air the next morning the commodore found himself half a dozen miles southwest of Kingston with three British vessels at anchor five miles farther to the southwest. A breeze was blowing from that direction, giving the British the advantage of the weather gauge. Chauncey immediately surmised that the enemy would sail down to engage him so he cleared the brig for action and began to take evasive manoeuvres. To his amazement, the three vessels, which he assumed were the *Royal George*, the *Prince Regent* and the *Duke of Gloucester,* continued to tug at their anchors, indifferent to his presence. Cautiously, Chauncey skirted between the enemy and the shoals at the western tip of Wolfe Island and crept toward Sackets. The conduct of the British mystified the commodore, who wrote to Secretary Hamilton: "I can only account for such strange conduct by seeing us at daylight in the morning stretching out ... from Kingston Harbor, he must have supposed us one of his own Vessels."[21] Chauncey was being too kind because there was no other vessel on Lake Ontario with the unmistakable profile of the *Oneida*. Whether due to a shortage of men, restrictive orders, or a lack of the energy and courage that their critics claimed they wanted, the officers of the Provincial Marine once more demonstrated their inability to handle their warships properly.

By 8 November Chauncey believed his squadron was strong enough to challenge the enemy.[22] The *Oneida's* armament had been increased to eighteen guns by the addition of either two more 24-pdr. carronades or a pair of long 12-pdr. guns that could provide some long-range bark to the bite of the carronades. The schooners, namely the *Hamilton, Governor Tompkins, Conquest, Growler, Julia* and *Pert,* had been equipped with an assortment of long guns and carronades, and of the original 700 men sent from New York, about 400 sea-

men and fifty marines had been distributed among the vessels – the others having been assigned to work at Sackets, at Oswego with Woolsey or at Black Rock
with Lieutenant Samuel Angus. Since his arrival on the lake, Isaac Chauncey
had not had an opportunity to reconnoitre the enemy in any detail or to hire
spies to obtain reliable information about the strength of the British squadron.
He had had a good look at three of his opponents, but he relied mainly upon
word of mouth when he wrote to Hamilton and Tompkins that he expected to
face six armed vessels carrying 106 guns and 880 men. In spite of these unfavourable odds, Chauncey sought to intercept part of the Provincial Marine
squadron and, as he mentioned to Tompkins, he hoped "before this month is
passed to be able to give you some account of the royal family upon this
Lake."[23]

At the commodore's bidding, the signal to "make sail" raced up a halliard on
the *Oneida.* The schooners slowly gained momentum, taking their places in
line behind the brig as it led them out of Black River Bay and west past the
shoals of Stony and Galloo Islands. Aboard the *Oneida* that morning was Ned
Myers. He had been assigned to the schooner *Scourge* (formerly Woolsey's
prize, the *Lord Nelson*), which was not yet ready for duty, so he and ten of his
mates had volunteered to join the brig for the voyage. Though he was part of
the first American squadron to make sail on the inland sea, Myers's reminis-
cences mentioned little about glory. Instead, he recalled that the schooners
were "scarcely fit for the duty on which they were employed" and that the
Oneida was "a warm little brig, ... but as dull as a transport. She had been built
to cross the bars of the American harbours, and would not travel to windward."[24]

The wind was favourable, and the squadron easily weathered Galloo Island
and continued westward toward a pair of islands known as the Ducks, twenty-
five miles west of Sackets. The passage was slow for the sun was near setting by
the time the Ducks were reached, and the commodore ordered the squadron to
anchor in the good holding ground off the main island, which would become a
regular station for American ships.

Early the next morning, 9 November, the squadron weighed anchor and began another slow voyage toward the spot where Chauncey intended to wait for
his quarry. This was a set of islands known as the False Ducks, a further seven
miles west and just off the southeast tip of the Prince Edward Peninsula. There
was no need for the Americans to await the British that day, for scarcely had the
enemy shore come into view when the *Royal George* was sighted making for
Kingston. Chauncey ordered a chase, but the wind was light and progress was
slow, the *George* maintaining a lead that even made shots from the 24- and 32-

pdr. long guns in the schooners impractical. Perhaps fearing that he might be cut off if he laid a course that would allow him to pass the eastern end of Amherst Island, Master and Commander Earl abruptly changed course and bore due north through the Upper Gap between the western end of Amherst Island and Indian Point on the Prince Edward Peninsula. Then he turned northeast to navigate the North Channel of the Bay of Quinte, heading toward Kingston. By this time darkness had fallen, and the weary eyes in Chauncey's squadron lost sight of the ship.

Although Chauncey's report to the Navy Department did not indicate how the night was spent, it is likely that the Americans anchored in the channel rather than risk proceeding in unknown waters. They had come into plain view

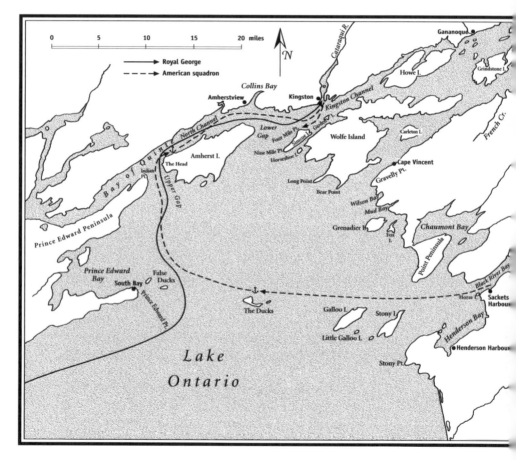

Squadron courses, 8, 9 and 10 November 1812. The sketchy details in Commodore Chauncey's report to Secretary Hamilton indicated this as the probable route of the American squadron as it chased the *Royal George* into Kingston.

Pursuit of the *Royal George*, 10 November 1812. Lieutenant Colonel Vincent reported that Commander Hugh Earl of the Provincial Marine had decided the American force was too strong for him to make a stand against it and so fled for Kingston, suffering damage to his rigging and receiving at least one 32-pdr. shot in the *Royal George's* hull. (By Owen Staples, courtesy of the Toronto Reference Library, T-15239)

of the locals, and word quickly spread down the shore that an invasion was imminent. The garrison at Kingston was alerted, and the militia hurriedly assembled, awaiting their deployment.

The squadron was in motion with the first light of dawn, 10 November 1812, inching northeastward through the channel. The village of Amherstview became visible and drew the commodore's attention. Through his telescope he examined a schooner lying beside a quay at the village and ordered Lieutenant Joseph Macpherson in the *Hamilton* to seize the vessel as a prize. Macpherson made for the village and captured the schooner *Two Brothers* without a struggle, confiscating its rigging, sails and other gear before setting it ablaze.

As the squadron left the North Channel, lookouts in the tops of the *Oneida* spotted the *Royal George* at anchor five miles to the east in the Kingston Channel. A new chase began, but this one was even slower than the previous day's because the wind fell away to barely a breeze, requiring every scrap of canvas to be set as the pursuit stretched toward Kingston Harbour. The intimidating spectacle was watched by all eyes along the shore, where preparations had been made to meet the enemy. "Persons of every age flocked into town from every quarter, eager to repulse the invaders from our peaceful shores," reported the *Quebec Mercury*.[25] Lieutenant Colonel John Vincent of the 49th Foot was the officer in command at Kingston and had at his disposal during this period 459 regulars and about 400 militia. In answer to the call to arms, 230 more citizens volunteered their services in the batteries and in the ranks being formed to oppose a landing. Through the morning and into the afternoon they stood at their posts watching the *George* as it crept into Kingston Harbour, fearful that the enemy's long-range shots might suddenly bring it up short.

The firing had started as the squadron passed Collins Bay, where a single British gunboat growled at the enemy. A little farther on the eager crew of a field gun took aim at the Americans from its vantage on Everett's Point and prompted them to give the shore a wider berth. The *Conquest*, Lieutenant Jesse Elliott, had taken the lead, firing round shot from its 32-pdr. and 24-pdr. in turn, hoping to disable the *George*. Close after it came the *Julia*, *Pert* and *Growler*, firing as their guns could bear, with the *Oneida* and *Hamilton* trailing and the *Governor Tompkins* so far back that it failed to get into the action. Despite their cannonade, the Americans were unable to damage the corvette sufficiently to allow them to catch up to it, and Earl finally came to anchor in the harbour around 3:00 p.m., more or less unscathed.

At this time the batteries on Points Murney, Mississauga and Frederick began to hurl their 9-pdr. shot at the enemy while the *Royal George* unleashed a broadside from its 32-pdr. carronades. This defence did not deter Elliott, who sailed on into the crossfire, supported by the other schooners. The *Oneida* entered the fray at about 3:20, drawing much fire from the British guns. Chauncey hoisted the signal for his gunboats to engage the enemy closely and the exchange became more intense. It stayed that way until 4:00, during which time a man was killed aboard the brig, a shot passed through the magazine of the *Growler* and the *Pert's* long gun burst, seriously wounding the schooner's commander, Sailing Master Robert Arundel. Ned Myers was busily employed, as he recalled: "The firing was sharp on both sides, ... I was stationed at a gun as her second captain, and was too busy to see much; but I know we kept our piece speaking as fast as we could, for a good bit."[26]

The fervour of the American attack convinced Earl that they intended to board his ship, so he ordered his men to slip the anchor about 4:00, and the *George* gradually drifted deeper into the harbour and closer to the protection of the shore. This manoeuvre, combined with the falling dark, an adverse change in the wind direction and the refusal of his pilots to approach any closer to the shore, led Chauncey to call off the fight and retreat with his schooners to an anchorage off Four Mile Point on Simcoe Island, four miles southwest of Kingston Harbour. There they spent a stormy night, attentive for signs of a small-boat attack, and licking their wounds. Eight men had been injured in the battle and two killed, one aboard *Oneida* and Sailing Master Arundel, who, in a dazed state, had been knocked overboard and drowned when the *Pert's* main boom swept across the quarterdeck as the schooner tacked its way out of the harbour. Some profit had been gained, however, for the British merchantman *Mary Hatt* unwittingly sailed into Kingston just as Chauncey was retreating, and Sailing Master Mervine Mix in the *Growler* had captured it, the squadron's second prize. At Kingston Lieutenant Colonel Vincent reported only one man killed aboard the *George,* which had received little material damage apart from its rigging being somewhat cut up.

When morning dawned, the lake was in a turmoil. Chauncey wanted to renew his attack on the British corvette, but fearing the turn in the weather, he ordered his schooners to follow him out to open water. Against a rising wind out of the west, the American squadron beat its way onto the lake, where around 10:00 a.m., 11 November, they spotted the schooner *Governor Simcoe* heading for Kingston. Another pursuit began, with some American shots striking home. James Richardson, senior, father of the young Provincial Marine lieutenant aboard the *Earl of Moira,* captained the *Simcoe.* He knew those waters well and evaded his pursuers by running his vessel so close to shore that the *Simcoe* scraped over a shoal and sank shortly after tying up to a wharf.

Chauncey's squadron remained off the Ducks until driven by a gale to find safety at Sackets late on 12 November. The next morning the *Growler* sailed in, escorting not just the *Mary Hatt,* but another prize, the sloop *Elizabeth.* When the weather had become too bad early on 11 November for Mix to follow Chauncey onto the lake, the commodore had instructed him to sail down the Kingston Channel and round the eastern end of Wolfe Island. Mix managed this and was on his way for a rendezvous at the Ducks when he perceived the *Elizabeth* in the distance under escort of the *Earl of Moira.* Unperturbed by the British ship's presence, Mix detained the *Elizabeth,* put a few hands aboard and sailed for Sackets.

When Chauncey heard this story, he departed immediately with the squadron in hopes of intercepting the *Moira,* but the weather worsened with squalls of snow and a gale that almost cast the brig and gunboats onto the Galloo shoals. The commodore persisted in his quest, perhaps trying to outdo his

Kingston, 1812. During the engagement with Chauncey on 10 November 1812, Commander Earl anchored the *Royal George* between Points Mississauga and Frederick, but, as the Americans pressed their attack, he slipped his anchor and drifted deeper into the harbour. (Based on chart of Kingston town and harbour, 1794, courtesy of the National Archives of Canada, NAC-19459)

young sailing master, and sighted Kingston Harbour on 14 November. By then, though, conditions had become too threatening, as Chauncey described to the navy secretary: "The ice making so fast upon the Slides of our Carronades that we could not have made use of them, I thought it prudent to make a Port."[27]

Following the engagement at Kingston, Chauncey proudly reported to Hamilton that he had secured "command of The Lake and that we can transport Troops and Stores to any part of it without any risk of an attack from the Enemy."[28] He had chased his main opponent off the lake, and after the *Moira* escaped his grasp, no other British shipping was seen in the waters around Kingston. News of the marauding Americans spread to York, where the *Prince Regent* and the *Duke of Gloucester* remained at anchor to spend the winter. Chauncey planned to ferry naval supplies to Fort Niagara for employment at Black Rock and he also wrote to Dearborn and Brigadier General Jacob Brown, in command of the local militia, to inform them that he was ready, at their request, to embark troops for raids against the British.[29] Three more former merchantmen, the *Scourge, Ontario* and *Fair American,* had been converted and were ready for action, and Chauncey considered making a landing at Kingston to destroy the vessels there or running down the St. Lawrence to attack Prescott. None of these plans came to fruition, however, for the weather worsened and the schooners he sent to patrol around the Ducks could not keep their station with safety. By the end of November Chauncey conceded that the navigation season was over and the time had come to batten down his squadron in winter moorings at Sackets.[30]

Pursuit of the *Governor Simcoe*, 11 November 1812. The *Quebec Mercury* noted that Chauncey's vessels fired more than fifty shots at the *Simcoe*, one of which holed the schooner, causing it to sink. It was also said that Captain Richardson had stove in his vessel's bottom by running over a shoal at the mouth of Kingston Harbour. (Watercolour, courtesy of the New York State Office of Parks, Recreation and Historic Preservation, Sackets Harbor State Historic Site)

Chase of the British schooner Simcoe by the U.S. Sch: Hamilton, Geo. Tompkins, and Julia

Although he had not destroyed the Provincial Marine, Commodore Chauncey had won control of Lake Ontario within eleven weeks of receiving his orders from Washington. His success was crowned on 26 November when the new corvette slid into the harbour at Sackets, just forty-five days after Henry Eckford had laid it down.[31] It was 112 feet long on the keel, 32½ feet abeam and would mount twenty-four 32-pdr. carronades, making the ship bigger and stronger than the *Royal George.* Named the *Madison* as a fitting opponent for the "royal family" on the other side, the corvette was one of only two warships launched by the U.S. Navy that year.

Chauncey's accomplishments were the only bright spots in an otherwise disastrous American campaign on the northern border in 1812. His administrative talents and the devotion to duty demonstrated by his command had started a new momentum upon which a more carefully planned operation against Canada could be made in the spring of 1813.

"Our Prospects Are Far … from Flattering"[1]

WINTER PROJECTS: DECEMBER 1812–MARCH 1813

*C*aptain James Brock, paymaster of the 49th Regiment of Foot, had the misfortune to be on the sloop *Elizabeth* en route from York to Kingston when the US Schooner *Growler* seized it from under the nose of a lackadaisical *Earl of Moira* on 13 November. Brock met Chauncey and found him "very communicative and full of confidence in his strength."[2] The Americans wrongly concluded that Brock was a relative (a brother, one observer noted) of Isaac Brock and had been conveying the general's personal effects to Quebec. They also claimed the captain revealed that 500 men of the 49th Foot were stationed at Kingston as well as other regular units and a body of militia – Brock later wrote a letter to the *Kingston Gazette* to deny the American stories. Bravado and gentility were the traits of honourable men, and when Lieutenant Colonel John Vincent politely requested, via a note carried under a white flag to Sackets, that Brock be returned to his friends, Chauncey generously complied. On 17 November the British officer sailed to Kingston on parole until a formal exchange could be negotiated.

Shortly after landing, Brock informed Vincent about what he had seen at Sackets Harbour, a "frigate" standing in the dockyard about to be launched with plans made to lay another keel as soon as the ship was in the water. Shipwrights crowded the yard, and seamen swarmed over the fleet of converted merchantmen. Two batteries protected the shipping, Fort Tompkins and the lately erected Fort Volunteer, situated just east of the village to cover the enclosed anchorage from the south shore. A hundred marines and nearly a thousand militia guarded the works, with rumour of reinforcements on the way.

Major General Sir Roger Hale Sheaffe, British Army (1763-1851). Commencing his military career in 1778, Sheaffe rose to the rank of lieutenant colonel in the 49th Foot (junior to Brock) twenty years later. He advanced to major general in June 1811 and was created a baronet of Great Britain in January 1813 in honour of his victory at Queenston Heights. (Courtesy of the National Archives of Canada, C-111307)

Vincent recorded Brock's impressions and dispatched them immediately to the new commander-in-chief in Upper Canada, Major General Roger Hale Sheaffe.

Following Brock's death at Queenston Heights, Sheaffe received command of the armed forces in the upper province and the position of head administrator of the government. At forty-nine years of age, Sheaffe had been in the British army since 1778 and had served more than twenty years in British North America.[3] Though he had orchestrated the victory at Queenston efficiently, Sheaffe lacked Brock's charismatic personality and was poorly regarded by many of his peers. When Vincent's letter arrived at his headquarters in the town of Niagara, the general was already puzzling over how to prepare for the impending American offensive in the spring. Opinions on the matter had been expressed to him by various individuals and by a special committee of the legislature that had observed: "By Land our success has exceeded our hopes – not so is our Warfare on the Lakes ... [and] to strengthen our Marine in the Lakes, is absolutely necessary, under existing circumstances; for the Defense and preservation of this Province."[4] With the information provided by James Brock at hand, Sheaffe wrote to Sir George Prevost on 23 November 1812, admitting that he hoped inclement weather would prevent the Americans from making another attack before winter set in. If the province survived into the new year, he gloomily forecast, only "exertions of the most energetic kind" would forestall defeat in the spring.[5]

Prevost had already addressed the state of the naval force on the lakes, send-ing Captain Andrew Gray to Upper Canada to assess the Provincial Marine and report on how it could be strengthened during the winter. Gray knew that the Marine was a weak link, but what he discovered at Kingston went beyond his worst fears. He found Master and Commander Hugh Earl and his officers "des-titute of all energy and spirit and are sunk into contempt in the eyes of all who know them."[6] The *Royal George* and the *Moira* were anchored in Navy Bay, their crews reduced to a couple of dozen seamen who could perform their duties. The batteries at Kingston possessed no more than eight small pieces of ord-nance, while the blockhouse that had been erected atop Point Henry covered the anchorage with only two long guns, a 9-pdr. and 6-pdr.

One of Gray's first recommendations was "to recover at a blow what we have lost" by attacking Sackets Harbour.[7] A unit from Montreal, either the 8th Foot, numbering 634 officers and men, or the 5th Battalion of Embodied Militia (567 effectives), could be marched to Kingston around the end of January, Gray sug-gested, where they would be trained in the use of snowshoes to facilitate the overland expedition. Gray assumed that three or four small field pieces, drawn on sleighs, would be capable of battering down any blockhouses in the way and, knowing Prevost's rigid policy about protecting the lower province first, he as-serted that the forces required from Montreal would not be absent longer than a month.

In later reports Gray tempered his views of the winter campaign as fears nagged him about the enemy reinforcing Sackets with men and defensive works. After voicing these concerns to Prevost in a despatch dated 11 December, Gray made two new recommendations, the first being that steps be taken to protect the vessels at Kingston and York against the kind of attack he had pro-posed. He advised that five or six guns (18- or 12-pdrs.) be transported from Quebec to each place along with gunners to handle them. To emphasize the need for defensive improvements, Gray added that "at Kingston there is but lit-tle protection afforded the vessels from the works on shore. Here [York] there is none."[8]

Gray's second suggestion was that an attempt be made to match the con-struction going on at Sackets Harbour by building two vessels on Lake Ontario, a ship at Kingston similar to the *Royal George* (with a second vessel of this type built at Amherstburg) and a thirty-gun frigate at York. Constructed of fir or whatever wood was available, they would be finished in time to receive their armament, provisions and crew in the spring. He estimated that up to sixty ad-ditional carpenters would be required for the work and, confident that this scheme would win approval, Gray asked John Dennis, the Provincial Marine's master shipwright, and former Provincial Marine commander John Steel to compile a list of materials that would be needed.

Sheaffe approved Gray's plan when they met at Fort George on 14 December[9] and wrote Prevost two days later to support the idea of building ships at York and Kingston and reiterate the urgency of having additional shore batteries mounted at each place. Sheaffe also suggested that gunboats be built if resources were available as he knew that there were going to be heavy demands for men and materiel during the winter, making the arrival of help from the Royal Navy in the spring all the more critical. Although Prevost's endorsement of these various recommendations was needed, Sheaffe did not wait for it, but instead sent Gray back to York immediately to begin the preparation of a yard big enough to build the thirty-gun frigate and then on to Kingston to start work there.

Prevost quickly approved the construction of two new ships on Lake Ontario and one on Lake Erie. To design the former vessels and superintend the projects he selected Thomas Plucknett, reputedly "an experienced officer in the Kings Naval Yards," and dispatched him and 120 shipwrights to Upper Canada.[10] Thirty-four seamen were also on the road to make up for the shortage at Kingston, and the Quartermaster General's Department had been ordered to find more. A company of the 49th Foot, plus a detachment of artillery, were ordered to march from Kingston to reinforce the garrison at York, their place being taken by a company of the Glengarry Light Infantry Fencible Regiment and regular gunners from Montreal. Four 18-pdr. long guns and four 12s would be transported from Quebec and Montreal as soon as arrangements could be made.

Prevost did not favour Gray's initial suggestion about an attack against Sackets Harbour, writing, "It will require some consideration before I can determine whether under all circumstances it would be proper to adopt it." He acknowledged that "the object is certainly highly important but whether it can be effected must depend upon the Force I shall have at my disposal at the period when you think it can be accomplished and the movements of the Enemy on our Frontiers."[11]

Prevost's hesitation made sense. Gray had proposed moving more than a thousand men across unfamiliar terrain in the dead of winter to fight an enemy that might have already managed to fortify himself against such an attack. At best, it would have been a risky business, but maybe worth the significant advantage to be gained by the destruction of Chauncey's Lake Ontario naval establishment. Prevost's concern about the strength of his force was harder to justify. Encamped in Lower Canada in late December 1812 were 6,320 regular

Commander Robert Barclay, RN (1785-1837). Barclay went to sea as a midshipman in 1798, serving off the coast of France and in the Mediterranean Sea until passing his lieutenancy exam in 1804. He was in HMS *Swiftsure* at the Battle of Trafalgar in 1805 and two years later received a wound in action against a French convoy that cost him his left arm. (Courtesy of the Toronto Reference Library, T-15259)

troops while the frontier of Upper Canada was defended by only 2,692 officers and men.[12] The detachment of 500 men from Montreal would have still left 1,300 men (including elements of two militia battalions) at that post, but Prevost's opinion about defending Lower Canada above all was resolute.

Although he was not much of a risk taker, Prevost demonstrated skill and energy in improving the defence of Canada. Having already written several requests to the home government for help from the Royal Navy, Prevost decided to seek assistance in a different direction. On 18 December he addressed a letter stating his situation and needs to Sir John Borlase Warren, Admiral of the Blue, who commanded both the North American station at Halifax and the West Indies station.[13] Two months went by before the despatch reached HMS *San Domingo* flying Warren's flag in his winter anchorage at Bermuda, but it received a prompt response. The admiral summoned three lieutenants who had been awaiting promotion (Robert Barclay, Robert Finnis and Daniel Pring) and advanced them to the rank of commander so that they could assume charge of Prevost's new ships. Next, Warren promoted six midshipmen to lieutenants and ordered them to take passage with the commanders, under Barclay as senior officer, for Halifax. From there they would proceed to Saint John, New Brunswick, and travel overland to Quebec rather than waiting until ships could navigate the ice-blocked Gulf of St. Lawrence. With the officers would go a pair of naval gunners, who would help prepare a shipment at Halifax of thirty 32-pdr.

carronades destined for the lakes, along with sails and rigging, as soon as the season would permit.

Warren reported these actions to the Admiralty and advised that an old frigate of fifty or sixty guns should be sent to Quebec manned by a crew of 550 and loaded with ordnance, provisions and other naval necessities. After arriving as early as possible in May, 350 of the men would travel inland to crew the warships on the lakes. At their head, Warren suggested, should be an "Intelligent, Steady, Active Master and Commander as Commodore."[14] He also recollected that during the Seven Years War and the Revolutionary War, naval officers had been encouraged to serve in the unpopular frontier regions with the enticements of extra pay and quick promotion.

Like-minded individuals in London had already reached similar conclusions. Prevost's pleas for reinforcements, which took between six and eight weeks to cross the ocean, had been addressed to his immediate superior, Henry Bathurst, the third Earl of Bathurst, Secretary for War and the Colonies. Bathurst presented Prevost's concerns during cabinet meetings convened by Prime Minister Robert Banks Jenkinson, Lord Liverpool. In his cabinet sat two veteran statesmen who, along with Bathurst, were chiefly concerned with events abroad: Robert Stewart, Viscount Castlereagh, the Secretary of State for Foreign Affairs, and Robert Saunders Dundas, the second Viscount Melville, First Lord of the Admiralty. These gentlemen discussed the situation in Canada and made decisions about the resources that could be spared from the war against Bonaparte. As a matter of protocol, the prime minister also consulted the Prince Regent, King George III's first son, George, the Prince of Wales, who was acting in his father's stead owing to the monarch's current derangement.

On 12 December 1812 Bathurst announced to Prevost that the 13th and 98th Foot and the 2nd Battalion of the 41st Foot would be convoyed to Bermuda and then to the St. Lawrence in the spring. Simultaneously, 200 seamen and an appropriate number of officers from the Royal Navy would be detached for the lake service. Out of consideration for the demands of the North American climate, the men would be selected from the flotilla that had just returned from duty in the Baltic Sea.

Shortly after these decisions were made a letter reached Bathurst written by Lieutenant Colonel Sir Howard Douglas, on the staff of the Royal Military College at Sandhurst. He had just returned from a tour of duty with Wellington in Spain and, hearing of the progress of the American war, offered Bathurst the insights he had gained while serving in Canada during the 1790s. Douglas echoed Prevost's insistence that "the possession of the upper and the protection of the lower province depend upon our maintaining a decided superiority on Lake Ontario." "Regularly bred naval officers" were necessary for the task, Douglas argued, and he recommended that components for warships be assembled in England and shipped across the Atlantic as had been done during the Revolutionary War.[15] Taking these views into consideration along with news in another despatch from Prevost about Chauncey's successes on Lake Ontario, Lord Bathurst obtained cabinet approval to increase the Great Lakes detachment to 300 men and wrote to Prevost on 13 January 1813 to inform him of the change.

Two months later the troopship *Woolwich* was about to depart from England with the naval detachment, which had grown to more than 400 in number. Further consultations among Liverpool's chief ministers, prompted perhaps by Admiral Warren's advice, had led to the addition of more men. Melville and the other lords of the Admiralty had assigned officers and men for the mission, and in conjunction with their colleagues at the Navy Board, had collected the ordnance, rigging, fittings and myriad other paraphernalia they speculated would be needed on the lakes.[16] To lead the expedition they had selected Sir James Lucas Yeo, a thirty-year-old post captain who had been at sea for more than half his life and had a reputation for intelligence and zeal.

While these decisions were being made abroad, trouble brewed in Upper Canada, with the first target of criticism being the Commissariat Department of the army. There were insufficient supplies of clothing, shoes, blankets and the material from which to make them on the spot. Forage for the artillery horses was lacking, firewood was scarce and there was barely enough coin in the military purse to buy essentials from local sources. Though small amounts of cash arrived, they did little to assuage the militia, who were doubly miserable for having been on duty throughout the autumn to the neglect of their farms and families; as a result, most of the units were sent home by mid-December. The man upon whose head a large portion of the blame was placed for failing to anticipate needs in Upper Canada was Deputy Commissary General Edward Couche. He and the other officers in the commissariat paid dearly for the fact that, before the war, the department had been undermanned and ill-prepared to cope with emergencies. Harangued by commanders at every post, Couche and his subordinates were forced to improvise a delivery system, but few who waited impatiently at the bitter end of the supply line had compassion for Couche's predicament. One of them, Lieutenant Colonel Robert Nichol, driven "crazy" by his assignment to distribute supplies in Upper Canada, was even moved to exclaim, "Couche should be hanged."[17]

A more reasoned explanation for the deficiencies came from the quill of Major Thomas Evans, 8th Foot, who had been the brigade major at Fort George since the outset of the war. Intimately familiar with the inner workings of the army and its problems, he pointed an accusatory finger at a most unlikely figure, Isaac Brock. To a confidant, Evans revealed that before the commencement of hostilities, the commissariat, as well as the militia and the barracks department, had been "without any system or arrangement whatever."[18] The people in charge of them were known to be uninformed and lazy and their weaknesses had been pointed out to Brock, but his "high spirit would never descend to particulars," asserted Evans, "trifles I may say in the abstract but ultimately essentials." Evans described how much of the groundwork required to support operations, such as Brock's hurried trip to Amherstburg and assault on Detroit in August 1812, had been arranged behind the scenes and in spite of the heel-dragging officials by individuals like Lieutenant Colonel Christopher Myers, 70th Foot, whom Evans considered a dedicated officer. Now the system was nearly out of control, and Evans feared that the blame would fall on Sheaffe's head. Greatly revered and universally mourned, Brock was above condemnation, but Sheaffe, a lesser man in many people's eyes, was a perfect target for invective.

As Evans feared, some people did take aim at Sheaffe, not only because of the disorder in the military, but because a wave of indignation had arisen after the successful repulse of an American invasion attempt between Chippawa and Fort Erie late in November. The commander of the British forces in that district, Lieutenant Colonel Cecil Bisshopp, whose conduct Sheaffe lauded in despatches, had requested reinforcements at Fort Erie to guard against further aggressions, but Sheaffe preferred instead to maintain a strong position at Chippawa and advised Bisshopp to consider retreating there if the Americans came again. Insulted by such a suggestion, the colonel and his closest officers took it to imply that they could not fight back against the invaders. When a rumour spread that Sheaffe had jokingly commented that allowing the Americans to have Fort Erie for a spell might satisfy their lust for victory, hackles rose on the necks of Bisshopp and his friends. They spread their disapproval of Sheaffe and by mid-December the general's behavior was being chastised throughout the province.[19]

Captain Andrew Gray of the Quartermaster General's Department was at the town of Niagara on Provincial Marine business at this time and heard the stories about Sheaffe. When he returned to York he publicly repeated accusations about the general's character and competence, suggesting that when Prevost heard about the matter Sheaffe was sure to be recalled. Gray openly repeated his slander in Kingston, unaware that the general might still possess a

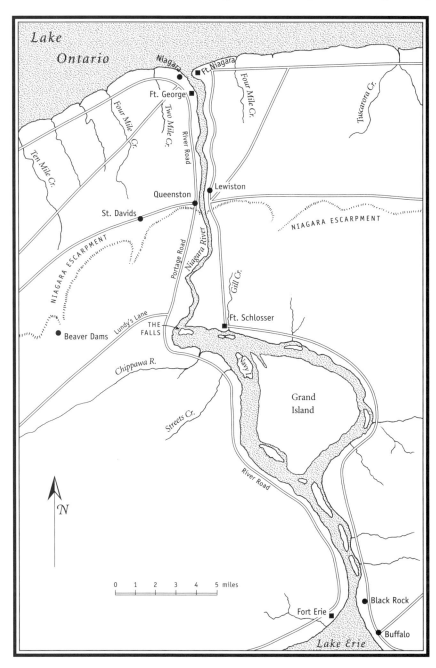

The Niagara Frontier, winter of 1812-1813. During the winter months the opposing sides held their ground at their posts along the course of the Niagara River. Black Rock's location across from Fort Erie made it an unfavourable place for Commodore Chauncey to establish a base for the squadron he wanted to develop on Lake Erie.

loyal friend or two. Such friends, William Powell, a leading citizen at York, and Lieutenant Colonel John Vincent at Kingston, brought the subject to Sheaffe's attention through his senior officers, Evans, Myers and Major John Glegg.[20] Informed about what was being said of him, the general protested directly to Prevost, enclosing pertinent correspondence.

In short order Gray received a stern reprimand from Prevost's adjutant general, Colonel Edward Baynes, but defended himself by denying that he had said anything personally critical about Sheaffe. The report of his comments at York, Gray claimed, had been made by someone who "wished to make me appear culpable in the eyes of Sir George." "I merely request," he wrote to Baynes, "you will not believe that I am quite so great a fool, as my enemies wish to make me appear."[21]

The controversy passed, but it had added to the pressure that Sheaffe shouldered as commander-in-chief in Upper Canada. Major John Glegg perceived "an irresistible melancholy on his mind, which is very distressing."[22] As January wore on, the general's health failed and he took to his bed, his aides actually fearing for his life.

In January 1813 another scandalous situation developed, this time at York, where it was hoped the headquarters for the Provincial Marine would eventually stand. The militia had been chopping timber since December for the new ship; barracks and workshops had been erected for the artificers; and seventy-eight of the shipwrights from Quebec had made their way to town. In December Captain Gray, John Dennis and Lieutenant William Fish, captain of the schooner *Prince Regent*, had chosen as the site where the corvette should be built a spot about half a mile east of the harbour's mouth, although the water was not deep enough at that point to launch the ship. To solve the depth problem, the three men had proposed the construction of a massive wharf that would extend like an inclined plane from the bank on the shore to deep water. The structure would measure 800 feet long, 100 feet wide and stand 25 feet tall at the embankment. The shipbuilders would construct the frigate, which was expected to be about 120 feet long and 35 feet abeam, on the wharf so that it could be launched into deep water when they were finished.

When Thomas Plucknett arrived at York, around 15 January, and saw what was intended, he stopped the work at once and made his own survey of the shoreline. "I am of Opinion," he later wrote, "that after an immense expense of money and the time that such a Wharf would take, it would be highly imprudent and dangerous to build the Ship on it."[23] Finding a better location about a quarter mile up the harbour, he set his labourers to digging out the embankment to create a more conventional building site. He had not advanced far when a despatch arrived from Gray at Kingston telling the superintendent that he must use the original location, whereupon Plucknett called a halt to the project and announced his intention to return to Quebec. Lieutenant Colonel Ralph Bruyeres, a Royal Engineer who had been inspecting fortifications in the province, arrived at York on 23 January before Plucknett could leave and found two building sites cleared, with wood stockpiled at each, while shipwrights and labourers sat idle. After calling upon the superintendent and hearing his vow that he would not "risk his reputation in building a ship on so uncertain a fabric (where the whole might in an instant fall to the ground)," Bruyeres convinced Plucknett to go with him to Niagara to consult with Sheaffe.[24]

At the town of Niagara the two men met with Lieutenant Colonel Christopher Myers, who, as deputy quartermaster general, oversaw Provincial Marine affairs in that region. Myers reported the dispute to the still-ailing general, and Sheaffe countermanded Gray's order to build on the site he had chosen, urging Plucknett to return to York and do what he thought best. Much appeased, the superintendent departed with the promise that the keel would be laid quickly and the project pushed ahead. Myers and Bruyeres were not completely comfortable with the arrangement. They noted that Plucknett had arrived without papers specifying his duties and place in the command hierarchy. "If he is a person of well known information and practical experience in such matters," wrote Myers to Prevost's military secretary, Lieutenant Noah Freer, Canadian Fencibles, it would be advisable that his authority be spelled out clearly so that further confusion would not occur.[25]

About ten days later Myers and Bruyeres journeyed to York to view the state of progress, only to be dismayed at the little that had been accomplished in the shipyard. The keel was down and some elements of the frames were being assembled, but materials lay scattered about in disorder, and the shipwrights seemed to be frittering their time away. Called upon to explain his plans and to present the proper paperwork, Plucknett was evasive, leaving Myers and Bruyeres to form the most depressing conclusions. "Whether Mr. Plucknett is a regular professional ship builder or not, it is not in my power to determine," reported Myers to Freer on 9 February, "but that he wants system and arrangement, I feel no hesitation in asserting."[26] Bruyeres seconded his opinion, "[Plucknett] appears to me to want method to keep his workmen employed to the best advantage."[27] Both men believed that a person was needed at York who understood how to direct the complicated undertaking involved in building a ship. That man was already present in the person of John Dennis, who had been designing and building ships for the government since 1799, including most of the warships on Lake Ontario, but he was employed as a glorified foreman on

Ordnance for the new ship at Kingston. This requisition for ordnance for the corvette at Kingston reveals that the ship (HMS *Wolfe*) was designed to carry its long guns facing forward and astern through bridle ports, gun ports cut in the bow and stern. There being no facility for casting ordnance in British North America, all guns and carronades had to be sent from Britain or the naval stores depot at Halifax. (Courtesy of the National Archives of Canada, C-138973)

Iron work for the new ships at Kingston and York. Since there was no iron foundry in Upper Canada before the war, all iron fittings had to be acquired in Lower Canada or stripped from shipping at Quebec. (Courtesy of the National Archives of Canada, C-138972) the project. In sweeping the Marine Department clean, Prevost and his advisors had pushed Dennis aside to allow new blood, namely Plucknett, to take over. The decision was a disastrous one, although it was not rescinded, in spite of the dire reports by Myers and Bruyeres, and Plucknett remained at York until the spring, bungling the construction of the ship that was supposed to match the might of the Americans and which was soon named the *Sir Isaac Brock* in honour of the hero of Upper Canada.

Evidence of another poor decision made by the military heads surfaced during the winter. Operating two separate shipyards (and a third at Amherstburg) at great distances from the storehouses of Quebec was virtually unsupportable and one symptom of the problem was a shortage of skilled labour at the outposts. During the third week of January Gray informed Prevost that up to ten sailmakers and someone to supervise them were needed in the province, as was a master rigger at each shipyard. Furthermore, Gray admitted to Prevost that not only was there an inadequate supply of naval ordnance in Canada for the two ships, but its delivery to York was going to be a problem.[28] The transport service was already greatly strained from having to move guns, rigging, sails, anchors and such to Kingston, let alone another 150 miles along winter roads that would break up late in February. Gray's solution was to hurry up the work at Kingston so that, as soon as the ice cleared, a supply convoy could sail to York with the essentials, though he failed to mention to Prevost that the disappearance of ice would also set Chauncey's powerful squadron free to attack the shipping or establish a blockade.

A more forthright analysis of marine arrangements in Upper Canada was offered by Bruyeres, who had been in the colonies since 1806 and had a wide knowledge of their resources. He had previously stated his low opinion of York and the idea of moving the marine establishment there, and he considered it a serious mistake to try to build one ship there and another at Kingston during the winter. Bruyeres repeated his criticisms in a report to Prevost in February. "It is much too remote and distant a Post to obtain the necessary resources to carry on any great undertaking ...," he wrote. "Nature has done very little to the position as a Military Post, or to the Harbor for the purposes of a Dock Yard; every thing must be created which will require considerable time, and Expence."[29] The thirty 32-pdr. carronades intended for the new ship would not reach York in time, Bruyeres concluded, so with Myers and Sheaffe he made arrangements to substitute twenty long guns and carronades taken from Fort George, the schooner *Prince Regent* and the shipment expected from Quebec. Despite Plucknett's assurances that the ship would be ready, the engineer had "great doubts of his success."[30]

Gray remained at Kingston, where he could watch over the progress on Point Frederick and monitor the state of Commander Hugh Earl's ships. The latter caused him even more concerns than they had in December – because when he visited the *Royal George* he found it filthy and disorganized, hardly capable of fending off an American raid; nearly an hour was needed to scale the carronades, as their vents were choked with debris and they misfired repeatedly. On the *Moira* conditions were slightly better, though Gray complained to Lieutenant Colonel Vincent that "the state of the *Moira* was *bad* and that of the *Royal George worse*."[31] In spite of the temptation to remove Earl and Lieutenant Theophilus Sampson from their positions, Gray let them be, knowing that a Royal Navy detachment was expected in the spring, at which time a "*radical reform* in the Provincial Marine" would take place.

Gray was required to relieve one individual of his authority early in February. As part of the reform of the Provincial Marine, he had hired James Morrison in Montreal to act as master shipwright in the dockyard at Kingston, but from the start Morrison showed a lack of knowledge and attention to his duties and progress on the ship was slow. Already frustrated by Plucknett's behaviour at York (and his long overdue requisitions), Gray abruptly dismissed Morrison and gave his job to Daniel Allen, the foreman of the shipwrights.[32] He then authorized an extensive overhaul of the *Moira's* rig, reducing its three masts to two, so that it would have more room on its deck to operate as a handy brig-of-war. Satisfied with the sight of Allen driving his men to raise frame after frame on the keel and the overall industry in the yard, Gray turned over its supervision to Captain J. B. Irwin, a deputy assistant in the Quartermaster General's Department, and headed for Montreal.

On 13 February Bruyeres stopped at Kingston, having completed his tour of the province. He was happy to report to Prevost that "very good progress is making here with the new Ship; also in the temporary Works of Defence."[33] This must have offered a glimmer of hope for Prevost as he pondered the dilemma-fraught conditions in Upper Canada. Preparations for the spring campaign had not begun well, but another two and a half months would pass before the ice broke up and that allowed plenty of time for a turnaround of the British fortunes.

During the first week of December 1812 Commodore Chauncey learned about preparations at Kingston when Sailing Master William Vaughan returned to Sackets Harbour in the sloop *Neptune* after taking Henry Murney, former master of the captured sloop *Elizabeth*, back to the British side. The commodore transmitted the information to Secretary Paul Hamilton with the

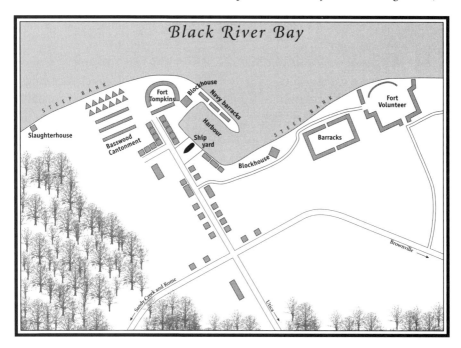

Sackets Harbour, winter of 1812-1813. The tiny village of Sackets Harbour took on the appearance of a military and naval stronghold during the winter of 1813 as Fort Tompkins was strengthened, barracks and blockhouses built and new fortifications rose on the shore east of the anchorage.

assurance that it was reliable because the details were "obtained from an officer on board of the *Royal George* whom Mr. Vaughan had known for several years and who is friendly disposed to us: therefore may be depended upon."[34] Kingston was defended by 600 men of the 49th Foot and 1,000 militia with a further 2,000 militia in the vicinity. The blockade that Chauncey's gunboats had maintained during the final, stormy weeks of November had succeeded in keeping the *George*, the *Moira* and a privately owned schooner, all of them loaded with clothing, munitions and food, from sailing to supply the garrisons on the Niagara Peninsula. They were now battened down for the winter, and the Glengarry Light Infantry, numbering about 500, had been forced to march to York. Vaughan had heard nothing about plans to attack Sackets; on the contrary, the British feared a visit from Chauncey and the military. The commodore took Vaughan's report at face value and, though relieved to find out that the British were actually worried about his offensive strength, Chauncey did not ease up on his plan to fortify Sackets. "We shall be prepared here at all events," he assured Hamilton, "to give them a warm reception if they should make any attempt upon us this winter."

The defence of the American base was now in the hands of an active and intelligent army officer, thirty-four-year-old Lieutenant Colonel Alexander Macomb of the Third Artillery Regiment. During his fourteen-year career Macomb had earned a reputation as a skilled engineer and he was eager for a chance to see action. Learning late in November that Macomb was on his way to the lake with his regiment, Chauncey wrote to express hope that they might combine in the attack on Kingston he was considering, but warned Macomb that he should hire barns near Brownville, eight miles east of the port, to house his men as there were no accommodations left at Sackets. Macomb would not be deterred and resolutely tramped into Sackets and set up his tents on 21 November, too late for the proposed attack. As snow fell and the soldiers shivered around their camp fires, their commanding officer met with Chauncey to discuss the fortification and accommodation needs at the post.

Henry Eckford had already constructed barracks, artificers shops and a mess hall for the shipwrights and work continued on a set of barracks for the marines. Forts Tompkins and Volunteer stood armed and ready, but in need of improvement. With Chauncey's approval, Macomb's men laboured through December and into the new year to erect two barracks facing the lake, one behind the other, just west of Fort Tompkins. These log structures, dubbed the "basswood cantonment," were big enough to house a thousand men and beside them were erected quarters for the officers. The soldiers put up a palisade around Fort Tompkins, expanded Fort Volunteer and added a blockhouse to it. In the enclosed harbour between the forts Chauncey moored his converted schooners in a line with the *Oneida* and the *Madison* at right angles across its ends so that their guns could oppose an attack from any direction.[35]

Chauncey was certain that his sailors could defend their vessels, but he considered the land forces too weak; combining marines and Macomb's regiment, there were 500 regular troops, augmented by about 600 serviceable militia. He asked Secretary Hamilton to convince army officials that a thousand more regulars were needed, and to strengthen his case he described how two or three thousand British might walk across the ice from Kingston to Wolfe Island to Gravelly Point, follow the shore around to Chaumont Bay and then charge across the ice of Black River Bay to Sackets. "If the Enemy by any desperate effort should succeed in obtaining possession of the Forts in this Town, the vessels must fall of course they could not be moved for the ice."[36] The commodore hoped to see the requisite reinforcements reach his base as early in the winter as possible.

The final days of November and first two weeks of December 1812 were taken up with various administrative chores. Chauncey directed Eckford to lay down the keel for a schooner that would resemble the speedy pilot boats in New York Harbour and arranged for its sails to be made by a master craftsman in that city. He ordered canvas to replace the worn sails of some of his gunboats and four more 32-pdr. carronades to complete the armament of the *Madison*. Certain that the army agent with whom he had made arrangements to feed the sailors and marines was charging too much for provisions, the commodore advertised for local farmers to sell directly to him. Chauncey contacted an agent in New York named James Heard about prize money for the crews involved in the seizure of the British merchantmen near Kingston. He answered an urgent request from John Jacob Astor, his old friend and former employer, who wanted to know what had happened to a shipment of furs, belonging to him, that had been in the British vessels captured by Lieutenant Jesse Elliott in the Upper Niagara River in October; Chauncey replied that he would trace the whereabouts of the shipment for the financier. Personnel matters wanted attention, and Chauncey granted leaves of absence to Dr. Walter Buchanan and Elliott, and summoned eight men to appear before courts martial for crimes ranging from the unofficerlike behaviour and drunkenness of Sailing Masters Joseph Gamble and John Hutton to desertion by three seamen. In dealing with these cases Chauncey demonstrated his belief in strict discipline and compassionate leniency: the three deserters were flogged while a fourth seaman was acquitted of disobedience because he had been provoked when a midshipman struck him with the flat of his sword – the midshipman was subsequently detained for future judgement.[37]

In mid-December Chauncey finally felt comfortable enough with the progress being made at Sackets Harbour to undertake his long-delayed visit to Buffalo. Before setting out he laid out clear instructions about how he wanted the establishment run during his absence. Alertness against a surprise attack was essential, and to this end the vessels were to be kept clear of snow and the guns and muskets ready for instant use. He ordered the removal and storage of the sails, rigging and upper spars of all the vessels. The lower spars of the *Madison* were to be stepped, the ship armed and manned, while carpenters completed its inner furnishings. The marines were instructed to move into their barracks and perform sentry duties, and the commanding officer of each vessel was required to muster his crew every four hours for a roll call in order to inhibit desertion.

Chauncey left the Harbour on 13 December 1812, leaving Lieutenant Melancthon Woolsey in charge until the arrival of Master Commandant James Leonard, who had been selected to command the *Madison*. Like his journey

from New York City, Chauncey's trip across the state was an arduous one because of the condition of the roads, but he was also dismayed at the deplorable
state of the army posts he passed along the way. "This frontier," he wrote to
Hamilton after he arrived at Black Rock, two miles north of Buffalo, "is left with
less protection than its importance requires from this place to Lewis Town a
distance of about 24 Miles there is not a single Sentinel."[38] Nothing had been
done to form a squadron on Lake Erie apart from collecting five merchant
schooners at the navy depot at Black Rock where Lieutenant Samuel Angus,
USN, commanded. The officer originally dispatched to achieve that goal, Jesse
Elliott, had favoured Black Rock as a site for a naval station, but Sailing Master
Daniel Dobbins, an experienced lakeman, had argued that the swift current of
the Niagara River and the British batteries at Fort Erie would make it difficult for
warships to enter the lake. He preferred Presque Isle Bay at Erie, Pennsylvania,
and was ready to build gunboats there, but lacked official authorization to begin.

Faced with the frustrations inherent in trying to organize two squadrons at
frontier posts separated by hundreds of miles of forest, swamps and rock,
Chauncey's temper got the better of him at Black Rock. As he and Angus
watched a slovenly conducted drill of a party of sailors and soldiers, "he got in a
passion and reflected on me [Angus] saying that they were in a state of D...d
insubordination."[39] Later, Chauncey contradicted one of Angus's orders, to
which the lieutenant responded by offering to resign his command. The commodore refused that request and, after more acrimonious exchanges, ordered
Angus's arrest. Given the disorder that had prevailed in the Niagara district following the failed invasions at Queenston and Fort Erie, Angus could hardly be
blamed for the poor performance of his men. Much disgruntled, Chauncey
headed for Erie, and Angus was soon re-assigned.

Arriving at Erie on 1 January 1813, Commodore Chauncey was pleased with
the knowledge and diligence demonstrated by Daniel Dobbins and approved
the construction there of four gunboats and a brig to carry twenty guns. He
headed back to Sackets and arrived on 19 January, disappointed to discover that
in his five-and-a-half-week absence the blockhouses had not been finished and
the army had not reinforced the garrison.[40] A daily routine had been established in the squadron with the men breaking ice around the vessels to form
ditches that might deter enemy boarders, working in gangs on the rigging of
the *Madison* and practising with the guns. "We had a target out on the ice," recalled Ned Myers, "and this we practised on, making ourselves rather expert
cannoneers." When away from their schooner to gather wood, Myers and the
other *Scourges* were allowed to keep an eye out for game and occasionally
"knocked over a deer."[41]

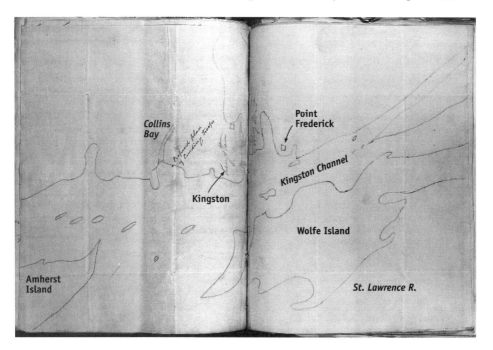

Chauncey's plan of attack, January 1813. Attached to the plan for an attack on Kingston that Chauncey proposed to the secretary of the navy on 21 January 1813 was a sketch that he apparently drew to indicate his intention to land the army midway between Collins Bay and Kingston Harbour. (Courtesy of the U.S. National Archives, RG45, M125, 26:29)

The day after his return, Chauncey learned about the state of affairs in the opposing camp when he interviewed four deserters who had run from the *Royal George* and professed to have accurate information about activity in the dockyard at Kingston. They said a thirty-six-gun ship was under construction there and two more ships, one of them a frigate, were said to be rising at York. "Every deserter that comes over (and there are many) gives the same account," Chauncey assured the navy secretary, and because of the potential improvement in British shipping, he asked for permission to lay down another strongly armed corvette.[42]

That night the commodore considered the implications of what he had been told about the British preparations and, assuming that the deserters' stories were "unquestionably correct," he wrote a confidential message to the secretary of the navy on 21 January in which he outlined, for the first time, the offensive operations he hoped to execute in the spring:

My plan is this, to prepare all my force this winter and in the spring as soon as the Ice breaks up to take onboard 1,000 picked troops and proceed to Kingston land them about three miles to the westward of the town in the bay which I have marked on the chart herewith enclosed leave two Vessels to cover their retreat (if such a measure should be found necessary) proceed with the remainder of the squadron to the Harbor of Kingston and attack the Forts and Ships at the same time the troops would attack in the rear with this force I have not doubts but that we should succeed in taking or destroying their ships and Forts and of course preserve our ascendancy upon this Lake.[43]

To obtain the army's best support, Chauncey planned to travel to Albany to discuss the attack with Dearborn as soon as he could clear his desk and ensure that everything at Sackets Harbour was in good order.

Among the correspondence that awaited the commodore's attention upon his return from Buffalo was an offer from Master Commandant Oliver Hazard Perry to serve on the Great Lakes with 150 seamen from his gunboat flotilla at Newport, Rhode Island. Having a high opinion of the twenty-seven-year-old officer, and eager to strengthen his command, Chauncey responded favourably to Perry and wrote to the Navy Department on his behalf. Perry received permission to join Chauncey and departed from Newport around the middle of February.[44]

Matters regarding a second master commandant were not quite so pleasing. James Leonard had arrived at Sackets during Chauncey's absence. He and

Master Commandant James Leonard, USN (d. 1832). Leonard entered the U.S. Navy as a midshipman in 1799 and earned his lieutenant's commission in 1807. He commanded the bomb ketch *Vesuvius* and a flotilla of gunboats at New York before being promoted to master commandant and sent to the lakes in November 1812. (Portrait by S. L. Waldo, courtesy of the U.S. National Archives, 428-KM-10896)

Chauncey had known each other for years and had clashed in July 1812 when Leonard had commanded a flotilla of gunboats at New York and had dared to sail past Chauncey's shipyard flying a commodore's pendant. When the latter sent a boat to remind Leonard that only Chauncey could fly such a flag in New York waters, the commandant replied that his actions were justified and continued on his way.[45] The man's reputation for being unafraid of confrontations had been established in 1807 when he fought a duel with Lieutenant Jacob Jones, USN, at a distance of nine feet and was nearly killed. He could hardly have been ruffled, then, when he was summoned to Chauncey's office at the Harbour to discuss a recent complaint about his behaviour.

Leonard had arrived at Sackets accompanied by a lady who everyone assumed was his wife, especially when they hired a room in a hotel and involved themselves in the local society. Suspicions soon arose about the lady's conduct and background, however, and a couple of ugly incidents involving comments made by a hotel manager and a store clerk soon brought allegations into the open that the woman was Leonard's mistress. As delicately as possible, Isaac Chauncey pointed out to his second-in-command that he had heard about the controversy and that such a living arrangement was inappropriate for a naval officer and a gentleman. Leonard responded that no impropriety had occurred, but agreed to send the woman away, which he did at least temporarily.[46]

There were several other, less controversial matters requiring Chauncey's attention before he could depart for Albany to meet with Dearborn.[47] Several officers arrived, and he assigned them to various vessels. The prizes *Elizabeth* and *Mary Hatt* were for sale, so the commodore instructed his secretary, and lately appointed purser, Samuel Anderson, to buy them, after which they would be altered into gunboats. Another court martial was held, this one involving a U.S. Marine private, Elizha Johnson, who had attempted to desert.[48] Johnson was found guilty, and the board of officers called for him to be executed by a firing squad, but since a death sentence required the president's approval, Chauncey wrote to the secretary with that request, adding "the frequency of this crime has rendered it necessary that an Example should be made to deter others from committing a Crime so fraught with Injury to the publick."[49] The president acceded, and early in April Johnson was executed at the Harbour in front of the assembled naval contingent.

On 1 February 1813 the commodore issued a general order meant to ensure that the squadron was kept on the alert and that everyone knew their quarters if the British launched a raid. He directed all guns and carronades to be kept loaded with one stand of grapeshot and one stand of canister each and that musket cartridges were to be made up to include one ball and three buck-shot.

He stipulated that the "men are not to leave their quarters at night on any account whatsoever not even to extinguish fires in the villages."[50] The burden of command during his absence would fall on the shoulders of Master Commandant Leonard, who, apart from maintaining discipline and harmony at the base, was to supervise the completion of the defensive works on land and the final carpentry and fitting out of the *Madison*. Perhaps concerned that Leonard might not rise to the challenge, Chauncey advised him on 1 February, "I am persuaded that you will use your best exertions to put it [the base] in that State that nothing but the annihilation of your whole force will enable the enemy to deprive you of it."[51]

After making these preparations, the commodore turned his back on his ice-locked squadron and headed south to meet Dearborn. Chauncey probably felt some anxiety at leaving his command when it seemed vulnerable to a surprise attack, but he must also have wanted to get to Albany to hear the latest news, for big changes were afoot on the political scene. In Washington there had been a major cabinet shuffle, and Chauncey must have been eager to find out what impact the changes would have on the war and on him.

CHAPTER 6

"Everything Shall Be Prepared"[1]

PLANNING THE CAMPAIGN: FEBRUARY–APRIL 1813

Secretary of War William Eustis paid the price for American military failures in 1812. His critics in Congress called for his removal, forgetting that the legislation they had drafted to prepare the country for war had done little to help his administration of the army. On 3 December Eustis handed his resignation to James Madison, but no immediate successor was readily available. The president offered the position to Secretary of State James Monroe, who agreed to conduct the War Department's business temporarily and, while Madison pursued other candidates, oversaw the first stage of the discussions that eventually set the goals for the 1813 campaign.[2]

In Monroe's view, the priority was the need to increase the size of the army beyond the current 19,000 men. The idea of invading Canada from the upper lakes to Halifax was still being promoted, but at the same time protests were being lodged about the lack of defensive forces in those states exposed to British incursions. Monroe dealt with that problem by obtaining approval for a plan that divided the nation into nine military districts, each with its own contingent of regulars and officers who would work with state officials and militia to prepare against attacks. The question of how big the army should become, however, was debated in detail, with Monroe anticipating a total of 70,000 troops at one point. Albert Gallatin, Secretary of the Treasury, brought those expectations down to earth by pointing out two critical realities. One was the shortage of funds available to pay for such an increase, and the second was the limited availability of provisions to maintain such a massive force. The New England states could not generate the produce needed to supply an ambitious movement from their region into Lower Canada, and the stockpiling of re-sources from New York and other states for such an undertaking would take until the autumn of 1813 to complete. Monroe accepted these conditions, realiz-ing that it was "not a question of what species of force [was] best, but a question of what we [could] get to take the field with early next spring."[3] Late in January Congress passed a bill approving the enlistment for one year of up to 20,000 men and giving more authority over appointments and instructions to officials in Washington. Among the key decision-makers it was also accepted that logis-tics would restrict offensive operations in the spring to the Upper Canadian frontier.

While these matters were being sorted out, President Madison tried to find a suitable man for the War Department. He offered the position to Henry Dearborn and Senator William Crawford, president *pro tem* of the Senate, who both turned him down. Next he assessed the qualifications of Daniel Tompkins and Brigadier General John Armstrong; with the former being the governor of New York State and the latter in charge of the defence of the city of New York, they were geographically well placed. The spring campaign would be launched, in part, through the state, so a local man running the War Department should garner popular support for the expedition. Armstrong, a fifty-four-year-old veteran of the Revolutionary War, was an acknowledged leader in American military thinking, but few people could tolerate his pugnacious character and reputation for unscrupulous behavior, least of all James Monroe, who looked

John Armstrong (1758-1843).
Armstrong's career began with his entry into the colonial army in 1775 and saw him serve in the state governments of Pennsylvania and New York and as the American minister in France during Napoleon's reign. Armstrong held the rank of brigadier general in the U.S. Army with the command of New York City when he accepted the position of secretary of war. (Portrait by Daniel Huntington, courtesy of the U.S. National Archives, 111-SC-94151)

upon Armstrong as a threat to his own political aspirations. Madison concluded that Tompkins was more valuable as a political ally at Albany (with a tough gubernatorial fight to take place in April) and invited Armstrong to take the job. As evidence of his low popularity, Armstrong's appointment narrowly won approval in the Senate by a vote of 18 to 15.[4]

A much less contentious adjustment in the cabinet was the selection of a new secretary of the navy. Although the naval arm had reaped glory on the oceans and the lakes, Paul Hamilton was blamed for confusion in his department and castigated for his chronic drinking. He resigned on 29 December and was replaced by Madison's first choice, William Jones, on 12 January. At fifty-two years of age, Jones, like most of the country's influential citizens, had fought in the Revolutionary War, serving not only with the army, but also on a privateer.[5] He later developed maritime business interests (which frequently required him to go to sea) and involved himself in politics, winning election to Congress in 1801. Jones's acceptance of the navy secretaryship was widely applauded, and he joined the inner circle of Washington decision-makers as a welcomed member.

Jones took a couple of weeks to become acquainted with his new portfolio (ousting the chief navy clerk, Charles Goldsborough, in short order), and it was not until 27 January 1813 that he opened correspondence with the commander-in-chief of the Great Lakes naval force. Chauncey received the letter at Albany on 10 February and was "much flattered in having been so fortunate as to have given satisfaction in my arrangements for the Lakes."[6] Indeed, the secretary congratulated the commodore on his "capacity, energy and judgement," and asserted his belief that "it is impossible to attach too much importance to our naval operations on the Lakes."[7] He approved what Chauncey had accomplished to date and endorsed his plans for the winter; a second corvette would be laid down at Sackets, requisitions for its components would be filled promptly, officers and seamen needed on the lake would be transferred without hesitation. Jones extended to Chauncey the same free hand that Hamilton had provided in his original instructions, informing him: "You are to consider the absolute superiority on all the Lakes, as the only limit to your authority."[8]

Evident in Jones's first despatch to Chauncey was his emphasis on gaining control of Lake Erie and the northern reaches of Lake Huron where its waters merged with Lakes Michigan and Superior and Georgian Bay. Whereas Paul Hamilton's concerns had been more evenly balanced between the squadrons above and below the Niagara River, Jones demonstrated a bias toward winning supremacy on Lakes Erie and Huron that dominated his subsequent correspondence with the commodore. Most of the letter written on 27 January was devoted to arrangements at the Erie, Pennsylvania, shipyard where he ordered a second twenty-gun brig to be built and which was supposed to be supplied by the industries in Pittsburgh. Creating a squadron on Lake Erie, Jones explained, would make it possible for Generals William Henry Harrison and James Winchester to recapture Detroit and seize Fort Malden at Amherstburg, which "would enable you to detach a part of your force to Lake Huron, to take post at the mouth of the French River on the N. E. Side of Lake Huron, where you will intercept the supplies for the western Indians."[9] Achieving control of that district would ruin the British alliance with the Indians in the northwest, argued Jones, and could be consolidated by the retaking of Mackinac Island and the resulting domination of Lake Michigan. "The command of Lake Ontario is no less important," Jones admitted, but seemingly as an afterthought.

Secretary Jones's preoccupation with attaining supremacy on the upper lakes may have been a reflection of his desire to champion fresh initiatives for the navy, to be a new broom after the ouster of Hamilton. In all likelihood, though, his concern about the upper lakes involved more complex issues. The protracted contest for dominion over the territories in the northwest had been one of the underlying causes of the war. William Hull's army was supposed to have chased the British out of southwestern Upper Canada, simultaneously breaking their alliance with the Indian nations of the northwest, but his shocking defeat and the loss of Detroit had clearly demonstrated the need for naval support for such an endeavour. Harrison and Winchester had moved brigades within striking distance of Detroit, though the policy-makers in Washington now understood the armies could not attack until the navy could help. Assuming that Chauncey would be able to manage that feat, and that the two generals would conquer their portion of Upper Canada, Jones wanted to disrupt the British-Indian alliance further by taking over their trading posts, especially the former American fort on Mackinac Island, which the British had seized in July 1812. There was a second reason for regaining that place. Having mercantile interests himself, Jones was aware of the losses that financiers like John Jacob Astor had suffered when Mackinac fell. In November 1812 Astor had written to Chauncey about a shipment of pelts aboard vessels captured by an American force in the Niagara River, but he was more concerned about a much larger store of furs confiscated by the British at Mackinac. It is reasonable to suggest that Astor, and others like him, pressured the government to act decisively on the upper lakes, for evidence does exist that Astor used his influence in Washington to reclaim those furs and other goods on the British side of the line.[10] Such requests from powerful individuals could not be ignored by President Madison and his ministers, especially since it was from Astor and other wealthy

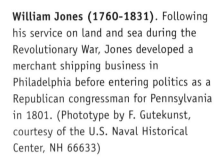

William Jones (1760-1831). Following his service on land and sea during the Revolutionary War, Jones developed a merchant shipping business in Philadelphia before entering politics as a Republican congressman for Pennsylvania in 1801. (Phototype by F. Gutekunst, courtesy of the U.S. Naval Historical Center, NH 66633)

merchants that Treasury Secretary Gallatin borrowed the $16 million needed in March 1813 to keep the treasury solvent.

Although Jones's firm opinions were influential during cabinet discussions, he did not dominate the choice of goals for the 1813 campaign. It was John Armstrong who played the leading role in this process and, when he moved into his new office, he acted quickly to advance his views by presenting a plan to the cabinet on 8 February. Montreal was too heavily defended, Armstrong asserted, and the army located along the Lake Champlain route to Canada was too small to stage a successful offensive. That left the cabinet with two alternatives: wait for a larger army to be assembled, trained and provisioned, or move early in the spring against a "secondary, but still an important object."[11] The secondary target was the extensive frontier between Prescott and Lake Erie. Armstrong recommended that 6,000 troops be gathered to attack first Kingston, then York, and finally Forts George and Erie. Preparations would have to be made quickly, for he viewed the period from 1 April until 15 May as the optimal time for launching the expedition because the ice remaining in the St. Lawrence would inhibit the British from moving reinforcements transported from England to the upper province. Although the point was not mentioned in Armstrong's discussion paper, the entire campaign would depend on the ability of Commodore Chauncey's squadron to provide transportation for the army. As well, the memo made no mention of the kind of campaign in the northwest that Secretary Jones was promoting.

The cabinet approved Armstrong's scheme, without realizing that their limited knowledge of conditions in British North America left them unaware of the errors in Armstrong's information. He calculated that 10,000 defenders stood in the environs of Montreal, when the number was closer to 7,400, including militia, but more significantly he underestimated the strength of the army in Upper Canada. Between Prescott and the Niagara Peninsula there were only 2,100 effectives, he claimed, which was true when regular units were mustered the previous December, but he failed to allow for militia and Indian warriors or any troops moved up from the lower province.[12] The most serious of Armstrong's mistakes was his assumption that ice would clog the St. Lawrence until mid-May but melt from the shores of Lake Ontario by 1 April. The secretary's plans would be difficult to follow.

Why was Washington so out of touch with conditions on the northern frontier? Just as Commodore Chauncey blindly relied on the assurances of deserters to learn about the enemy's machinations, Armstrong, Jones and the others based their decisions on word of mouth without confirming the reliability of the sources. They could hardly be blamed for their lack of knowledge since there was no instrument in place by which they could have become better informed. The Great Lakes were on the distant frontier, hundreds of miles away, sparsely populated, little known to the outside world. Few maps existed that offered, in the words of a young officer summoned to duty,

> more explicitness than to give Buffalo, Niagara, Oswego, etc. and stretched these few places over such a space that one would be led to suppose they occupied the whole of it…. Sacket's Harbor, particularly, had been much talked of in the news-papers, but probably not one person in a million could have fixed it within a hundred miles of its locality.[13]

The treachery of lakes that looked like duck ponds on large-scale maps could hardly be known to the wise heads in Washington (or London). Trackless forests, bogs and rocky escarpments could be imagined easily, but the true frustrations of hauling armies and navies over those sprawling wastes could only be understood first-hand. The inundation of business in Washington kept the president and his secretaries from gaining such insights, and so they set their goals and based their plans on incorrect and outdated information.

John Armstrong issued his first orders to Henry Dearborn on 10 February 1813.[14] While a brigade of 3,000 men would take post at Buffalo, a second brigade of 4,000 men would gather at Sackets Harbour, which the navy would carry across the lake to destroy the fortifications and shipping at Kingston, before attacking York, where the supplies and two new ships would be captured, and finally, an assault would be made against Forts George and Erie. Armstrong advised his senior general in the north to keep the troop build-up as quiet as possible, but to let it be known that he feared a visit from the British. Dearborn replied from his headquarters at Albany with a promise "to carry into effect the expedition proposed."[15] He suggested that a body of soldiers, such as the New Hampshire Militia, remain in the area of Lake Champlain so that the British would keep a large enough force in Lower Canada to defend against an attack down the Richelieu River, rather than committing everything they had to oppose Dearborn, once his true objective was identified.

Armstrong wrote to Dearborn on 24 February with a new wrinkle in his plan. Having heard about successful raids on British villages that had been launched by Major Benjamin Forsyth of the U.S. Rifle Regiment across the ice of the St. Lawrence from Ogdensburg, the secretary of war suggested that a similar mission be tried against Kingston. Colonel Zebulon Pike could travel with two brigades in sleighs from Lake Champlain to a point below Kingston, cross the river, sink the warships, capture the town and hold it until Chauncey ferried Dearborn's army to relieve them. If, at the worst, Prevost deployed a regiment to eliminate Pike, he could quickly slip over to the American side. "This would be the shorter road to the object," argued Armstrong, " and perhaps the safer one, as the St. Lawrence is now everywhere well bridged and offers no obstruction to either attack or retreat."[16]

Sitting at his desk in Washington, removed by the distance of a week or so from the latest news on the war front, the secretary could not have known how his conception of obstructions on the St. Lawrence was smashed on 22 February.[17] Early that day a British force of about 600 men, including detachments of the Glengarry Fencibles and the 8th Foot lately moved up from Lower Canada, seized Ogdensburg after a violent and bloody fight. Forsyth's riflemen and local militia, numbering about 500, had offered a brave resistance, but were soon put to flight, leaving twenty dead and seventy captured. The British lost seven killed and forty-eight wounded and occupied the town long enough to burn barracks and two schooners, plunder some residences and drag eleven artillery pieces, hundreds of shot and muskets, plus ammunition and two stands of colours back to Canada. At first, Forsyth aspired to counterattack, regain Ogdensburg and make Prescott pay dearly for British predations, but he ended up retreating to Sackets Harbour.

In spite of his disappointment with Forsyth's misfortune, on 25 February Dearborn portrayed the outcome of the incident to Armstrong as an opportunity to activate Brigadier General Jacob Brown and his New York militia to reinforce Forsyth at Sackets. He also ordered Pike to head in the same direction

Major General Henry Dearborn, U.S. Army (1751-1829). Trained as a physician, Dearborn joined the patriotic cause in the Revolutionary War, after which he settled in Maine Territory and was appointed major general for the Massachusetts militia. During Jefferson's presidency (1801-1809), Dearborn was the secretary of war, resigning in 1809 to take a civil post in Boston. (Courtesy of the National Archives of Canada, C-10925)

with some of his command, in the hope that the various elements could combine for an expedition across the ice to Kingston (like the one that Armstrong had devised the day before in Washington.) He believed the time was right for such a thrust, but that it was in danger of being lost because Chauncey had not returned to Albany from New York City. "If *he had arrived as soon as I had expected him,*" Dearborn complained petulantly, "*we might have made a stroke at Kingston, on the ice,* but his presence was necessary for having the aid of the seamen and marines."[18]

Having received Secretary Jones's permission to build a second ship at Sackets Harbour and also his urgent instructions to accelerate preparations on Lake Erie, Chauncey hurried to New York after meeting with Dearborn at Albany on 10 February.[19] Allowing himself one peaceful Sunday with his family, he then immersed himself in business at the New York shipyard, writing requisitions for the fittings, ordnance and provisions that had to be transported northward immediately to take advantage of the winter roads. He also began rounding up officers and men for his two squadrons, taking them from the frigate *John Adams,* the sloop *Alert* and the brig *Argus,* from which fifty men were detached under the leadership of Lieutenant Wolcott Chauncey, the commodore's brother. Chauncey completed this work by 24 February and departed for Albany, where he arrived four days later to learn that Dearborn had just hurried off to Sackets to superintend its defences against a threatened visit from the British.

In company with Master Commandant Perry, who rendezvoused with him at Albany, Chauncey reached Sackets on 3 March. There he found Dearborn in a lather over rumours of a massive concentration of British troops at Kingston under the direct command of Sir George Prevost. The general transmitted expresses to the officers who had not yet arrived to hasten their marches, and with each day the army encampments around Sackets swelled.[20] At first the commodore did not believe that an attack was imminent, but he passed along to Secretary Jones the stories of increased vigilance on the other side and the collection of up to 8,000 men at Kingston, and promised to be "ready to receive the enemy if he should think it proper to pay us a visit."[21]

Whether the anxiety expressed in Dearborn and Chauncey's correspondence during the first two weeks of March was genuine, or just part of the ruse that Armstrong had advised could be employed to justify the massing of troops at Sackets, is hard to determine. The expulsion of Forsyth from Ogdensburg had been a reminder of how determined and efficient the British army could be and had come hard on the heels of reports of the frightening defeat of Winchester's army at Frenchtown near Detroit on 22 January. Winchester had overreached himself by chasing a British garrison out of the Michigan village and been hammered by a retaliatory attack led from Fort Malden by Brigadier General Henry Procter. Winchester had lost more than 900 men killed and captured, himself included among the latter, and lurid tales had spread through the American lines of how Procter's native allies had massacred the wounded. Such events may have heightened apprehensions at Sackets, in addition to any tactical spreading of misinformation by Dearborn and the commodore. Proof of Chauncey's real concern was the fact that he detained Perry and all of his Newport seamen at Sackets until the presumed threat passed, which it did by 14 March. "From various sources," Dearborn wrote to Armstrong on that date, "I am satisfied that they are not in sufficient force to venture an attack on this place.... We are probably just strong enough on each side to defend, but not in sufficient force to hazard an offensive movement."[22]

After tensions had eased, Dearborn and Chauncey met with their senior officers in a council of war that examined the variables involved in attacking Kingston, York and the Niagara Peninsula in that order.[23] Since it was clear that the navy would have to transport the army to its destination, the size of the force would be governed by the number of men that could be safely carried in the squadron or towed in the large bateaux recently built by the army. Ice was also a matter for discussion; it usually broke up early in April in the western regions of the lake, but the surviving floes were blown down the lake by prevailing winds, jamming the harbours at the eastern end, namely Sackets and

Kingston, until at least mid-April. Even if the American squadron could leave its anchorage, it might not be able to get close enough to the shipping and batteries at Kingston to bombard them. The latest intelligence from Kingston was that upwards of 4,000 men were stationed there, posing a formidable defence force. Not surprisingly, the council of war concluded that York should become the first objective in the spring campaign, followed by Forts George and Erie, and then Kingston. Between 1,000 and 1,500 troops (out of close to 5,000 regulars and militia) would be embarked for the attack on York, while the balance would remain at Sackets as there was not enough room in the squadron to accommodate them and it was impractical to load them into flimsy bateaux and tow them 150 miles up the lake. In justifying the change, Chauncey pointed out to Jones that at York were "the *Prince Regent* of 18 guns, the *Duke of Gloucester* of 16 guns, and 2 brigs building calculated to carry 18 guns each."[24] By seizing them, and the naval stores known to be at York, he would greatly augment his squadron. The American invaders would hold the port until the British detached a force from Fort George to reclaim it, whereupon, after a lightning move across the lake, they would spring a raid on that fort in conjunction with the army at Buffalo, thereby securing the entire Niagara frontier. From there, the commodore intended to deploy a part of his squadron to blockade Kingston, while he went with as many men as he could spare to join Perry who had gone to Lake Erie. His scheme continued, reflecting perfectly the priorities that Secretary Jones had voiced in almost all the correspondence he had transmitted to Chauncey since taking office.[25] After getting "the whole Force into operation upon that Lake," explained the commodore, he would destroy the British squadron, "attack and take Malden and Detroit, and proceed into Lake Huron and attack and carry Machilimackinac [sic] *at all hazards*."[26] Admitting that his description of the proposed course of action was "sanguine," Chauncey assured the secretary that he had "thought much upon the subject and after making every Deduction of every possible contingency" he was convinced that they would succeed.

Five weeks passed as the despatches went south, where Madison and the others debated the change of course and issued their response. On 8 April, William Jones wrote to Chauncey that "the President has been pleased to express his approbation of the general outline, and his particular satisfaction with the judicious and zealous execution of the preparation arrangements under your direction."[27] Dearborn received a similar note of approval. "The alteration in the plan of campaign," wrote Armstrong, " ... would appear to be necessary, or at least proper."[28] Along with Jones, however, he had reservations. Both secretaries wanted a larger force to be committed to the action, even if it meant carrying them in the bateaux and risking the chance that they "may embarrass, or retard your movements."[29] Armstrong tried to argue from a historical perspective, reminding Dearborn that George Washington "carried his whole force against the Hessians in New Jersey, and beating them recovered that moral strength, that self confidence which he had lost by many preceding disasters." The current situation was similar, asserted the war secretary, and between 2,500 and 3,000 soldiers were required for the operation through which the nation "may soon get on our legs again if we can give some hard blows at the opening of the campaign."[30] To support his view further, while unconsciously revealing how poorly he had listened to Jones's reports to the cabinet about developments in and around the Sackets Harbour shipyard, Armstrong questioned why any men should be left at the navy yard, since the British would not care about it once the squadron had sailed.[31]

Apart from underlining their concerns about the size of the force involved, the secretaries endorsed Dearborn and Chauncey's decision to put off the visit to Kingston until later. Ever the political animals, they saw in an early and decisive victory at York positive effects for the Republican party in the New York gubernatorial voting which would begin on 27 April 1813 and last for three days. Perhaps an injection of "moral strength" under the skin of the public would translate into votes. At the very least, the profits earned by local farmers as their produce was purchased by the army's quartermasters would put the citizens in a mood favourable to the Republicans and their standard bearer, Daniel Tompkins. The decision was made to commence the 1813 campaign at York.

While these discussions were under way in Washington, day-to-day business continued at Sackets Harbour through March and April 1813. In the dockyard the schooner that Chauncey had ordered the previous December was assembled, its construction slowed by harsh weather, the absence of Henry Eckford, who went to New York to order materials for the next vessel, and the fabrication of parts for that project. On 5 April the labourers began cutting an opening in the ice at the foot of the slipway, and the next day the schooner was launched without mishap. Specifically built to carry messages up and down the lake in sixty or seventy hours, it was small (perhaps sixty-five feet in length), sharp-ended and armed by a single, brass 9-pdr. long gun.[32] Chauncey named the schooner the *Lady of the Lake,* and assigned Sailing Master Thomas Nichols to fit it out for service as fast as possible. Near by, the two prize vessels, which had been bought into the navy and renamed the *Raven* (*Mary Hatt*) and the *Asp* (*Elizabeth*), were being equipped with ordnance.[33]

Two days after the launch of the *Lady of the Lake*, a new keel was laid in its place for a large and powerful warship. Eckford had made his plans during the winter and directed the molding, cutting and shaping of the components for the backbone and its ribs with the intention of erecting the vessel as quickly as possible. This advanced work paid off, and within two weeks the frames were all in place and planking had begun. Isaac Chauncey admired Eckford's diligence and predicted that the ship would float by the first of June.[34]

Though usually referred to as a corvette like the *Madison*, the new vessel was conceived from the outset to be larger and more powerfully armed than that ship. Precise details about its dimensions were not recorded, but it was said to resemble closely the frigate *Essex*, measuring about 143 feet on the gundeck and thirty-eight feet abeam. Chauncey wanted long guns for it rather than the carronades on the *Madison* and *Oneida*, so that he could match their 500-yard range of broadsides with the one mile-plus effectiveness of the long guns. His decision later proved to be a significant one, but it was not made without a price. Long guns were more than double the weight of their shorter, stubbier brethren, and the commodore had to be mindful of overburdening a ship that would be as long as a frigate, but have a shallow enough draught to scrape over the shoals near the lake's shores. To this end, Chauncey ordered twenty-six of the short 24-pdrs. that had originally been cast for the frigate *Constitution* shipped to the lake. At eight feet in length, these weapons were about a foot shorter than the norm for their calibre, and with their wooden carriages would be lighter, take up less room on deck and require fewer men to handle them. Another difference in the new ship was the poop deck added to allow for extra officer accommodations at the rear of the quarterdeck. A second raised platform (referred to as a "topgallant forecastle") was laid above the gundeck from the foremast to the bow, providing an uncluttered space for handling the rigging.[35] On each of these decks a single 24-pdr. would be mounted on a circle, while twelve guns lined each side on the gundeck, giving the ship a broadside strength of fourteen guns.

From the inventories of materials on hand, Chauncey compiled requisitions for the vast array of items still needed for the station and transmitted them to John Bullus at New York.[36] Conducting the business of the squadron required 4 reams of best letter paper, 3 reams of common foolscap, 500 quills, 6 penknives, 6 dozen pencils, 100 papers of black ink powder, "Laws of the last Congress 2 Sessions," 5 boxes of candles and dozens of other particulars. The commodore also requested 14 hand trumpets, 50 deck scrapers, 10 compasses, 6 deep-sea lines, 5 pounds each of red, white, blue and yellow bunting and 100 pounds of yellow paint. Fourteen hundred sets of clothing (shoes, stockings, pants, frocks and handkerchiefs), plus 700 vests and 700 hats were ordered to outfit the seamen on both lakes. Rigging the new ship called for 5 18-inch cables in 120-fathom lengths, 12 different types of stays, 16,000 fathoms of rope varying in circumference from 7 inches to 1 inch, 18 coils of ratline, 500 yards of "old canvas," and 4 anchors each weighing 33 hundredweight. Ammunition of all calibres and types was needed: from 1,245 32-pdr. round shot (some of which was produced by a foundry at Rome, New York) to 1,058 18-pdr. stands of grapeshot and 66 canisters for 9-pdrs. One hundred barrels of powder, 1,000 pounds of match rope, 4,000 musket flints, 80 powder horns and 100 pistols were ordered. Chauncey's lists filled page after page and resulted in load after load of materiel proceeding from the Hudson to the Mohawk to the lake in a supply train that quickly surpassed the bulk of commerce that had been moved during the autumn.

Under the watchful eye of Lieutenant Colonel Alexander Macomb, the army had strengthened the defences at Sackets Harbour considerably. Fort Tompkins bristled with guns, including a 32-pdr. mounted on a raised platform known as a cavalier, and was protected by a light palisade, a blockhouse and the marine barracks. A short distance to the west, the basswood cantonment stood stout and defendable. On the spit of land that enclosed the harbour, now called Navy Point, there were barracks and three batteries, while on the shore just outside the basin the square earthen walls of Fort Volunteer were reinforced, backed by a blockhouse and adjoining barracks; not far off, the finishing touches were being put on a new hospital. In addition to these improvements, Macomb had ordered trees cut down in a wide ring around the village to create a tangle of foliage forming a natural abatis. Lastly, a camp had been set up on Horse Island, located almost a mile west of Fort Tompkins, where an advanced guard kept an eye out for invaders.[37]

Through March and April 1813 the population of Sackets grew as units of regulars arrived, raising the size of the military force to about 4,000. Elements from the Second Regiment of Light Dragoons, the Light Artillery Regiment, the Rifle Regiment, the Sixth, Ninth, Fifteenth, Sixteenth and Twenty-first Infantry Regiments, and volunteers from New York and Baltimore established their camps in and around the village. They were organized into two brigades, headed by the newly-promoted brigadier generals, Zebulon Pike and John Chandler, the latter, as senior officer, assuming overall command when Dearborn departed for Albany late in March.

By 10 April it was decided that Pike's brigade would be transported up the lake for the attack on York. Chauncey had anticipated that a problem over legitimacy of authority might develop when the commodore led seamen and marines ashore in cooperation with army units under the command of a brigadier general. Chauncey's rank as commodore was equivalent to that of a brigadier general, but he feared that a general would assume control of his sea-men once they were on land. To avoid such an unpleasant circumstance, he asked the navy secretary to have the president grant him "some brevet rank that the officers of the Army would recognize while I was acting on shore."[38] Chauncey discussed this issue with Macomb and Dearborn, but only the former agreed with his position. Jones supported Dearborn's view that such an arrangement was unnecessary and sent Chauncey a copy of the regulations stipulating division of authority between army and navy officers. Nevertheless, after a discussion of the sensitive issue in the cabinet, Secretary Armstrong in-structed Dearborn to return to Sackets and act as the senior military officer.[39] In the meantime, the commodore had reassured Dearborn that with "the arrangement made and making that we may calculate on success .... [and] eve-rything shall be prepared on my part."[40]

While decisions regarding strategy, tactics and construction filled Chauncey's days, he had to find time to deal with issues of a lesser sort that troubled his station. Sailing Master John Hutton, for instance, had become a troublesome individual; since coming to the lake in the fall, he had proven him-self to be a compulsive drinker and irritant. After arresting him several times, Chauncey finally called him before a court martial that sentenced him to be cashiered. Hutton appealed to William Jones and the president for his case to be reviewed, complaining that he, a warrant officer, had been confined in chains like a lowly criminal ("such is the tyranny practised here" by the com-modore, alleged Hutton). Months would pass before the matter would be re-solved.[41]

A more serious and complicated predicament, involving the squadron's pursers, had preceded Hutton's complaint. During the winter Chauncey di-vided the bookkeeping responsibilities of the pursers among three men, Alex-ander Darragh, Henry Fry and his secretary, Samuel Anderson. Darragh had been on the station since before the war, and although he agreed with the com-modore that the great increase in vessels and men would make his job more demanding, he preferred to hire assistant clerks rather than see other pursers reap the profits which pursers were entitled, by naval regulations, to make from shipboard transactions. Anderson's assignment was only temporary until a properly certified third purser, Edward Fitzgerald, arrived, but Darragh saw red when he learned of the arrangement and accused Chauncey of lining the pock-ets of his friend at the expense of Fry and him. Secretary Jones sent the commo-dore a copy of the complaint, to which Chauncey replied with a long and com-plex defence of his actions. He was incensed with the purser's "avarice and grasping disposition," which he said was prompted by the fact that Chauncey had forced him to follow the navy's rules when he arrived on the lake, thereby reducing Darragh's furtive money-grabbing. Had he not been within a few days of sailing, Chauncey vowed, he would have requested an inquiry into his own conduct, so that the truth would be known, and that Darragh could "receive the punishment due to the libeller of his superiors."[42] With Chauncey's explanation in hand, Jones solved the problem by pointing out that Anderson lacked the proper authority to have such a position, but that the division of purser duties was appropriate. Darragh, only partially vindicated, continued to serve at Sackets under a commander who clearly despised him.

These unpleasantries paled in comparison with the renewed scandal that flared up around Master Commandant Leonard. His "wife" reappeared at the Harbour late in the winter, to which Chauncey turned a blind eye, hoping to get on with waging war rather than become enmeshed in a bedroom farce. The spring campaign was close at hand on 10 April when seamen broke a path through the ice at the mouth of the harbour and hauled the *Madison* into deep water so that they could mount all its guns. The corvette's inner furnishings and lower rigging were complete, and, by the commodore's standing instructions, James Leonard should have slept in his ship. Instead, he went ashore before dark on 12 April to be with "Mrs. Leonard," and when a powerful wind arose late in the night and pushed heavy pans of ice around the *Madison*, knocking it off its anchorage, he was sleeping soundly in their rented love nest.

At dawn an alarm announced that the *Madison* was adrift in the ice. Chauncey hurriedly dressed and had himself rowed to the ship, where he spent the next four hours desperately trying to save it from foundering in the rolling ice. Leonard finally boarded the ship at 10:00 a.m. and was immediately arrested, charged by Chauncey with disobeying an order by sleeping ashore, neglecting his duty to ensure the safety and preparation of his vessel and "dissolute and immoral practices" unbefitting his gentlemanly and honourable profession.[43] Leonard rejected all of Chauncey's allegations and wrote a stinging rebuttal to the despatch he knew the commodore had already transmitted to William Jones. In it he claimed: "This unjust, ungrateful and passionate act of his [Chauncey's], has added another item to the list of his persecutions on this and other stations, where he commands."[44] Although Leonard was clearly culpable for the costs of his own passion, his remarks echoed those made by Sailing Master Hutton, Purser Darragh and, the previous December, Lieutenant Sam Angus at Black Rock. They cast a stain on Isaac Chauncey's otherwise competent command on the lakes; in Leonard's case, the stain would darken the commodore's thoughts for almost a year.

The strife that flared up at Sackets Harbour during the spring of 1813 was easily matched on the British side. As Chauncey sharpened his quills to describe the misconduct of his second-in-command, British heads were shaking over the disappointing state of the dockyard at York. Construction of the *Sir Isaac Brock* had been so slow and disorderly that most people did not expect to see it launched until June, blaming Thomas Plucknett, who, it was allowed, might have been "a scientific man and a good draughtsman," but was no master builder.[45]

Plucknett's dilatory approach to the project had combined with poor management skills to retard progress at every phase. Lieutenant Colonel Christopher Myers, the deputy quartermaster general, had visited the site in March and attempted to organize the men and materials and to give Plucknett orders, but the superintendent, who strutted around town in a uniform jacket topped with golden epaulets, either ignored the instructions or evaded their intent. When Prevost visited York during his quick tour of the Upper Canada posts in late February, Plucknett told him that he needed thirty more shipwrights to speed things up and that former master shipwright John Dennis was actually responsible for the poor showings. Unknown to Prevost was the fact that Plucknett had employed shipwrights to make extensive alterations to the house he had rented, was overdrawn on one of his accounts and had put his private servant on the public payroll. The pleas of local officers saved Dennis's job because it was only through him that they were able to ensure that anything was accomplished in the dockyard. In spite of his best efforts though, by mid-April the *Brock* was barely more than a skeleton. The shipwrights had erected all the frames, but only two of six or seven pieces of the keelson were in place. Eleven rows of planks were fastened to the frames on the starboard side, while on the larboard side there was nothing. The lower masts were planed down to size, but artificers were still squaring the upper masts and spars and enough canvas was ready to fashion only two topsails. Exasperated by Plucknett's "folly and misconduct," Captain Andrew Gray admitted, "as matters now stand it is very doubtful when [the *Brock*] will be ready."[46]

It had been intended to transport the ordnance for the new ship by sleigh from Kingston during the winter, but spring arrived before this could be managed. The alternative was to bring the guns by water so Lieutenant William Fish departed from York in the schooner *Prince Regent* as soon as the ice cleared in that district and arrived at Kingston late on 17 April – that harbour was still frozen shut and Fish anchored in Kingston Channel. Eager to hear the latest news from the Provincial capital, Captain Gray rowed out between the ice pans to the schooner but after climbing on board he was disgusted to find the vessel in

The *Sir Isaac Brock*. This modern interpretation of the York dockyard shows the *Brock* in the final stages of its external planking, with the dismantled *Duke of Gloucester* drawn up on shore and the masts of the schooner *Prince Regent* behind it. (By Owen Staples, courtesy of the Toronto Reference Library, T-15211)

filthy and disorganized condition, later protesting to Prevost that he had "never seen more palpable negligence in all the Duties of a Commander of an Armed Vessel." [47]

The next week Gray was even more horrified when he inspected the *Earl of Moira*, which shipwrights had altered from a ship to a brig during the winter. Gray had ordered its commander, Lieutenant Theophilus Sampson, to clean up the *Moira* after the extensive renovation and prepare it for active duty. Sampson had done so little by the time of Gray's inspection that the warship was still a mess and in addition there were only ten rounds of prepared ammunition in the magazine. His patience tried beyond control, Gray arrested Sampson on the spot, confining him to quarters until he brought his account books up to date, and turned the brig over to Lieutenant George Smith of the *Royal George*. [48]

Not everything was doom and gloom at Kingston, however, because the dockyard on Point Frederick was awhirl with productive activity. George Record was an experienced ship builder who had risen to the position of master shipwright in March after Daniel Allen was fired for urging his artificers to

British gunboat with partial lugger rig. This watercolour was based on plans for a gunboat proposed by Lieutenant Governor John Graves Simcoe. A true lugger-rigged craft would have had square sails on the foremast as well. The British gunboats were not decked, being equipped with rowing benches and fittings for mounting ordnance in the bow and stern. (Courtesy of the Toronto Reference Library, T-16944)

strike over working conditions. Edward Platt was supervising the flow of materials in the yard, and Colonel Thomas Pearson, a veteran officer whom one individual described as "a regular Tartar," laboured tirelessly to maintain discipline and order.[49]

Beside the corvette, which was rapidly approaching its launch, stood the skeleton of a new vessel. A survey early in March had revealed a large enough supply of wood in the yard to build an armed schooner, for which Record prepared a draft. After work commenced a change was made to the dimensions, and the vessel took on the proportions of a brig-of-war that would measure nearly seventy-two feet on the gundeck.[50] Andrew Gray looked upon the change as a valuable asset: "She will be fully competent to take her Station in our line of Battle, and this consideration is the more important as very little dependance [sic] can be placed upon any support from York."[51]

A second board of survey examined the merchant schooner *Governor Simcoe*, which had been refloated after its brush with the Americans in November.[52] Although the vessel was old and some of its woodwork was rotten, it was considered strong enough and big enough (seventy-four feet on the gundeck, twenty feet abeam, with a draught of twelve feet) to mount ten 18-pdr. carronades and two long 6-pdrs. To render it serviceable, the schooner's upper deck was to be lowered by three feet so that gunports could be cut, a task, which along with other necessary improvements, would take twenty men a month to complete.

Since enough hands and sufficient stores of building materials were on site, work on the *Simcoe* was soon in progress, as was a third project. This involved the building of as many as six gunboats (two at Kingston, four others at Prescott), each large enough to carry a single long gun in its bows. [53] They would be long, narrow, lugger-rigged craft, equipped with rowing benches and designed specifically "for the calms so prevalent on Lake Ontario ... [when they could] teaze and cut up the largest vessel in such a way as to force it to shift its station if not to perhaps capture it."[54] Although some bateaux appear to have been armed with light ordnance at this time, no purpose-built gunboats were reported to be attached to the Lake Ontario establishment. The gunboats' utility,

British gunboat with lateen rig. The large, triangular mainsail of this craft, another of Simcoe's designs, was known as a lateen. It appears that several such gunboats were built in the 1790s for use on Lake Ontario, but it is uncertain whether any were in service in 1812. (Courtesy of the Toronto Reference Library, T-16948)

especially in protecting the convoys of men and materiel transported on the upper St. Lawrence River, would be clearly demonstrated in the months ahead.

The main focus of the activity on Point Frederick was the new corvette, and by 25 April 1813 it was ready for launch. With Gray's approval, George Record tried an alternative method of attaching the vessel's launch cradle to its hull. Usually, the cradle was secured by ropes to cleats fastened to the underside of the hull, which could only be extracted by careening the ship right after launch. Record improvised a network of roping that required no cleats, which would allow the cradle to float free after launch, thereby avoiding its tedious removal, but as the hull began its slide down the tallow-slicked slipway, its weight stretched the ropes beyond expectations causing the keel to sag into the ways jamming against its cross-supports. Three days of hauling and wedging the ship were required to move it back up to its starting point, whereupon on 28 April the launch was attempted again, this time using cleats, and the ship backed gracefully into Navy Bay to the delight of hundreds of labourers and onlookers.

Gray could not contain his delight and he crowed to Prevost that the ship was "as fine a vessel of her Class as ever sailed under the British Pendant."[55] He named the ship the *Sir George Prevost,* in answer to Chauncey's *Madison,* but the commander-in-chief did not approve and within a week the name was changed to the *Wolfe,* to honour the hero of the Plains of Abraham. Gray predicted that only twenty days were needed to prepare the ship "for Sea," and immediately after the launch the hull was careened in the shallows so the cleats could be removed. Then it was hauled to the wharf so the riggers could begin setting up the standing rigging and the upper spars. Intended to be of the "class of the *Royal George,*" the *Wolfe* had only two decks, the flush upper or gun deck above and a berthing deck below, with a shallow hold between there and the keelson. As designed by Thomas Plucknett, it was longer and wider than its predecessor, measuring 107 feet on the gundeck and nearly thirty-one feet abeam, but it drew less water. The ship had also been pierced for twenty-two guns, though only eighteen 18-pdr. carronades and two 12-pdr. long guns were in store awaiting their placement as substitutes until the originally prescribed 32-pdr. carronades arrived from England or Halifax.[56]

During the latter half of April the British were constantly on the alert for a visit from the Americans. "We have had daily rumours of the enemy being out," Gray wrote to Noah Freer, Prevost's military secretary, on 29 April, "but have not yet seen anything of them."[57] Had the Americans followed their original plan and attacked Kingston, they would have faced a formidable opposition, though nothing equal in numbers to the two brigades at Sackets. By Gray's order the *Moira* was situated at the opening of Navy Bay and the *Royal George* lay between Point Frederick and the town, both of them with springs on their cables so that their broadsides could be aimed in any direction. Each night guard boats pulled through openings in the ice pack back and forth between the vessels and the land; Lieutenant Fish was ordered to patrol Kingston Channel in the *Prince Regent*. To reinforce the crews, and hopefully enhance their willingness to fight, Gray distributed a company of the Royal Newfoundland Fencibles on the vessels, raising the complements to 123 in the *George*, fifty-four in the *Moira* and fifty-three in the *Regent*.[58]

The Marine Department was backed by about 1,300 regular troops and as many militia. John Vincent, promoted in February to brigadier general, had gone to Fort George with the battalion companies of the 49th Regiment, but their places had been taken by detachments from the lower province.[59] The 104th Foot (numbering close to 600 officers and men) began arriving at Kingston on 12 April, having marched from New Brunswick that winter with only ten days rest at Quebec, and were joined soon after by four companies of the Canadian Voltigeurs (about 300 men). Both units supplemented the various companies of the 1st, 8th, 100th and Glengarry regiments already on post.

The new arrivals were generally impressed with what they discovered at Kingston. Lieutenant John Le Couteur of the 104th Foot kept a colourful journal of his war experiences and recorded this reaction:

> Some of us had been marching between eight hundred and a thousand miles … during which time we never lost sight of a forest, when suddenly there lay before our astonished and delighted view the town of Kingston, the magnificent Lake Ontario, and what was far more surprising still, a squadron of ships-of-war frozen on its bosom. It produced a striking and indescribable sensation.[60]

After finding accommodations in the town and resting briefly after the exhausting trek, Le Couteur and his comrades familiarized themselves with their environs. They considered the fortifications on Point Frederick too weak, apart from "a Capital blockhouse" overlooking the battery and the dockyard. They were on hand for the unfortunate first launch of the *Wolfe* and met Captain Gray, whom Le Couteur described as "a Half-horse, half-Alligator sort of soldier, sailor, carpenter, etc."[61] Gray's son, James, a seventeen-year-old ensign, had also arrived in town with the 104th.

Another officer, Captain Jacques Viger of the Canadian Voltigeurs, provided a more detailed description of Kingston's defences.[62] He noted the barracks and storehouses at the eastern end of town, a tower used as a magazine, an army hospital and a string of redoubts, fashioned of stone and wood, situated at intervals to protect the town's rear flanks. The batteries on Points Murney and Mississauga formed a crossfire at the harbour's mouth with the guns on Point Frederick, where troops now occupied barracks. Atop Point Henry the army was building a fortification and just offshore on Cedar Island, recently cleared of trees, stood a semaphore station that could communicate with lookouts posted at spots up and down Kingston Channel.[63]

On their rocky outcroppings, British sentinels shivered through the last, cold nights and rainswept days of April, peering into the gloom that covered the lake, but no enemy sails came into view. Instead, alarming information reached Kingston. Le Couteur wrote on 29 April: "Very disastrous news received from York, ... which was assaulted by the Americans and that our army was in full retreat."[64] The long-anticipated American offensive had finally begun.

PART III

Fighting for Supremacy

APRIL 1813 TO NOVEMBER 1813

HAIL to the Chief, the pure Son of the Ocean,
Who raises his flag on Ontario's wave;
Long may Canadians behold with emotion,
The Hero who's destin'd their Country to save.
    Let not a laurel fade,
    Gracious Heav'n lend him aid,
Every device of the Foe to withstand;
    Waft him to Victory
    Let the full Chorus be
"Yeo," the preserver the stay of our Lands.

KINGSTON GAZETTE, 1 OCTOBER 1814

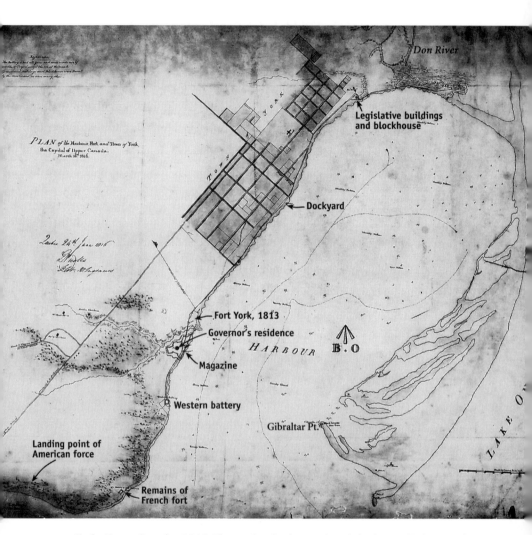

York, Upper Canada, 1813. The peninsula that enclosed the bay at York created a protected anchorage about two and a half miles long and a mile wide, but access was restricted to a narrow channel with a depth of about fifteen feet. The arrow indicates the location of Fort York during the American landings in 1813. Also shown is its location south of the original fort where it was rebuilt beginning late in 1813. (Based on a military chart of 1816, courtesy of the National Archives of Canada, NMC-17441)

CHAPTER 7

"Things Would Have Turned Out Better"[1]

THE ATTACK ON YORK: 27 APRIL 1813

Soon after the ice broke up in Black River Bay on 13 April, nearly upsetting the USS *Madison*, it moved in again and sealed Commodore Chauncey's squadron in place. A week passed during which Henry Dearborn returned to Sackets and oversaw the finalizing of plans for the offensive.[2] Everyone awaited the order to embark, but the destination was kept secret. Not so the latest developments at Kingston, where, it was said, a new warship had been launched and nearly a thousand reinforcements had arrived. "There are many conjectures relative to our destination," wrote Captain John Walworth of the Sixth Infantry to his father, "whither it is for Niagara, Little York, Kingston or some place on the River below is uncertain."[3] Even when the ice began melting away for good on 18 April and Brigadier General Zebulon Pike's brigade was told to prepare for departure, the truth remained hidden.

Embarkation began on 22 April and occupied all that day and part of the next. About 1,700 officers and men went out to the vessels, where they squeezed themselves into every available nook and cranny that kept them out of the way of the seamen. In concession to Jones and Armstrong's advice, the size of the force had been increased to dangerous proportions; on the *Madison* alone were 600 men, including the ship's crew – four times its normal complement. On no vessel could more than half the men get below deck at any one time.

Sailors and soldiers spent a cold night in the anchorage and awoke expecting to sail off to battle. Cocking an experienced eye at the horizon, Chauncey remarked to Dearborn that rough weather was imminent and that they should stay put. The general disagreed, and although Chauncey remonstrated with him, Dearborn's decision was final, and a signal soon shot up a halliard on the flagship telling the commanders to weigh anchor and make sail.[4] It was a mistake because a storm arose out of the southeast and by 2:00 p.m. the vessels were struggling through squalls and a rising sea near Stony Point. Worried about the state of his schooners lumbering under their heavy burdens, Chauncey finally overrode Dearborn and led his squadron back to Sackets, the troops being required to suffer through a miserable night beneath their sodden blankets.

After recuperating and waiting for a favourable wind, the squadron got under way again early on 25 April. In an order carefully diagrammed by Chauncey for his commanders, the thirteen vessels, each towing one or more of the army's bateaux, proceeded round Galloo Island, past the Ducks and into open water.[5] The *Julia* led the line and the *Growler* brought up the rear, with the *Madison* and *Oneida* holding positions in the centre. The weather was fair, the lake friendly, and the American armada sailed westward without incident.

Sentries atop the Scarborough Bluffs sighted Chauncey's sails early in the evening of 26 April and promptly relayed the news to the town of York by semaphore.[6] Sir Roger Hale Sheaffe was in the capital, having just finished legislative business and awaiting the arrival of Lieutenant Colonel Christopher Myers, who was to take command at the garrison. The British general was not surprised by enemy's appearance, since York's dockyard and weak defences made it a prime target. He immediately met with his senior officers and came to the conclusion that the Americans would land to the east and west of the town, trying to ensnare the British between their pincers (unless, of course, the squadron was bound for Niagara). Given the paucity of troops at his disposal, about 360 regulars and 300 militia and shipwrights, Sheaffe had few alternatives. To cover the eastern flank, he deployed two companies of militia in the town and at the blockhouse beside the legislative buildings, which stood near the edge of the marsh at the mouth of the Don River. He positioned the balance of his troops near the fort at the entrance to the harbour, which had been little improved since the outbreak of war and had only fourteen guns available for use. Adjacent to the fort was the government house, Sheaffe's temporary residence, in front of which was a battery containing two 12-pdr. guns. Nearby, in a hollow on the lake shore, was a large and well-stocked magazine, built of stone and earth. Two more batteries were located west of the garrison, but only one of them, half a mile up the shore, had guns, a pair of 18-pdrs. so ancient that they had been condemned and their trunnions broken off – lacking better equipment, the gunners had fastened the guns to wooden stocks.

Dawn on 27 April 1813 revealed the American vessels gathering near the eastern end of the long peninsula that enclosed the bay. They sailed westward and, rounding Gibraltar Point, aimed for a clearing a mile or so west of the fort, where the French had built a fortification in the previous century, a perfect spot to disembark their troops. Surprised that no flanking movement was being attempted, Sheaffe ordered the grenadier company of the 8th Foot to oppose the landing, supported by a body of native allies, a company each of the 8th and Glengarry Light Infantry, two weak companies of Newfoundland Fencibles and several militia companies. He sent no field guns with them, assuming that the narrow forest path would obstruct their passage.

Around 7:00 a.m. Chauncey's vessels dropped their anchors in front of the clearing, but nearly a mile offshore. The first wave of troops climbed down into the bateaux and ships' boats, which then gathered around the *Madison.* When Dearborn, Chauncey and Brigadier General Zebulon Pike felt the time was right, they gave the signal, and the flotilla struck for the beach, led by Major Benjamin Forsyth's riflemen in two of the larger boats. Dearborn had put Pike in command of the expedition and the young general had distributed precise instructions to his officers about how the landing was to proceed. The thirty-four-year-old Pike had spent more than half his life in the army, distinguishing himself during explorations of the west, and rising through the ranks, earning his promotion to brigadier general in March. In the eyes of his superiors, he was a zealous and dedicated officer, with a promising future in the military, but such admiration was not universal. Captain John Walworth, of the Sixth Infantry, mentioned to his father on 6 April, "Col. Pike has this day rec'd the appointment of Brigadier Gen. and is to command the 1st Brigade, the officers of his command almost detest him – none of them call to see him except one or two Sap heads."[7]

Seaman Ned Myers volunteered to help row the troops ashore from the *Scourge.* Up to that point he had been unimpressed with the soldiers, who were so sickened by the motion of the schooner that they refused their rations of grog. But as Myers and his mates bent to their oars and the British opened fire, his opinion changed as the infantry "became wide awake, pointed out to each other where to aim, and many of them actually jumped into the water, in order to get the sooner ashore."[8]

Hard fighting occurred as the Americans tried to gain a foothold on British soil. The rising wind out of the east had blown them along the shore during their long passage from the ships, causing them to ground nearly half a mile west of the clearing, in the vicinity of modern Dufferin Street. The Indians and the grenadiers hurried to oppose the landing alone as the troops intended to support them were delayed or became disoriented in the intervening forest.

Forsyth's Rifle Regiment was the first to land and quickly took cover among the trees, where their green uniforms blended into the undergrowth. They sniped at the British, who poured volleys into the boats as more Americans splashed ashore. Ned Myers did not enjoy being in the middle of the shooting gallery. "It is no fun to pull in under a sharp fire, with one's back to his enemy," he recollected, "and nothing but an oar to amuse himself with. The shot flew pretty thick, and two of our oars were split."[9]

During the middle of the melee, Pike arrived, conveyed in one of Chauncey's boats. The vanguard of his brigade inflicted heavy casualties on the British (nearly half the 8th Foot grenadiers were killed) and pushed them back, and Pike quickly organized his men to advance east toward the fort. Having delivered the army to the beach, the navy undertook its second objective, namely supporting the land attack. Several schooners moved closer to the shore, spraying the forest with canister from their long guns, chasing the British away and buying time for Pike's preparations. While the general began his march through the trees to the clearing and beyond, other schooners leapfrogged ahead and engaged the British 18-pdr. battery and the batteries at the government house and garrison. Being too deep of hull, the *Madison* and *Oneida* remained anchored well out from the land. Dearborn preferred the view from that distance and stayed put throughout the battle, but not so Isaac Chauncey. As an army officer noted, "the Commodore was through the whole of the action in his boat, encouraging and giving orders to the different schooners."[10]

The narrow paths through the thick forest slowed the eastward advance of the American column, which finally came to a full stop as round shot from the 18-pdr. battery whined by close overhead. Pike began to deploy infantry and artillery to attack the battery when it was suddenly removed from the contest by a mishandled match that detonated its magazine with a flash and a roar that killed and wounded dozens of British officers and men. When the survivors had regained their wits, they straggled back toward the garrison, and Pike resumed his movement on the garrison.

On the *Scourge*, Myers and his friends cheered at their enemy's misfortune. Sailing Master Joseph Osgood, their captain, steered to engage the garrison batteries just as Chauncey's gig came gliding by. He climbed onto the schooner to a round of cheers and spoke to the men, encouraging them. Round shot came whistling aboard, scattering a rack of boarding pikes and injuring a seaman. Chauncey ordered Myers to carry him below and a few minutes later as Myers's own gun crew hustled to remove and replace a disabled 6-pdr. long gun, he remarked, "That is quick work, my lads!" When Chauncey left, the men gave him three cheers again and watched "the old man … [as] he pulled through the fire

The attack on York, 27 April 1813. Though this modern depiction is inaccurate in its proportions and the number of American vessels on hand, it does present a reasonable illustration of how the navy supported Pike's brigade by landing his troops and covering their advance. The ship *Madison* and brig *Oneida* are shown at anchor off shore while the schooner gunboats tack back and forth as they engage the British batteries. (By Owen Staples, courtesy of the Toronto Reference Library, T-10271)

as coolly as if it were only a snow-balling scrape though many a poor fellow lost the number of his mess in the boats that day."[11]

About this time, noon, the event occurred that essentially ended the action. Having suffered heavy casualties and failed to repulse the landing, Sheaffe decided to retreat with his surviving regulars. He turned over command to two militia officer, Lieutenant Colonel William Chewett and Major William Allan, gave orders to blow up the main magazine and set fire to the *Sir Isaac Brock* and the dockyard storehouses, rallied his troops and marched out of York down the Kingston Road. Shortly thereafter the magazine exploded with an earsplitting roar, flinging debris hundreds of feet into the air amid a vast cloud of smoke. Chunks of stone and timber and earth rained down in a wide circle of death. Even on the *Scourge*, several hundred yards offshore, Ned Myers noted that "stones as big as my two fists fell on board of us, though nobody was hurt by them."[12] The same could not be said among Pike's troops, who had been standing at ease within 200 yards of the magazine. Thirty-eight Americans were killed outright, while another 222 were wounded by the explosion. Among the latter was Pike, who turned his back to the blast and was hit by a boulder that crushed his spine and left him gasping for life. He was carried quickly down to the beach and transported to the *Pert*, which in turn conveyed him to the *Madison*,where he soon expired, resting his head on a British flag captured on the battlefield and brought to him as proof of his victory.[13]

Brigadier General Zebulon Pike, U.S. Army (1779-1813). Due to his lofty rank and importance, Pike's remains were preserved in a cask of spirits and returned to Sackets Harbour early in May, where he was buried with full military honours in an iron casket. (Portrait by Thomas Gimbrede, courtesy of the Toronto Reference Library, T-15207)

A victory it was – at least superficially. The Americans had routed the British army and raised the Stars and Stripes over the capital of Upper Canada. The army and navy had demonstrated their ability to work cooperatively, by executing the largest joint operation in their nation's short history. The news of the first significant American military victory of the war spread through New York State, helping Daniel Tompkins trounce his opponent in the gubernatorial election.

There the celebrations ended, though, for the expedition was badly stained by an excess of blood and failed expectations. The explosion of the magazine had run up the butcher's bill to shocking proportions. Dearborn reported 55 dead and 265 wounded in all, while Sheaffe tabulated his losses at 66 killed and 71 wounded or missing.[14] The two brigs-of-war said to have been near launch in the York dockyard were not to be found. Instead, the rotten *Duke of Gloucester* lay unrigged and in mid-repair, while a mass of charred timbers showed where the *Brock* had stood. Blackened beams and mounds of ashes were all that remained of the storehouses containing large amounts of naval materiel. In their summaries of the action, Dearborn and Chauncey praised their men for their "great firmness" and "cool intrepidity," but employed no superlatives to describe the advantages gained at the cost of so many casualties. In tallying the captured goods, Chauncey listed "twenty cannon of different calibres from 32 to 6 pounders, a number of muskets, large quantities of fixed ammunition, shot, shells, and munitions of war of various kinds, a great deal of which was in boxes marked for Niagara and Malden."[15] Dearborn's men confiscated £2,500 from the provincial treasury.

After reading the official reports and unofficial narratives of the battle, Secretary of War Armstrong wrote a private letter to Dearborn on 15 May that contained none of the congratulations typical of the public announcements. Clearly composed as "an official censure," it pointed out the glaring disappointments of the battle: Pike's death, the loss of the new warship that "according to the Commodore's calculations" was supposed to have given him "a decided and permanent ascendancy on the Lake" and the escape of Sheaffe's troops. Although Armstrong admitted his "very insufficient knowledge of the topography of the country," he did not hesitate to suggest "that had the descent been made between the town and the barracks, things would have turned out better." The secretary expressed his hope that the next phase of the campaign would be orchestrated in such a way that the British force would "not be permitted to escape to-day that it may fight us to-morrow."[16]

The secretary had not learned yet of the other two great failures of the attack on York, the first being a remarkable lack of discipline in both services following the battle. For several days roving gangs of soldiers and seamen and local American sympathizers plundered and ravaged the town, freeing prisoners from the local jail, looting houses and harassing citizens. They burned the

Burning the bridge over the Don River, 27 April 1813. To forestall any American pursuers, General Sheaffe ordered the destruction of the Don River bridge as he headed out on the Kingston Road. His retreat preserved half his men to fight another day, but cost him overall command in Upper Canada. Thomas Plucknett and most of the shipwrights went with him. (Courtesy of the National Archives of Canada, C-6147)

legislature buildings, a library and the blockhouse by the Don River as well as the blockhouse at the garrison and the government house. Forsyth's riflemen were later accused of having done the worst damage as retribution for the sacking of Ogdensburg, but they were not the only culprits. Ned Myers admitted to going ashore, breaking into houses, stealing sugar, tea, liquor and enough other things to fill a purloined canoe twice over. He and his mates escaped punishment, and it was not until 3 May that the last of the American stragglers finally returned to the squadron. Representatives of the town protested repeatedly to Dearborn and Chauncey, and both officers tried to re-establish order in their ranks, and arranged for some of the captured provisions to be distributed among destitute families, but the length of time needed to get their carousing men under control was an indication of the poor discipline of the American force.

The other setback was initiated by the slow re-embarkation of the forces and worsened by adverse weather. Originally, it had been intended to remain at York until a British relief column departed from Fort George to recapture it. Then Chauncey would transport Dearborn's men to the Niagara Peninsula and attack Fort George in conjunction with an army waiting to storm across the Niagara River. This manoeuvre did not come to pass because by the time Dearborn's troops had all returned to the vessels, a persistent spring storm blanketed the vicinity, hammering the squadron with wind and rain and forcing it to remain anchored just west of Gibraltar Point for nearly a week. Only that superb little sea-boat *Lady of the Lake* was able to get away to deliver Dearborn and his staff to Fort Niagara on 3 May. [17] Some days earlier Chauncey had ordered Lieutenant Joseph Smith in the *Asp* to sail for Sackets Harbour with the worst of the wounded, in company with the transport *Gold Hunter*, but they could not make headway against the wind and were forced to anchor again until 4 May when the wounded could be carried to Fort Niagara instead. [18] It was not until 8 May that the rest of the squadron left York, crossed the lake and began landing the army down the coast from Fort Niagara at the Four Mile Creek anchorage. The men who stumbled ashore were in deplorable condition. As the commodore explained to Secretary Jones, "they had been so long crowded on board of the vessels without the opportunity of getting below or changing their wet clothes, that a fever was breaking out among the seamen and soldiers that was truly alarming. The soldiers were reduced to less than 1,000 effective men, and we had about 100 seamen sick in the fleet." [19]

A council of war involving Dearborn, Chauncey, Major General Morgan Lewis and Brigadier Generals William Winder and John Boyd decided that the troops needed at least a couple of weeks "to recruit their health and spirits." [20]

They postponed the attack on Fort George and Chauncey agreed to return to Sackets to bring up Chandler's brigade, during which time other units were expected to arrive at Fort Niagara. In part, Dearborn blamed the alteration in plans on the failure of the officers at Fort Niagara to complete preparations for the attack and the inclement weather, but he plainly held the navy responsible for the delay, as he explained to Secretary Armstrong on 13 May: "[Even] with all these defects, we should have made the attack on the 4th or 5th if the fleet had arrived with the troops in health on the 3d as expected."[21]

The *Madison* and seven schooners, including the prize *Duke of Gloucester,* soon to be renamed the *York* and used as an ammunition tender, returned to Sackets Harbour on 11 May. Lieutenant Woolsey had been detached in the *Oneida* with three schooners to pick up provisions that had arrived from New York. Three other schooners had been left at Fort Niagara, two of which, the *Governor Tompkins* and *Conquest,* participated in a raid on the British depot at Forty Mile Creek on 9 May, burning storehouses there.[22]

At Sackets Chauncey landed the casualties and sick from the York expedition at the hospital that had been set up in one of the barracks on Navy Point. The majority of the men recuperated and rejoined the squadron, but some, like Sailing Master Frederick Leonard, brother to the disgraced master commandant, died and were laid to rest in the village's cemetery. The crews had been further depleted at Niagara when fifty men went to Black Rock, where Commandant Oliver Perry and Henry Eckford were converting lakers into gunboats. Reinforcements had arrived at the Harbour, 147 officers and seamen sent from the *Constitution* at Boston by Captain William Bainbridge, but the shortage of manpower continued to be a concern to Chauncey since Perry needed several hundred additional hands and the new ship at Sackets had yet to be manned. That vessel was rapidly reaching completion; by 20 May it was all planked and half caulked, its launch date still on schedule for 1 June. Along with petitions for more men, Chauncey wrote to Jones to remind him that the ship lacked a commander and officers.[23]

As usual the commodore was anxious to hear about the latest developments at Kingston. He sent the *Lady of the Lake,* under Sailing Master Thomas Nichols, across on 14 May to return several prisoners, but the British intercepted it outside Kingston Harbour and prevented it from entering.[24] All Chauncey learned from Nichols was that the *Royal George, Earl of Moira, Prince Regent* and *Simcoe* appeared ready to sail, that the new ship was launched and almost rigged and that a Montreal newspaper had noted that eight Royal Navy officers, including a rear admiral, were on their way to the lake. This information increased Chauncey's anxiety about sailing from Sackets Harbour with

Chandler's brigade and leaving his base weakly defended against an attack. Nevertheless, it was his job to transport the army to Niagara, which he commenced on 16 May by ordering ten of his vessels to embark Chandler's men and head up the lake. Chauncey kept the *Lady of the Lake* cruising off Kingston Channel while he remained at anchor in the *Madison* waiting for reinforcements to reach the harbour.[25] To Dearborn he wrote, "I hope you will be perfectly prepared to act as soon as I arrive as I should not feel satisfied to keep the fleet long in that part of the Lake while the Enemy was in such force at Kingston and commanded by an experienced and enterprizing officer."[26]

The naval situation at Kingston had changed during the first week of May when Commander Robert Barclay and his colleagues from the Royal Navy arrived by boat at Point Frederick. He and the two other commanders, six lieutenants and two gunners from Admiral Warren's fleet had reached Halifax during the third week of March. Leaving the gunners and two lieutenants to oversee a shipment of ordnance, stores and rigging bound from Halifax to the lakes via Quebec when ice conditions allowed, Barclay and the others sailed to Saint John, New Brunswick, to begin the long overland trek. Barclay went on ahead, reaching Quebec on 20 April and presenting despatches to Sir George Prevost. Four days later he headed up-river with Commanders Robert Finnis and Daniel Pring, who had caught up to him.[27]

It appears that they had been warned about the sad state of the Provincial Marine, but what Barclay and the others discovered at Kingston was not so deplorable. "The Ships are I think as fine vessels of their kind as I have ever seen," Barclay wrote to Noah Freer, who had been promoted to captain. "The *Moira* is small, it is true, but she is by no means so despicable as was represented."[28] He considered the *Prince Regent* better suited for use as a dispatch boat than a warship. "The state in which I found the executive part of the Dock Yard reflects the highest credit on Capt. Gray," Barclay noted, although he recommended that a change in system was needed to limit "the abuse of public Stores."[29]

By the time of Barclay's appearance at Kingston, it was common knowledge that Sir James Lucas Yeo, an experienced officer, would soon arrive in Canada to take command on the lakes. Until then Barclay's main responsibility was to assess the situation at the naval establishment, make suggestions about its improvement and begin the process of reshaping it to meet Royal Navy standards. Without hesitation, he went to work, taking command of the *Wolfe* and assigning his companions to the other vessels. This, of course, meant that the officers of the Provincial Marine were displaced from their positions of authority. That such a change would take place had been formally announced in a general

The anchorage at Quebec. The St. Lawrence River at Quebec was crowded with warships and merchantmen during the war as depicted in this watercolour believed to have been done in 1814. The view is from Wolfe's Cove looking down river to Cape Diamond on the left and the citadel standing guard over the lower town. (Watercolour by H. T. Davies, courtesy of the National Archives of Canada, C-138099)

order from Prevost on 22 April. Prevost had assured the Marine officers that they would "be suitably provided for without dimunition of their salaries," but that failed to soothe their wounded pride.[30] As Barclay noted, they seemed "to feel the loss of their commands more sensibly than was expected" and virtually all quit the service.[31] Only three officers agreed to remain in the squadron, Surgeon Grant Powell and Lieutenants James Richardson and George Smith, while Master and Commander Hugh Earl leaned toward accepting a position as supervisor of the naval arsenal and Lieutenant Oliver Grace obtained permission to resign his commission for health reasons. Edward Platt indicated his eagerness to remain as master attendant in the dockyard, and James Richardson, Sr., master of the *Governor Simcoe*, volunteered to join the squadron. These men Barclay recommended highly to Sir George, but as for less cooperative officers like Lieutenants William Fish, Francis Gauvreau and Theophilus Sampson, he believed that they deserved little in the way of compensation, given their refusal to help their King and country in a time of need.

As he inspected the squadron and the dockyard, Barclay easily identified some missing necessities. At the top of his list were cables for the ships,

4 cabouses and their assorted equipment, and 20 barrels each of pitch and tar. Among the other miscellaneous items needed were white, black and yellow paint (7 hundredweight in all), 30 coils of various sizes of rope, 30 gallons of linseed oil, 6 compasses, 20 padlocks, 6 whipsaws and more than 5,500 yards of canvas. Barclay also emphasized that Royal Navy seamen were accustomed to an allowance of butter and cheese or cocoa and sugar as a substitute and that they expected a regular ration of tobacco, of which there was none at Kingston, a hardship that "would be severely felt." As for strengthening the squadron, he suggested the construction of between six and ten gunboats, large enough to carry a heavy long gun in the bow and a carronade in the stern. After consulting Andrew Gray, he also advised that sufficient wood remained in store on Point Frederick to lay down another ship in place of the one destroyed at York.[32]

The Royal Navy reached Kingston about the same time as Sheaffe and the survivors from York. After an exceedingly difficult march, Sheaffe finally composed his report and sent it to Prevost, who had left Quebec for Montreal as soon as he heard of the battle. Other versions of events in the provincial capital found their way to Prevost's attention during this time and the majority of them could not have reflected well on Sheaffe's conduct, for popular opinion was that he had defended York poorly. "He has lost entirely the confidence of the regulars and militia and his very name is odious to all ranks of people," declared a group of citizens at York, including William Chewett and William Allan.[33] Every aspect of his opposition to the invaders was castigated, from his slowness in deploying his troops, to the distance he kept between himself and the fighting and his failure to leave medical men behind to treat the wounded. "The general with the troops," wrote one observer, "pushed on to Kingston, and left us standing in the street, like a parcel of sheep."[34]

Although Prevost had been critical of Sheaffe's command in a recent despatch to Earl Bathurst, he did not take this opportunity to issue a formal reprimand for the defeat at York.[35] It also appears that neither Prevost nor anyone else congratulated the general for having saved half his regular troops rather than sacrificing them to a losing fight and for having the presence of mind to prevent the *Brock* from falling into Chauncey's hands. Instead, Prevost transmitted copies of the general's reports to Bathurst (as Sheaffe did himself) and attributed the defeat to the inferior size of the British force, the American ascendancy on Lake Ontario and Admiral Warren's neglect to send seamen sooner.[36] Prevost let a week pass before he announced to Bathurst that he was transferring Sheaffe to Montreal and giving his position as commander-in-chief of the armed forces in Upper Canada and head administrator of the government to Major General Francis De Rottenburg.[37] The change was publicly announced on 6 June and took effect on the nineteenth; Sheaffe remained at Montreal until the following November when, at Prevost's request, he was recalled to England.

Unmentioned in the official correspondence was the fact that the defences at York had been weak. There were only 200 regulars in the garrison – the two companies of the 8th Foot, on a march to Fort George, were only there by coincidence. The ordnance that Sheaffe had requested for the protection of the shipping (and that Prevost had promised would be transported) had not arrived. Reinforcing Kingston and the Niagara Peninsula had taken up all the available resources while York continued in a weakened state. As Lieutenant Colonel Ralph Bruyeres had pointed out during the winter, the decision to establish a naval base at York, long supported by Brock and Andrew Gray, and approved by Prevost, had been detrimental, except to divert American attention away from Kingston by presenting a sitting duck to the Americans. Prevost had actually aggravated the situation by selecting Thomas Plucknett as superintendent at York, which led to the delayed construction of the *Brock*. Prevost neither acknowledged these aspects of Sheaffe's defeat nor assumed any responsibility for the setbacks it created.

Like the maligned general, however, Prevost was soon the target of bitter resentment in the province's capital. Chewett, Allan and their friends openly criticized his management of the war, especially his devotion to a purely defensive policy despite the fact that they had warned him about the growing strength of the Americans. "This province," they wrote, "without a superiority on the water cannot be preserved." Prevost, in their opinion, should have gone on the offensive in the winter to reduce Chauncey's force. "In the capture of York," the dissidents declared, "behold the first fruits of that imbecility which prevented a vigorous attack upon Sackett's Harbour, an attack which … would have secured this Province during the whole war."[38]

The day after Prevost left for Montreal HMS *Woolwich* anchored at Quebec and Commodore Sir James Lucas Yeo set foot in Canada for the first time. Learning of the battle at York and Prevost's departure, the commodore ordered the 465 officers and seamen in his detachment to be ready to head up river at first light next morning. Well familiar with the vagaries of war, Yeo knew that speed was of the essence.

James Yeo's birthplace and family had strong connnections with the sea; he was born on 7 October 1782 in Southampton, the son of a naval victualling agent.[39] His formal education, received at an academy near Winchester, ended when at the age of ten he joined HMS *Windsor Castle* as a young gentleman thanks to the patronage of Admiral Phillips Cosby.[40] Few details are known about Yeo's early years in the Royal Navy, though his talents were recognized quickly and by the age of fourteen he had been advanced to acting-lieutenant in charge of the sixteen-gun sloop *Albacore*. Stationed in the West Indies, Yeo fell victim to Yellow Fever and went home in 1798 to recuperate. Within four years he was first lieutenant in HMS *Genereux* and publicly recognized for his leadership in action in the Adriatic Sea, but that distinction did not save him from demotion to half pay when the Peace of Amiens came in March 1802.

When Britain's war with France resumed, Yeo moved into Captain F. L. Maitland's frigate *Loire* as first officer. Patrolling off the northwest coast of Spain in June 1805, Maitland decided to attack enemy shipping at El Muros Bay and sent Lieutenant Yeo ashore with fifty men to silence a battery as the first step in the mission. Another more powerful emplacement soon opened a threatening fire upon the *Loire*, which prompted Yeo to attempt to seize it also. The naval party swarmed the battery, where they were outnumbered five to one, and carried it after a bloody fight in which the Spaniards suffered more than forty casualties; the British had six wounded, including Yeo, whose career nearly terminated on the end of a bayonet. El Muros quickly surrendered, and Maitland's men confiscated three vessels moored in the harbour, including a smart little corvette of twenty-two guns named the *Confiance*. In his report, Maitland declared that Yeo had "displayed as much gallantry as ever fell to the lot of any man," and to prove his high opinion of the lieutenant he placed him in command of the *Confiance*.[41] The ship was quickly bought into the navy and, Yeo was promoted to commander by the Admiralty before the end of June at the age of twenty-one.

In December 1807 the *Confiance* was part of Rear Admiral Sir Sidney Smith's fleet off Portugal. Commander Yeo conveyed Lord Strangford, the British ambassador, to Lisbon for negotiations that secured Portugal's alliance with Britain and arranged a passage to Brazil for the Prince Regent, Dom Joao, and his court. While the fleet sailed for Rio de Janeiro, Admiral Smith ordered Yeo home with news of the successful agreement, a privilege that led to him being posted to the seniority list of captains. As a "post" captain he should have moved into a larger ship, but Yeo must have expressed affection for the *Confiance*, because he was allowed to keep it and it was reclassified as a "post" ship.

During 1808 the *Confiance* was stationed at Rio de Janeiro with Smith, when Captain Yeo was instructed to carry despatches to General Jose Narcizo de Magles de Menez at the town of Para on the mouth of the Amazon River. Arriving at Para on 21 October, Yeo learned from de Menez that French privateers based at Cayenne in French Guiana had been attacking British merchantmen,

Commodore Sir James Lucas Yeo, RN (1782-1818). Sir Sidney Smith, one of Yeo's most important patrons, once described him as "a zealous, enterprising, laborious, daring, yet discreet public officer . . . [whose] Cayenne service [was] unequalled in the annals of our navy, except *by his own* similar audacious deed of arms at Muros." (After a painting by A. Buck, courtesy of the Toronto Reference Library, T-15241)

and the two men decided to put together a force strong enough to remove the threat. On 6 January 1809 a combined British and Portuguese expedition comprising the *Confiance*, 550 Portuguese infantrymen, two armed vessels and smaller craft arrived off the island of Cayenne. Within four days they had captured two forts, put a 1,000-man army to flight and orchestrated the capitulation of General Victor Hugues, governor of French Guiana, and his regime, thereby evicting the French from their last colony in South America. The brief campaign had been conducted during tremendously rainy and blustery weather, exhausting the British in particular and causing Yeo and many of his men to fall sick. Notable in the despatch Yeo wrote to describe the affair was his mention of two men who would later follow him to Canada, his twelve-year-old brother, George Cosby Yeo, and his first lieutenant and friend, William Howe Mulcaster. The latter had been especially important in the Cayenne campaign, often taking leadership of one wing of the offensive while Yeo led the other.

The Portuguese prince regent was so impressed with Yeo's accomplishment that, apart from giving him a diamond ring and distributing splendid gifts among his officers and crew, he bestowed upon the twenty-six-year-old captain a knighthood in the Order of St. Bento d'Avis, the first non-Catholic to be so honoured. In September 1809 Lord Strangford and Admiral Smith again delegated Yeo to carry despatches home, knowing well that his achievements would cause a sensation. He was summoned to the court at St. James, where King George III granted him permission to keep the Portuguese knighthood and then decreed him a knight commander of the Bath with authorization to assume his own coat of arms. The heraldic insignia was designed to represent his greatest achievements to date: the towers of Muros, the star of St. Bento and the name "Confiance."

Yeo was next placed in command of the frigate *Southampton*, 32, in which he arrived at Jamaica in March 1811 to join the fleet of Vice Admiral Charles Stirling. It took the young knight nearly a year to execute another of his daring exploits; on 3 February 1812 the *Southampton* captured a pirate flotilla comprising the *Amethyste*, 44, a brig and a corvette, manned by crews numbering more than 1,000 men.[42] After the declaration of the American war the *Southampton* cruised the eastern seaboard, and in September Yeo stopped a brig bound for New York, then sent it on its way having entrusted into the hands of a passenger a challenge to Captain David Porter of the frigate *Essex* to meet the *Southampton* off the Delaware Capes so that Yeo could "break [Porter's] sword over his damn'd head and put him down forward in irons."[43] Porter was willing to meet the challenge, but the meeting did not take place. Instead, the *Southampton* sailed southward and on 22 November outraced the US Brig *Vixen*, 14, seizing it in short order. Disaster soon nullifed the triumph because on the night of 27 November, the frigate and its latest prize ran upon a shoal near Concession Island in the Bahamas, broke their backs and sank. The British and their captives reached safety in ships' boats and a pair of tenders accompanying the *Southampton*.[44] The loss of his ship was the darkest hour in Yeo's otherwise unblemished career and it required him to return to England to explain his actions before a court martial. By coincidence, his good friend William Howe Mulcaster, who had been promoted to commander for his service at Cayenne, had wrecked his first command, the brig *Emulous,* on Ragged Island off the coast of Nova Scotia in August and had gone home to face a similar board of his superiors.[45]

Yeo and Mulcaster were acquitted of blame in the sinking of their ships, but they were left without immediate commands. Their misfortunes, however, had placed them in England at the very time when the Admiralty was looking around for an energetic, competent officer with a proven record of succeeding in the face of adversity. Lord Melville summoned Yeo and informed him about the situation on the Great Lakes, the weakness of the Provincial Marine, the escalation of American naval strength, the limited numbers of British troops and the vast geography of the war. If he agreed to lead the navy's detachment to the lakes, Melville told Yeo, his "first and paramount" concern would be "the defense of His Majesty's Provinces of North America," which he would maintain by cooperating "cordially" with Sir George Prevost, "not undertaking any operations without the full concurrence and approbation of him or of the Commanders of the Forces employed under him."[46] As well, Yeo would report frequently and thoroughly to the Admiralty about conditions on his station and he would also have to maintain regular communications with Admiral Warren. Although the position seemed to carry with it almost as many masters to please as enemies to face, Yeo did not back down from the challenge. His past experiences had prepared him for the chain of command that would link him to Quebec, London and Bermuda. Accepting the appointment also meant that Yeo could hoist a broad pendant as commodore and senior officer on a foreign station, commanding more than 450 officers and men and squadrons of vessels. It was a glorious opportunity, and the dauntless captain, whose thirtieth birthday had passed only five months before, accepted it with zeal – and gratitude for the confidence in his capabilities that his superiors clearly demonstrated.

Late February and early March of 1813 was a hectic time for Yeo. A vast number of preparations had to be made to equip the detachment for the lakes, but the personnel of the Royal Navy specialized in meeting such demands, and correspondence was soon flying back and forth across England calling in officers, seamen, ordnance, rigging and the myriad other items that would go into the troopship *Woolwich* for the voyage across the ocean. One of the perks of his new command was that Sir James could request the services of certain officers, if they were available. Since three commanders were to accompany him, Yeo chose William Mulcaster first. The record does not indicate that the other two commanders who joined the party, Francis Spilsbury and Thomas England, had sailed with Yeo, but a fourth man had.[47] He was Commander Richard O'Conor, who had been in the *Confiance* as a young lieutenant. O'Conor heard about the expedition to Canada and, being without a ship, asked permission from the Admiralty to volunteer to go along with Yeo. As he had done in the past, the commodore added his brother George to the muster as well as a handful of seamen who had followed him from the *Confiance* to the *Southampton*.

In all, four commanders, seven lieutenants, eight master's mates, thirteen midshipmen, two masters, two surgeons, four surgeon's assistants and 425 warrant officers and seamen, able and ordinary, embarked in the *Woolwich*.[48] They came from all parts of the service, lieutenants "on promotion," such as Charles Anthony and Alexander Dobbs, who were expecting to command one of the Great Lakes vessels, master's mates hoping to rise to acting-lieutenants, and midshipmen looking for advancement out of the crowded cockpit. The seamen came in scores from press gangs or from the receiving ship *Royal William* and in dozens from ships paying off or from captains looking to get rid of troublemakers. They were all veterans of the sea and of war; some, like Midshipman John Hill, had been with Nelson at the Battle of the Nile in 1798, while others, like Lieutenant Charles Anthony, had been at Trafalgar. Some had been captured by the French but had escaped back to England as Lieutenant Charles Cunliffe Owen had, or gone with Saumarez to the Baltic to face the Danes and Russians, as had Midshipman David Wingfield. The wealth of experience they brought to Canada would prove to be their most significant asset when they faced the Americans on the lakes.

Yeo joined the *Woolwich* at Portsmouth on 17 March 1813, and it left there a few days later for a brief stop at Plymouth before finally setting out across the Atlantic on 30 March. The *Woolwich*, specially fitted out as a transport, was crowded, carrying not only Yeo's force and naval materiel, but also a number of military officers. For some of the young men, the voyage was "a tolerable passage," because it brought the beginning of a great, new adventure. David Wingfield, eager to rise to a lieutenancy, recalled that "the vague idea we had of the Service, ... made us look upon it as pregnant with danger; but headed by an officer of our Commodore's known bravery, made us the more anxious to come in contact with the Enemy."[49] Another junior officer, Master's Mate John

A view of Montreal. Although drawn in 1830, this illustration indicates the variety of traffic on the St. Lawrence River, from bateaux and timber rafts to sloops and a steamboat, that operated between Quebec and Montreal during the War of 1812. (Ink drawing by R. A. Sproule, courtesy of the National Archives of Canada, C-100559)

Johnston, who had been impressed with Yeo's gentility when they met in the social circles of London, was shocked to discover that the commodore "quite altered his tone in Blue Water, particularly with us Mids, who he looks upon as a poor set of wretches sent out to be butchered for their Commissions and not worthy the name of Officers."[50] Yeo ordered Johnston out of the wardroom where he had originally been accommodated and down to the midshipman's berth, which the disappointed fellow found "a horrid place so crowded and Jam'd up in such a manner that I frequently feel suffocated; the passage home from India was completely Paradise compared to it."[51] By the time the *Woolwich* picked its way through the ice floes in the Gulf of St. Lawrence, poor Johnston was vowing to quit at Quebec and return home, never to sail again.

Before dawn on 6 May 1813 a flotilla of more than forty small boats gathered around the *Woolwich* at Quebec, and the officers with their parties of seamen began climbing down into them for the trip to Montreal. As Wingfield remembered, it was a less than orderly scene: "One vessel had all the biscuit, and another all the beef, which should have been divided among forty-two; the pork, we afterwards learned had been left on board the *Woolwich*."[52] Wingfield and his mates dined on eggs the master of their sloop gave them and playfully mocked their colleagues who lacked any dinner at all.

After reaching Montreal, where he met Prevost, Yeo split his men into three divisions for the journey by land and water to Kingston. The third division, supervised by Commander England, had the task of conducting two heavy gunboats up the rapids that interrupted the river at several places between Montreal and Prescott. Yeo and Prevost went ahead with the first group, arriving at Prescott around 15 May; from there they travelled in a flotilla of ships' boats and bateaux, escorted by the gunboat *Black Snake,* under the command of Provincial Marine Lieutenant Richardson, and sailed into Kingston Harbour the next day.[53]

Commander Robert Barclay welcomed Yeo to the lakes and handed over command of the naval establishment. Yeo was thankful for the work Barclay had done to improve the base, but the presence of the officers sent out by Warren left him with too many commanders and not enough ships. Barclay turned down the offer of the command of a gunboat flotilla on the upper St. Lawrence, so Yeo placed him in charge of the Provincial Marine squadron on Lake Erie. By 20 May Barclay left Kingston with three lieutenants, a surgeon, a purser, an ailing master's mate and nineteen seamen, most of whom, he later claimed, were the dregs of the Lake Ontario squadron.[54] Yeo picked Commander Daniel Pring to act as his flag captain in the *Wolfe,* though that term lasted less than two months. In July Pring was sent to command on Lake Champlain while the other commander, Robert Finnis, went to join Barclay.

With Barclay gone, Yeo hoisted his flag in the *Wolfe.* Mulcaster moved into the *Royal George* and Francis Spilsbury into the *Prince Regent* (which Yeo promptly renamed the *Beresford*). At first, Thomas England had the *Earl of Moira,* but the arduous job of hauling the gunboats up from Montreal had left him so sick that he was invalided home, and Lieutenant Alexander Dobbs received his eagerly awaited advancement to acting-commander in his place. The *Governor Simcoe* was ready for duty by this time, and after he changed its name to the *Sir Sidney Smith,* Yeo put Lieutenant Charles Radcliffe in charge of it. Perhaps owing to his status as a volunteer, Commander Richard O'Conor did not get a command afloat; instead, he agreed to remain on land acting as a commissioner at Point Frederick with the responsibility of instilling order into its administration.

Seventy members of the Provincial Marine remained in the squadron to supplement the Royal Navy draft. Yeo met with Lieutenants Richardson and Smith and asked if they would serve as pilots since their ranks did not equate to Royal Navy ranks, to which both men agreed. Throughout all the vessels the new commanders organized standard navy routines and systems, promoting the most capable seamen into positions ranging from boatswain to gunner, from quartermaster to captain of the foretop. Rather than creating an establishment in each separate crew, as was the Royal Navy habit, the entire squadron was listed on one set of books, kept by Purser John Marks with assistance from clerks in some of the vessels. The commodore kept close track of the many alterations and concluded that he lacked sufficient manpower to run the squadron the way it should be. As he had done in his first letter to the Admiralty, written at Quebec on 5 May, Yeo expressed concern that if he was able to take supremacy on Lake Ontario away from the Americans, "the superiority cannot long be maintained without an immediate reinforcement of seamen."[55] Although he was undermanned and commanded a squadron that he considered "in a very weak state," the commodore was determined "to proceed to sea to meet" the enemy within ten days of taking control at Kingston.

The arrival of the Royal Navy at Kingston excited much attention and, as Midshipman Wingfield recalled, "raised the drooping spirits of the inhabitants of that place, and generally, of the country at large."[56] Even Prevost was moved to write, "this most seasonable reinforcement will I hope enable us to regain an ascendancy on Lake Ontario."[57] That was the point of the whole exercise, and Yeo's early display of efficiency and zeal served to bolster those expectations.

CHAPTER 8

"They Fought ... Like Lions"[1]

FORT GEORGE AND SACKETS HARBOUR: MAY 1813

*A*s the third week of May ended, Commodore Isaac Chauncey was in a quandary. He had to transport the last of Dearborn's troops to Niagara for the assault on Fort George, but he was reluctant to leave his naval base improperly defended, especially since all signs indicated a sizeable British reinforcement at Kingston. Chauncey expressed his concerns to Henry Dearborn on 16 May, particularly mentioning the dockyard and "the new ship here [which] is in a state that she might be easily burned."[2] When Lieutenant Colonel Electus Backus and the unmounted First Light Dragoons, numbering between three and four hundred, marched into Sackets on 21 May with about 250 effectives of the Ninth and Twenty-first Infantry not far behind them, the commodore could no longer justify remaining at anchor. The next day Colonel Alexander Macomb and about 350 of his unit boarded the *Madison*, which set sail for Niagara. Chauncey left behind sealed instructions for Lieutenant Wolcott Chauncey, whom he expected to return to Sackets in the *Fair American*, accompanied by the *Pert*, putting him in charge of the place in his absence. "At all events," he advised his brother, "if this place should be attacked, let the defence of the new Ship be such, as to do yourself credit and silence clamour."[3]

The wind was light and contrary, and the *Madison* tacked up and down across the lake for two full days before reaching the anchorage at Four Mile Creek on 25 May. There, Chauncey found preparations for the attack on Fort George well in hand and an army of more than 4,000 men ready for battle.[4] Dearborn's council of war, including Major General Morgan Lewis, Brigadier Generals John Boyd, William Winder and John Chandler and Colonel Winfield

Scott (recently assigned to be Dearborn's adjutant general, or chief of staff), had decided on a massive landing on the shore of Lake Ontario about two miles west of the British post. It would be made in three waves, with Scott leading the way, backed by Boyd and then Winder. Chandler would land last to secure the beachhead, while Macomb's unit would be held in reserve and Colonel James Burn's mounted dragoons would cross the Niagara River near Queenston to cut off the British retreat. With Dearborn too sick and disabled to participate actively, titular command of the expedition went to Morgan Lewis, although the plan for the landing was actually the work of Scott, whose talents and energy outpaced those of his superiors. The naval role in the combined operation would be to cover the approach of almost 140 small craft carrying the troops and support their attack. To facilitate this aspect of the operation, Chauncey made a close examination of the enemy shore and went out after dark on 26 May in his gig to moor buoys that would guide the commanders of his schooners to positions from which they could bombard British batteries; Master Commandant Oliver H. Perry, who had come down from Erie to get into the fight, played an active role in these preparations. At 2:00 a.m. the next morning the embarkation commenced as the squadron slowly drew away from Four Mile Creek before a faint breeze, and the boats and bateaux, brimming with soldiers, gathered around them. Dearborn and Lewis boarded the *Madison*, waited for word that everyone was in place and then gave the order to steer for the enemy shore.

The British were ready and waiting. In no uncertain terms the American intentions had been announced by a bombardment through 25 and 26 May that had damaged Fort George, burning most of its buildings to the ground. The fort was not the only defensive work at Niagara, as two strong batteries were situated outside the palisade, one at the lighthouse on Mississauga Point and the other at the mouth of Two Mile Creek. As the new day revealed the American flotilla sweeping slowly out of a thin fog, Brigadier General John Vincent and his staff officers sat astride their horses at the lighthouse. About 1,000 regulars (from the 8th, 41st and 49th Foot, the Royal Artillery and the Glengarry and Royal Newfoundland Regiments), 350 militia and fifty native warriors were available to meet the Americans. Vincent had deployed Lieutenant Colonel Myers with about 600 men to oppose the landing at Two Mile Creek, where he expected the enemy to come ashore. The rest of his force guarded the river and the fort and remained as a reserve in a central location.

The American attack began with the launch of a rocket from Fort Niagara and a thirty-minute bombardment of Fort George and the town of Niagara by the American land batteries. After the guns fell silent, an hour crawled by

Colonel Winfield Scott, U.S. Army (1786-1866). A Virginian by birth, Scott joined the army after the *Leopard/ Chesapeake* incident in 1807. He played a leading role as lieutenant colonel of the Second U.S. Artillery Regiment during the battle at Queenston in October 1812, where he was captured. His active service resumed in 1813 and he was promoted to brigadier general at the outset of the 1814 campaign. (Courtesy of the National Portrait Gallery, Smithsonian Institution, Neg. 07910)

during which the small craft inched toward land, and the schooners, at Chauncey's signal, glided into the positions he and Perry had marked for them and began to hammer the British with their long guns. The *Julia*, mounting one 32- and one 12-pdr., and the *Growler*, a single 32-pdr. and four 4-pdrs., anchored in the mouth of the river and engaged the battery at the lighthouse. The *Ontario*, armed identically to the *Julia*, took up a position just north of the lighthouse, hitting the British position in a murderous crossfire. This same technique proved effective when the *Governor Tompkins*, carrying a 32-, a 24- and two 9-pdr. guns, plus a pair of 24-pdr. carronades, and the *Conquest*, with two 24s and a 6, enfiladed the battery near Two Mile Creek. Meanwhile the *Hamilton* (one 12-pdr. long gun on a circle and four 18-pdr. carronades along each rail), the *Asp* (two guns, a 24 and a 12), and the *Scourge* (four 6s and six 4s), anchored within 300 yards of the landing site and pummelled the British line waiting to resist the landing. Since most of the ordnance was mounted on circles, as many as twenty-four pieces of ordnance battered the defenders at close range, supported by more than a dozen guns on the American shore. The bombardment cut swaths through the redcoats and eventually silenced the British batteries.

From his quarters aboard the *Scourge*, Ned Myers recollected: "We now kept up a steady fire with grape and cannister, until the boats had got in-shore and were engaged with the enemy, when we threw round-shot, over the heads of our men, upon the English."[5] Winfield Scott splashed ashore with his troops about 6:00 a.m. and steadily pushed back Myers's line. The British regrouped and charged, threatening Scott, but Boyd's bateaux landed and the sheer number of Americans, their rolling volleys of musketry and the hail of naval fire devastated the British. Dozens of redcoats were killed, while Myers and others were wounded and captured. Although Vincent rushed reinforcements to the scene of action, the invaders could not be repulsed and slowly the British retreated toward and through Niagara, eventually forming ranks on the common west of Fort George.

As Scott and Boyd's command advanced beyond the beach, disappearing among the trees, the third wave and the artillery landed. Chauncey had placed his marines on alert and had assembled a reserve of several hundred seamen for use as a reserve, but the army needed no assistance. Around 10:00 a.m. the wind picked up and the abandoned boats on the beach were in danger of knocking each other to pieces as they rocked about in the surf. Chauncey signalled some of his gunboats to secure the craft and then follow him to an anchorage in the river. From his place on the common, Vincent watched the *Madison* sailing up the river while a fresh wave of American troops rowed across the Niagara to join the fight, and as noon approached he issued orders for a retreat to Queenston.

The attack on Fort George, 27 May 1813. In a simplistic style, this contemporary view shows Forts Niagara and George and the British batteries at the Mississauga Lighthouse and at Two Mile Creek. As divisions of small boats head for shore, the American gunboats cover their landing while the *Madison* and *Oneida* anchor offshore. This rare representation of the *Madison* underestimates the corvette's broadside batteries. (Courtesy of the Archives of Ontario, S-1439)

Fuses were laid to blow up the magazines in the fort and express riders raced away with orders for commanders to withdraw from all the posts between Queenston and Fort Erie and to rendezvous with Vincent at a supply depot he had established seventeen miles southwest of Fort George near Beaver Dams.

Colonel James Burn's Second Light Dragoons were supposed to stand in the way of a British retreat, but Burn did not cross the Niagara in time. After almost mimicking Pike's demise by breaking his collarbone when he was knocked off his horse by the detonation of a magazine at the fort, Winfield Scott gathered his troops to pursue Vincent, but a direct order from Lewis stopped him. As had happened at York, the British made their escape, and in this instance so successfully that Vincent was able to muster close to 1,600 men at Burlington Heights on 29 May. Nevertheless, Lewis and Dearborn were satisfied with the smooth execution of the amphibious assault. They had secured a toehold in Upper Canada and would deal with Vincent soon enough. As Dearborn explained to Secretary Armstrong, "The troops having been under arms from one o'clock in the morning were too much exhausted for any further pursuit ... tomorrow we shall proceed further on."[6] Another advantage for the Americans was not immediately apparent when the retreating British set fire to storehouses between Fort Erie and Point Abino; they were destroying provisions desperately needed by Brigadier General Procter's garrison at Fort Malden.[7]

In sweeping up after the action at Niagara, Boyd's men counted 107 British dead and 175 wounded, although British estimates of their losses were closer to 450. American casualties were much lower, thirty-nine killed, 111 wounded, with the naval count at one dead, two wounded. Chauncey was complimented by Dearborn for "his co-operation in all [the squadron's] important movements, and especially in its operations this day."[8] The commodore in turn praised his own men, who "all behaved so well it is difficult to select any one for commendation," although he made mention of Perry's help and the skill of Lieutenant Joseph Macpherson in the *Hamilton*.[9] As he had done at York, Seaman Myers found his way ashore with some of his mates, though this time they did no plundering, stopping instead to defend a group of civilians who were threatened by marauding soldiers shortly after the battle. Chauncey later sent the marines ashore to guard the town of Niagara from such depredations. While the army occupied the fort and its exterior batteries and established an encampment on the common, the seamen returned to their ships to prepare for the next stage of the campaign.

When the decision had been made in April to attack York first and Niagara second, Chauncey had intended as his third step to detach a part of his fleet to blockade Kingston while he led as many men as possible to join Perry at Erie.

As the great plumes of black smoke over Niagara dissipated, however, a different view of the campaign came into focus. Despite the showers of rain that the blustery weather blew off the lake on 28 May, Major General Lewis set out with Chandler and Winder's brigades to engage Vincent at Beaver Dams, but turned back when they learned the British had retreated all the way to Burlington Heights. The American senior officers next formed a plan to convey as much of the army as possible to land at York to cut off Vincent's route to Kingston.[10] Assuming he would be occupied with transporting the army again, Chauncey detached fifty-five seamen under Perry to sail the Black Rock vessels up to Erie since the Canadian side of the Niagara had now been cleared of British.

The voyage to York did not take place because late on 29 May a familiar sail came racing up the shore carrying a messenger, who delivered a hurriedly scribbled note from Lieutenant Wolcott Chauncey to his brother announcing that the British were on the lake and threatening Sackets Harbour. Anxious to return immediately to his base, Chauncey was detained in the narrow Niagara anchorage for two days as he waited for bad weather to clear and for a supply of ammunition to be brought down from Black Rock. Having embarked Colonel Macomb and 200 of his men, Chauncey finally weighed anchor on the morning of 31 May, but rather than dash straight for Sackets, he cut across the lake to York and sailed along the north shore in hope of encountering any British vessels that might be carrying provisions and reinforcements to Vincent.[11]

News of the departure of Chauncey's squadron from Sackets on 22 May had prompted Prevost to contemplate an attack on the American base. On 26 May he learned that Fort George was suffering from a tremendous bombardment that was, in all likelihood, the prelude to an assault by an army said to number 8,000. "The situation of Upper Canada becoming extremely critical," Prevost explained to Lord Bathurst, "I determined in attempting a diversion in General Vincent's favour by embarking the principal part of the small garrison of this place and proceeding with them to Sackett's Harbour."[12] He and his senior officers discussed this notion, the first major British offensive expedition in the Lake Ontario theatre since the outbreak of war, during a council at Kingston late on 26 May and formed a plan that would be under the direction of Colonel Edward Baynes, Prevost's adjutant general. During the night a boat, probably one of the sleek, Deal-built gigs Yeo had brought from England, raced across the lake, stood in close to the enemy base, surveyed the masts and the spires of smoke rising from the encampments and then scurried back to Kingston. It arrived at noon the next day with word that "the enemy's fleet was absent and that the garrison was weak."[13]

Within an hour elements of all the military units at Kingston were preparing and marching for their embarkation points.[14] Sails were loosed, and the *Wolfe* led the *Royal George, Earl of Moira, Beresford* (lately the *Prince Regent*) and *Sir Sidney Smith* (lately the *Governor Simcoe*) out to the prescribed assembly point near the eastern end of Simcoe Island.[15] The commodore later noted that the squadron was only "with much exertion and difficulty got ready," suggesting that he had not finished bringing the vessels up to his standards.[16] Nevertheless, thirty-three craft set out from the town around 5:00 p.m. and came alongside the vessels, carrying almost 800 men, comprising companies from the 1st, 8th, 100th and 104th Foot, plus the Glengarries and Voltigeurs, and a party of Mississaugas and Mohawks (about sixty Royal Newfoundland Fencibles were already serving in the squadron). Most of the soldiers climbed onto the vessels, but due to lack of space some unfortunates were forced to hunker down in the open and uncomfortable bateaux, all of which were towed behind the ships. A number of gunboats, including the *Black Snake, Glengarry* and *Quebec,* also joined the squadron, as did several canoes, one of which delivered Prevost and his suite to the flagship.[17] Lastly came a merchantman, the *Lady Murray,* employed to carry some of the infantry and two field guns.

An hour or so after sunset the squadron made sail, wore around Wolfe Island and steered southeast before a steady breeze. The wind faltered during the middle of the night so that as dawn broke, clear and beautiful, the expedition was still crawling across the lake with Wolfe and Grenadier Islands in full view. Lookouts in the tops of HMS *Wolfe* did not sight Sackets until the sun stood whole above the horizon, at which time the sound of warning guns came booming over the water and a schooner darted back from its patrol to the Harbour. Commodore Yeo climbed down into his gig and was whisked inshore for a closer look, as was Andrew Gray in Prevost's canoe. One of the gunboats covered them while a second trailed the Indians who shot off in their canoes to scout the enemy shore west of Henderson Harbour.

The coast had been visible for some time when Colonel Baynes ordered the troops into the boats around noon. By then clouds ruined the perfect day, threatening to bring bad weather. The boats gathered around the *Wolfe,* which had advanced past Stony Point, and at mid-afternoon they struck out eastward for a long, laborious pull to Horse Island, five or more miles distant. They were not yet near the beach when the wind suddenly arose from the north, blowing straight onshore with a heavy shower of rain. Aboard the flagship Baynes and Prevost expressed their anxiety about the safety of the ships and the heavily-loaded landing craft and debated recalling the troops and heading for open water. Midshipman David Wingfield was close enough to witness Commodore

Brigadier General Jacob Brown, New York Militia (1775-1828). Having tried his hand at teaching school and surveying, Brown bought a large plot of land in New York state near Lake Ontario in 1799 where he founded the village of Brownville and became a successful farmer. In 1809 he took command of a state militia regiment and was brigadier general of the militia guarding the upper St. Lawrence region when war broke out. Brown later advanced to the rank of major general in the U.S. Army as shown here. (Courtesy of the National Archives of Canada, C-100390)

Yeo's opposition to the proposal. "Sir James was obliged to obey though much against his will," wrote Wingfield, "this caused some altercation ... Sir James urging the expediency of an immediate attack and the Governor alleging the decline of the day to defer it."[18] Yeo lost the argument, and Baynes requested the fleet to make an offing while he signalled the landing craft to forget the enemy and steer back to the squadron.

While the boats struggled to regain the ships, the Mohawks and Mississaugas intercepted a flotilla of bateaux carrying men from the Ninth and Twenty-first U.S. Infantry Regiments to Sackets. After a sharp skirmish ashore, the surviving Americans, fearing a massacre, rowed out to the squadron to surrender and 115 were taken prisoner, though the unexpected capture did not compensate for the disappointing recall. A rumour spread that the squadron was returning to Kingston, which, as Captain Jacques Viger of the Voltigeurs recalled, "was greeted with general dissatisfaction and loud muttering."[19] The common belief was that a glorious opportunity of "taking the place ... without the loss of five men"[20] had been wasted, while "Sir George gave the Americans all that day and the next night"[21] to bolster their defences. A feeling of frustration and gloom, fueled by fatigue and discomfort, "put a great damp upon our spirits," wrote Wingfield, "as we plainly saw by our glasses, several boats well manned, enter the harbour to reinforce the garrison."[22]

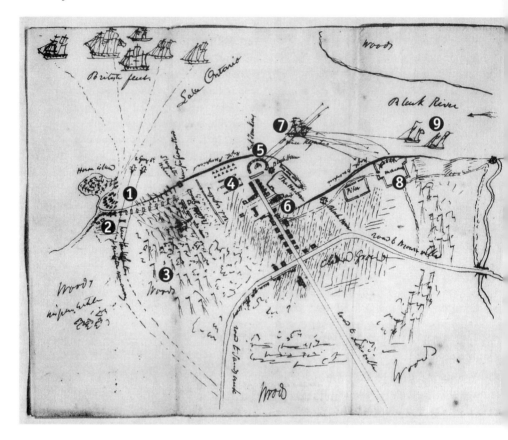

The Battle of Sackets Harbour, 29 May 1813. An unknown hand recorded this image of the attack, revealing the landing place of the British troops, the deployment of gunboats and the involvement of the *Beresford* (here labelled the *Prince Regent*, its former name). The vulnerability to destruction of Chauncey's new ship is clearly evident. 1. British landing point. 2. General Brown's initial position. 3. Macomb's abatis. 4. Basswood Cantonment. 5. Fort Tompkins. 6. New ship. 7. *Beresford*. 8. Fort Volunteer. 9. *Fair American* and *Pert*. (Courtesy of the U.S. Library of Congress)

Not surprisingly, the Americans took full advantage of the decision to postpone the attack. From the moment Wolcott Chauncey's *Fair American* had announced the approach of the British, the Harbour had been a whirlwind of activity. When Chauncey landed, he consulted Brigadier General Jacob Brown, Colonel Electus Backus and several others about the likely location of any British attack and how they would oppose it. Minute guns barked all day as express riders galloped down the neighbouring roads calling the militia to arms. As the enemy squadron tacked into the sunset, 190 men of the Ninth and Twenty-first

Infantry, who had trailed the flotilla of infantrymen captured earlier in the day, marched into the village. They increased to nearly 750 the number of regulars available (also including men from the Twenty-third Infantry, Light and Third Artillery and First Light Dragoons), all of whom were stationed under Backus in and around Fort Tompkins and the basswood cantonments and in Fort Volunteer. About 700 militia from Jefferson County went with Brown to establish a defensive line opposite Horse Island, where the Albany Volunteers were posted as the forward guard. Lieutenant Chauncey headed about 200 shipwrights, marines and sailors (many of the latter being convalescents from the naval hospital) at the batteries on Navy Point to defend the shipyard. As well, he had the *Fair American* and the *Pert*, Sailing Master Samuel Adams, free for deployment as the need arose. While sentries stared out at the lake through the night, everyone else at Sackets Harbour tried to get some sleep.

On board HMS *Wolfe* discussions continued about the attack and yielded a consensus late on 28 May for trying to land again. What provoked the change of heart is uncertain – perhaps the serendipitous capture of the American reinforcements or a moderation in the weather influenced Prevost and Baynes. Baynes did not offer an explanation in his later report, which, omitting any mention of the interrupted first attempt, began with "in conformity to a pre-arranged plan of operations with Commodore Sir James Yeo, the fleet of boats assembled astern of his ship at ten o'clock on the night of the 28th instant with the troops placed under my command … [and] proceeded towards Sackett's Harbour."[23] Scattered showers still fell as the seamen and soldiers, roused from an uneasy slumber, cranky and uncomfortable in their wet clothing, climbed down into the landing craft again. "Though there was no murmuring, or attempt to disobey orders," observed Wingfield, "their countenances … plainly shewed they did not obey the orders with that cheerfulness which confidence inspires."[24] From his place in a gunboat, Commander William Mulcaster guided the flotilla away from the squadron around midnight. The wind had disappeared again, and although a current pushed the boats off course, the first hint of dawn found them within striking distance of Horse Island.

Two American field guns and the long 32-pdr. at Fort Tompkins pitched round shot at the boats as they advanced. The gunboats pulled ahead to cover the landing by raking the beachhead with salvoes of grape and canister from their carronades. Jacob Brown, standing with his militia behind an embankment on the mainland, held his musketry while the Albany Volunteers on Horse Island opened fire on the British. A blizzard of ball and buckshot tore into the British, and within minutes Wingfield counted fifteen casualties in his boat. Lieutenant John Le Couteur of the 104th Foot saw a bateau split open by a round shot and sink almost instantly. The grenadiers of the 100th Foot splashed onto Horse Island and the American troops there fled to the mainland across a narrow, partially submerged causeway. The British swiftly occupied the island, and before the last of the bateaux reached land, the grenadiers fixed their bayonets and charged across the causeway toward the field gun and 700 militiamen who awaited them. It was the moment Jacob Brown had anticipated – a column of redcoats, clearly defined and easy to pick off – but the orderly, British advance and the sight of deadly bayonets drained the militia's valour and they fired one, misdirected volley and fled. Horrified, Brown tried to rally them, but failed as his men stampeded down the lake road and through the forest to safety in the village and beyond. Only a few stalwarts remained with Brown, taking cover behind the trees that skirted a large, cultivated field adjacent to his position.

When the boats had all reached land, followed by Prevost and aides in his canoe, Mulcaster positioned his gunboats east of Horse Island to fire their carronades into the foliage ahead of the army. After some confusion, Baynes formed up his troops in the field at the foot of the causeway. Harassing fire from the nearby woods prompted him to begin his advance on the fortifications and town rather than waiting for the two artillery pieces to be landed, the lack of wind having held up the schooner carrying them. The rain had passed, but the squadron lay motionless miles offshore unable to bring the destructive power of its broadsides to play on the American positions. Only one vessel managed to participate directly in the battle, the *Beresford*, under Commander Francis Spilsbury.[25] Probably propelled by ranks of men sweating at heavy sweeps mounted in portals in the vessel's sides, the *Beresford* crawled, spider-like, past Horse Island and the gunboat barrage to engage Fort Tompkins. If the *Lady Murray* was rowed to shore in similar fashion to unload its two field guns during this time, no one saw fit to mention it later. Even the schooner *Sir Sidney Smith* did not enter the fray, and the routine naval procedure of manning boats to haul one of the corvettes into action was likewise apparently not attempted.

Commodore Yeo did not remain in the *Wolfe* to supervise such operations. Unwilling to be left out of the excitement, he followed the troops, joining the 104th Foot as they marched toward the fortifications. Le Couteur later wrote:

> Sir James Yeo was running in front of and with our men, in a round Jacket and waving his cap, cheering the men on, without sword or pistol. His cockswain [sic] was hit by a musket bullet in the head – the Commodore desired him to go to the rear, to the Doctors. Not a bit, He swore He would not leave his Captain in a fight.[26]

The defences constructed during the winter by Macomb's men served their purpose admirably. The natural abatis created by felling hundreds of trees in the woods around Sackets hampered the British advance (as well as the ignominious militia retreat), forcing the main body to use the lake road and a path that branched around the right flank. As they neared the village, hidden sharpshooters sniped at the redcoats continuously, inflicting irksome casualties, which were aggravated when the leading units came under American artillery fire. Sometime between 7:00 and 8:00 a.m., the British were within sight of Fort Tompkins, the village and the shipyard. Baynes marshalled his troops just within the trees at the western extreme of the open plain in front of the cantonments and the fort. His men faced more than 700 American regulars under the command of Backus positioned in a drainage ditch that ran across the plain perpendicular to the lake and waiting behind the palisade outside the barracks and fort. After taking a short pause to dress his line, Baynes ordered the advance and the bloodiest fighting of the battle began.

Just then, the biggest blunder of the day was taking place on Navy Point. Although he had been specifically instructed by his brother to "defend the new ship to the last extremity," even if he had to abandon his gunboat and "retreat to the blockhouses," Wolcott Chauncey was not in the shipyard.[27] As Baynes's brigade approached Horse Island, he was directing the relocation of the *Fair American* and *Pert* from the Harbour to a position in front of Fort Volunteer. Next he went to the shipyard to supervise preparations there, but instead of remaining to observe the battle and command the defence of the Point himself, Chauncey left Lieutenant John Drury in charge and rowed back to the schooner.

Drury had arrived at Sackets during the previous January and was aboard the *Madison* during the attack on York.[28] He became so ill during the mission

Lieutenant John Le Couteur, British Army (1794-1875). Le Couteur's journal of his exploits during the war provides one of the few surviving accounts written by the young men who went to war for their respective nations. He was involved in some of the bloodiest fighting during 1813 and 1814. (Courtesy of the Société Jervaise, St. Helier, Jersey)

that he was invalided ashore, taking up residence in Brownville, from where he hurried to volunteer his services when he heard the alarm being raised the day before. Although referred to as a lieutenant, Drury was actually still rated as a midshipman (his warrant dated to January 1809) and would be until he was officially promoted in December 1814. Also posted to Navy Point were several convalescent warrant officers and Sailing Master John Hutton, the truculent inebriate who was awaiting the Navy Department's verdict on his court martial. Hutton had volunteered to help in the crisis, as had Master Commandant James Leonard. Despite Drury's obvious youth and inexperience, and the presence of an individual like Hutton, Lieutenant Chauncey decided to leave the young officer in command rather than supervise the defence of Navy Point himself.

As the battle raged, Sackets Harbour became shrouded in a cloud of white gunsmoke, growing more impenetrable by the minute. Amid the confusion spawned by poor visibility and the cacophony of battle, Drury made a critical error in judgement. Hearing a rumour that the army was in retreat, that the British were advancing and all was lost, he ordered the men to light their torches from the bonfire Wolcott Chauncey had instructed him to maintain and set everything on fire. Flame and smoke soon engulfed the blockhouse and storehouses, the heat growing so intense that the defenders in Fort Tompkins were almost forced away from their guns at the same time as the *Beresford* nosed its way past the bastions. Nearly everyone abandoned Navy Point; Drury and the others heading by boat to Fort Volunteer. Surprised to see them in retreat, Chauncey called out to Drury, demanding that he come aboard the *American* and explain himself, but spotting the *Beresford* creeping past the headland he ordered the schooners to engage it, as did the guns in Fort Volunteer. Round shot fell around the *American*, leading Lieutenant Chauncey to conclude that the British had captured the 32-pdr. in Fort Tompkins. He ordered Lieutenant Samuel Adams to slip the *Pert's* anchor, and the two schooners swept up the bay toward Black River. After anchoring again they hurled long-range shot at the *Beresford* without effect. In the meantime, the buildings in the shipyard went up in smoke, but not the new ship because Drury had performed his deed imperfectly. Though threatened by sparks and licks of flame, the vessel survived, thanks mainly to the fire brigade hurriedly organized by Major Samuel Brown, brother of the general.

While Drury had been ordering his men to torch the yard, the battle was still being hotly contested on the plain beyond the cantonments. The British charged and were pushed back. Backus withdrew his regulars from the ditch and consolidated his position in the barracks and fort, and Jacob Brown reassembled

New York State Militia captain. The single, silver epaulet, the sash, the sabre and the bicorn with cockade help to identify this officer's rank. His blue coat with scarlet facings was typical of most New York militia officers and rank and file. Called into service as needed, the militiamen were usually less well trained and equipped than the members of the regular army. (Painting by H.C. McBarron, courtesy of Parks Canada)

Private, 1st Regiment of Foot, British Army, c. 1812. Though the colour of their coats and trim varied from their enemy's (in this case brick-red with blue facings), the uniforms of the British soldiers were very similar to American uniforms. Extensive training and rigid discipline made British infantry regiments very dangerous opponents. (Painting by G.A. Embleton, courtesy of Parks Canada) some of the militia and brought them into action on the British right flank. Prevost and Baynes advanced with the troops, watching developments while musket balls slammed into the trees nearby. Rushing in the mob that thronged around the barracks, Le Couteur found himself without sword or pistol standing edgewise against a post in the palisade. "The Yankees were poking the muzzles of their guns, on each side of me while I made myself as flat as I could.... It was an uncomfortable position."[29] Jacques Viger watched the redcoats swarm between the barracks, the "frightful pass at which the heavy gun of the Fort was instantly aimed ... [discharging] canister that decimated them."[30] In this maelstrom, Captain Andrew Gray performed his last service to the King. Pausing to consult with Lieutenant Colonel Robert McDouall of the Glengarries about how best to dislodge the stubborn enemy, Gray "was shot thro' the body. On my hoping he was not badly wounded," reported McDouall, "he replied, 'They had done for me, it is all over with me.'" Moments later bugles announced the recall and the British slowly withdrew. Some of the wounded were helped off the field, and a grief-stricken Ensign James Gray had to be pried from his father's corpse.[31]

It had been a fearsome spectacle, but the primary goal of the venture, the destruction of the shipyard, appeared to have been achieved, if the vast plume of black smoke rising in that area was any indication. Rather than take more casualties, Baynes, with Prevost's approval, announced a withdrawal to the squadron. As on the previous day, Baynes's decision to curtail the attack was met with disbelief, but no open opposition. To buy time, he sent two flags across inviting the Americans to surrender and then seeking permission to treat the wounded. During these lapses, the British returned to the landing site, embarked in their boats about 10:00 a.m. and rowed back to the ships. Their retreat went unchallenged except for the late appearance of the *Fair American* and *Pert* sailing past Fort Tompkins to loft a few harmless shots into their wake.

As the British squadron stood out to the lake, the Americans celebrated their victory. They had repulsed the renowned British redcoats and saved the fort, shipyard and village and at a relatively low cost; twenty-two men were listed as killed in action, eighty-five others wounded. Among those who later died of their wounds was Backus, which left Jacob Brown as the officer who wrote the official report to the War Department. Although his militia had run and he had not been part of the hottest fighting, Brown's leadership was applauded and he was soon appointed a brigadier general in the regular army.

Apart from the casualties, the worst result of the action was the fire in the shipyard. Brown explained in his report that the new ship and the schooner *York* (lately the *Duke of Gloucester*) had been saved from the conflagration but that "the spoils of York and some few of Commodore Chauncey's effects" had been destroyed. The "few effects" later proved to include nearly every scrap of supplies, belongings and records owned by the marines and all the sails and rigging intended for the new ship. Brown pinned the blame for the mistake on unidentified individuals who had misled Wolcott Chauncey, "a brave honourable man," Brown wrote, "[who stood] higher in my estimation than before he was associated with me for the protection of this place."[32] Other observers were less certain about Chauncey's conduct. The bungled defence of the shipyard was widely discussed, provoking speculation and controversy about who was responsible for the mistake. While Wolcott Chauncey accused Drury of incompetence, others pointed at him. Among the people who questioned Chauncey's competence was James Leonard, who wrote a quick description of the battle and mailed it to Secretary Jones before noon that day, explaining later that he had assumed the secretary would want to have the latest news, but that Lieutenant Chauncey could not send it since he "was absent up the river when the express was making up."[33]

While the Americans celebrated, the British limped home. Forty-five men had died and 174 were wounded, more than 25 per cent of the landing force; among the naval party, there were only five wounded and one killed. The spoils purchased with all that blood included a single brass 6-pdr. field gun and 150 prisoners. It was soon learned that a large depot of naval stores had been accidentally destroyed by the Americans, but that Chauncey's new ship had survived the blaze. "The expedition has not been attended with the complete success which was expected from it," Prevost confessed in a despatch to Lord Bathurst. He extolled "the courage and patience of the small band of troops employed on this occasion, under circumstances of peculiar hardship and privation," detailing the difficulty of the terrain and the resolute conduct of the enemy, though offering no description of the interrupted assault on the first day of the expedition. Prevost justified his decision to order "the troops to leave a beaten enemy" by referring to the regretful light airs that had "prevented the co-operation of the ships" and the gunboats' inability "to silence the enemy's elevated battery or to produce any effect on their blockhouses."[34] His point was well taken because the Royal Navy had been unable to equal Commodore Chauncey's effective support of the American army at York and Fort George, a failure that hamstrung the whole operation at Sackets.

In his brief report to the Admiralty, Commodore Yeo did not mention the silence of his warships' guns nor the failed attempt on 28 May. Instead, he praised Mulcaster with a few words, criticized the inadequacy of the gunboats' armament and noted that "the troops, after gaining decided advantages, were reluctantly ordered to re-embark."[35] He gave no other hint of personal dissatisfaction with the way the fight had been waged, but in the squadron and ashore the private whispers of disaffection with Prevost began to spread. Pilot (formerly Lieutenant) James Richardson overheard one of the senior army officers mutter as he climbed aboard the flagship, "Oh, if he would but give me my own regiment, I would yet land again, and take the place."[36] "We gained a surprise and threw it away to allow the enemy to gain time," wrote Le Couteur. "The murmurs against Sir George were deep, not loud."[37] "This disgraceful affair," observed Midshipman Wingfield, "… caused a coolness between the Governor and Commodore, and at length broke out into an open rupture."[38]

At Kingston, where everyone had strained their ears to listen to the rumble of distant battle, the disappointing return of the squadron only served to exacerbate the news that the Americans had captured Fort George.[39] The situation seemed desperate, the fall of Upper Canada almost inevitable. One of the few saving graces was that Vincent had preserved most of his army after the battle at Fort George and had formed a post at Burlington Heights ready to oppose the inevitable American attack. If the army could be reinforced and provisioned, it stood a chance of surviving, and within days of its unhappy return to Kingston, Yeo's squadron was given the task of relieving Vincent's army and with it the opportunity to prove the efficiency of the British Navy.

The gloom that dominated the British camp obscured a significant advantage gained by the attack on Sackets. Realizing that he had come within a hair of losing all the shipping and facilities at his base, Isaac Chauncey was ever afterward hesitant to leave his base unless it was strongly defended, especially when an essential new ship stood on the stocks. As well, the commodore now had to contend with an enemy naval force that had been greatly enhanced by the arrival of Yeo and the Royal Navy detachment. His days of unchallenged cruising to York and Niagara were finished.

CHAPTER 9

"We Have the Lake Open to Us"[1]

THE ROYAL NAVY AT LARGE: JUNE AND JULY 1813

*I*n response to news that the British were threatening Sackets Harbour, Commodore Chauncey cruised the north shore of Lake Ontario and inspected the entrance of Kingston Channel from a distance at noon on 1 June 1813, looking for the British squadron, but when no opposition appeared he angled his course toward Sackets. As the squadron approached the base, officers squinting through their telescopes likely announced gaps and pockmarks in palisades, the disappearance of the marine barracks and storehouses and the ominous wisps of smoke still rising from their ruins. "What of the ship?" Chauncey might have wondered until it was finally spotted, its fresh, yellow planks safe within the protective clasp of the shipwrights' scaffolding. Around 4:00 p.m. the *Madison* came to anchor off Navy Point, and the commodore hurried ashore to find out what had happened.

Isaac Chauncey was generally relieved by what he saw and heard of the stalwart defence that Backus and Brown's troops had presented. The destruction of the barracks and storehouses he viewed as negligible, the buildings being "of no value."[2] The loss of their contents was a much more serious matter, since they included the fittings, canvas, rigging and the many other items that had been transported from New York during the spring, plus the materiel captured at York. Chauncey calculated that completion of the new ship would be delayed for three weeks while replacements for the destroyed property arrived from New York. As quickly as possible his clerks compiled an inventory of the necessaries and transmitted it to New York.

On 2 June Chauncey sent Sailing Master Thomas Nichols in the *Lady of the Lake* with a flag to Kingston.[3] From Nichols's observations and what he learned about the recent attack, Chauncey concluded that the British squadron was composed of seven ships and six gunboats, mounting 106 guns. His calculations were wrong; even accompanied by half a dozen gunboats, which was unlikely, Yeo's squadron carried no more than ninety carronades and long guns at the end of May 1813.[4] Though he had never seen his enemy's squadron in its entirety, Chauncey acted as if word-of-mouth reports were undeniably true and continued to repeat estimates about British strength that were the same as he had used the previous autumn, before the launch of the twenty-two-gun *Wolfe*. Whether the American commodore thought his estimates were accurate is uncertain. Inflated statistics certainly met his needs in an appeal to the Navy Department for more men and munitions, alleging that his fourteen vessels and eighty-two guns were greatly outclassed. Chauncey also utilized these numbers to explain to Secretary Jones and Commandant Oliver Perry that his previous intentions to join Perry at Erie, long postponed because of his operations with the army, would have to be shelved until he could attain uncontested ascendancy on the lake. "If [Yeo] leaves Kingston I shall meet him," vowed Chauncey on 4 June. "The result may be doubtful, but worth the trial." In the meantime Perry would have to look after his own affairs while the commodore hurried to get the new ship launched and outfitted, but, Chauncey complained to Jones, "she can be of no manner of use unless we have men."[5] His need for men was paramount, he complained to the navy secretary, naming inactive vessels at New York from which the men could be taken and requesting that Captain Charles Morris be transferred from the shipyard on the Potomac River to act as his second in command.

Chauncey was quick to start an investigation into the circumstances surrounding the fire on Navy Point. After discussing the incident with his brother and other principals involved he convened a board of inquiry headed by Lieutenant Melancthon Woolsey. After three days of testimony, during which neither Wolcott Chauncey nor John Drury made an appearance, the board concluded that Drury held command of the shipyard when the fire started and that "the conduct of the officers on the point [had been] dastardly in the extreme."[6] The commodore charged Drury with disobedience of orders and cowardice and ordered a court martial. Somehow overlooked in this initial inquiry were the commodore's original instructions to his brother on 20 May about the defence of Navy Point and the fact that Lieutenant Chauncey had boarded his schooner well before the fire broke out. An artillery major named Samuel Nye testified that the *Fair American* and *Pert* had moved too far down the bay to be of any use in the battle, which James Leonard corroborated, adding "I thought it was a dastardly act on the part of them all."[7]

In the days following the inquiry Chauncey abruptly placed his brother in command of the *Lady of the Lake*, its crew increased with thirty men from the *American*, and sent him to patrol off the British village of Newcastle on Presqu'ile Bay at the western extreme of the Prince Edward Peninsula with orders "to intercept the small vessels or boats of the Enemy going up or down the Lake with troops."[8] The lieutenant returned four days later with the transport *Lady Murray* under his wing, its hold full of ammunition and provisions, and was soon off again to snoop along the northern shore, though he captured no more prizes.

The commodore's report on the initial Navy Point fire inquiry took the better part of two weeks to reach Washington, so it was not until 8 July that Chauncey received Jones's response that a commodore did not have authority to convene such boards without approval from the Navy Department. Despite that condition, Jones accepted the inquiry results and approved Drury's subsequent trial, not knowing that the commodore had started proceedings that very day. This time the story became more convoluted with allegations being made that Lieutenant Chauncey had raised a red flag on the *American* as a previously agreed upon signal to destroy the shipyard. After eight days of testimony the court reached the verdict that Drury was innocent of cowardice and disobedience, though deserving of a private reprimand for a lapse in decision-making. Drury's career on Lake Ontario was ruined, however, and he was eventually moved to Lake Champlain, although the commodore delayed the paperwork, making the unhappy young officer remain at Sackets for several months. The troublesome sailing master, John Hutton, implicated in the events on Navy Point, also left the squadron during this period.[9]

Watching these developments was Master Commandant James Leonard whose frustration grew at the lack of concern the commodore had for his case. Since the middle of April, when Chauncey had arrested Leonard for failure to give proper attention to the *Madison*, and for his own personal life, the commandant had been waiting for a court martial to be convened.[10] He had appealed to the navy secretary for help, and Jones had twice directed the commodore to begin proceedings, but Chauncey had claimed he lacked time and sufficient officers to conduct it. After watching inquiries into the conduct of Wolcott Chauncey and John Drury, Leonard pointed out to the navy secretary that the time and officers were easily found when the issue concerned the commodore's brother. Jones responded by instructing the commodore again to resolve the Leonard case, but Chauncey persisted in ignoring the orders, and

Master Commandant Arthur Sinclair, USN (d. 1831). Like his fellow naval officers, Sinclair longed to win a ship-to-ship duel with the British. As commander of the brig *Nautilus*, he made an independent voyage late in 1812, taking a few small prizes, but failing to encounter any enemy warships, much to his bitter disappointment. He is shown here after he obtained his captaincy in 1813. (Courtesy of the U.S. Naval Historical Center, NH-44925)

Leonard lingered at Sackets. What the secretary thought of the commodore's inconsistent approach to meting out justice in his squadron is unknown, but that Chauncey's behaviour puzzled him seems likely. The controversy reflected badly on the commodore's leadership and seemed to validate the criticism voiced by unhappy officers on his station that the commodore could be a tyrant at times.

While the Navy Point issue dragged on, Chauncey's squadron continued its preparations for resuming operations. On 11 June, a party of eighty seamen and officers arrived led by Master Commandant Arthur Sinclair, another individual who would figure prominently in the months to come.[11] A Virginian by birth, Sinclair had begun his naval career in 1798, seeing duty as a midshipman during the Quasi-War with France and the Tripolitan War. He advanced to lieutenant in 1804 and later commanded the schooner *Enterprise* and the brig *Nautilus*. In July 1812 Sinclair received his promotion to master commandant and an appointment to the brig-sloop *Argus*, in which he made a cruise during the fall and early winter, narrowly evading capture by the Royal Navy and destruction in a tremendous month-long storm. He took over command of a squadron of gunboats on Chesapeake Bay the following February as he waited for appointment to a ship, which order finally came in May 1813 when William Jones informed him about the new vessel similar to the frigate *Essex* building on Lake Ontario. Assuming, perhaps, that Sinclair would be disappointed with a freshwater command, Jones wrote: "The service is of the utmost importance, combining enterprize and everything that can give character to an officer and effect our arms."[12] There was no mention in Jones's letter about the fact that Sinclair would be acting as second-in-command at Sackets Harbour or that James Leonard had lost that job; in all probability, the rumour mill of the service had already brought that tidbit to the commandant's ears. After acknowledging receipt of his orders at Norfolk on 22 May, Sinclair hurried to New York, where he met Lieutenant Edward Trenchard, also on his way to Lake Ontario at the head of eighty officers and men he had lately commanded aboard the sloop *Alert*.

Their arrival at Sackets Harbour was perfectly timed because on the next day, 12 June, the new ship, christened the *General Pike*, was launched. "Her launch excited great interest in this quarter," wrote Sinclair, "men, women and children came from *afar* to see it. It was a very beautiful one…. She is 3 feet longer and 1½ wider than the *Essex* pierced with 28 ports, tons near 1000 and is

USS *General Pike*. Heavily burdened as a ship like the *Pike* was, it was rigged to carry more than thirty square and fore-and-aft sails, not to mention the dozen or more stunsails (shown here attached to the spars on the foremast) employed in light airs. Though only half the sails were usually set, when speed was required and the wind was weak, thousands of square yards of canvas could be hauled into place. (Plan by C. Ware, courtesy of the U.S. Naval Historical Center, NH57006))

a most beautiful ship – what an elegant command on the attack."[13] Isaac Chauncey was delighted to see the *Pike* afloat. Fear that the British would spring a surprise raid to finish off what they had started in May had made him increase the nightly guard around the ship to 100 men while it still stood in the stocks; now he would at least be able to arm it while the carpenters and riggers finished their work. The vessel had been built in nine weeks and a day, faster than any similar ship in the country, Chauncey reckoned.[14] That same day the mail brought a letter from Washington containing Jones and Madison's praise and approval of the squadron's role during the attack on York and in helping the army invade Niagara. The commodore was grateful to receive their approbation and, in answering Jones, assured him that his "future exertions" would continued to justify the confidence placed in him.

Unfortunately, the launch of the *Pike* and the receipt of Jones's letter did little to dispel the bad news that reached Sackets on 10 June via a boat from Niagara. A battle had been fought near the Head of the Lake during the night of 6 June in which Generals John Chandler and William Winder had been taken prisoner, and Dearborn had hurried reinforcements in that direction from Fort George, leaving the garrison lightly manned. A squadron of ships had then appeared, which everyone at Fort George assumed at first was Chauncey's squadron. The commodore's first reaction to this report was to set sail immediately and rescue the army, but "upon more mature reflection" he opted to remain at Sackets to defend the new ship. He only needed four weeks to get it ready for service, whereas if he challenged the British now (they had "near a fourth more guns," he claimed), the odds would be against him, and a defeat would mean loss of supremacy on Lake Ontario, probable destruction of the army at Niagara and increased pressure on Perry at Erie. It was a decision over which Chauncey agonized at length, seeking the counsel of his officers, who agreed with him to a man. Nevertheless he petitioned Jones's approval for his "determination of putting nothing at hazard until the new ship is fitted."[15] By choosing to remain at his anchorage, Chauncey handed control of Lake Ontario to the British, who were already reaping the benefits of his absence.

Among the events in the War of 1812, the British acquisition of supremacy on Lake Ontario during June and July of 1813 was one of the most significant. Commodore Yeo's squadron departed from Kingston on 3 June, at Prevost's request, to deliver 220 men of the 8th Foot under Lieutenant Colonel Thomas Evans and a large supply of clothing, ammunition and food to Brigadier General John Vincent at Burlington Heights. Sir George watched the ships' slow departure from Kingston with some anxiety that they had "been obliged to Sail without being completely armed altho' our Batteries have been dismantled to arm them."[16] Accurate information about the strength of Yeo's squadron during this period is missing, though it appears to have comprised the *Wolfe*, 22, *Royal George*, 20, *Moira*, 18, *Beresford*, 12, and *Smith*, 12, in addition to a couple of gunboats with a single carronade each and probably the unarmed *Lady Murray* and *Lady Gore* At most Yeo possessed no more than ninety guns, or about "a fourth more" than his rival at Sackets mounted, but far short of Chauncey's earlier estimate of 106. Yeo commanded 545 officers and men who were making their first extended voyage as a squadron and for that reason they might have been easier for Chauncey to challenge than he speculated. That issue did not arise, however, as the British force fought adverse winds for the better part of five days, arriving off York late on 7 June, where they received notice of Vincent's victory at Stoney Creek the night before.[17]

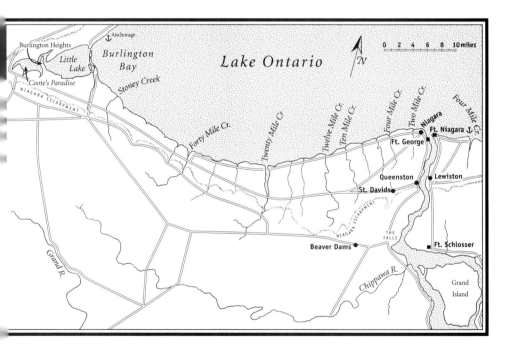

North shore of the Niagara Peninsula. Some of the heaviest fighting of 1813 took place within sight of Lake Ontario as battles raged around the town of Niagara, at Stoney Creek and near Beaver Dams. Commodore Yeo's appearance along this coast in June forced the Americans to restrict their activities to the vicinity of Fort George. (Based on an Admiralty chart of 1815, courtesy of the National Archives of Canada, NMC-18467)

After anchoring overnight near York, Yeo laid a course for Burlington Bay at dawn on 8 June, his pilots guiding him toward the plumes of smoke hanging over a large encampment near Forty Mile Creek. Telescopes soon revealed that the camp was American, so the commodore ordered the *Beresford* towed into range of the beach to bombard the site, backing it up with the *George*. The fire was returned, and as the exchange continued, the *Wolfe*, *Moira* and *Smith* sailed over toward the long spit of sand that separated Burlington Bay from the nearly isolated body of water known as Little Lake to find out when and where General Vincent wanted the 8th Foot deployed. After anchoring on the northern shore of Burlington Bay a couple of miles east of the inlet to Little Lake, Yeo and Lieutenant Colonel Evans went ashore to meet with their military colleagues.

From Vincent or his aides they received a quick briefing about the night action at Stoney Creek in which 700 British troops had confronted about 3,000 Americans from the two brigades, under Generals Chandler and Winder, sent by Dearborn to pursue and engage Vincent in the week following the battle at Fort George. Although the Americans repulsed the British, the casualties they suffered and the capture of their two generals threw them into disorder, causing them to withdraw on 7 June to a position near the mouth of the Forty Mile Creek. Henry Dearborn had instructed Major General Morgan Lewis to hurry there and take command.[18] As Yeo's fleet appeared, Vincent was deploying his troops and Indian allies to harass the Americans, and it was quickly decided that Yeo should land Evans's 8th Foot to act in conjunction with this force. By 5:30 p.m. on 8 July the *Wolfe* and its consorts were sailing back to Forty Mile Creek, where they disembarked the infantry.

In the meantime, the American army had withdrawn to Fort George, provoked by the appearance of the British squadron. From vantage points near the fort, Dearborn and his senior officers had sighted Yeo's vessels on 7 June, making the general think that either Chauncey had returned or that the British squadron had arrived to cover Vincent's retreat. Later, he watched two schooners moving along the shore as if examining it and he became concerned that Yeo intended to transport the army to attack Fort George before Lewis could return. Dearborn, therefore, scribbled a note to his subordinates to hurry back to the fort, but Lewis was already on his way, having abandoned his Forty Mile Creek camp, under pressure from the Indians, infantry and the *Beresford* and *George*.

So disorganized was the American retreat that a considerable amount of booty fell into the hands of the British, including 500 tents, 200 camp kettles, 140 barrels of flour, muskets, horses, boats and uncounted quantities of public and private baggage. Dearborn wrote to John Armstrong to explain his action:

"The enemy's fleet has passed, consisting of two ships and four heavy schooners. I have consequently deemed it prudent *to concentrate the forces at this point* [Fort George]."[19] By 10 June the brigades had returned to their encampment, Dearborn had withdrawn his detachments from Fort Erie, Chippawa and Queenston and had ordered improvements to the defences around Fort George and the town of Niagara. The American offensive on the Niagara Peninsula was at an end and, apart from one disastrous expedition to destroy a British depot near the hamlet of Beaver Dams on 24 June, Dearborn's army would remain in its armed camp by the mouth of the Niagara River for the rest of the summer.[20] Yeo's first appearance in that region of the lake, combined with Vincent's probing forces, had achieved a significant impact on the course of the summer campaign.

The British squadron remained at anchor off Forty Mile Creek until 11 June, partly due to bad weather. The spring of 1813 was notable for its persistent rain and low temperatures, prompting one longtime resident of York to remark at the end of May, "The weather is dreadful. We are now hovering over the fire as if it was March."[21] Yeo took advantage of the brief layover to load quantities of beef, pork, spirits and firewood, to make alterations in the arrangement of cabins aboard the *Wolfe*, as well as to paint the lower masts and one side of the hull, work that the shipwrights at Kingston had not had time to complete. Vincent and Deputy Adjutant-General Lieutenant Colonel John Harvey visited the commodore aboard his ship and pronounced it "a *war* vessel indeed," agreeing to lend Yeo sixty volunteers from the 8th Foot and a few gunners "for the heavy carronades," probably a pair or more of 68-pdrs.[22]

The army was fully expecting a clash to occur between Yeo and Chauncey imminently, which, if it brought good results, would make an attack on the Americans at Niagara possible. Yeo set sail during the evening of 11 June to seek the American squadron, laying a course for the southern shore. None of Chauncey's vessels was detected, but merchantmen carrying public and private stores were cruising there unaware that the British hounds were loose. By 16 June the fleet had captured three schooners and two sloops, burned a raft and gone ashore at the American Eighteen Mile Creek and the Genesee River to plunder storehouses. Well-burdened with prizes and confiscated provisions, Yeo anchored off Kingston on the morning of 17 June to discharge his booty.

At dawn the next day he was off again, having embarked a detachment of the 1st Foot since the object of this cruise required more ambitious activity on shore.[23] Propelled by light winds, the squadron approached Oswego under a cloudy sky on the morning of 19 June, where a cannonade from land batteries and gunboats in the harbour mouth greeted it. Lieutenant Melancthon

Woolsey was at the post, supervising the transfer of naval supplies to Sackets, and he moved quickly to discourage the British from landing. The British returned fire and some of the troops climbed down into boats, but Woolsey's resistance proved too intimidating, and, after retrieving the infantry, the squadron sailed away to the southwest.

Yeo's next target was the village of Sodus, twenty-five miles up the shore, where he landed the soldiers and a small naval party during a rain storm at dusk on 19 June. At first the place seemed deserted, but a band of militia waited until the British were close to their hiding place and then fired a single volley and fled. Five of the British fell wounded and one died on the spot, and, though the British returned fire, the fight was over. During the night Yeo's men ferried several hundred barrels of flour out to the squadron along with a few prisoners. The commodore explained to these unlucky fellows, before returning them to shore, that "wherever we came, if the residents remained quiet, private property and rights would be respected, but, in all cases, where the people made armed resistance and wantonly fired on us, they might expect to be punished."[24] Accordingly, Yeo ordered the storehouses at Sodus set aflame.

The Americans were not the only ones punished for the events at Sodus; beginning just before noon on 21 June, as the fleet headed westward before fresh breezes, seven British seamen were lashed in turn to a grating amidship on the *Wolfe* and flogged. Their crimes, drunkenness, missing the muster and theft, probably committed at Sodus, merited twelve to twenty-four lashes, and sent a message to the crew that the commodore was as strict with his own men as he was with the enemy.

Because of adverse winds, haze and rainy squalls, the squadron took three days to work up to an anchorage five miles off Forty Mile Creek. Early on 25 June Commodore Yeo went ashore to meet General Vincent, with whom he arranged for fresh provisions for his squadron and agreed to embark more than 150 American officers and men captured the previous day in the action at Beaver Dams. As well, Yeo handed over to the army the little schooner *Vincent* (lately the American laker *Lady Washington*, captured on 15 June) to serve as a tender, along with a small crew under David Wingfield, who had now advanced to the position of master's mate.[25] At dawn on 26 June the squadron weighed anchors and headed for Kingston, where it arrived two days later.

The failure to destroy the *General Pike* during the attack on Sackets Harbour had nagged Yeo for a month. He knew the *Pike* would give Chauncey a significant advantage and was determined to have another go at it. On the afternoon of 30 June 1813 a raiding force quietly assembled at the squadron's anchorage near Nine Mile Point on Simcoe Island.[26] It comprised Yeo's seamen and sol-

diers from the 1st and 100th Foot and Royal Newfoundland Fencibles, numbering in all close to 700. Leaving skeleton crews behind to handle the ships, they
departed in a flotilla of boats at 5:00 p.m. intending to arrive at Sackets Harbour before dawn, where they would do as much damage as possible, cut out
some of the vessels and return to Kingston. Unfortunately, they left too late, for
the flotilla was unable to cover the thirty-five-mile distance by sunrise even
though the lake was calm. Perhaps embarrassed that he and the other local pilots had not recommended an earlier departure to the commodore, James
Richardson placed the blame for the slow passage on "the sluggishness of the
gunboats, propelled by oars."[27] With dawn breaking and the American masts in
sight eight or nine miles away, there could be no thought of attack or of an immediate return to Kingston for fear of being spotted on the lake by one of
Chauncey's patrols and destroyed.

Yeo darted ahead in his gig to scout the shores of Chaumont Bay, finding a
location two miles in where they could seclude themselves during the day.[28] The
flotilla hurried to the spot, and the men worked frantically to hide their tracks.

Sackets Harbour, 1813. In less than a year the quiet village of Sackets Harbour had
turned into a heavily fortified camp as the army and navy combined their efforts to
strengthen their most important base of operations east of the Niagara River. Barracks,
blockhouses and storehouses surrounded the previously quiet basin where Chauncey
could anchor his ships in relative safety. (From the *Naval Chronicle*, 1818, courtesy of
the U.S. Naval Historical Center, NH-1696)

Richardson recalled: "We laid the boats broadside to the beach of a small bend in the shore, we cut saplings and bushes, and placed them in the water outside the boats, by means of which we were tolerably well screened."[29] The main body of the force moved back into the forest to await the day's end, but when a muster was called two men, a sergeant and a private of the 100th Foot, did not answer. Search parties fanned out to intercept the missing men but found no one, and Yeo turned to Richardson for advice: "Our Commodore ..., much exercised in mind, ... conversed with me as having more knowledge of these parts, relative to the practicability of their finding their way to some inhabitants and thus giving the alarm."[30] The depth of the forest and its remote location from towns gave the British hope that the deserters would be unable to warn the Americans of their presence. In the evening, though, Yeo's lookouts saw an enemy schooner anchor a mile down the shore from them and send in a boat. It returned with haste and the schooner quickly departed, its sails all set, firing its gun repeatedly as if to pass a warning that intruders were near.

Earlier that evening Isaac Chauncey and Arthur Sinclair had been enjoying a private dinner when they received news that a British deserter had been picked up on the lake by a canoe as he tried to make land with the help of a plank. When the man was brought to them, he divulged Yeo's scheme completely, explaining that the commodore himself intended to lead 400 men to seize the *Madison* while the remainder boarded other vessels. He also mentioned that the commodore was very familiar with their defences. As Sinclair later noted,

> although we keep guard Boats rowing every night and a vessel cruizing across the Bay, which has made us feel secure in the fleet, yet that enterprizing fellow, we are told, has been two nights in among us reconnoitering in his gigg [sic], and past by answering *guard Boat*, when challenged by the shipping.[31]

The alarm sounded immediately throughout Sackets Harbour, and the crews ran to their quarters, loaded their guns and carronades or set out in guard boats to sweep up and down Black River Bay. Sinclair suggested to the commodore that it might be a better idea to embark 1,000 of Macomb's troops, land them on Point Peninsula, then slip around to the north end of the peninsula to wait for the British to be flushed by land or water. Fearing that this would leave the *Pike* and the shipyard too lightly defended, Chauncey declined Sinclair's proposal, and the Americans waited at their guns through the night. Four or five hundred soldiers manned the *Pike*, and Sinclair declared that he "would have defied their whole army in Boats to have made a good landing on my decks."[32]

No nocturnal raid came so Chauncey set sail at first light on 2 July 1813. He searched the lake, which was shrouded in mist, sending his gunboats to peruse every inlet in Chaumont Bay and along the shores of Point Peninsula, but the British were gone, except for several more deserters (among them two Royal Navy seamen) who came out of the woods to surrender themselves.[33] Yeo had long since fled, deciding the night before that the mission had been betrayed. His squadron dropped down to meet the flotilla about 5:00 a.m. in the morning and then spent the rest of the day picking its way slowly through the fog back to Kingston.

Yeo never submitted an official report on this failed cutting-out expedition, although he discussed it with Prevost, who was still at Kingston. Yeo's tendency toward reticence had already begun to show itself; since arriving in Canada, he had composed only five reports to the Admiralty and none to Admiral Warren. During that same period his counterpart at Sackets had sent no fewer than thirty-nine despatches to Secretary Jones.[34]

The failure of his scheme left the British commodore in a foul humour. "We all felt it sorely," remembered Richardson, "but Commodore Yeo could hardly restrain himself."[35] Yeo's sour disposition did not improve when he reached his squadron because it was soon brought to his attention that two officers left in charge of vessels had become drunk and behaved in an ungentlemanly manner during the flotilla's absence. They were Lieutenant Robert Gibbs (aboard the *Wolfe*) and Lieutenant George Inglis (in the *George*), two of the officers Admiral Warren had detached with Robert Barclay, who had complained about them to Yeo. After a quick investigation, Yeo ordered Gibbs to Halifax under arrest, where, since Yeo had not been given authority to hold courts martial, Gibbs would have to be tried. Inglis was saved from a similar fate by the intervention of Commander Francis Spilsbury, but he remained in the squadron under a cloud until being sent to join Barclay on Lake Erie late in August.[36]

Three days after the return to Kingston, another round of punishments took place on the *Wolfe*. Ten men received between twelve and forty-eight lashes each for crimes ranging from drunkenness to contempt. Three days later two more men got a taste of the cat.[37] Whether the infliction of such severe penalties (with similar episodes probably occurring on the other vessels) was connected to the desertions in Chaumont Bay or was due to unconnected incidents is uncertain. It appears that the commodore and his officers were determined to maintain strict discipline among their crews that would prevent future operations from being disrupted by malcontents. Yeo wrote nothing about the matter and, in fact, in his sixth report to London on 16 July he noted, "I am happy to state that only one seaman has deserted to the enemy, and their conduct in

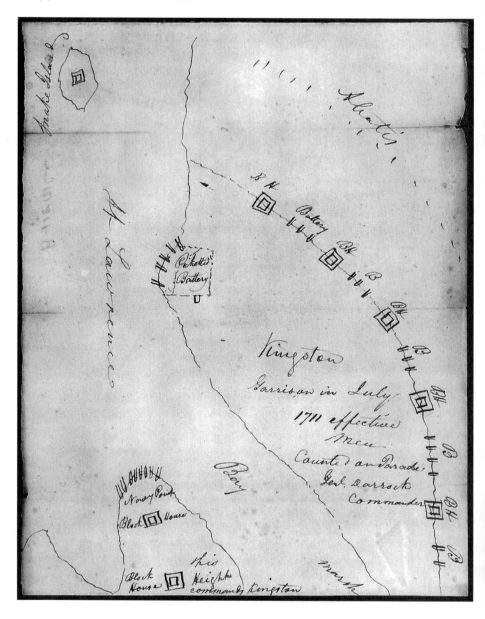

Defences at Kingston, July 1813. After his 600-man detachment was captured on 24 June 1813 at the battle of Beaver Dams, Colonel Charles Boerstler was sent as a prisoner to Quebec. Along the way he had enough time during a stopover at Kingston to record its defences in a sketch, which he later forwarded to the War Department. Boerstler mistakenly placed the Point Henry blockhouse on Point Frederick. (Courtesy of the United States National Archives, RG 107, B-118(7))

general has been orderly and good; every reasonable and proper indulgence has been given them to keep them in this temper."[38] At such a great distance, the Admiralty could not easily know the truth. Perhaps Sir James was hoping to be able to write a detailed account soon of how he had conquered Chauncey, the kind of report that had earned him his high reputation with the Lords of the Royal Navy.

Meanwhile, Chauncey's men were waiting impatiently to have a go at the British fleet. The *Pike* was slowly being prepared for service, but not fast enough for the commodore's wishes. "It is mortifying beyond expression to be obliged to remain here while the enemy is cruising," he wrote Jones on 3 July 1813.[39] Arthur Sinclair was similarly frustrated by the delays, as he expressed to his friend in Virginia: "I want to take this gallant Knight. I will if I do so, *bring him to Virginia in a Cage and shew him as a curiosity....* But joking apart, I expect d____d hard knocks."[40] Like Chauncey, Sinclair calculated that the British outgunned the American squadron and that any meeting on the lake would lead to a hard-fought contest. Nevertheless, they were looking forward to an engagement, especially since land operations had stalled and were dependent upon a resolution of who would control Lake Ontario.

The presence of Yeo's squadron had further aggravated troublesome conditions in the American camps. The unrelenting wet weather made transportation by land nearly impossible over the waterlogged roads and had sickened the troops, worsening Dearborn's own health to the point that Major General Morgan Lewis assumed command of the army at Niagara on 10 June. In light of the outcomes of the battles at York, Fort George and Stoney Creek, Dearborn's days as senior commander on the frontier were numbered. At mid-June Secretary Armstrong once more expressed his criticism of the aged general's leadership: "I cannot disguise from you the *surprise* occasioned by the *two escapes of a beaten enemy*, first on the 27th ultimo [Fort George], and again on the 6th instant [Stoney Creek]."[41] The hammer fell on 6 July when Armstrong notified Dearborn that President Madison wished him to withdraw from his command until he could regain his good health.

The secretary of war now began to promote the campaign objectives he had championed during the previous winter, namely Kingston and the St. Lawrence line of communication. He speculated that Yeo would retire under the guns of Kingston when the *Pike* finally emerged. If that happened, Armstrong proposed, it would be more productive to transport most of the troops from Fort George to unite with an army being assembled at Sackets, which in turn would move against Kingston or down the St. Lawrence to Montreal in coordination with Major General Wade Hampton's army in motion from Burlington,

Vermont. To this end, Morgan Lewis moved to Sackets Harbour to take charge of that post, leaving Fort George and the Niagara Frontier in the hands of Brigadier General John Boyd, who was instructed by the secretary to avoid any actions with the enemy unless absolutely necessary. On 9 July Armstrong told Lewis that "the moment Chauncey goes out, our stores along the south shore of the lake should be brought down to the harbor, and in that case your small posts ... drawn into your main body."[42]

Changes had also taken place in the British camp. Major General Francis De Rottenburg, a widely experienced officer who had served in Lower Canada since 1810, arrived on the Niagara Peninsula at the end of June to take control of military forces in the upper province. He soon after transmitted a censorious assessment of the province and the army to Prevost. He was far from satisfied with the wretched condition of the roads ("the worst I ever saw anywhere"), the competence of the department heads ("deficient in activity and cleverness") and the appalling rate of desertion. To discourage the latter, he planned to execute a fellow who had run from the 41st Foot, but as for the other problems he would have to make his "utmost exertions to keep affairs in some shape or other." De Rottenburg also had critical words for the navy, noting that "had Sir James time to spare to co-operate with the army, Fort George would have fallen. But I do not now possess means of attacking them on both sides of the river." [43] Accordingly, he decided to consolidate his forces at Burlington Heights, while keeping some pressure on the Americans with advanced pickets.

De Rottenburg's decision to fortify his position while badgering the enemy was in line with the main tenets of Prevost's overall strategy, which continued to be supported by the government in London. By the end of June 1813 the defeat at York was known by Prime Minister Liverpool's cabinet and the Prince Regent, on whose behalf Lord Bathurst wrote on 1 July to voice the government's reaction. No official blame was attributed to Prevost or Sheaffe, but Sir George was urged to establish a firm defence with the reinforcements sent to Canada since little more could be expected until late in the year. Opportunities were to be taken for turning "your defensive into offensive operations" as long as they did not "lead you to a great distance from your frontier." Bathurst also demonstrated his limited understanding of affairs by expressing his hope that, despite the loss of the ship and stores at York, "the British naval superiority on that lake, tho' diminished, is not lost."[44]

Unknown to the politicians in England, neither side held superiority on Lake Ontario during July, for while the armies held their positions the opposing squadrons remained at anchor in their harbours through most of the month. Both commodores were occupied with preparing their squadrons for the climactic engagement that would decide who controlled the lake and which army would prosper as a result.

At the Harbour Chauncey watched a new vessel sprout ribs and beams on the main slipway. After discussions with Henry Eckford, he had ordered the construction of a large schooner similar in size to the *Governor Tompkins,* intended to match the vessel nearing completion at Kingston.[45] As ordnance, rigging and other materials reached the Harbour by water from Oswego or overland from Rome, the *Pike* assumed the appearance of a warship. Twenty-six 24-pdr. long guns were mounted on the frigate, twelve along each side and two others on circles, one on the topgallant forecastle and one on the poop deck, making the ship the most powerful vessel on the lake.[46] The commodore's pleas for more men were answered during this period as nearly 400 officers and men arrived at the shipyard between the end of June and 15 July, with letters from the Navy Department indicating that several hundred more would follow.[47] Furthermore, by arrangement with Alexander Macomb and General Lewis, soldiers from the Third Artillery Regiment joined the squadron. Among the naval officers who arrived was Master Commandant William Crane, who had been ordered from New York with all the officers and men of the frigate *John Adams.*[48] Chauncey assigned Crane and his men to the *Madison* since they were familiar with each other and would not suffer the usual, new-ship confusions about stations and quarters, watch bills and pay rolls. The crew of the *Madison* and its temporary commander, Lieutenant Jesse Elliott, transferred into the new flagship, *Pike.*

The arrival of such ample reinforcements allowed Isaac Chauncey the leeway he needed to detach some of his seamen to Perry's station on Lake Erie. On 16 July the *Lady of the Lake* and the *Pert* left Sackets, each carrying sixty officers and men for delivery to Niagara, from where they would go by land and water to the shipyard at Erie, Pennsylvania.[49] By then, however, concern over the lack of men on Lake Erie was becoming a touchy matter between Perry and the commodore, with Secretary Jones acting as intermediary and advocate for action on Lake Erie. Perry had informed the secretary in June that he needed more than 400 men to operate his squadron and that the commodore had not instructed him on how to proceed when his vessels were ready for service. Jones responded with assurances that Chauncey would soon be sending him a large reinforcement, given the number of men on the road to Sackets. The secretary's undisguised emphasis that the British be first subdued on Lake Erie was obvious in his 3 July despatch to Perry as he openly over-rode Chauncey's command on the lakes by giving Perry permission to attack Barclay at Amherstburg at the earliest time, as long as Chauncey did not disagree. His prime motive was the

Master Commandant Oliver Hazard Perry, USN (1785-1819). Though he had been in the navy since 1799, Perry had little experience with an independent command. Before being assigned to the lakes, he had been the lieutenant commanding the schooner *Revenge* when it was wrecked in Long Island Sound in 1811 and, after his promotion to master commandant early in 1812, he was in charge of the gunboat station at Newport, Rhode Island. This portrait shows Perry as a captain later in his career. (From a portrait by J. W. Jarvis, courtesy of the U.S. Naval Historical Center, NH-47310)

same as it had been in the spring, namely to "induce the desertion of the Savages" by capturing Amherstburg and Fort Malden.[50]

On 3 July Jones also sent Chauncey a long and detailed analysis of his recent reports, beginning with his hope that control on Lake Ontario would soon be won because its delay was restricting operations on Lake Erie. The secretary then reviewed the numbers of men sent to Sackets Harbour and concluded that "our vessels are better manned than those in any other service, both in numbers and quality." In regard to Chauncey's estimates of the strength of Yeo's squadron, Jones scoffed, claiming that the size of the British force was "greatly overrated" by the commodore's informants. The reputation of the Royal Navy was of no importance, he argued, adding: "Although they are commanded by a *Knight* and *three Post Captains*, I feel that the untitled republican Commodore, and his gallant and able officers, though not 'Post Captains,' have nothing to apprehend from the charm of a name, or the fortuitous circumstance of superior grade."[51] Lastly, Jones revealed to Chauncey that he had given direct instructions to Perry, justifying his actions with the urgency of the situation on Lake Erie as opposed to an intention to usurp Chauncey's authority. He closed with assurances that President Madison continued to approve of everything the commodore was doing and waited eagerly to hear that naval superiority had been gained, especially since the army was suffering for lack of it.

The secretary's letter arrived at Sackets on 17 July. Without delay Chauncey composed a lengthy justification of the estimates of British strength compared to his own and the conditions he was facing on Lake Ontario, adding that he had just transferred men to Perry. If he felt any chagrin about being so blatantly challenged by Jones or by having Perry's station treated with such importance, Chauncey did not let on, except to offer his "regret that I have not more talents to execute the various and important duties of my command."[52] In all likelihood the commodore brooded about Jones's comments and waited for an opportunity to vent some spleen. Perry provided that opportunity by writing the following week to request more men to which Chauncey snapped back, "mortified" by Perry's complaints to Jones and alleging that Perry was urging the government to give him "a *separate command*."[53] When he received this letter nearly two weeks later, Perry indignantly offered his resignation so that he would not have to serve "under an officer who has been so totally regardless of my feelings."[54] Jones refused Perry's request and the commandant remained at Erie, but bad feelings had arisen between him and Chauncey that time would do little to assuage.

During this period Sir James Yeo also dealt with persistent appeals for more men from Commander Robert Barclay at Amherstburg, though their correspondence lacked the invective that flowed between Chauncey and Perry. Barclay had gone to Lake Erie with far fewer experienced hands than Perry had and, recognizing immediately the dire straits in which he would find himself once the American fleet was active, he penned a series of inquiries to Yeo, Vincent, Prevost, De Rottenburg and Brigadier General Henry Procter.[55] His efforts won him a sharp rebuke from the commodore and a reinforcement in late June comprising only Commander Robert Finnis and his servant. With the Lake Ontario squadron manned at a barely acceptable level, Yeo was unwilling and, essentially, unable to spare any personel. As well, Yeo was attending to the needs of the flotilla on the Richelieu River and Lake Champlain, where Commander Daniel Pring and several officers had gone in July.[56] Not until late August was a forty-man detachment transferred to Amherstburg.

His Majesty's Brig *Lord Melville* was launched at Point Frederick on 22 July. The twelve carronades and two long guns it was slated to carry would soon strengthen Yeo's line of battle, but the *Pike* continued to make the commodore anxious. When news reached Kingston that Chauncey had laid the keel for what was said to be a large brig, the commodore proposed to Prevost the building of a full-size frigate measuring 160 feet on the gun deck and 42 feet abeam.[57] This was the second time that Yeo had proposed the construction of a new ship; after the assault on Sackets Harbour in May he had recommended that a vessel be laid down similar to the lost *Sir Isaac Brock*, as had been suggested by Andrew Gray earlier that month. Ample quantities of wood were available and the shipwrights who had escaped from York bolstered the dockyard force, but the vessel was not started. Yeo's new proposal reaped no immediate results either, probably because he and Prevost knew that the men and arms needed for such a vessel, especially a frigate, could not be obtained during the current campaign. Point Frederick did not remain idle, as Commander Richard O'Conor, confirmed as commissioner of the shipyard, worked energetically to establish an efficient system of organization.[58] He oversaw the launch of several gunboats in June and July, and later had additional storehouses and barracks constructed, leading to the birth of a rumour at Sackets Harbour that the British planned to build and launch a twenty- to forty-gun vessel every forty days.[59]

The launch of the *Melville* and gunboats underlined the need for additional seamen, but unlike his counterpart at Sackets, who could name idle warships in New York harbour from which entire crews could be taken, Yeo lacked a resource that could readily reinforce him. Instead, his shortages were partly solved by assembling a draft of "volunteers" from the merchant fleet at Quebec. The arrangement for their transfer involved considerable negotiations, which restricted future impressment of merchant crews by Royal Navy ships at Quebec, provided wages and bounties for the men and defined the length and supervision of their service.[60] In all, sixty-five seamen, some of them troublemakers any master would be glad to be rid of, journeyed up the St. Lawrence,

Point Frederick Dockyard, 1813. Commander Richard O'Conor was largely responsible for bringing order to the former Provincial Marine dockyard by organizing its daily operations along traditional Royal Navy lines. In 1813 defences on the point were also improved. (Courtesy of Power Corporation)

reaching Kingston around the middle of July. In addition to the transport men, eighteen other individuals joined the squadron from Kingston and Quebec during this period, increasing the total complement to about 620.[61] Although this was a sufficient number to handle the vessels, it was not, in Yeo's estimation, enough to fight them. To make up the deficit, he arranged to increase the number of infantrymen serving as marines to 228, ninety-eight from the 100th Foot and 130 of the Royal Newfoundland Fencibles.[62]

In addition to the demands on Lake Erie and Champlain, the commodore was also asked to provide men to work in the gunboat flotilla that was convoying brigades of bateaux from Prescott to Kingston.[63] Apart from the occasional lieutenant and a few seamen, Yeo could only ask Commander O'Conor to supervise the operation of the nine boats, three of them being stationed at Prescott, three at Gananoque and three at Kingston. A couple of other gunboats appear to have remained with the fleet, their occasional manning and brief absences, crewed by Yeo's men, being noted in the logbook of the flagship. The scant records of the flotilla's service show that the *Black Snake* was joined by the *Thunderer, Retaliation* and *Spitfire* and that they were manned by elements of the Sedentary and Incorporated Militia, walking-convalescents from the 104th Foot and Canadian Voltigeurs, and a few gunners from the Royal Artillery.

It was the gunboats that fought the only engagements to take place during July 1813. A group of men, led by two New York militia officers named Dimock and Dixon, approached Chauncey and Lewis around the middle of the month for permission to make a voyage down the St. Lawrence River for the purpose of waylaying one of the British convoys.[64] The officers gave their approval and lent the would-be privateers fifty soldiers and two small sloops, the *Neptune* and the *Fox*, armed with a single long gun each. The adventurers set out on 18 July and late the next afternoon, halfway between Gananoque and Prescott, they sprang a trap on the *Spitfire* as it escorted a flotilla of bateaux loaded with 250 barrels of pork, 300 bags of bread, plus ammunition and other gear. So unsuspecting were the British that not a shot was fired during the capture, but one or more of the bateaux in the convoy must have escaped, for the Americans feared that their deed would soon be known at Kingston and took refuge up Cranberry Creek (opposite Wellesley Island, a short distance down the river from Wolfe Island) rather than darting home to Sackets. Their apprehensions were well founded because the alarm soon spread, and four gunboats converged at the northeast tip of Wolfe Island to intercept the raiders. Yeo's officers and seamen under Lieutenant John Scott manned three of them, while the fourth contained a detachment of the 100th Foot under Captain John Martin. They proceeded down-river, eventually learning that the Americans had sought shelter up Cranberry Creek, but by then darkness had fallen, prompting Martin and Scott to postpone any action until the following morning.

Before dawn on 20 July Major Richard Frend arrived on the scene from Prescott with a large detachment of the 41st Foot. Taking command of the assembled force, he immediately led the way through the marsh at the mouth of the stream and up its channel. Dimock and Dixon's men had spent the night building a barricade out of the barrels and bags from the bateaux they had seized and deploying their infantrymen to ambush their pursuers. Unwittingly, Frend rowed his force right into the snare, advancing up the narrowing creek until oarsmen could not get a purchase or turn their craft around. When the British stopped to clear trees that the Americans had cleverly felled to obstruct their movement, the signal to attack was given. Murderous fire raked the leading boat so badly that no one could stand to handle its gun. Frend landed some of his troops to outflank his opponent and succeeded in pushing them back so that he could make a slow and awkward retreat. Content with their successful defence, the Americans held firm while the British withdrew and departed for Kingston. The cost of the impulsive probe into confined and unfamiliar territory was four infantrymen killed and twelve wounded, plus injuries to Midshipman George Hugo and four seamen. On 21 July the *Neptune* and *Fox* arrived at Sackets with their prizes and more than sixty prisoners, having narrowly evaded the *Moira* at the entrance of the St. Lawrence. The incident was a pleasantly unexpected victory that Dimock and Dixon do not appear to have repeated, while, for the British, the incident at Cranberry Creek was a harsh lesson about vigilance on convoy duty and the dangers of venturing up narrow creeks. Subsequently, few bateau flotillas suffered the same fate.

As the triumphant privateersmen returned to Sackets, the American squadron was in the process of heading out on the lake. The *Madison, Oneida* and most of the schooners left the port on 21 July to cruise between the Ducks and Grenadier Island, watchful for a glimpse of enemy sails. Impatiently, Chauncey stayed at the Harbour, waiting for the mounting of the new flagship's last few guns. An outbreak of sickness had swept the *Pike*, prostrating Sinclair, most of the lieutenants and sixty of the crew.

Sackets Harbour had become a very unhealthy place for everyone, in part because of a lack of camp discipline that allowed filth and pestilence to spread unchecked. Morgan Lewis was shocked when he arrived there in June, writing to his wife: "You can form no conception of the abominable nuisances that everywhere assailed us on our arrival. It was difficult to breathe, and you could literally taste the putridity in the atmosphere."[65] Army surgeon William Ross later confirmed Lewis's references to the "septic vapour," although he also attributed a prevailing bowel inflammation to impure spring water and the effluvia in the Black River.[66] As well, Ross concluded, the men were laid low because the bread and whiskey served to them were made from grain containing the fungus ergot. Through July the number of naval invalids overflowed the hospital on Navy Point, and worsened crowded conditions in the army hospital near Fort Volunteer until Macomb complained to the commodore. Chauncey quickly assured him that he would hire a barn or some other building to house his disabled, at the same time as he prayed that a return to fresh air on the lake would heal his weakened crews.[67]

The *Pike* was finally ready on 22 July 1813 and set sail to rendezvous with the rest of the squadron off the Ducks. Having spent the better part of two months getting his command prepared to win decisive control on Lake Ontario, Chauncey was hoping for more than just fresh air and good health. He knew that the days ahead might lead to some of the most significant developments in the war.

The brig *Oneida* sets sail at Sackets Harbour. With one of the schooner/gunboats in company, the *Oneida*, commanded by Lieutenant Melancthon Woolsey, makes way past Fort Tompkins as the squadron prepares to sail in search of Yeo. (Oil painting by Peter Rindlisbacher, courtesy of the artist)

CHAPTER 10

"Deer, She's Gone!"[1]

THE COMMODORES MEET:
AUGUST 1813

*T*he American squadron sailed slowly westward and met the *Lady of the Lake* on 24 July 1813 with a despatch from Brigadier General John Boyd at Fort George informing the commodore of the general's interest in raiding the British depot at Burlington Heights. Thinking this to be a worthwhile venture, Chauncey sent the *Lady* right back to Niagara with his approval, but the winds were so weak and adverse that three days passed before the schooner reappeared carrying Colonel Winfield Scott and a company of regulars. Then the squadron was close to Fort Niagara and another day was taken as 150 additional infantry embarked from Four Mile Creek. Faint and baffling breezes continued to retard the squadron's movements and it was not until the evening of 29 July that it anchored on the north shore of Burlington Bay; the *Pert* had joined from Niagara raising the force's strength to thirteen vessels.[2]

Burlington Bay sprawled outside the isthmus of sand and marsh that enclosed Little Lake, known today as Hamilton Harbour. At the head of Little Lake, about seven miles west of the bay, stood Burlington Heights, the lofty peninsula where John Vincent, lately promoted to major general, had chosen to encamp his army. Little Lake emptied into the bay through a constantly shifting channel near the north end of the sandy isthmus, an outlet that Master's Mate David Wingfield and the crew of the tender *Vincent* were ordered to sound and buoy late in July 1813. By that date the channel was so shallow that Wingfield had to remove the *Vincent's* masts, its 18-pdr. and most of its provisions in order to enter Little Lake. Luckily, he had just completed this onerous task when Chauncey's squadron appeared in the offing around 26 July. Two boatloads of soldiers pulled over from Burlington Heights to help Wingfield reload his equipment and haul the schooner across the basin to a safe place below the battery on the hilltop. Three days later the Americans dropped their hooks at the anchorage three miles northeast of the outlet and began disembarking troops for what appeared to be an assault on the Heights.[3]

Having never navigated Burlington Bay before, Chauncey had no knowledge of the area, nor did Winfield Scott. Guides had been taken on from Niagara, but they could do little more than point out the general topography of the area and the best places to anchor. On the morning of 30 July Chauncey and Scott landed with 500 soldiers and sailors, and while one group swept the vicinity for livestock and information, a second party marched to the neck of land from where they could make a long-distance reconnaissance of the fortifications on Burlington Heights. Their telescopes showed their enemy "posted upon a peninsula of very high ground and strongly intrenched, and his camp defended by about 8 pieces of cannon;" local inhabitants also revealed that a large reinforcement had just arrived from York. The commodore and the colonel

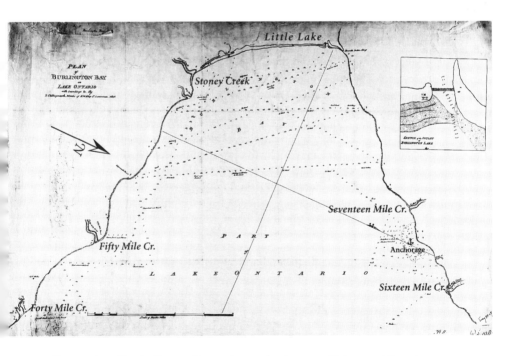

Burlington Bay. The Burlington Bay anchorage lay between Sixteen and Seventeen Mile Creek about seven miles east of the outlet from Little Lake. The depth of water in the outlet varied from four to seven feet when it was sounded in 1815. (Based on an Admiralty chart of 1815, courtesy of the National Archives of Canada, NMC-44763)

discussed various methods of attack, including storming the position in boats supported by the heavy ordnance of several schooners. They agreed, however, that the outlet was too shallow for the gunboats and that they lacked sufficient small craft to embark all 500 combatants at once. As a result, they returned to the shipping, upped anchor and sailed for York, having netted only a few head of cattle for their troubles.[4]

The American approach to York on 31 July was slow enough to allow many of the town's officials to flee for fear of being kidnapped as had been the fate of some Canadian inhabitants of Niagara. The Reverend John Strachan, who had conferred with Chauncey on behalf of the town during his visit in April, stood on the wharf by Fort York under a white flag awaiting the arrival, concerned that another week of plundering and vandalism was about to begin.[5] Chauncey's square-rigged vessels anchored off the harbour mouth while the schooners swept to shore and disembarked a landing party. Strachan, accompanied by another leading citizen named Grant Powell, met the Americans, asking to be taken to Chauncey to whom they explained that the town was defenceless, most of the male populace was on parole and the women and children were terrified of the depredations they might suffer. After admitting that the visit was in response to Yeo's raids of the communities on the south shore, especially the destruction at Sodus, the commodore assured the spokesmen that there would be no intrusions on private property since his purpose was to confiscate public goods.

Essentially, Chauncey kept his promise, for the Americans left the harbour before midnight without harassing the residents. During the afternoon Scott's troops had gone to the jail and hospital, rounding up willing prisoners and ambulatory invalids, looting two private stores and taking provisions and British army baggage. That would have been the end of the affair had local turncoats not whispered that a flotilla of bateaux had been hidden up the Don River. Early on 1 August 1813, several schooners sailed back into the harbour to land a search party, which soon found the bateaux. Later that day the squadron sailed for Niagara with eleven bateaux, 400 barrels of pork and bread, a pile of personal baggage and a 24-pdr. long gun. In their wake they left the barracks, woodyard and storehouses on Gibraltar Point in flames and a promise that a more destructive visit might be paid if Yeo took it in mind to assault other helpless American villages.[6] Ever the guardian of good manners, Chauncey also indicated to Strachan and Powell that he was troubled by the theft of York's lending library after the April battle and meant to return the books as soon as he could collect enough of them to make the trip worthwhile.[7]

The American squadron slipped across to its Four Mile Creek anchorage to disembark the troops and then swing idly at its moorings for several days.

Chauncey ordered Lieutenant Jesse Elliott to take 100 men from the *Pike* and head for Perry's squadron at Erie, and he borrowed from his other crews to make up for the shortage in the flagship.[8] On 5 August Winfield Scott returned to the *General Pike* in company with Brigadier General David R. Williams, an influential congressman recently appointed to active field duty.[9] They had been sent by Boyd, who had just received a letter from the War Department in which Secretary John Armstrong had reversed his 7 July instructions about holding fast at Fort George. Since Chauncey was once more on the lake, Armstrong advised Boyd, "it now becomes your business, in concert with the squadron, to harass and destroy the enemy whenever you can find him."[10] To this end Scott and Williams proposed a large-scale pincer action against De Rottenburg's army.[11] One thousand soldiers would board the squadron for a landing at either the Canadian Twelve Mile Creek or Forty Mile Creek, while another force would move from Queenston and Fort George to catch the British in between. Chauncey agreed with the scheme and instructions were issued for a brigade to embark early on 7 August. As the sun projected its first rays over the horizon on that day, however, Boyd's plan was unceremoniously dropped, for the light of dawn revealed sails approaching from the north. It was the circumstance for which everyone had been waiting – the "weighty conflict between the two fleets."[12]

The British squadron had departed with light opposing breezes from Kingston on 31 July to seek out Chauncey and engage him. Compared to the raid on Sackets Harbour and a handful of less ambitious undertakings, this was the most aggressive move the British had made since the beginning of the war. Prevost, the ever cautious commander-in-chief, must have watched the squadron's slow departure that day and the next with some trepidation before turning to his desk to express his thoughts to Lord Bathurst:

> It is scarcely possible that a decisive naval action can be avoided, and I therefore humbly hope that His Royal Highness the Prince Regent will approve of its being courted by us, as a necessary measure for the preservation of the advanced positions of his army, which I have determined to maintain until the naval ascendancy on Lake Ontario is decided.[13]

Yeo had made the best preparations possible for waging the battle. He juggled the ordnance in his squadron, replacing the 18-pdr. carronades in the *Wolfe* with a set of 32-pdrs. recently brought up from Quebec. The carronades and guns on most of the other vessels had also been changed during July, their overall weight of metal being increased considerably.[14] In addition, the commodore

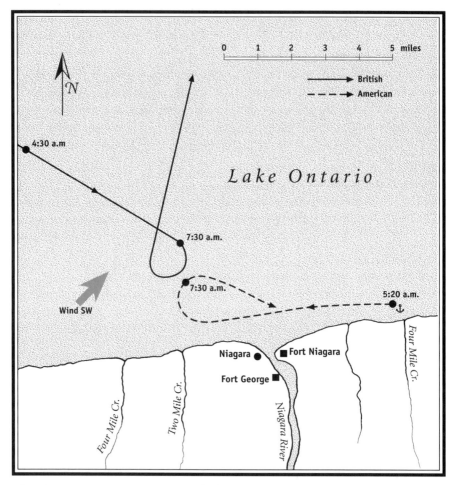

Squadron courses, 7 August 1813. The first encounter between the commodores occurred north of the mouth of the Niagara River, with the squadrons following these courses as indicated by the *Wolfe* logbook, official reports and eyewitness accounts.

had reinforced his seamen with the detachment of soldiers acting as marines who would play a key role if an action developed that allowed the British to board the American warships.

For a week, the British squadron, consisting of the *Wolfe, Royal George, Earl of Moira, Lord Melville, Beresford* and *Sir Sidney Smith,* plodded westward, making painfully slow headway against inconsistent and contrary winds.[15] A boat was sent ashore from the *Smith* on 5 August to gather news of the enemy's movements, and the next day the *George* sprang a leak that flooded its main powder magazine, ruining much of its contents. The powder was replaced from the other vessels, but the leak could not be found, resulting in the pumps on the corvette being constantly manned. The squadron sailed slowly across the lake in a southerly direction from York, and at 4:30 a.m. on 7 August 1813 was ten miles northwest of the Niagara River and in view of the American squadron at its anchorage.

The crews in both squadrons cleared for action within minutes, unnecessary equipment being stowed below, moorings cast off the guns, gunners assembling cartridge boxes, match tubs, rammers and sponges as the gun captains rolled shot in their hands to select those that would make the first broadside fly true. The combatants eyed each other warily, while alertly watching their respective flagships for signals. Yeo's squadron crawled southeastward on a starboard tack (the breeze being from the southwest), as Chauncey's force made way to the west on the opposite tack close to shore. The American squadron consisted of the *Pike, Madison, Oneida, Governor Tompkins, Conquest, Ontario, Fair American, Asp, Pert, Hamilton, Scourge, Julia* and *Growler*[16]

The convergence of the two squadrons, within full view of soldiers and citizens alike on both sides of the Niagara River, marked the first time the two commodores had come into contact. Chauncey opened the proceedings at 7:30 by asking Sinclair to fire a broadside from the *Pike*, which, owing to the large gap between the squadrons, plunged harmlessly into the depths. Nevertheless, Yeo answered with a single gun and a chorus of cheers, then bore up into the wind and led his line on an angle toward the Americans. The American squadron had already separated, unintentionally, into three divisions, the *Pike, Oneida* and two schooners pulling ahead of the *Madison* and two schooners, with six sluggish schooners lagging. Chauncey wore around and sailed back toward the east, standing "in under their batteries," as the *Wolfe's* log noted, but more likely trying to consolidate his force. Yeo turned north onto the larboard tack, and thus ended the first encounter. As Chauncey hovered near his shore, the British spent the rest of the day sailing slowly across the lake propelled by a light breeze.

To many of the spectators on the shore it must have been a disappointment to watch the two most powerful squadrons ever to appear on the Great Lakes manoeuvring toward each other and then turning away on divergent courses. It was a condition with which they were going to have to become accustomed, for the squadrons varied greatly in composition and required adroit handling if their respective commanders were to engage with a good hope of success.

The chief difference between the two squadrons lay in the armament that each carried.[17] The Americans possessed more long guns; of the 112 pieces of ordnance that Chauncey listed in his squadron at that time, sixty-six were long guns. Because some of these pieces were mounted on circles, forty-two of them, including six 32-pdrs. and nineteen 24-pdrs., could be brought to bear as a "broadside" on targets more than one mile away, under ideal conditions. In contrast, the British squadron carried nineteen long guns, out of a total of ninety-seven pieces of ordnance. With only one 24-pdr., fixed to a circle on the *Wolfe*, Yeo's long-distance broadside totalled ten guns, including the single 24, six 18s, two 9s and one 12-pdr. When the squadrons lay a mile or more apart, as they were when they first passed each other, the advantage was Chauncey's as his vessels could present a combined broadside of 779 pounds of metal compared with Yeo's broadside weight of 162 pounds.

At closer quarters, where Yeo's carronades added effectively to the destructive force of his long guns, the scales rode more evenly. The overall British broadside weight of metal rose to 1,392 pounds, due to the large number of carronades in Yeo's squadron. Chauncey had fewer of these weapons, so that when their weight of metal was added to that of the long guns his broadside totalled 1,387 pounds of iron. For obvious reasons, Yeo favoured an engagement within the 500-yard preferred range of the carronades, which were easier to operate, requiring fewer men and less powder, yet still packed a full-strength wallop at a faster rate than the ponderous long guns.[18]

All the naval and military men involved in the Great Lakes theatre of war understood the difference between the two squadrons and its influence on the commodores' tactics. James Richardson recollected that Yeo "was anxious to seek close quarters while it was the policy of the other to keep his distance."[19] During a lull, however, Chauncey's gunboats were well-suited to sweeping within range of the British and bombarding them at their leisure. Lieutenant Colonel John Harvey had noted this problem when he went aboard the *Wolfe* at Forty Mile Creek in June: "Sir James, I am happy to observe, is fully impressed with the necessity of having a *commanding* breeze ... [because] in a light one or calm the enemy's flotilla of small vessels would have an incalculable advantage."[20] "The object of Sir James," wrote Master's Mate David Wingfield, "was to engage them at close quarters and board, which would, in all human probability, have insured success ... [although the strategy depended upon] having the wind so in our favour, as to be enabled to maintain a distance, or come to close action."[21] One of the Americans watching the first encounter between the commodores believed he saw just such a plan in motion as he followed the manoeuvres off Niagara on 7 August: "Sir James's object just now appeared to be to get ours in a position where he could attack the *Pike* with two vessels at once, but Chauncey manoeuvred too well for him."[22]

The difference in armament carried by the opposing squadrons limited the options open to each commander, but other factors also influenced the course of Yeo and Chauncey's waltz. As in all operations, whether on sea or land, the natural elements contrived to disrupt the most carefully laid plans and to penalize carelessness. Such an incident occurred in the darkness after the first day of exchanges, producing a memorable event in Great Lakes history.

At sunset on 7 July the British lay close to their own shore west of York, while the Americans sat across the lake about six miles north of Twelve Mile Creek. Only a faint breeze propelled both squadrons and even that fell away so that Chauncey's gunboats, widely separated from the flagship, put out their sweeps to position themselves closer to the commodore. "It was a lovely evening," recounted Seaman Ned Myers of his view from the *Scourge*, "not a cloud visible, and the lake being smooth as a looking-glass."[23] Myers and George Turnblatt, the schooner's gunner, discussed the necessity of securing their guns, which had stood ready for action all day. Believing they should not be trussed up to the bulwarks with the enemy so near, the gunner went to get direction from the captain, Sailing Master Joseph Osgood. Osgood approved Turnblatt's plan and called the crew aft to tell the men that since he expected some action during the night, they should bed down next to their guns after having supper and a ration of grog. Lying on a rug pilfered during their first visit to York, Myers and his mess mate, Tom Goldsmith, soon fell asleep. Some time after midnight chilly splatterings of rain awoke Myers, who sat up in the pitch blackness and, finding Goldsmith awake, debated with him about going below to their mess chest for a bottle of liquor they hid there so they could fortify themselves against the sudden cold. Myers got up to feel his way forward to a narrow hatchway, but pulled up short. "A flash of lighting almost blinded me," he remembered. "The thunder came at the next instant, and with it a rushing of winds that fairly smothered the clap."[24]

Myers instantly saw the danger. Osgood had not reduced sail at sunset, thinking they would soon be under way. As a result most of the schooner's canvas abruptly billowed out as the gust of wind over the starboard side threatened to upset the vessel. Instinctively, Myers sprang to the forecastle, unfastening the jib sheet, the line that held the inside corner of the jib sail, so that the canvas could flap loose rather than catching the wind. He then released the larboard topsail sheet and grabbed its uphaul to clew up the sail, calling all the time to the helmsman to turn the schooner into the wind. A tempest had arisen out of nowhere, pounding the vessel with extraordinary ferocity and deluging it in a torrent of rain. "The water was now up to my breast," Myers recalled, "and I knew the schooner must go over."[25]

Aware of what must happen next, Myers struggled to the foremast to get out of the way when the guns, shot and other equipment slid down the canting deck. The great spread of canvas rocked the shallow-draught schooner, its stability lessened by the weight of the ordnance on its deck, and it fell over on its side. In flashes of lightning Myers saw his shipmates pinned beneath the debris or trying in vain to get through the hatchway, which seemed to have been blocked by a tumbled 4-pdr. The *Scourge* lay over on its larboard side, held to the water by its sodden canvas, buffeted by the roaring wind and waves. Myers climbed onto the upturned side of the vessel at the forechains. Two others were there, William Deer, the boatswain, and a young black sailor from Myers's gun crew. "'Deer, she's gone!'" cried Myers, but the boatswain did not answer, turning instead to walk out onto the rigging of the foremast, which now lay horizontal.[26] Myers left the boy and Deer behind and, unable to stand, crawled slowly aft.

At the stern he paused, debating whether to jump into the water or not. Looking down, he saw Joseph Osgood trying frantically to squeeze through one of the stern windows. Suspended beyond the stern of the schooner "there was a man visible on the end of the main-boom holding on by the clew of the sail. I do not know who it was. This man probably saw me, and that I was about to spring for he called out, 'Don't jump overboard! – don't jump overboard! The schooner is righting.'"[27]

Myers jumped. The schooner the Crooks brothers built before the war as the *Lord Nelson* sank. A non-swimmer, Myers thrashed to keep himself afloat and away from the vortex of the *Scourge* as it disappeared behind him. His hand struck something hard, which he recognized as the gunwale of the boat towed behind the schooner. He pulled himself in over its stern and then, fearing that the boat would be dragged below in the wake of the lost vessel, he struggled forward to untie it. The boat was free, however, for an unknown hand had loosened the rope. Myers lay there looking for the schooner and then calling out to any of his mates who might have made their escape.

Chauncey knew nothing of the disaster at first as the squally weather kept his attention fixed on trying to get to the windward of his enemy so that he could engage from a favourable position at first light. Around 2:00 a.m. on Sunday, 8 August, it was noticed from the quarterdeck of the *General Pike* that the *Scourge* and the *Hamilton* were not in sight. As dawn brightened Lieutenant Thomas Brown in the *Tompkins* hailed the flagship with news that he had picked up four seamen from the *Hamilton*, while the *Julia* soon arrived, rescuing four more from the *Hamilton* and eight *Scourges*. In the fatalistic way of a veteran seaman, Myers observed: "The lake had swallowed up the rest of the crews [more than eighty men]; and the *Scourge*, as had been often predicted, had literally become a coffin to a large portion of her people."[28]

Although the loss in life was shocking, the sinking of the *Hamilton* and *Scourge* did not seriously disable Isaac Chauncey's squadron. Their importance had been marginal, since the former had carried only a circle-mounted 12-pdr. long gun and eight 18-pdr. carronades while the latter mounted four 6-pdrs. and six 4-pdrs. The long-range punch of the squadron was still intact, but another significant aspect of the Great Lakes war had asserted itself again. Weather had caught the crews ill-prepared, robbing Chauncey of two vessels, just as the week of wind and rain after the battle at York had sapped the strength of Dearborn's army.

The violence of the weather during the early hours of 8 August was followed by a hot and sultry morning. Occasionally becalmed, the squadrons pivoted around each other between York and Niagara. Such conditions were perfect for the deployment of the American gunboats, and Chauncey signalled them to send the men to the sweeps in order to get close enough to the enemy to use their long guns. Just past noon, as the schooners were a mile and a half from Yeo's line, a breeze rose out of the south, bringing rain with it. Yeo steered after the schooners, but they returned to rendezvous with their commodore, and Yeo bore up, keeping his distance. With the weather threatening his heavily burdened gunboats again, Chauncey steered for the mouth of the Niagara River, where he anchored around 5:00 p.m. just before a sharp squall struck from the east.[29] Yeo remained on the open lake through the night under reduced sail.

Less happened the next day as the British hove to off York, their sails virtually unruffled until early evening, when a breeze rose and the enemy appeared twenty miles away to the southeast. Darkness fell without the opponents making contact.

On 9 August Sir James took time to report to Prevost. "Mr. Chauncey," he complained, "will not engage if he can help it except in his own port or in a calm, where his schooners would give him victory without his having a shot fired at him."[30] He also offered his assessment of the American squadron, declaring the *Pike* to be "a very fine large ship, but appears to be very unwieldy and unmanageable, and from the manner she is worked [I] should judge she is not complete with seamen." The *Madison* he considered similar to the *Wolfe* and well handled, whereas the *Oneida* was "small and sails bad," and the schooners, "though formidable in a calm, are very contemptible otherwise, as they have not the least shelter for their men." In his own ships Yeo noted growing frustration among the men because of the failure to do battle, but he was impressed with the enthusiastic way in which his crews functioned. One of the young master's mates who had just been advanced to acting-lieutenant, John Johnston, echoed his words in a letter home about the first brush with the

The British line of battle. A significant asset for the British was that Royal Navy officers and men were more experienced than their American counterparts in manoeuvring as part of a squadron or fleet. Though Yeo's warships were not equal in their seaworthiness, they were consistently handled with a precision that impressed Chauncey and his colleagues. Shown here are the *Wolfe, Royal George, Melville, Beresford, Moira* and *Smith*. (Oil painting by Peter Rindlisbacher, courtesy of the artist)

Americans: "All the Ships' Companys are in great Spirits and give us three Cheers whenever they pass us we intend boarding them if possible our men are well armed for the purpose."[31]

In the American squadron, similar assessments were being made. "Instead of finding Sir James Yeo that desperate hot headed boy which report has made him appear," wrote Commandant Sinclair, "we found him a judicious cautious and skillful commander."[32] Sinclair described the British squadron as "six regular built vessels of war, all sailing alike and able to support each other in any weather – capable of keeping the sea and acting efficiently when our Gunboats dare not cast their guns loose." Chauncey also noticed the superior manner in which the British squadron operated under the command of veteran Royal Navy officers and seamen as compared to the Provincial Marine crews hc had humbled during the previous November. Aggravating his problems was the fact that his manoeuvres were hampered by his "dull-sailing schooners."[33] Seaman Ned Myers shared that opinion: "Our squadron sailed very unequally, some being fast, and others dull as droggers."[34] Among the "droggers" were the *Asp*, the

Fair American and the *Oneida*, which Myers claimed "could not keep within a long distance of her proper berth."[35] In a desperate attempt to maintain some kind of order in his line of battle, Chauncey began towing the slower vessels behind the *Pike* and the *Madison*, hoping that another opportunity would arise that would justify keeping them in the squadron at all.

On 10 August that opportunity appeared. Yeo's vessels wandered into a lull six miles off Twelve Mile Creek during the afternoon and ground to a standstill, while the Americans, twenty miles to the northeast, reaped the benefit of a northerly breeze and steered to pounce on them. Their approach was slow, with Chauncey forming his ragged line of battle early in the evening and expectations rising that the sun would set on a momentous battle. With four miles still separating the squadrons, however, the wind suddenly shifted around to the southwest, filling the British sails and handing the advantage to Yeo. Presented so luckily with the "weather gauge," the tactical position that placed the wind at his back, Yeo formed line of battle and struck out after the Americans. Frustrated but perfectly composed, Chauncey signalled his squadron to tack around onto a northwesterly heading. Yeo followed on a roughly parallel course, gradually closing the gap.

As the sun sank the American commodore ordered his vessels to form two columns. The *Julia* led the *Growler, Asp, Pert, Ontario* and *Fair American* in the line closer to the British. Six hundred yards downwind, the *Pike* led the *Oneida, Madison, Governor Tompkins* and *Conquest*. It appears that this was a pre-arranged configuration, directed by signals from the flagship and supplemented with further signals instructing the six schooners in the windward division to engage the enemy as soon as their shot could reach. Once the firing had commenced, Chauncey wanted the gunboats "to edge down upon the line to leeward and pass through the intervals and form to leeward."[36] The first four schooners would sail between the larger vessels, while the last two would join the end of the *Pike's* line. It was the commodore's hope that, by offering up his vulnerable gunboats, he would make Yeo hungry enough to fall into the deadly range of the heavy American long guns.

Chauncey's plan was a good one and by 10:00 p.m. it seemed to be working. The *Wolfe*, demonstrating that the British vessels did not all possess the same sailing qualities, pulled ahead of its consorts and angled toward the *Ontario* and *Fair American*. The wind was rising and veering around to the northwest as the two squadrons converged less than ten miles southeast of York. The American windward crews turned their long guns around to bear on the *Wolfe*, waited until it was 1,200 yards away and opened fire at about 11:00 p.m. Almost half an hour passed before Yeo was in a suitable position for returning fire. The action

Chauncey's order of battle, 10 August 1813. To accompany his report to Secretary Jones, the commodore had one of his clerks sketch this illustration of his 10 August plan to lure Yeo into his grasp. At the inquiry into the capture of the schooners, it was revealed that the positions of the *Asp* and *Pert* were mistakenly reversed by the clerk. (Courtesy of the U.S. National Archives, RG 45, M125, 30:100) then became "general" as the British flagship, supported apparently by the *Lord Melville*, exchanged fire with the American windward division. After a few minutes Chauncey signalled those schooners to make their move, which the *Pert*, *Asp*, *Ontario* and *Fair American* did, slipping away to leeward, luring Yeo into Chauncey's trap. Unbelievably, however, the leading schooners, the *Julia*, Sailing Master James Trant, and the *Growler*, Lieutenant David Deacon, maintained their heading as if unaware of the commodore's intention.

On the *Pike* there were exclamations of surprise and anger and someone muttered, "They are lost."[37] Chauncey had to think fast. Yeo was too far off to engage him with any effect on the present course, although the *Wolfe* kept hurling long shots at the *Pike*. Chauncey might have turned into the wind and toward the British with his whole squadron, which almost certainly would have

Naval action on Lake Ontario, 10 August 1813. Midshipman Peter Spicer, stationed in the *Oneida,* was one of many observers in Chauncey's squadron who watched the *Julia* and *Growler* ignore the commodore's instructions. Without concern for scale, Spicer drew this view of the wayward schooners (at the top) being separated from their cohorts (bottom and right) by Yeo's squadron (middle). (Courtesy of the U.S. Naval Historical Center, NH-75733-KN)

led to a significant engagement. He rejected that option, fearing perhaps that his squadron would not be able to maintain formation as it struggled to windward, allowing the British, who commanded the weather gauge, to swoop down upon it. Instead, he let fall his main topsail and edged away two points on the compass so that the wind was directly astern.

This move was intended to offer a better target to Yeo, but the British commodore did not take the bait because the *Julia* and *Growler* had by then tacked as if they planned to circle around the British to attack them from the windward side. Yeo watched the gap grow between the schooners and their flagship, judged the opportunities presented to him and chose the surer thing, by bearing up and chasing after the wayward pair of schooners. Seeing that his own tactics were not working, Chauncey asked Sinclair to turn back toward the gunboats and the *Wolfe* as the rest of his squadron sailed away. The flagship approached Yeo and came to a virtual standstill as Sinclair backed the main topsail, inviting the knight to a duel. The invitation had no effect, and within minutes Chauncey reversed his decision and left the inattentive, or independently-minded, Trant and Deacon to their fate. "Finding that I must either separate from the rest of the squadron," he later wrote, "or relinquish the hope of saving the two which had separated, I reluctantly gave up the pursuit, [and] rejoined the squadron then to leeward."[38] Before a fresh breeze and under a clear sky, the American squadron gradually disappeared toward the southeast.

The *Julia* and *Growler* did not last long. Although they were among the best of Chauncey's converted lakers, they had turned toward the northern shore and were soon running out of water. As their leadsmen called out diminishing soundings, Trant and Deacon decided that rather than run aground they might as well try to run the gauntlet between the *Wolfe* and *Royal George* to the left, and the other vessels to the right. This attempt was futile, as the British flew down on them blasting away with guns and carronades. Ned Myers and the former *Scourges* cursed their bad luck. "We were within short canister-range, and got it smartly on both tacks," remarked Ned Myers. "Both of us kept up a heavy fire, swivelling our guns round, so as not to neglect anyone."[39] Trant shouted for the 18-pdr. to be filled to the muzzle and fired at the *Melville* as it closed on them, but some panic-stricken soul had mistakenly thrown the match-rope overboard. Minutes later a British boarding party was leaping onto their decks. Resigned to captivity, Myers sat down on the slide of the 32-pdr. and watched as the enemy seized the schooner even while fresh volleys of musketry rained down from the *Melville's* tops.

An officer approached Myers, asking, "'What are you doing here, you Yankee?'"

Capture of the *Julia* and *Growler*, 10 August 1813. The American schooners ran so close to land that they could see the lights of buildings, and their soundings revealed only two fathoms (twelve feet) of water. Believing their gunboats, known in the squadron for their speed, could evade the British squadron, the commanders opted to make a mad dash to open water. (By Owen Staples, courtesy of the Toronto Reference Library, T-15208)

Ned shot back, "Looking at your fools firing upon their own men."

"Take that for your sauce," snapped the officer, jabbing Myers's thigh with the point of his sword. [40]

Myers went below to bandage himself and found his mates had joined a group of British tars in trying to empty two barrels of whiskey as fast as possible. The scene was evolving into a party where international disputes had no place, when the same officer who had cut Myers rattled down the companionway and, seeing the "jollification," hollered, "Halloo! here's high life below stairs!"[41] As the seamen snuffed their candles and scuttled away, the officer tipped over the kegs and ended the festivities.

Myers and the other crew members were taken onto Commander William Mulcaster's *Royal George*, where they learned that the *Growler* had also struck its colours and, while no one had been wounded on the *Julia*, there had been casualties, including one death, on the other schooner. Although the British ship was screened off below, Myers was able to catch sight of a 68-pdr. carronade that appeared to have been dismounted. Later a pair of British sailors brought the prisoners some food and grog and wished them well.

In the meantime Sailing Master James Trant had been taken to the *Wolfe*, where he also took interest in the heavy carronades carried by the British. He saw four of the 68-pdrs. and evidence of the ammunition used in them – a five-pound charge, a sixty-eight-pound shot, a stand of grape and a large bag of musket balls meant for each one. As he stood on the deck he noticed an officer wearing a simple jacket and trousers attended by several other officers, and it took a minute or two for Trant to realize that he was in the company of the renowned Sir James Lucas Yeo. When they were introduced, Yeo demanded, "What does your Commodore mean by running away from me always?"[42] Trant had no answer. The next day he and the others landed at York to begin their long march to imprisonment at Quebec and Halifax. For most of the men, Ned Myers included, the war was over.[43]

On the day after the capture, Tuesday 11 August 1813, Yeo made no effort to seek out his adversary. Chauncey's squadron was barely visible to the southeast at dawn and the wind was fair for York, so the British steered for that destination and rounded Gibraltar Point at noon. Across the lake Chauncey's lookouts watched their enemy sail out of sight. The wind was blowing harder than it had for days, and the *American* and *Asp* were struggling to keep station. The commodore finally signalled them to head for the Niagara River and anchor there while the rest of the squadron continued eastward. Chauncey laid a course for the Genesee River, intending to give his schooners some relief from the buffeting they were suffering. En route, Commandant William Crane and Lieutenant Melancthon Woolsey informed him that they were almost out of provisions, and since the wind threatened to rise to gale strength, Chauncey bypassed Genesee and laid a course for Sackets Harbour. As fate would have it, the wind vanished the next morning, delaying their return to Sackets until 13 August. Just before noon Chauncey anchored close in to his shipyard so that provisioning could be handled quickly. He must have been uncomfortable knowing that everyone on shore had noted the depletion of his numbers and would soon know that his great aspirations to conquer "the British knight" had met with defeat and disappointment.

Lieutenant David Deacon, USN

(d. 1840) After their exchange from captivity, David Deacon and James Trant appeared before a court of inquiry in September 1814 concerning the loss of the *Julia* and *Growler* and were absolved of blame. Deacon was promoted to master commandant the following December. He is shown here after 1826 when he had advanced to the rank of captain.
(Courtesy of the Kennedy Galleries, Inc. and the U.S. Naval Historical Center, NH-50509)

CHAPTER **11**

"Give the Vapouring Dog
a Sound Drubbing"[1]

ENGAGEMENT AT THE GENESEE:
11 SEPTEMBER 1813

While his crews worked frantically to replenish the limited holds of their shallow-draught warships on 13 August, Commodore Chauncey wrote a long and detailed report to Secretary Jones about his first unsuccessful meeting with James Yeo. He began by admitting how "distressed and mortified" he was to have lost four of his vessels and then offered a blow-by-blow account of the encounters. The tragic foundering of the *Scourge* and *Hamilton*, Chauncey explained, gave Yeo "decidedly the superiority," although the British knight persisted in avoiding action. The loss of the *Julia* and *Growler* further reduced his strength due to "an error in judgment and excess of zeal" on the parts of the two commanders who, Chauncey stated, "disobeyed my positive orders." He considered the British commodore to have been lucky so far and hoped "that it will be my turn next, and although inferior in point of force I feel very confident of success."[2]

Elsewhere in the American squadron less optimistic quills were busy during this period. One correspondent copied portions of the logbook for one of the vessels and submitted them, without comment, to the *United States Gazette* on 15 August. A week later a second summary of the actions near the western end of Lake Ontario was sent to the same paper, but this time the anonymous officer injected his critical perception of the handling of the *General Pike* on the night the two gunboats were captured. "Every gun was pointed, every match ready in hand," he wrote, "when to our utter astonishment the Commodore wore and stood S.E., leaving Sir James to exult in the capture ... which was certainly a very fortunate one for him."[3] A third individual, an anonymous mid-

181

shipman, wrote a letter to his uncle, which eventually found its way to William Jones's desk. Regarding the initial activity off the Niagara River on 7 August, this young officer noted: "The Com. fired five or six guns which they [the British] did not return but continued bearing down upon us. The Com. thunder struck (and no doubt frightened) at their coolness and determined bravery tacked ship and left them under pretense of endeavouring to get the weather gage."[4] This writer blamed the loss of the *Hamilton* and *Scourge* on Chauncey's passive tactics "for which the Com. is answerable and perhaps highly censurable (you know he is a peace man)." Of the midnight meeting on 10 August, he added, "We kept closing, two of our schooners were in the midst of the enemys fleet when the Com. wore ship and left the enemy! The two schooners were taken. They fought like heroes."

Complaints like these soon reached the ears of Major General Morgan Lewis, commanding at Sackets Harbour, who was so disturbed that he penned an outline of Chauncey's voyage for the benefit of Daniel Tompkins, the governor of New York, to allay concerns provoked by stories that might be reaching Tompkins's quarter: "Rumor will, do doubt, be disposed in these days of miss representation very much to exaggerate it," he wrote, referring to the loss of four gunboats. "Scoundrels will exult and Essex men perhaps sing a Te Deum in honor of *Sir James the Deliverer*."[5] Citing a conversation with the commodore and an examination of the *Oneida's* logbook as his sources, Lewis explained how Chauncey had sought battle repeatedly while Yeo avoided it. When the "Te Deums" for Yeo began to appear in print, Arthur Sinclair took up the quill of outrage, complaining bitterly about a copy of one of Yeo's despatches that appeared in a newspaper published in Ogdensburg. "It is, as usual, an egregious falsehood - scarsely a word of truth in it," he claimed, "[because] this inhuman Monster of an Editor, remarks at the bottom of his publication - after exulting in our losses, that those two vessels [the *Hamilton* and *Scourge*] in carrying sail *to get away from the Enemy* had upset and drowned 100 men.... What does such fellows deserve? Hanging is too good for them."[6] Sinclair was concerned as to how Chauncey's leadership would be perceived by the public. "I never pityed a man more in my life than I do him," he confided to a friend before adding a hint of criticism. "He is a brave enterprising man but has had rather too high an opinion of those confounded gunboats."[7]

After the squadron had resupplied, the *Pike* led the *Madison, Oneida, Governor Tompkins, Ontario, Pert* and *Lady of the Lake* on the customary course toward the Ducks at sunset on 14 August 1813.[8] No military reinforcements or provisions had been taken on board, for Chauncey intended to rendezvous with the two schooners he had sent to Niagara and then to seek out his adversary.

The British squadron had anchored close to York on 11 August and spent the next two days making repairs to the *Growler* (renamed *Hamilton*) and *Julia* (renamed *Confiance*) and to one of the *Wolfe's* topmasts.[9] Attention was paid to the leak in the *Royal George* and to another leak that had opened in the *Melville*, while the prisoners from the American schooners were landed and fresh provisions embarked. Just after noon on 13 August the squadron, now comprising eight vessels, cruised away toward Fort Niagara and then steered over to the Canadian Ten Mile Creek. Under reduced canvas and light airs, it remained in this area until late the next day, when anchors were dropped and Yeo went ashore to meet with Prevost, who had made a quick trip up from Kingston to visit De Rottenburg's headquarters at St. Davids, near Queenston. He returned at 5:00 p.m. on 15 August, and at dawn the next morning the squadron crept away on an easterly course paralleling the shore. At mid-morning seamen and marines manned the boats to cut out a large bateau attempting to reach Fort Niagara. Soon after taking the prize in tow, lookouts announced the appearance of sails in the northeast twelve or so miles away. Once more, the crews cleared decks and ran to their quarters, their expectations rising.

Yeo ordered his line to close up, then came around to a larboard tack, following a northerly course before southwest winds that were slowly increasing in force. As evening turned to night the squadrons stayed well apart under double-reefed topsails; 17 August dawned with rain and steady, high winds out of the southwest, and, since he could see nothing of Chauncey, Yeo let the squadron have its head. Between 5:00 a.m. and 7:00 p.m. it covered 125 miles of open water eastward, passing the Ducks on a course for Kingston. The Americans, who had followed, came into view the next day, seemingly intent on returning to Sackets, which allowed Yeo to continue toward Kingston, where his squadron anchored early in the afternoon of 19 August.

Yeo's warships remained in port for the next five days. While the rest of the squadron swung at moorings in Kingston Harbour, the *Melville, Confiance* and *Hamilton* moved into Navy Bay so the dockyard crews could complete necessary refits. Six weeks of provisions were stored in all the vessels, the *Wolfe* alone receiving 3,600 pounds of pork, 880 pounds of fresh beef, 603 gallons of rum, 612 pounds of sugar and 672 pounds of rice. The squadron's muster was supplemented by the arrival of ten transport men from Quebec and two Royal Navy men, a gunner and Lieutenant James Groves, who had missed the *Woolwich's* departure from Plymouth the previous March. When preparations were completed, the squadron assembled at Nine Mile Point, where it was joined on 24 August by three transports carrying supplies and reinforcements for Major General De Rottenburg's army, as well as a naval detachment for Commander

Robert Barclay at Amherstburg. This latter group included thirty-eight seamen and junior officers from HM Troop Ship *Dover* and Lieutenant George Bignal. The *Dover* had been one of three transports that had delivered De Meuron's Regiment to Quebec, and while the others carried American prisoners to Halifax, the *Dover's* Captain Augustus Drury received orders to lay his ship and proceed with his crew to Kingston. When the first division reached Kingston under Bignal, Yeo embarked them and set sail for Niagara at 9:00 a.m. on 24 August.[10]

A fair and steady wind quickly propelled the British squadron up the lake. It halted off the Gibraltar lighthouse at 8:00 a.m. on 26 August long enough to leave one transport at York while the other two parted company for the Head of the Lake to disembark supplies, troops and Lieutenant Bignal's party.[11] Within two hours the eight warships were off again, steering for the Canadian Four Mile Creek, where they anchored that evening. Early next day Prevost and his suite rowed out to the *Wolfe*, which then led its consorts in toward Fort Niagara. The commander-in-chief wanted to have a close look at his enemy's position, so at 6:30 a.m. he, Yeo and their staffs transferred to the *Hamilton* and slipped far enough into the mouth of the Niagara River to exchange shots with the American batteries. The schooner returned from its reconnaissance before noon, and the squadron turned back toward York. As the senior officers of both services enjoyed dinner and discussion, the warships stood across the lake to the capital. Prevost went ashore just before sunset, having agreed with Yeo that "an action on the lake must 'ere long be unavoidable," and that any combined operation of the army and navy should be delayed until the contest was decided.[12]

While the British appeared satisfied to maintain their current position on the Niagara Peninsula as the naval issue remained unresolved, plans were afoot in the American camp to retake the offensive; the scheme that Secretary Armstrong had begun to promote vigorously in July was now taking substantial form. On 20 August Major General James Wilkinson arrived at Sackets Harbour to assume overall command of the northern theatre and the proposed campaign down the St. Lawrence River. Aged fifty-six years, he was a veteran of the Revolutionary War whose subsequent career through a maze of diplomatic and political intrigue had earned him a reputation for questionable ethics.[13] Armstrong considered Wilkinson a friend, whereas Major General Wade Hampton (who commanded the Lake Champlain army meant to move in conjunction with Wilkinson's) hated the man.

Wilkinson's appointment had actually been approved in the spring, but he had taken his time getting to Washington and proceeding to Sackets. On his arrival, however, the general initiated a flurry of correspondence, planning and action. At his direction, a council of war involving Morgan Lewis, Chauncey,

Brigadier General Jacob Brown and Brigadier General Robert Swarthout, the quartermaster general, concluded that the main strength of the U.S. army in the north should be concentrated at Sackets Harbour, and "a bold feint on Kingston" should be made while the main thrust would move down the St. Lawrence River to meet Hampton and "take possession of Montreal."[14] Wilkinson planned to sail for Niagara, knowing that the British would soon hear of his destination and assume that a fresh attack was planned for that quarter. Having created this ruse, he then hoped to return to Sackets with Boyd's army (leaving a militia force in its place), where a huge flotilla of bateaux, gunboats and scows and a mountain of provisions were being prepared for the expedition down the St. Lawrence. While the navy would play the critical role of covering the army, Wilkinson saw the immediate "necessity of settling the point of *naval* superiority before we commit ourselves."[15] If Chauncey could vanquish Yeo, the new campaign could be executed without interference.

The American squadron limped back into port on 19 August, after being knocked around by the strong winds and rough seas that had arisen on 16 August. Most of the vessels had suffered damage in spars or rigging or sprung planks, and sickness had laid low eighty seamen in the *Madison*. The *Conquest* was towed to the dockyard, leaking at such a rate that it had to be emptied and careened so that the hull could be completely recaulked. There were plenty of shipwrights ready to perform that chore because they had launched the new schooner *Sylph* at 7:00 a.m. the previous day. It lay beside the wharf, as a crew of riggers stepped its masts and began setting up the rigging. The commodore was pleased with his new vessel. "From her construction," he assured William Jones, "she must sail fast, she will add very much to my present force, and in point of force fully counterbalance the vessels which I have lost."[16] The schooner's bulwarks had ten gunports a side, a feature that would lead the British to think it carried twenty guns when they first saw it. Instead of filling those ports though, Chauncey ordered four 32-pdr. guns mounted on circles and only six 6-pdrs. at the ports, giving the *Sylph* a broadside of 146 pounds of long-range iron.

The commodore decided to remain at the Harbour until the *Sylph* was ready for duty, which permitted his crews a brief respite after a month of almost continuous sea service and standing to quarters. Despite any fatigue some of the officers might have felt, a number of the young gentlemen had reason to celebrate shortly after dropping anchor. On 24 July Congress had approved a long list of promotions and since the squadron's last visit to the Harbour a stack of new commissions had arrived from Washington. With pleasure Commodore Chauncey welcomed Arthur Sinclair to the select circle of U.S. Navy captains,

congratulated Melancthon Woolsey on his advancement to master and commandant and presented certificates to six newly-confirmed lieutenants and
three surgeons.[17] Later, a group of officers gathered to celebrate the good news
over dinner and drink. The party released pent up spirits and drowned frustrations, but it also worsened the misery of at least one young hopeful. Twenty-
three year old Francis Gregory had been at Sackets Harbour since the previous
autumn. Already a midshipman for four years with battle experience in gunboats at New Orleans, Gregory had served as an acting-lieutenant for months
and, indeed, had been the lone officer on watch on the April morning when the
Madison had almost foundered as the harbour's ice broke up. Chagrined at the
sight of other acting-lieutenants being formally promoted, and fuelled by liquor and the tactless remarks of his comrades about his having been snubbed,
Gregory hurriedly composed a bitter letter of resignation and mailed it off to
the Navy Department. The next day, when his mind cleared and his passions
cooled, Gregory meekly went to the commodore to beg his assistance in retrieving his carelessly discarded career. After undoubtedly giving the young
man a stern lecture about sobriety and gentlemanly deportment, Chauncey
compassionately wrote to the secretary on Gregory's behalf. "If, sir, … you
would have the goodness to … forgive him his false step," the commodore suggested, "I would be willing to pledge myself for his future good conduct, and
whenever you may deem him worthy of a commission, he will I know show
himself worthy of it."[18] Chauncey was right to rescue Gregory, for the young
officer shortly proved his worth and went on to a distinguished career in the
service.

Like Gregory, a second officer suffered disappointment and dismay as the
squadron lay at Sackets, but his discomfort had actually been increased by the
receipt of a very prestigious commission. From the moment he had reached the
lake in June, Arthur Sinclair had not been happy with his appointment. "On my
arrival here," he explained to William Jones on 22 August, "I was much disappointed and mortified to find that the Comdr. intended shifting his Flag onto
[the *General Pike*] and that I was, consequently, to lose the command of *the
ship*." Such a post, Sinclair believed, was better suited to a junior master commandant, and the rank of captain that he now held "placed it out of my power,
with anything like justice to myself or respect for the grade I hold, to remain
longer in this situation."[19] Sinclair acknowledged his respect for Chauncey and
the Navy Department, but asked for a re-assignment. For a month he waited to
hear back from Jones during which time he was "in hourly expectation of being
ordered to the command of one of the new Frigates" as he explained to a
friend.[20] Late in September Jones's response arrived at Sackets, clearly stating

the secretary's view of the matter: "The pretentions of Officers are extravagant, and unwarrantable, and entirely unsupported by the practice of the Navy."[21] The secretary made no offer of another ship, and Sinclair continued in the *Pike* until December without raising his bone of contention again.

Final preparations for another cruise were completed on 29 August and at 7:00 p.m. that evening Chauncey led his squadron out of Black River Bay before a light easterly breeze.[22] Eight vessels formed the line that stood out to the lake, the *Pike, Madison, Oneida, Sylph, Tompkins, Ontario, Pert* and *Lady of the Lake*. Still under repair, the *Conquest* would soon join the squadron as would the *Fair American* and *Asp*, which had remained at Niagara after seeking shelter there from the rough weather experienced at the end of the previous cruise.[23] The recently promoted Master and Commandant Melancthon Woolsey commanded the *Sylph*, now classed a sloop because of Woolsey's rank, on its maiden voyage, his position in the *Oneida* having been given to Lieutenant Thomas Brown. Alterations had been made to the ordnance of some of the vessels, prompting the commodore to note that his squadron now carried ninety-one guns in all.[24] The *Sylph's* four 32-pdrs. had come from the *Ontario, Pert, York* and Fort Tompkins, with the 6-pdrs. taken from the *Oneida, Pert, Conquest* and a battery on Navy Point. The only vessel to receive replacements was the *Pert*, into which was moved the *York's* other gun, a long 24-pdr.[25] Overall, the clout of the American broadsides, reduced somewhat by the loss of the four schooners earlier in the month, had been restored with the addition of the *Sylph*. In time the schooner confirmed Henry Eckford's talents as a master designer by sailing quickly and dependably, making it a greater asset to the squadron than the converted lakers had ever been.

Just before the squadron's departure Chauncey had sent Sailing Master William Vaughan to Kingston in the sloop *Union* to deliver a message to Yeo. Vaughan returned with the news that the British were not in port, so rather than sailing north to inspect Kingston, Chauncey set a course for the western reaches of the lake, intending "to fall in with the enemy between this and the head of the lake."[26] The voyage was a slow one; westerly winds, squalls and light airs combined to retard the progress of the squadron, making it necessary to tack repeatedly, setting sail only to reef or reduce it altogether shortly thereafter. The commodore's aspirations were met, however, in the middle of the afternoon of 3 September 1813 when seven sails were sighted to the northwest. The American squadron was about fifteen miles due north of the Niagara River, and Chauncey turned to chase the British for a couple of hours, but then tacked around and sailed southward toward Niagara, dropping his bowers in the river opposite Fort George at 8:00 p.m.

After depositing Prevost at York on 27 August, Yeo had remained near the provincial capital for the better part of the week, making only one slow trip across the lake and back. The *Fair American* and *Asp* chased the sloop *Vincent*, which had been snooping into the mouth of the Niagara River after a Durham boat on 1 September, but they fled back to their anchorage when Yeo appeared to rescue the army's tender. The commodore summoned Master's Mate David Wingfield to the *Wolfe* and gave him a place in the ship, since he wanted to employ the sloop as a transport. Besides, as Wingfield recalled, "Sir James ... told me he had sent for me as he thought I should prefer being in the squadron if an engagement ensued, to going to Kingston and lying inactive."[27]

Two days later, as the squadron cruised south of York, Chauncey was seen fifteen miles or so to the southeast. Later that day, as the American squadron took up its anchorage in the Niagara River, the British turned toward York, then dropped down to their Four Mile Creek on the morning of 4 September. The weather was too rough to make a good anchorage, although a boat did come out from the shore carrying despatches and two American deserters. From these "most intelligent fellows," as Lieutenant Colonel John Harvey termed them, Yeo heard that the new American schooner carried twenty-two long 18-pdrs., that the U.S. squadron was short of men, that Chauncey had been placed under arrest and Isaac Hull, captain of the USS *Constitution* when it conquered HMS *Guerriere*, had replaced him. Yeo was pleased to learn about the change in command – as he explained to Prevost on 5 September:

> I have very little doubt that a new commander will produce new measures, and that as soon as he comes out we shall have a general action, which, as I consider it the first and great object, I shall remain in this quarter (as long as my provisions last,) to watch their motions and give countenance to the Centre Division[28]

Whether Chauncey heard that the criticisms of his conduct had been sensationalized to include his outright expulsion is uncertain. Apparently undeterred by popular opinion, he stuck to the Niagara River for four days, exercising the crews at quarters and meeting with Wilkinson, who had reached the post on 4 September somewhat exhausted and ill after an unpleasant trip from Sackets in an open boat.[29] At dawn on Tuesday, 7 September, the commodore signalled for his squadron to prepare to sail and to clear for action, and at 7:00 a.m., the squadron left Niagara, steering a northerly course. Yeo had kept on the lake since picking up the deserters and led his vessels on a course to parallel Chauncey. Through that day and the next they mirrored each other's manoeuvres over toward the Scarborough Bluffs, southward from York, westward toward Burlington. On 10 September, the wind blew faint but steady and the squadrons bore nearly due east all day, with Chauncey four miles off Yeo's starboard quarter as they passed within ten miles of Fort Niagara that evening. After dusk the wind picked up so that the adversaries covered sixty miles in the dark.

The sunrise of 11 September revealed the two squadrons west of Braddock Bay, nine miles apart, their headway reduced by a weakening breeze out of the southwest. Rather than continuing eastward, Yeo, who still held the lead, bore up on a starboard tack, steering close in to shore. He might have been hoping to catch a land breeze, but there was none to be found. At about 9:00 a.m. the sails of all eight British warships began to fall limp as the ships passed Braddock Bay eight miles northwest of the Genesee River. Positioned several miles off shore, the Americans kept the wind, though their progress was slow – as the British inched toward the mouth of the Genesee. At 2:30 p.m. the *Pike* opened fire on the British, followed soon after by the *Sylph*.

11 September 1813 The commodores provided little information about the exact location of this engagement. The logbook of the *Wolfe* placed the British squadron about eight miles west northwest of the Genesee River at 9:00 a.m. with the breeze dying away. The *Sylph* logbook noted that the Americans were still making chase at noon. Yeo and Chauncey both mentioned the calm that halted the British off the Genesee River and that the Americans drew within long gun range ($^3/_4$ mile stated Chauncey) before a land breeze helped Yeo escape.

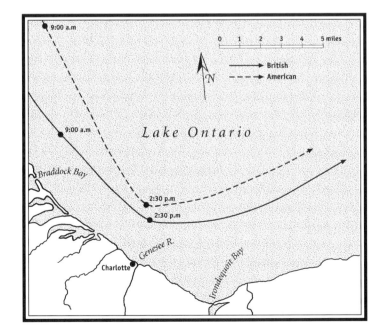

Engagement at the Genesee River, 11 September 1813. The *Pike* and *Sylph* loft their shot at the becalmed *Melville, Royal George* and *Sir Sidney Smith*. The British set as much sail as they can and send some of their men into boats to haul the ships away from the Americans and find a breeze that will allow them to escape the bombardment. (Oil painting by Peter Rindlisbacher, author's collection)

The tactical situation that had evolved near the Genesee was perfectly suited to the strength of Chauncey's squadron. With the British lying becalmed, all their ships' boats out trying to tow them out of range, their schooner-men straining their backs at the sweeps, the American long guns, especially the 32-pdrs., could knock them over like sitting ducks. It was the opportunity for Chauncey's converted lakers to finally return the investment of time and energy spent keeping them with the squadron. Unfortunately for the American commodore, such was not to be the case as the wretched gunboats gave everyone another reason to condemn their existence. "Had our Schooners done their duty we must have had him," claimed Arthur Sinclair. "The time was calm and smooth and just suited to them; but they are commanded by a set of boys without the least experience or judgment."[30] "Owing to the dullness of the sailing of most of our Schooners we were unable to bring the Enemy to close action," noted the log of the *Sylph*.[31]

In spite of the gunboats' inability to enter the fight, the engagement off Genesee proved to be a warm one. Closing to within three quarters of a mile of his enemy, allowing only the *Pike* and *Sylph* to use their ordnance to effect, Commodore Chauncey was able to bombard the British for ninety minutes. On the *Pike*, the 24-pdr. on the topgallant forecastle had been replaced with a mortar under the direction of Captain Samuel Archer of the Second Artillery Regiment and a crew of the army volunteers serving in the squadron. As the ship's other weapons blasted away as they could bear, Archer lofted a dozen shells over the 1,200 yard range to burst among the British crews, but the mortar's recoil was so strong that after its twelfth round it burst its bolts and tumbled onto the deck. Sinclair quickly had the long gun hauled back into place and the fight resumed. As the widely separated vessels worked frantically to evade their pursuers, the British could bring only six guns to bear, which inflicted damage to the rigging of the *Pike*, but caused no casualties. The *Royal George* and the *Melville* were nearest to the Americans and suffered torn sails and rigging, four

"A View of the Running Fight" on 11 September 1813. Midshipman Peter Spicer, posted to the *Sylph*, drew this illustration of Chauncey's squadron (above) chasing Yeo's ships (below) from the Genesee River to the False Ducks. The *Pike* leads the *Sylph*, *Madison*, schooners *Lady of the Lake*, *Ontario* and *Tompkins*, the *Oneida* and the *American*, its two circle-mounted long guns plainly visible amidship. Spicer confused the names of the British vessels, listing the second and fifth vessels as the *Beresford* and *Prince Regent* (two names of the same schooner) and omitting the *Melville*. It appears that the *Wolfe* is ahead of the *Melville*, towing the *Confiance/Julia*, followed by the *Moira*, *Beresford*, *Royal George*, *Smith* and *Hamilton/Growler*. Note the square topsails on both masts of the schooners *Beresford* and *Smith*, which were occasionally misidentified as brigs. (Courtesy of the U.S. Naval Historical Center, NH-75734-KN)

Shot damage in a man-of-war. Although iron shot were deadly in themselves, the jagged splinters torn up by their passage through the stout timbers of a ship inflicted devastating wounds on crews. The "live-fire" of fully-loaded carronades at a full-scale replica of a portion of the US Brig *Lawrence's* hull and bulwarks produced the damage shown in these photographs. The calibre of ordnance used was: top – 12 pdr. round shot with some grape shot; middle – 24-pdr. round shot; bottom – 24-pdr. round shot. (Photographs by the author, with permission of the Erie Maritime Museum and the Pennsylvania Historical and Museum Commission)

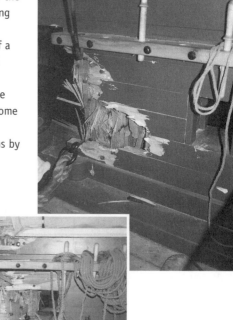

men killed and five wounded. The damage might have continued, but a breeze rippled across the still water from the land around 4:00 p.m., restoring life to the British ships. They began to make way, gathering up their boats as they headed for open water.

Frustrated to see such an opportunity yield no grand result, Chauncey steered to follow the British. The breeze freshened and the pursuit grew more lively. Just after 5:00, Chauncey signalled the *Sylph*, which had already proved its speedy seaworthiness, to hurry forward in an attempt to capture their former schooner *Growler*, which had fallen to the rear of Yeo's line. Perceiving Chauncey's intent, Yeo signalled Mulcaster in the *George* to cut back and take the inefficient *Hamilton* in tow. The American long guns had continued to try their luck, but the commodore ceased firing at 6:20 and soon signalled his larger warships to tow the most sluggish schooners in his line.

There was a deep, communal sigh of relief in all the British ships except the *Wolfe*, for one of the last of the *Pike's* round shot had created a nightmarish scene on the quarterdeck. A young midshipman named William Ellery had forlornly predicted his own death as he sat with his fellows in their quarters that afternoon. As the American sails fell slowly behind them in the early evening, David Wingfield crossed the deck to congratulate Ellery on having escaped his doom. "Well, Bill," said Wingfield, "you are still in the land of the living." The youngster had only time to reply with a "melancholy smile" before a shot "took him about the navel and literally cut him in two; we caught him in our arms but he was a corpse in an instant."[32]

The two squadrons sped on a northeasterly course before a wind out of the southwest through the falling dark and past midnight, covering seventy miles by half past three of 12 September. At that time the British rounded the False Ducks and anchored in the mouth of South Bay on the southeast edge of the Prince Edward Peninsula. Yeo hoped that Chauncey would carelessly follow him around the islands, allowing Yeo to get to windward of him, but Chauncey was unwilling to sacrifice the weather gauge. He pulled up short of the islands, preferring to tack back and forth to windward rather than approach Yeo's anchorage. Once more a promising situation produced nothing of merit. Of the manoeuvres of the two squadrons since 6 September and the action off the Genesee, Yeo wrote to Prevost, "I found it impossible to bring him to close action;" while Chauncey wrote to Jones, "I was much disappointed that Sir James refused to fight me."[33] Control of Lake Ontario remained in a stalemate, which did not seriously infringe on the campaign plans then afoot in the American camp. For James Yeo, however, his inability to resolve the issue had begun to try Prevost's patience.

CHAPTER 12

"All or None"[1]

THE BURLINGTON RACES:
28 SEPTEMBER 1813

Since his arrival in May, it had been the general expectation in Upper Canada that Sir James Yeo would win control of Lake Ontario. In part he had been successful. The unopposed operation of his squadron in June had helped to stifle the Americans at Niagara and harass the communities on the southern shore of the lake. When he had sailed westward late in July, he had gone with Prevost's approval to confront Chauncey and do battle, but by the time he returned to Kingston in mid-September, after another indecisive excursion and somewhat battered by Chauncey's squadron, Prevost's patient wait for something decisive to occur had ended. On 15 September, just three weeks after affirming his support for Yeo's efforts, Sir George wrote to Lord Bathurst: "I cannot disguise from Your Lordship that I feel some disappointment at the return of our squadron after being so many days in sight of the enemy's squadron without having obtained a decided advantage."[2]

Yeo received notice of Prevost's changing attitude on the morning of 15 September as his squadron lay in the mouth of South Bay, where it had remained since eluding the Americans three days before. A boat scurried up from Kingston bearing Commander Richard O'Conor, who relayed the commander-in-chief's views to the commodore personally. O'Conor explained to Yeo that Prevost wanted him to return to Kingston to escort a supply convoy to relieve De Rottenburg's army. The commodore was then to meet with De Rottenburg to plot a joint operation against the enemy garrisons at the mouth of the Niagara River – in short, Yeo's free rein was being hauled in. How Yeo reacted as he sat with his colleague in the cramped cabin of the *Wolfe* and listened to the verbal instructions was not recorded, but his official response revealed a clear reluctance to terminate attempts to beat Chauncey. "*Without a written communication on the subject*," he wrote to Prevost, "I do not think myself justified in giving up watching the enemy."[3]

Later that day the squadron upped anchor and sailed slowly toward Kingston, though Chauncey's sails were still in sight to the west beyond the False Ducks. Occasionally, a schooner dropped down to have a closer look, just as the *Melville* had remained under sail to watch Chauncey's movements. No contact was made between the squadrons, and after spending a night anchored near Amherst Island, the British vessels reached Kingston on 16 September.

Yeo moored close to the dockyard, having decided to make alterations in some of the vessels to improve their sailing and fighting qualities. The *Sir Sidney Smith* was brought alongside the *Wolfe* and stripped of its rigging. Its lower masts were hoisted out of their steps, by means of tackle fixed to the *Wolfe's* mainyard. Artificers then sawed off a portion of each mast and restepped it, which reduced the weight of the schooner's top hamper, making the vessel less unwieldy. A new foretopmast was set up on the flagship, and carpenters also rebuilt the ship's magazine. Ordnance was shifted, resulting in the *Royal George* and *Beresford* each receiving a circle-mounted 24-pdr. long gun. To compensate for the addition of that heavy gun and carriage, the *Beresford* lost its two long 9-pdrs. and two carronades. Pairs of carronades were also taken from the *Wolfe* and the *Earl of Moira*, probably to relieve their burden and to increase space on deck. Presumably, the superfluous ordnance went into the gunboats, although some of it, namely the 32-pdrs. from the *Hamilton* and *Confiance,* were earmarked for use in the land batteries. Yeo had been unimpressed by the two prizes, especially the *Confiance,* which "only retards me when the enemy have the weather-gage ... [and] gives me more anxiety and trouble than she is worth."[4] He removed both schooners from his line of battle, consigning them to convoy duty as transports. The alterations to the British squadron diminished its overall weight of metal, but increased the long guns in the six warships, which could now throw a long-range broadside of 201 pounds. Given the constraints of shipping and available ordnance, it was the best Yeo could do to match Chauncey's overpowering long guns.[5]

While this work was in hand Yeo met with Prevost and received the written order he had requested. He was to escort a convoy of supplies to the Head of the Lake, participate in a combined operation against the Americans at Niagara, or, if that mission seemed too risky, cover De Rottenburg's retrograde movement to Burlington Heights or beyond. The transports were to be kept in motion carrying provisions for the army as long as the season permitted; "they are to

receive from your [Yeo's] force the necessary protection."[6] As well, Prevost instructed Yeo "to impress" upon Commander Robert Barclay that his squadron,
further reinforced by the second division of seamen and marines from the *Dover* being carried up in the convoy, must regain control of Lake Erie and keep
the supply line open between Long Point and the Detroit River.

News of Barclay's defeat at the hands of Perry near Put-in-Bay on 10 September had not reached Kingston by dawn on Sunday, 19 September when the
British squadron left Navy Bay. All that day the six warships fought a westerly
breeze as they strove to gain the lake and at first light the next morning they
were still only eight miles southeast of the False Ducks. Several leagues to the
southwest the sails of the American squadron could be dimly seen. Occasionally one of Chauncey's vessels came downwind to reconnoitre, then turned
back. Yeo, following his instructions closely, tacked toward the Ducks, keeping a
wary eye on his adversary. His squadron remained in that vicinity, following a
roughly triangular route until early Tuesday morning when the convoy of eight
transports finally appeared rounding the False Ducks. Yeo made way to intercept them, taking the worst-behaved in tow, and steered a course toward the
west.

In the American squadron, the intervening time had been taken up with determined preparations for the fall campaign. Chauncey had quit the lake on
17 September, certain that the British commander did not want to fight him
and that the strong westerlies would keep his opponent penned in at Kingston.
He had also heard that Secretary of War Armstrong himself had arrived at
Sackets Harbour and the commodore was eager to discuss the current situation. While the men in his squadron once more hurried to stock their vessels,
Chauncey went ashore to meet with Armstrong.

The secretary had arrived at Sackets on 5 September to consult with Major
General James Wilkinson directly about the fall campaign. While he waited for
Wilkinson to arrive, Armstrong improved his familiarity with local conditions
and went over his plans for the invasion he had long promoted. As was his way,
however, he persisted in debating the options open to his commanders in the
field. To Wilkinson, on 15 September, he noted the advantages of attacking at a
point down the St. Lawrence or going for Kingston directly, but, in his typical
ambiguous style, left the decision to his general: "Think of this, if you like it,
choose your part, go first or last, sever the communication or take Kingston."[7]
Just before Chauncey arrived at Sackets two days later, Armstrong's sources had
convinced him that the only regular forces defending Kingston were ten dis-
contented companies of De Watteville's Regiment, a polyglot of European mer-

cenaries lately arrived from Spain. Unaware that there were actually 3,200 regular troops at the British base, the secretary discussed strategy with Chauncey, stressing the vital role that his squadron would play in the imminent operation.[8] He repeated the gist of his advice in a letter to Wilkinson after Chauncey had sailed: "Let not the great objects of the campaign be hazarded by running after Yeo; these accomplished, his race is run. Kingston or the point below seized, all above perishes because the tree is then girdled."[9] Several days later the secretary reported to President Madison, who was recovering from the illness that had incapacitated him through most of the summer, that he had impressed upon the commodore the importance of preserving his squadron for convoying Wilkinson's army to Sackets and beyond, rather than chasing the elusive Yeo around the lake.[10]

With the immediate needs of the new campaign foremost in his thoughts, Chauncey led his squadron away from Sackets before dawn on 18 September, scarcely fifteen hours after dropping his hooks there. The breezes continued to blow from the west, rising and falling away to calm, retarding the squadron's progress so that two days passed and the Ducks were still in sight to the northeast. That morning they sighted the British near the Ducks, but Chauncey made no move to engage them, although he had the weather gauge. With Armstrong's advice in mind, he continued his frustrating struggle to windward, hoping, as he later explained to William Jones, to entice Yeo to the western end of the lake.[11]

Unaware that their instructions were virtually identical, the two commodores kept their distance while they worked their way up the lake, hugging their respective shorelines as closely as possible. When he approached Niagara, Chauncey sent a note ahead to Wilkinson to determine his state of readiness, but the army was not ready for the trip to Sackets, and after dark on 24 September the squadron crept into the Niagara River and anchored. Chauncey immediately went ashore to meet the general, who, he discovered, had recovered sufficiently from his illness to begin the transfer of his 4,000-man army. A council of war held on 20 September had chosen Kingston as its first "great object in view," rather than simply a diversion as Wilkinson had stated a month before, and 25 September had been picked as the day to set out for Sackets, but the weather closed in and the embarkation was postponed.[12]

Shortly after reaching Niagara, Isaac Chauncey heard the latest news from Lake Erie – Perry had met and beaten the British two weeks before, capturing Barclay's entire squadron. "If this should prove true in all its details (and God grant that it may)," the commodore wrote to Secretary of the Navy William Jones, "he has immortalized himself." Given his acrimonious relationship with

Perry leaves the stricken flagship *Lawrence*, 10 September 1813. Perry was criticized by the British for appearing to have surrendered the brig *Lawrence*, 20, after fire from Barclay's vessels had shattered it, and then leaving it to take command of the relatively undamaged brig *Niagara*, 20, with which he broke the British line and secured his victory. Throughout the United States, however, Perry's success was celebrated, and he instantly became a heroic figure who was feted wherever he went. (Courtesy of the Ohio Historical Society)

Perry and the many frustrations he had endured on Lake Ontario, Chauncey did not spend many words expressing jubilation over Perry's success. Whether to cover his chagrin or promote his own case, Chauncey went on to detail a rumour of the death of Yeo's chief subordinate, Commander William Mulcaster, in the *Royal George* during the engagement near the Genesee on 11 September. He regretted having been unable to bring Yeo to a close contest on that occasion, which, he assured the navy secretary, "would have been as complete as that upon Lake Erie" and, almost pathetically, ended his despatch with the plaint: "If we did not succeed it was not our fault."[13]

Across the lake, word of the disaster on Lake Erie had been confirmed for more than a week by the time the British squadron and its convoy anchored inshore at Burlington Bay on 26 September.[14] Characteristically, Yeo did not hurry to respond to the news in writing. Master's Mate David Wingfield later claimed to have brought him a despatch announcing Barclay's defeat, but of Yeo's state of mind or the mood in the squadron nothing appears to have been recorded.[15] Elsewhere, blame was already being attributed to the commodore, as Prevost wrote to Bathurst on 22 September:

> I deplored the protracted contest on Lake Ontario for the naval ascendancy, Sir James Yeo having detained for this important object nearly the whole of the officers and seamen which were sent from England with himself, leaving Captain Barclay on Lake Erie to depend almost entirely on the exertions of soldiers belonging to the 41st Regiment and Royal Newfoundland.[16]

Having landed all the stores and materiel carried by the squadron, and incorporating the *Dover's* men into his own musters, Sir James raised the signal to set sail early on the afternoon of 26 September and departed from Burlington Bay leaving behind most of the transports. One or two of the schooners, including the *Confiance* now commanded by Wingfield, trailed behind the squadron as it slowly moved into open water on a northeasterly course. Dawn found the ships maintaining that heading under easy sail twenty miles or so southwest of York. In the wake of Barclay's defeat, and with signs of activity among the Americans along the lower Niagara River, all thoughts of a combined operation with De Rottenburg's army vanished. Yeo noted that he had left the transports to go in search of the enemy, which made their appearance in the form of a single, small schooner at mid-afternoon on Monday, 27 September.[17] At great distance, the schooner was seen to fire two guns, but nothing else was detected before the sun set upon the squadron ten miles south of York.

The American squadron got under way that evening. The day before, it had loaded large quantities of shot, shell and other stores for Wilkinson's army, and between thirty and sixty soldiers had embarked in each vessel.[18] Aware that Yeo had been off York the previous day, a nervous Wilkinson asked Chauncey to dispatch the *Lady of the Lake* and the *Neptune* to keep an eye out for the British squadron. "What may be the views of the Knight?" pondered the general in a note to Armstrong, "to gasconade, to retard my movements, or to enable De Rottenburg to follow me?"[19] Chauncey agreed to a cruise into the western waters, watching for Yeo, ready either to meet him or to protect Wilkinson's flotilla as it moved toward Sackets. Under cover of darkness that night the army was supposed to commence its voyage down the lake shore, carrying 3,500 men and two weeks of provisions straight to Grenadier Island, near Sackets Harbour, as quickly as possible, but the wind rose and conditions on the lake became so rough that the soldiers hauled their boats up on the beach and took shelter around their campfires.

The American squadron slowly angled in a wide, curving route toward Burlington Bay, seeing nothing of the British until first light on 28 September. Yeo had already spotted his adversary and reversed his southerly course to close with York so that a boat could be sent ashore with despatches. Around 10:30 a.m., when it returned, the British turned onto the larboard tack, steering almost due south, propelled by a fresh gale out of the east. The Americans had laid a northerly course to intercept their foe, and when the *Wolfe* led its consorts south, Chauncey signalled for his warships to wear in succession onto a roughly parallel route.

At midday both commodores ordered preparation for battle and formed their lines.[20] The *Pike*, towing the *Asp*, led the way; after it came the *Sylph*, burdened by the *Ontario*, the *Madison*, also hauling a schooner, the *Oneida*, *Tompkins*, and the three remaining schooners. The *Wolfe* had the van of the British line, presumably followed by the *George, Melville, Moira, Beresford* and *Smith*. Wingfield stood off in the *Confiance* and later recollected that "it blew a stiff top gallant breeze which gave them both an excellent opportunity of manoeuvring."[21] Despite the instructions and advice they had received at Kingston and Sackets Harbour, both commodores seemed "determined to engage … [to make] the decisive blow."[22] With the implications of Perry's victory and Barclay's loss foremost in their thoughts, Chauncey and Yeo must have viewed the opportunity developing before them as their own chance to win fame and redemption.

The two squadrons moved southwards, twelve to fifteen miles from York, but Chauncey took advantage of the weather gauge to adjust his course and edge down upon the British line. He assumed that Yeo's intention was to slip away from him and then tack to windward, but as the *Pike* drew nearly opposite the *Wolfe* around 12:30 on a path that posed a threat to the *Beresford* and *Smith*, Yeo abruptly changed course. Hoisting the signal to tack in order, the commodore whipped the *Wolfe* around to present the ship's starboard side to the wind and drove northward aiming to avoid the *Pike* and engage the middle and rear of Chauncey's line.

To the Americans it appeared that Yeo meant not only to cover his trailing vessels but to pass the main elements of Chauncey's line and then intercept the schooners at its rear. Chauncey would have nothing of it, and asked Sinclair to wear to the west in order to meet Yeo at right angles. With the *Wolfe's* opening fire, the gap between the two flagships narrowed while the *George* and others turned toward the action. All the British guns that would bear were directed at the *Pike*, which could respond with only the circle-mounted guns on its

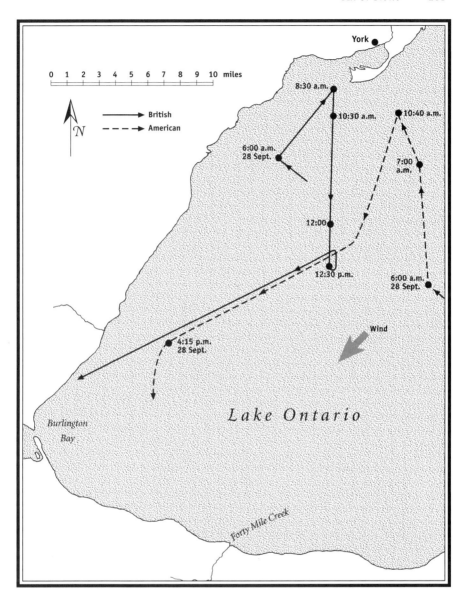

Squadron courses, 28 September 1813. According to logbook entries, the British appear to have sighted the Americans at first light and then laid a course for York so that the commodore could communicate with the shore. Once he had sighted Yeo, Chauncey eased slowly towards York and then turned south to follow his adversary. After their clash, they both tore before the wind toward Burlington Bay.

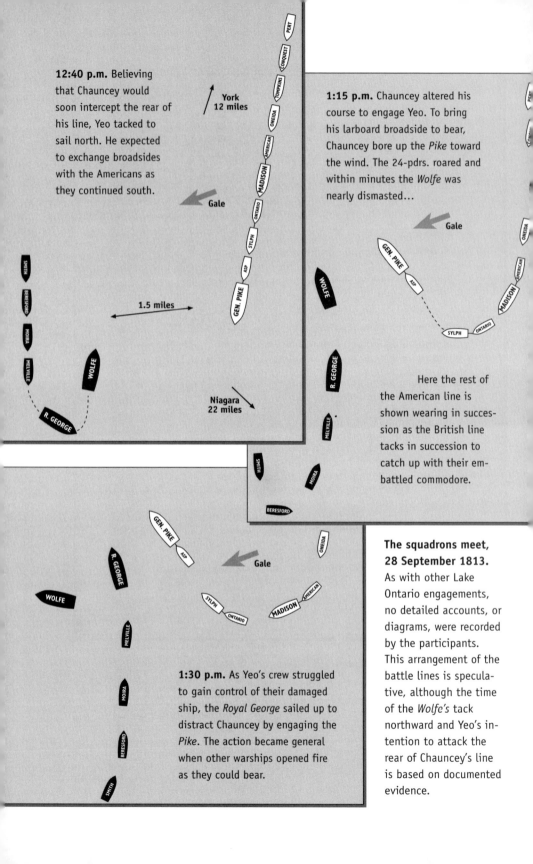

12:40 p.m. Believing that Chauncey would soon intercept the rear of his line, Yeo tacked to sail north. He expected to exchange broadsides with the Americans as they continued south.

York 12 miles

Gale

PERT
CONQUEST
TOMPKINS
ONEIDA
AMERICAN
MADISON
ONTARIO
SYLPH
ASP
GEN. PIKE

1.5 miles

SMITH
BERESFORD
MOIRA
MELVILLE
WOLFE
R. GEORGE

Niagara 22 miles

1:15 p.m. Chauncey altered his course to engage Yeo. To bring his larboard broadside to bear, Chauncey bore up the *Pike* toward the wind. The 24-pdrs. roared and within minutes the *Wolfe* was nearly dismasted...

Gale

PERT
CONQUEST
ONEIDA
AMERICAN
MADISON
GEN. PIKE
ASP
SYLPH
ONTARIO
WOLFE
R. GEORGE
MELVILLE
SMITH
MOIRA
BERESFORD

Here the rest of the American line is shown wearing in succession as the British line tacks in succession to catch up with their embattled commodore.

GEN. PIKE
ASP
R. GEORGE
WOLFE
SYLPH
ONTARIO
MADISON
AMERICAN
ONEIDA
MELVILLE
MOIRA
BERESFORD
SMITH

Gale

1:30 p.m. As Yeo's crew struggled to gain control of their damaged ship, the *Royal George* sailed up to distract Chauncey by engaging the *Pike*. The action became general when other warships opened fire as they could bear.

The squadrons meet, 28 September 1813. As with other Lake Ontario engagements, no detailed accounts, or diagrams, were recorded by the participants. This arrangement of the battle lines is speculative, although the time of the *Wolfe's* tack northward and Yeo's intention to attack the rear of Chauncey's line is based on documented evidence.

topgallant forecastle and poop, but Chauncey and Sinclair were undaunted. "Covering our whole fleet," Sinclair recalled, "[I] run right down for him disregarding his fire, until within good distance when I hauled up and opened an elegant fire on him."[23]

As the *Wolfe* raced northward, every eye was on the big American flagship as it veered around so that its long 24-pdrs. could bear. The *Pike* suddenly disappeared behind a cloud of white smoke, licked with flame, as fourteen long guns erupted, sending a deadly hail of round- and chain-shot across the several hundred yards separating the two ships. Yeo's vessel reeled under the blow and fell a couple of points off its course, then answered in kind as the commodore called for the helmsmen to bring the ship around to close with the *Pike*. About 1:20 p.m. the main topgallant mast of the American flagship shuddered in its spider web of rigging and buckled over onto the topsail, damaged by British shot fired on the upward roll in the rising waves. Again broadsides were exchanged and, then – disaster. American metal sliced through thick stays supporting the mizen topmast of the *Wolfe*, collapsing it with the press of wind, and it pulled the main topmast with it down on deck and over the side.

In the battle for control of Lake Ontario, this instant may have been the most pivotal. Yeo's flagship staggered and lost its heading, half its top hamper gone by the board, its deck a scene of chaos. It was the danger Yeo had sought to avoid all summer by never approaching too close to the ominous broadsides of the *Pike*. He did not have any time, however, to congratulate himself for past prudence or to criticize himself for allowing his ship to get too near its adversary. Chauncey and Sinclair resumed their westerly heading and bore down on their wounded prey, with visions of victory crossing their minds. Their gun crews hurried to reload as the decisive rounds in the contest for supremacy of the lake were about to be fired, and then it all changed. Up came Mulcaster's *Royal George* between the *Pike* and the *Wolfe*. Yeo's trusted friend calmly backed his sails, bringing his ship to a virtual stop and slammed broadside after broadside into the *Pike*. Wingfield described the manoeuvre as "most admirable." Sinclair thought it "elegant," and Yeo acknowledged that Mulcaster saved the day "with his accustomed energy and zeal." As the *Melville* and *Moira* added their fire to the battle, the *Pike* veered away, continuing its cannonade. The *Madison, Oneida* and *Governor Tompkins* all participated in this hottest and most confused phase of the action, receiving damage from the British bombardment. In the space of fifteen minutes or less, the crew of the *Wolfe* recovered from their shock, hacked away the debris that could be abandoned, slipped their dead overboard and carried the wounded below. The helm was turned to let the ship have its head, and with the remnants of the main course and the

The *Royal George* saves the *Wolfe*, 28 September 1813. Commander William Mulcaster covered his commodore's escape by backing his sails and holding a position that allowed him to blast the *Pike* with his starboard carronades at a close range that made them a match for Chauncey's long 24-pdrs. Meanwhile, Yeo raced away from the danger as the rising forceful wind dead astern filled his foremast sails. (Oil painting by Peter Rindlisbacher, courtesy of the artist)

sails of the foremast drawing fully, the *Wolfe* recovered its grace and sped away straight downwind, bound for Burlington Bay.

Now began the pursuit that later became known as the "Burlington Races," watched by straining eyes from the shores of the lake.[24] The *George* and the others turned to follow their commodore with the American squadron snapping at their heels; regular battle order seems to have disappeared, and a pell-mell action evolved. Commandant Jacob Crane in the *Madison* and Lieutenant Thomas Brown in the *Oneida* strove to get close enough to the British to employ their carronades, but the former was retarded by having to tow a schooner and the latter again re-affirmed its reputation as a clumsy sailer. Woolsey in the *Sylph*, hamstrung by the *Ontario*, also failed to make a noticeable impact, and only the *Pike* maintained continuous contact, hammering away at whichever vessel offered the best target.

Sinclair later admitted, "This was the most trying time I ever had in my life." The *Beresford* came within his grasp, apparently as it turned to follow the recovered *Wolfe*. About the same time the *Melville* also nipped close to the *Pike's* bows, barely escaping. "I beged [sic] the Comdr. to let me take them, but he was so sure of all, he *exclaimed all or none.*" Rather than cutting out those two vessels, Chauncey urged Sinclair to press the pursuit. "Had she [the *Pike*] not borne the Flag," Sinclair regretted, "I might have, as a Captain, immortalized myself."[25] Things soon got worse for Sinclair. With damage to his ship starting to mount (the main topgallant mast down, the rigging of the bowsprit and foremast badly cut up and several hits below the waterline), one of the 24-pdr. guns on the forecastle burst, hurling a deadly swath of iron shards in all directions, hitting men as far away as the quarterdeck. More than twenty were killed or wounded and the topgallant forecastle was so badly damaged that the gun there was rendered useless. Four other pieces of ordnance were taken out of commission when ominous cracks appeared in their muzzles.

The Americans pursued the British past 2:00 p.m., propelled by a wind that rose to a full gale. While Chauncey's best vessels were restrained by the schooners from which he would not free them, the others struggled to keep up. Overall weight of metal did not matter in this circumstance as only the *Pike* maintained contact with its foe, staying close enough to pound away at the *Wolfe* when its guns would bear, but leaking so badly that seamen rocked the pumps up and down sending a non-stop stream of water over the side. The fifteen or so miles that separated the scene of the first exchanges and the anchorage on the northern shore of Burlington Bay were covered in ninety minutes, during which time Sinclair's guns were unable to inflict a killing stroke on the British flagship. The

Commander William Howe Mulcaster, RN (1785-1837). Mulcaster had earned a reputation for courageous and intelligent conduct well before he joined Yeo's detachment. In 1806 he participated in a cutting-out expedition on the Spanish coast that prompted Earl St. Vincent, one of Britain's most distinguished admirals, to refer to the pride he felt at seeing one of his students prosper. Mulcaster attained the rank of captain during the war and was later knighted. (Origin unknown, taken from Way, *Crysler's Farm*)

The *Wolfe* limps into the anchorage at Burlington Bay, 28 September 1813. After a three-hour race from the scene of its battle with the *General Pike*, the *Wolfe* finally reaches safety close to the northern shore of Burlington Bay. In the distance the rest of the British vessels fight the gale as they approach the anchorage. (Oil painting by Peter Rindlisbacher, courtesy of the artist and the *Hamilton–Scourge* Foundation)

other British warships sped along in the intervening space, but their involvement appears to have been minimal, and Chauncey refused to unleash the *Madison* and *Sylph* so that they could get into the fight, perhaps to save his wallowing gunboats from capture.

Just after 3:00, when the American flagship was within six miles of the lee shore of Burlington Bay, Chauncey faced a critical decision. With Yeo apparently bound for the anchorage at Burlington, he faced several options. He could bring his ships to anchor as well and continue the battle, but some of his vessels might end up on shore among similarly wrecked British ships; "he amongst his friends," reasoned the American commodore, "and we amongst our enemies."[26] Even if he did not maintain the fight, the easterly gale was pushing his squadron toward the hostile shore of the bay, where De Rottenburg's artillery would soon be in place to hit it. In addition, the loss of some or all of Chauncey's warships would have a doubly detrimental effect because survival of an intact squadron was essential to Wilkinson's forthcoming campaign. Given these circumstances, Chauncey saw his dreams of "all or none" vanish as he signalled his squadron to haul up onto the larboard tack and quit the pursuit. He wrote, "I, without hesitation, relinquished the opportunity of acquiring individual reputation at the expense of my country."[27]

Surprised and relieved, Yeo brought his squadron to anchor at Burlington, the *Royal George* losing its foretopmast as it came head to the wind. A military detachment had hurried to the shore opposite the anchorage, and work was already under way to erect a battery in case Chauncey pressed his attack further. With barely a pause, the weary crews in the squadron began repairing their damaged ships. Dead men, five in all according to Yeo, who had not already been thrown overboard were sewn into their hammocks for burial at sea, while at least eleven seamen and two privates from the Royal Newfoundland Regiment received attention from the surgeons and their assistants.[28] Through the cold, stormy night that followed and all the next day the crews laboured to fit new masts and spars. After dark a seaman fell to his death from the topmast of the *Wolfe* and was committed to the deep the following morning, after which his shipmates returned to their tasks for another forty-eight hours of repairs. In the meantime, the *Melville* and *Beresford* kept daylight patrols in the offing, watching Chauncey's movements.

After turning back from the chase, the American squadron started a battle against the elements. The temperature dropped and the wind and waves rose higher as if determined to throw Chauncey's warships onto the beach at Burlington. No sooner had the commodore hauled down his order to swing around into the wind than the foremast of the *Tompkins* tore itself out of its rigging and lurched over the side. Immediately Chauncey signalled Woolsey to cast off the *Ontario* and take the crippled schooner in tow, which he managed to do by 5:00 p.m., forty-five minutes after receiving Chauncey's message. The strength of the wind required Woolsey to reduce sail and send down the *Sylph's* topgallant yard as the whole squadron struggled to avoid the lee shore, managing a heading that remained west of north. As the heaviest of the converted merchantmen, the *Tompkins* proved a difficult burden for the *Sylph*; in the darkness at nine o'clock the hawser that connected the two schooners suddenly parted, and fifteen minutes later a large vessel, that soon proved to be the *Madison*, came looming out of the night nearly running the *Sylph* under. The violence of the storm prevented Woolsey from rejoining the *Tompkins*, although Chauncey was finally able to gain some easterly ground by tacking the squadron at midnight and then wearing around to the south and east at three o'clock in the morning. After three more hours, as the cloud cover lightened, Lieutenant William Finch, who later earned the commodore's praise for his expert handling of the *Tompkins*, fired its guns to signal the stricken schooner's distress. Once more, the *Sylph* bore down to its rescue, re-attached the hawser, then set a single-reefed foresail and followed the squadron as it tacked to the north-northeast, still within sight of Yeo's anchorage, fourteen miles away.

All through Wednesday, 29 September, and on into Thursday the American squadron fought the weather. The winds fell and rose again but finally subsided enough for the warships to reach the anchorage off the American Four Mile Creek on the morning of 1 October. Chauncey counted his total casualties at twenty-seven, and apart from expressing disappointment in not having captured his knightly foe, the commodore assured the navy secretary in the despatch he wrote on 1 October that his officers and men were still anxious to get at the British. With a suggestion that Perry's victory pervaded his thoughts, Chauncey vowed "if he [Yeo] ever gives us an opportunity for close action they [Chauncey's crews] will show that they are not inferior to any of their countrymen."[29]

The naval action of 28 September had been watched by interested eyes on shore, the keenest of which belonged to Major General James Wilkinson. So extreme had been the tempest on the lake that his flotilla had remained on the beach, soaked and frozen by the horrid weather until Friday, when a lull permitted their departure. Wilkinson exchanged notes with Chauncey in which they agreed that the navy could best serve the army by keeping Yeo bottled up at the Head of the Lake. If Yeo should escape, Chauncey warned the general, and "slip past me in the night and get 18 or 20 hours start of me down the lake … I shall lose no time in following him."[30] Accordingly, the American squadron weighed its anchors at noon on 2 October and stood northward across the lake while Wilkinson set sail about the same time for Sackets Harbour, leaving behind more than 900 regulars under Winfield Scott and 600 militia at the Niagara forts.

That same day, HMS *Wolfe*, restored to fighting trim, led the squadron over to the Canadian Four Mile Creek so that Yeo could communicate with his land counterparts. A withdrawal to Burlington Heights was under way, and De Rottenburg had also sent part of his force to Kingston to prepare for the anticipated attack on that place.[31] The American squadron was in sight all day and the next when Yeo returned to the Burlington anchorage. The rest of Sunday and all of Monday, 4 October, was taken up with erecting a battery on land using a 12-pdr. from the *Smith* and one or more of the *Wolfe*'s 18-pdr. guns. The next morning, 5 October, the guns and ammunition were retrieved from the shore and the squadron set off toward the east.

In the meantime a curious event had taken place. As Wilkinson had requested, Chauncey had kept Yeo in his sight until the morning of 4 October when the wind failed and no progress could be made into Burlington Bay. Chauncey signalled the *Lady of the Lake* to sweep to the west during the afternoon in search of the enemy. The weather was cloudy with occasional squalls, and the American schooner's appearance and a signal for the large brig *Melville* to give chase were noted in the *Wolfe's* log. Distant gunfire was noted in the *Sylph's* logbook about 6:00 p.m., and several hours later the *Lady* returned to the squadron, but Sailing Master Mervine Mix did not report to Chauncey that he had seen Yeo. Instead, he led Chauncey to believe that "the fleet was not there. [Mix] saw but two gunboats."[32] Assuming the British had given him the slip in the night, Chauncey ordered his officers to cram on every stitch of fabric their vessels could carry. With a freshening breeze from the northwest, the squadron dashed down the lake in one of its rare bursts of uninterrupted speed.

Chauncey's mistake led to his most productive attack on British shipping and to one of Yeo's greatest embarrassments. A convoy carrying wounded men and the two flank companies of De Watteville's Regiment had departed from York on the third under the command of Lieutenant Hector Maclean, RN, in the cutter-rigged *Drummond*.[33] In the convoy were also the *Confiance*, captained by David Wingfield, the sloop *Betsy* under Master Theophilus Sampson, formerly the Provincial Marine commander of the *Earl of Moira*, plus four schooners, the *Hamilton, Mary Ann, Lady Gore* and *Enterprise*. Held up by adverse winds until late on 5 October, they were nearing the False Ducks at mid-afternoon the next day, Wednesday, when sails appeared in the southwest, powered by a strong wind out of the north-northwest.

The sight of the convoy at first raised Chauncey's hopes that he had caught Yeo, but closer examination revealed it to be a pack of small transports, which suddenly broke formation and fled on individual headings. Chauncey signalled the *Sylph* to cast off the *Ontario* and join the *Lady of the Lake* in pursuit, then threw off the *Pike's* tow and, leaving the squadron in Crane's hands, joined the chase. A dejected Wingfield watched the warships charge down upon him and, knowing that capture was imminent, he resolved to jettison anything that could be useful to the Americans. All muskets, ammunition and stores were thrown overboard, and Yeo's gig (one of two prized boats he had brought with him from England), which was being returned to Kingston for repairs, was hacked in two and dumped over the side. Then Wingfield called out to Sampson in the *Betsy*, which the *Confiance* was towing, to haul his sloop up to the schooner's stern so its crew could jump on board after setting the *Betsy* aflame. By that time the *Sylph* had ranged up on their beam and fired a gun, and Wingfield, knowing the game was over, cast his sword to the deck and went below to the schooner's tiny cabin. In his memoirs he recollected:

all hope of promotion vanished at once, expecting the worst of treatment, … I either sat, or laid down, and could scarcely refrain from shedding tears; … as the American Lieutenant [Francis Gregory] came into the cabin; I believe he perceived my agitation, which I endeavoured to conceal, for he came up to me and offered his hand, at the same time returning my sword, telling me not to regret, for it might not be long ere he was in the same situation.[34]

Gregory (acting as a lieutenant though still officially a midshipman) had apparently been sent from the flagship because Commandant Woolsey was ordered by the commodore to press on after the rest of the convoy in the *Sylph*. This he did, filling his sails and barreling up to the *Hamilton* and *Mary Ann*, stopping their flight with warning guns. Then he raced into the darkness after the *Drummond* and captured it, sending one of his own officers aboard. Although the *Lady Gore* managed to find seclusion by sneaking inshore of the Ducks during the night, at 6:00 the next morning, 6 October, Melancthon Woolsey expertly sniffed out the schooner and took it into custody. Only the schooner *Enterprise*, carrying a couple of dozen De Wattevilles, managed to elude capture and brought the news of the lost convoy into Kingston.

With the lake growing wild again, making the safe transfer of prisoners impossible, Chauncey brought his squadron to anchor at Sackets at noon on 6 October. The parcel of schooners trailing his various warships made an impressive appearance; "all gun vessels," he reported to Jones, "mounting one to three guns."[35] About 252 prisoners, including eighteen army and navy officers, had been taken and of the De Wattevilles, Arthur Sinclair remarked, "They are the finest looking men I have ever seen." They had been warned by the British that the American conduct toward prisoners was despicable, and Sinclair perceived that "the poor devils trembled like criminals when they came onboard."[36] He soon used his Virginian charm to assuage their fears to such an extent that he claimed they later told him that they regretted not being able to join the American ranks.[37]

David Wingfield had also learned a surprising lesson about his adversaries. After boarding the *Pike*, which he discovered "in excellent order" despite the damage it had received on 28 September, he was accommodated in an officer's cabin and invited to dine in the wardroom. Some days later, as he and a fellow prisoner strode the poop deck lamenting their lack of negotiable currency, they were interrupted by Isaac Chauncey himself. The commodore "entered familiarly into conversation with us, and from him we learned that we should most likely get our [otherwise worthless British army] bills cashed at Albany, through which city we should pass."[38] Within days Wingfield and the others were on their way south. Their eventual destination was a series of villages in Massachusetts, where they lived like officers and gentlemen in private accommodations while waiting for their exchange.

Yeo's squadron was only a few hours behind Chauncey. It anchored in the mouth of the Bay of Quinte on 6 October and remained there while the commodore proceeded to Kingston in the *Smith*. Late in the day he learned of the loss of the convoy, which caused his temper to flare as he sought to escape culpability for the incident. Yeo blamed the calamity on "the obstinacy or stupidity or Lieut. Maclean, who instead of keeping in with our shore as he was ordered … stood over to the Real Duck Islands and the wind coming from the NNE he could not regain his own shore."[39] No one, it seems, publicly corrected the commodore's misinformation about wind direction and the convoy's route, but his failure to follow Prevost's precise instructions about protecting the transport service was noted by his superior. Prevost asked De Rottenburg for information about the circumstances under which the De Wattevilles had been detached to Kingston and the general replied that he had ordered the movement and that "an application was made to Commodore Sir James Yeo to afford those vessels the necessary protection."[40] When Prevost wrote to the Horse Guards in London, late in October, for troops to replace these losses, he hinted his displeasure by stating that it had been "expected that the necessary protection would have been afforded to them [the troops in the transports] by Sir James Yeo's Fleet."[41]

Within a four-week period Yeo had suffered a succession of failures unlike anything he had experienced during his previously brilliant career. Having been battered off Genesee, defeated on Lake Erie, dismasted near Burlington and now found to be remiss in following his superior's *written communication*, the British commodore had reached his nadir and, with the Americans appearing ready to launch a major offensive, the future looked even more bleak.

CHAPTER 13

"A Mere Attendant
upon the Army"[1]

THE ST. LAWRENCE CAMPAIGN:
OCTOBER–NOVEMBER 1813

*D*espite the many setbacks and frustrations he had experienced, Commodore Isaac Chauncey had not given up trying to perform the duty for which he had been sent to the lakes. As the *General Pike* tugged at its anchor at Sackets Harbour on 6 October 1813, Chauncey must have felt content to know that his perseverance had helped him regain the upper hand over his adversary. The rumours of his dismissal, so prevalent a month before, had died away. Indeed, shortly after stepping ashore Chauncey took delivery of a lengthy despatch from the Navy Department in which the secretary praised the efforts he had made during the summer. "Your Country and its entire Government," William Jones had written on 19 September, "have seen nothing in your conduct but proofs of zeal, skill and intrepidity." He decried Chauncey's critics and impugned Yeo's tactics, adding, "In everything which constitutes real efficiency you are his equal and I trust will be found his superior."[2] Jones's vote of confidence was much needed by the war-weary commodore, and Chauncey assured the secretary that his praise "was truly grateful to my feelings, particularly at this time, and will stimulate to still greater exertions (if greater is possible) for the accomplishment of the object and wishes of the Executive."[3]

Madison's cabinet did have an important objective for Chauncey to achieve, which Jones relayed in his letter of congratulations. He was to provide "prompt and zealous cooperation" to Secretary of War Armstrong in his plans for the army's final campaign of the year.[4] Chauncey was eager to support the expected landing of Major General Wilkinson's army near Kingston, since he anticipated that such action would provoke Yeo into a proper sea battle. Wilkinson had arrived at Sackets Harbour on 4 October, well ahead of most of his army and sick once again with the "fever" he had contracted early in September. He conferred immediately with Armstrong and the two men disagreed about the initial target of attack, Wilkinson now preferring Montreal, Armstrong still wanting to seize Kingston. The alternatives were debated in a council of war on 5 October, with Armstrong's goal being chosen provided several conditions remained the same: Yeo did not return to Kingston; the garrison at Kingston was not reinforced too greatly; and the weather stayed calm enough for the flotilla of open boats carrying the troops to navigate the lake. Although each of these conditions appeared to be contravened during the first week of October, Wilkinson discussed with Chauncey arrangements for moving against Kingston; the commodore argued in favour of landing west of the port rather than down-river from it.[5]

During an exchange of notes on Sunday, 9 October, Wilkinson informed Chauncey that the army, numbering roughly 6,000, would set out for Kingston the following day, but the wind and rain that descended on the Harbour that day continued into the next and worsened – aboard the *Sylph* the officer of the watch noted in the logbook that the schooner was pelted by "hail," though it was more likely sleet or freezing rain. Activity at Sackets Harbour ground to a

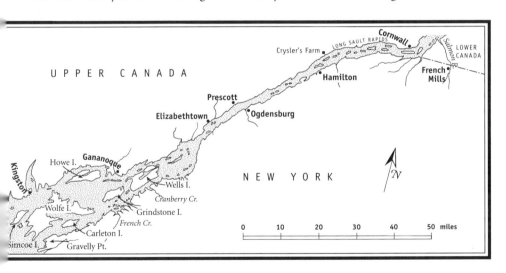

The Upper St. Lawrence. The final American offensive of 1813 involved transporting a large army to invade Upper Canada somewhere along the St. Lawrence River. While locations above and below Kingston were considered, it was finally decided to descend the river to Montreal, though that operation required a long and difficult trip down the narrow waterway, the northern bank of which was hostile territory. (Based on a contemporary map by John Melish, 1813)

halt as the thousands of soldiers and sailors huddled in their tents or sought warmth and dry clothes below decks while the gales blew and the clouds unleashed rain, snow and sleet for the rest of the week. One officer wrote that the village "was full of soldiers and of mud. We waded (for when one sinks up to the knees it is not walking) through the streets to head quarters."[6] Major General Morgan Lewis reported to a correspondent that two feet of snow fell in the vicinity and that the severity of the weather retarded the progress of the army's movement from Niagara. The vast assortment of boats that had brought the first brigade of Wilkinson's soldiers to Sackets had been battered by the elements, some foundering, others being cast ashore, one unlucky boatload of men ending up on the British side of the lake at Ernestown in the Bay of Quinte. The experience afloat was typified by this description of the struggle aboard a heavily laden Durham boat, hauling an equally overburdened barge:

> The wind blew high and blew strong and handled the barge in tow as if it had been an egg shell. We eased off the line and gave it full swing; still when the gust took it on top of a wave, while the Durham was for a moment becalmed in the trough below, it would shoot ahead with such accelerated velocity, as to threaten to dash into our stern.[7]

On 16 October the heavy weather let up, and at 10:00 a.m. the squadron got under way, proceeding out of Black River Bay under fair skies with a breeze veering around to the southeast. The first division of the army, comprising forty boats and commanded by Brigadier General Jacob Brown, also departed that day to establish a staging camp on Grenadier Island for the attack on Kingston. Unfortunately, this movement was hampered by misunderstandings among the senior officers. Chauncey had sailed with the intention of rendezvousing, at Armstrong's request, with a large detachment of soldiers at the Genesee River, Colonel Winfield Scott's 950-man Second Artillery Regiment, which had left the forts at Niagara in the hands of 1,000 militia under Brigadier General George McClure, and set out for Sackets. When Wilkinson heard of Armstrong's request to Chauncey, he dashed off a note to the commodore announcing that the mission was devised "without my privity or approbation, and I hold myself therefore irresponsible for consequences."[8] Chauncey received both this message and a second memo from Armstrong retracting his first request. Accordingly, he anchored his squadron at the Ducks late on 16 October, expecting that he would soon be covering the army's drive against Kingston. Unknown to Chauncey were new turns in the battle of wills being waged between Wilkinson and Armstrong. Even as the squadron cruised onto the lake, the secretary was explaining to Major General Wade Hampton, the commander at Lake Champlain, that "the manoeuvre intended is lost so far as regards Kingston," owing to a military build-up there, and that Hampton should march his army to the mouth of the Châteauguay River to meet Wilkinson on his way to Montreal.[9] On 18 October Wilkinson challenged the secretary's order to Hampton, urging him to tell Hampton to aim for a point closer to Kingston, to which objective Wilkinson still seemed committed.[10]

At Kingston every possible preparation was being made for the expected visit from the Americans, said to number in excess of 6,000 effectives at Sackets Harbour and another 5,000 with Hampton. Elements of the 49th and 104th Foot and the Canadian Voltigeurs, somewhat reduced by illness and fatigue, had reached the port, swelling its defenders to more than 4,000 men. The defences had been significantly improved since Chauncey had blasted his way into the harbour in November 1812. Fifty-five pieces of ordnance were in batteries around the harbour and the town, and atop Point Henry, and a floating battery was under construction. While most of the reinforcements from above remained at Kingston, some companies marched down-river to garrisons at Gananoque, Prescott, Cornwall and places in between, all connected by a system of signal relays and dragoon despatch riders. Sir George Prevost had departed late in September to his headquarters at Montreal, and on 12 October Major General Francis De Rottenburg arrived at Kingston from the Head of the Lake in the schooner *Vincent* to take command of what was commonly believed to be the most threatened point in Upper Canada.[11]

The British squadron had anchored in the harbour late on 7 October and remained there for a full week.[12] Three new gunboats were being fitted out, and Yeo directed that all the other gunboats currently on the Upper St. Lawrence be assembled at Kingston.[13] He assigned the *Wolfe's* first lieutenant, Charles Anthony, to oversee their operation and gave him the former *Dover* men and, apparently, some of the original detachment from England to crew the boats. Anthony, a twenty-year veteran who had received a Turkish medal of honour for participation in gunboat actions on the Nile in 1801, had won Yeo's high regard and received an acting commission as commander from the commodore when he took charge of the gunboats. The removal of 160 officers and seamen caused a shortage of manpower in the squadron, which was exacerbated by the fact that the temporary volunteers from the Quebec transports were reaching the end of their term of service. Yeo asked them to join the squadron full time, but, to a man, they refused and eventually left Kingston at the end of October.[14] Fortunately for the commodore, a detachment of about 110 Royal Navy officers and men came up the Kingston Channel on 13 October. Formerly of HMS

Marlborough, 74, at Halifax, they had been ordered to the lakes by Admiral Warren in response to an entreaty for reinforcements made to him by Prevost in June. Their timely arrival compensated for the withdrawal of the merchant volunteers and allowed Yeo to keep his squadron adequately manned while Anthony put the gunboat service on an effective footing.

De Rottenburg asked Yeo to make a supply voyage to relieve the army on the Niagara Peninsula, which had been left under the command of Major General John Vincent. About the same time orders were received from Prevost stipulating that Yeo's vessels be deployed at either end of Wolfe Island to guard against the expected American invasion. Yeo and De Rottenburg discussed Prevost's instructions at length and, after deciding that they could not abandon Vincent "without equally compromising the honour of the British army," informed Prevost that the squadron would be committed to another trip up the lake.[15] The commodore set sail on 15 October with this purpose in mind, but a stiff southwest breeze kept him from making any appreciable headway, which turned out to be an unexpected blessing as the same wind brought Lieutenant John Johnston back from Sackets Harbour, where he had been sent several days earlier under a flag of truce. Johnston revealed that the enemy port was filled with small craft of every description, a new brig had been launched, and Kingston would soon be attacked. He had also heard the strong rumour of an American military victory at Burlington. This intelligence caused De Rottenburg and Yeo to cancel the trip up the lake and direct their energies to the defence of Kingston.

Although the commodore did not like the idea of dividing his squadron, he indicated to Prevost on 17 October that the *Wolfe* and *Royal George* would remain at Kingston while the other four vessels would be deployed along with the gunboats at the eastern end of Wolfe Island. "Nothing but your Excellency's pointed instructions on that head could have induced me to do it," he explained, although the truth was that he ignored the commander-in-chief's orders by keeping all six vessels at Kingston until the end of the month.[16] Along with De Rottenburg, Yeo suspected that York might be the actual target of the American campaign, especially since Major General Henry Procter's defeat at Moraviantown on 5 October meant that the invading army in that quarter might link up with the force occupying the Niagara Peninsula.[17] Through the third and fourth week of October British sentries from Burlington Bay to Prescott scanned the horizon straining to perceive the first evidence that would confirm that their position was the target of the massive American attack.

What the British could not know was the pandemonium on the American side. After a few hours of friendly skies over Sackets Harbour, the elements turned vicious again late on 16 October and hammered the army and navy relentlessly for two weeks. The squadron sought refuge at the Harbour on the night of 17 October and then returned to cruise between Stony and Grenadier Islands. Daily, groups of small boats braved the steep waves and showers of wind-swept rain and snow to reach the Grenadier Island encampment. Scores of bateaux, scows, gunboats and most of Chauncey's converted merchantmen struggled over the ten miles of stormy seas, running dangerously close to the bows of the patrolling squadron, losing their way and crashing ashore or disappearing without a trace. Morgan Lewis commented to his wife on 25 October: "They have suffered much and are not yet all collected. God knows when we shall set out from hence."[18]

Wilkinson and Armstrong continued their exchange of confusing correspondence.[19] The secretary explained to Wilkinson that Kingston was no longer a feasible objective, given its reinforcement and the difficulty of crossing in such horrible weather, and he argued in favour of going down the St. Lawrence to Montreal, an operation that would allow access to supplies and an eventual junction with Hampton's army. Although Wilkinson had tried to convince Armstrong of this earlier, he now refused to accept the secretary's advice at face value and asked for direct and specific written orders for an attack on Montreal. With his characteristic ambiguity, Armstrong evaded the request but offered a list of reasons supporting the drive down the river. During the fourth week of October, however, the secretary abruptly packed his bags and rode out of Sackets Harbour, with the apparent intention of going to meet with Hampton. His path soon turned toward Washington, and his advice for Wilkinson grew sparser with distance. "Again, adieu," Armstrong wrote on 27 October. "All kinds of prosperity attend you."[20] By that time Wilkinson had decided to advance on Montreal. A portion of his force reached Ogdensburg several days before the main body pushed off from Grenadier Island and entered the St. Lawrence on 30 October.[21] His troops were badly weakened by exposure to the elements and barely capable of operating as a coherent force. The first wave of the armada, a gangling mass of boats and scows, directed by inexperienced and weary officers, sailed past Wolfe Island toward an encampment at French Creek (now, Clayton, New York). Few could have been confident of victory, but no one was yet aware that their fate was virtually sealed by a battle fought on 26 October along the Châteauguay River when a largely French-Canadian force under Lieutenant Colonel Charles de Salaberry had defeated Hampton's march northward. Hampton used this setback as an opportunity to turn away from a campaign he had never liked and abandoned the plan to unite with Wilkinson.[22]

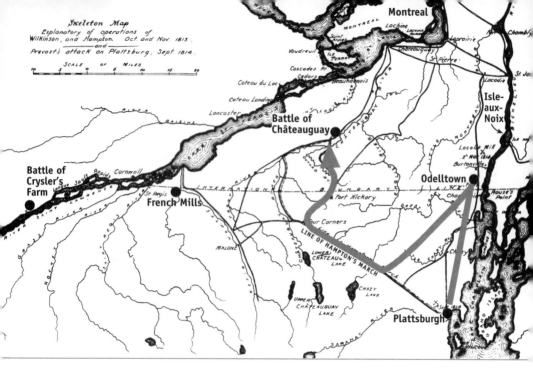

Hampton's movement toward Montreal, October 1813. Having been ordered to rendezvous with Wilkinson on the banks of the St. Lawrence above Montreal, Major General Wade Hampton marched his army from Plattsburgh, but turned back to American territory after British troops opposed his advance at Châteauguay on 26 October 1813. (Based on contemporary chart, courtesy of the National Archives of Canada, NMC-6755)

An indication of the disorder that prevailed among the senior American commanders is that Chauncey remained uninformed about the decision to avoid Kingston until 29 October. For two weeks he had fought the stormy lake while faithfully covering the army's disorganized progress to Grenadier Island and making the occasional reconnaissance of the British port. On Friday, 29 October, he visited Wilkinson at his headquarters on Grenadier Island to find out when the attack would be made, only to hear that the general wanted his support as the army navigated the St. Lawrence toward Montreal. The commodore was livid and expressed his rage and feelings of betrayal in a long letter to William Jones. "In all consultations upon this subject for the last four weeks," he wrote, "Kingston was fixed upon as the point to be first attacked."[23] Armstrong had assured him of this plan, but now the navy was to provide transport to the army without hope of participating in a critical battle with the British and then return to Sackets Harbour, which was to be left virtually unprotected. After expounding his opposition to the Montreal operation and his preference for Kingston, Chauncey calmly concluded this missive with a firm promise to do his duty as required. He tempered that promise, however, by saying that he would not keep his squadron in the St. Lawrence any longer than was absolutely necessary for fear of being trapped in the ice that would soon seal it from bank to bank. The commodore waited until 2 November, when the last part of Wilkinson's army was about to set out from Grenadier Island for the perils of the upper St. Lawrence.[24]

By delaying, Isaac Chauncey missed a chance to catch a part of his adversary's squadron as it ventured beyond the safety of the Kingston Channel. The parade of American boats down the river southeast of Wolfe Island did not escape the eyes of the British, nor did their congregation at French Creek, which emptied into the St. Lawrence opposite Grindstone Island. On Monday, 1 November, with De Rottenburg's approval, Yeo sent the *Earl of Moira, Lord Melville* and four gunboats to meet with the *Beresford* and *Sir Sidney Smith*, which had taken up a position at the northeast end of Wolfe Island two days before. William Mulcaster, recently promoted by Yeo to post captain in recognition of his conduct on 28 September, was given command of this flotilla with orders to attack the Americans at French Creek.[25] Amid a driving snowstorm, the warships passed through the gap between Wolfe and Grindstone Islands during Monday afternoon and across the two-mile width of the river to engage a body of infantrymen perched on the headland that protected the entrance to the creek.[26] Mulcaster led the vessels close enough to shore to hear the enemy's cries as broadsides of grapeshot and cannister raked their ranks and sent them packing.

The squadron tacked around the headland and came into view of the American camp. Mulcaster perceived his foe to be "in great force drawn up in three columns with a battery of two brass 18-pdrs. in front and a numerous train of artillery on their flanks."[27] Unable to squeeze all four warships into the narrow bay, he anchored the *Melville, Moira* and *Smith* in a line and opened fire on the Americans, holding the *Beresford* and gunboats in reserve. The American commander Brigadier General Jacob Brown viewed the exchange with delight, noting that many of the American shots smashed home into the British ships. So strong was the fire from shore that Mulcaster cancelled an intended gunboat attack on the American flank and withdrew into the falling dark. Early next morning he returned to engage the batteries, hoping to destroy the boats and scows hauled up on the beach, but the ferocity of the American defence, now including shot heated in a hastily improvised shot oven, forced him to withdraw. Having lost one killed and five injured, the disappointed British sailed back to the Kingston Channel and up to the anchorage at Point Frederick, leaving the American flotilla more or less unharmed. On shore up to ten casualties were reported along with the observation that one of the enemy brigs had been so badly damaged that it had to be towed out of the action.

Early on 2 November the American squadron steered into the St. Lawrence River, coming to anchor off Gravelly Point twenty-four hours later. The next morning it sailed to the northeast end of Wolfe Island, where it dropped anchor again. For the naval officers, the narrow passage of the river was not a pleasant situation, especially since they had been left out of the grand scheme of things. Captain Sinclair wrote: "We were in daily expectation of the ice setting in, strong westerly winds prevailing, every point capable of being fortified by the Enemy and our pilots ignorant of the navigation."[28] As the ships rode at anchor or shifted position, the last of Wilkinson's troops passed on their way to French Creek, spurred on by blue skies and uncommonly mild weather.

Beginning shortly after dawn on 5 November, the army struck out from French Creek on its expedition downstream. The last of the boats had barely disappeared that afternoon when the British squadron, accompanied by gunboats, sailed down the Kingston Channel and anchored several miles north of the Americans. The gap between Wolfe and Grindstone Islands, which separated the two squadrons, was lined with shoals and shallow passages that made navigation by large ships difficult. Chauncey ordered his vessels cleared for action and, the weather being pleasant, he sent a boat off to sound the gap so that the *Sylph* and *Pike*, lightened of some of their burden, might be hauled closer to the British. The plan was frustrated the next morning when Yeo, for reasons never explained, returned to Kingston without firing a shot.

The American commodore was now left in a dilemma. The army had begun its descent upon Montreal, while his enemy had gone up the Kingston Channel with the possible intention of rounding the western end of Wolfe Island and blockading the mouth of the St. Lawrence. Furthermore, Chauncey feared that the British would send a force to occupy Carleton Island, which dominated the south channel of the St. Lawrence at Wolfe Island. By mounting a few guns in old Fort Carleton, a relic of the Revolutionary War, they could control the river, preventing Chauncey's vessels from returning to Sackets. The commodore used these reasons to justify his decision to withdraw the squadron from the river in stages, first to Carleton Island and then to Gravelly Point, where, on 10 November, the weather turned bad again, prompting him to return to the Harbour. From that place, he wrote to Secretary Jones on 11 November, describing the interval of pleasant weather and assuring the secretary that "the Army could not have asked for a more favourable time, which I have no doubt, but that the General has taken advantage of and I presume by this time is in Montreal."[29]

Chauncey had been wrong about British intentions. Their prime concern was not his squadron, but the invasion force streaming down the St. Lawrence. Prevost had ordered "a corps of observation" formed at Kingston and sent to follow Wilkinson.[30] Placed under the command of Lieutenant Colonel Joseph Morrison of the 89th Foot, the force consisted of 550 men from his own regiment, the remnants of the 49th Foot (about 300 effectives) and twenty gunners with two field pieces. Transport was provided by the *Beresford* and *Smith*, a half dozen or so gunboats and a host of bateaux, manned in part by the Royal Navy and commanded by the intrepid Captain Mulcaster. Late on 6 November, Morrison departed from Kingston, thirty-six hours behind Wilkinson.

That night the Americans slipped past the batteries at Prescott in the darkness, suffering only a handful of casualties. The next day, Sunday, Wilkinson ordered Colonel Alexander Macomb to land a 1,200-man detachment on the Canadian side below Prescott, to sweep the shoreline along their route clean of any further batteries or pockets of militiamen that might impede the expedition's progress. Brigadier General Brown and his brigade were sent to join Macomb on Monday and clear the way to Cornwall. The following morning, 9 November, Morrison reached Prescott and increased his strength to more than 1,000 by adding the garrison's troops to his force. Since the river shoaled dangerously below Prescott, the schooners were left there while the British continued in gunboats and bateaux after a party under Mulcaster seized the American village of Hamilton, New York, briefly, carrying off a large amount of materiel. First contact between the opposing forces occurred on Wednesday, 10 November when the British gunboats drew within range of Wilkinson's rearguard and opened fire. Field guns were landed by the Americans to return the compliment and succeeded in damaging the gunboat *Buffalo*, which sank upon withdrawing to Prescott. That night Morrison disembarked his troops and established a camp on and around the farm belonging to John Crysler, several miles upstream from the treacherous Long Sault Rapids.[31]

Thursday, 11 November 1813, dawned grey and miserable after a heavy storm of rain and sleet.[32] Confusion reigned in the American camp, which had been pitched on the Canadian shore, just down the river from Crysler's farm. Wilkinson was so ill that he was barely able to raise his head off his pillow and issued conflicting orders to his commanders, at first appearing ready to run the flotilla down the rapids and then hesitating when news arrived of the British infantry harassing his rear. To stifle that nuisance, Wilkinson ordered Brigadier General John Boyd to lead a force that eventually numbered 2,400 rank and file, including artillery and cavalry, against Morrison's men well positioned on John Crysler's muddy fields. The battle raged all afternoon, ending with Boyd's withdrawal after sustaining nearly 350 casualties compared to about 185 among the British. On 12 November, the Americans shot the Long Sault rapids and united with Brown at Cornwall, where Wilkinson learned of Hampton's

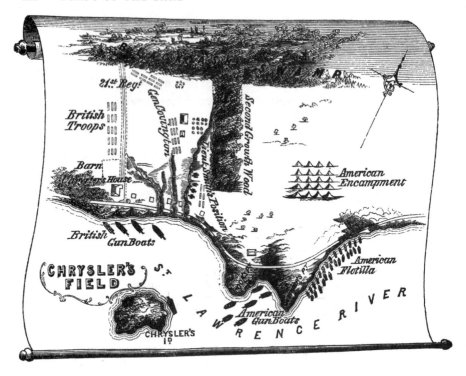

Positions of the adversaries at Crysler's farm, 11 November 1813. This engraving depicts the positions of the two armies when they engaged at Crysler's farm. Note the location of British gunboats, which supported Morrison's army, and the American gunboats, which did not participate in the battle. (From Benson Lossing, *A Pictorial Field-book of the War of 1812*)

defeat at Châteauguay and his refusal to march into Canada. Concluding that all hope of a successful campaign against Montreal was gone, the American general ordered the removal of his force from British soil. The next day, his crestfallen and exhausted army descended the next stretch of rapids to Lake St. Francis and, crossing to the American side, rowed up the Salmon River eight miles to the village of French Mills. The long, drawn-out, weatherbeaten, indecisive autumn campaign thus stumbled to its ignominious end, with James Wilkinson declaring to Armstrong that to "General Hampton's outrage of every principle of subordination and discipline may be ascribed the failure of the expedition."[33]

Not entirely convinced that Wilkinson was beaten, the British maintained their vigilance. On 15 November, Mulcaster shot the rapids with his gunboats, cruised the length of Lake St. Francis and tied up at the garrison at Coteau du Lac, a post recently reinforced in anticipation of the invasion.[34] From there, he kept a wary eye on Americans until it could be confirmed that they had no intention of leaving their camp.

By the time Mulcaster reached Coteau du Lac, the curtain had risen on the final drama of 1813. When he brought his squadron back to the Harbour, Chauncey took delivery of a message from Secretary Armstrong asking the navy to transport a detachment of the northwestern army from Niagara to Sackets. The commodore was eager to meet the request since Wilkinson's campaign had deprived his shipyard of its military protection, but he warned Armstrong of the "boisterous"conditions on the lake, adding that he would make an attempt to reach Niagara but could not guarantee success.[35] The squadron sailed from Sackets during the afternoon of Sunday, 13 November, and with a steady and strong breeze out of the northeast, whisked up the lake, arriving off Niagara the following evening. By then the wind was too strong for a safe passage into the river in the dark, so the squadron hove to or wore back

Climax of the action at Crysler's Farm, 11 November 1813. As the American army withdraws from the battlefield (toward the left of this painting), the Second U.S. Light Dragoons (upper left) make a charge to cover the retreat of the artillery only to be devastated by British infantry (upper right) and artillery fire. In the distance can be seen one of the British gunboats, which were close enough to bombard the entire range of Crysler's farm. (Painting by A. S. Scott, courtesy of the St. Lawrence Parks Commission)

and forth through the night, waiting until noon the next day to navigate the channel and come to anchor between Forts Niagara and George.

Within twenty-four hours provisions had been landed and a brigade of infantry embarked, part of the army with which Major General William Henry Harrison had invaded southwestern Upper Canada and beaten Procter at the Battle of Moraviantown. Numbering about 1,400, the infantry crowded aboard the ships, the *Sylph* alone taking on 160 men. They had already experienced a voyage down Lake Erie in Captain Perry's squadron and so were accustomed to cramped conditions and shipboard routines, but nothing had prepared them for the ride they were about to face.

The squadron left the Niagara River during the afternoon of Tuesday, 16 November, and congregated around the *Pike*, which had not entered the river with the others and now took on groups of soldiers from the various vessels. That night the wind rose from the east, preventing any headway being made toward Sackets, and the squadron stayed close to the flagship, making and shortening sail as necessary, wearing in its wake. Some progress was gained on Wednesday, but by nightfall a full gale was blowing and squalls of rain and snow soon separated the warships, the familiar pattern of men against the sea taking priority as each crew fought the elements independently struggling to keep their vessel afloat. The *Pike*, being the biggest and most seaworthy, faced the tempest with the least discomfort and reached Sackets Harbour on 20 November. "The Troops and Seamen suffered extremely," wrote the commodore, "as they were wet from the commencement of the Gale untill [sic] their arrival here – the Water so deep on the birth deck, that we were obliged to scuttle it [cut holes in the side] to let the Water off."[36] The rest of the squadron battled against the violent weather less successfully – the *American* ran ashore near Fort Niagara and the *Tompkins* scraped over the river's bar and tore off its rudder, while a steep following sea broke over the stern of the *Sylph*, stove in the boat hanging in the stern davits, snatched it from its fittings and swallowed it whole. The schooner *Julia* (given its original name after recapture as the *Confiance*) was pushed into Burlington Bay, where its crew, in a final attempt to save it, dropped both of its anchors and rode out the gale within a mile of the enemy's shore. Not until 27 November did the last of the squadron reach the safety of the Harbour, the seamen exhausted, the soldiers prostrate with sickness, cold and outright terror. Chauncey then wisely decided to lay his squadron up for the winter, with the exception of the *Lady of the Lake* and the *Sylph*, which he kept on patrol as long as they could do so with safety.[37]

The 1813 naval campaign thus came to an disappointing end on Lake Ontario with no decisive battle having been fought, and no unchallengeable mastery of the lake having been won.

PART IV

The War of the Dockyards

NOVEMBER 1813 – APRIL 1814

THE WOLF AND THE PIKE
(sung to the tune of "The Cobbler")

A Wolf once met a Pike,
  And vow'd that he would eat her,
Did you e'er dream the like;
  That little Pike should beat her;
Says Wolf I'm tir'd of beef and veal,
  And fish is finer feeding,
But little Pike with fins of steel,
  Set her great mouth a bleeding.

When Wolf first felt her wound,
  She scamper'd up from table,
And ran upon dry ground,
  As fast as she was able;
Says she this was a cursed dish,
  For Wolf to think of ever,
And Pike from this day is a fish
  I ne'er will taste – no never.

But Pike, who from the deep,
  With scorn beheld her canting;
Now feigns to be asleep,
  And for more sport is panting.
If ugly Wolf invade her bed,
  Her limpid bed of water,
The pretty Pike will strike her dead,
  Unless she cry for quarter.

WAR JOURNAL, 12 NOVEMBER 1813

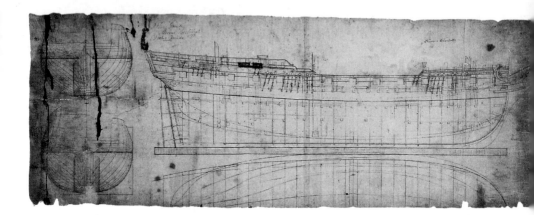

HMS *Princess Charlotte*. Named for one of the king's daughters, the *Princess Charlotte* was considered a fifth rate according to the Royal Navy rating system due to its forty-gun armament. Although it resembled its saltwater cousins closely, the *Charlotte* required a shallower draught of water than they did. This view is one of very few extant plans drawn by a master shipwright during the war. (Courtesy of the National Archives of Canada, NMC-97256)

CHAPTER 14

"Such a Force . . .
May Save the Country"[1]

BRITISH NAVAL ESCALATION:
NOVEMBER 1813 – MARCH 1814

*W*hile the American squadron struggled to remain afloat amid the tremendous November 1813 gale, Commodore Sir James Yeo's ships lay inactive at Kingston. Several gunboats joined the squadron from Gananoque on 12 November, followed later that day by the *Beresford* and *Sir Sidney Smith*, which had tacked up-river from Prescott. The two schooners were soon off again, each of them making a couple of cruises into the Bay of Quinte or up the lake with supplies for the army. On one of its return trips, the *Beresford* hauled a large raft loaded with timber out of the bay, one of at least two such rafts sent from that district during November. The *Wolfe, Royal George, Earl of Moira* and *Lord Melville* made their final, brief trips of the season on 3 December and then took up moorings in Navy Bay, where the schooners soon joined them. Over the next few days the crews aired and dried the squadron's sails, struck them below or sent them ashore with the running rigging and upper spars, as they closed up the vessels for the winter or cleared them out so that the shipwrights could commence refits and repairs.[2]

Yeo also remained, relatively inactive, at Kingston during the period. A rumour about him circulated on the American side with enough credence for Captain Arthur Sinclair to repeat it for the benefit of his correspondent: "He [Yeo] was dangerously wounded in the action on the 28th Septr. by a 24 pdr shot from this ship. It carried off a large part of the flesh from one of his thighs and he just now begins to hobble upon crutches."[3] True, the commodore had not led his gunboats in pursuit of Wilkinson with the same zeal that had spurred him into action on land at Sackets Harbour the previous May, but no evidence has come to light about any wound that Yeo might have suffered. It seems more likely that he chose to remain with the main part of his squadron early in November while giving William Mulcaster the opportunity for distinction he had earned by his competence and loyalty.

There was no end of business requiring the commodore's attention, however, and among the first of these matters was the loss of the British squadron on Lake Erie. Never one to devote much energy to correspondence, Yeo did not react in writing to the news of Robert Barclay's defeat until 10 October when he sent a despatch to Admiral Warren. Even at that date he had not received Barclay's official account of the battle and so claimed ignorance of that officer's reasons for sailing to meet Perry's squadron. Major General Henry Procter, it was popularly alleged, had ordered Barclay to sail as a means of re-establishing the supply route to Long Point and gaining relief for the starving post at Amherstburg. Yeo claimed that he could not in propriety comment on whether "that very great scarcity did or did not exist," which was less than honest of him because from the time of Barclay's arrival at Amherstburg in June, the commander had detailed the shortages that hampered his operations and repeatedly sought men and materiel from Yeo's squadron, as had Procter.[4] In addition, on 19 September, unaware that the battle on Lake Erie had been fought, Prevost had asked Yeo to recommend strongly to Barclay that he make an attempt to reopen the supply line. Finally, Yeo asserted to Warren that a "reinforcement" was on its way to Lake Erie for which Barclay should have waited, but neglected to explain that it comprised only the remaining fifty officers and men from HMS *Dover*, which would have brought the total number Yeo had deployed on Lake Erie to about one hundred.

Early in November Barclay's official report reached Yeo, requiring him to comment on its implications. The severely wounded commander's despatch, published widely on both sides of the border, described the privations at Amherstburg that had justified his actions and revealed that he had been able to muster "not more than fifty British Seamen" in his squadron and had not received definite assurance of reinforcements from Yeo.[5] On 14 November Yeo submitted to Admiral Warren (but not directly to the Admiralty) a copy of the report with a covering letter in which he unequivocally stated his view that Barclay "was not justified in seeking a contest."[6] The commodore accused his subordinate of not waiting for the reinforcements promised to him and challenged the protests about tight rations, citing as supporting evidence Procter's admission that he had burned a store of grain before retreating from Fort Malden. Yeo summarized his critique of the situation on Lake Erie by asserting that there had been insufficient reasons "for General Procter to urge Captain

Barclay to so hazardous and unequal a contest."[7] The next day he sent a copy of Barclay's despatch to Prevost enclosed with a letter in which he admitted that the Lake Erie squadron had been deficient in men and guns.[8] Rather than criticizing the commander's decision to engage Perry in this document, Yeo suggested that the battle had been lost because of the heavy casualties suffered by the British officers.

Prevost had taken a different stance on the defeat, suggesting in a despatch to Bathurst on 22 September that, considering the scant information available by that date, Barclay's decision seemed to have been a reasonable one, given the problems at Amherstburg.[9] Adroitly, Sir George also revealed that Yeo had kept nearly all of his original Royal Navy detachment at Kingston, leaving Barclay to depend on the army to complete his ship complements. In November, after Barclay and Procter's reports had reached him, Prevost issued a general order in which he openly called for the "reproach and censure" of Procter's actions, while extolling the "gallant daring and self devotion to their country's cause" demonstrated by Barclay and his seamen.[10] Along with Yeo's despatches to Warren, Prevost's commentaries and enclosures found their way to England, where they became the subject of discussions among senior officials. Word of the unprecedented loss of an entire squadron had reached London early in November, and in announcing the defeat *The Times* had absolved the Admiralty of blame, choosing to castigate Perry while dismissing the provincial "inhabitants" who had reportedly manned Barclay's ships.[11] More accurate depictions of the engagement and the context in which it had occurred would not reach England until Barclay returned to appear before a court martial at Portsmouth the following September, where his version of events would lay blame at Yeo's feet, adding weight to the doubts about the commodore that were forming at the Admiralty.

Of greater import to Yeo, as he considered his situation at Kingston in November of 1813, was the problem of winning control of Lake Ontario. Six months of war had taught him that his chances of gaining mastery over the Americans were extremely tenuous. His enemy outmanned him and, after the launch of the *General Pike* and the *Sylph* with their heavy armament, his force was significantly outgunned. To rectify that situation he had appealed for help from Warren and the Admiralty, and his requests had been seconded by Prevost. During the autumn of 1813 those requests began to reap results as a sharp escalation took place in the strength of the shipping and crews under Yeo's command. It was upon these matters that commodore focused his attention as winter ended the navigation season.[12]

Since assuming the position of commissioner at the Point Frederick dockyard, Commander Richard O'Conor had regulated its operations and extended its facilities. There were new storehouses and barracks, some still under construction, as well as a loft for sail and mold making, a hospital, a floating battery and a flying bridge connecting the dockyard to the town. The shipwrights had launched several gunboats recently and had repaired others while they made preparations for the winter refit of the squadron. The wharves needed improvement and a new wharf was planned large enough to support a set of shears for lifting masts and ordnance and for careening the ships so that their hulls could be scraped, patched and caulked. O'Conor had sailed with the squadron on 19 September and spent several weeks with the army on the Niagara Peninsula. Upon his return he was disappointed with the slow progress of the numerous projects and, frustrated by the enormity of his responsibilities, suggested to Prevost that he was unfit to handle the "considerable trouble and fexation" inherent to the job of commissioner.[13] The commander-in-chief would hear nothing of such talk, and O'Conor steadfastly continued to deal with the demands of his job; by December 1813 he had gained effective control once more of the wide range of projects on Navy Point.

The most ambitious enterprise at Point Frederick involved the two vessels rising on the spacious slipways that had been cleared in the yard. Since the burning of the *Sir Isaac Brock* at York in April, various individuals had recommended building larger warships, but, after the July launch of the brig *Melville*, work had been limited to the fabrication of gunboats. Late in September Yeo and his senior officers addressed the notion of enhancing the squadron's power again, and, with Prevost's approval, considered building a brig to serve as a transport, but they soon shelved that project and decided to lay the keels for two frigates instead.[14]

The first was to become HMS *Princess Charlotte*, 42, although it was originally named the *Vittoria* to honour Wellington's recent victory in Spain.[15] Even before the dockyard workers raised its stem and stern posts Yeo awarded a commission for the ship to Mulcaster, which was the circumstance he used to advance his friend to the rank of post captain. The *Charlotte's* keel, pieced together about the first of October, measured 121 feet, 6 inches in length. With a backbone of those dimensions, the structure would bear a gundeck five feet longer than the keel and attain a breadth of more than thirty-seven feet. It would carry sixteen 32-pdr. carronades, two 68-pdr. carronades and two dozen 24-pdr. long guns, making it more than a match for Chauncey's *General Pike*. As master builder in the yard, George Record designed the frigate and directed the 150 shipwrights and artificers employed in giving shape to his plans.

During the third week of October work began on a second frigate, destined to become HMS *Prince Regent*, 56.[16] Based on the plans of a master shipwright named Patrick Fleming, this vessel was thirty feet longer and five feet wider than the *Charlotte*. Its broadsides would also be more substantial, mounting twenty-four 32-pdr. carronades, four 68-pdrs. and twenty-eight 24-pdr. long guns. George Record appears to have overseen its construction, although a second person, John Goudie, was involved in the Point Frederick projects. Based at Quebec, Goudie had hired labourers for the dockyard at a rate of pay that provoked a near-strike among Record's shipwrights, who received wages according to the government's lower salary scale. When O'Conor returned from the Niagara Peninsula he discovered a whirlwind of "cabals and jealousies" hampering the smooth flow of business in the dockyard; to add to these headaches, Record resigned his position, believing that O'Conor had mistreated him and that it would be inappropriate for him to direct privately-contracted workers while he was still a publicly-paid master builder.[17] In spite of such obstacles, O'Conor kept the work going, enlisting Prevost's assistance in settling the various grievances in the yard. The commissioner was so successful in his efforts that the two frigates stood framed and partially planked by the end of November, and O'Conor feared the shipwrights would soon outpace the supply of materiel.

There was no opportunity for idleness among the Point Frederick shipwrights as spare hands were kept busy with the construction of three large gunboats (while a fourth was privately built at Ernestown).[18] As November ebbed, Yeo and the others debated the wisdom of starting a third frigate, owing to a rumour that Chauncey had already laid down two heavy frigates at Sackets. O'Conor went so far as to compile a list of items that would be required for such a ship, but nothing further was done for the time being. Yeo was very pleased with his friend's accomplishments and praised him to Prevost. "A great credit is due to Captain O'Conor," Yeo wrote on 2 December, "for his very zealous exertions in the Dock Yard – both Ships are in a very forward State and everything goes on with a spirit which is highly satisfactory."[19]

Obtaining crews for these new ships and the rest of the squadron was one of Yeo's priorities. The arrival of the *Marlborough* draft had compensated for the loss of the volunteers from the Quebec transports, but Yeo considered the *Marlboroughs* a poor addition to his complement; they were mainly "Americans, who have been taken this war, a number of old infirm Men, and Boys."[20] Within a few weeks the picture brightened considerably when Yeo learned that the Admiralty had sent a large reinforcement from England in response to his pleas for help.

On 5 August 1813, just days after a package of Yeo's despatches had reached the Admiralty, Commander Stephen Popham, already, at age thirty-three, an eighteen-year veteran of the service, was ordered to lead a 350-man RN detachment to the lakes.[21] A month later HMS *Æolus* departed from England carrying Popham, his men and a hold full of war materiel. It arrived at Quebec with the transport *Hydra* on 24 October, and Yeo sent orders for Popham to place the *Æolus* in ordinary after stripping it of every usable fixture, and head for Kingston with his crew and cargo as quickly as possible.[22] The alarm created by Wilkinson's descent down the St. Lawrence delayed the journey of Popham's division, and after the Americans withdrew to French Mills Prevost split the detachment, sending 170 of them to Isle-aux-Noix on the Richelieu River, where Commander Daniel Pring was struggling to maintain the Lake Champlain squadron. The remaining 180 officers and men reached Kingston on 16 December. Since the crews of the *George* and *Wolfe* had moved into barracks ashore, and Mulcaster had the commission for the *Charlotte*, Yeo gave the *George* over to Popham, dividing his men between that ship and the *Wolfe*. Sir James was unhappy about the diminution of Popham's detachment, believing that transportmen would have met Pring's needs quite adequately, but he considered the new hands to be of "fine" quality, though "very wild." A good number of them had wandered off into the wilds en route to the lake, prompting Yeo to remark, "it is inconceivable the difficulty of bringing up the seamen by land - they are guilty of every species of folly and extravagance."[23]

About the time the *Æolus* arrived at Quebec, six troop transports took up their moorings below the town. They carried the 1st and 2nd Royal Marine Battalions, as well as two companies of Royal Marine Artillery with a rocket detachment. Admiral Warren had sent these units, numbering more than a thousand officers and men, from Halifax to Quebec in answer to Prevost and Yeo's appeals for reinforcements. The 2nd Battalion was soon on the march and progressed as far as Prescott, where it took up quarters for the winter. In January the Admiralty formally assigned the battalion, minus its artillery company, to Yeo.[24]

The slowness with which Warren had responded to the requests from Yeo and Prevost had sparked frustration. Prevost, in particular, had voiced his complaints about the late arrival of the *Marlboroughs* and the marines, while Warren tried to explain his own shortages in manpower.[25] Realizing he would need hundreds more men to operate his new ships, Yeo decided during the first week of December to send an emissary to Halifax to provide Warren with a first-hand account of the situation on Lake Ontario. The job went to Lieutenant John Scott, who had travelled the overland route from Saint John with Robert Barclay in the spring and become the first lieutenant in the *Wolfe*, impressing

Lieutenant General Gordon Drummond, British Army (1772-1854). Drummond entered the army as an ensign in 1789 and within five years had risen to lieutenant colonel of the 8th Regiment of Foot, which he led into battle in Flanders and Holland. He also saw action in Egypt before being assigned to diplomatic posts in Jamaica, Canada and Ireland. (Courtesy of the McCord Museum of Canadian History, Montreal, M400)

the commodore with his competence and zeal.[26] Yeo also hoped that Warren's previous knowledge of Scott would help that officer convince the admiral of the need for 200 or more seamen at Kingston. Scott left the *Wolfe* on Tuesday, 7 December, facing a 900-mile journey down the frigid St. Lawrence and across the snowy forests of New Brunswick.

Scott departed from Kingston several days after the arrival at that place of a man who would become a central figure in the subsequent events of the war. Lieutenant General Gordon Drummond reached Kingston on 3 December almost a month after HMS *Ethalion* had delivered him to Quebec. Drummond was appointed to command in Upper Canada. Born at Quebec in 1772, the son of the deputy paymaster general to the forces in Canada, Drummond had been in the army from the age of seventeen.[27] He had seen action in the Netherlands and Egypt and had advanced to brigadier general in 1804, after which he had served in Jamaica for two years and on the staff of Governor-in-Chief Sir James Craig at Quebec between 1808 and 1811. Shortly after being advanced to the rank of lieutenant general, Drummond assumed command of a district in Ireland, which post he held when instructed to return to Canada during the summer of 1813. Competent, but lacking panache, Drummond had developed the efficient administrative skills that were badly needed to command in the upper province. As his second-in-command, the Horse Guards had selected Major General Phineas Riall, another seasoned veteran and a capable officer.

Drummond and Riall met Prevost in Montreal to discuss the developments of the late campaign before travelling up to Kingston to confer with Yeo. By 14 December Drummond had moved on to York to be sworn in as president of the provincial government and so was close at hand when news reached the capital that Brigadier General George McClure had withdrawn all American troops from the Niagara Peninsula after burning the town of Niagara to the ground. Drummond's response to McClure's universally condemned behaviour was swift. In the next two weeks he orchestrated what Isaac Brock had wanted to do at the outbreak of the war, namely destroy the American forces and fortifications along the Niagara River.[28] On 18 December Lieutenant Colonel John Murray led 600 British soldiers to capture Fort Niagara and its large depot of supplies after a violent and bloody clash, and the following day Riall crossed the river to Lewiston at the head of nearly 1,000 men to ravage that village, then do the same to several other settlements, a Tuscarora encampment and Fort Schlosser. On 29 December, Riall attacked Buffalo and Black Rock, razing those settlements as the final act of retribution for the injury done to the Canadian inhabitants of Niagara. The year 1813 ended with all American invasion schemes defeated, except for the meagre force remaining on British territory along the Detroit River.

Heartened by his success at Niagara, Drummond was open to ideas about how to reclaim control of Lake Erie and the lost western territories. Yeo had initiated discussion of the topic with Prevost late in November, proposing an ambitious and inventive scheme for striking against Perry's squadron and its prizes. He had learned that the captured corvettes *Detroit* and *Queen Charlotte*, yet unrepaired following the Battle of Put-in-Bay, lay at South Bass Island, while most of the rest of the American squadron was moored within the protective arm of the Presque Isle Peninsula at Erie. Yeo suggested that, as soon as the ice broke up, 200 seamen and twice that number of soldiers could slip across the lake to Erie from Long Point in small boats, destroy the American brigs *Lawrence* and *Niagara,* and seize the smaller vessels. In their prizes, the raiders would then sail up to South Bass Island and recapture the former British corvettes. Since sufficient craft were not available on Lake Erie and the building of small boats would draw attention to the plan, Yeo proposed that prefabricated vessels be employed. "My idea," he explained to Prevost on 11 December, "is to have the frame of the Boat, as light as possible to go with bolts and screws – the outside to be covered with hides instead of Plank – which cover is to be made exactly to fit the bottom of the Boat and can be put on in a few hours."[29] Oars would be fashioned at York, the parts for fourteen such boats sent ahead in sleighs to be followed when the time was right by the raiding party. After two or three days of preparations at Long Point, the assault could be launched. Though it depended on endless contingencies, Yeo considered this plan more likely to succeed than an attempt to build a new squadron at a place like Long Point. Prevost appreciated Yeo's inventiveness but pointed out a number of potential defects. Regaining superiority on Lake Ontario was more important in his view and he advised Yeo "to consult Lieutenant General Drummond and maturely to consider whether the object you have in view is to be attained without the sacrifice of higher interests."[30]

When Drummond returned to Kingston in January 1814, Yeo discussed the matter with him, probably showing him the model of the collapsible boat built by one of his carpenters. Drummond was already familiar with the scheme, having received word of it in a letter from Prevost, and he liked the basic premise, but preferred the use of 1,500 regulars, militia and Indians, plus Yeo's 200 seamen.[31] He wrote to Prevost on 21 January, laying out an elaborate plan for an overland march to Fort Malden, detailing the use of sleighs and the rations that would be needed. An attack would be made across the ice of the Detroit River to capture Detroit and then over forty miles of ice to seize the ships at South Bass Island. No mention was made of raiding Erie, and Drummond revealed one of the weaknesses in the plan, which was the lack of snow that had accumulated thus far that winter.

In response, Prevost agreed with Drummond's concern that there might not be enough snow for sleighs to be used in transporting the force, but he also pointed out the difficulty that might exist in procuring adequate supplies in the districts through which the expedition would pass. In spite of his reservations, Prevost approved the expedition as long as Drummond and Yeo got it moving by the second week of February.

The relatively mild winter of 1813-1814 rang the death knell on this bold venture. Too little snow fell and Drummond formally cancelled the excursion on 19 February.[32] The British took no large scale action to win back control of Lake Erie; instead, a party of seamen and artificers under Lieutenant Newdigate Poyntz, RN, one of Popham's officers, set out for Georgian Bay via the Lake Simcoe route to establish a dockyard at Penetanguishene Bay where they would build gunboats. Difficulties of terrain soon showed Penetanguishene to be an impractical depot, and the detachment cleared an alternate site near the mouth of the Nottawasaga River on the southernmost shore of Georgian Bay. It was hoped that Poyntz would be able to render support to the lonely British outpost at Mackinac when the sailing season opened.[33]

Although the weather during January and February 1814 was mild by local standards, its "hard frosts" and occasional snowstorms provided new experiences

**Commander Alexander Dobbs, RN
(ca. 1784-1827).** Dobbs came to Canada
as a lieutenant hoping from promotion.
He had been in the navy since 1797,
serving in the West Indies and the
Mediterranean, and had spent a brief
period in HMS *Confiance*, Yeo's first
command. Dobbs was one of Yeo's best
officers on the lakes and was promoted to
commander soon after their arrival at
Kingston in May 1813. (Courtesy of the
Ontario Archives, ACC 6988, S-12772)

for the British seamen. They constructed plank roofs over the decks of the ships
to keep the snow off as ice ("six to eight feet thick," Master's Mate David
Wingfield later claimed) fixed them in place.[34] Freed from the burden of endless duty afloat, the officers enjoyed skating on Navy Bay or sleighing over the
roads and fields at speeds that would allow a man to travel seventy miles in a
day. Some military units drilled on the ice, which groaned in complaint, keeping everyone alert. Yeo used the ice to solve disputes among his officers with at
least one duel being fought by having the combatants fire muskets at each other
as they stood in sentry boxes set eighty yards apart on a frozen pond. In ordering this arrangement, the commodore made the duel seem so ludicrous that no
one wanted to repeat it, and duelling effectively ended in his squadron.

"The Navy are in great vogue at Kingston, though they think us a very curious sort of fellows," bragged Lieutenant John Johnston, RN. "We have made a
very beautiful Theatre and the Officers of the Navy act."[35] He and his friends
formed the Amateur Theatre at Point Frederick, performing a play called "The
Poor Gentleman" for the public, accompanied by their own band and even a
couple of young ladies whom they convinced to take speaking parts. The officers' mess was "a first rate one both for style and company – all Captains and select society."[36] Army officers joined the navy for meals and celebrations;
Stephen Popham brought Lieutenant John Le Couteur of the 104th Foot to one
event, and Le Couteur and a large host of officers and gentry attended the wedding of Commander Alexander Dobbs and Mary Cartwright, the daughter of a
prominent citizen of Kingston, on the evening of 17 February 1814. Afterwards
the dancing went on until the wee hours, though a false alarm about an

impending enemy attack prevented the newlyweds from travelling to Montreal for their honeymoon. "So you see," Johnston wrote to his family, "we are quite gay in the Wilds of America."[37]

Life was not as frivolous for the seamen, although they too were spared the gruelling tedium of watches around the clock. Many of the men lived in the new barracks, from which they issued each morning to help in the dockyard, fit gun tackles and make wads, pick oakum or set up lines and blocks. Musters were held weekly as were church services, with alternating groups enjoying liberty every second Sunday. Sickness was not common and even cases of frostbite were rare. The commodore worried that since the ice had joined his station to the enemy's shore he would lose men to desertion, but though some of the seamen and soldiers at Kingston did "run" to the American side, the occurrences were rare enough to make mention of them in despatches unnecessary. All in all, the naval establishment appears to have been a smooth-running and comfortable station during this period.[38]

And an industrious one, too: despite the officers' assertions of endless good fun, everyone worked hard completing the new construction at the dockyard. The moderate weather made working outside easier, and the slipways and workshops were abuzz with activity. "I have been over at the yard yesterday myself to see them [the new ships]," observed a visitor on 16 January, "and the progress made in the last week is truly astonishing. I cannot but think that they will be nearly finished in the course of the ensuing month."[39] Although that individual's estimation about the completion date was optimistic, the *Princess Charlotte* and *Prince Regent* had literally sprung up from their keels. By the final week of January 1814 they were planked, their beams nearly all in, the wales on and the masts and spars one third fashioned.[40] Caulking began around the middle of February, but there was a shortage of oakum that worried Yeo, and his growing anxiety was obvious in the number of letters he wrote asking that essential materials be procured: iron in large enough dimensions to meet the demands of his frigates, canvas that could be cut into sails and prepared for quick installation along with all the standing and running rigging right after the ships were launched. He had the *Æolus* surveyed to determine what cables, rigging and sails could be salvaged from it. The shortage of snow made transportation of the ordnance difficult, but by the end of February ninety-one carronades and long guns had arrived at Kingston.[41]

From various sources rumours reached Kingston that Chauncey was building either a pair of powerful brigs or a frigate, a brig and a schooner or two frigates and a large brig (more likely a third frigate) at Sackets Harbour. If the worst of these scenarios was true, the Americans would have the upper hand

HMS *Prince Regent*. Captain Henry Davies, newly sent from England, assumed command of the *Prince Regent* during the spring of 1814 and appears to have painted this view of his frigate, considered a fourth rate by Royal Navy standards. The ship was slightly smaller than the famous American frigate *Constitution*, though its firepower was about the same. (Watercolour by Henry T. Davies, courtesy of the National Archives of Canada, C-138986)

after the navigation season opened, forcing Yeo to fight an unequal battle or remain penned up at Kingston with his two new ships lying idle. In light of the rumours, discussion began again about laying down another frigate similar to the *Prince Regent*, with the commodore predicting that it could be launched in June. In short order the inventories of needs were completed and transmitted to Montreal, Quebec and Halifax. Commissioner O'Conor took out advertisements in the *Kingston Gazette*, seeking proposals from persons interested in filling the Navy's orders for 20,000 feet of red pine, 10,000 feet of red cedar, and later, lengths of rock elm squared to fourteen inches and knees of oak, elm and spruce. Wishing to avoid problems like those experienced with Record and Goudie, Yeo and his colleagues picked Master Shipwright William Bell to design the ship. Bell had lately arrived at Kingston, having fled the shipyard at Amherstburg, where he had been the master shipwright since the turn of the century. Whatever his first drawings for a frigate looked like, they were soon scrapped, for as February passed into March Yeo's original intentions were abandoned. The proportions of the third ship increased immensely, growing a gundeck that was almost forty feet longer than the *Regent's*, rising to present two solid tiers of 24- and 32-pdr. long guns and a third deck of heavy carronades. It would eventually become the first rate *St. Lawrence*, pierced for 102 guns. The material for such a behemoth, however, would sap the Royal Navy's resources and strain the supply routes through the spring and summer, affecting the tide of the war during that period. Whether Yeo, Drummond, Prevost and the others foresaw the implications of their commitment to such a prodigious undertaking is uncertain, but it is clear that they wanted to avoid the naval imbalance that had hindered Yeo's encounters with Chauncey and they viewed this drastic escalation of their armada as the means to that end. The commodore, it seems, was passionate about his desire to win control of the lake, as he earnestly expressed to Sir George on 28 February: "I pledge myself to Your Excellency that every exertion of my body and mind shall be devoted to defeat the enemy's views, and that the force entrusted to my command never shall surrender to the enemy while *I have life*."[42]

In this same despatch Yeo also noted his pleasure at learning from Prevost that 200 seamen were on the march to Kingston thanks to the success Lieutenant John Scott had achieved in his mission to Halifax.[43] Scott had completed his journey down the valley of the Saint John River in January, arriving at the port

Relics from HMS *Prince Regent*. In 1938 divers visited the remains of the *Prince Regent* on the bottom of Deadman Bay and removed artifacts for display in Old Fort Henry, then under development. Shown in these photos are a 24-pdr. long gun from the frigate's lower deck and a filling table from the gunner's room next to the magazine. On the table, topped with copper to resist sparks, the gunner made up the cartridges for use in the ordnance. (Photographs by the author)

of Saint John and taking passage to Halifax. Since Warren was at sea, the lieutenant met with his second-in-command, Rear Admiral Edward Griffith, and the lieutenant governor of Nova Scotia, Sir John Sherbrooke. In December Warren had insisted that he could not spare another soul from his squadron, but Scott convinced Griffith and Sherbrooke of the dire situation at Kingston, and they decided to detach 210 officers and men from four warships at Halifax.[44] Commander Edward Collier, captain of one of the vessels, HM Brig *Manly*, 14, volunteered to lead the expedition, which departed from Halifax on the brig *Fantome* on 22 January.

Collier's detachment reached Saint John on 26 January after enduring a horrendous winter storm that so encrusted the *Fantome* with ice that it nearly foundered. Collier split the seamen into three divisions, which set off for Fredericton in sleighs provided by the locals, but at that place the men escaped their barracks during the night and ran amok in the town, prompting a reorganization of the party into two groups, one following a day or so behind the other. They headed north by sleigh for another eighty miles, at which point the transport service ended, and it was snowshoes for all and a toboggan for the equipment and supplies of every four men. Entire regiments had followed the cross-country route to the St. Lawrence River previously, but for such a large group of seamen the trek was a unique one. A description of the journey by Lieutenant Henry Kent, RN, who commanded the second group, appeared in the *Naval Chronicle* in 1815. In it he itemized the outfit he had procured for the trip:

> I provided myself at Halifax with a jacket, trousers, and a waistcoat, lined with fine flannel, so that with those, three flannel shirts, and a linen one on, three pairs of stockings, and a square piece of blanket wrapped on my feet, with moccasans [sic] over all, I felt pretty warm.[45]

The naval parties tramped across a snowy wilderness, sleeping around campfires at night when they could find no other shelter, nearly surrendering to the elements on one occasion when a fierce blizzard struck from the north. Collier's men reached the St. Lawrence at Rivière-du-Loup first and were relieved to find their hardships eased as they climbed into sleighs for conveyance to Quebec. They arrived there on 19 February, taking up lodging in HMS *Æolus* until Kent's division caught up to them eight days later; without further delay, for fear the men might find a way to get into trouble again, Collier marched them off the next day for Kingston.

There were more men from the Royal Navy about to head to the Great Lakes, but no one in Canada had yet heard of their expedition. News of Barclay's defeat and Yeo's lack of success in subduing Chauncey had caused some consternation in London. Lord Bathurst immediately wrote to Prevost and urged him to re-establish a naval force on Lake Erie and destroy the American squadron.[46] About the same time the Admiralty and Prime Minister Lord Liverpool's cabinet considered the advice of an anonymous "Loyalist" who suggested that components for as many as five small frigates could be fabricated in England and transported to Quebec for assembly on the lakes.[47] The scheme was almost identical to the one put forth late in 1812 by Sir Howard Douglas and may have come surreptitiously from his own quill. Basing his proposal on the use of prefabricated vessels on Lake Champlain during the American revolution, Douglas had advised that "vessels with the frames and such other parts and stores as are sent from England may arrive at Quebec by the 10th or 12th of May, and their contents reach Lake Ontario by the first of June."[48]

Similar propositions reached London from two other sources. On 1 December 1813 Admiral Warren recommended to the Admiralty that three ships and three brigs be built, "in frame," presumably at Kingston, and then transported to Long Point on Lake Erie or to Matchedash Bay, also known as Penetanguishene Bay, on the eastern shore of Georgian Bay. Apparently unaware of the difficult topography between Montreal and the upper lakes, Warren implied that the guns, sails, men and rigging sent from England would reach the distant sites in time for the vessels to be ready the following spring.[49] Another suggestion came from Canada. On 23 November 1813 James Kerr, a member of the legislative council at Quebec, transmitted to Lord Melville the ideas of James Campbell, whom Kerr knew to be "an experienced and ingenious man."[50] Kerr predicted that Lake Erie could be won back and victory gained overall if the navy built six ships each on Lakes Ontario and Champlain from components prepared in England. He submitted Campbell's design for a twenty-three-gun vessel with a 125-foot keel and drawing only three and a half feet of water. It would carry two masts rigged with huge lateen sails, giving it the appearance of the xebec frigates preferred by the Mediterranean corsairs. "They may be put together in a month or six weeks at farthest [and] ... master the Lakes and keep them for ever in possession of the British Empire," wrote Kerr.[51]

Warren and Kerr's ideas added fuel to a fire that was already burning by the time their letters crossed the ocean. The year 1813 had ended on the upswing for Britain. Napoleon had been beaten back across the French border and an allied offensive was being planned to topple him from his throne. Liverpool's government was turning its attention to the war in America and committing larger land and sea forces to that theatre, which had a direct impact for the Royal Navy on the Great Lakes. The proposals by Douglas and the

"Loyalist" struck a note with the cabinet and the Admiralty, whose knowledge of the distant and isolated posts in the wilderness of Canada was too limited to challenge assumptions about ship-building kits being delivered and assembled with alacrity.

By the third week of December 1813 the government decided that the Chatham shipyards would construct the hull of a frigate except for its planks and decks and send the pieces to Canada. On New Year's Day, 1814, a second frigate was ordered, and, three days later, two brigs were added to the list, all of them to be built of fir. The frigates, fifth rates named the *Prompte* and the *Psyche,* were to carry thirty 24-pdr. long guns and eight 32-pdr. carronades on their gundecks, forecastles and quarterdecks. The brigs, sixth rate sloops named the *Goshawk* and the *Colibri,* would mount eight 24-pdr. long guns, two 12-pdrs. and eight 24-pdr. carronades. By 22 February the fir components for the vessels had been completed at the Chatham complex and their rigging and ordnance was nearly all collected. A squadron of transports, chosen because their shallow draughts would permit them to deliver their cargoes straight to Montreal, prepared for a March sailing date.[52]

Because of their ratings, each frigate and brig-sloop was to be manned by a crew of 300 and 140 respectively, so, with its "ships-in-frame" project, the government committed nearly 900 more officers and men to the Great Lakes war. The Admiralty chose Captain George Downie to lead the expedition with Commanders Frederick Hickey, Henry Thomas Davies and Peter Fisher, the latter three being promoted to post rank with their new appointments; .[53]

This increase would nearly double the size of the British naval force on the lakes, the administrative implications of which were not missed by the heads of government. To allow Yeo the latitude he would need to cope with his increasing responsibilities, management of the naval establishment in Canada was revamped. Originally, Yeo was expected to keep his men on the books of one establishment and to work in close cooperation with the army's quartermaster general's department under Prevost. The government swept that system aside, and the Admiralty issued orders in January 1814 that made Yeo's command independent from the army.[54] Sir James's official title was changed from "Senior Officer on the Lakes," to "Commander-in-Chief of His Majesty's Ships and Vessels employed on the Lakes." He would be allowed a flag captain on his ship and would take control of all aspects of civil administration ashore, acting in the manner of a Royal Navy commissioner at a foreign yard. To avoid conflicts with names of ships already on the navy's list, the Admiralty re-classified and re-named the vessels on Lakes Ontario and Champlain and added them to the official Navy list. The books for the original establishment were to be closed and each vessel, gunboat squadron and dockyard would become a separate establishment with its own records.

Bathurst explained the sweeping reform in a despatch to Prevost on 20 January:

> It has been determined … to extend the Scale of Naval Exertions; and feeling that to impose upon you the Conduct of Naval Operations so much more extended than heretofore, would be to increase unnecessarily the Responsibility of your Situation, I have thought it expedient, both with a View to your Convenience and the Advantage of the Public Service, to submit to the Lords Commissioners of the Admiralty, the Necessity of taking charge of all the Naval Establishments on the Lakes, and placing the Fleets and Dock Yards there on a similiar Footing with His Majesty's Fleets and Dock Yards in other Parts of the World.[55]

The naval reinforcement being sent to Canada soon became public knowledge in Britain and prompted one anonymous observer to voice his support of the plan to the editor of the *Naval Chronicle*. Signing himself as "Serus," this writer hoped the reinforcement would mean that the people at home would "not again be distressed at the recital of misfortune or failure from want of men, long guns or indeed from any cause that may be foreseen."[56] "Serus" lauded the merit of Yeo and Mulcaster and praised the selection of Downie and the others. He described the qualities of the ships in frame, pointing out that their heavy armament would prevent incidents like the long-range bombardment Yeo had suffered at the Genesee River in September. Adding that a large frigate was expected to be launched in the spring at Kingston and that 200 seamen were marching overland to the lakes, " Serus" concluded that "I pray we may soon be gratified with the glad tidings that his [Yeo's] efforts have been crowned with success." Likely a member of Liverpool's inner circle who used the pages of the *Chronicle* to extol the wisdom of the government's own policies, "Serus" put the onus for victory squarely on Sir James Yeo's shoulders. Now that such resources had been put at his disposal, Yeo was equipped to win the day and any other outcome would hardly be excused.

CHAPTER 15

"An Augmentation
of Our Naval Force"[1]

PREPARATIONS AT SACKETS HARBOUR:
NOVEMBER 1813 – APRIL 1814

Commodore Isaac Chauncey anchored his squadron safely at Sackets Harbour on 2 December 1813, arranging them in two perpendicular lines so that their broadsides and the batteries ashore would cover all angles against a surprise attack. Chauncey took the *Conquest, Fair American, Pert* and *Julia* out of commission, sending their crews into the *Sylph, Madison* and *General Pike*, in order to "add, to the safety of the fleet and insure a more rigid and better discipline among the officers and men."[2] The commodore wanted to go to Washington to meet with Secretary of the Navy Jones, but before he could leave he had to deal with an assortment of administrative matters.

At the top of Chauncey's list was the long-delayed court martial of Master Commandant James Leonard. Despite Leonard's complaints about his protracted confinement at Sackets and Jones's repeated instructions to hold a trial since the morning in mid-April when ice floes had nearly carried away the *Madison*, the commodore had never found time to convene the court. Finally, the irate commandant's day of judgement came, beginning on 1 December at the home of Sailing Master William Vaughan (where there was sufficient room) with Captain Arthur Sinclair serving as president of the board. Sinclair, Commandants William Crane and Melancthon Woolsey and ten lieutenants listened to eight days of testimony about Leonard's culpability for the poor care of the *Madison* and about his relationship with his "wife," the notorious "Mrs. Leonard." On 9 December the board retired to consider the case, returning quickly with a verdict of guilty on all counts, after which Leonard was free to head for New York and await the Navy Department's sentence. It came on 15

January, denouncing the commandant and suspending him from duty for one year, dating back to the time of the infraction. Although he had only three months to remain officially inactive, Leonard's active service afloat was finished.[3]

After the court martial Arthur Sinclair also left Sackets Harbour. He had discussed with the commodore the discomfort he felt in holding the rank of full captain while serving as the flag officer in a ship of the *Pike's* class. Chauncey understood and let him go with regret "that I am to lose the society of an agreeable Companion and the Services of an Officer who has shown on all occasions so much zeal and ability."[4] Sinclair's time on Lake Ontario had earned him the commodore's respect, but none of the laurels for which he yearned. "How much more hard cruizing and d_____d hard fighting have we had," he asked his correspondent in a thinly veiled reference to Oliver Hazard Perry, "than many who have received publick [sic] thanks – freedom of the citys [sic] in gold Boxes – swords and dinners and lord knows what."[5] Sinclair journeyed to Washington to apply to Secretary Jones for a command on the ocean, but spent the winter in Virginia with his wife and two young children apparently recovering from a case of rheumatic gout, which had helped hasten his departure from the lake.

Lieutenant Wolcott Chauncey had sought permission from the Navy Department to leave his brother's command and finally received it in December. In a request written in November, he had cited a "bilious fever" and a "disease of the lungs" as his reasons for wanting a posting to a southern station so he could recover his health.[6] Other ills might have been troubling him, however. In September he had written to Jones complaining that people were still criticizing him for allowing the fire to be set in the shipyard during the British attack on 29 May 1813. He had asked that the findings of the inquiry held after the battle to investigate his conduct be made public, to which Jones replied that they had been. The commodore had kept the *Fair American*, Wolcott Chauncey's schooner, detached at the Niagara River for most of the summer, but its return to Sackets with the squadron in October must have caused the lieutenant too much pain as he tried to mingle in the unforgiving society of the naval officers at the base. In December the Navy Department transferred Lieutenant Chauncey to the US Sloop *Erie* at Baltimore, where he took up quarters, relieved to be away from the freshwater navy.

Poor health and the need to attend to family matters drove other officers from Sackets, although only on leaves of absence. Melancthon Woolsey was among them, afflicted with an illness that had caused him to be replaced in the *Sylph* by Lieutenant John Pettigrew late in October. Chauncey granted Woolsey some well-deserved time with his family to restore his vitality.[7]

One officer the commodore would have preferred to see at his post through-out the long, cold, lonely winter was Captain Oliver H. Perry. On 13 October, just days after finally receiving a copy from Perry of his official report on the battle at Put-in-Bay, Chauncey had been flabbergasted to receive a notice from Secretary Jones stating that he had given Perry permission to return to New-port, Rhode Island. Jones's approval had come as a result of Perry's request to be posted to a sea-going ship appropriate to the rank of captain, a promotion dated retroactively to the day of his victory. Knowing that Mackinac Island had still not been reclaimed from British hands, one of Jones's prime objectives, and that Perry's job on the upper lakes was therefore only half done, Chauncey felt that Jones had made a regrettable error in judgement. A naval officer, he argued to the secretary, "has no right to select for himself a particular service or to be dissatisfied with that assigned to him," adding with more than a smidgeon of hyperbole, "... I should have accepted the command of a half dozen bark canoes on Lake Superior with as much alacrity as I did the command on these Lakes."[8]

Allowing Perry to leave Lake Erie so easily (and without asking for Chauncey's opinion on the matter) was a precedent that the commodore be-lieved would prompt other officers to seek convenient and comfortable post-ings. Chauncey's angry response did not change anything, and Perry departed from the scene of his triumph to reap the tributes befitting a hero as he trav-elled home to Rhode Island. Chauncey appointed Master Commandant Jesse Elliott to take his place, but as the snow fell at Sackets, the commodore was still complaining to Jones that Perry had never submitted to him the proper lists of prizes and prisoners nor an accurate muster of the officers and men under his command, nor had he sought Chauncey's advice about promotions made after the battle. Chauncey's relationship with the talented young officer he had wel-comed so heartily the previous winter thus ended bitterly, although the acri-mony might have been neutralized in some small part by the fact that Perry's accomplishments would eventually put nearly $13,000 of prize money in the pocket of his immediate superior at Sackets Harbour.[9]

Of greater importance to Chauncey than courts martial, exits and leaves of absence was the British construction program at Kingston. Information that he considered reliable had reached his ears late in November telling of two ships rising in the Point Frederick dockyard, one with a keel measuring 150 feet, the other with a keel of 123 feet.[10] Two weeks later the return from Kingston under a flag of truce of an American named Shoemaker, who had been captured by the British the previous June, brought confirmation of the first two ships building and word that a third had already been laid down.[11]

By comparison, nothing was under construction at Sackets. Secretary Jones had discussed the topic in a long despatch to Chauncey in September, perhaps prompted by rumours of the British building a warship every forty days at Kingston. If the question of supremacy on the lake was not resolved, he had advised, Chauncey should replace the converted lakers with "vessels of a more formidable class."[12] Jones suggested that three sloops built along the lines of the newly launched *Peacock*, which was equipped with twenty 42-pdr. carronades and two long 24s, would fit the bill; he had already discussed the idea with the *Peacock's* builders, Adam and Noah Brown, who were enthusiastic about setting up shop at Sackets. Chauncey liked Jones's suggestions and acknowledged the Browns' skill - they had been instrumental in the preparation of Perry's squadron - but declared his unconditional support for Henry Eckford as the man who should conduct the work at Sackets. "As to his talents as a Ship Carpenter I am bold to say, that there is not his equal in the U. States, or perhaps in the World," claimed the commodore before proceeding to itemize Eckford's achievements of the past year.[13]

Since that exchange nothing had been decided about the American building program, although Jones continued to ponder the alternatives, and on 30 November he instructed John Bullus, the navy agent at New York, to get ready to transport enough equipment and materials to the lake to support an ambitious winter construction program. "Request the Gentleman," wrote Jones, "who built the *General Pike* (I do not at this moment recollect his name) to proceed to Sacketts Harbour and confer with Commodore Chauncey on the subject of building a Frigate 175 feet between perpendiculars 40 feet abeam … Also two Sloops of War of the size of the *Peacock*."[14] The forgotten "gentleman," Henry Eckford, arrived at Sackets on 9 December and, after meeting with Chauncey, prepared contracts for timber and accommodations for shipwrights, while the commodore arranged for two additional building sites to be cleared. Eckford departed for New York three days later with the usual long lists of supplies, fittings, ordnance and rigging required, but as late at 18 December there was still no certainty about when work would commence.[15] By that date Chauncey had written once more to Jones with news from Kingston, where two ships would be ready to launch early in the spring. He calculated that four vessels would actually be needed to match the increase in Yeo's squadron, but also allowed that if the government planned to take a defensive stance, it could save money by waiting until the spring to construct ships at Sackets.[16] Approval to begin building reached Chauncey around 23 December, and he wrote to Bullus asking him to hurry Eckford and his artificers back to the lake, but three more weeks passed before the keels for three vessels were set up.[17] On 26 December, after turning over command of the squadron to Commandant William Crane, Isaac Chauncey left Sackets intending to spend a day with his family in New York and then go on to Washington.

The commodore devoted more than a week to his family and public business in New York before travelling to Washington to meet with Jones on 13 January. The secretary was also eager to know the details of Wilkinson's campaign on the St. Lawrence, asking Chauncey to describe his own involvement in writing.[18] Washington was a hotbed of political intrigue, and his visit gave the commodore some insight into why approval for building on Lake Ontario had been delayed.[19]

Wilkinson's failed campaign and the British desolation of the Niagara frontier late in December 1813 had eclipsed some of the glory won earlier in the year by American forces at York, Fort George, Put-in-Bay and Moraviantown. In response, Secretary of War John Armstrong recommended increasing the size of the army and navy on the lakes and, to fellow Republicans in New York State, he promised a winter campaign that would drive the British back across the Niagara River. Secretary of State James Monroe openly opposed Armstrong's plans and called for his removal on grounds that he was responsible for the failure of the St. Lawrence expedition, but President Madison stepped between them to wield his authority, forbidding the winter campaign and refusing to support Monroe's protests.

Other problems dominated the president's time. American envoys had gone to Russia the previous May, at the invitation of the Russian government, to meet with British representatives to discuss peace. This initiative had failed, but in the autumn the British offered to meet American emissaries face to face in London or in Gothenburg, Sweden. Somewhat strengthened by their success against Napoleon, the British implied that any settlement would sacrifice American claims to sovereignty on the high seas. "Free Trade and Sailors' Rights" had been the rallying cry of supporters of Madison's original declaration of war, and he feared losing their votes. Monroe and William Jones favoured peace talks, but Armstrong argued that discussing peace meant giving in to the British and made redundant any further efforts to wage war. The president finally decided to send a delegation to Gothenburg, but insisted that the war would continue. To maintain support among his political allies, he picked Henry Clay, a confirmed War Hawk who would never bow to British demands, to lead the negotiating team, which departed from New York on the frigate *John Adams* in January.

The financing of the war once more became a matter of contention in Washington. Secretary of the Treasury Albert Gallatin had been part of the original peace delegation (and continued in that role in the new negotiations), his duties at the treasury being assumed by William Jones. The navy secretary persevered through the trials of managing two ministries at once, acknowledging to Madison that the workload had limited his attention to naval affairs, as well as threatening his personal finances. Much to his relief, Senator George Campbell from Tennessee took over the treasury post during the winter and tackled the problem of raising the funds Jones had projected would be needed in the ensuing year – $24.5 million for the army and $7 million for the navy. A loan to supplement regular government income was obviously needed, but being as distasteful to the legislators as it had been the year before, the issue resulted in a lengthy debate before Congress approved it in March 1814. Finding lenders was the next hurdle and that was not resolved until May when Campbell finally secured enough subscribers and institutions. During the interim the president's key advisors, including William Jones, urged him to rescind legislation enacted late in 1813 to restrict the outrageous commerce going on between Atlantic ports, especially in New England, and the British. The resumption of trade would help to refill government coffers by means of duties, it was argued, and entrepreneurs like John Jacob Astor and David Parrish might be more willing to risk loans to the treasury. Madison grudgingly submitted to his advisors in April and, after bitter congressional debates, the infamous embargo died.

The impact of all these developments upon the war on the northern border was that a clear and concise plan of operations for 1814 was not made in Washington during the winter and early spring. At one point William Jones had recommended ceasing operations in the north altogether, since he considered it incongruous to renew trade with British commercial interests sailing from Europe while fighting British forces in Canada. He preferred to harass those carriers through a stepped-up naval program on the Atlantic seaboard. It was an idea that he repeated in late May when he asked Madison if there was "an adequate object" for all the men and munitions going to the lakes. "I do not understand," he concluded, "that we are prepared for or have any view to offensive military operations."[20] American objectives for 1814 would not be set until June, a delay that was to be fatal to the aspirations of the United States in that year.

Although campaign goals for 1814 had not been confirmed by spring, the American government expended considerable energy, money and resources on the improvement of the military and naval establishments in the north. George Izard received a promotion to major general and replaced Hampton at Plattsburgh, while Jacob Brown also advanced to the rank of major general about the time that James Wilkinson lost his command following an abortive attempt to invade Lower Canada in March – the remnants of Wilkinson's army

were divided between Sackets Harbour and Plattsburgh. Other officers recommended for promotion by Secretary of War John Armstrong included Alexander Macomb, Edmund P. Gaines, Eleazar W. Ripley and Winfield Scott, all promoted brigadier generals. These changes meant that, for the first time in the
war, a group of young, aggressive and experienced commanders led the U.S.
Army in the north. Steps were also taken to increase the size of the army. Early
in the winter it had been feared that the end of an enlistment period would
sharply reduce the forces they would command, but Congress approved an increase in bounties and the official strength of the army rose past 31,000 men.

Secretary Jones may have had doubts about pursuing another expensive
campaign on the lakes, but he continued to endorse Chauncey's work at Sackets
and to pay his shopping bills.[21] Eckford and his shipwrights laid down two
brigs, modelled after the *Peacock*, and a large frigate at Sackets during the second week of January 1814. Storekeepers at New York assembled the myriad materials needed for new ships and put them on the road up the valley of the inter-
mittently frozen Hudson River.[22] Along with them went more than one
hundred pieces of ordnance and thousands of tons of shot, procured from gunboats, land batteries, idle warships and foundries.[23] Jones approved an increase
in the bounty for naval enlistments and a number of Chauncey's lieutenants
opened rendezvous at Philadelphia, New York and Boston to enlist men.[24] As
before, entire crews transferred from inactive warships on the seaboard to
Sackets Harbour. The officers and men of the *Ontario* and *Erie*, including Lieutenant Wolcott Chauncey, laid up their sloops, at the secretary's order, and
headed north under the command of Commandant Charles Ridgely. Captain
Jacob Jones received similar instructions to remove the crew and marines from
the *Macedonian* at New London and go with them to Sackets Harbour. Eventually nearly 2,000 personnel would serve on Lake Ontario, far more than were
employed at any other American station.[25]

Despite his uncertainty about a northern campaign, Jones still viewed control of the upper lakes as a priority, and men and munitions travelled to Erie to
prepare the ships there for another campaign. The events of 1813 having shown
that it was unreasonable to expect Commodore Chauncey to coordinate two
such widely separated commands, William Jones decided to divide the naval
organization on the lakes. He called upon Arthur Sinclair, inviting him to take
charge of the Lake Erie squadron as commodore, which he accepted and which
Chauncey graciously seconded.[26]

Chauncey returned to Sackets Harbour on 23 February 1814. To his eye,
things were in good order, and he applauded William Crane for his management of the base. Actually, the Harbour had been a hellish place over the winter,

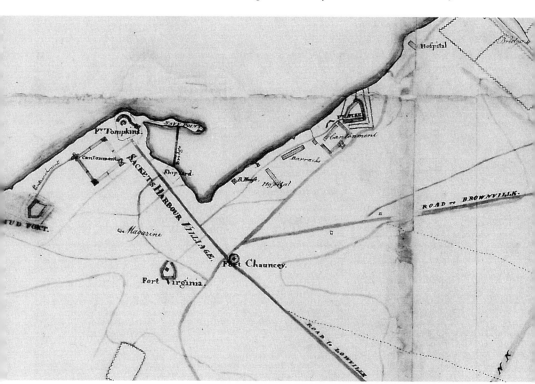

Sackets Harbour, 1814. During the winter of 1813-1814 the defences at Sackets Harbour were strengthened by the construction of the Mud Fort, Fort Virginia and Fort Chauncey. Fort Volunteer had been renamed Fort Pike and the navy had fashioned a shortcut to Navy Point by building a floating bridge between there and the village side of the basin. (Courtesy of the U.S. National Archives, RG 77, D15-2)

proving once again to be an extremely unhealthy environment.[27] So many soldiers had died in December that funeral dirges had been prohibited for fear of further depressing the despondent troops. Crane reported 1,700 men in the army camps in January of which he figured only five or six hundred could actually turn out when called to duty. In the squadron more than 200 men were ill with only two surgeons and three surgeon's mates to care for them. Chauncey and Crane had both enacted strict regulations for the maintenance of proper hygiene and for the treatment of the sick, but to little avail.[28] The cul-de-sac location of Sackets Harbour lacked the fresh breezes and cleansing currents of the Kingston Channel, and the effluent of thousands of men eventually took its toll. The previous September, William Ross, an army surgeon, had remarked that the bakery at Sackets was located "on a stagnant part of the lake and [because of] the numerous privies which surround it, ... the water thereabouts is impregnated with ... excrementious matter."[29] Ross later reported that the ground upon which new fortifications were constructed during the winter of 1814 held its own peril. Trench-diggers unearthed shallow graves, one of which held a box, buried after the May 1813 battle, labelled "British arms and legs." The surgeon warned that "from such incautious proceedings ... armies have been swept away."[30] Rather than being carried off by the fetid conditions under which they were forced to live, soldiers and seamen deserted at an alarming rate.

Like most of his peers, Master Commandant Crane wanted to leave the lake. He had asked Jones in November to return his crew and him to the frigate *John Adams*, which they had painstakingly prepared for sea the previous spring.[31] When Jones denied his request, however, Crane accepted the order and re-mained to superintend the defence of the squadron and to facilitate the work in the shipyard. The spread of illness and the shortage of officers had made his ef-forts difficult, but he made sure that the vessels were in order and ready to fight and that canals were cut in the ice around them. He also completed improve-ments to Fort Tompkins and the naval blockhouses and built a new battery on the edge of town, which he named Fort Chauncey.[32] Through the weeks of Chauncey's absence, Crane kept the healthy hands hard at work and reported them in fine spirits, establishing himself as one of the most competent officers to serve on Lake Ontario. Crane's abilities and devotion to duty so impressed the commodore that Chauncey appointed him "Captain of the Fleet '*pro tem*'" on 2 March.[33]

The sight of the two brigs and the frigate rising on the stocks also excited Chauncey's admiration for his master shipwright. Henry Eckford had worked his miracles again; though the brigs had been only six weeks on the ways, his men had completely planked and half caulked them, while the ship looked to be ready by early May.[34] The dimensions of the latter vessel had been increased so that it would be able to mount thirty-two 32-pdr. long guns on its gun deck and thirty 32-pdr. carronades on its spar deck, giving it the most powerful broadsides on the lake. This augmentation had been stimulated by the steady stream of information from deserters and from individuals retained to observe the enemy's winter works, who had divulged the size and weight of metal of the *Prince Regent* and *Princess Charlotte* and confirmed that the third ship at King-ston would be at least a seventy-four-gunner.[35] Faced with this raising of the ante in his contest with Yeo, Chauncey soon set Eckford's labourers to work cutting out the parts for a second frigate that would carry twenty-six 24-pdr. long guns and be built on the slipway of the first brig that swam.[36]

Chauncey intended to challenge Yeo for mastery of the lake, though it soon became evident that his objective was threatened by the long delay in making the commitment to improve his squadron. The British had been moving men and munitions since October and would be ready as soon as the lake cleared of ice, but as Chauncey's requisitions stacked up he worried that the transportation of essentials from New York had begun too late. The approaching dilemma was obvious to the commodore as he journeyed north, and he reported to Jones on 24 February: "The roads are dreadful, and if the present mild weather continues we shall experience difficulty in getting in our stores."[37]

Within ten days Chauncey learned that a shipment of heavy ordnance had sunk into the mud at Poughkeepsie and that the teamsters had abandoned it. He urgently sent out directions to his agents to wrestle the guns to landings on the Hudson, load them into sloops and get them up to Albany. From there he hoped they could be brought in sleighs as much of the rest of his supplies were, or be carried by scows up the Mohawk.[38] On 17 March the commodore instructed his transporters at Schenectady to hold the guns there as they arrived, but to send on carronades and anything else that could be hauled in sleighs from Utica and Rome. Chauncey expected to have to wait until the ice on the Mohawk River allowed transport of his long 24- and 32-pdrs. to Sackets by way of Oswego, but his impatience got the better of him. He continued to pester his representatives at Schenectady, advising them to do whatever was necessary to forward the ordnance and other stores, double-manning the boats, running cascades and offering bonuses for accelerated delivery.[39]

Besides the ponderous ordnance, Isaac Chauncey submitted indents for a dozen kedges and sixteen anchors, the largest of which weighed fifty-five hundredweight each. He ordered miles of rigging, thousands of shirts, trousers and shoes, nearly 300 bolts of canvas for sails and another 260 bolts of cheaper fabric for hammocks, and approved contracts with "furnaces" at Onondaga and Rome to cast shot of all types and tons of pig for ballast. Also itemized was a complete set of cabin furniture, from a full place setting for twelve, to a single soup ladle and a looking glass. Chauncey asked Navy Agent Bullus to multiply that particular indent by five to equip his new ships and, presumably, the *Sylph*. As March gave way to April, the pressure built with requisitions flying south and shipments crawling north.[40]

On 7 April 1814 the first of the two new brigs, named the *Jefferson*, was launched through a hole cut in the ice of the basin. With its twin, it had been sitting ready for ten days, and the commodore could not wait any longer for nature to melt the frozen cover. As fate would have it, a storm dumped fifteen inches of snow on Sackets Harbour that day and the next, but it had little effect on Eckford's riggers. They had the lower masts in within twenty-four hours and five days later the brig was ballasted and equipped with a makeshift battery of carronades and long guns. On 13 April the second brig, the *Jones*, slid down its ways into the basin, but there was no armament for it and no iron ballast to keep it properly upright, while the officers and seamen who would form its crew were still on the road north. The *Jones* sat impotently beside the wharf while the nearly-complete frigate, now named the *Superior*, towered in the stocks nearby. Eckford's shipwrights had already begun assembling the backbone and ribs of the second frigate, eventually known as the *Mohawk*, but the commodore did not know when or if he would be able to arm and man it.[41] "Figure to yourselves my situation," he wrote to his transport agents, trying to explain his predicament, "and then judge whether I have not cause for anxiety and almost for mental derangement."[42]

Adding to the commodore's trepidations was the threat of a British attack. Deserters and spies had warned of various schemes during the winter, and as the ice thinned in April the stories persisted.[43] Three thousand redcoats were said to be ready to embark at Kingston on 14 April, and, a week later, Sir James was said to be ready to employ his squadron for an attack, having learned that Chauncey had sailed for the Head of the Lake. By way of defence, the American navy could muster about 1,000 seamen and marines, while the army, headed by the recently arrived Brigadier General Edmund Gaines, numbered about 1,500 men of whom 800 or so were considered "effective." Chauncey asked Jones to persuade Secretary of War Armstrong to send reinforcements to the Harbour and at least 500 men to Oswego, through which his heavy ordnance would have to pass.[44]

The defence of Sackets Harbour might not have been a worry for Chauncey during his fretful April if it had been Armstrong's habit to issue instructions in a forthright and direct manner. In February Armstrong had ordered Jacob Brown to march his division of 2,000 men from the winter camp at French Mills to Sackets. They arrived on 16 February, whereupon Brown learned he had been promoted a major general and given command of the border from Sackets to Detroit. On the last day of the month Armstrong sent Brown a despatch with two sets of instructions: one recommended an attack with Chauncey across the ice to Kingston, "what I last year intended Pike should have done without aid;" and the other told him to march to Niagara and push the British back to Canada.[45] Armstrong's true priority was Kingston, and the second message was meant to be released as a ruse, but Brown, in consultation with Chauncey, missed Armstrong's meaning. They agreed that, because of the mild winter, no crossing of the St. Lawrence was secure, so Brown folded his tents and set off for Buffalo around 15 March to pursue Armstrong's optional objective. He was nearly there when another note from the secretary arrived.

The USS *Superior.* No image was made of Commodore Chauncey's largest frigate during its brief period of service. This view of the ship *in ordinary* (before it was sold for scrap in 1825) was based on information obtained by Benson Lossing for his book *The Pictorial Field-book of the War of 1812.*

This one sought an explanation for the departure from Sackets, but with his usual knack for ambiguity the secretary encouraged Brown to press on with his march and see what he could accomplish. Confused, the general, who had been joined by Brigadier General Winfield Scott, continued to Buffalo. In April, when Brigadier General Gaines informed him of a threatened British attack at Sackets, Brown left his army in Scott's hands and returned to the Harbour, remaining there until late in May.[46]

Throughout April 1814, Chauncey paced the floor, distressed by the unprepared state of his squadron. "I am at a loss to know," he wrote to Bullus on 10 April, "how I am to get the stores to this place for the Roads at this time are really impassable for empty waggons and the Oneida Lake is still froze – this harbor and Bay broke up yesterday and I should not be astonished if we had a visit from Sir James in the course of a few days."[47] Never a man to concede easily, Chauncey had his captains haul their vessels out of the basin and prepare them for service. He sent out Francis Gregory (still only an acting-lieutenant) in the *Lady of the Lake* with orders to patrol across the lake and back, looking for the enemy. To his trusted subordinate Melancthon Woolsey, Chauncey gave instructions to travel overland with thirty seamen to organize the transhipment of ordnance and other heavy gear to the Harbour.[48] Beyond these measures, all he could do was wait.

Raising the frames. Master ship designer Melbourne Smith walks along the keelson during reconstruction of the US Brig *Niagara* (similar in design to the brigs *Jefferson* and *Jones*) at Erie, Pennsylvania, in 1988. Most of the frames, called bends when fully assembled, have been fastened between the keelson and the keel and raised to their full height. Temporary timbers known as crosspales brace the frames above, to be replaced later by heavy beams underlying the upper and berthing decks. (Courtesy Flagship Niagara League, photo by Lynda Lee)

PART V

Conflicting Priorities

APRIL 1814 – DECEMBER 1814

A lady so gay, and a lover so bold,
Oft cruised in the maze of the fashion,
The lady was anxious her love to behold
And the youth to declare all his passion

[but] the maiden was coy and unsteady
The moment the knight came near hand,
And altho' she appear'd always ready
He ne'er could her presence command.

For under the lee of her guardian she sail'd
Who swore to the knight she ne'er should be wed,
And I trust that next year his aim will have fail'd
And the lady be plac'd on the knight's bridal bed.

KINGSTON GAZETTE, 15 JANUARY 1814

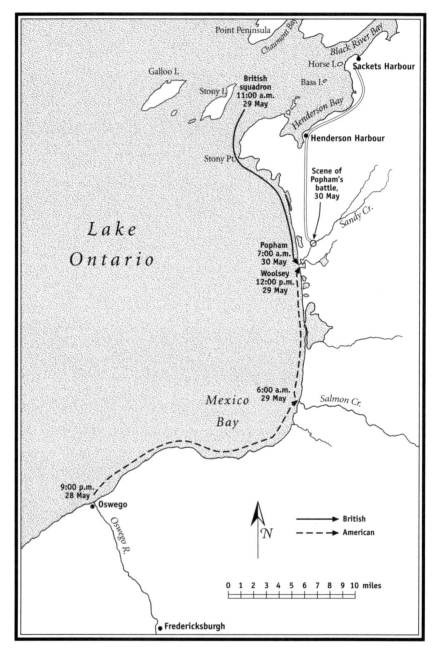

From Oswego to Sackets Harbour. The importance of Oswego as the key transhipment point on Lake Ontario for supplies from New York continued to be evident during 1814. The shoreline of Mexico Bay was the route taken by American convoys of boats headed for Sackets Harbour under cover of darkness, stopping at Salmon and Sandy Creeks to rest their crews during the day.

CHAPTER 16

"Wary Measures and Occasional Daring Enterprises"[1]

ACTIONS AT OSWEGO AND SANDY CREEK: APRIL – JUNE 1814

Commander Edward Collier's reinforcement from Halifax arrived at Kingston on 22 March 1814 to a rousing chorus of three cheers from Yeo's officers and seamen. Several days were allowed for the weary detachment to recuperate before being distributed among the ships and gunboats. Collier took command of the *Sir Sidney Smith*, while Lieutenant Kent became first lieutenant in Mulcaster's *Princess Charlotte*.[2]

The influx of new faces bringing news of the outside world to the naval establishment may have served to disrupt the otherwise tranquil situation at Kingston. As the winter faded, the seamen had become concerned about their rations, a matter that suddenly flared into a controversy shortly after the men from Halifax arrived. A week after Collier arrived a delegation of petty officers approached the commodore with their grievances, explaining that the men believed their rations had been cut when biscuit was substituted for bread and pork was provided after the supply of beef dried up. Yeo tried to explain to them that no reductions had been made, but he soon heard that a poll was being taken among the ranks "in a most unreserved manner" over support for a protest against the alleged grievance. Late on 30 March the commodore reported the "alarming spirit of discontent" raging among his men to Lieutenant General Gordon Drummond, who acted quickly to settle the dispute.[3] The next day he convened a board of inquiry and immediately issued a memo with its findings and his order to increase the daily ration of bread, or a substitute (flour or biscuit), and the weekly ration of pork when beef was not attainable.

Lieutenant Colonel James Malcolm, Royal Marines (1766-1849). Malcolm had seen action in the West Indies and Spain before being sent with the 2nd Battalion of Royal Marines to Halifax in 1812 for service with the Royal Navy fleet along the eastern seaboard. After a brief period with Yeo on Lake Ontario, Malcolm's battalion was ordered back to Halifax where it participated in the attack on Washington in August 1814. Following the war Malcolm was knighted for his extensive service. (Portrait courtesy of the Town Hall, Langholm, Dumfrieshire, Scotland)

Drummond's action apparently satisfied the seamen because they did not raise the issue again.

Yeo and Drummond could not afford any disturbance in their preparations to resume action as soon as the lake would allow. The *Prince Regent* and *Princess Charlotte* were ready for launching by the first week of April, their ballast and stores arranged in tidy piles by the main wharf, their guns and carriages lined up nearby and all their spars laid out in the yard, rigged and ready to install. The new gunboats *Nelly, Lais* and *Cleopatra* stood outfitted and waiting as were the vessels that had formed the squadron the year before, including the *Royal George*, which had been careened, and the schooner *Beresford*, which had been converted to a brig. The entire 2nd Marine Battalion, plus its rocket detachment, under the command of Lieutenant Colonel James Malcolm, would soon be on the march from Prescott to Kingston for employment on the squadron.[4]

Despite the success of their efforts, Yeo and Drummond were not certain that their winter building program had been adequate. Deserters and spies had provided them with information that, as of the first week of March, the Americans had "two of their new ships nearly ready to launch, and a third will be ready the 1st of May and a fourth by the end of that month."[5] The vessels, it was said, were to be outfitted with heavy ordnance, including 32-pdr. long guns and 42-pdr. carronades. Based on this type of sketchy information, Yeo tabulated the force he expected Chauncey would be able to muster and compared it to what he hoped to command. He assumed that Chauncey's brigs and his second frigate would be armed exclusively with long guns that would out-range him, as the *General Pike* had done the previous season, even with the addition of the two new Kingston frigates.[6] Yeo shared his views with Drummond and Prevost, submitting them also to the Admiralty and to Warren at Halifax, with a warning that without "immediate reinforcements … I cannot expect success against the enemy."[7] Drummond echoed the commodore's uncertainty, though with more optimism, as he explained to Prevost on 2 April: "It is impossible at present to ascertain to which side the naval superiority on the lake will preponderate, … [but] we have, in my opinion, as much right to look for its possession as the enemy."[8]

Prevost was not entirely convinced by Yeo's calculations. In the same way that he had responded to a similar comparison prepared by Yeo in February, Sir George questioned the likelihood of the Americans being able to increase their strength so dramatically after such a late start in their preparations. Ignoring Prevost's argument, Yeo complained to the Admiralty that Prevost believed an "officer should see His Enemy before he makes up his mind that he is to be beat by them."[9] On 13 April the British naval commander penned a long explanation to Prevost about Chauncey's new vessels, their strengths and weaknesses and his expectations about an engagement: "I shall be able either to bring Chauncey to a decisive action or should I find him too superior … manoeuvre with him until the Third Ship is ready."[10] Though later evidence would show that Yeo overestimated both the firepower of his opponent and his ability to be prepared by May, his fear of being out-ranged was well founded. Had Chauncey been able to put his improved squadron on the lake to confront the British during the first week of May, his broadsides would have been marginally stronger than Yeo's, even without his second frigate, the difference lying in the long-range power of the 32-pdr. guns slated for the lower deck of the first frigate.[11]

Concern over the narrow margin in potential strength between the naval forces heightened Yeo's resolve to give the third ship "a description to look down all opposition."[12] Master Shipwright William Bell had directed the laying of its 170-foot keel late in March, and the commodore and his senior officers soon agreed that the ship would carry thirty-two 32-pdr. long guns on its lower deck, thirty-four 24s on its middle deck and thirty-six 32-pdr. carronades on its flush spar deck.[13] Its broadsides would be as powerful as the Royal Navy's newest first rates but, built for the shallow waters of Lake Ontario, it would lack the deep hold and towering stern quarters of its saltwater cousins. All attention at Point Frederick now focused on the first rate; local contractors hauled quantities of pine, cedar, oak and elm to the dockyard and Commissioner Richard O'Conor dispatched his requisitions for guns, anchors, iron, rigging and sails to

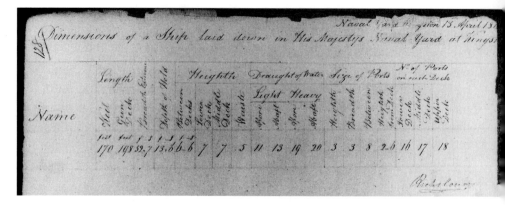

Dimensions for a first rate. By mid-April 1814 the dimensions of the new ship at Point Frederick had been confirmed and Commissioner O'Conor submitted this tabulation to Prevost. The configuration of the decks was later changed to have seventeen gunports per side on each deck. (Courtesy of the National Archives of Canada, C-107048)

Quebec and beyond.[14] Drummond had earlier suggested the forces needed a pair of "light and fast sailing vessels" to facilitate communication and transportation among the key posts on the lake.[15] Prevost had approved his proposal and passed an order to O'Conor to do the work, but as the needs of the three-decker predominated, only a single small schooner began to take shape in the shadow of the first rate as resources could be spared.

Two factors complicated the work at Point Frederick. The first was the proposal of an armistice between the combatants, which had originated during negotiations about prisoner exchanges. In April 1814 President Madison gave his representatives permission to discuss an armistice with the British, and Prevost queried his senior officers on their views. Drummond and Yeo both denounced such negotiations, the commodore asserting that any pause in hostilities would allow Chauncey more time to prepare his squadron. Others thought that an armistice was attainable, given the fact that peace negotiators would be meeting soon in Sweden, and it was even suggested that a cessation in hostilities would mean that a third deck would not be needed for the new ship at Kingston, at great savings to the public purse. With these possibilities in mind, and in spite of what Drummond and Yeo believed, Prevost sent an emissary to meet with the Americans, but the mission failed. Nevertheless the possibility of an armistice had influenced Prevost's thoughts on how the spring campaign should be pursued.[16]

About the same time that an armistice was debated, despatches reached Quebec announcing the home government's intention to send prefabricated warships to the lakes. Prevost's attitude to this idea had not changed since he had rejected it the previous spring, and he wasted no time in convening a board of officers to evaluate the plan and forwarded its findings to Yeo and Commander Daniel Pring at Isle-aux-Noix. The board declared the scheme impractical for several reasons: the ordnance and rigging for Yeo's third ship were, or would soon be, in transit, and their arrival would be delayed by the need to transport the components of four more vessels; there was not enough wood on hand to plank and deck the ships, nor could it be delivered in sufficient quantity before the winter of 1814-15; artificers would have to construct special barges to carry the large and unwieldy members of the hulls; and their carriage up the rapids beyond Montreal, which was always very difficult, would likely be harrassed by the Americans. Yeo agreed with the board's assessment and declared, "It does not take a moment's deliberation to most respectfully coincide with Your Excellency as to the almost impossibility of bringing up ships in frame."[17] Prevost packaged up the reports and letters and sent them off to England, where they arrived midway through the summer and two months after the first components of the prefabricated warships had been landed at Montreal.

On the afternoon of Thursday, 14 April 1814, everyone who could find his or her way there gathered at the Point Frederick dockyard and waited eagerly, despite a steady drizzle, for the launch of the new ships. At 5:30 p.m., wrote Lieutenant John Le Couteur of the 104th Foot,

> the blocks were knocked away and the pretty Frigate *Princess Charlotte* glided into the smooth fresh water, dashing the white foam before Her in her plunge. The gallant Mulcaster, her Captain, was launched with Her. Half an hour later, the *Regent*, a Noble Sixty-gun Frigate followed the *Princess*, as a Lover to guard his Belle. He, not *she*, went off beautifully, plunging in the calm waters then rode in Triumph a real Lord of the Lake.[18]

Within two weeks, provisioning, arming and rigging of the ships was complete and they took up moorings with the rest of the squadron and the new gunboats. Only the *Beresford* had ventured onto the lake by this time, having been sent to Niagara on the day of the double launch to deliver a company of the 103rd Foot, some ordnance and other stores.[19]

The despatches that had brought news of the government's intention to transport ships in frame to Canada also enclosed the Admiralty's orders for Commodore Yeo to revise the organization of his command. He chose the first day of May for the commencement of the new arrangement; on 30 April his purser closed the books of the original establishment, and the following morning the new establishment came into existence.[20]

Sir James Yeo, Commander-in-Chief of His Majesty's Ships and Vessels on the Lakes of Canada, now took up quarters in the spacious cabin of his new flagship, HMS *Prince Regent*, 58. Richard O'Conor paced the frigate's quarterdeck, promoted by Yeo to become captain of the powerful warship, which immediately qualified him to be "posted" to the all-important captains' seniority list. John Scott was first lieutenant, supported by the lately-advanced Lieutenants Charles Griffin, George Hugo and George Cosby Yeo, all of whom had come to the lake with the commodore as midshipmen. A short distance away floated HMS *Princess Charlotte*, 40, with Mulcaster in command. Next came the "old" squadron, all its vessels given new names so they would conform with the conventions of the Admiralty's list. The former *Wolfe*, now renamed HMS *Montreal*, 21, and HMS *Niagara* (the former *Royal George*), 21, were reclassified from sloops to sixth rates, causing their commanders, Francis Spilsbury and Stephen Popham respectively, to qualify for inclusion on the post captains list. Commander Alexander Dobbs kept the *Charwell* (former *Earl of Moira*), 13, and Commander Charles Anthony, who due to ill health had been replaced in the gunboats by newly-promoted Commander Charles Cunliffe Owen, moved into the *Star* (former *Lord Melville*), 14; with commanders on their quarterdecks, the brigs now became classed as brig-sloops. Lieutenant Charles Radcliffe had the *Netley* (former *Beresford*), 9, and Commander Collier remained in the *Magnet* (former *Sir Sidney Smith*), 11, also classed as a sloop. Each vessel now formed a separate establishment with its own purser or clerk to keep track of its complex records in consultation with the captain, but this change did not guarantee universal improvements. Yeo later explained to the Admiralty that he lacked enough commissioned and petty officers to fill the positions prescribed by the new organization and that there were not sufficient, dependable artificers in the dockyard for him to administer it according to regulations. He also lobbied the Admiralty on behalf of his seamen who he believed deserved an increase to their normal pay because of the many privations they had to suffer on the remote shores of Lake Ontario.[21]

On 1 May 1814 the new squadron sat ready for action. It possessed a strength that far exceeded the weight of metal Yeo had employed in the previous season. Now his long guns could throw a long-range, single-shotted broadside of 795 pounds as opposed to the weaker 201 pounds of September 1813; the total broadside weight, with carronades, exceeded 2,800 pounds. His complement had nearly doubled with the arrival of Popham and Collier's men, and the addition of Malcolm's marines would greatly enhance his chances of success if he

Captain Francis Brockell Spilsbury (1784-1830), RN. At the age of twelve Spilsbury went to sea with his father (Francis, Sr.), a surgeon in the Royal Navy who arrived at Kingston with Downie's detachment in June 1814. The reclassification of HMS *Montreal* (neé *Wolfe*) as a sixth-rate on the Admiralty list meant that Spilsbury, its commander, was automatically advanced to the rank of post captain as he is shown in this portrait. (Courtesy of the Massey Library, Royal Military College of Canada, Kingston)

ran his ships alongside the Americans. All that remained was to map out what this impressive new squadron was to do.

Early in March the British began to develop plans for specific operations in the 1814 campaign. Yeo wanted to beat his opponent in a proper engagement, although if it looked that Chauncey held too much of an upper hand, he intended to play "cat and mouse" with him around the lake until his powerful first rate was launched. A naval action was not Lieutenant General Drummond's first priority, since he felt that an effort should be made to bring relief to Major General Riall's army, which had spent a difficult winter on the Niagara Peninsula. He expressed his wishes to the commodore on 9 April, asking him to deliver the 103rd Foot to the Head of the Lake and provisions, stores and ordnance to Forts George and Niagara. Drummond then recommended that the squadron make a cruise along the southern shore, inspecting creeks and rivers for American coastal traffic, especially near Oswego, before conducting a careful reconnaissance of Sackets Harbour.[22] Sir James and the general met to share their views and settled on Chauncey's naval base as their prime objective. Based on the notion that the American squadron would not be able to operate as early as Yeo could, the two senior officers drew up a plan that would see the squadron carry 4,000 soldiers and artillery, including a pair of 24-pdr. brass field guns, to Sackets to execute a massive attack on the American base. Some delay would result from bringing the brass guns and various detachments down the lake from Niagara and in having the 800 men needed to make a forced march from Montreal. During that interval they could embark a smaller force in the squadron for an attack on the vast depots said to have been accumulated at Oswego.[23]

Drummond and Yeo sent this plan to Prevost at Montreal on 13 April. Ten days later Sir George transmitted a "confidential" note to Drummond describing a combined operation of another sort against Sackets Harbour. He agreed with his senior officers that a pre-emptive strike against the naval base was the best way to achieve mastery on the lake because if Chauncey was allowed to complete his ships in peace, he could soon gain control of the water, hampering British operations on land. To this end, Prevost submitted an alternate proposal for Drummond's consideration, involving an attack by land some time after Yeo imposed a "a strict blockade."[24] Prevost credited Major General Francis De Rottenburg and informed agents for the details behind his scheme.

At Kingston the senior officers debated and rejected Prevost's ideas and resubmitted their original plan, in detail, but Sir George was not convinced and replied on 30 April that he did not want to detach troops from Lower Canada for fear of leaving that province vulnerable. Furthermore, he reminded Drummond that the home government had supported a cautious approach to fighting the war, never "exposing too much at one stake … and from that policy I am not disposed to depart."[25] As an extra reason, he offered the possibility that peace talks were about to commence and any rash movement by the army and navy might derail them. Finally, the commander-in-chief underscored his position by stating that Drummond and Yeo should not initiate any large-scale offensive without his approval, although he was not opposed to the pursuit of an objective of lesser proportions.

Unwilling to give up an operation that seemed vital and absolutely practical, Drummond presented his case to Prevost yet a third time on 3 May, enclosing the latest intelligence from Sackets. As it looked as if Chauncey's second frigate would be launched in six weeks, he argued, time was of the essence and a reinforcement of 800 men from Quebec was essential to the operation. "The only way to completely secure the Upper Province," he continued, "is a vigorous combined attack of army and navy against the enemy's chief means of annoyance, their fleet and stores at Sackett's Harbor."[26] The general also announced that he was going ahead with the first part of the plan Yeo and he had devised by embarking 900 troops in the squadron to pay a visit to Oswego. The squadron was ready, and it was time to take the war to the Americans.

At 4:00 a.m. on Tuesday, 4 May 1814, the British squadron weighed anchor and let fall its great sheets of canvas.[27] About 900 seamen, supplemented by 400 marines, put their backs into the task of getting the four ships, two brigs and two schooners in motion while 550 soldiers crowded the warships' decks, and bateaux and gunboats were towed in their wakes. Commodore Yeo ordered a thunderous salute fired as his ships cleared the harbour; at noon the guns sounded again as the crews drilled at their quarters. Toward evening the wind rose out of the southwest, threatening a gale, and the commodore laid a course for the lee of the False Ducks, where he anchored as darkness fell. At 2:00 a.m. the following morning the squadron resumed its journey, gliding southward before a light westerly, with studding sails set.

At first light on 5 May, lookouts on the ramparts of the fort at Oswego sighted the British and passed the word quickly to Melancthon Woolsey and Lieutenant Colonel George Mitchell, Third U.S. Artillery Regiment, who hurried to see for themselves what the new day was bringing. This situation was a difficult one since their duty was to protect the naval stores that had been accumulated at the port, but their defensive force was small and their tactical position weak.

Mitchell commanded 290 men.[28] He had been with a part of Major General Brown's army at Batavia when ordered to assemble four companies from his regiment and one company of the Light Artillery Regiment and march to Oswego to form a guard for the naval stores at that place. This detachment arrived at the mouth of the Oswego River on 30 April and took up quarters in the fortification atop the hill on the eastern shore of the bay. When built by the British nearly half a century before, the site had been formidable, with high earthen ramparts and a deep fosse on three sides of a spacious square, but its exterior pickets and gates had long since disappeared and only a low embrasure protected the rear of the fort. A handful of barracks and other low buildings still stood within the compound, while five small-calibre guns were on hand, all of them lacking proper carriages and three of them without trunnions. Mitchell's gunners had constructed carriages and platforms for the ordnance, installing three to face the lake and the others toward the long glacis that stretched to a landing place east of the fort. They had also replaced some of the picketing skirting the fort. When the British hove into view, Mitchell decided to keep his men out of sight until the intentions of the enemy could be determined, although he delegated one of his companies to be ready to man the guns, while the rest would act as infantry. He also gave instructions for tents to be pitched on the village side of the bay near an empty battery on the shore to suggest that it had guns and that a larger detachment was present.

Commandant Woolsey had only Lieutenant George Pearce and twenty-five seamen in his detachment, which had been waiting since late April for the arrival of naval supplies.[29] So far they had collected a shipment of seven guns, a large cable and sundry shot and sent it on successfully to Sackets and were just loading a second delivery, including a dozen or so guns with their accoutrements

Yeo inspects the landing of troops at Oswego, 6 May 1814. The pendant on the bow of this boat is a smaller version of the broad pendant flying from the mainmast of the flagship *Prince Regent*, which suggests that this boat is conveying Commodore Yeo as he uses his telescope to inspect preparations for the landing at Oswego. A midshipman in the stern appears to be signalling the squadron. The ships are (left to right) the *Montreal* or *Niagara*, the *Magnet* and *Princess Charlotte*. (Detail from a drawing by Captain William Steele, Royal Marines, courtesy of the Toronto Reference Library, T-15225)

and about seventy coils of rigging with blocks, into several schooners and bateaux. Also stacked in the Oswego storehouses were more than 1,000 barrels of food, apparently belonging to the army, while another cache of naval materiel was being assembled above the lower cataract that interrupted navigation of the Oswego River twelve miles from the lake at the hamlet of Fredericksburgh. When the British appeared, Woolsey ordered some of the guns and shot thrown into the river immediately and arranged for the schooners, one of which was the *Growler*, captured and lost by Yeo the previous year, to be scuttled if the need arose.

Woolsey and Mitchell decided to make the best stand they could, but acknowledged that, if threatened with capture, they would retreat to Fredericksburgh. Together they watched the enemy squadron make its slow advance all morning, then take a position beyond artillery range, backing its sails and hauling the boats around to receive troops.

Aboard the *Regent*, plans had been carefully prepared for the expedition. Although Drummond and Yeo commanded the overall operation, Captains O'Conor and Mulcaster and Lieutenant Colonel Victor Fischer, of De Watteville's Regiment, each commanded parts of the operation. O'Conor's task was to marshall the boats that would carry the infantry ashore. Mulcaster was to lead a party of 200 seamen to assault the fort from the western flank while Fischer was at the head of the main force landed by O'Conor's boats to attack up the glacis east of the fort. This detachment included 400 Royal Marines, 100 De Wattevilles and about fifty Glengarries; the balance of the troops were to remain on the ships as a reserve.

Before the attack went in, it was decided that the enemy's strength should be probed. For this purpose, the heavy gunboats and the sloops cruised close to shore to draw fire (the schooner *Netley* appears to have left the squadron at this time, bound for Niagara). Commander Collier commanded the gunboats and earned himself a mention in despatches for so effectively testing the American position. Mitchell satisfied the purpose of the British advance by ordering his gunners into action, but one of his guns soon burst, leaving him with a 4-pdr. and a 9-pdr. facing the lake and two 4-pdrs. protecting the eastern flank. Nevertheless, they made their mark by holing one of Collier's gunboats seriously enough for the British to abandon it before they slipped back to the flagship after 4:00 p. m.

The infantry and marines now climbed down into their boats, but their debarkation was soon stopped as a northeast wind swept mountains of dark clouds toward the fleet, threatening bad weather. The abrupt change in the weather provoked alarm on the overcrowded ships; on the *Prince Regent*, Lieutenant Joseph Mermet of De Watteville's later described the scene: "At 6 o'clock, we dine, confused noise, screams, whistle blows, a thousand god dams, all hands, all Royal Marines, upon deck, god damn! all foreigners below: god damn! out and run; be quick! be quick!"[30] Unwilling to leave his squadron so close to a lee shore, Yeo advised Drummond that they must seek a seaway, and so the warships, under close-reefed topsails, drew away from the land in such a hurry that some of the small craft were left behind. Later the townspeople went to confiscate them, as they did the half-sunk gunboat.

It was all reminiscent of the attack on Sackets Harbour the previous May, but this time no reinforcements joined the American garrison, which numbered less than a quarter of the force that had opposed Yeo and Prevost at that place, and the weather soon changed, permitting Yeo's ships to return inshore so that they could cover the landing. By midnight the squadron had worn around toward Oswego, and two hours later O'Conor began loading the landing craft with soldiers from every vessel except the *Charlotte* and the *Magnet*, where the reserves remained. The *Montreal* and *Niagara* crept through the darkness toward the land until they were well within a thousand yards of the fort, whereupon, at 6:00 a.m. they opened fire with their guns, hoping to enfilade Mitchell's lakeside battery. Close behind came the *Magnet*, firing its guns, and possibly some of the Royal Marine rockets, at the town and Mitchell's false encampment, where enemy troops had been seen in motion. Around 9:00 a.m. Mulcaster eased the *Charlotte* to an anchorage at long shot range before making his final preparations for leading the naval party ashore.

The ferocity of the naval bombardment chased the American militia away to safety, but Mitchell's two meagre batteries kept up a steady fire while he held his infantry in safety behind the thick walls of the fort. Under Captain Stephen Popham's watchful eye, the *Niagara* crept within close range of the fort, "not much beyond musket shot," claimed Lieutenant Rufus McIntire of the Third Artillery.[31] This was due to the skill of its pilot, lately promoted to master in the Royal Navy, James Richardson. "Not without some degree of diffidence did I perform the task," he admitted, "for not since I was a lad had I been there, and then only in small vessels, with very light draught of water."[32] The *Niagaras* anchored their ship and pounded the Americans with their broadside of nine 32-pdr. carronades and single 24- and 18-pdr. guns. Using a shot oven to heat their shot until they were nearly red hot, Mitchell's gunners returned the British fire in kind, if not in weight of metal, and succeeded in setting fire to the *Niagara* three times. Popham burned his hand seriously while helping to extinguish one blaze, while Master Richardson gave up more than his hand. In reaching out to pick up something, he suddenly realized that one of the enemy shot had "made so free with me as to carry off my left arm just below my shoulder, which rendered amputation at the shoulder joint necessary."[33] Crew members carried him below, where the surgeon quickly performed the operation, saving Richardson's life.

The final preparations for landing the troops were so slow that the *Star* and the *Charwell* did not begin to escort the bateaux and gunboats toward the beach until noon, firing their long guns as they approached to hold the enemy back. By that time some of the marines and infantrymen had been in the small craft for ten hours. There was yet time for them to think about the impending battle because another hour passed before the *Charlotte's* starboard battery of twelve long 24s commenced its bombardment of the fort.

Mitchell and Woolsey watched this second ominous approach, probably praying that a gale or some such tempest would arise to sink Yeo. Without further help from the elements, however, the defenders had to rely on their own efforts. The two guns in front of the fort had been engaged with the British through the morning, the officer in charge of the 4-pdr. ordering his gun carried outside the rampart so that he could get a clearer shot at his foe. Thinking

The British attack at Oswego, 6 May 1814. Lieutenant John Hewett of the Royal Marines drew this depiction of the British fleet as the troops went ashore under protection of the smaller vessels and the frigates anchored in deep water. Of special note are Mulcaster's party landing to the right of the fort and the details in the rig and design of the British vessels, (left to right) *Prince Regent, Star, Princess Charlotte, Charwell, Niagara, Montreal* and *Magnet*. (Engraved from a drawing by Hewett, courtesy of the National Archives of Canada, C-794)

that the British meant to land on the village side, Mitchell sent one of his companies across the river to support 200 militia who had just arrived. When he realized the attack would actually come up the glacis, he recalled those men and deployed them with another company in a line part way down the glacis where they were exposed to salvoes of grapeshot from the advancing brigs. A third company took up its place in the woods behind the expected landing point, about one third of a mile east of the fort. The gunners at the remaining 4-pdrs. did their best to support their comrades.

The British boats grounded in the shallows quite a distance from the shore just before 2:00 p.m. To set an example for their men, the officers stepped over the gunwales first and most immediately sank nearly out of sight; "Mermet's ears served him like fins," recalled the lieutenant of his plunge into the cold water.[34] The lakeshore became a mass of sodden, red-coated Royal Marines and De Wattevilles and green-jacketed Glengarries struggling ashore, streaming with water, shaking themselves, and checking their cartridge boxes to determine how much of their ammunition was ruined. "The cartridge boxes were full of water," wrote Mermet, "never mind, we have bayonets."[35] The Americans greeted them with well-aimed volleys from the woods and the glacis so Lieutenant Colonel Fischer ordered the Glengarries to clear the enemy from the forest, which they accomplished in short order. Yeo and Drummond came ashore about this time to participate in the adventure, while on the other side of the fort Mulcaster's men were making their landing and preparing to charge up the steeper incline to storm the main battery.

Mitchell now called his companies back to take up a position in the eastern fosse of the fort where Lieutenant Pearce joined them with the naval party. They fired down upon the British line, which was forming for an attack. The Glengarries were in the bush, the marines arranged in rank and file perpendicular to the lake with the De Wattevilles between them and the trees. Fischer gave the order to advance, and the whole force made a fast-step charge up the hill. Their dunking in the cold lake while coming ashore had rendered the British ammunition so undependable that no firing was possible, and while the Americans continued to pour a hail of fire down upon their adversaries, the redcoats strode forward, bayonets fixed. They fell by the dozens. Captain William Holtaway and six fellow marines were killed outright, while thirty-three others suffered wounds. The De Wattevilles lost eight men, with twenty wounded, among whom was Lieutenant Victor May, one of their favourite officers; more fortunate were the Glengarry Fencibles, who had only nine wounded. Moving forward with the troops, Commodore Yeo almost gave up his command as a musket ball pierced his cocked hat and another clipped one of his heels. Only the unceasing long-range bombardment from the gunboats, sloops and ships covered the silent British advance up the glacis.

On the opposite side of the fort Mulcaster's seamen landed and hurried up toward their objective. Armed with cutlasses and pikes, they sought to swarm over Mitchell's gunners, who defended themselves with muskets. Leading the charge, Mulcaster watched one of the figures take careful aim and pull the trigger, but the captain was unable to move quickly enough to avoid the ball, which sliced through his leg and sent him sprawling on the ground. John Scott, Yeo's faithful lieutenant, assumed the command and led the seamen up and into the battery under heavy fire.

On the eastern side the British line faltered, and the Americans took heart, but covered by a rise in the slope, a wave of marines surged forward to the northeast corner of the fosse, mounted the rampart and ran down into the fort while at the same time the sailors beat their way into the main battery. Realizing that further resistance was futile, Mitchell ordered a retreat.

Aftermath of the battle at Oswego, 6 May 1814. The ground around the fort at Oswego is strewn with the casualties of the battle as the British storm over the ramparts just before Lieutenant John Hewett of the Royal Marines scaled the flag pole. Note the two British gunboats in the foreground with long guns in their bows and carronades in their sterns. (Engraved from a drawing by Hewett, courtesy of the Toronto Reference Library, T-15228)

Barely half an hour after they came ashore, Royal Marine Lieutenant John Hewett and a burly sergeant were in the van of the raiders as they fought their way toward the lofty flag pole in the centre of the fort. Hewett leapt up to the foot rests and scaled the pole, drawing the fire of insulted Americans who succeeded in hitting him several times. Unfazed, Hewett tore the massive Stars and Stripes flag from the nails that held it aloft and it fluttered to the ground to the cheers and huzzahs of his comrades. The Americans disappeared into the forest, virtually unharassed by musket fire, dragging whatever wounded could scramble to their feet. By that time, Woolsey's party had scuttled the last of the boats and joined the retreat toward Fredericksburgh.

The British secured the perimeter around the fort and village, the reserve being conveyed to shore to help with the task. The wounded were tended to and taken to the squadron, as were the dead. An American officer and more than twenty rank and file were found dead on the field and buried, while another twenty-five or so uninjured prisoners were transported to the warships (Lieutenant Colonel Mitchell later reported six killed, thirty-eight wounded and twenty-five captured). The Royal Marines and other units that had been engaged in the fighting retired to a field south of the fort to recover from their exertions, where they scrounged up food, drink and cigars and established an impromptu bivouac. Drummond and Yeo joined the men to congratulate them on their success.

Sir James may have put on a smile for the rank and file, but at least part of his mind was preoccupied with depressing news. He had been to see his friend Mulcaster, who had been carried to the guard house within the fort and laid upon a wooden bed. Surgeon Francis Carlisle, one of the few former Provincial Marine officers still employed in the squadron, examined Mulcaster's wound and discovered that the ball had passed right through the captain's upper leg, just missing his groin muscle, but too high up to allow amputation. Mulcaster had bled heavily and was suffering from intense spasms of pain. He managed to ask Carlisle, "Well, doctor, what do you think?"

"Sir, I fear it is a most severe wound," the surgeon answered.

"Do you think it mortal?" inquired Mulcaster. "You may without hesitation tell me, for I am prepared for the worst."

"Then, Sir, I am sorry to say *it is.*"

"How long do you suppose I shall have to live."

"About two hours."

"Then make haste," groaned Mulcaster, "give me a sheet of paper and let me write a letter." One of Drummond's aides, Captain William Jervoise, stepped forward to offer his back as a desk, and the captain managed, between paroxysms of pain, to write a letter to his mother, bidding her adieu and entreating her to take care of his fiancée, Sophia Sawyer, to whom he had become betrothed before leaving for Canada.[36]

His friend's plight might have been on Yeo's mind when he encountered Alvin Bronson, one of Chauncey's key contractors, in the village. The removal of captured goods had begun and it appears that some of the navy's boats had gone aground on the river's bar soYeo demanded that Bronson find pilots who knew how to navigate the channel, but the merchant refused. "Go yourself," retorted the commodore angrily, "and if you get the boat aground, I'll shoot you." Lieutenant Colonel John Harvey intervened to inform Yeo that Bronson, being a local businessman, might have particular information about the navy's depots, whereupon Sir James demanded that Bronson reveal anything pertinent that he knew. Again the American declined, and Yeo ordered him seized and taken to the flagship; for his obstinacy, Alvin Bronson earned himself a month of detention in the British squadron.[37]

Through the afternoon and evening and into the darkness of 6 May, the British hauled their captured goods to the warships. Tallies varied as to the amount of booty taken, but at least three 32-pdr. and four 24-pdr. long guns and more than 300 shot of all descriptions and calibres were seized.[38] Some of this ordnance came from the submerged schooners *Growler* and *Penelope* and boats that had been scuttled, but were refloated by the British and added to the profits. Another vessel, the *Henrietta*, escaped capture as did at least eight pieces of ordnance, which had been dumped into the river. Besides rigging and miscellaneous naval gear, the British also took between 1,100 and 2,400 barrels of bread, salt, pork and flour, most of it apparently intended for the soldiers at the Harbour.

While the last of the troops and seamen re-embarked (along with the most seriously wounded, including the resilient Captain Mulcaster), the landing force set fire to the buildings within the fort and the public storehouses in the village. Yeo's ships upped anchor around 4:00 a.m. on 7 May, setting a course for Kingston. The officers' next responsibility was to prepare their reports of the action, which they universally evaluated as a "compleat success."[39] Drummond emphasized the "gallant cool, and judicious conduct" of Lieutenant Colonel Victor Fischer, who lauded the Royal Marines and the way in which they "formed their Column in the most regular manner, and by their steady and rapid advance, carried the fort."[40] Yeo described "the Forts and Town of Oswego" as "the most formidable I have seen in Upper Canada."[41] He praised Lieutenant Colonel James Malcolm of the marines, O'Conor, Popham and other naval officers and lamented the wounds suffered by Mulcaster and Richardson. Drummond had shown him "the support and attention which never fail in securing perfect cordiality between the two Services."[42] Everyone took notice of the good conduct of the troops during and after the battle when they ignored the temptations of drunkenness and desertion that the enemy territory held out to them.

Everyone at Kingston had heard the roll of gunfire with some trepidation, but fear dissipated when the squadron arrived in the Kingston Channel early on 8 May. "It was a proud sight to see the nobel [sic] ship [*Prince Regent*] entering the harbour with the American below the Broad pendant, signalling Victory," wrote John Le Couteur.[43] The glorious news of the victory soon came ashore, but along with it came the casualties. "On Sunday we buried poor Holtaway," noted Le Couteur, adding later, "The Flower of De Watteville's Regiment, De May, died this morn."[44] Most of the wounded, including William Mulcaster, survived their brush with death, yet they were evidence of the cost of the assault on Oswego. Backed by tons of naval ordnance, 650 men had gone ashore to subdue a garrison holding only four, small, serviceable guns and 300 effectives. The cost of that victory was ninety casualties in return for fewer than a dozen pieces of ordnance, some small schooners and rigging, and a large quantity of provisions. Such results did little to support Drummond and Yeo's proposal for a full-scale attack on Sackets Harbour, a place that was far better fortified than it had been when Prevost and Yeo visited there the previous May. It now bristled with ordnance distributed among well-built batteries, manned by more than a thousand regulars, not to mention the increased strength of Chauncey's ships and their crews. The scheme was doomed anyway because before Drummond and Yeo returned from Oswego Prevost had reiterated his reluctance to transfer 800 troops from the lower province to make up the 4,000 needed for the Sackets expedition.[45] No further mention was made of the idea, except for an insinuating comment from Drummond in a despatch to Lord Bathurst. The raid on Oswego, he explained early in July, had come about because, when he presented his ideas ("which I did not think in the least chimerical") to Prevost, he had been turned down. Drummond added, "I turned my thoughts to the destruction of the depot at Fort Oswego, by which the American fleet had been retarded beyond measure."[46]

Just as Yeo had exaggerated the strength of the "Forts and Town of Oswego," Drummond also overstated the impact of the raid. After the American forces withdrew, Master Commandant Woolsey and Lieutenant Colonel Mitchell assembled their men at Fredericksburgh and waited for the British to march the twelve miles up river to seize the goods collected there, expecting that Drummond and Yeo also meant to advance a further dozen miles to plunder the richer depot at Three River Point, but such was not to be the case. Instead, a lonely British deserter, Quartermaster John Miller, one of Popham's men, gave himself up and revealed everything he knew about the squadron and its operations. Within a day of the battle a reinforcement of dragoons and riflemen sent from Sackets by Chauncey and Brown arrived at Fredericksburgh. The commodore and general praised their subordinates for the resistance they had displayed at Oswego; Brown extolled Mitchell's "*steady discipline*, and gallant conduct," while Chauncey professed that "the gallant band that defended Oswego deserve immortality."[47] In somewhat of a lather over the loss of his guns, however, Chauncey could not help but point out to his ever-dependable subordinate, Woolsey, that the delay in the attack during the night of 5 May had provided him with more than enough time to ferry all the naval goods up the river to Fredericksburgh. That, and the army's failure to burn its stores of food, were the only two lapses in the gallant defence of Oswego.

With the British controlling the lake, Chauncey decided to alter his plans.[48] He ordered Woolsey to collect at Three River Point all the 24- and 32-pdr. long guns and large-dimension rigging that the rivermen delivered, but to send the boats back to North Bay on Lake Oneida or to Rome with all other materials, carronades included. From those places 200 teams were soon carting the most ponderous equipment and stores over the muddy roads to Sackets. In the meantime, he ordered Woolsey and his seamen down to Oswego to raise any sunken ordnance and equipment they could find and remove them to Fredericksburgh, where he was to keep them in boats, ready to run the falls at a moment's notice when the coast was clear enough for another shipment to be made to Sackets.

The American base was now a frenzy of activity. The United States Ship *Superior* had been launched on 1 May, and the men and materiel needed to sail it and the new brigs were rolling into town in an endless train.[49] Master Commandant Charles Ridgely arrived with the officers and crews of the *Ontario* and *Erie*; with them came Lieutenant Wolcott Chauncey, who immediately found his circumstances unbearable and obtained a transfer to Lake Erie. Commandant Jesse Elliott and Edward Trenchard returned for second tours of duty with the commodore and independent commands in the squadron. The men from the US Frigate *Macedonian*, numbering more than 250, also reached the Harbour in several separate detachments, led by their captain, Jacob Jones. Since he was senior to William Crane, Chauncey was obliged to appoint Jones captain of the squadron, but not before publicly recognizing Crane's "zeal and ability."[50]

Sackets Harbour was on alert for a surprise attack from the British. Just before the assault on Oswego, there had been an attempt by a single boatload of Royal Navy men to carry a bomb into the Harbour and lay it beneath the *Superior*. Chauncey later heard from the deserter, John Miller, that two similar missions had been tried, one of which involved rocketeers in a specially outfitted ship's boat.[51] Guard boats patrolled the outlying waters of Black River Bay, while the *Lady of the Lake* ventured farther afield. On 19 May the schooner came racing into the Harbour, pursued by the British squadron, which then took up an anchorage off Stony Island to observe activity in the shipyard while choking off communication with Oswego by water. "This is the first time," Chauncey wrote with regret to Secretary William Jones, "that I have experienced the mortification of a Blockade since I have been on the Lake."[52]

After landing the ordnance and other goods captured at Oswego, Yeo sailed from Kingston on 11 May.[53] During the next week he had cruised along the south shore of the lake, searching for signs of war materiel in transit. Twice the squadron approached Oswego, but seeing no activity veered away. Boats went in to examine the villages of Charlotte and Pultneyville, where the militia greeted them with such intense fire that the British abandoned attempts to land and returned to the squadron. A couple of days were spent near the Ducks until the *Lady of the Lake* was spotted and chased, and Yeo decided to take up a position to watch over his adversary. As the *Regent, Charlotte* (now commanded by Edward Collier in Mulcaster's place), *Montreal* and *Niagara* maintained station off Stony Island, the smaller vessels came and went, some carrying troops to Burlington and Niagara, others patrolling for enemy traffic. Sir James took ill during this period with an undisclosed malady. Only a few passing references were ever made to his poor health, which seems to have lingered into July and may have been a reoccurrence of the fevers he had contracted during his tours of duty in the West Indies.

Drummond was with the squadron after the imposition of the blockade, but Yeo was too sick to accompany him on 25 May when Drummond went inshore in a gig, covered by a gunboat, to view Sackets Harbour at close hand. The British conducted similar inspections all along the American coast, and it was one of these that was soon to present Yeo with a frustrating setback.

With the British squadron breathing down his neck, Isaac Chauncey kept writing fretful instructions for Woolsey about loading the heavy ordnance into boats above the falls and being ready to depart at a moment's notice. He was to send the boats in divisions down the coast in stages, stopping the first night at Salmon Creek and the second at Sandy Creek. Six men from the First Rifle Regiment were to guard each boat, and, at Woolsey's suggestion, Oneida Indians agreed to act as escorts on shore. To confuse the enemy, Chauncey wanted Woolsey to spread rumours of his intention to return all the long guns to Lake Oneida.

On 26 May the commodore mistakenly perceived the British squadron to be leaving its anchorage and quickly worded a message to Woolsey to start a division of boats on its way. He negated that command the next day, but, given the time lost in delivering these messages, it did not arrive in time to stop the movement.[54] Early on 28 May, Woolsey dispatched Sailing Master Samuel Dixon down the coast to watch out for the British while he and his men ran nineteen boats over the cascade at Fredericksburgh and on to Oswego. The convoy was transporting twenty-one 32-pdr. long guns and ten 24-pdr. long guns, plus three 42-pdr. carronades, ten large cables and a variety of other materials. For protection, Woolsey arranged with Major Daniel Appling to have 130 of his regular riflemen in the boats, while 150 Oneida warriors were to meet them along the way. At nightfall the flotilla left the Oswego River, reaching Salmon Creek shortly after sunrise, where it intended to take cover for the day. Unfortunately, one of the boats was missing, and, apprehensive that the British would find it and come looking for the rest, Woolsey pushed his flotilla on to Sandy Creek, passing two miles up its winding course to a landing near a road that ran the twelve miles into Sackets Harbour. Arriving at that point around noon on 29 May, Woolsey scribbled a note to Chauncey and gave it to an express rider to take to the commodore.[55]

At 7:00 a.m. on 29 May, lookouts on the *Regent* sighted the wayward boat, and the British soon captured it. Easily intimidated by the stern-faced Royal Navy officers and the hundreds of gawking seamen, the boatmen quickly revealed their mission and that they had become separated from a much larger flotilla with a strong escort. Yeo decided to intercept the American flotilla, and at 11:00 a.m. Stephen Popham left the squadron with two gunboats and three cutters manned by 160 seamen and marines intent on hunting down Woolsey's convoy. Apparently as an afterthought, Captain Spilsbury followed eight hours later in two heavily-manned ship's boats, one of which was the commodore's remaining Deal-built gig.

Melancthon Woolsey's messenger reached Sackets Harbour before the end of the day. Chauncey asked Brigadier General Edward Gaines for assistance, and a troop of dragoons with a couple of artillery pieces soon headed west along the road to Sandy Creek.[56] The next morning Captain Richard Smith of the U.S. Marines marched out with 100 officers and men, followed later by Commandant Charles Ridgely and a party of seamen. At the landing Woolsey received an acknowledgement from the commodore at 2:00 a.m. on 30 May just as a heavy rainstorm deluged the vicinity. A short time afterward he instructed Lieutenant George Pearce to scout along the lakeside in a boat with Dixon to see if the British were snooping around. As the clouds were beginning to lighten with the new day, Pearce's boat returned with news that a flotilla of heavy boats had been sighted making its way for the creek. Woolsey conferred with Appling about preparing a reception for the British. They deployed the seamen, boat handlers, riflemen and Oneidas on both sides of the creek about half a mile below the landing. At nine o'clock the dragoons and the artillery arrived from Sackets in time to take up positions.

Spilsbury had caught up with Popham during the night. They had sighted Pearce's boat and given chase, pausing at the mouth of Sandy Creek only long enough to debate whether or not to go any further. Commodore Yeo later claimed to have warned Popham about going up narrow, unfamiliar waterways, citing the unpleasant experience that Lieutenant John Scott had suffered the previous July at Cranberry Creek on the St. Lawrence River. Despite this warning, Popham favoured a pursuit, and assuming overall responsibility for the expedition, led the way up the waterway in his gunboat.

The creek followed a looping path through a swamp that eventually mingled with dry land and trees. The British moved upstream, firing the gunboat

Rocket boat. With the addition of the rocket unit of Royal Marines to his squadron, Commodore Yeo hoped to create chaos in the American shipyard by launching a rocket attack from his blockading squadron. The loss of seven boats and more than 200 men at Sandy Creek forced him to cancel such plans as he could no longer spare boats for that specialized use. (Courtesy of the Museum Restoration Service)

carronades into the undergrowth as they went. Around 10:00 a.m., after rounding a bend, they caught sight of the masts of the eighteen bateaux standing half a mile away beyond a stretch of bullrushes and scrub. Popham ordered a halt, then deployed the marine detachment on the left bank and a portion of the seamen with a cohorn mortar under Spilsbury on the right, leaving his smaller boats behind under a light guard. With a continuation of blasts of canister or grape from the 68-pdr. carronade in the bow of his gunboat, Popham gave the signal to advance.

A cluster of Indians suddenly sprang up when one of the salvoes raked their hiding place and fled before the carronade could be fired again; it now became fouled with burnt powder, and Popham ordered the gunboat turned about so that its long 24-pdr. would bear on the foliage ahead. The confines of the creek made the manoeuvre nearly impossible, and as the British struggled to turn the boat Woolsey and Appling decided the time was right to spring their ambush. There was a storm of musketry as the Americans and the Oneidas leapt up, taking the British by surprise. Popham's men put up a stiff opposition but, surrounded by their adversaries, stood little chance. Two of the marine lieutenants fell wounded, while a young master's mate from the *Montreal* named Charles Hoare was killed outright. Seventeen others died on the spot and up to fifty were also wounded. The Americans moved forward, pressing their attack and soon encircled both detachments and the gunboats themselves. With no options available, Popham, himself wounded, signalled a surrender and the fighting stopped. The Oneidas were not satisfied, however, and approached their opponents with the intention of taking additional trophies and it was only with some strenuous effort that the American officers managed to save the survivors from mistreatment.

For the British the action at Sandy Creek was a sudden and shocking defeat. In a matter of minutes, Popham's aspirations of returning to the squadron with a convoy of Chauncey's precious ordnance were blown. The Americans stripped them of their weapons and marched them off to Sackets and eventual imprisonment in New England. In his report to Yeo, Popham explained that "the importance of the Lading of their Boats to the Equipment of their Squadron, was a strong Motive for me to risk the Attack."[57] He admitted to being surprised by the strength of the resistance and weakened by the loss of the lead carronade, but he praised his officers and men for their conduct and made no attempt to shift blame to anyone else's shoulders. An officer who encountered Popham during his confinement in Massachusetts noted: "Captain Popham is a steady, brave, and I think, a good man, and is very much chagrined at being captured, as the whole responsibility rested on him; he was blamed for following them up so narrow a creek."[58]

For the Americans, the result was a joyful victory. Woolsey, in particular, must have felt relief at its outcome – he had survived the attack on Oswego,

Cohorn mortar. This type of ordnance threw a 5.5-inch shell and was designed to be carried and handled by two men. Captain Popham apparently wanted Spilsbury's cohorn mortar crew to distract the American bateaux-defenders with shells exploding over their heads while his armed party stormed their position. (Photograph by the author)

supervised the handling of the critical guns and stores for weeks under a continuous barrage of cranky notes from his commodore, and now had managed
to save a significant shipment from capture. Chauncey praised his efforts to
Secretary Jones, but did not waste any congratulatory words in writing on his
diligent subordinate Woolsey. He did send other officers to take over supervision of the flotilla, with plans to move most of its cargo overland if necessary.
Woolsey, it appears, returned to Sackets for a much-deserved rest and soon assumed command of the brig-sloop *Jones*.

News of Popham's disaster struck the British squadron like a hammer. "Sir
James in a horrible rage at their imprudence," noted John Le Couteur. "So
much for taking boats full of men up a wooded creek."[59] The commodore submitted to Prevost a tabulation of the impact that losing 220 seamen and marines had on his command.[60] Nearly the entire crews of the *Montreal* and
Niagara had been killed or captured, so Yeo transferred men from the *Magnet*
and *Netley* into them, leaving only a handful in each of the smaller vessels,
which rendered them useful only as transports. He wrote to Drummond, asking for his advice on how the squadron could be best utilized to defend the
province, given the rising strength of Chauncey's squadron and the precarious
weakness of his own. Drummond replied: "There exists at present no motive or
object connected with the security of this Province which can make it necessary
for you to act otherwise than cautiously on *the defensive*."[61]

On 5 June Yeo lifted the blockade of Sackets and repositioned his squadron
in the mouth of the Bay of Quinte near Amherst Island. During the next week,
however, the first divisions of the Royal Navy detachment sent from England
the previous March began making their appearance, thereby solving his manpower shortage. As the reinforcements arrived through June, the crews filled
up, even to the point of enjoying surpluses. Recently vacated stern cabins were
reoccupied as Captain George Downie moved into the *Montreal* and Captain
Henry Davies took over the *Niagara*. The Admiralty had officially appointed
Richard O'Conor commissioner of the dockyard, which meant a raise in pay,
but deprived him of command in the *Regent*, which went to Captain Frederick
Hickey. The fourth new captain, Peter Fisher, soon went to Isle-aux-Noix as
senior officer, superseding Commander Pring, who remained on that station.
Edward Collier kept his post captain appointment in the *Prince Charlotte*,
Radcliffe stayed in the *Netley* and a lieutenant named George Hawkesworth ad-
vanced to the *Magnet*. Alexander Dobbs took over command of the *Star* from
Charles Anthony, who was invalided home. To replace Dobbs, Yeo posted Lieu-
tenant Henry Spence into the *Charwell*.[62]

The squadron anchored at Kingston on 13 June and Yeo went ashore to meet

Drummond. The revitalization of the warships' companies having made their proper employment more feasible, the two officers discussed the options of renewing the blockade at Sackets or transporting a large reinforcement to Niagara. The latter choice was taken, as it seemed likely that the summer's fighting would centre on that frontier. Accordingly, the remainder of the 103rd Foot and the Royal Artillery and a portion of the 100th Foot embarked along with a vast amount of supplies, and the main components of the squadron sailed on 15 June; some of the smaller vessels had already gone up. They made an uneventful round trip to Niagara and back by 24 June, whereupon the commodore took up moorings off Point Frederick.

Resumption of the blockade at Sackets Harbour did not take place, for reasons that remain unclear. Yeo and Drummond agreed that the "Enemy are not in sufficient force to undertake any expedition in the face of our present Squadron," but they did not consider it essential for the squadron to be anchored off Stony Point even as a nagging deterrent to Chauncey.[63] Instead, the commodore and the general mutually decided that it was better to keep the frigates and corvettes at Kingston while work on the three-decker continued at a steady pace. "Circumstances may arise," wrote Drummond on 6 June, anticipating his own needs in the near future, "which may render it expedient and necessary to adopt a widely different system, such for instance as the relief of the necessities of the advanced Divisions, an Expedition against Sacketts Harbour, etc., etc."[64]

Several weeks later when more was known about the strength of the American squadron, Drummond explained to Lord Bathurst that Yeo did not possess the power to oppose Chauncey and "was obliged to remain in port until his new ship is finished."[65] This reservation was well founded, for Chauncey eventually sailed with nearly twice the long-range weight of metal that even the enhanced British squadron could muster.[66] Unless Yeo could engage Chauncey at close quarters, his squadron would be in peril.

While the ships anchored off Point Frederick, the sloops and schooners, under the charge of Commander Dobbs, remained in contact with the "advanced Divisions" on the Niagara Peninsula, and the gunboat flotilla laboured without cease on the St. Lawrence. Yeo waited impatiently at Kingston, and Chauncey was allowed to get ready to sail. As it turned out, a harassing blockade by the British was not needed to hamstring the American squadron or to keep it from providing essential support to its army, when such support was vitally necessary for a campaign that was so poorly conceived.

CHAPTER 17

"For God's Sake
Let Me See You"[1]

STRIFE AMONG THE SENIOR OFFICERS:
JUNE–NOVEMBER 1814

On 7 June 1814 President James Madison sat down with his cabinet to discuss the direction the war should take.[2] He had asked his secretaries to attend the meeting with the latest information they could collect about the strength of their departments, the situation in Europe and the peace negotiations at Gothenburg. What they brought to the table shed a gloomy light on American fortunes. At last report, Napoleon was about to surrender, which meant that Britain would soon be able to focus all its attention on the American war. Albert Gallatin and the others had reported from Europe that there was no willingness on the part of the British representatives to compromise on the issues that Madison's government wanted addressed in a treaty, namely impressment and free trade. Secretary of the Treasury George Campbell noted that sufficient funds were not available to support an ambitious summer campaign against the St. Lawrence River and Montreal, although less expensive schemes might be undertaken to harass the British and uphold national pride. Secretary of War John Armstrong, who had proposed various courses in the preceding months, revealed that the army on the northern border was stronger and better officered than in the previous two years, while Secretary of the Navy William Jones listed the improvements in the freshwater squadrons and the state of the seaboard forces, but added that he still had doubts about the value of a northern war.

Although there was disagreement about the best way to proceed, by the end of their deliberations Madison and his secretaries had hammered out a four-step plan for a summer campaign that would save face for the nation and, they hoped, improve the American position in the peace negotiations. Commodore Arthur Sinclair, in cooperation with an army force, would sail to unseat the British from their domination of Lake Huron's northern passage and destroy the shipyard rumoured to be under development on Georgian Bay in a secluded inlet known to the Americans as Matchedash and to the British as Penetanguishene. Major General Jacob Brown would invade Upper Canada at Long Point on Lake Erie, presumably with transportation provided by Sinclair before his voyage to Lake Huron, and then march on Burlington Heights, from where he could go on to capture the Niagara Peninsula and York. The cabinet recognized the fact, however, that Brown's invasion was dependent "on Commodore Chauncey's getting the command of the L[ake]. without which supplies could not be secured."[3] The third element of the plan involved building about fifteen large gunboats at Sackets Harbour to use against the British supply route on the St. Lawrence with help from Major General George Izard's division. Lastly, Izard was to make diversions in the Lake Champlain valley that would distract Prevost's attention from movements in the western part of Upper Canada. Madison and the others continued to debate and even quarrel throughout the summer about how best to manage the war and their relations with Britain, but their sketchy and unfocused scheme remained as the guideline for the final American offensive in the north.

On 11 June, the United States Ship *Mohawk* slid down its tallow-greased ways and plunged into the basin at Sackets Harbour, just thirty-four days after Henry Eckford had laid its keel. With a gundeck measuring about 145 feet, the frigate would mount twenty-six long 24-pdrs. and sixteen 32-pdr. carronades.[4]

Jacob Jones (1768-1850). On 18 October 1812 Jones's sloop *Wasp*, 18, beat HMS *Frolic*, 18, off the Atlantic seaboard only to fall victim to HMS *Poictiers*, 74, later in the day. After his exchange Jones was awarded a gold medal by Congress and command of the former British frigate *Macedonian*. A British blockade kept Jones at anchor at New London, Connecticut, until the Navy Department finally ordered the *Macedonian's* crew to the lakes. (Portrait by A. Rosenthal, courtesy of the U.S. Naval Historical Center, NH-48739)

Three days before the launch Master Commandant Charles Ridgely had arrived at the Harbour with the convoy of guns and rigging from Sandy Creek, as well as the British craft captured by Woolsey and Appling on 30 May. Together with the ordnance brought overland from the Mohawk River and Lake Oneida, the guns that had been saved from the British completed the number that Chauncey needed to arm his squadron. In addition, almost all the rigging, shot, powder and other stores required to outfit the new brigs and ships had reached the Harbour by 10 June. "I therefore begin to feel," Chauncey asserted to Jones, "as if we should soon be in a situation to take the Lake in fact there will be nothing to prevent my sailing on the first of July if Seamen arrive to man that vessel."[5] The secretary had anticipated this need and had ordered Captain John Smith to the lake with his 340-man crew from the frigate *Congress*, 36, blockaded at Boston. The first detachment marched into Sackets on 19 June, followed over the next ten days by the others, except for Smith, whose health had broken down.[6] Nine days later Chauncey revised his estimated departure date when he reported to Jones that the guns of the *Mohawk* had been mounted and he expected to set sail in a week.[7]

The stage was now set for Chauncey to assume mastery on the lake and help Major General Jacob Brown in his drive against the British. Brown wrote to the commodore on 21 June to make that very point: "I shall consider the Lake as yours, the moment you have your new vessels in condition to appear upon it."[8] He assumed that Yeo would not "honestly and manfully" confront Chauncey and he wanted to know "when you will be out and if I may expect you in the neighbourhood of Fort George by the 10th of July? or what day?" An alternative was for the navy to rendezvous with the army at Burlington, but in either case Brown wanted Chauncey to bring the U.S. Rifle Regiment from Sackets and a pair of the army's 18-pdr. field guns that could be used against the forts. He posed these possibilities with some trepidation, however, because he learned that Commodore Sinclair meant to set out for Lake Huron without transporting Brown's army to Long Point, which was the general's only reasonable way of accomplishing that part of the cabinet's plan. "I am yet to learn," he admitted to Chauncey on 21 June, "that the Fleet on either Lake will cooperate with the Army under my command."[9]

Brown's reservations were well founded because Chauncey had no intention of racing to the Head of the Lake to work in concert with the army. He had received notice of the cabinet's wishes and had assured Secretary Jones that Henry Eckford would build the large gunboats that were wanted and that the navy would arm some of them with the surplus of ordnance that had been accrued.[10] As for cooperating with the army, Chauncey took the campaign objec-

Ridiculing the Royal Navy. During the late spring of 1814 American privateers captured British transports carrying ordnance and pieces for the fir frigates. After Commandant Thomas Macdonough's squadron won the Battle of Plattsburgh in September, American cartoonists took up their pens to invite King George III to cook up more ships for the lakes. (Courtesy of the Toronto Reference Library, T-14654)

tives at face value, particularly in relation to the cabinet's specific statement about the importance of "Commodore Chauncey's getting command of the L[ake]."[11] He explained to Brown on 25 June:

> I shall proceed in quest of Sir James and offer him battle if he accepts the invitation I shall either go to *Kingston* [presumably, as a prisoner] *or be at leisure* to cooperate with you upon any enterprize against the Enemy. But if Sir James pursues the policy that he did last Year of avoiding a general action I should be obliged to watch his movements to prevent his doing mischief. I shall therefore be governed by circumstances if he visits the head of the lake with his fleet you may expect to see me there also if he returns to Kingston I shall remain in this vicinity to watch his movements.[12]

A second issue influenced the commodore's decision. He had heard that 700 seamen, 2,000 marines and 300 shipwrights had lately reinforced Yeo and that a large number of troops had arrived at Quebec from the European battlefields. Such a congregation of strength caused Chauncey to fear a raid on Sackets, which he still believed was not adequately protected by the army. Because of this threat, he was even hesitant about following Yeo up the lake, if the British commander dared to come out of Kingston. Without forthrightly stating that the general should not soon expect help from the navy, Chauncey dispensed with Brown's question by concluding his letter: "In your contemplated enterprize may your most sanguine wishes be realized and may the God of battles preserve you and give you victory."[13]

For the first time during his command on the lake, Commodore Isaac Chauncey had turned his back on the needs of the army. His original orders had required him to cooperate with the generals and he had always done what they had asked, from Van Rensselaer's requests in September 1812, through Dearborn's campaigns of the following spring and Wilkinson's needs that autumn. Perhaps still smarting from the wounds inflicted by the near-loss of his shipyard in May 1813 or by Wilkinson's failure to attack Kingston, Chauncey now chose to make his squadron's status upon the lake his chief priority, although his attitude was also affected by a growing friction with Brown.[14] During the spring they had disagreed about Yeo's likely response to the sailing of the improved American squadron, the British strength at Kingston and the possibility of an attack on Sackets, and after Brown departed from the Harbour, he scolded Chauncey for not keeping him informed of his progress. Even before he heard that Sinclair would not transport his army across Lake Erie, Brown was openly doubting that the navy would provide the assistance his army would need in its upcoming campaign; on 7 June he had complained to Armstrong: "*I do know* that the Navy of Lake Ontario is under great obligation to the Army, for its preservation and support, the last and the present campaign and have not seen in this navy a magnanimous expression of the obligation."[15]

Letters travelled by express in three days from Sackets Harbour to Buffalo, so Brown had almost certainly received the commodore's letter of 25 June before the end of the month. By then he had also received a letter from Armstrong, dated 9 June, in which the secretary pointed out the difficulty of attempting to cross to Long Point without the help of Sinclair's whole squadron. Even if Brown could seize Burlington, Armstrong admitted, getting provisions would be impossible without American control of Lake Ontario and, citing William Jones's informed prediction that Chauncey would not sail before 15 July, Armstrong concluded that the expedition to Burlington "must be *suspended* 'till Chauncey shall have gained the command of the Lake." He suggested, however, as an alternative, and "to prevent their [Brown's troops] blood from stagnating, why not take Fort Erie and its Garrison stated at 3 or 400 men?"[16]

Brown had already decided to attack Fort Erie, but he was not yet ready to postpone the march on Burlington Heights. On 17 June, the same day that he wrote Chauncey about his state of readiness, the general informed Armstrong of his intention to cross the Niagara River at Buffalo and capture Fort Erie, Chippawa, Queenston, Fort George and Burlington. Though he had plainly expressed his scepticism in other letters about the support he could expect from the navy, Brown nonetheless told Armstrong that he expected "the arrival of Chauncey as circumstances should dictate."[17] Brown's 4,500-man division entered Upper Canada on 3 July, easily taking Fort Erie and then defeating the British under Major General Phineas Riall in a hard-fought battle at Chippawa two days later. By 10 July the army had advanced to Queenston.

While skirmishers infiltrated the environs of Fort George, Brown stood on Queenston Heights, scanning the lake in hope of seeing American sails. The commodore had written on 8 July to congratulate him on the successful beginning of his operation and to pass along what he had heard about the movement of British troops. Chauncey was hoping to sail "in a few days," but, despite rumours that Yeo would not leave Kingston until his new ship was built, he meant to remain in the vicinity of the Duck Islands unless Yeo did sail up the lake, in which case "I hope to have the pleasure of seeing you at Fort George or Niagara."[18] These words might have given Jacob Brown hope that Chauncey was finally ready to work in conjunction with him, for he waited impatiently at Queenston until 13 July until penning a note to the commodore. "I have looked for your fleet with the greatest anxiety since the 10th." he wrote, obviously exasperated. "Meet me on the lake shore north of Fort George with your fleet, and we will be able … to settle a plan of operations that will break the power of the enemy." The defences at Kingston were weak, Brown argued, implying that the commodore did not need to guard his shipyard. "Sir James will not fight," he declared, so Chauncey should ignore that threat. "Meet me at the head of the lake," Brown offered as an alternative, and together they would conquer Burlington and York, "your fleet carrying for me the necessary supplies."

The general's plea showed that he had forgotten, or was ignoring, the fact that Chauncey had explained that he would not join with the army until he had gained uncontested control of the lake. In contradiction to Armstrong's advice about delaying operations until Chauncey achieved his goal, Brown had committed his army to a campaign designed to seek the objectives of the Washington cabinet's original scheme. Now he found himself in a predicament. Lacking the heavy artillery that he needed to capture Fort George, he pointed his finger to the lake and pleaded with Chauncey: "For God's sake, let me see you."[19]

The squadron was still tugging at its anchor lines at Sackets Harbour as Brown waited at Queenston. Two weeks overdue on the sailing date he had promised in June, the commodore held his ships back for two reasons. There was a shortage of iron and suitable blocks for the gun carriages on the *Mohawk*, the installation of which was further complicated by an outbreak of sickness among the key artificers.[20] As well, difficulties arose when newly-arrived officers whom he had assigned to the various vessels complained about being separated from their former shipmates. Just about everything else was ready – the vessels were provisioned and armed, rigged and waiting – and questions began to be raised in the squadron about why they were not on the lake. Later, in his defence, Chauncey's replied to his critics by pointing out that "a man-of-war may appear to a landsman perfectly ready for sea, when she is deficient in many of the most essential points of her armament."[21] This was not written, however, until the second week of August because another situation developed that prolonged the squadron's idleness; on or about 15 July Isaac Chauncey fell victim to "a violent fever" that confined him to his bed for more than two weeks. Though Jacob Jones, at age forty-six, was officially captain of the squadron and a recognized man of action (his sloop *Wasp* had beaten the British sloop *Frolic* in October 1812), Chauncey had issued no orders for Jones to assume command of the squadron in the event of the commodore's indisposition by illness.[22] As a result, while Brown went head to head against Lieutenant General Gordon Drummond at the bloody battle of Lundy's Lane on 25 July, and the *Mohawk* was finally ready for service, Isaac Chauncey lay in his quarters at Sackets Harbour, just beginning to recover from a malady brought on by what he described as a "great anxiety of mind and severe bodily exertions."[23]

Still so weak that he had to be carried, the commodore went on board the frigate *Superior* on 31 July, and the next morning the squadron sailed. It presented a prodigious sight, more powerful and impressive than Yeo's squadron had appeared in May. The flagship *Superior*, 58, had the van, with Chauncey as its captain in lieu of the invalided John Smith of the *Congress*. Next came the *Mohawk*, 42, under Jacob Jones and the *Pike*, 26, under Crane. Master Commandant Edward Trenchard had the *Madison*, 23, Charles Ridgely commanded the brig *Jefferson*, 20, and Melancthon Woolsey had its twin, the *Jones*, 21; the latter two vessels were now classed as sloops owing to master commandants being in command. Following them came the *Sylph*, 18, (lately altered into a brig, though also classed a sloop) in the hands of Master Commandant Jesse Elliott, and the *Oneida*, 14, Lieutenant Thomas Brown. Accompanying the

The US Brig *Jefferson* and consorts. With their 42-pdr. carronades and assorted long guns, the brig *Jefferson* and its twin, the *Jones*, were the most heavily armed vessels of their type on the lakes. Their ponderous batteries, lofty rigs and shallow draughts made them susceptible to upset in rough weather. Shown to the left is the *Sylph*, one of Chauncey's fastest vessels. (Oil painting by Peter Rindlisbacher, courtesy of the artist)

squadron was Chauncey's speedy messenger, the *Lady of the Lake*, captained by Lieutenant Mervine Mix.[24]

Rather than proceeding immediately to blockade Kingston, Chauncey diverted from his stated course and sailed up the lake, reaching the western waters on 5 August. There, he oversaw the only significant damage that his powerful new squadron ever inflicted on its adversary.[25]

Under Commander Alexander Dobbs, the *Star*, *Charwell*, *Netley*, *Magnet* and *Vincent* had taken up moorings in the Niagara River in July to provide quick transportation from York to Niagara for Drummond's army. As the American ships came into view at noon on the 5 August, the *Magnet* was caught midway across the lake bound for Niagara. The schooner's captain, Lieutenant George Hawkesworth, attempted to outrun the *Lady of the Lake* and the *Sylph*, but failed to negotiate his tacks properly and was left with no other choice than to drive his vessel hard aground at Ten Mile Creek. Men from the warships at Niagara and a company of artillerymen raced overland to support the stranded schooner and managed to strip it of some of its cargo of ammunition. When the Americans appeared ready to send in boats to retrieve the *Magnet*, the British laid a fuse and escaped to shore, and the schooner, formerly the aging merchantman *Governor Simcoe*, blew up with an enormous roar. At York, an observer recorded the incident: "I felt a violent concussion of the air, and ... an explosion towards Niagara, much greater, than the explosion of our magazine [during Pike's April 1813 attack]" and ... "saw a prodigious cloud of smoke rising to great height."[26] When he heard of the loss of the *Magnet*, Drummond deemed it "an act of unpardonable precipitation."[27] Though the record is not clear on this matter, Lieutenant Hawkesworth appeared at Sackets Harbour in November, declaring himself a deserter, having apparently run to avoid a court martial.

Rather than landing at a safe point such as the Genesee River and going overland to meet with Brown, who was recovering from wounds received at Lundy's Lane, Chauncey detached the *Jefferson*, *Sylph* and *Oneida* to blockade the British vessels in the Niagara River and set a course for Kingston.[28] His only acknowledgement of the army was to transmit a brief note to the general, stating: "I do not feel myself justified to remain longer absent from the lower end of the Lake."[29] En route, he took time to respond to Brown's pleading note of 13 July, posing several questions for the general. Had Brigadier General Gaines not informed him of Chauncey's likely timetable, he asked? Had Brown forgotten a conversation with the commodore about the role to be played by the squadron and, if not, then why had Brown "thrown out to the public in your despatch to the Secretary of War, that you expected the fleet to cooperate with you?" Chauncey then accused Brown of misleading anyone who read the newspaper copies of his letters to Armstrong that Chauncey had promised to meet the army at Burlington and he reminded the general that the squadron's purpose was not to serve as "an agreeable appendage" of the army, but rather to accomplish "a higher destiny ... to seek and to fight the enemy's fleet."[30]

The commodore had learned by this time that Brown's despatches were in print in newspapers, leading to criticism of the squadron's actions, or lack of them; "you can but perceive how much has been lost by the delay, and the command of Lake Ontario being with the Enemy," Brown had explained to Armstrong on 25 July (and to the general public in the following weeks).[31] On 10 August, Chauncey wrote at great length to Secretary Jones, detailing the expectations, setbacks, sickness, misconceptions and outright falsehoods that had developed since the beginning of the summer. He proudly compared his accomplishments with those of any other commander and professed that his "zeal and exertions" were not wanting.[32] Although he did not refer specifically to the matter, Chauncey had certainly heard that William Jones had instructed Captain Stephen Decatur to take over at Sackets during Chauncey's illness. Not willing to hurt his colleague's feelings, Decatur had reluctantly travelled at a snail's pace as far as Albany before the news of Chauncey's recovery allowed him to return to New York.

The navy secretary levelled his own complaints at the commodore in a letter received on the *Superior* on 19 August. It contained what Chauncey termed "the first censure I have received from the Navy Department after more than fifteen years constant service." Jones expressed his personal dismay, and the president's disapproval, about the recent management of the squadron, which led Chauncey to request that his conduct be formally reviewed by a board of inquiry as soon as it was practicable. He did not take the criticism lying down, however, and responded with another extensive description of conditions and parallel situations. Chauncey also stepped up his condemnation of Brown, labelling him akin to "a *political Demagogue*," and complaining that Brown had "succeeded in deceiving you as well as the President and nation by his *insidious letters*."[33] The long simmering dispute between the two senior officers had now turned into an open conflict. Brown would soon lambast Chauncey with the allegation of acting as if "the fleet of Lake Ontario was your private property, over which the government had no control" and upon his return to Sackets Harbour late in the autumn, he and the commodore carefully avoided each other's company.[34]

Chauncey made his appearance off Kingston on 10 August. He observed the activity in the dockyard, though a view of the new ship was obscured by storehouses. Captured mail revealed to him that the British shipwrights believed the massive vessel, said to exceed the proportions of the first rate HMS *Nelson*, 120, was not being built with enough braces and supports to keep it from breaking its back upon launch. Chauncey dispatched the *Jones* to patrol the supply line from Oswego to Sackets against British raids and hoped that his reduced numbers (only the *Superior, Mohawk, Pike* and *Madison* remained) would entice Sir James to meet him. His aspirations were denied, and he soon hauled off for the Ducks, where he anchored his four ships and carried on his blockade at a comfortable distance to the end of August and beyond.[35] Brown's campaign on the Niagara, which now centred around the American position at Fort Erie, was far removed from Chauncey's squadron, and the commodore made no effort to shorten the distance. Only an invitation from Izard to meet his 4,000-man division at Ogdensburg, ferry it across the St. Lawrence and then launch a joint attack upon Kingston linked Chauncey again with the army's operations. The commodore rejected the plan, asserting that his ships could not descend the river to meet Izard and recommending that the general march to Sackets. In reciting these circumstances to Jones, Chauncey wearily admitted, "I have no pretension to military science."[36]

The British attack on Washington, 24 August 1814. While controversy raged between the senior commanders in the northern theatre, chaos reigned in Washington. A British army led by Major General Robert Ross and Royal Navy forces under Rear Admiral George Cockburn stormed into the city on 24 August, burning the navy yard and numerous public buildings and forcing President Madison and his government to flee. (Courtesy of the U.S. National Archives, 148-GW-478)

The American commodore might have enjoyed a smidgeon of vindication if he had known that Sir James Yeo was also under pressure from his military colleagues, though without such acrimonious exchanges. Chauncey's arrival on the lake combined with misfortune to place Riall's Right Division of the British army in jeopardy, and though the Royal Navy's help was urgently requested, its own projects stood in the way.

The *Prince Regent*, *Princess Charlotte*, *Montreal* and *Niagara* had remained at their moorings in Kingston through the summer. The corvettes patrolled the offing in turns, but the appearance of Chauncey's squadron chased them back to their holding ground near Point Frederick, where activity centred on the new ship. Anticipated launch dates in June, July and August slipped by as the enormity of the task involved in building a first rate vessel at such great distances from suitable resources took its toll. Workers slowly plundered three seventy-four-gun ships at Quebec, the *Ajax, Centaur* and *Warspite,* for the variety of gear required at Kingston, everything from clew garnets and hammocks, to compasses and a barge.[37] Tons of materiel floated up the St. Lawrence, over and around the treacherous rapids and past enemy outposts, consuming the efforts of hundreds of men, at escalating costs to the public purse.

As if building the three-decker was not enough, there was another extensive naval construction project going on throughout the summer. The transports carrying the prefabricated components for two ships and two sloops from the Chatham dockyard in England reached Montreal in June. Trying to appease the home government without burdening the supply line beyond its bounds, Prevost approved the transportation of one of the vessels to Kingston for construction.[38] Insufficient government boats and personnel were on hand to meet this additional challenge, so the job was awarded to a private contractor named William Forbes, who promptly hired enough men and craft to get things going. After sorting out the parts for Frigate B, Forbes's people loaded them into bateaux and started for Point Frederick, where presumably they were stock-

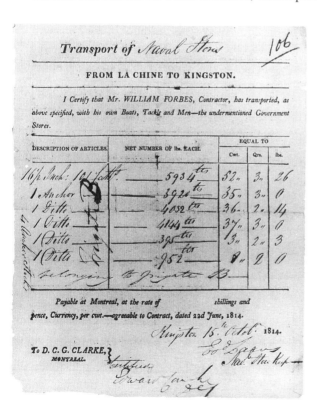

Transporting the parts of Frigate B. Storekeepers carefully recorded the successful transportation from Montreal to Kingston of each of the thousands of pieces of timber, rigging and equipment belonging to "Frigate B." After signing the contract late in June to transport the material, William Forbes kept his gangs hard at work for more than four months to complete the task. (Courtesy of the National Archives of Canada, C-107047)

piled until enough had arrived for construction to begin. Unknown to anyone in Canada, the Admiralty, upon receiving Prevost and Yeo's condemnations of the ships-in-frame scheme in July, had decided to cancel the project. Their Lordships' deliberation revealed that, while the sloops' components were good enough for them to be sent to Halifax and constructed there, the frames of the frigates were "chiefly of the most inferior Fir," which forbade their use in vessels meant "for general sea duty."[39] The board's decision did not reach Canada until the fall, by which time Frigate B was nearly ready for launch.

Commander Dobbs's vessels had maintained communication between Kingston and Niagara through July carrying men, munitions and food to the front. After Chauncey's squadron took to the lake and caused the loss of the *Magnet*, the *Star*, *Charwell*, *Netley* and *Vincent* remained penned up in the Niagara River for the better part of two months. With the *Jefferson*, *Sylph* and *Oneida* curtailing his activities, Dobbs took a detachment of his seamen and travelled up the river road to join Drummond near Fort Erie, where the latter was engaged in a protracted siege of Brown's position near the fort. Soon after reaching Drummond's camp, Dobbs saw an opportunity to strike a blow against the enemy by capturing three schooners from Commodore Sinclair's squadron, which had been left behind to help the army. With Drummond's blessing, Dobbs succeeded in cutting out two of the schooners, the *Ohio* and *Somers*, from their anchorage off Fort Erie late on 12 August after a bloody hand-to-hand struggle, which ended in the death of Lieutenant Charles

Capture of the *Somers* and *Ohio*, 12 August 1814. On 12 August 1814 Commander Alexander Dobbs's Royal Navy detachment transported a gig and five bateaux eight miles overland from the Niagara River to a point west of Fort Erie. After dark they attacked three American armed vessels, the *Porcupine*, *Somers* and *Ohio*, lying close to the fort, carrying the latter two after a brief but bloody fight. (By Owen Staples, courtesy of the Toronto Reference Library, T-15221)

Radcliffe, RN; Dobbs's men piloted the prizes down the Niagara River to the British post at Chippawa.[40]

Drummond had more ambitious objects in mind than a single cutting-out expedition. In the early hours of 15 August, he sent nearly 2,000 men to attack Fort Erie at both ends of its half-mile-long ramparts simultaneously. Misfortune, human error and poorly reasoned tactics led to total failure and the loss of 905 men killed, wounded and missing; among them were more than four dozen Royal Navy seamen and marines (Dobbs was numbered among the wounded).[41] This calamity left Drummond reeling, his dismay aggravated by the fact that Lake Ontario was no longer a freeway for reinforcements or the provisions and stores that were running low on the Niagara Peninsula. In his report about the attack Drummond advised Prevost to describe the plight of his army to Yeo and ask him to convey men, food and munitions to the peninsula as soon as possible. Two days later he urgently repeated this request for his superior to "impress on the Commodore's mind, that the Right Division, …, depends almost entirely on his prompt, and vigorous, exertions, for its relief, nay perhaps even for its safety."[42] That same day, 18 August, Drummond wrote directly to Yeo, describing his dire situation and imploring him to sail at the earliest possible time and "to push up to this point with every article of provisions and stores which the department of the army at Kingston can apply to you to receive."[43]

Drummond kept up his appeals for assistance from the squadron, though he soon admitted, "I really begin to fear that relief by this mode may not reach us in time."[44] The best he could rely on was a convoy of bateaux under Dobbs coasting around the end of the lake to York or the occasional voyage by one of the schooners when the American blockaders temporarily left their post. At his headquarters in Montreal, Prevost also had doubts about the quickness with which the navy would be able to assist Drummond's army. He reported to Lord Bathurst on 27 August that the "vacillating communications I have received from Sir James Yeo" prevented him from knowing when the squadron would be ready to sail.[45] It was only through a verbal report from Major Foster Coore, an aide-de-camp who had recently visited Point Frederick, that he came to conclude that the squadron would not sail until early October. The commodore himself seems not to have become involved at this point in the discussion about the employment of his frigates and corvettes. Instead he expressed concern over the casualties suffered by so many seamen at Fort Erie on 15 August and asked Sir George to send up more marines from the 1st Battalion to replace them as Lieutenant Colonel Malcolm and the 2nd Battalion had returned to duty on the Atlantic seaboard late in the spring.[46] Yeo showed no inclination, however, to risk a battle with Chauncey's powerful squadron in order to open the supply line to Niagara. While the USS *Superior* and its companions rode at their anchors off the Ducks, HMS *Prince Regent* and its consorts rocked gently at Kingston, and the generals were left to fight their own battles.

A t a time when warships of unprecedented size were on the lake, there is irony in the fact that, apart from the chase of the *Magnet*, the only engagements between Chauncey and Yeo's forces involved daring young officers in small boats. Lieutenant Francis Gregory, USN, and Master's Mate David Wingfield, RN, were destined to meet once again, bringing criticism and congratulations from their respective commodores.

An advocate of Gregory's potential as an officer, Commodore Chauncey had sent him on a mission in June to harass the convoys of bateaux passing through the maze of islands below Kingston. Commanding three small boats, one of which was Yeo's Deal gig captured at Sandy Creek, and assisted by Sailing Masters William Vaughan and Samuel Dixon, Lieutenant Gregory hid out among the islands for several days, watching convoys pass up and down until he spotted a solitary gunboat on 19 June. This proved to be the *Black Snake*, operated by a crew of militia, who halted their vessel when a skiff containing Gregory and several men flagged them down. As the skiff came alongside the British, the three larger American boats suddenly darted out from behind the neck of land where they had been waiting, their crews armed with muskets, and surrounded the *Black Snake*. The capture was made without resistance, but observers on shore spread the alarm about the marauding Americans, which was repeated by semaphore posts to Kingston, and Commander Charles Owen was soon in hot pursuit in two heavily armed and manned gunboats. Gregory and his mates tried to make their escape, but when Owen started lofting round shot at them, the lieutenant ordered his men to scuttle the *Black Snake*. Relieved of that burden, they easily outpaced the heavy gunboats, leaving Owen to organize the retrieval of their near-prize.[47]

The commodore was so impressed with Gregory's zeal and cleverness that he sent him on another expedition, this time to lie in wait near the village of Newcastle (at the western extreme of Prince Edward Peninsula), looking for supply convoys. In two gigs and accompanied by Vaughan and Dixon, Gregory left Sackets on 26 June and skimmed across the lake, pitching camp on Nicholson Island, seven miles offshore from the village. The next morning they spotted some traffic and began to approach it, when they spied a gunboat and scurried back to cover. After nightfall, Gregory went to shore with one boat and kidnapped a local citizen, who revealed that an alarm had been announced along the coast about American raiders. Fearing that he could spend no more time in that area, Gregory went back for the other boat and then led his whole party ashore that night to perform the second objective of the voyage. Chauncey had heard that a stout little schooner was being built for the navy at Newcastle and Gregory discovered that there was indeed a vessel nearly ready for launch. Under cover of darkness, he and his men stole up to the hull, which had been left unguarded, and set it aflame. In short order, they were in the boats and whisking back across the lake. The commodore lauded his accomplishment and informed the navy secretary that his skilful lieutenant had "performed a most difficult service with his usual gallantry and good sense."[48]

While Francis Gregory basked in the glow of his commodore's praise, Master's Mate David Wingfield was nearing the end of his confinement at Pittsfield, Vermont. Officially "on leave," Wingfield returned to Kingston with several other officers in mid-July. They reported to the commodore and were surprised to find him in poor health, though he welcomed the young men graciously and gave them accommodations in the *Regent* until their exchange could be confirmed. Wingfield was impressed with the changes made on Point Frederick since the previous October. There was now "a spacious dockyard, with every convenient store house, a great number of new faces among the officers who'd arrived from England, and the town twice as large again as formerly."[49]

When notice of his formal exchange arrived at the end of July, Wingfield sought employment by the commodore, who permitted him to participate in one of the small boat excursions being made along the American shore. He sailed with two cutters full of officers and seamen from Kingston to Grenadier Island, from where they could observe movement on the mainland. They were at this post when Chauncey's squadron sailed from Sackets on 1 August and they noticed a pair of small vessels near the squadron as it anchored off Stony Island. With darkness falling, Wingfield and the others silently approached the vessels: "We could see the men assembled on the Quarter deck, comfortably smoking their segars quite unconcerned and got close to them before we were noticed, a boat was run up either side and she became an easy conquest."[50] The next day the cutters escorted a schooner and a sloop into Kingston Harbour, where Wingfield was delighted to learn that the commodore had enacted a new and immediate system of awarding prize money without the services of an agent.[51]

Late in August Yeo dispatched a number of boats to search out the American raiding party that was making a nuisance of itself along the north shore of the Bay of Quinte and, to add insult to injury, employing Sir James's former gig for the purpose. Wingfield took part in this venture and hid out with a company of men for a couple of days until the suspect craft came into view, hotly pursued by another British boat. He and his crew pushed their boat into the water and barely missed intercepting the Americans, who raced by them, gaining a good lead. Wingfield's coxswain fired a musket at them and knocked over the man pulling the stroke oar. Then Wingfield fired several shots and hit a midshipman who had taken the stroke oar's place. As the gig began to lose its speed, an officer suddenly stood up and, with the assistance of one of his crew, manhandled another fellow out of the bottom and hurled him overboard. Recognizing this as a ploy to get him to stop, Wingfield instructed his men to throw the swimmer an oar and pressed on. Within several minutes, the Americans gave up their flight, having had five wounded and the midshipman killed. The man clinging to the oar turned out to be a prisoner, a local who had been on a raft of wood destroyed by the Americans that morning.

At that point David Wingfield received one of the biggest surprises of his Great Lakes career because the American officer who offered his sword was none other than Francis Gregory, the same person who had accepted Wingfield's surrender on the schooner *Confiance* the previous autumn. Gregory's comforting words to Wingfield on that occasion that "it might not be long ere he was in the same situation" had thus proven to be prescient.[52] The British put their prisoner in Yeo's reclaimed gig and hurried to Kingston, where the commodore expressed his gratitude to Wingfield and the dejected Lieutenant Gregory soon received a stinging rebuke from Chauncey.

After five months of construction, HMS *St. Lawrence* slid into Navy Bay at 10:00 a.m. on 10 September 1814. Measuring 194 feet along its main gundeck with a beam of nearly fifty-one feet, it made the plunge without incident, thereby confirming Master Shipwright William Bell's engineering skills and denying the cynical predictions of some of his carpenters. Commodore Yeo proudly announced the successful launch to Prevost and the Admiralty, asserting: "Every effort shall be used to get her ready for service and ... I fervently hope, and look forward to a glorious culmination of this campaign."[53]

The next morning Chauncey brought his four ships into the Kingston Channel and hove to. The Stars and Stripes rose on each vessel as an invitation to do battle, but the only response the British made was to turn their four ships around on their springs to offer a line of broadsides. Yeo intended to risk nothing, and why should he; his first rate was within weeks of sailing now, and Chauncey had nothing to oppose it. The American commodore remained long enough to make a thorough observation of Kingston's defences and then tacked around to regain the lake, chased by a heavy gale that rose out of the east.[54]

The nasty weather was a portent of dreadful news that would soon reach Kingston from the lower province. Barely twenty-four hours after the launch of the *St. Lawrence*, Captain George Downie had died in battle on board HMS *Confiance* in the bay at Plattsburgh, New York, and the largest British invasion of the northern states was about to falter.

During the summer 13,000 officers and men from Wellington's army in Europe had arrived at Quebec, somewhat worn out and disappointed not to have gone home.[55] Lord Bathurst had instructed Prevost to make use of this reinforcement by effecting the "entire destruction of Sackets harbour and the Naval Establishments on Lake Erie and Lake Champlain."[56] Though Drummond and Yeo had promoted the importance of destroying the American base at Sackets, Prevost selected Plattsburgh as his objective, forming three divisions numbering more than 10,000 men, and crossed the border on 1 September. Fewer than 3,000 men under Brigadier General Alexander Macomb and a naval squadron commanded by Master Commandant Thomas Macdonough defended Plattsburgh. Prevost's plan, to orchestrate a joint operation against the Americans, depended on the British squadron being ready for the engagement, a condition that he had been warned was not likely to be achieved before the middle of September. A brig, two sloops and twelve gunboats had comprised the British squadron until 25 August when the frigate *Confiance,* 37, was launched at the Isle-aux-Noix shipyard. The shipwrights and naval personnel were working frantically when Captain George Downie suddenly arrived from Kingston to take over command from Captain Peter Fisher, whom Yeo had recalled to Lake Ontario. Though hampered by shortages of materiel and manpower, Downie was able to equip the frigate adequately enough to rendezvous with the rest of his squadron on Lake Champlain late on 9 September.

Prevost had been waiting in the neighbourhood of Plattsburgh since 6 September and was anxious to commence his attack. He wrote to Downie, explaining, somewhat emphatically, the importance of the navy's part in the expedition. Downie replied that the *Confiance* required more work before it could participate. Late on 9 September he wrote to Prevost with his intention to advance on Macdonough's squadron the next day, but adverse wind sprang up and prevented his sailing. This delay irritated Sir George, who peevishly wrote to Downie: "I ascribed the disappointment I have experienced to the unfortunate change of wind, and shall rejoice to learn that my reasonable expectations have been frustrated by no other cause."[57] Insulted by the insinuation that he had held back for any but the most justifiable causes, Downie responded to Prevost's aide: "I am surprised that Sir George should think it necessary to urge me upon this subject."[58]

The Battle of Plattsburgh, 11 September 1814. The battle between the British and American squadrons in the bay at Plattsburgh, New York, provided a spectacle for spectators around the shore. Here the anchored American warship *Saratoga* returns fire from the British flagship *Confiance* and the *Linnet* at the *Saratoga's* stern. (Courtesy of the National Archives of Canada, C-10928)

The next morning the British squadron sailed up to Plattsburgh and engaged the Americans at about 9:00 a.m. Within an hour Downie was dead and the squadron was in disarray. While Macdonough's men effectively battered their opponents and won a glorious victory, Prevost looked on, allowing only a partial assault on Macomb's defences. Sticking firmly to his belief that Macdonough's destruction was crucial to the success of any land operation, Prevost observed the American crews taking possession of the British vessels and concluded that all was lost. That evening, he astounded his senior officers by issuing instructions for the army to retreat back to Canada, ending his brief campaign "because the most complete success," as he explained to Lord Bathurst, "would have been unavailing, and the possession of the Enemy's works offered no advantage to compensate for the loss we must have sustained in acquiring Possession of them."[59] With the same caution that had dominated nearly every aspect of his military command since the outbreak of the war,

Prevost chose to leave a goal ungained rather than pay for it with any more blood. In this instance, though, he was to pay a heavy price for his decision.

It was Daniel Pring who conveyed the news of the disaster to Yeo and raised the questionable conduct of Prevost. "Captain Downie [was] urged by Sir George Prevost," alleged Pring, "… relying on his promise that the works abreast of which the Enemy's Fleet lay moored, should be stormed at the same moment the Naval Action should commence."[60] The commodore packaged up copies of the relevant correspondence for delivery to England and then mulled the matter over for several days, probably discussing the issue with his senior officers and military confidantes. On 29 September he wrote a brief letter to the Admiralty in which he laid the groundwork for the charges that would eventually lead Prevost to request an inquiry into his conduct, namely that "Captain Downie was urged and even goaded on to his fate by his Excellency who appears to have assumed the direction of the naval force."[61]

Yeo's comments would arrive in England nearly two months later, on the heels of a second but less significant controversy involving his command. This one concerned Peter Fisher, who was so indignant at his removal from Isle-aux-Noix that he aggressively challenged Yeo's decision after he returned to Kingston early in September. The commodore had informed him originally that George Downie had asked for an independent command and that Yeo was trying to accommodate him. Downie denied this upon his arrival at the Richelieu River dockyard, and Fisher boldly proclaimed to Yeo that he viewed his transfer as an indication that Sir James felt he was unfit for such a position. To make matters worse, Fisher believed that Yeo shunned him in the re-assignment of officers prompted by the launch of the *St. Lawrence*. Intended to take effect around the first of October, the slate of positions put Frederick Hickey into the new flagship, Henry Davies in the *Regent*, Richard O'Conor in the *Charlotte* and Edward Collier in the *Niagara*.[62] Meanwhile Fisher fumed in the *Montreal*, Downie's former ship, a vessel he considered greatly inferior to the *Confiance*, which he had helped build and launch. He was especially incensed to see O'Conor, whom he termed "an officer under the Rank of Post Captain; and taken from half pay," advanced to such an impressive frigate as the *Charlotte*.[63] Through notes and a face to face encounter, Fisher pleaded his case to the commodore, who did not alter his arrangement but did agree to submit Fisher's complaint to the Admiralty, adding his own observations that the captain's comments had been "very intemperate" and that his "temper [was] too violent to entrust him with a separate command."[64]

During this time work continued from dawn to dusk to prepare HMS *St. Lawrence* for service. The seamen lifted its lofty masts into place and set up its

LIEU^T GEN^L SIR GEORGE PROVOST
GOVERNOR OF CANADA.

Prevost as commander-in-chief in the field. Sir George Prevost's term in Canada fell to its lowest point following the debacle at Plattsburgh. Veterans especially reviled him; one of them wrote that he was "heartily tired of this Country, as every military man must be, who has any reputation to lose, under such a Goose as our little nincompoop."[2] (Courtesy of the Toronto Reference Library, T-15460) miles of rigging, 102 guns and carronades plus a pair of 68-pdr. "smashers" soon lined the decks, and tons of ballast and stores filled the ship's hold. The commodore moved into his spacious cabins within a week of the launch, while the decks in front of and below his accommodations gradually became the home to more than 600 men. Manning the huge flagship had been one of Yeo's nagging concerns all summer, but his persistent requests and the cooperation of authorities near and far allowed him to crew the first rate with seamen from the transports and warships at Quebec, the gunboat flotilla in the upper St. Lawrence and the other vessels in the squadron.[65] As September passed into October the labour continued, occasionally observed from a distance by Chauncey's patrol. Expectations arose that, despite the presence of the *St. Lawrence*, the American squadron would challenge the British as soon as they sailed and that the long awaited, climactic battle would finally occur.[66]

Prevost arrived at Kingston on 10 October and visited the squadron four days later to inspect its state of readiness. He also met with Yeo to discuss the squadron's employment during the quickly fading navigation season, but their conversations sparked another disagreement since Prevost wanted the ships to carry men and munitions to the Niagara Peninsula, and Yeo hesitated to encumber his squadron if Chauncey might offer to fight. Prevost's request was based on his concern for the situation of Drummond's army, which had suffered another setback at Fort Erie during an American sortie on 17 September in which the British took more than 600 casualties. Having lifted his siege of the fort a few days later, Drummond believed that the Americans were making a last ditch effort to destroy his army before the *St. Lawrence* and the rest of the squadron could sail. When he learned that a 4,000-man reinforcement had been landed by Chauncey east of Fort Niagara, he declared in a letter to Prevost on 6 October that "nothing but the Squadron can relieve us."[67] Several days later he announced to his chief that an additional 1,000 men had arrived from Detroit in Commodore Sinclair's squadron and that the word was out that the Americans planned to take over the peninsula and occupy it through the winter. On 11 October Drummond reiterated his need for a strong reinforcement to be landed at Fort George immediately and four days later bluntly warned Prevost:

Should the 90th Regiment (or some strong Regt.) and the requisite supply of provisions and Stores, not come up in the Squadron, and should any disaster happen to this Division (in consequence) and above all should Commodore Chauncey (as is probable) decline an Action, His Majesty's Naval Commander will in My Opinion have much to answer for.[68]

Drummond's stinging indictment of Yeo's commitment to the common good of the British armed forces was remarkably similar to the complaints Brown had levelled at Chauncey. It read like a preamble to charges that Drummond could ultimately lay against the commodore in the event of a disaster at Niagara similar to the defeat at Plattsburgh.

Sir George was acutely aware of the privations being suffered by the army on the Niagara Peninsula and he made his case strongly to Yeo, asking him again, as he had done frequently since August, to transport the entire 90th Regiment of Foot (950 men) and a mountain of supplies to Drummond. Yeo refused on the grounds that he was anticipating a battle with Chauncey and did not want his warships crowded with infantry and baggage.[69] Unstated were Yeo's doubts about Prevost and his own hesitation to be "goaded" into a voyage that might leave him unsupported in defeat as had happened to Downie. Yeo had obviously reached a point in his tenure where, like his counterpart at Sackets, he was no longer willing to have his squadron utilized like "an agreeable appendage" to the army.[70]

Prevost pressed Yeo to consider the needs of Drummond's army and finally succeeded in persuading him to embark a portion of the 90th Foot and some provisions, which by no means overburdened the squadron. Prevost's exasperation found its voice when he wrote to Bathurst on 18 October, alluding to the similarity between Yeo and Downie's conduct. It had always been accepted during this war, he wrote, that operations of the army were tied to naval support. However, the escalation of the naval department, Prevost argued, had caused its commanders to believe that they could "by a trial of strength ... decide the fate of the war." They had forgotten "their necessary identity with the land force for the general prosperity of the common cause." Now, instead of manifesting a "zealous, prompt, and cheerful co-operation" when asked to move men and equipment, they viewed such requests "as hampering the powers of the fleet and endangering its safety."[71]

Prevost also pointed out to Bathurst that in addition to naval operations being delayed by the protracted construction of the *St. Lawrence*, the needs of that ship had dominated the supply lines during the summer, to the detriment of all else. In time, Prevost came up with a solution to the problem he believed arose when commanders like Yeo and Downie became too proprietary about their squadrons. In November he proposed to Bathurst that the Admiralty appoint a rear admiral to take overall command of the Great Lakes command, who would work in concert with the army staff to develop campaign goals and direct the operations of the separate squadrons accordingly. In this way, Prevost suggested, a squadron's activity would not depend on the officer commanding it, "whose situation might on some occasions give him a bias incompatible with the real good of the service."[72]

Prevost's recommendation that an admiral would help to unify the forces had more to do with his frustration over Yeo's persistent opposition than it had to do with reality. Admirals and generals were just as likely to differ in their campaign preferences even when the loss of a squadron did not have as far-reaching impact as it would have had on Lake Ontario. During the British campaign against Washington and Baltimore, for instance, Vice Admiral Sir Alexander Cochrane, Rear Admiral George Cockburn and Major General Robert Ross differed over operations and tactics, which, after Washington had been captured, led to a delay in the attack on Baltimore and resulted in a disappointing end to the operation.[73] In Canada an ambitious, risk-taking officer like Admiral Cockburn would have been exasperated by the conservative Prevost unless a single, superior officer had been on hand to give each of them direct orders based upon well-focused objectives. Unfortunately, the notion of "unified command" had yet to become common in military thinking, resulting in the confused goal-setting that produced disputes between the services on both sides of the border during the summer of 1814. Prevost thought he had the solution when he blamed Yeo, who, having been made commander-in-chief on the Lakes of Canada, responded with allegations of military interference. At the same time Jacob Brown ignored his own decision to undertake an extensive march into Upper Canada, contrary to the advice of Secretary Armstrong, and attributed his problems to Chauncey's failure to employ his fleet as "an arm" to the land forces, while the commodore hung Brown out to dry by narrowly pursuing the authorized goal of seeking mastery of the lake. In Washington and London the decision makers continued to rely on a tradition of "cooperation" between the services with the result that their war efforts stumbled and bumbled through the second half of 1814.

Though the purpose for which it had been built was barely a factor any more, HMS *St. Lawrence's* grandeur was no less when it set sail on its maiden voyage on Sunday, 16 October, accompanied by the *Regent, Charlotte, Montreal* and *Niagara*. According to Jesse Elliott, who observed the squadron from a distance on the US Sloop *Sylph*, two brigs and a larger schooner, which he assumed had arrived the previous day from Niagara, also joined the procession. As soon as the squadron cleared Kingston Channel Yeo ordered two hours of gun drill and then called the captains to his ship.

Two days later Niagara was in view from the mastheads, but a southwest wind brought showers of rain, and Yeo decided not to approach the shore immediately. Through most of 19 October, the weather remained contrary, and in the evening a series of squalls swept across the lake, causing the crews to reduce sail in a hurry. Thunder boomed and lightning slashed at the squadron, striking both the *Prince Regent* and the *St. Lawrence*. Master's Mate Wingfield once more saw death come within a hair's breadth of him. Posted to the flagship, he was on the quarterdeck when a bolt of lightning struck the mainmast, splitting the heavy iron hoops binding it and killing and wounding a handful of men. What caused Wingfield and his colleagues to bless their lucky stars was the fact that a magazine was situated just aft of the mainmast's step, which contained several hundred prepared cartridges, and, as Wingfield recollected, "had the lightning communicated to them we should all have taken our departure."[74]

Conditions did not moderate on 20 October, but Yeo was impatient to deliver the troops and supplies. The squadron clawed up toward the mouth of the Niagara River and finally succeeded in anchoring at a point three miles off shore. Debarkation began late in the afternoon as the *Star*, *Charwell* and *Netley* came out from the river to ferry the infantrymen ashore, a transfer made difficult by high winds and a heavy swell. Despite the persistent bad weather, the process continued until the afternoon of 22 October, when the last of men and stores were set down on land and the squadron could up its anchors and gain a seaway.

Lieutenant General Drummond visited the squadron during its stopover. He had been unhappy to learn that only half of the 90th Foot had been transported and then disappointed when Yeo rejected his request to leave some of the Royal Marines to make up for the inadequate reinforcement. "The enemy's fleet may very possibly engage the squadron under my command," Sir James explained to Drummond's messenger, "and the marines compose the most efficient part of their crews."[75] On 21 October the general rode down to Fort George and went out to the *St. Lawrence* to converse with the commodore personally. What words passed between the two men are unknown, although before the meeting Drummond had stated his intention to "urge him [Yeo] to apply his ships to the only service which they can render us during the remainder of the season," namely, bringing up two full regiments to replace worn out troops at Niagara and Burlington.[76] Drummond succeeded in convincing Sir James to embark several exhausted companies of the 8th and 104th Foot for Kingston and he left with him "a memorandum" stipulating his need for the additional regiments. Some days after the squadron had sailed, however, the general was still complaining about the navy's lack of cooperation, predicting that a famine would occur if Yeo refused to remove the rest of the worn-out and retired units, and their hungry bellies, from the resource-strapped Niagara Peninsula.[77]

More agreeable weather guided the squadron's quick return to Kingston. It anchored off the town on 24 October and the troops on board were sent ashore to be replaced almost immediately by others waiting to embark. The commodore's apprehension about an encounter with the American squadron had been unfounded. Except for the occasional distant sail, nothing got in the way of Yeo's potent force and nothing ever would.

At Sackets Harbour the majority of the warships rode at their anchors during the last week of October. The rough weather that had arisen after the launch of the *St. Lawrence* kept Chauncey on the lake until 17 September, when he was finally able to gain the safety of his anchorage. The next day the *Jefferson* and *Jones* had reached Sackets, both of them somewhat knocked about by the stormy weather. So close had the *Jefferson* come to foundering, as it strove to avoid the lee shore in Burlington Bay, that Commandant Charles Ridgely had been forced to jettison ten of his 42-pdr. carronades to reduce the sloop's wallowing.[78]

Major General George Izard had completed his march to Sackets by this time, but instead of boarding the squadron for an attack on Kingston, the general wanted transportation up the lake for his 4,000 men. This service Commodore Chauncey was willing to perform, and on 21 September his entire squadron, supplemented by some of the laid up schooners and a separate flotilla under the charge of the army's quartermaster general's department, set out with most of Izard's men aboard. They arrived off the Genesee River on 22 October, disembarked the land force and turned back to the Harbour.[79]

The American squadron resumed its watch over Kingston on 25 September and hopes soon soared that Yeo was coming out to fight when the *Niagara* and *Montreal* appeared making way from the Kingston Channel. Chauncey ordered his commanders to clear for action and beat to quarters, but to no avail; the corvettes were simply making a scouting run and returned to their port without firing a gun. On 29 September Chauncey again led his warships in a line off Kingston, showing the American standard, inviting Yeo to fight. When nothing stirred in the British anchorage, the commodore put back to the lake.[80] That day he wrote to Henry Eckford: "I begin to despair of meeting Sir James on equal terms he is determined to put nothing to hazard.... I shall be obliged to take up my Quarters at Sackett's Harbor untill you build me a 74."[81] Having failed to induce his adversary to fight frigate-to-frigate, Chauncey remained on the lake until he knew the three-decker was completely rigged and ready for action. Then, accepting that his squadron could never match Yeo's firepower once the *St. Lawrence* sailed, he laid a course for Sackets, anchoring there on 7 October.[82] Except for occasional patrols by the smaller vessels, the American squadron's career had come to an end. Once ashore, Chauncey worked quickly to ensure that the land defences at the Harbour were capable of withstanding an attack, despite the inadequate force he claimed the army had placed there.[83] Though he seemed certain, at first, that the attack was imminent, the commodore relaxed his apprehensions by the end of October, having heard that Yeo's squadron had shown no penchant for aggressive activities.

HMS *St. Lawrence* began its second voyage on 1 November 1814. The passage to Niagara was made in a day and a half, but again bad weather made things difficult. While the larger ships maintained an offing of twelve miles, the *Niagara*, *Montreal* and the other smaller vessels ferried 1,200 men from the 6th and 37th Foot and the Canadian Fencible Regiment and the Royal Artillery ashore at Fort George. The process took two days of cautious manoeuvring, after which the *St. Lawrence* and the frigates sailed over to York to await the arrival of the 1,100 exhausted troops Yeo had agreed to convey back to Kingston.

The navy's arrival managed to irritate Drummond once more. Ignoring the problems posed by inclement weather, he complained to Prevost that "after throwing the troops hastily on shore Sir James has gone over to York with the 9-pdr. artillery brigade, the ordnance, provisions and other stores which were embarked in the large ships. I hope he will send them over to Niagara by the smaller vessels, as they might have almost as well been left at Kingston as be landed at York."[84] Drummond also asked Yeo to participate in an attack against Izard's force near Lewiston, but the commodore declined, citing the dangers posed to his squadron by the disagreeable weather. As it was, Drummond's time on the Niagara war front was nearing an end. Realizing that Yeo's mastery of Lake Ontario would prohibit any further military action, the Americans blew up Fort Erie and withdrew from Canadian territory on 5 November. This allowed Drummond, who had made several requests to be relieved because of poor health, an opportunity to leave the frontier; by the time the last of the worn-out troops had embarked in the squadron at York, Drummond and his suite had also boarded the *St. Lawrence*. On 10 November the ships came to anchor off Point Frederick and began discharging their passengers, the general going ashore to be greeted by an artillery salute and "the most lively sensation of joy, by all classes of people."[85] The scene offered a gratifying end to what had been a long and frustrating campaign.

PART VI

The Curtain Falls

From On the Death of Commodore
Sir James Lucas Yeo, k.c.b.

Oh weep for the Hero! for where shall we find –
A fond heart so devoted and brave –
'Twas Britannia's glory which brighten'd his mind, –
And he prov'd that she rul'd on the wave.

NAVAL CHRONICLE, 1817

Two first rates building at Point Frederick, 1815. By the spring of 1815 the new first rates, later named *Wolfe* and *Canada*, stood with their frames complete in the Point Frederick dockyard. The masts and upper decks of the *St. Lawrence* are visible to the left of the new ships with the Point Henry fortifications beyond. To the right is the commodore's house. (Watercolour by E. E. Vidal, courtesy of the Massey Library, Royal Military College of Canada, Kingston)

CHAPTER 18

"Returning Peace at Length Is Heard"[1]

WINTER ARRIVES AND THE WAR ENDS

The British squadron swung at its moorings in Kingston Harbour, the crews mainly involved in disembarking troops and artillery and taking on provisions while parties of seamen left their ships to work in the dockyard. As fresh breezes blew clouds and squalls in off the lake on 13 November Lieutenant General Drummond approached Commodore Yeo with a request to make another supply run up to Niagara. A large American raiding party had stormed from Detroit to the Grand River, burning barns, mills and homesteads and thereby ruining stores that the army had planned to use through the winter.[2] Yeo refused to take his largest vessels onto the lake again, owing to the bad weather, but he did allow the *Montreal, Niagara, Star, Charwell* and *Netley* to sail on 28 November. The *Montreal* returned in three days; Yeo had stated earlier that the corvette was in such need of repair as to be unserviceable, and it is likely that the ship limped back into port without completing its mission. The smaller vessels returned to Kingston safely on 9 December, without the *Niagara*, which had gone to York. Discussions had been held throughout the fall about shipbuilding projects on Lake Erie and Georgian Bay in preparation for action in 1815. When the American raid north of Lake Erie dampened plans to build ships near Long Point, Yeo instructed Captain Edward Collier to establish a naval base at Penetanguishene Harbour on Georgian Bay. For that reason Collier had gone to York with the *Niagara* heavily loaded with twenty of the *Princess Charlotte's* 24-pdr. long guns, plus their carriages, shot, powder and accoutrements. It was intended that this ordnance be carried overland to Georgian Bay during the winter, followed closely by all the other materiel to build a forty-four-gun frigate.[3]

A similar warship was taking form at Point Frederick. William Forbes had delivered the parts for Frigate B with such efficiency that a board of officers voted to award him a bonus of £1,000.[4] Two new people were managing the project; the Admiralty had ordered Master Shipwright Thomas Strickland to Canada, deposing William Bell. Captain Sir Robert Hall, RN, had superseded Richard O'Conor as commissioner early in the fall, and O'Conor left Kingston in November, carrying despatches to England on Yeo's behalf, with the intention that he would explain the naval situation fully to the Admiralty.[5] After discussions with the commodore, Hall ordered the upper deck of Frigate B to be completely planked, creating a spar deck that would allow the ship's armament to be increased from thirty-eight to fifty-six guns. As well, he called for three gunboats and a pair of large transports to be laid down, predicting later that twenty gunboats and fifty bateaux would be ready for operation by the spring. In December the senior officers also decided to construct a seventy-four-gun ship at Point Frederick, and on 26 December, one day after the launch of Frigate B, named HMS *Psyche*, the shipwrights began piecing together the keel of the seventy-four in its place.[6]

Commodore Yeo had long since made his recommendations about how the Great Lakes navy should be strengthened for a campaign in 1815 and had put them in the hands of his trusted colleague, Captain O'Conor. He wanted two ships-of-the-line sent to Quebec so that their entire crews could join the freshwater squadrons, bringing with them a familiarity with each other that would help ensure their effectiveness. Later he asked the Admiralty to send him officers who were eager to gain promotion, adding: "I must confess with regret that I have observed a weariness and discontent in those who lately came out (with the exception of Captain Hickey)."[7] Sir James had every expectation of continuing the war against Chauncey. Even when he received a letter from the Admiralty around 1 January stating their Lordships' disappointment with the paucity of information he had provided about the administration of his command, Yeo showed no willingness to surrender his wearisome and stressful position. He energetically compiled all the relevant data he could and mailed it off, blaming his difficulties on the lack of a suitable support staff.[8] At the same time he and Robert Hall were forming their plans to construct a second ship-of-the-line; within weeks, the two sister ships would grow into 104-gunners.

Isaac Chauncey's thoughts paralleled those of his adversary. Asked by Secretary Jones late in October to offer his opinions on how the war might be continued in this spring, Chauncey had replied that two ships capable of carrying ninety or one hundred guns each should be built at Sackets Harbour. He would have preferred a third vessel of the same strength, but figured that there would be only enough timber left over to build a frigate. He also argued heartily in favour of an ambitious operation against the St. Lawrence region, an idea he had long championed. The premise behind the 1814 campaign, he wrote, "to take Kingston by crossing at Erie in preference to being landed a few miles of the spot is a species of military policy much beyond my comprehension."[9] The commodore submitted reports on the status of his establishment and indents of materials required to complete the projects he proposed. Trying to avoid the situation he had experienced the previous spring, he advised Jones to grant early approval to the work so ordnance and equipment would arrive in time to allow the ships to sail in May. Apparently confident that he would continue to enhance the strength of the navy on Lake Ontario, Chauncey quickly put his winter organization into effect, handed command over to Captain Jacob Jones and headed south on 3 December to confer with his constructors at New York and his superiors in Washington.[10]

Across the ocean much had happened to alter the situation on the Great Lakes. The controversy arising from the battle at Plattsburgh came to the attention of the British government late in the autumn of 1814, but, before receiving that news, Liverpool's cabinet and Admiralty had found other reasons to be critical about the state of naval affairs in Canada, beginning with the inquiry into the loss of the Lake Erie squadron.

Commander Robert Barclay appeared before a court martial on board HMS *Gladiator* at Portsmouth on 9 September. In his written deposition he shed light on some previously misunderstood circumstances concerning his defeat at the hands of Oliver Hazard Perry. The commander bluntly explained that Yeo's friend, Mulcaster, had turned down the Lake Erie command, that Yeo had sent Barclay to Amherstburg with a weak and motley crew and had later rebuked him for too forcibly asking for reinforcements. Prevost, not Yeo, had dispatched the detachment of men from the *Dover*, Barclay claimed, directly challenging Yeo's comment that Barclay had not waited long enough for the rest of the *Dover* men to arrive and that he had acted as if he had nothing to lose. "I had not only my own Character as an Officer to support," asserted Barclay, "but also to uphold the honor of the British Navy."[11] Barclay's words were well supported by his war-torn appearance. He had lost his left arm in the line of duty years before and now stood before the court with his right arm still badly hampered by one of the wounds he had received at Put-in-Bay. The commander's testimony and that of his fellow officers led the court to conclude that Barclay and the others had done their best in a most difficult situation. The court absolved them of blame, concluding that, in part, the shortage "of able Seamen whom he [Barclay] had repeatedly and earnestly requested to be sent to him" had caused the defeat.[12] By so doing, the board of officers indirectly placed a portion of the blame for the loss of the Lake Erie squadron squarely upon the shoulders of Sir James Yeo.

What effect the findings of the Barclay court martial had on the Admiralty's deliberations about the Great Lakes station is uncertain. It was the lowest point in an operation that had brought other disappointments: Yeo had been unable to master Chauncey, despite spending weeks manoeuvring with him during the summer of 1813; the Americans had battered his squadron near Burlington in September of that year; Yeo had failed to provide adequate cover for a convoy carrying troops to Kingston the next month; though extravagantly reinforced during the winter of 1814, Yeo had accomplished only one successful raid in the spring before losing more than 200 men in a foolish undertaking on Sandy Creek; he had spent the summer building a first rate line-of-battleship for war on a mere lake, while simultaneously making redundant the government's expensive shipment of prefabricated vessels; and, while his new flagship was on the ways, Yeo's other heavily armed frigates had swung idly at their moorings, during which time Prevost's concerns about the lack of support received from the navy by Drummond's army found their way to the colonial department in London.

If the Lords of the Admiralty discussed these matters, they did not deem it necessary to inform Yeo about their dissatisfaction in regards to them. They did point out an inadequacy in the commodore's conduct, however, by instructing Yeo late in October to submit information about his proceedings in more detail and on a more regular basis. Their Lordships repeated the reprimand three weeks later when the correspondence regarding Peter Fisher's dispute with Sir James over his removal from Isle-aux-Noix and placement in the *Montreal* reached London. After reviewing the letters exchanged by the principals, they remarked that, like Fisher, they did not understand either why the captain had been posted in the *Montreal* because Yeo had not kept them adequately informed about his previous appointments. They reiterated their request for information, emphasizing the importance of commanders on remote stations maintaining frequent contact with the Admiralty.[13]

About the same time that the Admiralty reacted to Fisher's situation, news of the loss of the British squadron on Lake Champlain reached England, along with a deluge of reports and letters about Prevost's failed expedition. Among the despatches was Yeo's observation that Prevost had "urged" and "goaded" Downie into action, and a letter from Prevost himself in which he justified his "reasons for not discouraging a Naval Contest in which if all had done their duty I might have had a very different report to make."[14] Such blatantly conflicting criticisms provided undeniable proof of a rupture in the relationship between Prevost and his naval chief. Other communications from Canada during this period made it clear that Prevost had lost the confidence of too many officers and civil authorities to remain in his post.[15] After some deliberation about this unpleasant state of affairs, Lord Liverpool's government decided to use Yeo's allegations as the fulcrum against which to force Prevost's removal. On 12 December John Croker, the first secretary at the Admiralty, wrote a brief note to the commodore requiring him to return to England to deal with the charges he had made against Prevost, who was also being ordered home and replaced at Quebec by Drummond.[16]

The commodore received no other explanation for his recall, although a different justification was given to his successor. On 12 December the Admiralty issued instructions to Captain Sir Edward W. C. Owen to travel to Canada and assume control of the Great Lakes station. The Lords advised Owen simply that they had found it necessary on "frequent occasions to express to Sir James Yeo their regret at the unsatisfactory and insufficient communications which he has made to them."[17] Just as Arthur Sinclair had heard about James Leonard's transgressions when Secretary Jones ordered him to Sackets Harbour in April 1813, Owen most certainly learned more about the command he was going to assume from naval scuttlebutt.

Twelve days after Yeo's recall was sent, a peace treaty was signed at Ghent. Negotiations had been conducted since early August and had dealt with issues ranging from the establishment of an extensive Indian nation south of the western Great Lakes to fishery rights. The British had held the upper hand and their representatives pressed their demands on Albert Gallatin and his colleagues, who had been ordered to give up the stand against impressment. News of the failed attacks on Baltimore and Plattsburgh weakened British resolve, however, as estimates predicted staggering costs for a renewed campaign in 1815. In the end, the emissaries agreed to a return to *status quo ante bellum.* Maritime concerns were not mentioned, though both sides agreed to make peace with the Indian nations who had participated in the conflict, and commissions were established to examine boundary concerns and a reduction of the slave trade. War officially ended with the signing of this document, dependent on ratification by each nation's legislature; on 2 January 1815, the ship *Favourite* left England to carry the terms across the ocean for the consideration of Congress.[18]

Isaac Chauncey returned to Sackets Harbour on 25 January 1815 in the company of his midshipman son, John, who had been ordered to the lake. The Navy Department, where Benjamin Crowinshield was now the secretary, had approved his ideas about building warships to rival HMS *St. Lawrence*. After months of seeking permission from President Madison to resign his position in

Signing the Treaty at Ghent, 25 December 1814. Representatives of Britain and the United States finally agreed on conditions to end the war on Christmas Eve 1814 at Ghent. Prominent figures depicted here are Lord Gambier (left) shaking hands with John Quincy Adams, behind whom stands Albert Gallatin. (Courtesy of the National Archives of Canada, C5996)

order to resurrect his failing personal finances and seek relief from the bombardment of his critics, William Jones finally convinced the president to replace him in December.[19] Before leaving the department he had held for nearly two years, Jones appears to have made no effort to remove Chauncey from his Great Lakes command, despite the fact that he had been plainly critical of the commodore during the summer. Jones's opposition to escalating the contest for control of the lakes was still strong, and as his retirement from Madison's cabinet neared, he argued about the impracticality of building bigger ships and committing more seamen to the freshwater service.[20] Nevertheless, the building continued at Sackets Harbour, and Jones left his office after writing a congratulatory letter to Chauncey praising him for his devotion to duty and thanking him for his faithful service.[21]

By the time Chauncey returned to the Harbour, Henry Eckford's gangs had cleared a new slipway on Navy Point and set up the keel of a monstrous vessel that was already sprouting ribs.[22] Two and a half miles away at a new shipyard near Stony Point, Noah and Adam Brown had begun work on a similarly huge ship. Hundreds of shipwrights climbed among the structures while equally large numbers of axemen chopped down the timber that went immediately to the yards. The winter roads were in good condition, by and large, and supplies reached the Harbour in an almost unbroken train of wagons and sleds. A third ship had yet to be started, but the commodore was already recommending that its dimensions be increased. Assessing the size of his new ships and their needs in the upcoming year, Chauncey calculated that he would require nearly 3,000 additional officers, seamen and marines in the spring and sent Commandant Charles Ridgely to Washington with despatches to answer Crowinshield's questions after he had read the commodore's indent.

Rumours of peace interrupted the shipbuilding machine at Sackets Harbour during the third week of February. When confirmation reached Chauncey's hands on 23 February, he immediately ordered a suspension to all work and at eleven o'clock that morning sat down to write to his opposite number. "I have much pleasure," he announced to Yeo, "in enclosing the Treaty concluded at Ghent on the 24th December last with the Ratification of the President of the United States."[23] The note went into its envelope and was soon on its way under flag of truce to Kingston.

Sir James was not at his base to receive the good news.[24] He had departed near the end of January to make a quick tour of inspection of Long Point and Penetanguishene. The former site he condemned, upon his arrival at Kingston on 25 February, as not even suitable for building schooners, but he approved of the Georgian Bay location. The news of peace swept the implications of his evaluations aside, however, and Yeo issued instructions for Collier to cease construction at Penetanguishene, though he decided to continue building the two new ships on Point Frederick, which were later named the *Canada* and the *Wolfe*.[25]

The British squadron in ordinary. With their upper spars and rigging removed, (left to right) *St. Lawrence, Prince Regent, Princess Charlotte* and *Psyche* swing at their moorings in Navy Bay between Point Frederick and Point Henry in the spring of 1815. The wooden roof raised over the decks of the *Psyche* for the winter remains in place. (Watercolour by E. E. Vidal, courtesy of the Massey Library, Royal Military College of Canada, Kingston)

During Yeo's absence rumours had reached Kingston that he would no longer command the squadron on Lake Ontario in the spring. As well, a Montreal newspaper had printed extracts of his and Prevost's despatches concerning the loss of the Lake Champlain squadron. A commentary by a British observer noted that "it is quite evident from the tone of these despatches, that Sir George Prevost and Sir James Yeo cannot long continue to act together with benefit to the public service."[26] One of Prevost's aides-de-camp, Major Foster Coore, fired off a letter to Yeo, reprinted in the *Montreal Gazette*, "deprecating" the commodore's "presumptions" about the state of Downie's squadron and the effect that Prevost's correspondence had on him.[27] The controversy between Sir James and Sir George was now openly revealed, casting a malignant pall over the armed forces in the Canadas when jubilation at the news of peace should have prevailed.

Commodore Edward Owen arrived at Kingston on 19 March, receiving a salute of thirteen guns from the ships and raising his broad pendant in the *Psyche*. Yeo struck his pendant at sunset two days later and on 23 March boarded the *Netley* for his final voyage on Lake Ontario.[28] Chauncey had invited him to visit Sackets Harbour, which matched Yeo's plans perfectly as he intended to travel

The American squadron in 1815. During a visit to Sackets Harbour in 1815 Lieutenant Emeric Essex Vidal, RN, painted this panoramic view of the American squadron. Only the brig *Jones* (foreground below) and the *Lady of the Lake* (partly obstructed, right below) were in commission, while the *Sylph* and *Pike* (centre below) lay dismantled. Named for Andrew Jackson's victory in January 1815, the *New Orleans* (facing page) stood in the stocks on the new slipway on Navy Point surrounded by other warships in ordinary: (left to right) *Mohawk*, *Jefferson*, *Superior*, *Madison* and *Oneida*. A gunboat glides into Black River Bay carrying stones for the foundation of the *Orleans's* slipway. (Drawing by E. E. Vidal, courtesy of the Massey Library, Royal Military College of Canada, Kingston)

south to New York and take passage from there to England rather than waiting until ships could reach Quebec in May. Among the commodore's party were Commander Charles Owen (no relation to the new commodore) and Captain Frederick Hickey.[29] They met Chauncey, who so graciously entertained them that they prolonged their stay at Sackets until 2 April. Left unrecorded were the private conversations between the two commodores or the after-dinner toasts and discussions about the tense days spent hiding out in the forest near the Harbour or waiting for consistent breezes near the Head of the Lake.

Yeo's journey to New York brought him more social calls from American officers, though not all of them were congenial. Master Commandant David Deacon challenged him to a duel to resolve an insult the commodore had done him during Deacon's confinement after the capture of the gunboat *Growler* in August 1813. Yeo claimed to have no knowledge of such an individual, and Charles Owen visited Deacon and his representatives, one of whom was Stephen Decatur, to sort out the misunderstanding. The Americans were not appeased, and although the record of this incident is incomplete, Yeo may have actually agreed to a duel with Decatur, who offered to stand in for Deacon as an officer of suitable rank to oppose the commodore.[30] Frederick Hickey also ran into trouble in New York. The captain of a commercial schooner with which Hickey had accidentally collided while he commanded the sloop *Atalante* accosted the captain, declaring his intention to sue him for his losses. A prominent lawyer in New York agreed to sign a bond for the amount of the supposed damages to the vessel until Hickey was at leisure to return to resolve the matter (which he did in 1820).[31] Much farther afield, Prevost's defenders at Quebec heard that Yeo had taken the American route and spread it around that his purpose was to gather more damaging evidence about Prevost's conduct at Plattsburgh. Sir George reportedly mentioned this in a letter to the Duke of York, which provoked an angry denial from Yeo.[32]

Yeo reached Liverpool on 15 May 1815 and went directly to London to explain his management of the freshwater naval war to the Admiralty and to offer his advice on how a similar conflict with the United States in the future should be waged. As well, he presented his justifications for the accusations he had made about Prevost's conduct at Plattsburgh. Captain O'Conor had preceded him, providing the Lords of the Admiralty with insight about the circumstances in Canada, which might be the reason Yeo did not have to endure a barrage of criticism about his management of the Great Lakes command. Just the opposite occurred; any disapproval of his lack of communication or his role in Barclay's defeat or his failure to subdue Chauncey was forgotten, and within weeks of arriving home the Admiralty instructed Yeo to raise his broad pendant again as a commodore in HMS *Inconstant*, 36, and to lead a squadron to the west coast of Africa to oppose the slave trade.[33] This acknowledgement of Yeo's competence was the most obvious proof that the accomplishments of his tenure on the Great Lakes, seen in the context explained by O'Conor and Yeo himself, had won the approval of his superiors. His immediate appointment was all the more significant in light of the fact that the Royal Navy had begun such an extensive reduction of its forces that even a vindicated veteran like Robert Barclay lingered on half pay for the better part of a decade.

As he prepared the *Inconstant* for sea during the summer of 1815, Yeo also spent time in legal consultations convened to word formal charges against Prevost. When Commander Daniel Pring and other officers from the Lake Champlain squadron appeared before a court martial in August, Yeo was one of the prime interrogators, helping to clarify the conditions of Downie's squadron and the promises of support from Prevost.[34] The date of 12 January 1816 was set for Prevost's court martial, but the session did not take place. Exhausted from the rigours of his Canadian service, Sir George contracted a severe case of dropsy and died on 5 January at the age of forty-eight. Though debated at great length thereafter, Prevost's responsibility for the defeat at Plattsburgh remains unresolved.[35]

Commodore Yeo sailed to Africa early in 1816 and returned later in the year with prizes and hundreds of liberated slaves. He next moved into the frigate *Semiramis* and continued to patrol the slave trade lanes. The ship was at Jamaica during the summer of 1818 when fever struck Yeo and quickly ruined his health. On 21 August, as the *Semiramis* was sailing to England, Sir James Lucas Yeo succumbed, aged thirty-six. His crew preserved his body in spirits until they reached home, where they laid him to rest in the Garrison Chapel at Portsmouth on 7 September. Chief among the mourners was Lieutenant George Cosby Yeo, who had continued to follow his brother to sea.[36]

Isaac Chauncey enjoyed twenty-five years of service after the war. He remained at Sackets Harbour until June of 1815, slowly putting the warships in ordinary and selling off the schooners he had converted from merchantmen three years before. Like Yeo, Chauncey did not have to wait long for employment. Although his actions during the summer of 1814 had been publicly castigated in the newspapers and privately questioned by William Jones and President Madison, prompting Chauncey to invite an inquiry into his conduct, no such investigation was undertaken. Quite the contrary, the Navy Department soon appointed him to the USS *Washington*, 74, the line-of-battleship that had been built at Portsmouth, New Hampshire, during the latter stages of the war. In that ship Chauncey sailed in March 1816 to assume command of the naval squadron in the Mediterranean Sea. If Madison and the new faces in his cabinet had any doubts about Chauncey's abilities, they did not show them. Though only ten places from the top of the captains' list in the U.S. Navy, Chauncey was still junior to Hull, Bainbridge, Decatur and Stewart, men who had all fought and won glorious ship-to-ship victories against the British. His quick reassignment as commodore was proof that his faithful and industrious administration of the war on the lakes had not gone unrecognized.

After a three-year stint in the Mediterranean, Chauncey's days afloat ended. He spent the rest of his career as a member of the newly created Board of Naval Commissioners and commandant of the naval yard at New York. He died on 27 January 1840 in Washington at the age of sixty-seven and was buried in the Congressional Cemetery. Chauncey was survived by his wife and two sons, both of whom earned commissions in the navy.[37]

Like the commodores, the officers and men who had sailed the warships on Lake Ontario maintained their contact with the navy through careers that were long and prosperous or sadly brief. Melancthon Woolsey, though greatly hampered by the debts he accrued by not keeping careful records of his transactions before and during the war, lived to become the commodore of the U.S. Navy squadron at Brazil between 1832 and 1834. Released from a British prison after the war, Seaman Ned Myers sought employment before the mast and, after suffering an injury in 1840, ended up in a home for retired seamen. There he encountered James Fenimore Cooper, whom he had known as a midshipman before 1812, and recounted his life story. After the publication of Cooper's book, Myers returned to a life dominated by alcohol and dropped out of sight. Oliver Hazard Perry's deeds also gained him plenty of fame, but he did not have long to enjoy it. While commanding the frigate *John Adams* in 1819, he contracted yellow fever in Venezuela and died. Henry Eckford also fell victim to a fever in a far away place. Though he continued his successful shipbuilding career after the war, his finances fell apart because of poor investments and he accepted a job building for the sultan of Turkey, where he passed away in 1832. Arthur Sinclair does not appear to have enjoyed a command at sea after the war; the evidence suggests that he was in charge of the naval station at Norfolk, Virginia, until his death in 1831. Of all the American officers who served on Lake Ontario, Francis Gregory had one of the longest and most successful careers. He survived to become an admiral in 1862, helping the Union to build ironclads and seeing his nation make peace with itself before his death at age seventy-six.[38]

The grave of William Vaughan. A citizen of Sackets Harbour, Sailing Master William Vaughan was an asset to the U.S. Navy during the war. Like a number of his contemporaries, he was laid to rest in one of the cemeteries at the Harbour. (Photograph by the author)

Among the British, one of the longest lived was also among the few who served from the beginning to the end of the war. This was James Richardson who gave up the nautical life shortly after the peace to become a Methodist minister. Through a life of toil and devotion to his beliefs, Richardson became a revered bishop who ended his days in Toronto in 1875. Few, if any, of his shipmates managed so many years. Lieutenant John Johnston was killed during the Royal Navy's bombardment of Algiers in 1816. His companion, David Wingfield, left Canada that year, having been stationed on the upper lakes and then Kingston. Though he had gained his lieutenant's commission, he did not win another ship and remained on half pay through the 1840s. Barclay and Mulcaster passed away within weeks of one another in 1837 after enjoying productive family lives despite the crippling wounds that all but ended their careers. Daniel Pring and Edward Collier eventually raised commodores' pendants and survived into the 1840s. Richard O'Conor, knighted in 1836, retired from the navy nine years later as a rear admiral and lived until January 1855. Some of the Royal Navy men retired from the service shortly after the war and returned to Canada. Among them was Francis Spilsbury, who settled in Cramahe Township near Cobourg and took on the trappings of a gentleman farmer with indifferent success until his death in 1831.[39]

The Royal Military College. Taken from the hillside below Old Fort Henry, this photograph shows the RMC complex that now occupies Point Frederick. The four-storey stone building left of centre dates to 1820, when it was used as a storehouse for naval gear and became known as the "Stone Frigate." (Photographs by the author)

(Left) **Fishing access point on Sandy Creek.** At the point where Woolsey and Appling caught Popham's naval party in the deadly ambush in May 1814, the State of New York has filled in part of the marsh to create a landing for anglers.

Navy Point Marina. While the area occupied by Fort Tompkins and most of the ground that was hotly contested in May 1813 has been preserved for historic purposes, Navy Point at Sackets Harbour is home to a thriving marina. Beneath the docks lie the remains of the 1814 brig *Jefferson*.

The *St. Lawrence* swivel gun. The smallest piece of ordnance on the largest sailing warship built on the Great Lakes was retrieved from the remains of the *St. Lawrence* at Kingston in the 1930s for display in the museum at Old Fort Henry.

Only one of the ships outlasted the oldest veteran. Henry Eckford's final project, named the *New Orleans*, was planked to its upper decks before work was stopped after news of peace reached the lake. It sat for decades upon its slipway at Sackets Harbour, preserved by the government within a protective ship's house, which finally sagged and collapsed around 1880; four years later labourers demolished the ship. The death knell for the other warships had sounded in 1817 when Britain and the United States signed the Rush-Bagot Agreement for the purpose of limiting active armed vessels on the lakes to a handful of schooners. The Navy Department ordered most of the American warships broken up and sold for scrap, while the *Oneida* was sold for use as a laker, lasting until 1837, and the *Sylph* continued a similar career up to 1843. That same year the remains of the *Netley* (launched in 1812 as the *Prince Regent*) finally fell victim to the scrappers at Kingston. A couple of its contemporaries were already sunk in nearby Deadman Bay, but the rest had disappeared. Yeo's unique flagship, *St. Lawrence*, had lain idle and rotting at its wharf until 1832, when the British government began the last phase of its withdrawal of naval forces from the inland waters of Canada. The Royal Navy's one and only freshwater first rate was sold for £25 and a promise to haul the sad old hulk away.[40]

And by the time the last sailor was buried and the final hull was dismantled, what was being said about the battle for control of Lake Ontario? In truth, not very much. There had been no climactic engagement and so there was no glorious hero like Perry or Macdonough. Instead of a single decisive action that produced a rivetting and concise story, the contest had been long and tedious, complicated and frustrating. The naval historians of the period treated the affairs of Chauncey and Yeo with polite respect, but their activities lacked the colourful anecdotes reserved for the winners of engagements. One of their contemporaries went so far as to condemn their entire regimes. In his autobiography, Winfield Scott, who, like Chauncey, had fought in the Lake Ontario theatre through each year of the war, wrote: "The two naval *heroes of defeat* held each other a little more than at arm's length – neither being willing to risk a battle without a decided superiority in guns and men."[41]

Scott's condemnation was unfair. As professional officers and proven seamen, Yeo and Chauncey would gladly have fought each other to the death and often set out from their ports with that goal in mind. Apart from a few brief months during the summer of 1813, however, the operations of the squadrons on Lake Ontario had been tied inextricably to the fortunes of their respective armies. Through most of the war, the commodores fulfilled their responsibilities with dedication and competence, sacrificing their own predilections for the common good; only in the third year did they falter in this regard – Chauncey more so than Yeo – having lost faith in their military colleagues. Nevertheless, both men were forging ahead to renew the contest when news of peace arrived. Though neither commodore won a crown of laurel on Lake Ontario, their devotion to duty was recognized by their grateful nations. Through tempest and doldrum, broadside and accident, they had wrestled tirelessly to win mastery of what one recent historian has termed "the most important theatre in the war."[42] Given the complexities of their commands, the two commodores, their officers and seamen had done their duty as well as any nation could expect.

Appendices

APPENDIX A

Overview of the British and American Squadrons on Lake Ontario, 1812-1814

Table 1: British Squadron

The information in this table is based on Admiralty surveys of the vessels in the Lake Ontario squadron in 1814 and 1815. No data was available for the schooner *Duke of Gloucester*, launched in 1807.[1]

Vessel	Rig	Launch	Tons	Length of Keel	Length of Gun Deck	Extreme Beam	Depth of Hold	No. of Gunports	Designer
Earl of Moira/ Charwell	ship/ brig	28-05-05	168	61'	70'	23' 8"	2' 3"	14	John Dennis
Royal George/ Niagara	ship	-07-09	330	87'	101'	27' 7"	5'	20	John Dennis
Prince Regent/ Lord Beresford/ Netley	schooner	-07-12	142	60'	71' 9"	21'	2'	8	John Dennis
Sir George Prevost/ Wolfe/ Montreal	ship	22-04-13	426	103'	107'	30' 10"	4' 6"	22	Thomas Plucknett
Governor Simcoe/Sir Sidney Smith/ Magnet	schooner	29-10-93	137	-	74'	18' 6"	-	14	uncertain
Lord Melville/ Star	brig	-07-13	186	71' 6"	72' 10"	24' 3"	2' 6"	14	George Record
Prince Regent	ship	14-04-14	1293	150'	160' 9"	43'	9' 2"	56	Patrick Fleming
Princess Charlotte	ship	14-04-14	755	121' 6"	126' 9"	37' 4"	8' 8"	40	George Record
St. Lawrence	ship	10-09-14	2304	172' 6"	194' 2"	52' 7"	18' 6"	102	William Bell
Psyche	ship	25-12-14	743	121'	130'	36' 7"	10' 3"	52	uncertain
New ships No.1 & No.2/ *Canada* & *Wolfe*	ship	not	2158	172'	193' 6"	50' 8"	18' 3"	104	Thomas Strickland

Table 2: The American Squadron

No comprehensive surveys appear to have been made of the American squadron. Information here is based on a individual reference. Instead of length of gundeck, American data shows length between perpendiculars at the bow and stern, a comparable dimension. Very little information could be found about the schooners *Lady of the Lake* (89 tons, launched 6 April 1813) and *Sylph* (340 tons, launched August 1813) or the frigate *Superior* (launched 1 May 1814), all of which were designed by Henry Eckford. [2]

Vessel	Rig	Launch	Tons	Length of Keel	Length of Gun Deck	Extreme Beam	Depth of Hold	No. of Gun-ports	Designer
Oneida	brig	31-03-09	262	77' 6"	85' 6"	23'	8'	16	Christian Bergh[3]
Madison	ship	26-11-12	580	112'	120'	32' 6"	11' 6"	24	Henry Eckford[4]
General Pike	ship	12-06-13	900	120'	143'	38'	15'	26	Henry Eckford[5]
Jefferson & Jones	brig	07-04-14 13-04-14	600	108' 9"	122' 11"	33' 2"	10' 5"	22	Henry Eckford[6]
Mohawk	frigate	11-06-14	1200	130'	145'	38'	12'	42	Henry Eckford[7]
New Orleans	ship	-	3200	183' 8"	212'	56'	30'	110	Henry Eckford[8]

Table 3: American Converted Lakers

Commodore Chauncey's squadron included the following "gunboats" that had been merchantmen prior to the war. Captured British lakers are indicated with (P) and their "prize" value is shown.[9]

Original Name	Gunboat Name	Burthen	Date of Purchase	Price
Charles & Ann	*Governor Tompkins*	96	24 Oct. 1812	$5,800
Genesee Packet	*Conquest*	82	?	$5,500
Diana	*Hamilton*	76	10 Nov., 1812	$5,250
Fair American	Same	82	10 Nov. 1812	$5,250
Ontario	same	81	?	$4,000
Julia	same	53	10 Nov. 1812	$3,800
Collector	*Pert*	50	?	$3,700
Experiment	*Growler*	53	?	$3,200
Lord Nelson (P)	*Scourge*	45	1 Oct. 1812	$2,999
Elizabeth (P)	*Asp*	57	6 Feb. 1813	$3,500
Mary Hatt (P)	*Raven*	50	6 Feb. 1813	$2,500

APPENDIX B

The Opposing Squadrons, Autumn 1812

Table 1: The British Squadron

The Provincial Marine warships appear to have been equipped in this manner during the first navigation season of the war, as described in reports completed by Andrew Gray between February 1812 and March 1813. Crew numbers are approximate.[1] Abbreviations are used for officer ranks in the appendices. See Table 4 in this appendix for full spellings.

Vessel and Commander	Total Guns	Carronades No. & Type	Long Guns No. & Type	Crew
Royal George Mstr. & Cmdr. H. Earl	20	20-32s	0	100
Earl of Moira Lt. T. Sampson	14	10-18s	4-6s	50
Prince Regent Lt. W. Fish	12	10-12s	2-6s	35
Duke of Gloucester Lt. F. Gauvreau	6	0	6-6s	20
Total Numbers	52	40	12	205

Table 2: The American View of the Provincial Marine

Commodore Chauncey anticipated the strength of the Provincial Marine to be as shown here. His information was quite wrong, though it resembles a list Lt. Woolsey had submitted to the Navy Department in 1811. The *Governor Simcoe* was not armed until the spring of 1813 and the *Toronto* was broken up at York by January 1812. The *Seneca* is not mentioned among relevant British documents.[2]

Vessel	Ordnance	Crew
Royal George	26	260
Earl of Moira	18	200
Prince Regent	18	150
Gloucester	14	80
Toronta	14	80
Gov. Simcoe	12	70
Seneca	4	40
Totals	106	880

Table 3: The American Squadron

Shown here are the American vessels that participated in the attack on Kingston on 10 November 1812. Their ordnance is based upon several conflicting reports. On 6 November Chauncey informed Secretary Hamilton that he was about to sail with the *Oneida* and six schooners, "mounting altogether 40 guns of different Calibres and 430 men including Marines." Two days later he wrote to General Dearborn that his squadron comprised the *Oneida* and nine schooners carrying 56 pieces of ordnance, 500 seamen and 100 marines., three of which (the *Scourge, Ontario* and *Fair American*) did not participate in the attack. Lieutenant Elliott named specific vessels and their ordnance. An asterisk (*) indicates ordnance that is mounted on a circle.[3]

Vessel and Commander	Total Guns	Carronades No. & Type	Long Guns No. & Type
Oneida Lt. M. Woolsey Com. I. Chauncey	18	18-24s	0
Governor Tompkins Lt. T. Brown	6	4-32s	1-32* 1-24*
Hamilton Lt. J. Macpherson	11	10-18s	1-24*
Pert S. Mstr. R. Arundel	3	0	1-32* 2-6s
Conquest Lt. J. Elliott	1	0	1-32*
Julia S. Mstr. J. Trant	3	0	1-32* 2-6s*
Growler S. Mstr. M. Mix	1	0	1-32*
Totals	43	32	11

Table 4: Abbreviations for Officer Ranks

Com.	Commodore
Capt.	Captain
Mstr. & Cmdr.	Master and Commander
Cmdr.	Commander
M. Cmdt.	Master Commandant
Lt.	Lieutenant
S. Mstr.	Sailing Master

APPENDIX C

British Gunboat Flotillas During and After 1813

Table 1: Upper St. Lawrence Flotilla, July 1813

Commodore Yeo prepared this plan on 21 July 1813 for a gunboat flotilla to operate between Kingston and Prescott.[1]

Gunboat #	Carronades	Long Guns	No. of Oars	Crew
1	1-24	-	36	40
2	-	1-18	36	40
3	-	1-18	36	40
4	1-24	-	24	27
5	1-24	-	24	27
6	-	1-6	24	27
7	-	1-6	24	27
8	-	1-6	24	27
9	-	1-9	26	30
Totals	3	6	254	285

Table 2: Gunboats Between Coteau du Lac and Kingston, January 1814

Commander Richard O'Conor submitted this report on 16 January 1814 showing gunboats stationed upriver of Montreal following the Wilkinson campaign. The gunboats *Crysler*, *Queenston* and *Niagara* were renamed the *Nelly*, *Lais* and *Cleopatra* by April 1814. Nine other gunboats were listed as stationed at Isle-aux-Noix (*Sir George Prevost*, *Sir James L. Yeo*, *Lord Wellington*, *General Simcoe*, *Marshal Beresford*, *Sir Home Popham*, *General Brock*, *Tecumseh*, *Lord Cochrane*).[2]

#	Name	Rig	Size	Carronades	Long Guns	No. of Sweeps	Where Built	Current Station	Condition
1	*Nelson*	Schooner	60' x 13'6"	1-32	1-24	36	Pt. Fred.	C. du Lac	New, good repair
2	*Quebec*	Lugger	44' x 8'3"	1-32	-	26	Quebec	C. du Lac	Serviceable
3	*Kingston*	Lugger	60'9" x 13'6"	1-24	-	24	Pt. Fred.	C. du Lac	Serviceable
4	*Glengarry*	Sloop	48' x 8'7"	1-24	-	24	Quebec	C. du Lac	Serviceable
5	*Thunderer*	Lugger	40' x 8'	-	1-6	22	USA	C. du Lac	Wants repair
6	*Retaliation*	Sloop	44' x 8'3"	-	1-6	24	USA	Prescott	In a bad state
7	*Brock*	Sloop	58' x 8'2"	-	1-6	22	USA	C. du Lac	In a bad state
8	*Black Snake*	Lugger	44' x 8'6"	-	1-6	22	USA	C. du Lac	In a bad state
9	*York*	Sloop	36' x 8'	1-12	-	22	USA	C. du Lac	In a bad state
10	*Cornwall*	Sloop	58' x 8'2"	1-12	-	24	USA	C. du Lac	In a bad state

Table 2 (continued)

#	Name	Rig	Size	Carronades	Long Guns	No. of Sweeps	Where Built	Current Station	Condition
11	Crysler	Lugger	48' x 12'	-	1-24	30	Pt. Fred.	Pt. Fred.	New and will be
12	Queenston	Lugger	48' x 12'	-	1-24	30	Pt. Fred.	Pt. Fred.	ready for launch
13	Niagara	Lugger	60' x 14'	1-32	1-24	36	Pt. Fred.	Pt. Fred.	in the spring
14	Buffalo	Lugger	58' x 16'	1-32	1-24	36	Pt. Fred.	Pt. Fred.	sunk 10 Nov. now under repair
15	not named	Lugger	55' x 12'	-	1-24	36	C. du Lac	C. du Lac	under construction
16	"	Lugger	55' x 12'	-	1-24	36	C. du Lac	C. du Lac	" "
17	"	Lugger	55' x 12'	-	1-24	36	C. du Lac	C. du Lac	" "
18	"	Lugger	55' x 12'	-	1-24	36	C. du Lac	C. du Lac	" "
19	"	Lugger	55' x 12'	-	1-24	36	C. du Lac	C. du Lac	" "
20	"	Lugger	55' x 12'	-	1-24	36	C. du Lac	C. du Lac	" "

Table 3: Gunboats in Service late in 1814

The following gunboats were in operation on the St. Lawrence between Prescott and Kingston during the autumn of 1814 as noted (along with twelve others) in the logbook of Lt. Daniel Salter, RN.[3]

Name	Size	Carronades	Long Guns	Oars
Muros	60' x 14'	1-32	1-18	36
Kingston	60' x 14'	1-32	1-18	36
Drummond	60' x 14'	1-32	1-18	36
Helena	60' x 14'	1-32	1-18	36
Sydney	60' x 14'	1-32	1-18	36
Gananoque	60' x 14'	1-32	1-18	36
Cleopatra	5'4" x ?	?	?	?

Other gunboats named by Salter: *Prescott, Spitfire, Thunderer, Retaliation, Eleanor, Dreadnought, General Conran, Sir George Prevost, General Robinson, General Kempt, Nelson, Wellington*

APPENDIX D

The Opposing Squadrons in May and June 1813

Table 1: The British Squadron

The precise depiction of the ordnance the squadrons is difficult due to the lack of complete contemporary documentation and the common practice of changing ordnance. The description of the British broadsides below is based upon several documents written before and during this period, but it is not meant to be definitive.[1]

Vessel and Commander	Total Guns	Carronades No. & Type	Long Guns No. & Type
Wolfe Cmdr. D. Pring Com. J. Yeo	22	2-68s 18-18s	2-12s
Royal George Cmdr. W. Mulcaster	20	18-32s	2-9s
Earl of Moira Lt. A. Dobbs	18	18-18s	-
Beresford Cmdr. F. Spilsbury	12	10-12s	2-6s
Sir Sidney Smith Lt. C. Radcliffe	12	10-32s	2-12s
Total Numbers	84	76	8

Table 2: The American Squadron

This table is based on a list Commodore Chauncey compiled on 18 July 1813. On 4 June he stated that his squadron mounted 82 guns, which differs from the number shown here. That tally may not have included informal alterations like the two brass 4-pdrs. that Sailing Master Joseph Osgood purloined for use on the *Scourge* after the battle at York in April. Omitted from this list is the US Schooner *York* (formerly the British *Duke of Gloucester*), which was armed with two long guns, a 32 and a 24 at Sackets, but never used in the squadron. An asterisk indicates a gun that was mounted on a circle.[2]

Vessel and Commander	Total Guns	Carronades No. & Type	Long Guns No. & Type
Madison Lt. J. Elliott Com. Chauncey	24	20-32s	4-12s
Oneida Lt. M. Woolsey	18	16-24s	2-6s
G. Tompkins Lt. T. Brown	6	2-24s	1-32* 1-24* 2-9s

Table 2 (continued)

Vessel and Commander	Total Guns	Carronades No. & Type	Long Guns No. & Type
Conquest Lt. J. Pettigrew	3	0	2-24s* 1-6*
Ontario S. Mstr. J. Stevens	2	0	1-32* 1-12*
F. American Lt. W. Chauncey	2	0	1-32* 1-24*
Asp Lt. J. Smith	2	0	1-24* 1-12*
Pert Lt. S. Adams	3	0	1-32* 2-6s
Lady of the Lake S. Mstr. T. Nichols	1	0	1-9*
Raven S. Mstr. J. Bowers	1	0	1-18*
Growler S. Mstr. M. Mix	5	0	1-32* 4-4s
Julia S. Mstr. J. Trant	2	0	1-32*x 4-4s
Hamilton Lt. J. Macpherson	9	8-18s	1-12*
Scourge S. Mstr. J. Osgood	10	0	4-6s 6-4s
Totals	88	46	42

APPENDIX E

The Opposing Squadrons , 8-11 August 1813

Table 1: The British Squadron

Detailed reports prepared late in July 1813 showed the British squadron armed and crewed in this way during engagements in the second week of August 1813.[1]

Vessel and Commander	Total Guns	Carronades No. & Type	Long Guns No. & Type	Crew		
				Seamen	Marines	Total
Wolfe Com. J. Yeo	23 10-32s	4-68s 8-18s	1-24*	175	49	224
Royal George Cmdr. W. Mulcaster	20 16-32s	2-68s	2-18s	155	49	204
Lord Melville Cmdr. F. Spilsbury	14	12-32s	2-18s	60	38	98
Earl of Moira Cmdr. A. Dobbs	16	14-24s	2-9s	92	35	127
Beresford Lt. C. Radcliffe	12	10-18s	2-9s	70	28	98
Sir Sidney Smith Lt. C. Owen	12	10-32s	2-12s	80	29	109
Total Numbers	97	78	19	632	228	860

Table 2: The American Squadron

Commodore Chauncey compiled a report on 18 July 1813 showing this arrangement for his squadron. This summary lists only the thirteen vessels involved in the engagements between 8-11 August, omitting the others – the *Lady of the Lake, Raven* and *York* (which never sailed with the squadron).[2]

Vessel and Commander	Total Guns	Carronades No. & Type	Long Guns No. & Type	Crew		
				Seamen	Marines	Total
General Pike M. Cmdt. A. Sinclair Com. I. Chauncey	26	0	24-24s 2-24s*	392	40	432
Madison M. Cmdt. W. Crane	24	20-32s	4-12s	240	34	274
Oneida Lt. M. Woolsey	18	16-24s	2-6s	132	14	146
G. Tompkins Lt. T. Brown	6	2-24s	1-32* 1-24* 2-9s	53	11	64
Conquest Lt. J. Pettigrew	3	0	2-24s* 1-6*	57	9	66

Table 2 (continued)

Vessel and Commander	Total Guns	Carronades No. & Type	Long Guns No. & Type	Crew Seamen	Marines	Total
Ontario S. Mstr. J. Stevens	2	0	1-32* 1-12*	26	3	29
F. American Lt. W. Chauncey	2	0	1-32* 1-24*	52	11	63
Asp Lt. J. Smith	2	0	1-24* 1-12*	27	0	27
Pert Lt. S. Adams	3	0	1-32* 2-6s	26	9	35
Growler Lt. David Deacon	5	0	1-32* 4-4s	30	1	31
Julia S. Mstr. J. Trant	2	0	1-32* 1-12*	35	1	36
Hamilton Lt. W. Winter	9	8-18s	1-12*	44	9	53
Scourge S. Mstr. J. Osgood	10	0	4-6s 6-4s	32	1	33
Total Numbers	112	46	66	1146	143	1289

Table 3: Broadside Strengths of the Two Squadrons, 8-11 August 1813

To tabulate broadside strengths of the opposing squadrons, the total number of pieces of ordnance that could fired on one side of each vessel was counted, assuming that circle-mounted guns could fire on both sides and other guns could fire on only one side. It is assumed that each gun was single-shotted.[3]

	American Squadron					British Squadron				
Calibre	Carronades		Long Guns			Calibre	Carronades		Long Guns	
	No.	Weight	No.	Weight			No.	Weight	No.	Weight
68s	-	-	-	-		68s	3	204	-	-
32s	10	320	6	192		32s	24	768	-	-
24s	9	216	19	456		24s	7	168	1	24
18s	4	72	-	-		18s	5	90	6	108
12s	-		6	72		12s	-	-	1	12
9s	-	-	1	9		9s	-	-	2	18
6s	-	-	5	30		6s	-	-	-	-
4s	-	-	5	20		4s	-	-	-	-
Totals	23	608	42	779			39	1230	10	162

Strength after the loss of:

Hamilton & Scourge	19	536	36	743	
Julia & Growler	19	536	31	659	

APPENDIX F

The Opposing Squadrons at the Engagement near the Genesee River, 11 September 1813

Table 1: The British Squadron

No changes in ordnance appear to have been made between the August engagements and the engagement off the Genesee River, so this table merges the information of Appendix E, Table 1 with the two schooners captured on 10 August.

Vessel and Commander	Total Guns	Carronades No. & Type	Long Guns No. & Type
Wolfe Com. J. Yeo	23	4-68s 10-32s	1-24* 8-18s
Royal George Cmdr. W. Mulcaster	20	2-68s 16-32s	2-18s
Lord Melville Cmdr. F. Spilsbury	14	12-32s	2-18s
Earl of Moira Cmdr. A. Dobbs	16	14-24s	2-9s
Beresford Lt. C. Radcliffe	12	10-18s	2-9s
Sir Sidney Smith Lt. C. Owen	12	10-32s	2-12s
Confiance (*Julia*) unknown	2	0	1-32* 1-12*
Hamilton (*Growler*) unknown	5	0	1-32* 4-4s
Total Numbers	104	78	26

Table 2: The American Squadron

The addition of the *Sylph* to the squadron compensated for the loss of the four schooners, although it entailed the removal of ordnance from several other vessels. Commodore Chauncey noted on 28 August that his squadron mounted ninety-one guns, which is the arrangement shown here for the vessels present at the engagement on 11 September.[1]

Vessel and Commander	Total Guns	Carronades No. & Type	Long Guns No. & Type
General Pike Capt. A. Sinclair Com. I. Chauncey	26	0	24-24s 2-24s*
Madison M. Cmdt. W. Crane	24	20-32s	4-12s

Table 2 (continued)

Vessel and Commander	Total Guns	Carronades No. & Type	Long Guns No. & Type
Sylph M. Cmdt. Woolsey	10	0	4-32s* 6-6s
Oneida Lt. T. Brown	16	16-24s	0
G. Tompkins Lt. W. Finch	6	2-24s	1-32* 1-24* 2-9s
Conquest Lt. J. Pettigrew	2	0	2-24s*
Ontario S. Mstr. J. Stevens	1	0	1-12*
F. American Lt. W. Chauncey	2	0	1-32* 1-24*
Asp Lt. J. Smith	2	0	1-24* 1-12*
Pert Lt. S. Adams	1	0	1-24*
Lady of the Lake S. Mstr. M. Mix	1	0	1-9
Total Numbers	91	38	53

Table 3: Broadside Strengths of the Two Squadrons on 11 September 1813

	American Squadron					British Squadron			
Calibre	Carronades		Long Guns		Calibre	Carronades		Long Guns	
	No.	Weight	No.	Weight		No.	Weight	No.	Weight
68s	-	-	-	-	68s	3	204	-	-
32s	10	320	6	192	32s	24	768	2	64
24s	9	216	20	480	24s	7	168	1	24
18s	-	-	-	-	18s	5	90	6	108
12s	-	-	4	48	12s	-	-	2	24
9s	-	-	2	18	9s	-	-	2	18
6s	-	-	3	18	6s	-	-	-	-
4s	-	-	-	-	4s	-	-	2	8
Totals	19	536	35	756		39	1230	15	246

APPENDIX G

The Opposing Squadrons at the "Burlington Races," 28 September 1813

Table 1: The British Squadron

Commodore Yeo restructured the ordnance in his squadron (and removed the *Confiance* and *Hamilton*) prior to the engagement on 28 September according to a statement by Yeo on 8 October. Precise information regarding the presence of marines was not shown in this document.[1]

Vessel and Commander	Total Guns	Carronades No. & Type	Long Guns No. & Type	Crew
Wolfe Com. J. Yeo	21	4-68s 8-32s	1-24* 8-18s	200
Royal George Cmdr. W. Mulcaster	21	2-68s 16-32s	1-24* 2-18s	158
Lord Melville Cmdr. F. Spilsbury	14	12-32s	2-18s	95
Earl of Moira Lt. C. Anthony	14	12-24s	2-9s	90
Beresford Lt. C. Radcliffe	9	8-18s	1-24*	70
Sir Sidney Smith Lt. C. Owen	12	10-32s	2-12s	75
Total Numbers	91	72	19	688

Table 2: The American Squadron

Chauncey does not appear to have made changes in his squadron following the engagement on 11 September. The information shown here is the same as that in Appendix F, Table 2.

Vessel and Commander	Total Guns	Carronades No. & Type	Long Guns No. & Type
General Pike Capt. A. Sinclair Com. I. Chauncey	26	0	24-24s 2-24s*
Madison M. Cmdt. W. Crane	24	20-32s	4-12s
Sylph M. Cmdt. M. Woolsey	10	0	4-32s* 6-6s
Oneida Lt. T. Brown	16	16-24s	0

Table 2 (continued)

Vessel and Commander	Total Guns	Carronades No. & Type	Long Guns No. & Type
G. Tompkins Lt. W. Finch	6	2-24s	1-32* 1-24* 2-9s
Conquest Lt. Henry Wells	2	0	2-24s*
Ontario S. Mstr. J. Stevens	1	0	1-12*
F. American Lt. W. Chauncey	2	0	1-32* 1-24*
Asp Lt. J. Smith	2	0	1-24* 1-12*
Pert Lt. S. Adams	1	0	1-24
Lady of the Lake S. Mstr. M. Mix	1	0	1-9*
Total Numbers	91	38	53

Table 3: Broadside Strengths of the Two Squadrons on 28 September 1813

	American Squadron					British Squadron				
Calibre	Carronades		Long Guns		Calibre	Carronades		Long Guns	
	No.	Weight	No.	Weight		No.	Weight	No.	Weight
68s	-	-	-	-	68s	3	204	-	-
32s	10	320	6	192	32s	23	736	-	-
24s	9	216	20	480	24s	6	144	3	72
18s	-	-	-	-	18s	4	72	6	108
12s	-	-	4	48	12s	-	-	1	12
9s	-	-	2	18	9s	-	-	1	9
6s	-	-	3	18	6s	-	-	-	-
4s	-	-	-	-	4s	-	-	-	-
Totals	19	536	35	756		36	1156	11	201

APPENDIX H

The Opposing Squadrons in 1814

Table 1: British Squadron

Commodore Yeo described this arrangement for his squadron in April 1814.[1]

Vessel and Commander	Total Guns	Carronades No. & Type	Long Guns No. & Type
Prince Regent Capt. R. O'Conor Com. J. Yeo	58	8-68s 20-32s	30-24s
Princess Charlotte Capt. W. Mulcaster	40	16-32s	24-24s
Montreal/ Wolfe Capt. F. Spilsbury	21	18-32s	1-18* 2-18s
Niagara/ Royal George Capt. S. Popham	21	18-32s	1-24* 2-18s
Star/ Lord Melville Cmdr. C. Anthony	14	12-32s	2-18s
Charwell/ Earl of Moira Cmdr. A. Dobbs	13	12-24s	1-18*
Netley/ Beresford Lt. C. Radcliffe	9	8-18s	1-24*
Magnet/ Sir Sidney Smith Cmdr. E. Collier	11	10-24s	1-9*
Total Numbers	187	122	65

Table 2: American Squadron

Commodore Chauncey described this arrangement for his squadron on 15 July 1814.[2]

Vessel and Commander	Total Guns	Carronades No. & Type	Long Guns No. & Type
Superior Com. I. Chauncey	58	26-42s	30-32s 2-24s
Mohawk Capt. J. Jones	42	16-32s	26-24s
General Pike M. Cmdt. W. Crane	26	0	24-24s 2-24s*
Madison M. Cmdt. E. Trenchard	23	8-32s	14-18s 1-18*
Jefferson M. Cmdt. C. Ridgely	20	16-42s	4-24s
Jones M. Cmdt. M. Woolsey	21	18-42s	2-24s 1-18*

Table 2 (continued)

Vessel and Commander	Total Guns	Carronades No. & Type	Long Guns No. & Type
Sylph M. Cmdt. J. Elliott	18	16-24s	2-9s
Oneida Lt. T. Brown	14	0	14-12s
Lady of the Lake Lt. M. Mix	1	0	1-9*
Total Numbers	223	100	123

Table 3: Broadside Strengths of the Squadrons on 31 July 1814

If the squadrons had fought an engagement on 31 July (before the destruction of the *Magnet*), their weight of metal would have been as shown here.

	American Squadron					British Squadron			
Calibre	Carronades		Long Guns		Calibre	Carronades		Long Guns	
	No.	Weight	No.	Weight	No.	Weight	No.	Weight	
68s	-	-	-	-	68s	4	272	-	-
42s	30	1260	-	-	42s	-	-	-	-
32s	12	384	15	480	32s	42	1344	-	-
24s	8	192	31	744	24s	11	264	29	696
18s	-	-	9	162	18s	9	162	5	90
12s	-	-	7	84	12s	-	-	-	-
9s	-	-	2	9	9s	-	-	1	9
Totals 50	1836	64	1488	Totals	66	2042	35	795	

Strength after the addition of:

St. Lawrence	18	612	34	952
(minus *Magnet*)	- 5	-120	-1	-9
Totals	96	2534	68	1738

Glossary

abatis An obstruction consisting of sharpened stakes sticking out of the ground side by side or fastened to fence-like supports arranged in a long line.

a taste of the cat To be punished by being flogged with a cat-o'-nine-tails.

abeam When calculating a ship's dimensions the measurement "abeam" is the width or breadth of the hull. A wind blowing toward a ship's side is "abeam," as is any vessel located to the side of the ship as opposed to ahead or behind (abaft).

admiral A senior officer in the Royal Navy commanding a fleet or a portion of a fleet. In ascending order of seniority, they were rear admirals, vice admirals and admirals, each class of which was subdivided into blue, white and red squadrons. The most senior officer was admiral of the fleet, while an admiral of the yellow squadron was on half pay and deemed unsuitable for future employment afloat. The USN did not adopt admiral ranks until the Civil War. The Provincial Marine did not have admirals.

admiral of the blue An officer, like John Warren, whose seniority had raised him to the seventh level among admirals. His flagship wore a blue flag at the truck of the main mast.

artillery Heavy weapons, including guns, carronades, howitzers and mortars. See ordnance.

backbone In a vessel, its keel.

ball The projectile fired by a musket, .71 inch in diameter in British muskets and .65 inch in diameter in American muskets.

bar An obstruction to navigation consisting of sand and gravel in the mouth of a stream or river.

bar shot A projectile consisting of an 8"-14" bar connecting two solid hemispheres, also known as dismantling shot as it was used to damage rigging.

bastion A four-sided work which projects from the main rampart of a fort or fortification which permits the defenders to fire along the face of the main rampart.

bateau An open, flat-bottomed boat powered by oars and/or a simple rig, commonly used for transportation of troops, arms and provisions.

battalion In the British army, an infantry unit consisting of between 500 and 1,000 men, commanded by a lieutenant colonel. In the British army of the period, the terms "battalion" and "regiment" were used interchangeably.

beam A heavy squared timber joining the frames across the hull and supporting the deck.

bear up To turn into the wind.

berthing deck The deck where the majority of the crew members sleeps.

block A "pulley" through which lines are run.

blockhouse A military structure, typically two storeys high, used for storage, accommodation or defensive purposes.

B.O. British Board of Ordnance. These letters and an arrow were marked on material belonging to the British armed forces.

boarding party A group of seamen or marines delegated to capture another vessel by storming over its sides either from boats or from their own ship.

boom A spar to which is fastened the lower edge of a fore and aft sail or studding sail.

bower The heaviest anchor (usually two per vessel) carried at the bow, permanently fixed to its cable and ready for instant use.

bowsprit The spar extending forward from the forecastle over the bow.

brig A two-masted, square-rigged vessel.

brig-sloop A brig commanded by a commander (RN) or master commandant (USN).

broadside All of a vessel's ordnance that can bear on a target to one side of the vessel.

buckshot Lead shot measuring 0.24 to 0.31 inches in diameter added to a musket cartridge.

bunting Light, woollen fabric from which flags may be made.

cable Heavy rope used for fastening an anchor to a vessel and for other lifting and towing, its size usually based on the ratio of one inch in circumference to every two feet in the vessel's beam.

cabouse The stove used for preparing meals in the vessel's galley.

canister A projectile fired by ordnance, consisting of a tin can filled with small lead bullets, referred to by the Royal Artillery as "case shot.".

capstan A large, cylindrical winch fitted with bars against which seamen apply pressure to turn the capstan to raise or lower heavy objects such as anchors, spars or boats.

captain Officially, the senior, commissioned officer in a ship below the rank of admiral (in the USN at this period the highest ranking officers in the service), but also the honorific title given to officers of any other rank who commanded warships or merchant vessels. Also see **post captain**.

careen To haul a vessel as far over on one side as possible, without upsetting it, so that its hull can be repaired or scraped clean.

carriage The wooden framework upon which a piece of ordnance is mounted so that it may be fired and moved.

carronade A piece of ordnance with a short barrel and a wide, smooth bore, developed in the 1770s and employed on warships because it was lighter in construction than a long gun, required a smaller gun crew and smaller charges than a long gun, and could fire large-calibre projectiles, though its effective range was limited to about 500 yards.

cartridge The container of propellant used to fire a projectile, for a musket a paper tube holding about six or eight drams of black powder, for a long gun a paper or flannel bag holding about one-third the weight of the projectile in black powder, for a carronade the same package holding on average one-ninth the weight of the projectile in black powder.

case shot See canister.

cat-o'-nine-tails A whip made from nine lengths of cord, each with three knots tied near its end, fastened to a thick rope handle.

caulk To seal the joints between planks by driving oakum or rope junk into them using a hammer and caulking iron.

cavalier A raised, interior battery, usually in the middle of a bastion.

chain shot A projectile consisting of a piece of chain 8" to 12" long connecting two round shot, also known as dismantling shot and used to damage rigging.

circle A pivot mount for ordnance, consisting of a gun carriage fastened to a skid with rollers on its underside that fit into a circular track in the deck, allowing the gun to be rotated to fire in virtually any direction.

cleat A two-armed block of wood around which a rope made be temporarily fastened by taking several overlapping turns around the arms of the cleat.

clew The lowermost corners of a square sail or the aftermost corner of a fore and aft sail.

clew garnet The tackle fastened to the clews of a course sail. Clew lines are used for all other sails.

clew up To raise up the lower corners of a square sail or aftermost corner of a fore and aft sail using the clew garnet or clew line.

cockpit The accommodations for midshipmen and master's mates and, in some vessels, for the surgeon and his mates aboard a vessel.

commander In the RN, a commissioned officer ranked between lieutenant and post captain. Any vessel that he moved into was known as a sloop during his commission.

commission The document issued to officers of lieutenant rank and above in the RN, and including surgeons, surgeon's mates and pursers in the USN after 1812, certifying them to serve in specific positions until replaced and/or transferred to other positions.

commission pendant A long, slender flag flown at the masthead of a vessel commanded by a commissioned officer, white with the red St. George's cross in the RN. Also spelled "pennant."

commodore A temporary position of responsibility awarded to a naval captain, involving the overall command of more than one warship for a specific assignment.

commodore's pendant The short, wide, swallow-tailed commission pendant flown by a commodore from his mainmast. In the RN its coloured indicated seniority among commodores, similar to the system among admirals, in ascending order blue, white and red. Contemporary artwork shows Commodore Yeo's pendant to be blue.

company In naval terms, a vessel's crew. In military terms, a sub-unit of an infantry battalion or regiment, with between 50 and 100 men, commanded by a captain.

corvette A ship, smaller than a sixth rate (RN) or frigate (USN), and a suitable command for a commander or master commandant. It generally carried up to 20 guns on one deck, although HMS *Wolfe*, 22, and the USS *Madison*, 24, were both referred to as corvettes.

course The sail fastened to the lower yard on a mast, the one closest to the deck.

coxswain The helmsman of a ship's boat. A captain's coxswain was in charge of ensuring that the captain's launch or gig was always ready for service and often followed the captain from commission to commission.

cradle The structure constructed around the lower stern section of the hull to keep it upright during its launch.

cutter A type of ship's boat. Also a decked vessel with one mast having a fore and aft rig, except for a square topsail.

deck scraper A device, usually a block of sandstone, used to clean a deck by scraping its surface, after which it is washed down; also known as holystones, likely because seamen had to do their work on their knees and referred to such scrapers as "bibles" or "prayer books.".

deepsea line A lead line used in deep water.

driver A long narrow square sail raised on a gaff to the outer peak of the spanker gaff and set to draw just aft of the spanker.

Durham boat A large bateau-like craft.

edge away To gradually move away from a specific point or specific course.

fathom A length or depth of six feet.

fifth rate In the RN, a warship with 30 to 44 guns on one or two decks.

first rate In the RN, a warship with more than 100 guns on three decks.

fittings All the individual pieces of equipment used to operate a vessel.

fleet The whole of a nation's navy or a portion of that navy assembled for a specific purpose.

floor The large timber fastened across the keel to which the futtocks are fastened.

flotilla A group of small boats, such as bateaux or gunboats.

forecastle The portion of the upper deck between the foremast and the bow.

foremast The mast closest to the bow of the vessel.

fore and aft rig A vessel has a fore and aft rig when most of its propulsion is achieved through the use of sails set along the midline of the vessel rather than athwart the vessel, as with square sails.

forechains The long horizontal board jutting out from a vessel's hull to which the lower shrouds of the foremast are fastened.

foresail The course fastened to the lower yard on the foremast.

fosse The defensive ditch on the outside of a fortification.

foundry An establishment for melting iron and pouring it into molds.

fourth rate In the RN, a warship with between 50 and 60 guns on two decks.

frames The riblike components of a vessel's hull, consisting of overlapping timbers known as futtocks (up to four on each side of the hull), fastened to the keel and secured by the keelson longitudinally and beams athwart the hull.

frigate A ship (RN fifth and sixth rates) originally developed to carry around 30 guns, but later improved to carry more than 40 guns. Too small to fight in the traditional line of battle, it was used as an extension of a fleet or on independent missions. A frigate was an appropriate command for a captain and in the RN an officer's initial commission in a frigate, also considered a "post"-ship, meant automatic appointment to the Admiralty's seniority list.

futtock A component of a frame, overlapped with other futtocks (up to four on each side of the hull) to form the frame.

gaff A spar to which is fastened the upper edge of a fore and aft sail.

galley The "kitchen" aboard a vessel.

gig A light, narrow ship's boat, built for speed.

glacis The downward sloping plain outside of a fortification.

grapeshot A projectile fired from ordnance consisting of a canvas shroud quilted over nine small round shot (resembling grapes, of notably large proportion) positioned around a iron spindle fitted into a circular iron plate.

grenadiers In the British army, the soldiers in a specific company (usually one per battalion) selected for their military prowess and intimidating size.

gunboat A small armed vessel, varying considerably in size, rig and strength from a bateau fitted with a carronade or small-calibre long gun, to a purpose-built craft with rowing benches and two or three guns on slides or circles, to converted merchantmen outfitted with one or more pieces of heavy ordnance. On the lakes the British gunboats were commanded by midshipmen, master's mates or militia officers and belonged to a flotilla under the supervision of a lieutenant or commander, while the American gunboats, mainly converted lakers, were commanded by sailing masters and occasionally by lieutenants.

gun-brig A brig commanded by a lieutenant (RN or USN).

gundeck A deck with guns located along its entire length.

gunport The opening through which guns are fired, usually between two feet, six inches and three feet square and closed with a hinged cover on vessels with more than one deck of guns.

gunroom The accommodations for the gunner under whose supervision young midshipmen (RN) were placed prior to 1805. After that the term applied to the wardroom in a frigate or smaller warship.

gunwale In a vessel, the wide cap fastened to the top of the bulwark. In a boat the cap fastened to the topmost planks in the sides.

halliard A line for raising or lowering sails except for the courses, which, being heavy are raised by a heavier tackle known as jeers.

hand trumpet A long, funnel shaped device used for amplifying instructions. Also called a speaking trumpet.

hawser A heavy cable.

headsails The fore and aft sails set between the foremast and the bowsprit and its booms.

howitzer A short-barrelled piece of ordnance with a wide bore, mounted on a field carriage used to fire explosive projectiles (see shells) on a higher trajectory than a field gun, its calibre being determined by the diameter of its bore.

hundredweight A unit of measurement, equivalent to 112 pounds.

instant (inst.) From the Latin *instantem*, meaning, in a letter, the present or current month.

impressment The practice of enlisting unwilling individuals for service in a warship.

jib The fore and aft sail usually set foremost on a vessel, set from the foremast to the jib boom, which is attached to the bow sprit. A flying jib could be set ahead of the jib.

keel The backbone of a vessel, made from up to seven pieces of large dimension timber joined (scarphed) together to which are attached the stem- and stern-posts and the frames.

keelson An assembly of several large dimension timbers joined together and laid over the floors of the frames to fasten them to the keel.

larboard The left, or port, side of a vessel facing forward.

lateen A large triangular shaped sail fastened to a long yard that is set with one end of the yard secured low to the deck so that the other end holds the other wide end of the sail aloft.

launch The largest boat carried on a warship, also called a longboat.

lead line A weighed line used to measure depth.

leeward The downwind side of a vessel. A lee shore was a shore towards which the wind was propelling a vessel.

lieutenant The first rank of commissioned officers involving increased responsibilities in a vessel, such as being in command of a watch, or independent command of a vessel. A "first" lieutenant was in charge of making sure all elements of the vessel and its crew were in optimum condition. Seniority descended through second, third, fourth and fifth lieutenant, depending on the size of the vessel.

long gun Commonly known improperly as a "cannon," a piece of ordnance with a long, smooth-bore barrel, the calibre of which being determined by the weight of shot it fired.

lower mast The bottom, and thickest, section of the mast assembly.

lugger A small vessel, usually having two masts upon which are raised square sails on yards, or lugs, which are about two-thirds the length of the lower edges of the sails.

magazine A compartment in which black powder and "fixed" cartridges, which have been prepared for use, are stored.

main boom The spar extending over the stern of a schooner to which is attached the lower edge of the mainsail, the largest fore and aft sail on a schooner.

mainmast The tallest mast on a vessel, located behind the foremast.

mainsail The course fastened to the lower yard of the mainmast.

mast A vertical spar to which are attached smaller spars (the yards) and their sails. The term refers to entire structure from the step to the truck and may also refer to each of the component parts of the mast since most masts consist of a lower section to which are attached one or two upper sections.

master The senior warrant officer in the RN in charge of navigation and pilotage, among other tasks, equal in status to the lieutenants and accommodated with them, but rarely promoted from his position.

master and commander A rank used only in the Provincial Marine during this period equivalent to a RN commander. The RN had used this term until 1794.

master commandant A rank used only in the USN during this period equivalent to a RN commander. The vessel under his command was classed a "sloop" regardless of its rig.

master's mate A superior midshipman being groomed for advancement to lieutenant in both services, but more often mentioned in RN records. Also, in both services, a highly skilled seaman or mate from a merchantman with potential to become a master or, rarely, to gain a commission.

match rope A rope with its tips kept smouldering for use in igniting a piece of ordnance.

match tub A partially closed tub of water into which match ropes are dangled to prevent acidental fire.

mess The location where naval officers take their meals and socialize. The crew of a vessel is divided into groups of about eight men each who dined and socialized together around a mess table on the berthing deck(s).

midshipman A "young gentleman" who had three year's experience at sea could be rated a midshipman and thereby be in line to attain a commission in the RN. In the USN this was an entry level appointment, certified with a warrant, which provided training necessary to earn a commission.

mizen The aftermost mast of a three-masted vessel. Also mizzen.

moor To anchor using two anchors, one to either side of the bow with their cables fastened to a swivel so that the vessel can swing with the wind and current, or with one anchor ahead and one behind, or, in modern usage, secured afore and abaft to a quay.

mooring A permanent location in a harbour where vessels can be secured without having to use their own anchors.

mortar A short, squat piece of ordnance designed to fire explosive projectiles (see shells) in a high, curving trajectory, its calibre determined by the diameter of its bore.

naval ordnance Artillery used aboard ships, usually long guns and carronades, but also swivel guns and mortars.

oakum Tarred fibres picked from condemned ropes.

ordnance All "artillery" used aboard vessels or on land, including long guns, field guns, carronades, swivel guns, howitzers and mortars.

orlop deck A deck below the waterline used for accommodations and storage.

palisade A wooden wall constructed of upright sharpened posts or plain poles.

petty officers In both services, generally, assistants to warrant officers, such as quartermaster's, master's mates, gunner's mates, master-at-arms.

pilot An individual hired to share his knowledge of local waters.

pilot boat A speedy sloop or schooner employed to transport pilots to vessels entering a port on the seaboard.

poop deck A deck built above the aft portion of the quarterdeck to create additional accommodations and as a platform for ordnance. Also termed the "roundhouse.".

port The left, or larboard, side of a vessel, facing forwards.

post captain In the RN, the rank above commander whereby the officer was granted a commission for a sixth rate warship, or better, and was posted to the seniority list, which meant that he could attain the rank of admiral if he lived long enough to rise to the upper echelons of the list. The seniority of captains in the USN was noted, but since that service had no admiral ranks advancement to the rank of captain did not hold the additional perk of being "posted.".

post ship In the RN, generally a sixth rate warship, although a smaller vessel entered that class, temporarily, if its commander was advanced to "post" rank.

powder horn A container, often fashioned from a cow horn, worn by a gunner in which a supply of fine black powder was kept for priming the vent or touch hole of his ordnance.

press gang A group of seamen, headed by an officer, delegated to impress suitable individuals for employment upon a warship.

privateer A privately owned vessel outfitted and manned as a warship and employed to capture enemy shipping for the profit of the owner and crew.

proximo (prox.) From the Latin *proximo mense*, next month

purser A warrant officer (RN) or commissioned officer (USN) responsible for supplying provisions, clothing, coal, candles, etc., who was allowed to supplement his wage through frugality and an authorized commission on some transactions.

quarterdeck The area of the upper deck of a vessel between the mainmast and the stern.

quartermaster A petty officer assigned to assist the master in such tasks as steering, stowing goods in the hold and handling cables.

quarters The places to which members of a crew are assigned during an engagement.

rating The seamen in a warship, including boys, ordinary and able seamen.

ratline The heavy lines woven horizontally to the shrouds, like ladders, by which seamen ascended to operate the sails and spars.

receiving ship A old warship moored in a harbour to provide temporary accommodation for seamen awaiting reassignment. HMS *Royal William*, launched in 1719 as a 100-gunner, was still in use as a receiving ship at Portsmouth, England in 1813.

ribs The frames of a vessel.

rig The type of masting and sail configuration.

rigging The lines attached to spars and sails.

rope junk Fibres picked from condemned ropes for use in caulking.

round shot A solid, spherical, iron projectile, its calibre determined by its weight. A typical 9-pdr. shot measured 4 inches in diameter, whereas a typical 24- pdr. shot measured 5.33 inches in diameter.

royal The sail fastened to the royal yard, the fourth yard above the deck.

running rigging All the lines employed in operating the sails and spars.

sailing master In the USN, equivalent to the RN master.

scale the guns To fire a charge of powder from a piece of ordnance in order to remove any rust that might have formed in its bore.

schooner A two-masted vessel, rigged primarily with fore-and-aft sails. It was considered a topsail schooner when square topsails and topgallants were added to its foremast. Contemporary art shows such sails on the mainmasts of British schooners on Lake Ontario.

seaway To make a seaway is to get some headway on the vessel.

second rate In the RN, a warship with 90 to 98 guns on three decks.

semaphore An apparatus for conveying signals by spelling out words using one or more movable arms, or an alternate system (i.e. flags).

sheet A line attached to the lower corners of a square sail or the lower trailing corner of a fore-and-aft sail or a boom.

shell A hollow, iron projectile filled with powder and ignited by a fuse so that it will explode near the enemy.

shipwrights Labourers skilled in the multifaceted craft of building vessels.

shot A round projectile fired by a piece of ordnance.

shrouds The heavy lines in the standing rigging that brace the lower masts to the sides of the hull and brace the topmast and topgallants masts to their tops.

sixth rate In the RN, a warship with 20 to 30 guns, and "post ships" with fewer guns.

slide A flat platform, the slide, with a centre-slot in which the ordnance, fastened to a conventional carriage or a flat "bed," slid when it recoiled. It was often attached to a pivot in the gunport and had a pair of small wheels at the rear for traversing the gun.

slip the anchor To buoy the deployed anchor cable and then detach the cable so that a vessel can leave its morring quickly.

slipway The platform upon which a vessel is built, commencing with its keel, and down which the vessel slides during its launch.

sloop Commonly, a one-masted vessel with fore and aft rig. When applied to a warship, this term indicated that a commander or master commandant had charge of the vessel, which could be rigged as a schooner, a brig or a corvette.

smashers Large calibre carronades, usually 68-pdrs.

snow A two-masted vessel with square sails on both masts (much like a brig) and with an additional, short mast (termed the trysail mast) located right behind the mainmast from which a trysail (similar to a spanker) was set.

sound To measure the depth of water.

spanker The fore and aft sail set behind the mizen and used in place of a mizensail, or mizen course.

spar deck The uppermost deck of a flushed-deck vessel, that is one where the waist is planked over to create a level deck from bow to stern.

spars All the "poles" (masts, yards, booms, gaffs) employed in the rig of a vessel.

spring Used for turning a vessel in a desired direction, a spring consisted of a cable run out through one of the sternmost ports and carried to second cable attached to an anchor that has been dropped ahead of the vessel. By hauling in the first cable (using the capstan) and letting out the second cable, the vessel can be turned.

squadron A small number of warships directed by a senior officer.

square rig A vessel has a square rig when most of its propulsion is achieved with sails set athwart the vessel rather than along its midline as in fore and aft rigs.

stand of grape A single round of grapeshot.

standing rigging All the lines used to brace and support the masts and yards.

starboard The right hand side of a vessel, facing forward.

stations The places to which crew members are assigned to conduct manoeuvres in sailing a vessel.

stays The heavy lines in the standing rigging which brace the masts to the deck behind (backstays) and ahead to the deck and to the other masts and bowsprit.

staysails Fore and aft sails suspended from the stays when in use or furled to the mast ahead when not in use.

step The wooden structure built on and around the keelson to receive the foot of the lower mast.

step the mast To set a mast in its step.

stream anchor A spare anchor weighing about one third the main anchor or bower.

studding sails Supplementary sails used when wind conditions were extremely light and blowing from the stern. They were laced to booms extended past the yardarm of the topsail and topgallant sail yards (usually) and fastened to similar booms on the yard below.

sweep A long, heavy oar used to row or "sweep" a small warship or gunboat.

swivel gun A short, small calibre long gun-like weapon mounted on a pivot located in the bow of a small boat or on the gunwale of a vessel.

tack To change a vessel's course so that the bow of the vessel passes across the eye of the wind causing the wind to blow from over the starboard side (starboard tack) to over the larboard side (larboard tack) or vice versa.

tackle When pronounced *taykle*, the ropes and pulleys (blocks) used to move heavy objects like guns or to trims sails and yards; when pronounced *tackle*, the rigging and general equipment of a ship, including cables and anchors.

third rate In the RN, a warship with 64 to 80 guns on two decks.

topgallant breeze A wind of up to 5-6 knots that allows the topgallant sails to be set safely.

topgallant mast The mast section fastened to and standing above the topmast.

topgallant sail The sail fastened to the topgallant yard, the third yard above the deck.

topgallant forecastle A deck built to cover the forecastle.

topmast The mast section fastened to and standing above the lower mast; the middle portion of the mast assembly.

top The platform built around the assembly used to fasten the topmast to the lower mast and the topgallant mast to the topmast. It provided a structure to which the upper shrouds could be fastened and it was also the quarters of sharp shooters during an engagement.

topsail The sail fastened to the topsail yard, the second yard above the deck.

touch hole See **vent**.

troopship A vessel delegated for transporting troops, often a warship that had had most of its guns removed to accommodate large numbers of passengers.

truck The cap of a mast, fitted with sheaves through which halliards run to raise flags and pendants.

trucks The heavy, small-diameter "wheels" on a naval, or garrison, gun carriage.

trunnions The two cylinder pivots mounted opposite each other near the middle point of a gun's length, which support the gun on its carriage and allow it to be elevated.

ultimo (ult.) From the Latin *ultimo mense*, last month.

vent The narrow hole in the rear of a piece or ordnance through which a priming tool may be inserted to pierce the cartridge so that a priming tube, containing a train of fine powder, may be inserted for igniting the weapon. Also known as the touch hole.

waist The part of the upper deck between the forecastle and the quarterdeck, often open, apart from gangways along the sides, to the gundeck below.

wales A band of heavy planking between the water line and gundeck that strengthened and stiffened the vessel fore and aft. Wales were also installed between gundecks.

warrant officer Officers warranted by the Navy Board (RN) with specialized skills, including masters, surgeons, pursers, chaplains, boatswains, carpenters, gunners and schoolmasters. In the USN, boatswains, carpenters, sail makers and gunners.

wardroom The officers' "mess" aboard a large warship, located between the rows of officers' cabins (situated against the hull in the stern).

watch bill The list delegating jobs and timetables to the members of a crew.

wear To change a vessel's course so that the stern of the vessel passes across the eye of the wind causing the wind to blow from over the starboard side (starboard tack) to over the larboard side (larboard tack) or vice versa.

xebec frigate An armed vessel, favoured by the Barbary States (currently Morocco, Algiers, Tunisia and Libya), with two masts featuring a lateen rig and armed with about twenty guns. It was powerful and fast, and could be rowed in a lull.

yard A spar attached to a mast, usually athwart the vessel in a horizontal position, to which a sail is fastened.

yardarm The outside end of a yard.

Endnotes

Abbreviations Used in Endnotes

ADM	British Admiralty Files
ASP:MA	*American State Papers: Military Affairs*
ASP:NA	*American State Papers: Naval Affairs*
BHS	Buffalo and Erie Country Historical Society Museum
CL	Chauncey Letterbook
CO	British Colonial Office
DAB	*Dictionary of American Biography*
DCB	*Dictionary of Canadian Biography*
DHC	E.A. Cruikshank, ed., *The Documentary History of the Campaign upon the Niagara Frontier*, document cited first, followed by volume:page
DNB	*Dictionary of National Biography*
M125	Letters received by the Secretary of the Navy from Captains, USNA, RG 45, microcopy 125, document cited first, followed by reel:item
M147	Letters received by the Secretary of the Navy from Masters Commandant, USNA, RG 45, microcopy 147, document cited first, followed by reel:part:item
M148	Letters received by the Secretary of the Navy from Commissioned Officers below the rank of Commander and from Warrant Officers, USNA, RG 45, microcopy 148, document cited first, followed by reel:volume:page
M149	Letters sent by the Secretary of the Navy to Officers, USNA, RG 45, microcopy 149, document cited first, followed by reel:page
M273	Records of General Courts Martial and Courts of Inquiry, USNA, RG 45, microcopy 273, document cited first, followed by reel:page.
M625	Area File of the Naval Records Collection, Area Seven, document cited first, followed by reel (no pagination)
MG	Manuscript Group
NAC	National Archives of Canada
NBD	William O'Byrne, *A Naval Biographical Dictionary*
NWDH	William Dudley, ed. *The Naval War of 1812: A Documentary History*, document cited first, followed by volume:page
PM	Provincial Marine
PRO	Public Record Office
RG	Record Group
RM	Royal Marine
RN	Royal Navy
RNB	John Marshall, *Royal Navy Biography*
USN	United States Navy
USNA	United States National Archives

Preface
1. Graves, *Merry Hearts*, 158.
2. Roosevelt, *Naval War of 1812*, 334. Cruikshank, "The Contest for Lake Ontario in 1812 and 1813" and "The Contest for the Command of Lake Ontario in 1814." James, *Naval Occurrences of the Late War*. Mahan, *Sea Power in Its Relation to the War of 1812*.
3. Scott, *Memoirs of Lieutenant-General Scott*, 1:113.

Chapter 1: "On the Banks of the Lake": Lake Ontario Before the War
1. Campbell, *Life of De Witt Clinton*, 79.
2. Campbell, *Life of De Witt Clinton*, 79. Description of the lake's physical characteristics based upon: *The Canadian Encyclopedia*, 3:1576-7.
3. 11 Nov. 1807, *York Gazette*, Firth, *The Town of York*, 132.
4. This description of the *Lord Nelson* and the other lakers based upon: Cain, "Building the *Lord Nelson*," and Cain, "Provisioning Lake Ontario Merchant Schooners." The large hold of the *Governor Simcoe* exceeded the legal limit of 120 tons when it was launched in 1793: Cartwright to Hamilton, 2 Nov. 1793 and MacKay to Beckwith, 25 April 1794, Preston, *Kingston Before the War of 1812*, 202 and 203.
5. Description of the lake ports is based upon: Campbell, *Life of De Witt Clinton*, 28-184; Bouchette, *A Topographical Description of Lower Canada with Remarks upon Upper Canada*; Gourlay, *Statistical Account of Upper Canada*, vol. 1; Wilder, *The Battle of Sackett's Harbour*, 1-5.
6. At this period a village named Newcastle was located on the landward side of the Presqu'ile Peninsula where Presqu'ile Provincial Park is found today. The village was already in decline and eventually disappeared. It should not be confused with the current town of Newcastle, located about 45 miles west. See O'Brien, *Speedy Justice*, 120.

Chapter 2: "Opposing Force to Force": War is Declared: 18 June 1812
1. Madison's message to Congress, 1 June 1812, Hunt, *The Writings of James Madison*, 8:200.
2. Clay to Bledsoe, 18 June 1812, Hopkins, *The Papers of Henry Clay*, 1:600. Thomas Jefferson later predicted: "The acquisition of Canada this year, as far as the neighbourhood of Quebec, will be a mere matter of marching, and will give us experience for the attack on Halifax the next and the final expulsion of England from the American continent," in a letter to William Duane, 4 Aug. 1812, Ford, *The Works of Thomas Jefferson*, 11:264.
3. This discussion of the events leading up to the war is based upon: Hickey, *The War of 1812. A Forgotten Conflict*, 5-50; Hitsman, *The Incredible War of 1812*, 14-23, 41-44; Coles, *The War of 1812*, 1-37; and Brant, *Madison, The President*, 355-483 and *Madison, Commander In Chief, 1812-1836*, 13-54.
4. Casey, "The Potash Rebellion and the Embargo of 1807-09." See also Strum, "A Gross and Unprovoked Outrage: Niagara Incident."
5. Brant, *The President*, 357.
6. Report on Relations with Great Britain, 29 Nov. 1811, Meriwether, *The Papers of John C. Calhoun*, 2:67-8.
7. Clay to Morrison, 21 Dec. 1811, Hopkins, *Henry Clay*, 1:600.
8. *Ibid.*
9. Bayard to Rodney, 9 March 1812, cited in Hickey, *War of 1812*, 35.
10. Speech of Seybert, 18 Jan. 1812, cited in *ibid.*, 34.
11. Armstrong to Eustis, 2 Jan. 1812, *DHC*, 3:30.
12. Hull, *Memoirs of the Campaign of the Northwest Army of the United States, A.D. 1812*, 18- 24.
13. Madison's War Message, 1 June 1812, cited in Brant, *The President*, 472.
14. For a biography of Woolsey, see *DAB*, 10:517-8.
15. For a description of the dimensions of the *Oneida*, see Appendix A, Table 2.
16. For a discussion of naval ordnance, see Tucker, *Arming the Fleet*, 73-130.
17. Woolsey to Robert Smith, 2 April 1809, USNA, M148, 6:11:3. For a description of the *Oneida*, see: Chapelle, *The History of the American Sailing Navy: The Ships and Their Development*, 229-30; and Palmer, "James Fenimore Cooper and the Navy Brig *Oneida*."

18. For Woolsey's correspondence with the Navy Department between Aug. and Nov. 1810, see USNA, M148, 8:15:5, 64, 79, 117, 163, 180.

19. For Woolsey's correspondence between Sep. 1811 and Jan. 1812, see *ibid.*, 9:17:140, 144, 188, 236, 268; and 9:18:5.

20. Woolsey to Hamilton, 9 June 1812, *ibid.*, 10:19:19.

21. Wharton to Hall, 10 May 1812, *NWDH*, 1:108.

22. Woolsey to Hamilton, 4 July 1812, USNA, M148, 10:19:82.

23. "Not a moment should be lost in gaining possession of Niagara and Kingston, and cooperating with General Hull in taking Upper Canada," wrote William Eustis to Dearborn on 15 Aug. 1812, *DHC*, 3:180. Similar messages were sent to Dearborn on 29 July and 1 Aug., *ibid.*: 156, 159.

24. Hamilton to Woolsey, 2 July 1812, USNA, M149, 10:85.

Chapter 3: "Our Navy … Is Worse Than Nothing": The Failure of the Provincial Marine: July-November 1812

1. Strachan to McGill, Nov. 1812, Spragge, *Strachan Letter Book*, 27-8.

2. Douglas, "The Anatomy of Naval Incompetence," 3-25. Muster numbers are those expected to be attained in 1812, according to a report by A. Pye, Proposed Establishment of the Provincial Marine Department … for the Year 1812, 30 Aug. 1811, NAC, RG 8, I, 728:60.

3. Information about the Provincial Marine vessels is based upon the following: Report of the Provincial Marine of the Canadas, 7 Dec. 1811, NAC, RG 8, I, 373:29; Gray to Prevost, 29 Jan. 1812, *ibid.*, 728:77; Report upon the P. M. Establishment …, 24 Feb. 1812, *ibid.*, 728:86; and, A Statement of Naval Forces on Lake Ontario, 14 Oct. 1814, NAC, MG 12, ADM 106, 1997. For further descriptions of the vessel, see Appendix A, Table 1.

4. Like wooden ships everywhere, the vessels on the Great Lakes suffered from rot. Vessels on the lakes appear to have been made from a variety of woods from oak to pine and occasionally cedar. One technique employed on Lake Ontario to inhibit decay was to pack the spaces between frames with salt, as was done with varying effect on the *Oneida* and the *Moira*. See: Note by William Gamble, enclosed in Woolsey to Smith, 4 Dec. 1808, USNA, M148, reel 5, 9:185; Proposed Establishment … 1812, 30 Aug. 1811, NAC, RG 8, I, 728:60; Gray to Prevost, 29 Jan. 1812, *ibid.*, 728:77.

5. Gore to Craig, 14 Nov. 1808, NAC, RG 8, I, 673:147. Craig to Gore, 24 Jan. 1809, NAC, RG 5, A1, 9:18.

6. For a biography of Prevost, see *DCB*, 5:693.

7. Prevost to Bathurst, 18 May 1812, Hitsman, *Incredible War*, 247. Returns of troops in Upper and Lower Canada, 4 July 1812, *DHC*, 3:98-9.

8. For a biography of Brock, see *DCB*, 5:109.

9. Brock to Prevost, 2 Dec. 1811, *DHC*, 3:21. Prevost to Brock, 24 Dec. 1811, *ibid.*, 26.

10. Biographical information about Hugh Earl is scanty. See a petition for financial settlement from Earl to Prevost, 15 October 1813, NAC, RG 8, I, 731:42 and Preston, *Kingston Before The War of 1812*, 251n.

11. Gray to Prevost, 29 Jan. 1812, NAC, RG 8, I, 728:77.

12. Oliver Grace and Timothy Shay were assigned to be officers in the Provincial Marine, apparently by Brock's authority, but under informal arrangements. Memorial by Grace, 7 Dec. 1812, *ibid.*, 729:92. Memorial by Shay, 6 March 1813, *ibid.*, 106. Regarding Grace and others, see Prevost to Bathurst, 24 July 1814, NAC, MG 11, CO 42, 157:79; Freer to W. Drummond, 16 Sept. 1813, *ibid.*, 81; and Report of a Board of Officers, 4 Sept. 1813, *ibid.*, 83.

13. Prevost to Liverpool, 14 April 1812, *DHC.*, 3:52.

14. Woolsey had also erroneously listed two vessels among the British squadron: the *Toronto*, a government yacht lying dismantled at York, and the *Governor Simcoe*, an unarmed merchant laker. See: Woolsey to Hamilton, 23 July 1811, USNA, M148, reel 9, 17:144. The inaccuracy of "intelligence" sources plagued both sides throughout the war.

15. Prevost repeated his warning against offensive operations to Brock in several letters: 7 July 1812, *DHC*, 3:113; 10 July 1812, *ibid.*, 120; 2 Aug. 1812, *ibid.*, 160.

16. The attack on Sackets based upon the following: Woolsey to Hamilton, 21 July 1812, USNA,

M148, reel 10, 19: 100; Preston, "The First Battle of Sackets Harbour;" and Lossing, *Pictorial Field-book*, 367-9.

17. Lossing, *Pictorial Field-book*, 367-8.

18. Robert to Baynes, 17 July 1813, NAC, RG 8, I, 676:183.

19. Prevost to Brock, 12 Aug. 1812, *DHC.*, 3:168.

20. *New York Gazette*, 14 July 1812, cited in *DHC*, 3:126. *Buffalo Gazette*, 21 July 1812, cited in *ibid.*, 135.

21. Woolsey to Hamilton, 21 July 1812, USNA, M148, reel 10, 19:100.

22. Earl had been in the Provincial Marine since 1793, Report of a Board of Officers, 16 Sept. 1813, NAC, MG 11, CO 42, 157:81.

23. Muster rolls for the Provincial Marine squadrons are lacking, but the "scanty supply of sailors at Quebec" is mentioned in Prevost to Bathurst, 17 Oct. 1812, NAC, MG 11, CO 42, 118:273. Although returns for Upper and Lower Canada, dated 4 July 1812, indicate that 368 Royal Newfoundland Fencibles were in the upper province and none were in the lower province (*DHC*, 3:98-99), pro-ceedings from a council at York attended by Brock and others on 3 Aug. 1812 showed only 200 Newfoundlanders in the province (*ibid.*, 162) and later correspondence showed a further 110 of the regiment in transit from Quebec (Prevost to Brock, 12 Aug. 1812, *ibid.*, 167). The regiment was sent in detachments for service in the garrisons along the Detroit and Niagara rivers (District General Order, 14 Aug. 1812, *ibid.*, 179 and Myers to Lethbridge, 22 Aug. 1812, *ibid., 200).

24. Woolsey to Hamilton, 3 Aug. 1812, plus enclosures: Woolsey to Wells, 30 July 1812; Wells to Woolsey, 1 Aug. 1812, USNA, M148, reel 10, 19:138. Woolsey to Hamilton, 8 Aug. 1812, plus enclo-sures: Wells to Woolsey, 4 Aug. 1812; Woolsey to Vaughan, 5 Aug. 1812; Woolsey to Dixon, 5 Aug 1812, and; Ford to Van Rensselaer, 2 Aug. 1812, *ibid.*, 142.

25. The armistice was arranged by Prevost and Dearborn on 9 Aug. for the purpose of allowing Madison's cabinet time to contemplate the news that the British had rescinded its trade restric-tions just days before the war had been declared. Hostilities were renewed on 4 Sept.

26. The raid on Charlotte is based on: Phelps to Tompkins, 4 Oct. 1812, *DHC*, 4:32-3; *National Intelligencer*, 20 Oct. 1812, *ibid.*, 33, *New York Evening Post*, 14 Oct. 1812, *ibid.*, 35, and; Lovett to Alexander, 6 Oct. 1812, *ibid.*, 39. Earl to Prevost, 10 Oct. 1813, NAC, RG 8, I, 731: 43. Royal Navy complements are shown in Comparative Statement of the Force of His Majesty's Squadron and that of the enemy employed on Lake Ontario, 24 July 1813, enclosed in Prevost to Bathurst, 1 Aug. 1812, NAC, MG 11, CO 42, 151:95.

27. Strachan to McGill, Nov. 1812, Spragge, *Strachan Letter Book*, 27-8.

28. Prevost to Bathurst, 17 Oct 1812, NAC, MG 11, CO 42,147:215. Prevost repeated his appeal to Bathurst, recommending his brother, Captain Thomas James Prevost, RN, for command of the detachment, 26 Oct. 1812, *ibid.*, 148:3. See also Prevost to Bathurst, 5 Nov. 1812, *ibid.*, 7.

29. Richardson Memoirs, Malcomson, *Sailors of 1812*, 22-3.

Chapter 4: "The Command of Lake Ontario": Chauncey's Season of Success: September–December 1812

1. Chauncey to Hamilton, 13 Nov. 1812, USNA, M125, 25:176.

2. Brant, *Madison, Commander in Chief*, 73-5.

3. Biographical information about Chauncey may be found in: Pratt, *Preble's Boys*, 170-198; *DAB*, 2: 40-1; Baillie, *American Biographical Index*, items 336-62.

4. For a description of the War with Tripoli, see Gardiner, *The Campaign of Trafalgar*, 14-7.

5. Hamilton to Chauncey, 31 Aug. 1812, *NWDH*, 1:300. A supplement to these instructions was sent five days later: Hamilton to Chauncey, 4 Sept. 1812, *ibid.*, 301.

6. Chauncey to Hamilton, 3 Sept. 1812, USNA, M125, 25:14. Copies of most of Chauncey's corre-spondence is also found in the volumes of the Isaac Chauncey Letter Books held by the New-York Historical Society in New York City and the Clements Library at the University of Michi-gan in Ann Arbor. In researching this topic, the USNA letters were accessed prior to the letter books, so they are utilized as the main source for Chauncey's correspondence with the navy sec-retaries. Other correspondence is referenced to the letter books.

7. For a biography of Eckford, see *DAB*, 3: 4-5.

8. Chauncey to Woolsey, 3 Sept 1812, CL.

9. Woolsey to Hamilton, 7 Sept. 1812, USNA, M148, 10:20:25.
10. Chauncey to Sailing Masters Watts, Grenell, Arundel and Sisson, 20 Sept. 1812, CL. See also Chauncey to Lt. Pettigrew, 24 Sept. 1812; Chauncey to S. M. Gamble, Mix and Osgood, 26 Sept. 1812; and Chauncey to S. M. Mallaby, 26 Sept. 1812, *ibid.* Correspondence regarding the marines is Chauncey to Tarbell, 5 Sept. 1812; Chauncey to Hall, 5 Sept., 1812; and Chauncey to Smith, 20, 24, Sept. and 2 Oct. 1812, *ibid.*
11. For a biography of Elliott, see *DAB*, 3:96-7.
12. Elliott to Chauncey, 8 Oct. 1812, enclosed in Chauncey to Hamilton, USNA, M125, 25:127.
13. Cooper, *Ned Myers*, 53.
14. Materials sent to the lakes are summarized in Chauncey to Hamilton, 26 Sept. 1812, USNA, M125, 25: 79.
15. A detailed survey of this route made in 1810 by De Witt Clinton and others was described in Campbell, *Life of De Witt Clinton*, 29-94.
16. Chauncey to Van Rensselaer, 8 Sept. 1812, CL; Chauncey to Dearborn, 8 Sept. 1812, *ibid.*; Chauncey to Tompkins, 11, 15 & 22 Sept. 1812, *ibid.*
17. Chauncey to Anderson, 25 Sept. 1812, CL; Chauncey to Arundel, 8 Oct. 1812, *ibid.*; Chauncey to Sanford and Lusher, 8 Oct. 1812, *ibid.* Anderson to Hamilton, 8 Oct. 1812, *NWDH*, 1:322.
18. Chauncey to Angus, 8 Oct. 1812, CL.
19. Relevant correspondence for this period includes: Chauncey to Trant, 8 Oct. 1812, CL; Chauncey to Noon, 12 Oct. 1812, *ibid.*; Chauncey to Ludlow, 13 Oct. 1812 *ibid.*; Chauncey to Woolsey, 24 Oct. 1812, *ibid.*; Chauncey to Bullus, 26 Oct. 1812, *ibid.* Chauncey to Hamilton, 12 Oct. 1812, USNA, M125, 25:114. Chauncey to Hamilton, 18 Oct. 1812, *ibid.*, 127. Chauncey to Hamilton, 21 Oct. 1812, *ibid.*, 137. Chauncey to Hamilton, 22 Oct. 1812, *ibid.*, 138. Chauncey to Hamilton, 27 Oct. 1812, *ibid.*, 148.
20. Purchases on Lake Ontario, enclosed with Chauncey to Hamilton, 8 Dec. 1812, USNA, M125, 33:31. For a list of the purchased schooners, see Appendix A, Table 3.
21. Chauncey to Hamilton, 4 Nov. 1812, USNA, M125, 33:161.
22. Details about the November encounters are based on: Chauncey to Hamilton, 6 Nov. 1812, USNA, M125, 33:168; Chauncey to Hamilton, 13 Nov. 1812, *ibid.*, 176; Chauncey to Hamilton, 17 Nov. 1812, *ibid.*, 183; Chauncey to Tompkins, 7 Nov. 1812, CL; Chauncey to Vincent, 16 Nov. 1812, *ibid.*; Elliott to Porter, 3 Nov. 1812, *DHC*, 4:177-8; Letter from an American Officer, *New York Statesman*, 15 Nov. 1812, *ibid.*, 213-4; *Quebec Mercury*, 8 Dec. 1812, *ibid.*, 220-1; Vincent to Sheaffe, 11 Nov. 1812, NAC, RG 8, I, 228:80; Distribution of the Forces in Canada, 12 Nov. 1812, *ibid.*, 1707:61; Gray to Prevost, 3 Dec. 1812, *ibid.*, 728:135; Stacey, "Commodore Chauncey's Attack."
23. Chauncey to Tompkins, 7 Nov. 1812, CL. Chauncey to Hamilton, 6 Nov. 1812, USNA, M125, 25:167. Chauncey to Dearborn, 8 Nov. 1812, CL. Chauncey Chauncey's information about the strength of the Provincial Marine was inaccurate. In both of the above letters he stated the incorrectly calculated sums of 108 guns and 890 men, which have been corrected in the text. For a comparison of the two squadrons, see Appendix B.
24. Cooper, *Ned Myers*, 56-7. Later testimonies would also reveal that the brig's shallow draft made it difficult for the vessel to sail close to the direction of the wind because on such an angle, the force of the wind pushed the brig off course to leeward or downwind.
25. 8 Dec. 1812, *Quebec Mercury*, *DHC*, 4:220.
26. Cooper, *Ned Myers*, 57.
27. Chauncey to Hamilton, 17 Nov. 1812, USNA, M125, 25:183.
28. Chauncey to Hamilton, 13 Nov. 1812, *ibid.*, 176.
29. Chauncey to Dearborn, 17 Nov. 1812, CL; Chauncey to Brown, 18 and 27 Nov. 1812, *ibid.*
30. Chauncey to Dearborn, 30 Nov. 1812, *ibid.*
31. Chauncey to Hamilton, 26 Nov. 1812, USNA, M125, 25:192. For a description of the *Madison*, see Appendix A, Table 2.

Chapter 5: "Our Prospects Are Far … from Flattering.": Winter Projects: December 1812–March 1813
1. Glegg to ?, 10 Jan. 1813, *DHC*, 3:31.
2. Anderson to Hamilton, 13 Nov. 1812, *DHC*, 4:210. American reports were false as there were 459

regular officers and men at Kingston on 12 Nov. 1812, of which 262 were in the 49th Reg., Distribution of Forces in Canada, 12 Nov. 1812, NAC, RG 8, I, 1707:60. Chauncey to Hamilton, 17 Nov. 1812, USNA, M125, 25:183. 9 Jan. 1813, *Kingston Gazette*. Chauncey to Vincent, 16 and 17 Nov. 1812, CL. Chauncey to Vaughan, 17 Nov. 1812, *ibid.*

3. For a biography of Sheaffe, see *DCB*, 8:793. Notes about Sheaffe's character and behaviour may be found in *DHC*, 5:35-9.

4. Scott to Sheaffe, 17 Nov. 1812, NAC, RG 8, I, 728:113.

5. Sheaffe to Prevost, 23 Nov. 1812, *ibid.*, 115.

6. Gray to Prevost, 3 Dec. 1812, *ibid.*, 135.

7. *Ibid.* See Distribution of Forces in Canada, 12 Nov. 1812, NAC, RG 8, I, 1707:60.

8. Gray to Prevost, 11 Dec. 1812, *ibid.*, 728:119.

9. Sheaffe to Prevost, 16 Dec. 1812, *ibid.*, 677:260.

10. Prevost to Gray, 19 Dec. 1812, *ibid.*, 728:125.

11. *Ibid.*

12. Distribution of Forces in Upper Canada and Distribution of Forces in Lower Canada, 21 Dec. 1812, NAC, RG 8, I,1707:127. This return also showed close to 3,700 militiamen in five large battalions and several other groups in Lower Canada. The Upper Canada return did not list militia units although more than 10,000 men were available for the call to duty, see Gray, *Soldiers of the King*, 33.

13. Prevost to Warren, 18 Dec. 1812, enclosed with Warren to Croker, 21 Feb. 1813, NAC, MG 12, ADM 1, 503:163.

14. Warren to Croker, 21 Feb. 1813, *ibid.*, 170.

15. Douglas to Bathurst, 20 Dec. 1812, *DHC*, 4:332. For a biography of Douglas, see *DNB*, 5:1203. Prevost to Bathurst, 5 Nov. 1812, NAC, MG 11, CO 42, 148: 7. Bathurst to Prevost, 13 Jan. 1813, *ibid.*, 160:357

16. Bathurst to Prevost, 12 March 1813, *ibid.*, 359.

17. Nichol to Talbot, 12 Dec. 1812, *DHC*, 4:299. Other correspondence relating to shortages includes: Sheaffe to Prevost, 16 Dec. 1812, NAC, RG 8, I, 677: 260; Nichol to Talbot, 18 Dec. 1812, Cruikshank, *DHC*, 4:327; Sheaffe to Prevost, 22 Dec. 1812, NAC, RG 8, I, 677:288; Sheaffe to Bathurst, 31 Dec. 1812, *DHC*, 4:338; Sheaffe to Prevost, NAC, RG 8, I, 117:1. For a description of the problems in the Commissariat Department, see Steppler, *Logistical Considerations in the Canadian War of 1812.*

18. Evans to Powell, 6 Jan. 1813, *DHC*, 5:29. Although Evans did not name the Marine Department as a weak link ignored by Brock, some of its unimproved deficiencies may be attributed to his lack of attention.

19. For correspondence and a description of this matter, see *DHC*, 5:35.

20. Glegg to confidential, 10 Jan. 1813, *ibid.*, 31. Sheaffe to Powell, 20 Jan. 1813, *ibid.*, 45.

21. Gray to Baynes, 24 Jan. 1813, NAC, RG 8, I, 729:26.

22. Glegg to confidential, 10 Jan. 1813, Cruikshank, *DHC*, 5:31. Regarding Sheaffe's illness, see: Bruyeres to Prevost, 28 Jan. 1813, NAC, RG 8, I, 729: 71.

23. Plucknett to Myers, 27 Jan. 1813, *ibid.*, 62.

24. Bruyeres to Prevost, 28 Jan. 1813, *ibid.*, 69.

25. Myers to Plucknett, 27 Jan. 1813, *ibid.*, 56. Myers to Freer, 27 Jan. 1813, *ibid.*, 58.

26. Myers to Freer, 9 Feb. 1813, *ibid.*, 86.

27. Bruyeres to Prevost, 13 Feb. 1813, *ibid.*, 387:15.

28. Gray to Prevost, 19 Jan. 1813, *ibid.*, 729:34.

29. Bruyeres to Prevost, 13 Feb. 1813, *ibid.*, 387:15. See also Bruyeres to Prevost, undated, presumably enclosed in Prevost to Liverpool, 3 March 1812, Firth, *Town of York*, 77; and Bruyeres to Prevost, 19 Jan. 1813, NAC, RG 8, I, 387:10.

30. Gray to Prevost, 19 Jan. 1813, *ibid.*, 729: 34.

31. Gray to Vincent, 16 Jan. 1813, *ibid.*, 729:28.

32. Gray to Myers, 9 Feb. 1813, *ibid.*, 729:99. Short of skilled labourers, Gray was immediately forced to rehire Morrison to build the spars for the ship at Kingston.

33. Bruyeres to Prevost, 13 Feb. 1813, *ibid.*, 387:15. In his report about the province's fortifications, Bruyeres pointed out the many weaknesses of Fort George, its ruinous and unfinished state, its

need for extensive improvements, additional defences and men to prepare to face the enemy. Fort Erie was only marginally better.

34. Chauncey to Hamilton, 9 Dec. 1812, USNA, M125, 25:210. As he had done previously, Chauncey allowed himself to be misled by information provided about the strength of the British. According to a return taken on 21 December 1812 (NAC, RG 8, I, 1707:127) there was a total of 547 regular officers and men at Kingston, including 291 from the 49th Foot and 60 Glengarries. Only one member of that regiment was stationed above Kingston. At Prescott there were 130 of the latter regiment, the balance (368) being at Montreal. 8 Dec. 1812, *Quebec Mercury, DHC*, 4:220. Chauncey to Vincent, 16 Nov. and 5 Dec. 1812, CL. Chauncey to Vaughan, 5 Dec. 1812, *ibid*. Regarding use of the *Neptune*, see Chauncey to Brown, 31 Oct. 1812, *ibid*. The *Neptune* was never listed among the naval vessels.

35. For a biography of Macomb, see Everest, *The Military Career of Alexander Macomb*. Chauncey to Macomb, 20 Nov 1812, CL. Chauncey to Dearborn, 30 Nov. 1812, *ibid*. Chauncey to Hamilton, 12 Dec. 1812, USNA, M125, 25:211. See also Wilder, *Sackett's Harbour*, 30-32.

36. Chauncey to Hamilton, 1 Dec. 1812, USNA, M125, 25:200. Chauncey to Dearborn 30 Nov. 1812, CL.

37. Chauncey to Bullus, 29a and 29b Nov., 10 Dec. 1812, *ibid*. Chauncey to Hamilton, 8 Dec. 1812, USNA, M125, 25:209. Advertisement to farmers, 1 Feb. 1813, CL. Chauncey to Heard, 18 Nov. 1812, *ibid*. Chauncey to Astor, 27 Nov. and 8 Dec. 1812, *ibid*. Chauncey to Elliott, 9 Dec. 1812, *ibid*. Chauncey to Buchanan, 10 Dec. 1812, *ibid*. Chauncey to Gamble and Hutton, 17 Nov. 1812, *ibid*. Chauncey to Woolsey, 7 Dec. 1812, *ibid*. Circular, 10 Dec. 1812, *ibid*. Chauncey to Billings, 10 Dec. 1812, *ibid*.

38. Chauncey to Hamilton, 25 Dec. 1812, CL.

39. Angus to Hamilton, 27 Dec. 1812, *NWDH*, 1:372. Regarding the Dobbins-Elliott debate, see Dobbins to Hamilton, 12 Dec. 1812, *ibid.*, 369.

40. Chauncey to Hamilton, 1 Jan. and 8 Jan. 1813, USNA, M125, 26:1 and 13. Chauncey to the navy secretary, 20 Jan. 1813, *ibid.*:25. This latter note and others of this period were addressed to the "navy secretary" only since it was known that Hamilton had resigned, but the name of his successor was not known yet at Sackets.

41. Cooper, *Ned Myers*, 58. Only two pieces of correspondence include references to illness during this period: Chauncey to Dodge, 23 Jan. 1813 (asking for militiamen to stand guard in place of sick Marines), CL and Chauncey to Downing, 28 Jan. 1813 (allowing the midshipman to go home to regain his health), *ibid*.

42. Chauncey to the navy secretary, 20 Jan. 1813, USNA, M125, 26:28.

43. Chauncey to the navy secretary, 21 Jan. 1813, *ibid.*:29.

44. Chauncey to Perry, 20 Jan. 1813, CL. Chauncey to the navy secretary, 21 Jan. 1813, USNA, M125, 26:28. Jones to Chauncey, 11 Feb. 1813, USNA, M149, 10:248. Perry to Jones, 17 Feb. 1813, USNA, M147,5:1:20.

45. Chauncey to Hamilton, 14 July 1812, CL. Regarding Leonard's career, see Leonard to Jones, 23 April 1813, M147, 5:1:51 and Wilder, *Sackett's Harbour*, 31-32.

46. This conflict is described in Leonard to Jones, 23 April 1813, USNA, M125, 28:2. Leonard's behaviour is described in Wilder, *Sackett's Harbour*, 31-32 and McKee, *A Gentlemanly Profession*, 441-2.

47. Chauncey to Conkling, 25 Jan. 1813, CL. Chauncey to Drury, 26 Jan. 1813, *ibid*. Chauncey to Wetmore, Chauncey to Fry and Anderson, 1 Feb. 1813, *ibid*. Chauncey to Kemper, 1 Feb. 1813, *ibid*. Chauncey to Lowe, 2 Feb. 1813, *ibid*. Chauncey to Leonard and Anderson, 4 Feb. 1813.

48. Chauncey to Smith, 3 Feb. 1813, CL.

49. Chauncey to Jones, 4 Feb. 1813, USNA, M125, 26:48. Chauncey to Jones, 9 April 1813, *ibid.*, 27:158.

50. General Order by Chauncey, 1 Feb. 1813, CL.

51. Chauncey to Leonard, 1 Feb. 1813, *ibid*.

Chapter 6: "Everything Shall Be Prepared": Planning the Campaign: February–April 1813

1. Chauncey to Dearborn, 10 April 1813, CL.

2. This discussion about changes in the cabinet and its policies based upon Brant, *Commander in Chief*, 114-168 and Stagg, *Madison's War*, 270-303.

3. Monroe to Dearborn, 31 Jan. 1813, cited in Stagg, *Madison's War*, 281.

4. For studies of John Armstrong's career, see: C. Edward Skeen, *John Armstrong, Jr., 1758- 1843, A Biography*; C. Edward Skeen, "Mr. Madison's Secretary of War;"; C. Edward Skeen, "Monroe and Armstrong;" and *DAB*, 1:355.

5. For studies of William Jones's career, see: Charles Oscar Paullin, "Naval Administration Under Secretaries of the Navy;" Edward K. Eckert, "William Jones: Mr. Madison's Secretary of the Navy;" and *DAB*, 5:205.

6. Chauncey to Jones, 10 Feb. 1813, CL. The commodore's first letter to Jones was written on 4 February.

7. Jones to Chauncey, 27 Jan. 1813, USNA, M149, 10:231.

8. *Ibid.*

9. *Ibid.*

10. Astor got help from Gallatin and Attorney General Pinkney to reclaim goods trapped in Canada by the declaration of war. When Captain Arthur Sinclair, USN, complained to Jones in 1814 that Astor's agent was retrieving furs from Mackinac, Jones turned a blind eye to the transaction with the enemy. Astor's involvement in the war is described in John Denis Haeger, *John Jacob Astor: Business and Finance in the Early Republic*, 138-169. Astor, David Parish and Stephen Girard loaned the U.S. government more than $10 million in April 1813.

11. The ultimate failure of the American military campaign of 1813 led to an investigation and report by John Armstrong, which was presented to the second session of the Thirteenth Congress on 2 Feb. 1814. It contained correspondence relevant to the topic. The report (identified as No. 127, "Causes of the Failure of the Army of the Northern Frontier") was published in *ASP:MA*, 1: 439-88. Armstrong's cabinet notes of 8 Feb. 1813 are on *ibid.*:439.

12. Distribution of the Forces in Lower Canada, 21 Dec. 1812, NAC, RG 8, I, 1707:129. Distribution of the Forces in Upper Canada, 21 Dec. 1812, *ibid.*:127.

13. This commentary comes from the anonymous journal of an officer attached to one of the regiments put into motion during the spring of 1813, published as a series in "The First Campaign of an A.D.C.," in *Military and Navy Magazine*. This quote is from 1:155.

14. Armstrong to Dearborn, 10 Feb. 1813, *ASP:MA*, 1:439.

15. Dearborn to Armstrong, 18 Feb. 1813, *ibid.*, 440.

16. Armstrong to Dearborn, 24 Feb. 1813, *ibid.*, 440.

17. Macdonnell to Baynes, 22 Feb. 1813, enclosed in Prevost to Bathurst, 27 Feb. 1813, NAC, MG 11, CO 42, 150: 76. Forsyth to Macomb, 22 Feb. 1813, *DHC*, 5:74. Macomb to Dearborn, 23 Feb. 1813, *ibid.*, 77.

18. Dearborn to Armstrong, 25 Feb. 1813, *ASP:MA*, 1:440.

19. Chauncey to Leonard, 10 Feb. 1813, CL; Chauncey to Jones, 15 Feb. 1813, *ibid.*; Chauncey to Perry, 16 Feb. 1813, *ibid.*; Chauncey to G. Harrison, 17 Feb. 1813, *ibid.*; Chauncey to N. Brown, 18 Feb. 1813, *ibid.*; Chauncey to Decatur, 23 Feb. 1813, *ibid.*; Chauncey to W. Chauncey, 23 Feb. 1813, *ibid.*; Chauncey to Hatfield, 28 Feb. 1813, *ibid.*; Chauncey to Jones, 28 Feb. 1813, *ibid.* Decatur complained about the detachment of 50 men from the *Argus* to Lake Ontario under Wolcott Chauncey, Decatur to Jones, 18 Feb. 1813, USNA, M125, 26:89. Chauncey to Jones, 5 and 21 Feb. 1813, *ibid.*:50 and 99.

20. Dearborn to Armstrong, 3 and 9 March 1813, *ASP:MA*, 1:441.

21. Chauncey to Jones, 3 March 1813, USNA, M125, 27:8. See also: Chauncey Jones, 5 and 8 March 1813, *ibid.*:12 and 20.

22. Dearborn to Armstrong, 14 March 1813, *ASP:MA*, 1:442.

23. This interpretation of the council of war is based upon the correspondence that resulted from it, as shown below.

24. Chauncey to Jones, 18 March 1813, USNA, M125, 27:58. Chauncey's information about the British shipping was mainly incorrect. The *Prince Regent* was at York, but was armed with ten 12-pdr. carronades. The *Duke of Gloucester* had six guns, but was lying dismantled at York, and there was only one 30-gun corvette under construction at the port. Dearborn sent similar messages, Dearborn to Armstrong, 16 March 1813 and undated, *ASP:MA*, 1:442.

25. Correspondence from Jones to Chauncey on these dates 2, 11, and 27 Feb 1813, and 27 March 1813 (USNA, M149, 10:242, 251, 285 and 323) was dominated by information, advice and questions

about the Lake Erie squadron. Other letters in the period dealt briefly with isolated matters regarding both squadrons.

26. Chauncey to Jones, 18 March 1813, USNA, M125, 27:58.

27. Jones to Chauncey, 8 April 1813, *NWDH*, 2:433. Chauncey and Dearborn's letters of 16 March and 14 March respectively were received, discussed and responded to by Jones and Armstrong on 8 April and 29 March respectively. These messages were received by Chauncey and Dearborn on 22 April (at Sackets) and 5 April (at Albany) respectively.

28. Armstrong to Dearborn, 29 March 1813, *ASP:MA*, 1:442.

29. Jones to Chauncey, 8 April 1813, *NWDH*, 2:433.

30. Armstrong to Dearborn, 29 March 1813, *ASP:MA*, 1: 442. He repeated his concern about the use of bateaux to transport a larger force in Armstrong to Dearborn, 5 April 1813, *ASP:MA*, 1:442.

31. For a discussion of the election's influence on the campaign, see Stagg, *Madison's War*, 285- 8. Some Republican supporters had actually printed hand bills announcing victory at York (which was supposed to be an absolute secret) before the squadron sailed. Not everyone was adamant about winning a victory before the election. In his letter to Chauncey on 8 April, William Jones suggested that it might be better to "await a more favourable state of things" so that a larger force could be transported using the bateaux.

32. Precise information about the dimensions of this vessel is lacking. See Appendix A, Table 2.

33. Chauncey to Jones, 6 April 1813, USNA, M125, 27:135. The only data about the *Lady of the Lake* shows its burthen as 89 tons. For a brief discussion of pilot boats, see Chapelle, *Sailing Navy*, 235- 8. The prize vessels were purchased for $3500 (*Elizabeth*) and $2,500 (*Mary Hatt*), Chauncey to Bullus, 17 March 1813, CL.

34. Chauncey to Jones, 8 April, USNA, M125, 27:152. Chauncey to Jones, 23 April, *ibid.*, 28:39.

35. Chauncey noted the gun deck was 142 feet in length in a requisition for materials, Dimensions of Spars for Ship building at Sackets Harbor, enclosed with Chauncey to Bullus, 16 April 1813, CL. Master Commandant Arthur Sinclair noted the vessel was 3 feet longer and 1½ feet wider than the *Essex* (Sinclair to Cocke, 4 July 1813, Malcomson, *Sailors of 1812*, 45) which was 141 feet, 9 inches long and 37 feet abeam, Chapelle, *Sailing Navy*, 165-6, 539. For the vessel's dimensions, see Appendix A, Table 2. Regarding the short 24-pdrs., see Chauncey to Bullus, 16 April 1813, CL and Tucker, *Arming the Fleet*, 88-89.

36. Chauncey to Bullus, 20 March, 16a and b, 21 April 1813, CL; Chauncey to Buttsell, 26 March 1813, *ibid.*; Chauncey to Anderson, 7 April 1813, *ibid.*

37. Wilder, *The Battle of Sackett's Harbour*, 45, 97.

38. Chauncey to Jones, 18 March 1813, USNA, M125, 27:58.

39. Jones to Chauncey, 8 April 1813, *NWDH*, 2: 433. See also Armstrong to Dearborn, 14 April 1813, cited in Stagg, *Madison's War*, 287.

40. Chauncey to Dearborn, 10 April 1813, CL.

41. Hutton to Jones, 25 April 1813, USNA, M148, 11:21:209. Hutton memorial to Madison, *ibid.* Chauncey to Jones, 21 April 1813, USNA, M125, 28:26. Hutton does not appear to have served in the squadron again. He is listed as last noted on Lake Ontario in 1815 by Callahan, *List of Officers*.

42. Chauncey to Jones, 18 April 1813, USNA, M125, 28:12. Chauncey to Fry, 18 April 1813 and Fry to Chauncey, 18 April 1813, enclosed with above. Jones to Chauncey, 2 April 1813, M149, 10:333.

43. Chauncey to Leonard, 13 April 1813, USNA, M125, 27:176. Chauncey to Jones, 16 April 1813, *ibid.*, 28:2. Details of this incident are found in Leonard Court Martial 1–7 Dec. 1813, USNA, M273, 6:151.

44. Leonard to Jones, 23 April 1813, USNA, M147, 5:51.

45. Clerk to Gray, 25 March 1813, NAC, RG 8, I, 729:175.

46. Gray to Freer, 29 April 1813, *ibid.*:173. Gray was enclosing a copy of Clerk's detailed and accusatory letter to him so that Freer could show it to Prevost for his information about Plucknett, but not for "any public use."

47. Gray to Freer, 18 April 1813, *ibid.*:162.

48. Gray to Sampson, 24 April 1813 and Gray to Smith, 24 April 1813, enclosed with Gray to Halkett, 24 April 1813, NAC, RG 8, I, 729:168.

49. Pearson was described by Lieutenant John Le Couteur, Graves, *Merry Hearts*, 109. Gray to Freer

(?), 29 April 1813, *ibid.*:169. Allen's expulsion is detailed in Pearson to Freer, 11 March 1813, *ibid.*:111 and Irwin to Pearson, 11 March 1813, *ibid.*:113.

50. For the dimensions of this vessel, the *Lord Melville*, see Appendix A, Table 1.

51. Gray to Freer (?), 29 April 1813, NAC, RG 8, I, 729:169. A survey of the schooner *Simcoe* conducted by Record and Allen pointed to the surplus wood, Record and Allen, to ?, 6 March 1813, *ibid.*:110. Record was credited with design of the vessel, Statement of the Naval Force on Lake Ontario, 14 Oct. 1814, NAC, MG 12, ADM 106, 1997 (the volumes in this series were unpaginated).

52. Proceedings of a Board of Survey …, 24 Feb. 1813, NAC, RG 8, I, 729:104. See Appendix A, Table 1.

53. For details regarding British gunboats, see Appendix C.

54. Irwin to Freer, 28 March 1813, NAC, RG 8, I, 729:148. Lt. Col. Myers noted that the six 6-pdrs. of the *Gloucester* had been mounted in the bateaux at York, Myers to Freer, 2 April 1813, *ibid.*:153. Thirteen gunboats were proposed to be added to the establishments at Quebec and Lake Ontario during 1812, but no reference was made to their existence on the lake until May 1813, Proposed Establishment of the Provincial Marine …, by Pye, 30 Aug. 1811, *ibid.*, 728:60. Plans were being made late in April 1813 to man a gunboat squadron in the Montreal section of the St. Lawrence River, Plan proposed for raising a Marine Corp …, by Eliot, 21 April 1813, *ibid.*, 729:180.

55. Gray to Freer, 29 April 1813, NAC, RG 8, I, 729:169. For the dimensions of this vessel, see Appendix A, Table 1.

56. The depth of the *Royal George* (13 feet, 11 inches) was considered too great for the shallow Lake Ontario ports, Report on the Provincial Marine …, by Pye, 7 Dec. 1811, NAC, RG 8, I, 373:29. Regarding the substitute ordnance, see: Myers to Freer, 2 April 1813, *ibid.*, 729:153.

57. Gray to Freer, 29 April 1813, *ibid.*:169.

58. Regulations to be observed …, by Gray, 19 April 1813, NAC, RG 8, I, 722:92. Gray to Freer, 29 April 1813, *ibid.*, 729:169.

59. Prevost to Sheaffe, 27 March 1813, NAC, MG 11, CO 42, 150:122. Numbers of men are based upon Graves, *Merry Hearts*, 102, showing 550 rank and file of the 104th and Distribution of Troops in Canada, 21 Dec. 1812, NAC, RG 8, I, 1701:124, showing 301 Voltigeurs.

60. Graves, *Merry Hearts*, 103.

61. *Ibid.*, 112.

62. J. Neilson, "Diary of an Officer in the War of 1812."

63. Gray illustrated the semaphore station and its signals and indicated that he wanted it placed on the blockhouse atop Point Henry. Viger describes it on Cedar Island. Gray to Freer, 18 April 1813, NAC, RG 8, I, 729:162.

64. Graves, *Merry Hearts*, 112.

Chapter 7: "Things Would Have Turned Out Better": The Attack on York: 27 April 1813

1. Armstrong to Dearborn, 15 May 1813, Armstrong, *Notices of the War*, 228.

2. Lieutenant Elliott was given command of the *Madison*, in the place of the disgraced Leonard, Chauncey to Elliott, 17 April 1813, CL. The offer of a detachment of soldiers to serve in the squadron was accepted, Chauncey to Chandler, 18 April 1813, *ibid.* Five weeks' provisions were put aboard the ships, Chauncey to Darragh, Fry and Anderson, 18 April 1813, *ibid.* The seamen at Black Rock were summoned for embarkation at Niagara, Chauncey to Pettigrew, 19 April 1813, *ibid.* The squadron's commanders were told to prepare for receiving troops, 22 April 1813, *ibid.* The *Lady of the Lake* was despatched to transport a rigger and his men to Niagara, Chauncey to Nichols, 22 April 1813, *ibid.*.

3. J. Walworth to father, 19 April 1813, NAC, MG 24, F 16, Jonas Simonds, 1813-1814. Simonds was the colonel of the 6th Regiment.

4. Chauncey to Jones, 24 April 1813, USNA, M125, 28:51.

5. Order of sailing instructions, by Chauncey, 23 April 1813, CL.

6. Description of the Battle of York based on: Chauncey to Jones, 28 April 1813, USNA, M125, 28:63; Dearborn to Armstrong, 28 April and 3 May 1813, *ASP:MA*, 1: 443 and 444; Sheaffe to Prevost, 5 May 1813, NAC, MG 11, CO 42, 150:158; Terms of capitulation, 27 April 1813, *ibid.*:163; Return of casualties, 10 May 1813, *ibid.*:165; Pike's Brigade Order, 25 April 1813, *DHC*, 5:162; Various ac-

counts and anecdotes by: Powell, n.d.; Meeting of Magistrates, n. d.; Allan to Sheaffe, 2 May 1813; letter by Fraser, May 1813, *ibid.*:179-82; by Chewett, Allan *et al.*, 8 May 1813; by Powell, n.d., by Finan, n.d., *ibid.*:192-207. Benn, *Historic Fort York*, 50-64. Stacey, *The Battle of Little York*.

7. J. Walworth to father, 6 April 1813, NAC, MG 24, F 16.

8. Cooper, *Ned Myers*, 59.

9. *Ibid.*, 60.

10. Letter by Fraser, *DHC*, 5:180.

11. Cooper, *Ned Myers*, 61. "Lost the number of his mess" means that the seaman was killed and therefore his numbered place among the men with whom he ate, or messed, was given to someone else.

12. *Ibid.*

13. Chauncey presented the flag to Pike's widow, who had travelled to Sackets with her husband, and also offered her financial assistance. Chauncey to Pike, 15a and 15b May 1813, CL.

14. These figures appear to apply to the regulars only, as Sheaffe left before a full muster could be made of the militia companies and Indians.

15. Chauncey to Jones, 7 May 1813, USNA, M125, 28:101.

16. Armstrong to Dearborn, 15 May 1813, Armstrong, *Notices of the War*, 228.

17. The *Lady of the Lake* was not involved in the landing at York. It had been sent to deliver Henry Eckford to Niagara so that he could assist Perry in preparing the vessels at Black Rock for service. The *Gold Hunter* (mentioned only at this time) also arrived after the battle. Chauncey to Jones, 7 May 1813, USNA, M125, 28:101.

18. The *Lady of the Lake* carried wounded to Niagara on 4 May, Chauncey to Jones, *ibid.* Chauncey to Smith, 30 April and 4 May 1813, CL; Chauncey to Nichols, 4 May 1813, *ibid.*

19. Chauncey to Jones, 11 May 1813, USNA, M125, 28:136.

20. Dearborn to Armstrong, 13 May 1813, *ASP:MA*, 1:444.

21. *Ibid.*

22. Chauncey to Jones, 11 May 1813, USNA, M125, 28:136. 18 May 1813, *Buffalo Gazette*, *DHC*, 7:233.

23. Chauncey to Jones, 11, 16a and 16b May 1813, USNA, M125, 28:136,143 and 144. Chauncey to Brown, 9 May 1813, CL; Chauncey to Bainbridge, 16 May 1813, *ibid.*

24. Chauncey to Nichols, 14 May 1813, *ibid.*; Chauncey to the commanding officer at Kingston, 14 May 1813, *ibid.*

25. Chauncey to Jones, 15 and 17 May 1813, USNA, M125, 28:141 and 148. Chauncey to Woolsey, Macpherson and W. Chauncey, 16 May 1813, CL.

26. Chauncey to Dearborn, 16 May 1813, CL.

27. Barclay to Warren, 23 March 1813, NAC, MG 12, ADM. 1, 503:261. Barclay's arrival at Quebec was recorded by Prevost's daughter with whom he danced at a dinner party, NAC, MG 24, A 9, Select Papers Relating to Major General Augustyn and Sir George Prevost and Family, Recollections: Extracts from Journals, etc., by Miss A. E. Prevost, 134-6.

28. Barclay to Freer, 9 May 1813, NAC, RG 8, I, 729:183.

29. *Ibid.*

30. General Order by Baynes, 22 April 1813, NAC, RG 8, I, 1170:177.

31. Barclay to Freer, 9 May 1813, NAC, RG 8, I, 729:183. Barclay to Prevost, 16 May 1813, *ibid.*:193. For Carlisle, see *ibid.*, 731:43 and Mulcaster Biography, NAC, MG 24, F95:36-38.

32. Regarding Barclay's recommendations about material needs, see: Barclay to Sheaffe, 5 May 1813, NAC, RG 8, I, 678:236; Barclay to Freer, 9 May 1813, NAC RG 8, I, 729:183; Required to Complete Fitting ..., by Barclay, 8 May 1813, *ibid.*:189; Ordnance Required, by Barclay, 9 May 1813, *ibid.*:191; Slop Clothing required, by Barclay, 9 May 1813, *ibid.*:192.

33. Account by Chewett, Allan *et al*, 8 May 1813, *DHC*, 5:192.

34. Berkie to Macdonell, 5 May 1813, NAC, MG 24, G 59, John Macdonell, 1813.

35. Prevost to Bathurst, 21 April 1813, NAC, MG 11, CO 42, 150:143. Prevost criticized Sheaffe for failing to follow up. the victory at Queenston by destroying Fort Niagara in the way that Ogdensburg had been attacked in February.

36. Prevost to Bathurst, 18 May 1813, *ibid.*:156. Sheaffe to Bathurst, 18 May 1813, *DHC*, 5:232.

37. Prevost to Bathurst, 26 May 1813, NAC, MG 11, CO 42, 150:171. Prevost to Bathurst, 24 June 1813, *ibid.*, 151:37. General Order by Baynes, 6 June 1813, NAC, RG 8, I, 1170:229. General Order by

Baynes, 18 June 1813, *ibid.*:266. For a description of the Prevost-Sheaffe conflict, see Sheaffe's biography, *DCB*, 8:793.

38. Account by Chewett, Allan *et al*, 8 May 1813, *DHC*, 5:192.

39. For biographies of Yeo, see: "Memoir of the Public Services of Sir James Lucas Yeo," *The Naval Chronicle*; Spurr, "Sir James Lucas Yeo," *Historic Kingston*; *DNB*, 21:1234; *DCB*, 5:874.

40. Why Cosby sponsored Yeo is uncertain, although he may have been related to the Yeo family. Yeo's younger brother was named George Cosby Yeo.

41. Maitland to Drury, 4 June 1805, *Naval Chronicle*, 13:499.

42. Yeo to Stirling, 3 Feb. 1812, NAC, MG 12, ADM 1, 2736:51.

43. "Naval Defiance," 18 Sept. 1812, *Naval Chronicle*, 28:372. (Illustration of Yeo (p. 117), Smith's comment from Smith to de Rothesay, 6 Jan. 1829, Barrow, *Life of Admiral Smith*, 1:333.)

44. Yeo to Stirling, 11 Dec. 1812, *NWDH*, 1:595.

45. *Ibid.*:216*n*.

46. Yeo's formal instructions were packaged in three documents: The Admiralty to Yeo, 19 March 1813, NAC, RG 8, I, 729:132; Croker to Yeo, 19 March 1813, *ibid.*:135, and; The Admiralty to Yeo, 16 March 1813, NAC, MG 12, ADM 2, 1376:283 (this letter indicated that Yeo was also to take orders from Admiral Warren). Two historians have pointed out that Yeo was hampered by having too many masters. As subsequent events revealed, Yeo was most directly affected by Prevost and only remotely influenced by direct orders from Warren or the Admiralty. As well, a man with the go-for-the-jugular attitude like Yeo had could hardly have been intimidated by such circumstances. See Spurr, "Yeo: A Hero," and Drake, "Commodore Sir James Lucas Yeo and Governor General George Prevost."

47. Contemporary biographies of some of the RN officers who sailed with Yeo include: Mulcaster, *RNB*, supplement 3:215 (see also an informal biography of Mulcaster done in 1851, NAC, MG 24, F 95); Spilsbury, *RNB*, sup. 4:89 (also *DCB*, 6:730); Anthony, *RNB*, vol. 4, part 1:147, Dobbs, *ibid.*, sup. 4:216; O'Conor, *ibid.*, sup.3:400; Dobbs, *ibid.*, sup. 4:216; Owen, *ibid.*, vol. 4, pt. 1:342; O'Conor, *NBD*, 829; Owen, *ibid.*, 844; Hill, *ibid.*, 514; Wingfield, *ibid.*,1310 (also Wingfield's memoir of his lake service, NAC, MG24, F 18).

48. The men who sailed with Yeo as well as the Provincial Marine personnel who remained with his Lake Ontario squadron and other individuals who joined that squadron between May 1813 and April 1814 are listed in The Muster for the Lake Ontario Establishment, PRO, ADM 37, 5000 (unpaginated). For relevant correspondence regarding preparations for Yeo's detachment see: Barrow to Goulburn, 4a and 4b March 1813, NAC, MG 11, CO 42, 152:206 and 208; Croker to Goulburn, 6 and 11 March 1813, *ibid.*:218 and 242; Barrow to Goulburn, 12 March 1813, *ibid.*:254; Croker to Goulburn, 19 March 1813, *ibid.*, 153:31. Croker to Spilsbury, *et. al.*, 8 March 1813, NAC, MG 12, ADM 2, 1376:182; Admiralty Board to Navy Board, 8 March 1813, *ibid.*:183; Establishment of Officers and Seamen for a Particular Service, n.d., *ibid.*:185; Croker to Transport Board, 8 March 1813, *ibid.*:186; Croker to Navy Board, 8 March 1813, *ibid.*:187; Croker to Victualling Board, 9 March 1813, *ibid.*:189; Croker to Sullivan, 9 March 1813, *ibid.*:190. Yeo to Croker, n.d., 13, 17, 18, 19, 6, 21 and 30 March 1813, NAC, MG 12, ADM 1, 2736: 18, 20, 22, 24, 26, 32, 50 and 52.

49. Wingfield, NAC, MG 24, F 18:2. A portion of Wingfield's memoir was published in Ellison, "David Wingfield and Sacketts Harbour."

50. Johnston to J. Johnston, 28 April 1813, *NWDH*, 2:444. This letter and others by Johnston are part of the Johnston Family Papers, contained in the Halsey Papers (ref. 16221-16356) held by the County Record Office, Hertford, Hertfordshire, UK. Some of the correspondence was originally reprinted in Ritchie and Ritchie, "A Laker's Log."

51. *Ibid.*

52. Wingfield, NAC, MG 24, F 18:2.

53. *Ibid.*, 3-4. "Richardson Memoirs," Malcomson, *Sailors of 1812*, 23-4. For details about the dimensions of the *Black Snake* and the two other gunboats mentioned here (probably the *Glengarry* and *Quebec*), see Appendix C.

54. This was the beginning of Barclay's struggle to obtain reinforcements for the weak Lake Erie squadron. Yeo's priority was to maintain strength on Lake Ontario, to the detriment of Barclay. See Barclay's Narrative during his court martial in Sept. 1814, NAC, MG 12, ADM 1, 5445:2; and

Malcomson, "The Barclay Correspondence." Pring's temporary command in the *Wolfe* was mentioned in Prevost to Bathurst, 18 July 1813, NAC, MG 11, CO 42, 151:69.

55. Yeo to Croker, 26 May 1813, NAC, MG 12, ADM 1, 2736:70. Yeo to Croker, 5 May 1813, *ibid.*:66. Regarding promotions, see: enclosures with: Yeo to Croker, 26 May 1813; Board of Health Survey on England, 24 May 1813, *ibid.*:72; Yeo to Croker, 16 July 1813, *ibid.*: 93. For numbers of Provincial Marine seamen and other promotions, see Lake Ontario Muster, PRO, ADM 37, 5000.

56. Wingfield, NAC, MG 24, F 18:5.

57. Prevost to Procter, 7 May 1813, NAC, RG 8, I, 678:216.

Chapter 8: "They Fought … Like Lions": Fort George and Sackets Harbour: May 1813

1. Viger to his wife, 12 June 1813, NAC, MG 24, L8, Ma Sabredache, vol. 8. From manuscript translation and notes (done by Stuart Sutherland) provided by Donald E. Graves, June 1995. Viger referred to the Americans at Sackets Harbour in this context, but the epithet suits both sides in the two battles depicted in this chapter.

2. Chauncey to Dearborn, 16 May 1813, CLB.

3. Chauncey to W. Chauncey, 20 May 1813, *ibid.*

4. Description of the assault on Fort George based on: Chauncey to Jones, 27 and 28 May 1813, USNA, M125, 28:187 and 190; Harvey to Baynes, 25 May 1813, NAC, RG 8, I, 678:311; Vincent to Prevost, 28 May 1813, *ibid.*:318; Fowler to Baynes, 29 May 1813, *ibid.*:338; Vincent to Baynes, 31 May 1813, *ibid.*:354; Return of Troops at 40 Mile Creek, 30 May 1813, *ibid.*:355; Dearborn to Armstrong, 27 and 29 May 1813, *ASP:MA*, 1: 445; Return of British Casualties, 27 May 1813, *DHC*, 5:248; List of Casualties in 1st U.S. Brigade, 26 July 1813, *ibid.*:248; Noon to Tompkins, 27 and 28 May 1813, *ibid.*:249 and 263; Dearborn to Tompkins, 27 May 1813, *ibid.*:250; Lewis to Tompkins, 27 May 1813, *ibid.*:254; Holcroft to De Rottenburg, 15 Aug. 1813, *ibid.*:259; Notes by Merritt, *ibid.*:261; Lewis to Tompkins, 28 May 1813, *ibid.*:264; McDonogh to parents, 30 May 1813, *ibid.*:269; *Buffalo Gazette*, 1 June 1813, *ibid.*:272; J. Walworth to father, 29 May 1813, NAC, MG 24, F 16. Cooper, *Ned Myers*, 66-74. E. A. Cruikshank, *The Battle of Fort George.*

5. Cooper, *Ned Myers*, 66-7.

6. Dearborn to Armstrong, 27 May 1813, *ASP:MA*, 1:445.

7. Vincent to Baynes, 4 June 1813, NAC, RG 8, I, 679:19.

8. *Ibid.*

9. Chauncey to Jones, 28 May 1813, USNA, M125, 28:190.

10. Dearborn to Armstrong, 29 May 1813, *ASP:MA*, 1: 445. Dearborn and Noon to Tompkins, 29 May 1813, *DHC*, 5:265. Chauncey to Jones, 29 May 1813, USNA, M125, 28:196. Chauncey to Jones, 2 June 1813, *ibid.*:29:8.

11. *Ibid.* Dearborn to Armstrong, 8 June 1813, *DHC*, 6:55.

12. Prevost to Bathurst, 1 June 1813, NAC, MG 11, CO 42,150:175.

13. Viger to his wife, 12 June 1813, NAC, MG 24, L8.

14. Description of the assault on Sackets Harbour based on: General Order by Baynes, 30 May 1813, NAC, RG 8, I, 1170:216; Baynes to Prevost, 30 May 1813, NAC, MG 11, CO 42, 150:179; Return of Killed and Wounded on 29 May 1813, *ibid.*:183; Prevost to Bathurst, 1 June 1813, *ibid.*:175; Yeo to Croker, 31 May 1813, NAC, MG 12, ADM 1, 2736: 82; Wingfield, NAC, MG 12, F 18:6-10; Viger to his wife, 12 June 1813, NAC, MG 24, L8; Graves, *Merry Hearts*, 115-8; "Richardson Memoirs," Malcomson, *Sailors of 1812*, 28-9; Brown to Armstrong, 1 June 1813, *NWDH*, 2:473; Brown to Tompkins, 29 May 1813, and Brown to Tompkins, 1 June 1813, *DHC*, 5:283; Chauncey to Jones, 2 June 1813, $\frac{1}{3}$, M125, 29:8; Chauncey to Perry and Dearborn, 3 June 1813, CL; Smith to Wharton, 11 June 1813, *NWDH*, 2:478; Wolcott Chauncey Inquiry, 8, 9, 11 June 1813, USNA, M273, 6: 4:141; John Drury Court Martial, 8–19 July 1813, *ibid.*:143; Wilder, *Sackett's Harbour*, 69-123.

15. For a description of the ordnance of the British fleet, see Appendix D, Table 1.

16. Yeo to Croker, 31 May 1813, NAC, MG 12, ADM 1, 2736:82.

17. References were made to two gunboats employed by the British, but no document names them. They were armed with carronades of varying calibres. Circumstantial evidence suggests that more than two were used, possibly even armed bateaux in addition to the three named here. See Appendix C.

18. Wingfield, NAC, MG 24, F 18:7.

19. Viger to his wife, 12 June 1813, NAC, MG 24, L8.

20. "Richardson Memoirs," Malcomson, *Sailors of 1812*, 28.

21. Graves, *Merry Hearts*, 115.

22. Wingfield, NAC, MG 24, F 18:7.

23. Baynes to Prevost, 30 May 1813, NAC, RG 8, I, 678:347.

24. Wingfield, NAC, MG 24, F 18:7.

25. Although only a schooner, Royal Navy procedure dictated that the *Beresford* was properly classed as a "sloop" while commissioned to Commander Francis Spilsbury.

26. Graves, *Merry Hearts*, 116. Yeo wisely left his dress uniform aboard, preferring to wear a small coat and round hat so that his rank would not be readily apparent to enemy sharp shooters. The coxswain was George Barnett.

27. Chauncey to W. Chauncey, 20 May 1813, CL.

28. Facts about Drury's career are found in: Chauncey to Drury, 25 January and 22 April 1813, CL; Woolsey to Dr. J. Drury, 17 April 1813, a letter of reference enclosed with Dr. J. Drury to Jones, 14 May 1813, USNA, M148, 11:1:196; Callahan, *List of Officers*.

29. Graves, *Merry Hearts*, 116.

30. Viger to his wife, 12 June 1813, NAC, MG 24, L8.

31. Many of the British dead, including Gray, were not retrieved by the British. It appears that they were buried in a hurriedly dug communal grave. Gray's death was noted by correspondents on both sides. General Brown presented Gray's sword to Electus Backus before he died, Brown to Armstrong, 1 June 1813, *NWDH*, 2:473.

32. *Ibid.*

33. Leonard to Jones, 3 June 1813, USNA, M147, 5:1:69. Leonard to Jones, 29 May 1813, *ibid.*:66.

34. Prevost to Bathurst, 1 June 1813, NAC, MG 11, CO 42, 150:175.

35. Yeo to Croker, 31 May 1813, NAC, MG 12, ADM 1, 2736:82.

36. "Richardson Memoirs," Malcomson, *Sailors of 1812*, 29.

37. Graves, *Merry Hearts*, 117.

38. Wingfield, NAC, MG 24, F 18:10.

39. Graves, *Merry Hearts*, 118.

Chapter 9: "We Have the Lake Open to Us": The Royal Navy at Large: June and July, 1813

1. Vincent to Prevost, 8 June 1813, NAC, RG 8, I, 679:53.

2. Chauncey to Jones, 2 June 1813, USNA, M125, 29:8. Chauncey to Jones, 11 June 1813, *ibid.*:47. Chauncey to Bullus, 3 and 5 June 1813, CL.

3. Chauncey to Nichols and Prevost, 2 June 1813, *ibid.* Nichols carried the wives of Colonel James Dennis and Captain James Brock from Sackets to Kingston. Since their husbands had retreated with General Vincent and the ladies were destitute at the town of Niagara after the battle on 27 May, they asked the Chauncey for conveyance to Kingston. Ever the gentleman, he complied. In return, Chauncey asked Prevost (who agreed) to return Lieutenant James Dudley who had been captured in April while hunting on supposedly neutral territory on an island in the Niagara River; see Sheaffe to Prevost, 19 April 1813, NAC, RG 8, I, 678:170.

4. For a comparison of the two squadrons, see Appendix D.

5. Chauncey to Jones, 4 June 1813, USNA, M125, 29:14. Chauncey to Perry, 3 June 1813, CL.

6. Wolcott Chauncey Inquiry, 8, 9 and 11 June 1813, USNA, M273, 6:4:141.

7. *Ibid.*

8. Chauncey to W. Chauncey, 14 June 1813, CL. W. Chauncey to Chauncey, 18 June 1813, enclosed in Chauncey to Jones, 18 June 1813, USNA, M125, 29:82.

9. Jones to Chauncey, 8 July 1813, USNA, M149, 11:9. Chauncey to Jones, 18 July 1813, USNA, M125, 30:13. Drury Court Martial, 8-19 July 1813, USNA, M273, 6:4:143. Chauncey did not send the court martial results to Washington until 4 Aug. 1813 and then waited until Jones acknowledged them to carry out the verdict, Chauncey to Jones, 4 Aug. 1813, USNA, M125, 30:68. Drury complained to Jones about his mistreatment by Chauncey, Drury to Jones, 14 Oct. 1813, M148, 11:24:33. Drury was transferred to Lake Champlain in 1814 where his excessive drinking got him into trouble

(see McKee, *Honorable Profession*, 454). He was lost at sea in 1815 aboard the US Brig *Epervier*. Hutton had complained about his treatment by W. Chauncey after the fire, Hutton to Jones, 5 June 1813, USNA, M148, 11:22:120.

10. Leonard to Jones, 7 and 26 July, 5 Aug. 1813, USNA, M146, 5:1:87, 89 and 94. Jones to Leonard, 17 July 1813, USNA, M149, 11:21. Jones to Chauncey, 27 April 1813, *ibid.*,10:378. Chauncey explained the delay in Leonard's court date on the same day John Drury's court martial began, see Chauncey to Jones, 8 July 1813, USNA, M125, 29:172.

11. There is no biography of Arthur Sinclair. A good source of information about his life is the "Kennon Letters," a series published in 26 separate instalments in *The Virginia Magazine of History and Biography*, vol. 30-40 (1922-32). Letters written by Sinclair to the brother of his first wife, John Hartwell Cocke, are part of the Cocke Papers (#642) in the Special Collection Department, University of Virginia Library. A portion of those letters forms "Private Correspondence of Arthur Sinclair," Malcomson, *Sailors of 1812*, 38-71.

12. Jones to Sinclair, 18 May 1813, USNA, M149, 10:426. Sinclair to Jones, 22 May 1813, USNA, M146, 5:1:64. Jones to Trenchard, 21, 29 and 31 May 1813, USNA, M149, 10:435, 446 and 447. Trenchard to Jones, 25, 26a and 26b May 1813, USNA, M148, 11:22:79, 80 and 81.

13. Sinclair to Cocke, 4 July 1813, Malcomson, *Sailors of 1812*, 45.

14. Chauncey to Jones, 12 June 1813, USNA, M125, 29:57. Chauncey to Jones, 13 June 1813, *ibid.*:59.

15. Chauncey to Jones, 11 June 1813, *ibid.*:47.

16. Prevost to Warren, 5 June 1813, NAC, MG 24, A9, Prevost's Military Letter Book, 2:89.

17. Details about the movements of the *Wolfe* for the period from June until December 1813 are found in the ship's log book, which appears to have fallen into enemy hands and ended up in the USNA. For this chapter see 8 June 1813–28 July 1813, Logbook, HMS *Wolfe*.

18. Vincent to Prevost, 6 June 1813, NAC, RG 8, I, 679:27. Chandler to Dearborn, 18 June 1813, *DHC*, 6:25. Lewis to Armstrong, 14 June 1813, *ASP:MA*, 1:446. Four notes from Dearborn to Lewis, 6 and 7 June 1813, *ibid.*:447.

19. Dearborn to Armstrong, 8 June 1813, *ASP:MA*, 1:445. Evans to Harvey, 10 June 1813, NAC, RG 8, I, 679:80.

20. More than 500 Americans under Lieutenant Colonel Charles Boerstler were captured after a three-hour fight with Indian allies from the Grand River and Lower Canada near Beaver Dams on 24 June, Hitsman, *Incredible War*, 138-9.

21. A. Powell to W. Powell, 31 May 1813, *DHC*, 5:289. Mrs. Powell remarked a week later, "A drizzling summer rain with fog and calm impeded the progress of our ships, and every moment increases the importance of their speedy movements." A. Powell to W. Powell, 8 June 1813, *ibid.*, 6:56.

22. Harvey to Baynes, 11 June 1813, NAC, RG 8, I, 679:76.

23. Regarding the cruises on the American shore 11-20 June, see: Logbook, HMS *Wolfe*, USNA; Yeo to Croker, 29 June 1813, NAC, MG 12, ADM 1, 2736:89; General Order by Baynes, 17 June 1813, *DHC*, 6:90; 20 and 30 June, 22 July 1813, American Daily Advertiser, *ibid.*:93-4; Bennett to Tompkins, 26 June 1813, *ibid.*:154. Chauncey to Jones, 18 June 1813, USNA, M125, 29:77. Woolsey to Chauncey, 19 June 1813, enclosed with Chauncey to Jones, 20 June 1813, *ibid.*:93. Chauncey to Woolsey, 20 and 22 June 1813, CL.

24. "Richardson Memoirs," Malcomson, *Sailors of 1812*, 34.

25. Wingfield, NAC, MG 24, F 18:11. Wingfield notes that his vessel was a hired schooner, but later events showed it to be the *Vincent*. Having an independent command like this showed that Wingfield was almost ready for promotion to lieutenant, until which time he would be considered a master's mate, a senior midshipman of sorts. In 1818 Samuel F. Hooker submitted a losses claim to the government for the loss of his private property among public property on the *Lady Washington*, *ASP:C*, 1:609. The arrival at Kingston of the prisoners aboard the squadron was mentioned on 29 June 1813, in the *Kingston Gazette*.

26. Sinclair to Cocke, 4 July 1813, Malcomson, *Sailors of 1812*, 39; "Richardson Memoirs," *ibid.*,34; Chauncey to Jones, 3 July 1813, USNA, M125, 29:147; Prevost to Bathurst, 3 July 1813, NAC, MG 11, CO 42, 151: 46. Yeo did not mention the failed raid in any of his reports.

27. "Richardson Memoirs," Malcomson, *Sailors of 1812*, 35.

28. Richardson referred to Chaumont Bay as Hungry Bay.

29. "Richardson Memoirs," Malcomson, *Sailors of 1812*, 35.

30. *Ibid.*

31. Sinclair to Cocke, 4 July 1813, Malcomson, *Sailors of 1812*, 43.

32. *Ibid.*

33. Chauncey noted that six men, in all, deserted, Chauncey to Jones, 3 July 1813, USNA, 29:147. Richardson noted two from the 100th Foot, two seamen were marked "R" for "Run" on 1 July 1813, Lake Ontario Muster, PRO, ADM 37, 5000 and Prevost remarked that two Newfoundlanders had deserted, Prevost to Bathurst, 3 July 1813, NAC, MG 11, CO 42, 151:46.

34. Yeo's letter to Croker on 29 June (NAC, MG 12, ADM 1, 2736:89) was his fifth piece of correspondence, including several enclosures, whereas Chauncey wrote 39 letters to Jones between 5 May and 3 July (USNA, M125, reels 28 and 29). Late in 1814 the Admiralty complained about Yeo's reticence, Admiralty to Owen, 12 Dec. 1814, NAC, MG 12, ADM 2, 1381:67.

35. "Richardson Memoirs," Malcomson, *Sailors of 1812*, 36.

36. Gibbs was discharged from the Lake Ontario squadron on 7 July 1813 and Inglis on 26 August, Lake Ontario Muster, PRO, ADM 37, 5000. Yeo did not have authority to convene court martials. In 1815 George Inglis brought charges against Yeo for his mistreatment on Lake Ontario. See Yeo to Croker, 3, 11, 18, Oct. and 17 and 18 Nov. 1815, NAC, MG 12, ADM 1, 2738:155, 171, 180, 187, and 200. The story of Gibbs and Inglis is detailed in Malcomson, "George Inglis: Insights About the Man Who Hauled Down the British Flag at Put-in-Bay."

37. Punishments noted on 5 and 8 July 1813, Logbook, HMS *Wolfe*, USNA.

38. Yeo to Croker, 16 July 1813, NAC, MG 12, ADM 1, 2736:93.

39. Chauncey to Jones, 3 July 1813, USNA, M125, 29:147.

40. Sinclair to Cocke, 4 July 1813, Malcomson, *Sailors of 1812*, 43.

41. Armstrong to Dearborn, 19 June 1813, *ASP:MA*, 1: 449. Dearborn to Armstrong, 20 June 1813, *ibid.* Armstrong to Dearborn, 6 July 1813, *ibid.* General Order by Scott, 10 June 1813, *DHC*, 6:70.

42. Armstrong to Lewis, 9 July 1813, *ibid.*:451; Armstrong to Lewis, 3 July 1813, *ibid.* Armstrong to Boyd, 7 July 1813, *ibid.* Armstrong later sketched out campaign alternatives in his characteristic obtuse manner in a document entitled "Plan of Campaign," said to be approved by Madison's cabinet on 23 July 1813, *DHC*, 6:266.

43. De Rottenburg to Prevost, 7 July 1813, *DHC*, 6:199.

44. Bathurst to Prevost, 1 July 1813, NAC, RG 8, I, 679:164.

45. Chauncey to Bullus, 27 June 1813, CL. Little is known about the size of the *Sylph*. Chauncey noted that Eckford had built the *Governor Tompkins* during the summer of 1812 and intended to make the new vessel similar to it.

46. This arrangement is described in A View of the Force of the Squadron ..., by Chauncey, 15 July 1814, CL.

47. Thirty-five men arrived on 29 June enlisted at New York and 94 men came from Boston on 1 July, Chauncey to Jones, 1 July 1813, USNA, M125, 29:137. The 200-man crew of the *John Adams* arrived on 10 July, Chauncey to Jones, 10 July 1813, *ibid.*:182. Forty-five more arrived from New York on 15 July, Chauncey to Jones 15 July 1813, *ibid.*:198. Several officers were individually ordered to Sackets, Jones to Chauncey, 31 May and 8 June, USNA, M149, 10:447 and 458. Lieutenant Renshaw was ordered to enlist and send 250 in addition to those already sent, Jones to Renshaw, 14 June 1813, *ibid.*:465. One hundred and ten marines under Captain Robert Wainwright were also ordered to the lake, Jones to Chauncey, 3 July 1813, *NWDH*, 2:509. Regarding the soldiers, see Chauncey to Jones, 8 July 1813, USNA, M125, 29:171.

48. Jones to Crane, 26 June 1813, USNA, M149, 10:487. For a biography of Crane, see *DAB*, 2:510. Chauncey to Jones, 8a July 1813, USNA, M125, 29:170.

49. Chauncey to Mix, Adams, Champlin and Forrest, 15 July 1813, CL.

50. Estimate by Hambleton, 20 June 1813, enclosed with Perry to Jones, 19 June 1813, *NWDH*, 2:481. Jones to Perry, 3 July 1813, *ibid.*:487.

51. Jones to Chauncey, 3 July 1813, *NWDH*, 2:509.

52. Chauncey to Jones, 17 July 1813, USNA, M125, 30:11.

53. Chauncey to Perry, 30 July 1813, CL.

54. Perry to Jones, 10 Aug. 1813, *NWDH*, 2:532. Jones to Perry, 18 Aug. 1813, *ibid.*:533.

55. Barclay's correspondence is examined in detail in Malcomson, "The Barclay Correspondence."

56. Prevost to Bathurst, 20 July 1813, NAC, MG 11, CO 42, 151:84. Promotions List enclosed with Yeo to Croker, 16 July 1813, NAC, MG 12, ADM 1, 2736:93. Lake Ontario Muster, PRO, ADM 37,5000. Isaac Chauncey had no connection to Lake Champlain where Lieutenant Thomas Macdonough had been put in charge in September 1812, Hamilton to Macdonough, 28 Sept. 1812, *NWDH*, 1:319.

57. Yeo to Prevost, 22 July 1813, NAC, RG 8, I, 730:55. Yeo to Prevost, 31 May 1813, *ibid.*, 729:201. Gray to Sheaffe, 4 May 1813, *ibid.*, 678:232.

58. General Order by Baynes, 23 July 1813, NAC, RG 8, I, 730:63. O'Conor to Freer, 27 July 1813, *ibid.*:71.

59. Very little was recorded about the construction of gunboats at Point Frederick or elsewhere on the British side, although paroled prisoners and spies informed Chauncey that between six and ten were being built late in June, Chauncey to Jones, 24 June 1813, USNA, M125, 29:104. See Appendix C for details regarding gunboats. For constructions on Point Frederick, see Enclosures with O'Conor to Freer, 3 Sept. 1813, NAC, RG 8, I, 730:119. Chauncey reported that work on three ships at Point Frederick began on 3 Aug., with a launch every forty days in Chauncey to Jones, 20 Aug. 1813, USNA, M125, 30:129.

60. Kempt to Freer, 6 June 1813, NAC, RG 8, I, 730:7. Davis to Freer, 19? June 1813, *ibid.*:16. List of Transport Men, 18 June 1813, *ibid.*:20. Kempt to Freer, 18 June 1813, *ibid.*:21.

61. Lake Ontario Muster, PRO, ADM 37, 5000. The transport men only served until 31 October. Among the others who joined was Lieutenant James Groves who had missed the *Woolwich* at Plymouth. For sizes and distribution of crews, see Appendix E, Table 1.

62. General Order by Baynes, 26 July 1813, *DHC*, 6:281. See also General Orders by Baynes, 10 and 24 July 1813, *ibid.*:213 and 281.

63. Yeo to Prevost, 21 July 1813, NAC, RG 8, I, 730:52. Proposed Plan for Manning the Gun Boats by Darroch, 21 July 1813, *ibid.*: 48. Plan for Gun Boat Service by Yeo, 21 July 1813, *ibid.*:51. Gunboats leaving and returning to the fleet are noted on 19, 22, 24, 25 and 26 July, Logbook, HMS *Wolfe*, USNA. Regarding manning the boats and their appearance, see General Order, 8 June 1813, *DHC*, 6:53; Garrison Order, 22 June 1813, *ibid.*:104; General Order by Baynes, 24 July 1813, *ibid.*:273.

64. Description of the Cranberry Creek incident based upon: Extract of Lewis to Armstrong, 20 July 1813 and extract of letter from a gentleman at Sackets Harbour, 28 July 1813, in 10 Aug. 1813, *Buffalo Gazette*, *DHC*, 6288; General Order by Baynes, 24 July 1813, *ibid.*:271; 7 Aug. 1813, *Niles Register*, *ibid.*:273; Chauncey to Jones, 21 July 1813, USNA, M125, 30:24. Baynes's report referred to the event occurring at Goose Creek, another rivulet several miles west of Cranberry Marsh. Captain Henry Milnes, aide-de-camp to Prevost, was mortally wounded in this incident. On 31 May 1814 more than 200 British seamen and marines were captured during a similar event at Sandy Creek, near Oswego.

65. Lewis to Mrs. Lewis, 9 Aug. 1813, *DHC*, 6:328.

66. Remarks on weekly sick report by Ross to Brown, 18 Sept. 1814 and Ross to Gaines, 15 June 1814, Wilkinson, *Memoirs*, 3: APPENDIX 12.

67. Chauncey to Macomb, 13 July 1813, CL. Chauncey to Jones, 21 July 1813, USNA, M125, 30:24.

Chapter 10: "Deer, She's Gone!": The Commodores Meet: August 1813

1. Cooper, *Ned Myers*, 82.

2. Chauncey to Jones, 4 Aug. 1813, USNA, M125, 30:69. Chauncey to Boyd, 24 and 25 July 1813, CL. The *Lady of the Lake* had been carrying 20 British prisoners to Sackets. They were transferred to the *Raven* and then sent back to Niagara. Chauncey to Mallaby, Lewis, Adams and Mix, 24 July 1813, *ibid.* Boyd to Porter and Armstrong, 24 July 1813, *DHC*, 6:281 and 282. The *Pert* had been at Niagara discharging a detachment of men for Lake Erie and had then bombarded the British camp at Four Mile Creek, Upper Canada, around 24 July (as mentioned in Chauncey to Boyd, 25 July), MacEwen to Mrs. MacEwen, 26 July 1813, *ibid.*:279.

3. Wingfield, NAC, MG 24, F 18:14-5. Wingfield provides an informative description of Burlington Bay and Little Lake as does an Admiralty chart of the area drawn in 1815, NAC, MG 11, CO 42,172: MAP reference 58. The anchorage was located between Sixteen and Seventeen Mile Creek (now apparently Bronte Creek), which were named by their distance up the shore from York.

4. Chauncey to Jones, 4 Aug. 1813, USNA, M125, 30:69. Scott to Boyd, 3 Aug. 1813, *ASP:MA*, 1:450. Battersby to Baynes, 31 July 1813, NAC, RG 8, I, 679:517.

5. Powell and Strachan to Baynes, 2 Aug. 1813, *ibid.*:324. Allan to Baynes, 3 Aug. 1813, *ibid.*, 688c:84. Scott to Boyd, 3 Aug. 1813, *ASP:MA*, 1:450.

6. In June Powell had complained, "there is some regret expressed that it became necessary for the Commodore to destroy the town of Sodus from the apprehension that this place may be the subject of retaliation," see Powell to Prevost, 28 June 1813, NAC, RG 8, I,679:148.

7. Some of the purloined books were returned in the autumn, see Chauncey to Scott and Powell, 14 Nov. 1813, CL.

8. Chauncey to Elliott, Smith and Conklin, 3 Aug. 1813, *ibid.*

9. Williams, chairman of the House Military Committee, was present on the northern battle line for only a brief period, Brant, *Commander in Chief*, 167.

10. Armstrong to Boyd, 30 July 1813, *ASP:MA*, 1: 450. Armstrong to Boyd, 7 July 1813, *ibid.*:449.

11. Boyd to Porter, 5 Aug. 1813, *DHC*, 6:312. Boyd to Armstrong, 8 Aug. 1813, *ASP:MA*, 1:451.

12. De Rottenburg to Prevost, 1 July 1813, NAC, RG 8, I, 679:218.

13. Prevost to Bathurst, 1 Aug. 1813, NAC, MG 11, CO 42,151:95.

14. Changes in the carronades on the *Wolfe* were mentioned in the note of 6 July, Logbook, HMS *Wolfe*, USNA, RG 45. See Appendix E, Table 1 and compare it to Appendix D, Table 1.

15. Details of events between 31 July and 16 Aug. 1813 based *ibid.*; Yeo to Prevost, 9 and 11 Aug. 1813, NAC, RG 8, I, 730:78 and 81; Chauncey to Jones, 13 Aug. 1813, USNA, M125, 30:99; Lewis to Tompkins, 15 Aug. 1813, *DHC*, 7:24; letters from naval officers, 27 Aug. and 6 Sept. 1813, *United States Gazette*, *ibid.*:26 and 28; letter from Deacon, 25 Sept. 1813, *Niles Weekly Register*, *ibid.*:4. Yeo to Warren, 10 Aug. 1813, *ibid.*:5.

16. The *Raven* had been sent to Sackets (Chauncey to Mallaby, 24 July 1813, CL) as had the *Lady of the Lake* (Chauncey to Mix, 6 Aug. 1813, *ibid.*). The *York* never served with the squadron.

17. This discussion of ordnance based on reports by Yeo and Chauncey as in Appendix E.

18. For a comparison of broadside strengths, see Appendix E, Table 3.

19. "Richardson Memoirs," Malcomson, *Sailors of 1812*, 36.

20. Harvey to Baynes, 11 June 1813, NAC, RG 8, I, 679:76.

21. Wingfield, NAC, MG 24, F 18:16.

22. Mcdonogh to his sister, 9 Aug. 1813, *DHC*, 6:325.

23. Cooper, *Ned Myers*, 78.

24. *Ibid.*, 81.

25. *Ibid.*

26. *Ibid.*, 82.

27. *Ibid.*, 83.

28. *Ibid.*, 90. Nineteen survivors were noted by Cain, *Ghost Ships, 111*, but Myers stated sixteen men were picked up as did Chauncey in Chauncey to Jones, 13 Aug. 1813, USNA, M125, 30:99. Myers's account is supported by Nelson, "The Sinking of the *Hamilton* and *Scourge*." Underwater examination of the wreck of the *Scourge* does not substantiate Myers's claim that all the guns of the schooner were left unsecured, nor that a hatch was obstructed by a gun, see Nelson, "*Hamilton* and *Scourge*."

29. As the American squadron lay at anchor off Niagara, 150 infantrymen were embarked on the vessels from Boyd's army to serve as marines in repelling boarders, Chauncey to Jones, 13 Aug. 1813, USNA, M125, 30:99.

30. Yeo to Prevost, 9 Aug. 1813, NAC, RG 8, I, 730:78.

31. Johnston to his mother, 25 July 1813 (which was a log-like letter containing this quote under the date of 9 Aug.), County Record Office, Hertford, Hertfordshire, UK, Halsey Papers, Johnston Family Papers, #16295.

32. Sinclair to Cocke, 25 Aug. 1813, Malcomson, *Sailors of 1812*, 48.

33. Chauncey to Jones, 13 Aug. 1813, USNA, M125, 30:99.

34. Cooper, *Ned Myers*, 75.

35. *Ibid.*, 77.

36. Chauncey to Jones, 13 Aug. 1813, USNA, M125, 30:99.

37. Various testimonies, Court of Inquiry into the Loss of the *Julia* and *Growler*, 2 Sept. 1814, USNA, M273, 6:5:171.
38. *Ibid.*
39. Cooper, *Ned Myers*, 97.
40. *Ibid.*, 99.
41. *Ibid.*
42. Trant Testimony in Deacon and Trant Inquiry, 2 Sept. 1814, USNA, M273, 6:5:171.
43. Since all prisoners of war were eligible to be exchanged, or prone to escape, a close examination and record was made of their physical attributes. Ned Myers, identified himself as Edward Myers from Dresden, aged twenty years. He measured five feet, seven inches tall with a medium build, a "long, sallow" face, fair hair, grey eyes and a scar on his left fore finger. Sailing Master James Trant, was fifty years old, a native of New York, standing five foot, nine inches with a stout frame, a dark, oval complexion and dark hair and eyes. Lieutenant David Deacon was a thirty-one old from New Jersey, five feet, ten inches, thin, dark-haired, with hazel eyes in a face like Trant's, tanned a deep brown by years at sea. Information was taken for thirty-six seamen and soldiers from each schooner who were on average twenty-six years of age and five feet, seven inches in height. See Prisoner of War Records, NAC, RG 8, I, 694A.

Chapter 11: "Give the Vapouring Dog a Sound Drubbing": Engagement at the Genesee: 11 September 1813

1. Wilkinson to Armstrong, 24 Aug. 1813, Wilkinson, *Memoirs of My Own Times*, 4:app. 29.
2. Chauncey to Jones, 13 Aug. 1813, USNA, M125, 30:99.
3. Letter from an officer (written 22 Aug. 1813), 6 Sept. 1813, *United States Gazette, DHC*, 7:28. Extract from a journal (15 Aug. 1813), 27 Aug. 1813, *United States Gazette, ibid.*:26.
4. Anonymous to his uncle (J. Jones), 13 Aug. 1813, enclosed (among Chauncey's letters to the Navy Department) with J. Jones to William Jones, 25 March 1814, USNA, M125, 35:78.
5. Lewis to Tompkins, 15 Aug 1813, *DHC*, 7:24. "Essex men" would seem to mean "traitors" in the context of the mutineers who attempted to take over the USS *Essex* in 1800, but failed. A *"Te Deum"* is a hymn of praise.
6. Sinclair to Cocke, 25 Aug. 1813, Malcomson, *Sailors of 1812*, 50-1.
7. *Ibid.*, 49.
8. Chauncey to Jones, 19 Aug. 1813, USNA, M125, 30:119.
9. Daily events in the British squadron based upon 11 Aug.–11 Sept. 1813, *Wolfe* Log, USNA, RG 45.
10. Yeo to Prevost, 22 Aug. 1813, NAC, RG 8, I, 730:96. The second division of men from the *Dover*, numbering 45 officers and men and 8 marines, (*ibid.*:156) did not reach Kingston until 14 Sept. 1813. Lt. W. Lutman, Master's Mate C. Pynsent and 36 seamen joined Yeo's squadron at that time. See also Lake Ontario Muster, PRO, ADM 37, 5000.
11. Yeo used this opportunity to get rid of Lieutenant George Inglis, who had caused the disruption in the squadron during the failed cutting out expedition to Sackets Harbour at the end of June.
12. Prevost to Bathurst, 25 Aug. 1813, NAC, MG 11, CO 42, 151:138. Yeo to Prevost, 22 Aug. 1813, NAC, RG 8, I, 730:96.
13. For a biography of Wilkinson, see *DAB*, 10:222. Also see Brant, *Commander in Chief*, 203-9 and Stagg, *Madison's War*, 336-47.
14. Council of War Minutes, 26 Aug. 1813, Armstrong, *Notices of the War*, 2: APP. 8. Wilkinson to Armstrong, 21 and 26 Aug. 1813, *ASP:MA*, 1:465. Wilkinson to Tompkins, 21 Aug. 1813, *DHC*, 7:46. Tompkins to McClure, 27 Aug. 1813, *ibid.*:75. Wilkinson to Armstrong, 24 Aug. 1813, Wilkinson, *Memoirs of My Own Times*, 3:29. Armstrong to Swarthout, 25 Aug. 1813, *ibid.*:app.56.
15. Wilkinson to Armstrong, 26 Aug. 1813, *ASP:MA*,1:465.
16. Chauncey to Jones, 19 Aug. 1813, USNA, M125, 30:119.
17. For promotions list, see List of Naval Officers, *ASP:NA*, 1:300-1. Chauncey to Jones, 20, 25a, 25b and 28 Aug. 1813, USNA, M125, 30:123, 149, 150 and 164. Chauncey forwarded Elliott's commission as master commandant to Erie. Edward Trenchard, posted to the inactive *York, was* also advanced to master commandant, but a mental derangement he suffered had become so severe that Chauncey sent him to New York ostensibly to arrange for the transportation of naval gear,

but actually in hopes that his friends there would be able to help him. The new lieutenants were: James Dudley, Joseph Wragg, Charles Skinner, Samuel Bullus, Samuel Adams, and P. A. Jones. The new surgeons were: Walter Buchanan, William Caton and Walter Campbell.

18. Chauncey to Jones, 23 Aug. 1813, USNA, M125, 30:143. For a biography of Gregory, see *Dictionary of American Naval Fighting Ships*, 3:154. Gregory lived to become a rear admiral in the U.S. Navy serving four years of duty with the Union Navy during the Civil War.

19. Sinclair to Jones, 22 Aug. 1813, USNA, M125, 30:140.

20. Sinclair to Cocke, 25 Aug. 1813, Malcomson, *Sailors of 1812*, 51.

21. Jones to Sinclair, 16 Sept. 1813, USNA, M149, 11:90.

22. Time and place references from this point in the study are taken from the logbook of the US Sloop *Sylph* (Burton Historical Collection) in addition to the logbook of HMS *Wolfe* (USNA, RG 45). The *Sylph's* log notes that Chauncey's squadron sailed at 7:00 p.m. on 30 Aug. 1813 because in these vessels a calendar day began at noon of the day prior to the actual calendar date (Monday, 30 Aug 1813 began at noon of what was Sunday, 29 Aug. to the rest of the local world and lasted until noon the next day, which was noon of 30 Aug. elsewhere). British logbooks from vessels on the lakes followed the conventional calendar. From this point, American log dates will be altered to agree with conventional calendar records.

23. The later presence of the *Conquest* does not appear to have been mentioned anywhere other than a note made in the logbook of the *Sylph* on Sunday, 12 Sept. 1813.

24. For a description of the squadron's ordnance, see Appendix F, Tables 2 and 3.

25. The transfer of ordnance is noted in the logbook of the USS *Sylph*, 18–30 Aug. 1813, Burton Historical Collection.

26. Chauncey to Jones, 28 Aug. 1813, USNA, M125, 30:162. Chauncey to Vaughan, 24 Aug. 1813, CL.

27. Wingfield, NAC, MG 24, F 18:15-6.

28. Yeo to Prevost, 5 Sept. 1813, NAC, RG 8, I, 730:134. Harvey to Yeo, 4 Sept. 1813, *ibid.*:129. Depositions of Quin and Brown, enclosed above.

29. Dawson to Porter, 5 Sept. 1813, *DHC*, 7:107. 7 Sept. 1813, *Buffalo Gazette*, *ibid.*:107.

30. Sinclair to Cocke, 10 Oct. 1813, Malcomson, *Sailors of 1812*, 59.

31. Logbook, US Sloop *Sylph*, 12 Sept. (11 Sept. British) 1813, Burton Historical Collection.

32. Wingfield, NAC, MG 24, F 18:17.

33. Yeo to Prevost, 14 Sept. 1813, NAC, RG 8, I, 730:159. Chauncey to Jones, 13 Sept. 1813, USNA, M125, 31:43.

Chapter 12: "All or None": The Burlington Races: 28 September 1813

1. Sinclair to Cocke, 10 Oct. 1813, Malcomson, *Sailors of 1812*, 63.

2. Prevost to Bathurst, 15 Sept, 1813, NAC, MG 11, CO 42, 151:146. Prevost to Bathurst, 25 Aug. 1813, *ibid.*:138.

3. Yeo to Prevost, 15 Sept. 1813, NAC, RG 8, I, 730:164.

4. *Ibid.* Alterations to the squadron are noted in that letter and the record of 16 Sept.–19 Sept. 1813, Logbook, HMS *Wolfe*, USNA, RG 45. For a description of the British squadron after the changes see Appendix G, Tables 1 and 3.

5. For a comparison of ordnance in the two squadrons in August and early September 1813, see Appendix E, Table 3 and Appendix F, Table 3.

6. Prevost to Yeo, 19 Sept. 1813, *DHC*, 7:148. Daily events for this period based upon the record of 19 Sept.–8 Oct. 1813, Logbook, HMS *Wolfe*, USNA, RG 45.

7. Armstrong to Wilkinson, 15 Sept. 1813, Wilkinson, *Memoirs*, 3:377.

8. General Weekly State of the Left Division ..., by Darroch, 16 Sept. 1813, NAC, RG 8, I, 1708:51.

9. Armstrong to Wilkinson, 18 Sept. 1813, *ASP:MA*, 1:468.

10. Armstrong to Madison, 21 Sept. 1813, *NWDH*, 2:583.

11. Daily events for this period based upon the record of 12 Sept.–8 Oct. 1813, Logbook, US Sloop *Sylph*, Burton Historical Collection.

12. Minutes of Council of War, 20 Sept. 1813, Wilkinson, *Memoirs*, 3:app.12.

13. Chauncey to Jones, 25 September 1813, USNA, M125,31:80.

14. De Rottenburg to Prevost, 17 Sept. 1813, NAC, RG 8, I, 680:78.

15. Wingfield, NAC, MG 24, F 18:19.

16. Prevost to Bathurst, 22 Sept. 1813, NAC, MG 11, CO 42,151:154.

17. Yeo to Warren, 29 Sept. 1813, NAC, MG 12, ADM 1, 2736:127.

18. General Orders by Chauncey, 26 Sept. 1813, CL.

19. Wilkinson to Armstrong, 27 Sept. 1813, *ASP:MA*, 1:459. De Rottenburg to Prevost and Darroch, 28 Sept. 1813, NAC, RG 8, I, 680:119 and 126.

20. Description of the action on 28 September based on: Chauncey to Jones, 1 Oct. 1813, USNA, M125, 31:85; Yeo to Warren, 29 Sept. 1813, NAC, MG 12, ADM 1, 2736:127; De Rottenburg to Prevost, 28 and 29 Sept. 1813, NAC, RG 8, I, 680:119 and 123; Cameron to Markland, 29 Sept. 1813, *ibid.*:131; Wilkinson to Armstrong, 29 Sept. and 2 Oct. 1813, *DHC*, 7:178 and 187; Extract of the Logbook of the *Madison*, *ibid.*:211.

21. Wingfield, NAC, MG 24, F 18:18.

22. *Ibid.*

23. Sinclair to Cocke, 10 Oct. 1813, Malcomson, *Sailors of 1812*, 60.

24. Lieutenant Le Couteur, 104th Foot, almost fell out of a tree at Four Mile Creek as he gave a play-by-play account of the action to Colonel John Harvey (Graves, *Merry Hearts*, 135). Commander Richard O'Conor, visiting De Rottenburg's headquarters, watched the action from Queenston Heights (De Rottenburg to Prevost, 28 Sept. 1813, NAC, RG 8, I, 680:119). Captain Tito Lilièvre, Royal Newfoundland Regiment, made observations from York (*ibid.*:128). Americans studied the action from Lewiston Heights (Wilkinson to Armstrong, 29 Sept. 1813, Cruikshank, *DHC*, 7:178).

25. Sinclair to Cocke, 10 Oct. 1813, Malcomson, *Sailors of 1812*, 61, 63.

26. Chauncey to Jones, 1 Oct. 1813, USNA, M125, 31:85.

27. *Ibid.*

28. Enclosed with Yeo's 29 Sept. despatch (NAC, MG 12, ADM 1, 2736:54) to Prevost was the list of British killed and wounded, showing five dead and thirteen wounded. The 28 Sept. entry in the Logbook of HMS *Wolfe*, lists one of the seamen from that list killed and two listed seamen wounded, plus one "marine" killed who does not appear on Yeo's list. The Lake Ontario Muster (PRO, ADM 37, 5000) lists an additional seaman killed at this time. Wingfield noted "25 killed and wounded throughout the whole squadron" (NAC, MG 24, F 18:19).

29. Chauncey to Jones, 1 Oct. 1813, USNA, M125, 31:85.

30. Chauncey to Wilkinson, 1 Oct. 1813, CL. Wilkinson to Chauncey, 1 Oct. 1813, *DHC*, 7:183. Wilkinson to Armstrong, 2 Oct. 1813, *ASP:MA*, 1:470.

31. De Rottenburg to Prevost, 30 Sept. and 3 Oct. 1813, NAC, RG 8, I, 680:123 and 137.

32. Chauncey to Jones, 8 Oct. 1813, USNA, M125, 31:126.

33. Maclean's name does not appear in any of the available musters. Why he was chosen to command the squadron is uncertain.

34. Wingfield, NAC, MG 24, F 18:20. In August 1814, shortly after Wingfield returned to the lakes, he returned the favour by capturing Gregory in a small boat chase near the mouth of the Bay of Quinte (*ibid.*:43). See also, Malcomson, "The Captures of the Schooner *Julia/Confiance*."

35. Chauncey to Jones, 8 Oct. 1813, USNA, M125, 31:126.

36. Sinclair to Cocke, 10 Oct. 1813, Malcomson, *Sailors of 1812*, 57.

37. Two hundred and fifty-two prisoners are counted in Return of Prisoners of War landed … on 6 and 7 Oct. 1813, *DHC*, 7:210. Thirty-seven individuals were taken from two of schooners each, while 72 individuals were taken from a third (including two women from the first and the third) by the *Sylph*, 5 and 6 Oct. 1813, Logbook, US Sloop *Sylph*, Burton Historical Collection.

38. Wingfield, NAC, MG 24, F 18:21.

39. Yeo to Prevost, 7 Oct. 1813, NAC, RG 8, I, 731:5. Maj. Gen. Duncan Darroch informed Yeo of the loss late on 6 Oct. as noted in Darroch to Prevost, 7 Oct. 1813, *ibid.*, 680:151.

40. De Rottenburg to Freer, 17 Oct. 1813, *ibid.*:680:229.

41. Prevost to Torrens, 30 Oct. 1813, *ibid.*, 1221:216.

Chapter 13: "A Mere Attendant upon the Army": The St. Lawrence Campaign: October–November 1813

1. Chauncey to Jones, 30 Oct. 1813, USNA, M125, 32:63.
2. Jones to Chauncey, 19 Sept. 1813, *NWDH*, 2:581. Jones also discussed shipbuilding plans at length, which are discussed in a following chapter.
3. Chauncey to Jones, 8a Oct. 1813, USNA, M125, 31:146.
4. Jones to Chauncey, 19 Sept. 1813, *NWDH*, 2:581.
5. Council of War, 5 Oct. 1813, Wilkinson, *Memoirs*, 3:190. Wilkinson to Chauncey, 9a and 9b Oct., 1813 and Chauncey to Wilkinson, 9a and 9B ⅔CT. 1813, *ibid.: app.* 13.
6. Anonymous, "The First Campaign of an A.D.C.," 5:87-8. Other notes about weather conditions during this period: Wilkinson to Chauncey, 9a Oct. 1813, Wilkinson, *Memoirs*, 3:190; 9 Oct.–9 Nov. 1813, Logbook, US Sloop *Sylph*, Burton Historical Collection; Lewis to Livingstone, 16 Oct. 1813, *DHC*, 7:71; Johnston to Cartwright, 17 Oct. 1813, *DHC*, 8:74.
7. Anonymous, "First Campaign of an A.D.C.," 4:27. See also the letters of J. Walworth to his father during the fall of 1813, NAC, MG 24, F 16, Jonas Simonds, 1813-1814.
8. Wilkinson to Chauncey 16 Oct. 1813 and Chauncey to Wilkinson, 16a and 16b Oct. 1813, *DHC*, 8:69, 70 and 72. Scott to Wilkinson, 11 Oct. 1813, *ASP:MA*, 1:482. Chauncey to Jones, 16 and 17 Oct. 1813, USNA, M125, 32:5 and 10. Chauncey to Armstrong, 16 Oct. 1813, CL.
9. Armstrong to Hampton, 16 Oct. 1813, *ASP:MA*, 1:461.
10. Wilkinson to Armstrong, 18 Oct. 1813, Armstrong, *Notices of the War*, 2:206.
11. Pearson to Baynes, 12 Oct. 1813, NAC, RG 8, I, 680:171. The size of the force at Kingston, Gananoque and Prescott based upon: General Weekly Statement of the Left Division …, by Darroch, 16 Sept. 1813, *ibid.*, 1708: 52; and, General Weekly Distribution of the Troops forming the Centre Division …, by De Rottenburg, 15 Sept. 1813, *ibid.*:50. Return of Royal Artillery, Ordnance … round Kingston, by Darroch, 9 Oct. 1813, *ibid.*, 680:163. Pearson to Baynes, 17 Oct. 1813, *ibid.*:226.
12. Daily events for this period based upon the records of 9 Oct. to 9 Nov. 1813, Logbook, HMS *Wolfe*, USNA, RG 45.
13. Yeo to Croker, 14 Oct. 1813, NAC, MG 12, ADM 1, 2736:144. An Admiralty response on the corner of this document notes that Anthony's commission was confirmed. Anthony's commission by Yeo was dated 21 Sept. 1813, *ibid.*:143. For a biography of Anthony, see *NBD*, 16.
14. Yeo to Croker, 14 Oct. 1813, NAC, RG 8, I, 731:21. In this note Yeo mentioned his dissatisfaction with the *Marlborough* men who he claimed included "a number of old, infirm Men, and Boys." The transport volunteers departed on 31 October and close to 110 *Marlboroughs* were admitted on 13 October according to the Lake Ontario Muster, PRO, ADM 37, 5000. Other relevant correspondence includes: Warren to Prevost, 21 Aug. 1813; Griffith to Prevost, 7 Sept. 1813; Warren to Prevost, 21 Sept. 1813, NAC, MG 24, A9, Prevost's Military Letter Book, 2:73, 75 and 78. According to these orders, the sloop *Indian* was also supposed to go to Quebec and send its crew (the vessel was rated at 121 men: Ships in Sea Pay, 1 July 1813, *NWDH*, 2:168) to the lakes, but appears to have been delayed.
15. De Rottenburg to Prevost, 14 Oct. 1813, NAC, RG 8, I, 680:188.
16. Yeo to Prevost, 17 Oct. 1813, *ibid*, 731: 47.
17. *Ibid.* De Rottenburg to Prevost, 18 Oct. 1813, *ibid.*, 680:241.
18. Lewis to his wife, 25 Oct. 1813, *DHC*, 8:94.
19. Armstrong to Wilkinson, 19 Oct. 1813; Wilkinson to Armstrong, 19 Oct. 1813; and, Armstrong to Wilkinson, 20 Oct. 1813, Armstrong, *Notices of the War*, 2:207, 209 and 210.
20. Armstrong to Wilkinson, 27 Oct. 1813, Wilkinson, *Memoirs of My Own Times*, 3: APP. 41.
21. Totten Diary, *ibid.*, 3:224. Wilkinson to Armstrong, 1 Nov. 1813, *ASP:MA*, 1:474.
22. Hampton to Armstrong, 1 Nov. 1813, *ibid.*:461.
23. Chauncey to Jones, 30 Oct. 1813, USNA, M125, 32: 63.
24. Chauncey to Jones, 4 Nov. 1813, *ibid.*:76.
25. Yeo to Melville, 31 Oct. 1813, NAC, MG 24, F 14, Melville Letters. Yeo managed Mulcaster's promotion by placing him in command of one of the two frigates then under construction at Kingston. Mulcaster's place in the *Royal George* was assigned to Commander Stephen Popham, who was known to be on his way to Kingston with a detachment of RN officers and men.

26. Details of the French Creek engagement based on: Mulcaster to Yeo, 2 Nov. 1813, enclosed in Yeo to Warren, 3 Nov. 1813, NAC, MG 12, ADM 1, 2736:186; De Rottenburg to Baynes, 2 Nov. 1813, NAC, RG 8, I, 681:11; Brown to Dennis, 2 Nov. 1813, *DHC*, 8:125. Wilkinson Journal, 2 Nov. 1813, *ASP:MA*, 1:476.

27. Mulcaster to Yeo, 2 Nov. 1813, enclosed in Yeo to Warren, 3 Nov. 1813, NAC, MG 12, ADM 1, 2736:186.

28. Sinclair to Cocke, 30 Nov. 1813, Malcomson, *Sailors of 1812*, 66. See also, Chauncey to Jones, 11 Nov. 1813, USNA, M125, 32:93.

29. Chauncey to Jones, 11 Nov. 1813, *ibid.*

30. Prevost to Bathurst, 15 Nov. 1813, NAC, MG 11, CO 42, 152:10.

31. Description of progress down the St. Lawrence, based on: Wilkinson Journal, 21 Oct.–13 Nov. 1813, *ASP:MA*, 1: 476; Lewis to his wife, 13 Nov. 1813, *DHC*, 8:175; J. K. Paige Diary, *ibid.*:148. Capitulation of Hamilton by Ogden and Richards, 10 Nov. 1813, enclosed with Morrison to De Rottenburg, 11 Nov. 1813, NAC, RG 8, I, 681:78.

32. Events surrounding the Battle of Crysler's Farm based on: Morrison to De Rottenburg, 12 Nov. 1813, NAC, RG 8, I, 681:76; Boyd to Wilkinson, 12 Nov. 1813, *DHC*, 8:170; Way, *The Day at Crysler's Farm*; Graves, *"Brilliant Little Affair," Battle at Crysler's Farm, 1813*.

33. Wilkinson to Armstrong, 24 Nov. 1813, *ASP:MA*, 1:430.

34. Morrison to Baynes, 15 Nov. 1813, NAC, RG 8, I, 681:44.

35. Chauncey to Armstrong, 12 Nov. 1813, CL. Chauncey to Jones, 12 Nov. 1813, USNA, M125, 32:99. Chauncey to Harrison, 14 Nov. 1813, CL. Chauncey had already heard that 1400 officers and men of the northwestern army under Major General William Henry Harrison (the victor of Moraviantown) had reached Niagara in a letter from Perry, 24 Oct. 1813, enclosed in Chauncey to Jones, 31 Oct. 1813, USNA, M125, 32:64.

36. Chauncey to Jones, 21 Nov. 1813, *ibid.*:114.

37. Chauncey to Jones, 21, 24 and 28 Nov. 1813, *ibid.*:114, 123 and 138. See also, Sinclair to Cocke, 30 Nov. 1813, Malcomson, *Sailors of 1812*, 64; Bacon to Tompkins, 21 Nov. 1813, *DHC*, 8:222.

Chapter 14: "Such a Force … May Save the Country": British Naval Escalation: November 1813– March 1814

1. Yeo to Beckwith, 10 Feb. 1814, NAC, RG 8, I, 732:32.

2. Daily events for this period based on the record of 12 Nov.–20 Dec. 1813, Logbook, HMS *Wolfe*, USNA, RG 45. The logbook ends at this latter date below which are the signatures of Isaac Chauncey and Melancthon Woolsey, suggesting that the book was captured after being sent to Quebec, ostensibly for subsequent delivery to the Admiralty in England. Notes on the record of the document show that it was sent to the Navy Department in 1814 by Captain Thomas Macdonough at Plattsburgh.

3. Sinclair to Cocke, 30 Nov. 1813, Malcomson, *Sailors of 1812*, 69.

4. Yeo to Warren, 10 Oct. 1813, NAC, RG 8, I, 731:124. See also Malcomson, "Controversial Relations among the British," and "The Barclay Correspondence." Prevost to Yeo, 19 Sept. 1813, *DHC*, 7:148.

5. Barclay to Yeo, 12 Sept. 1813, NAC, RG 8, I, 731:116.

6. Yeo to Warren, 14 Nov. 1813, NAC, MG 12, ADM 1, 2737:2. Chauncey had informed Yeo of the severity of Barclay's wounds in a letter on 12 Oct. 1813 and that Barclay had been paroled and was recuperating in Queenston in a letter on 23 Nov. 1813, CL.

7. Yeo to Warren, 14 Nov. 1813, NAC, MG 12, ADM 1, 2737:2.

8. Yeo to Prevost, 15 Nov. 1813, NAC, MG 11, CO 42, 152:47.

9. Prevost to Bathurst, 22 Sept. 1813, *ibid.*, 151:154.

10. General Order by Baynes, 24 Nov. 1813, *ibid.*, 152:59.

11. 8 Nov. 1813, *The Times* of London, 3; 12 Nov. 1813, *ibid.*, 3.

12. Yeo to Croker, 5, 26 May and 15 July 1813, NAC, MG 12, ADM 1, 2736:66, 70 and 96. Yeo to Melville, 18 Sept. 1813, NAC, MG 24, F 14. Prevost to Bathurst, 18 May 1813, NAC, MG 11, CO 42, 150:156. Prevost to Warren, 5 June 1813, NAC, MG 24, A9, 2:89.

13. O'Conor to Freer, 22 Oct. 1813, NAC, RG 8, I, 731:64. Report and Progress of the Naval Yard, by McCulloch (acting commissioner in O'Conor's absence), 10 Oct. 1813, *ibid.*:18. The purpose of

O'Conor's trip to the Head of the Lake is uncertain. He visited with De Rottenburg, observing the Burlington Races from atop Queenston Heights, De Rottenburg to Prevost, 28 Sept. 1813, *ibid.*, 680:119.

14. Record to Freer, 21 Sept. 1813, NAC, RG 8, I, 730:181. Darroch to Prevost, 27 Sept. 1813, *ibid.*:182. Yeo to Prevost, 8 Oct. 1813, *ibid.*, 731: 8. Report by Darroch, 10 Oct. 1813, *ibid.*:18. O'Conor to Freer, 15 Oct. 1813, *ibid.*, 731:35. O'Conor to Freer, 22 Oct. 1813, *ibid.*:64.

15. For dimensions and ordnance of HMS *Princess Charlotte*, see Appendices A and G. A draught of the ship was signed by John Goudie (NAC, Cartographic and Architectural Archives Division, NMC-97256), but Royal Navy records (see Appendix A) give credit for its design to George Record. Regarding Mulcaster's commission, see Yeo to Prevost, 2 Dec. 1813, NAC, RG 8, I, 731:157; Yeo to Melville, 31 Oct. 1813, NAC, MG 24, F 14.

16. For dimensions and ordnance of HMS *Prince Regent*, see Appendices A and G.

17. O'Conor to Freer, 22 Oct. 1813, NAC, RG 8, I, 731:64. O'Conor to Freer, 30 Oct., 3, 5, 9, 11, 19 and 24 Nov. 1813, *ibid.*:86, 96, 100, 103, 111, 112, 131 and 133. Record to Freer, 24 Nov. 1813, *ibid.*:140.

18. Yeo to Melville, 31 Oct. 1813, NAC, MG 24, F 14. Return of the State of Forwardness ..., by O'Conor, 16 Dec. 1813, NAC, RG 8, 731:178.

19. Yeo to Prevost, 2 Dec. 1813, *ibid.*:157.

20. Yeo to Prevost, 14 Oct. 1813, *ibid.*:21.

21. Croker to Popham, 5 Aug. 1813, NAC, MG 12, ADM 2, 1377:226. Croker to Goulburn and Warren, 3 Aug. 1813, *ibid.*:219 and 220. Croker to Yeo and Popham, 2 Sept. 1813, *ibid.*:322 and 326. Bathurst to Prevost, 14a and 14b Aug. 1813, NAC, MG 11, CO 42,151:134 and 136. For a biography of Popham, see *RNB*, sup. 4, 85.

22. Yeo to Popham, 30 Oct. 1813, NAC, RG 8, I, 731:85.

23. Yeo to Melville, 6 Dec. 1813, NAC, MG 24, F 18. Yeo to Prevost, 2 Dec. 1813, NAC, RG 8, I, 731:157. Crew transfers: 16 Dec. 1813, Logbook, HMS *Wolfe*, USNA, RG 45. Pring's establishment at Isle-aux-Noix was becoming more important during this period, given the naval build-up by the British and Americans. The establishment at Coteau du Lac was also of importance, given the proximity of Wilkinson's winter camp. It appears that Yeo and O'Conor visited both places during the winter: Yeo to Prevost, 10 Jan. 1814, NAC, RG8, I, 732:1; O'Conor to Prevost, 8 Feb. 1814, *ibid.*:31; Yeo to Prevost, 8 Feb. 1814, *ibid.*:26; Yeo to Beckwith, 10 Feb. 1814, *ibid.*:32.

24. Prevost to Bathurst, 31 Oct. 1814, NAC, MG 11, CO 42, 153:29. Beckwith to Prevost, 21 Sept. 1813, NAC, MG 24, A9, 2:70. General Order by Baynes, 3 Nov. 1813, NAC, RG 8, I, 1171: 81. Drummond to Prevost, 5 April 1813, *ibid.*, 683:8. Bathurst to Prevost, 28 Jan. 1814, NAC, RG 8, I, 732:14. Regarding the Royal Marine Battalions, see Lavery, *Nelson's Navy: The Ships, Men and Organization, 1793-1815*, 152.

25. Prevost to Beckwith, 26 Sept. 1813, NAC, MG 24, A 9, 2:72. Prevost to Warren, 17 Oct. and 13 Nov. 1813, *ibid.*:81 and 84. Warren to Prevost, 24 Aug., 19 Oct. and 1 Dec. 1813, *ibid.*:73, 80 and 94.

26. Yeo to Prevost, 6 Dec. 1813, NAC, RG 8, I, 731:169. 7 Dec. 1813, Logbook, HMS *Wolfe*, USNA, RG 45. Yeo estimated that he would need nearly 300 more men to man his improved squadron. This figure is based on his reduction of crews aboard the existing vessels and minimum numbers in the frigates and the arrival of the *Marlboroughs*, see: Yeo to Prevost, 25 Oct. 1813, NAC, RG 8, I, 731:76.

27. For a biography of Drummond, see *DCB*, 8:236. For a biography of Riall, see *ibid.*, 7:744. See also Graves, *Where Right and Glory Lead! The Battle of Lundy's Lane, 1814*, 51-7.

28. For a description of the events at Niagara in December 1813, see Cruikshank, *Drummond's Winter Campaign*.

29. Yeo to Prevost, 11 Dec. 1813, NAC, RG 8, I, 731:172. Yeo to Prevost, 29 Nov. 1813, *ibid.*:143.

30. Prevost to Yeo, 17 Dec. 1813, *ibid.*:181.

31. Drummond to Prevost, 21 Jan. 1814, NAC, MG 11, CO 42, 156:77.

32. Prevost to Drummond, 29 Jan. 1814, NAC, RG 8, I, 1222:32. Drummond to Prevost, 3 and 19 Feb. 1814, *ibid.*, 688:90 and 120. Prevost to Drummond, 28 Feb. 1814, *ibid.*, 1222:55.

33. Yeo to Prevost, 8 Feb. 1814, *ibid.*, 732:29. Yeo to Croker, 13 April 1814, NAC, MG 12, ADM 1, 2737:132. Drummond to Prevost, 24 Jan. 1814, NAC, RG 8, I, 682:67. Bruyeres to Prevost, 23 Jan. 1814, *ibid.*, 732:10. Freer to Drummond, 4 Feb. 1814, *ibid.*, 1222:38. Prevost to Bathurst, 8 Feb. 1814, NAC, MG 12, CO 42, 156:87. For a biography of Poyntz, see *NBD*, 920.

34. Wingfield, NAC, MG 24, F 18:6.
35. Ritchie and Ritchie, "A Laker's Log," 208. An advertisement for the play appeared in *The Quebec Mercury* on 10 March 1814, noting that the play had been written by a "military amateur" and that proceeds would be donated to the Patriotic Fund.
36. Graves, *Merry Hearts*, 157.
37. Ritchie and Ritchie, "A Laker's Log," 209. The Dobbs-Cartwright wedding was announced in the *Kingston Gazette* on 22 Feb. 1814.
38. Master John Harris, RN, came to Kingston with Yeo's detachment and served in HMS *Royal George*. On 1 January 1814 he began a logbook of his service, which he kept daily for the entire year as he was transferred from vessel to vessel. The description of daily life noted here is taken from that log, (NAC, MG 12, Adm. 52, Master's Log, *Princess Charlotte, Star, Niagara,* and *Prince Regent*, 3928) 1 Jan.–28 Feb. 1814, Harris Logbook, HMS *Princess Charlotte*. Harris's life story and that of his family is recorded in Harris and Harris, *The Eldon House Diaries*. Casualties and desertions for this period were also examined in the Lake Ontario Muster, PRO, ADM 37, 5000. Yeo to Croker, 14 Jan. 1814, NAC, MG 12, ADM1, 2737:11.
39. McMahon to Jarvis, 16 Jan. 1814, *DHC*, 9:119.
40. A Statement of His Majesty's Naval Force …, by O'Conor, 26 Jan. 1814, NAC, MG 11, CO 42, 156:99.
41. Yeo to Beckwith, 10 Feb. 1814, NAC, RG 8, I, 732:32. Yeo to Beckwith and Prevost, 28 Feb. 1814, *ibid.*:43 and 44.
42. Yeo to Prevost, 28 Feb. 1814, NAC, RG 8, I, 732: 44. Yeo to Prevost, 11 Dec. 1814, *ibid.*, 731:176. Yeo to Prevost, 8 Feb. 1814, *ibid.*, 732:26. Yeo to Beckwith, 10 Feb. 1814, *ibid.*:32. De Rottenburg to Freer, 7 Jan. 1814, *ibid.*, 682:14. Drummond to Prevost, 25 Jan. and 5 Feb. 1814, *ibid.*: 49 and 93. Creighton to Prevost, 7 Feb. 1814, *ibid.*:23. O'Conor to Freer, 8 Feb. 1814, *ibid.*:25. O'Conor to Prevost, 3 Feb. 1814, *ibid.*, 732:20. Yeo to Prevost, 8 and 28 Feb. 1814, *ibid.*:26 and 44. Yeo to Beckwith, 10 and 28 Feb. 1814, *ibid.*:32 and 43. Bell had reached Kingston in November and had been considered as a supervisor for Record and Goudie's men (O'Conor to Freer, 24 Nov. 1813, *ibid.*, 731:133). He later wrote a memorial to Prevost in which he provided information about his career and time at Kingston (Memorial from Bell, 7 July 1814, NAC, MG 24, A 9, 1:359). O'Conor's *Kingston Gazette* ads appeared on and after 14 Jan. 1814, 2 Feb. 1814, 1 March 1814, 2 June 1814. O'Conor had first mentioned a "small frigate," (O'Conor to Prevost, 3 Feb. 1814, NAC, RG 8, I, 732:20), whereas Yeo soon gave its dimensions as: keel – 136; gun deck – 150 feet; beam – 44 feet, depth of hold – 13 feet, 6 inches; draught – 17 feet, dimensions that were almost identical to those of the *Prince Regent* (Yeo to Prevost, 8 Feb. 1814, *ibid.*:26). For dimensions and ordnance of HMS *St. Lawrence*, see Appendices A and H. For a description of the evolution of HMS *St. Lawrence*, see Malcomson, "HMS *St. Lawrence*: The Freshwater First-Rate."
43. Prevost had been notified that the first of two divisions of RN officers and seamen had reached Quebec from Halifax, (Collier to Prevost, 19 Feb. 1814, NAC, RG 8, I, 732:39).
44. Griffith to Croker, 19 Jan. 1814, NAC, MG 12, ADM 1, 505:11. Griffith had already informed Warren of his decision, basing his actions on orders left by Warren, who was not pleased to be deprived of more men, (Griffith to Warren, 11 Jan. 1814, enclosed in Warren to Croker, 26 Jan. 1814, *ibid.*:14). For biographies of Collier, see *RNB*, sup. 3, 412 and *NBD*, 215.
45. "Extraordinary March of Lieutenant Henry Kent …," *Naval Chronicle*. Kent's letter also appears in Malcomson, *Sailors of 1812*, 73-80. For a biography of Kent, see *NBD*, 608.
46. Bathurst to Prevost, 5 Nov. 1813, NAC, RG 8, I, 731:97.
47. A "Loyalist" to Croker, 23 Nov. 1813, enclosed in Barrow to Bunbury, 25 Nov. 1813, NAC, MG 11, CO 42, 155:198.
48. Douglas to Bathurst, 20 Dec. 1812, *ibid.*, 149:175. Prevost to Bathurst, 21 April 1813, *ibid.*, 150:143.
49. Warren to Croker, 1 Dec. 1813, NAC, "Report #9: Copies of all Correspondence and Orders …," *Papers Relating to the War with America*, Extracts of House of Lords, Accounts and Papers, vol 75, 1815, [hereafter: Report #9], 11. An investigation into the costs incurred in sending two frigates and two brigs in frame to Canada was ordered by the House of Lords in 1815, resulting in the report cited above.
50. Kerr to Melville, 23 Nov. 1813, The Melville Papers, William L. Clements Library.

51. Campbell to Kerr, 2 Nov. 1813, enclosed in *ibid*. See also Malcomson, "Xebecs for the Great Lakes War."

52. The decision to build the vessels in frame was announced in Bathurst to Prevost, 15 Dec. 1813, NAC, MG 11, CO 42, 160:373 and amplified in Bathurst to Prevost, 29 Jan. 1814, *ibid.*:379 and in Croker to Yeo, 29 Jan. 1814, NAC, Report #9, 11. Other relevant correspondence includes: Croker to Goulburn, 29 Jan. 1814, *ibid.*:12; Admiralty to Navy Board, 10 Feb.1814, *ibid.*:12; Admiralty to Croker, 11 Feb. 1814, *ibid.*:13; Admiralty to Navy Board, 14 Feb. 1814, *ibid.*:13; Admiralty to Croker, 21 and 22 Feb. 1814, *ibid.*:14; Admiralty to Croker, 4 March 1814, *ibid.*:14; Croker to Yeo, 17 March 1814, *ibid.*:15. See also T. Malcomson, "HMS *Psyche*: A Frigate in Frame."

53. Croker to Yeo, 22 Feb. 1814, NAC, MG 12, ADM 2, 1379:217. For biographies, see: Davies, *NBD*, 267 and *RNB*, sup. 3:235; Fisher – *ibid.*:237; Hickey – *ibid.*:227.

54. Croker to Yeo, 29 Jan. 1814, NAC, MG 12, ADM 2, 1379:131. Other details are in Yeo to Croker, 21 May 1814, *ibid.*, ADM 1, 2737:96.

55. Bathurst to Prevost, 20 Jan. 1814, NAC, MG 11, CO 42, 160:377. Admiralty to Bathurst, 10 Jan. 1814, *ibid.*, 158: 8. Recommendation for such a revision had been made the previous July in Canada by Commissariat General W. H. Robinson to Prevost, 16 July 1813, NAC, MG 13, WO 57, 14.

56. Serus to the editor, 7 March 1814, *Naval Chronicle*, vol. 31 (1814), 214.

Chapter 15: "An Augmentation of Our Naval Force": Preparations at Sackets Harbour: November 1813–April 1814

1. Jones to Bullus, 30 Nov. 1813, *The New American State Papers*, 4:328.

2. Chauncey to Jones, 24 Dec. 1813, USNA, M125, 33:101. Chauncey to Jones, 11 Dec. 1813, *ibid.*:38. Chauncey to Wells, Adams and P. Jones, 12 Dec. 1813, CL.

3. Jones to Chauncey, 19 Sept. 1813, *NWDH*, 2:581. Chauncey to Jones, 8 Oct. 1813, USNA, M125, 31:146. Leonard Court Martial, 1-9 Dec. 1813, USNA, M273, 6:4:151. Chauncey to Jones, 11 Dec. 1813, USNA, M125, 33:36. General Order by Jones, 15 Jan. 1814, USNA, M149, 11:288. Promoted to captain in February 1815, Leonard's next command after the *Madison* affair was to supervise the laid-up Lake Champlain squadron at Whitehall, New York, where he remained until his death in 1832, see Crisman, *The* Eagle: *An American Brig on Lake Champlain*. Several other courts martial were held during this period: Chauncey to Jones, 30a and 30b Nov. 1813, USNA, M125, 32:145 and 146.

4. Chauncey to Sinclair, 14 Dec. 1813, CL. Chauncey to Jones, 14 Dec. 1813, USNA, M125, 33:53.

5. Sinclair to Cocke, 30 Nov. 1813, Malcomson, *Sailors of 1812*, 70. Sinclair to Jones, 17 Jan. 1814, USNA, M125, 34:40.

6. W. Chauncey to Jones, 14 Nov. 1813, USNA, M148, 12:24:101. W. Chauncey to Jones, 5 Sept. 1813, *ibid.*, 12:23:147. No correspondence appears in the CL regarding this matter. W. Chauncey's appointment to the *Erie* is mentioned in Jones to Ridgely, 7 Dec. 1813, USNA, M149, 11:162.

7. 26–28 Oct. 1813, Logbook, US Schooner *Sylph*, Burton Historical Collection. Chauncey to Woolsey, 17 Dec. 1813, CL. Chauncey to Macpherson, 9 Dec. 1813, *ibid*. Chauncey to Flinn, 10 Dec. 1813, *ibid*. Chauncey to Caton, 12 Dec. 1813, *ibid*. Chauncey to Sterne, 15 Dec. 1813, *ibid*. Chauncey to Hall, 16 Dec. 1813, *ibid*. Chauncey to Vaughan, 19 Dec. 1813, *ibid*. Chauncey to Hubbard and Mallaby, 20 Dec. 1813, *ibid*. Chauncey to Gregory and Kroom, 22 Dec. 1813, *ibid*.

8. Chauncey to Jones, 13 Oct. 1813, NAC, M125, 31:168.

9. Howell, "Purser Samuel Hambleton." Perry and Elliott received $7,140 in prize money, although Congress voted to increase Perry's share to equal Chauncey's. Chauncey's complaints about Perry are found in: Chauncey to Elliott, 8 Dec. 1813, CL and Chauncey to Jones, 17 Dec. 1813, USNA, M125, 33:67. For Elliot's assignment to Erie, see Chauncey to Elliott, 13 Oct. 1813, enclosed in *ibid.*, 31:168. Elliott asked for a leave from Erie, but Chauncey forbade it: Chauncey to Jones, 8 Dec. 1813, *ibid.*, 33:29; Chauncey to Elliott, 8 Dec. 1813, CL.

10. Chauncey to Jones, 25 Nov. 1813, *ibid.*, 32:128.

11. Chauncey to Jones, 11 Dec. 1813, *ibid.*, 33:38.

12. Jones to Chauncey, 19 Sept. 1813, *NWDH*, 2:581.

13. Chauncey to Jones, 8 Oct. 1813, USNA, M125, 31:146.

14. Jones to Bullus, 30 Nov. 1813, *The New American State Papers*, 4:328.

15. Chauncey to Jones, 12 Dec. 1813, M125, 32:40. Chauncey to Bullus, 18 Dec. 1813, CL.

16. Chauncey to Jones, 17 Dec. 1813, USNA, M125, 33:67.

17. Chauncey to Bullus, 23 Dec. 1813, CL. Chauncey to Jones, 24 Dec. 1813, USNA, M125, 33:101. Chauncey to Crane, 20 Dec. 1813, CL.

18. Chauncey to Jones, 2 and 14 Jan. 1814, USNA, M125, 34: 7 and 33.

19. Material regarding the political scene in Washington during this period based on: Stagg, *Madison's War*, 362-84; and Brant, *Commander in Chief*, 227-61.

20. Jones to Madison, 25 May 1814, Historical Society of Pennsylvania, William Jones Papers, Box 4, 1814. Jones's earlier queries cited in Stagg, *Madison's War*, 380.

21. Hundreds of thousands of dollars were spent to support the Lake Ontario squadron. A sample of the expenditures include: Jones to Chauncey, 13 Dec. 1813, USNA, M149, 11:179. Chauncey to Bullus, 11 Dec. 1813, 19 Jan. and 28 Feb. 1814, CL. Chauncey to Jones, 29 March 1814, USNA, M125, 35:86.

22. Indents for rigging, stores and shot, enclosed with Chauncey to Bullus, 4 Feb. 1814, CL. Chauncey to Bullus, 12 and 18 Feb. 1814, *ibid.*

23. Chauncey to Jones, 25 Jan. 1814, USNA, M125, 34:72. Chauncey to Jones, 11 March 1814, *ibid.*, 35:33. Chauncey to Harrison, 10 Feb. 1814, CL. Chauncey to Bullus, 11 March 1814, *ibid.* Chauncey to Evans, 12a, 12b and 28 Feb. 1814, *ibid.* Chauncey to Woolsey, 1 March 1814, *ibid.* Jones to commanding officer of USS *President*, 10 April 1814, USNA, M149, 11:274.

24. Able-bodied seamen were offered $12 a month with a $15 signing bounty if they enlisted, although these amounts were increased to $15 and $30. William Bainbridge at Boston thought the rates were excessive and complained to Chauncey who asked Jones to inform Bainbridge that he had approved the rates: Chauncey to Jones, 7 March 1814, USNA, M125, 35:20. Chauncey to Jones, 9 Feb. 1814, *ibid.*, 34:103. Chauncey to Macpherson, 20 Jan. and 9 Feb. 1814, CL. Chauncey to Harrison, 21 Jan. 1814, *ibid.* Chauncey to Yarnell, 22 Jan. 1814, *ibid.* Chauncey to Bullus, 29 Jan., 10 and 13 Feb 1814, *ibid.* Chauncey to Stewart, 9 Feb. 1814, *ibid.*

25. Jones to Spence and Ridgely, 4 April 1814, USNA, M149, 11:261 and 263. R. T. Spence was the commander of the *Ontario*, but did not go to the lakes due to illness (Spence to Jones, 9 April 1814, USNA, M146, 5:2:102). Jones to Jacob Jones, 6 April 1814, USNA, M149, 11:266. A tabulation showing the distribution of naval personnel, dated 31 Aug. 1814, showed 1961 men on Lake Ontario, with New York having the next highest number at 1305 men, Historical Society of Pennsylvania, William Jones Papers, Box 4,1814.

26. Sinclair to Jones, 9 April 1814, USNA, M125, 35:136. Chauncey to Jones, 26 April 1814, *ibid.*:185.

27. Crane to Chauncey, 6 Jan. 1814, enclosed in Crane to Jones, 6 Jan. 1814, USNA, M147, 5:2:3. Crane to Jones, 10 Jan. 1814, *ibid.*:8. Crane to Chauncey, 11 Jan. 1814, enclosed in Crane to Jones, 11 Jan. 1814, *ibid.*:10. Crane to Jones, 13 Feb. 1814, *ibid.*:52. Wilkinson noted the prohibition of funeral bands in his *Memoirs*, 3: app. 12.

28. General Order by Chauncey, 12 Dec. 1813, CL. Chauncey to Crane, 20 Dec. 1813, *ibid.* Chauncey to Pettigrew, 25 Dec. 1813, *ibid.* Rules for Regulation of Shipboard Life on board USS *Madison* by Crane, 19 Dec. 1813, *NWDH*, 2:616.

29. Report by Ross, 18 Sept. 1813, *ibid.*

30. Ross to Gaines, 15 June 1814, *ibid.*

31. Crane to Jones, 13 Feb. 1814, USNA, M147, 5:2:52.

32. Crane to Chauncey, 1 Feb. 1814, enclosed in Crane to Jones, 1 Feb. 1814, *ibid.*:40.

33. Memo by Chauncey, 2 March 1814, CL. All paper work was now to be presented by officers to Crane, who would then discuss the matters with the commodore.

34. Chauncey to Jones, 24 Feb. 1814, USNA, M125, 34:138. Chauncey to Jones, 7 March 1814, *ibid.*, 35:21.

35. Crane to Chauncey, 13 Jan. 1814, enclosed in Crane to Jones, 13 Jan. 1814, USNA, M147, 5:2:12. Chauncey to Jones, 7 March 1814, USNA, M125, 35:21.

36. A View of the American Squadron on Lake Ontario ... by Chauncey, enclosed with Chauncey to Jones, 15 March 1814, *ibid.*: 47 (the enclosure appears in CL, but not in M125).

37. Chauncey to Jones, 24 Feb. 1814, USNA, M125, 35:138.

38. Chauncey to Anderson and Bullus 4 March 1814, CL. Chauncey to Walton and Co., 5 March 1814, *ibid.*

39. Chauncey to Walton and Co., 17 and 21 March 1814, *ibid.* Chauncey to Anderson, 21 March 1814, *ibid.*

40. Chauncey to Bullus,18, 25, 29 and 31 March, 4 and 6 April 1814, CL. Chauncey to Woolsey, 1 March 1814, *ibid.* Chauncey to Lynch, 17 March 1814, *ibid.* Indent for Standing Rigging, Indent for Slop Clothing, late March (?) 1814, *ibid.* Chauncey to Townsend and Bronson, 4 April 1814, *ibid.* Chauncey to Jones, 29 March 1814, USNA, M125, 35:87.

41. Chauncey to Jones, 7, 8 and 14 April 1814, USNA, M125:100, 101 and 102.

42. Chauncey to Walton and Co., 9 April 1814, CL.

43. Crane to Chauncey, 11 Jan. 1814, enclosed in Crane to Jones, 11 Jan. 1814, USNA, M147, 5:2:10. Crane to Jones, 18 Jan. 1814, *ibid.*:18. Chauncey to Jones, 14 and 22 April 1814, USNA, M125, 35:102 and 104. Chauncey to Tompkins, 14 April 1814, CL. Chauncey to Brown, 15 April 1814, *ibid.*

44. Chauncey to Jones, 4 April 1814, *ibid.*:114. Chauncey refers to "800 effective men," while informants to the British described the military strength at 1500 or 1600: Drummond to Prevost, 21 March 1814, NAC, RG 8, I, 388:41; and Deposition of Robert Christie, 24 March 1814, *ibid.*, 682:246.

45. Armstrong to Brown, 28 Feb. 1814, *DHC*, 9:201.

46. This section on Brown's movements based on Graves, *Where Right and Glory Lead*, 18-21.

47. Chauncey to Bullus, 10 April 1814, CL.

48. Memo by Chauncey, 30 March 1814, *ibid.* Chauncey to Gregory, 13 April 1814, *ibid.* Chauncey to Anderson, 23 April 1814, *ibid.*

Chapter 16: "Wary Measures and Occasional Daring Enterprises": Actions at Oswego and Sandy Creek: April–June 1814

1. Prevost to Drummond, 30 April 1814, NAC, RG 8, I, 1222:112.

2. "Extraordinary March …," by Kent, *The Naval Chronicle*, vol. 33 (1815), 1123-7.

3. Drummond to Prevost, 2 April 1814, NAC, RG 8, I, 732:90. Harvey to Yeo, 1 April 1814, *ibid.*:86. Yeo to Harvey, 1 April 1814, *ibid.*:87. District General Order by Harvey, 31 March 1814, *ibid.*:88. Robinson to Prevost, 7 April 1814, *ibid.*:113. General Order by Baynes, 20 Jan. 1814, NAC, MG 12, ADM 106, 1997. News of an impending mutiny reached Sackets Harbour as mentioned in Chauncey to Jones, 26 March 1814, USNA, M125, 35:76. Yeo later described the seamen's hardships (Yeo to Croker, 21 May 1814, NAC, MG 12, ADM 1, 2737:96), mentioning that their last beef day had been 24 February 1814 with no hope of another until July.

4. Drummond to Prevost, 22 March 1814, NAC, RG 8, I, 732:74. Drummond to Prevost, 5 April 1814, *ibid.*, 683:8. Prevost to Drummond, 6 April 1814, *ibid.*, 1222:85.

5. Yeo to Warren, 5 March 1814, enclosed in Yeo to Croker, 5 March 1814, NAC, MG 12, ADM 1, 2737:32. Deposition of Robert Christie, 24 March 1814, enclosed with Drummond to Prevost, 24 March 1814, NAC, RG 8, I, 682:244.

6. Statements estimating the strength of the opposing squadrons, by Yeo, enclosed in Yeo to Croker, 5 March 1814, *ibid.*:35.

7. *Ibid.*, p. 32. See also Yeo to Prevost, 10 March 1814, NAC, RG 8, I, 732:59.

8. Drummond to Prevost, 2 April 1814, *ibid.*, 683:1.

9. Yeo to Croker, 14 April 1814, NAC, MG 12, ADM 1, 2737:74. Prevost to Yeo, 7 April 1814, enclosed in *ibid.*:75. Yeo mentioned Prevost's doubts in Yeo to Beckwith, 26 Feb. 1814, NAC, RG 8, I, 732:41.

10. Yeo to Prevost, 13 April 1814, *ibid.*, 683:19.

11. For a comparison of ordnance in the squadrons, see Appendix H.

12. Yeo to Prevost, 13 April 1814, NAC, RG 8, I, 683:19.

13. Dimensions of a Ship …, by O'Conor, enclosed in O'Conor to Freer, 13 April 1814, NAC, RG 8, I, 732:128. O'Conor to Freer, 10 April 1814, *ibid.*:121. For the dimensions and ordnance of HMS *St. Lawrence*, see Appendices A and H.

14. Yeo to Freer, 29 March 1814, NAC, RG 8, I, 732:84. Wodehouse to Prevost, 9 April 1814, *ibid.*:118. Griffith to Prevost, 14 April 1814, NAC, MG 24, A9, 2:114. Sherbrooke to Freer, 19 April 1814, NAC, RG 8, I, 834:5.

15. Drummond to Prevost, 5 March 1814, NAC, RG 8, I, 682:163. Prevost to Drummond, 22 March 1814, *ibid.*, 1222:67. A schooner in frame was reported to be on the ways in O'Conor to Freer, 21

May 1814, *ibid.*, 732:171. Although little is known about this vessel, it was likely named the *Julia*, of 77 tons burthen. See Statement of Naval Forces on Lake Ontario, 14 Oct. 1814, NAC, MG 12, ADM 106, 1997.

16. Drummond to Prevost, 2 April 1814, NAC, RG 8, I, 683:1. Prevost to Yeo, 7 April 1813, NAC, MG 12, ADM 1, 2737:75. Yeo to Prevost, 13 April 1814, NAC, RG 8, I, 683:19. Prevost to Macomb, 25 April 1814, *ibid.*:47. O'Conor to Freer, 13 April 1814, *ibid.*, 732:129. Prevost to Drummond, 30 April 1814, *ibid.*, 1222:112. Prevost to Baynes, 29 April 1814, *ibid.*, 683:88. Baynes to Prevost, 1 and 3 May 1814, *ibid.*:81 and 83. See also Stagg, *Madison's War*, 385-6.

17. Yeo to Prevost, 13 April 1814, NAC, RG 8, I, 732:133. Robinson, Clarke and Freer to Prevost, 6 April 1814, *ibid.*:97. Prevost to Bathurst, 9 May 1814, NAC, MG 11, CO 42, 156:241. Yeo to Prevost, 22 April 1814, *ibid.*:22 April 1814. Pring to Prevost, 24 April 1814, *ibid.*:249.

18. Graves, *Merry Hearts*, 158. Drummond to Prevost, 13 April 1814, NAC, RG 8, I, 732:132. Yeo to Croker, 15 April 1814, NAC, MG 12, ADM 1, 2737:70.

19. Drummond to Prevost, 15 April 1814, NAC, RG 8, I, 683:25. The schooner *Vincent* appears to have sailed with the *Beresford*: Drummond to Prevost, 28 April 1814, *ibid.*:61. Memo by Glegg, undated, *DHC*, 9:291. Gordon to Merritt, 17 April 1814, *ibid.*:297.

20. For a description of the British squadron's ordnance, see Appendix H, Table 1.

21. Croker to Yeo, 29 Jan. 1814, NAC, MG 12, ADM 2, 1379:131. Yeo to Croker, 21 May 1814, *ibid.*, ADM 1, 2737:98. Instructions for administration of the squadron, 29 Jan. 1814, *ibid.*:93. Promotion lists enclosed in Yeo to Croker, 13 April, 20 July and 17 Aug. 1814, *ibid.*:132, 135 and 139. Other promotions: Yeo to Croker, 9 May 1814, *ibid.*:105. The muster of the Lake Ontario Establishment indicated transfer of all individuals to newly named ships on 30 April 1814, PRO, ADM 37, 5000. Issuance of commissions suggests that the paper work for the change was not completed in one day: Yeo to O'Conor, 1 May 1814, NAC, MG 12, ADM 1, 2261; Yeo to Popham, 2 May 1814, *ibid.*, 2347; Yeo to Spilsbury, 2 May 1814, *ibid.*, 2543. O'Conor offered his resignation as commissioner, but Prevost refused it: O'Conor to Prevost, 16 March 1814, enclosed in Prevost to Bathurst, 27 March 1814, NAC, MG 11, CO 42, 156:161. Though Commodore Chauncey later referred to the *Magnet* as a brig (Chauncey to Jones, 10 Aug. 1814, USNA, M125, 38:84), there is no notice in British records of a conversion having been made. A sloop could have as few as ten guns (Lavery, *Nelson's Navy*, 98), so the *Magnet*, though still a schooner, fit that classification with Collier as commander.

22. Harvey to Yeo, 9 April 1814, NAC, RG 8, I, 732:147. Previously, Drummond had shown his concern about Riall's needs and the use of the squadron to supply him: Drummond to Prevost, 11 March 1814, *ibid.*, 682:192; Drummond to Prevost, 22 March 1814, *ibid.*, 833:119; and Drummond to Prevost, 2 April 1814, *ibid.*, 683:1.

23. Plans written on 13 April 1814 were amplified in Drummond to Prevost, 27 and 28 April 1814, NAC, RG 8 , I, 683:57 and 61.

24. Prevost to Drummond, 23 April 1814, *ibid.*, 1222:107.

25. Prevost to Drummond, 30 April 1814, *ibid.*:112.

26. Drummond to Prevost, 3 May 1814, *ibid.*, 683:93.

27. Description of the Battle of Oswego based on: 3 May–10 May 1814, Harris Logbook, HMS *Princess Charlotte*, NAC, MG 12. Drummond to Prevost, 3 May 1814, NAC, RG 8, I, 683:93. Fischer to Harvey, 7 May 1814, *ibid.*:101. Return of Ordnance ..., by Cruttendon, enclosed with Fischer to Harvey, *ibid.*:104. Drummond to Prevost, 7 May 1814, *ibid.*:105. Return of Killed and Wounded, by Harvey, enclosed with Drummond to Prevost, *ibid.*:113. Memo of Stores ..., enclosed with Drummond to Prevost, *ibid.*:118. Yeo to Croker, 9 May 1814, NAC, MG 12, ADM 1, 2737: 43. List of Killed and Wounded, by Yeo, enclosed with *ibid.*:50. Ordnance Stores Brought Off ..., by Yeo, enclosed with *ibid.*:51. Woolsey to Chauncey, 7 May 1814, enclosed in Chauncey to Jones, 9 May 1814, USNA, M125, 36:41. Chauncey to Jones, 6, 7a, 7b, 8, 12 and 16 May, *ibid.*:26, 28, 29, 37, 55 and 69. Brown to Armstrong, 6 and 8 May 1814, Jacob Brown Manuscripts, BHS. Mitchell to Brown, 7 May 1814, 14 June 1814, *Quebec Mercury*. Mermet to Viger, 23 May 1814, Viger Papers, NAC, MG 24, L 8. Mulcaster Biography, NAC, MG 24, F 95:35-40. General Order by Baynes, 12 May 1814, *DHC*, 9:344. 19 May 1814, *New York Evening Post*, *ibid.*:344. General Order by Jones, 12 May 1814, *ibid.*:346. Biographical sketch of Hewett, *ibid.*:347. McIntire to Holmes, 9 May 1814, John C.

Frederiksen, "The War of 1812 in Northern New York: The Observations of Captain Rufus McIntire." Loss of the schooner *Penelope, ASP*, Claims, 1:732, 761. Henry B. Dawson, "Attack on Oswego, 5-7 May 1814." Lossing, *Pictorial Field-book*, 792-8.

28. Although Lieutenant Colonel Mitchell mentioned 290 men in his detachment (Mitchell to Brown, 7 May 1814, *Quebec Mercury*), Captain McIntire reported 342 men: McIntire to Holmes, 9 May 1814, Frederiksen, "The Observations of Captain Rufus McIntire," p. 312. McIntire addressed his letter from "Oswego Falls, Volney," the latter place being a nearby village he seems to have confused with Fredericksburgh.

29. Woolsey's orders, Chauncey to Woolsey, 21 April 1814, were enclosed in Chauncey to Jones, 16 May 1814, USNA, M125, 36:69. Regarding the first shipment, see Chauncey to Jones, 3 May 1814, *ibid.*:12.

30. Mermet to Viger, 23 May 1814, Viger Papers, NAC, MG 24, L 8.

31. McIntire to Holmes, 9 May 1814, Frederiksen, "Observations of Rufus McIntire," 315.

32. "Richardson Memoirs," Malcomson, *Sailors of 1812*, 81-2.

33. *Ibid.*, 82.

34. Mermet Viger, 23 May 1814, Viger Papers, NAC, MG 24, L 8.

35. *Ibid.*

36. This dialogue taken from Mulcaster Biography, NAC, MG 24, F 95:36-9.

37. The Yeo–Bronson exchange based upon Lossing, *Pictorial Field-book*, 796-7. Bronson was released near the end of May: Chauncey to Bronson, 28 May 1814, CL, Chauncey to Yeo, 29 May 1814, *ibid.*

38. Yeo reported seven heavy guns, ordnance stores, three schooners, 2,400 barrels and some "barge" rope taken and six guns and a schooner sunk: Enclosed in Yeo to Croker, 9 May 1814, NAC, MG 12, ADM 1, 2737: 43. Military reports noted two guns destroyed and nine guns confiscated along with ordnance stores, two schooners and a Durham boat, plus others, rope and blocks and 1045 barrels of goods: Report by Cruttendon, enclosed in Fischer to Harvey, 7 May 1814, NAC, RG 8, I, 683, 101. Woolsey also supplied Chauncey with an itemized list of materials that agreed, more or less, with Yeo's report (enclosed in Chauncey to Jones, 16 May 1814, USNA, M125, 36:69).

39. Drummond to Prevost, 7 May 1814, NAC, RG 8, I, 683:105.

40. Fischer to Harvey, 7 May 1814, *ibid.*, 101.

41. Yeo to Croker, 9 May 1814, NAC, MG 12, ADM 1, 2737:43.

42. *Ibid.*

43. Graves, *Merry Hearts*, 161.

44. *Ibid.*

45. Prevost to Drummond, 7 May 1814, NAC, RG 8, I, 1222:117.

46. Drummond to Bathurst, 3 July 1814, *DHC*, 1:24.

47. Brown to Armstrong, 12 May 1814, Jacob Brown Manuscripts, BHS. Chauncey to Jones, 9 June 1814, USNA, M125, 37:37. The deserter's report is mentioned in Woolsey to Chauncey, 7 May 1814, enclosed in Chauncey to Jones, 9 May 1814, USNA, M125, 36:41. Chauncey to Jones, 6 May 1814, *ibid.*:26. Chauncey to Woolsey, 10 May 1814, CL.

48. Chauncey to Woolsey, 7, 9, 10, 11, 13, 14, 19a and 19b May 1814, CL Chauncey to Anderson and Walton, 9 May 1814, *ibid.* Chauncey to Foreman, 17 May 1814, *ibid.* Chauncey to Jones, 16, 20 and 25 May 1814, USNA, M125, 36:69, 82 and 101.

49. Chauncey to Jones, 25 and 30 April 1814, USNA, M125, 35:172 and 203. Chauncey to Jones, 2, 4, 11, 12, 15, 21, 22, 24, 27a and 27b May 1814, *ibid.*, 36:7, 14, 52, 56, 67, 85, 91, 100, 107 and 108. Chauncey to Elliott, 13 May 1814, CL. Chauncey to W. Chauncey, 26 and 27 May 1814, *ibid.* Chauncey to W. Chauncey, 11 and 14 June 1814, *ibid.* Chauncey to Jones, 15 June 1814, USNA, M125, 37:63. Wolcott Chauncey obtained the rank of master commandant in 1817 and died in 1835, Callahan, *List of Officers*.

50. Memo by Chauncey, 27 May 1814, CL.

51. Chauncey to Jones, 27 April 1814, USNA, M125, 35:186. Woolsey to Chauncey, enclosed in Chauncey to Jones, 9 May 1814, *ibid.*, 36:41. See also reference to a letter from Owen to Johnston in which a comment is made about one of their friends being absent on a secret raid, Ritchie and Ritchie, "A Laker's Log," 209-10.

52. Chauncey to Jones, 20 May 1814, USNA, M125, 36:82.

53. Daily events for the period 11 May–24 June based on: Harris Logbook, HMS *Princess Charlotte*, NAC, MG 12; Collier Logbook, HMS *Princess Charlotte, ibid.;* Hickey Logbook, HMS *Prince Regent, ibid.* Hickey did not take command until 9 June, but the logbook is noted as being his from 14 May. Drummond to Prevost, 21 May 1814, NAC, RG 8, I, 683:191.
54. Chauncey to Woolsey, 26 and 27 May 1814, CL.
55. The description of the battle at Sandy Creek based on: Chauncey to Smith, Woolsey and Ridgely, 30 May 1814, *ibid.* Chauncey to Ridgely, 1 June 1814, *ibid.* Chauncey to Jones, 2 June 1814, USNA, M125, 37:3. Woolsey to Chauncey, no date, enclosed with *ibid.* Drummond to Prevost, 2 June 1814, NAC, RG 8, I, 683: 226. Prevost to Bathurst, 8 June 1814, NAC, MG 11, CO 42, 156:327. Popham to Yeo, 1 June 1814, *ibid.*:331.
56. Gaines took command of the military at Sackets after Brown departed for Buffalo during the last week of May.
57. Popham to Yeo, 1 June 1814, NAC, RG 8, I, 156:327.
58. William Hamilton Merritt, "Journal of Events Principally on the Detroit and Niagara Frontiers," 3:640.
59. Graves, *Merry Hearts*, 162.
60. State of HM Ships and Vessels on Lake Ontario, by Yeo, 2 June 1814, NAC, MG 11, CO 42, 156:339. Yeo reckoned his total deficit in men stood at 279 and that he would need 640 more for the new ship. The total, 919, was nearly made up by Downie's detachment from England.
61. Drummond to Yeo, 6 June 1814, NAC, RG 8, I, 683:242.
62. Commodore Yeo did not itemize the changes in one succinct table. Placements shown here are gleaned from a number of sources, including: Boards of survey on the health of various officers and seamen and promotion lists, enclosed in Yeo to Croker, 13 June, 11, 20 and 30 July, and 17 August 1814, NAC, MG 12, ADM 1, 2737:114, 124, 135, 139 and 162. For a biography of Spence, see *NBD*, 1102. Hawkesworth had arrived at Kingston on 13. Oct. 1813 from HMS *La Mutine* at Quebec (PRO, ADM37, 5000) and was praised by Yeo for participation in a small raid in January 1814 (Yeo to Croker, 1 Jan. 1814, NAC, MG 12, ADM 1, 2737:15). See also musters for the following vessels during this period: *Prince Regent*, PRO, ADM 37, 5128; *Princess Charlotte, ibid.*, 5245; *Niagara, ibid.*, 5377; *Star, ibid.*, 5636; *Charwell, ibid.*, 5629; *Netley, ibid.*, 5642; and gunboats, *ibid.*, 5002.
63. Yeo to Drummond, 3 June 1814, NAC, RG 8, I, 683: 239.
64. Drummond to Yeo, 6 June 1814, *ibid.*:242.
65. Drummond to Bathurst, 3 July 1814, *DHC*, 1:24.
66. For a comparison of the squadrons, see Appendix H.

Chapter 17: "For God's Sake Let Me See You": Strife Among the Senior Officers: June to November 1814

1. Brown to Chauncey, 13 July 1814, Brown Manuscripts, BHS.
2. This section about the deliberations in Washington based on: Stagg, *Madison's War*, 387-407; and Brant, *Commander in Chief*, 262-85.
3. Cabinet Memorandum, 7 June 1814, Hunt, *The Writings of James Madison*, 8:280.
4. Chauncey to Jones, 11 June 1814, USNA, M125, 37:54. In this letter Chauncey mentioned that the *Mohawk* was larger than the frigate *New York*. For details about the *Mohawk's* dimensions and ordnance, see Appendices A and H.
5. Chauncey to Jones, 8 June 1814, USNA, M125, 37:31. Chauncey repeated his confidence that he would be able to sail by 1 July in Chauncey to Jones, 9 and 11 June 1814, *ibid.*:39 and 54.
6. Chauncey to Jones, 9 June 1814, *ibid.*:39. Smith to Jones, 9 June 1814, *ibid.*:42. Hull to Jones, 16 and 25 June 1814, *ibid.*:68 and 102. Chauncey to Jones, 19, 21 and 28 June 1814, *ibid.*:78, 85 and 108. Officers and seamen also arrived from enlistment stations during this period: Chauncey to Jones, 15 June and 1 July 1814, *ibid.*:64 and 108.
7. Chauncey to Jones, 28 June 1814, *ibid.*:108.
8. Brown to Chauncey, 21 June 1814, Brown Manuscripts, BHS.
9. *Ibid.* Brown had heard by 17 June that Sinclair's squadron would not be at his service, Brown to Armstrong, 17 June 1814, *ibid.*

10. Chauncey to Jones, 15d June 1814, USNA, M125, 37:67.

11. Cabinet Memorandum, 7 June 1814, Hunt, *The Writings of James Madison*, 8:280.

12. Chauncey to Brown, 25 June 1814, CL.

13. *Ibid.*

14. Brown to Chauncey, 18 April and 21 June 1814, Brown Manuscripts, BHS. Brown to Gaines, 18 April 1814, *ibid.* Brown to Armstrong, 25 April, 21 May, 15 and 7 and 17 June 1814, *ibid.* A dispute also arose between Chauncey and Brigadier General Gaines after the battle at Sandy Creek over prize money rights to the captured British boats and ordnance: Chauncey to Gaines, 4, 6, 10a, 10b and 10c June 1814, CL. Appling's survivors attempted to obtain some of the prize money after the war: No. 494, British Flotilla Captured by a Detachment of the Army in 1814, *ASP:Claims*, 1:678.

15. Brown to Armstrong, 7 June 1814, Brown Manuscripts, BHS.

16. Armstrong to Brown, 9 June 1814, *ibid.*

17. Brown to Armstrong, 17 June 1814, *ibid.* Armstrong's letter of the 9th was acknowledged by an undated letter (late June) of Brown to Armstrong, in which the general discussed his invasion plans, *ibid.*

18. Chauncey to Brown, 8 July 1814, CL.

19. Brown to Chauncey, 13 July 1814, Brown Manuscripts, BHS.

20. J. Jones to W. Jones, 25 July 1814, USNA, M125, 38:34. Chauncey told his captains to be ready to sail by 17 July: Memo by Chauncey, 13 July 1814, CL. Gun carriages on the *Mohawk*, and some on the *Superior*, constructed at New York by Adam and Noah Brown had proven to be defective and Chauncey refused to pay their bill because of it (Chauncey to the Browns, 8 July 1814, *ibid.*).

21. Chauncey to Jones, 10a Aug. 1814, USNA, M125, 38:84.

22. For a biography of Jacob Jones, see *DAB*, 5:176.

23. Chauncey to Jones, 10a Aug. 1814, USNA, M125, 38:84.

24. Smith's absence is explained in Smith to Jones, 24 June 1814, *ibid.*:46. Commanding officers on various ships based on: Chauncey to Woolsey, 9 June 1814, CL; Chauncey to J. Jones, Crane and Trenchard, 9 July 1814, *ibid;* Chauncey to Ridgely, Elliott and Brown, 7 Aug. 1814, *ibid;* Chauncey to Mix, 26 Aug. 1814, *ibid.* In this last note Chauncey addressed Mix, previously a sailing master, as a lieutenant, although that position was not confirmed until Dec. 1814 (*ASP:NA*, 1:367). Promotion from sailing master to lieutenant was rare, and indicated the high esteem in which the commodore held Mix. For a description of ordnance, see Appendix H, Table 3.

25. Daily events for the period July–September 1814 based on: Logbook, US Sloop *Jones*, Burton Historical Collection; Harris Logbook, HM Sloop *Star*, NAC, MG 12, ADM. 52, 3928: Harris was transferred to the *Star* from the *Princess Charlotte* late in June); Collier Logbook, HMS *Princess Charlotte*, *ibid.*, ADM 51, 2700; Hickey Logbook, *ibid.*, 4488.

26. T. Ridout to T. G. Ridout, 9 Aug. 1814, Firth, *Town of York*, 332.

27. Drummond to Prevost, 8 Aug. 1814, *DHC*, 1:124. Hawkesworth's desertion is mentioned in Chauncey to Smith, 3 Jan. 1815, CL. Hawkesworth had arrived at Kingston on 13 Oct. 1813 from HMS *La Mutine* at Quebec, PRO, ADM 37, 5000 as a midshipman and been promoted to lieutenant in the *Magnet* under Collier, taking over that vessel following Collier's transfer to the *Princess Charlotte* after the attack on Oswego.

28. Chauncey to Ridgely, Elliott and T. Brown, 7 Aug. 1814, CL.

29. Chauncey to Brown, 7 Aug. 1814, *ibid.*

30. Chauncey to Brown, 10 Aug. 1814, *ibid.*

31. Brown to Armstrong, 25 July 1814, Jacob Brown Manuscripts, BHS.

32. Chauncey to Jones, 10 Aug. 1814, USNA, M125, 38:84. Decatur to Jones, 2, 4,,5, 8 and 10 Aug. 1814, *ibid.*:57, 62, 63, 75 and 83.

33. Chauncey to Jones, 19 Aug. 1814, *ibid.*:113.

34. Brown to Chauncey, 4 Sept. 1814, *DHC*, 2: 444. The absence of civilities between the men is mentioned in Brown to Spencer, 27 Nov. 1814, Gratz Papers, Historical Society of Pennsylvania.

35. Chauncey to Jones, 10c, 18 and 29 Aug. 1814, USNA, M125, 38:85, 111 and 145. Chauncey to Woolsey, 14 Aug. 1814, CL.

36. Chauncey to Jones, 27 Aug. 1814, USNA, M125, 38:142. Izard to Chauncey, 11 Aug. 1814 and Chauncey to Izard, 20 Aug. 1814, enclosed in Chauncey to Jones, 20 Aug. 1814, *ibid.*:121.

37. An Account of the Stores furnished …, Summer of 1814, by the Navy Office, 18 April 1815, NAC, MG 11, CO 42, 160:132.

38. Smyth to Beckwith, 16 June 1814, NAC, RG 8, I, 733:17. A Tender for Bringing Four Ships in Sections from Montreal …, by William Forbes, no date, *ibid.*:21. Beckwith *et al.* to Prevost, 22 June 1814, NAC, MG 11, CO 42, 160:345. Prevost to Bathurst, 8 June and 1 July 1814, *ibid.*, 160:341 and 343.

39. Croker to Yeo, 26 July 1814, NAC, Report #9, 17. Admiralty Board to Navy Board, 18 and 21 July 1814, *ibid.*, 15 and 16. Admiralty to Croker, 20 July 1814, *ibid.*, 16.

40. Dobbs to Yeo, 13 April 1814, Cruikshank, *DHC*, 1:135. Conkling to Kennedy, 16 Aug. 1814, *ibid.*:136. District Order by Harvey, 13 Aug. 1814, enclosed in Yeo to Croker, 24 Aug. 1814, NAC, MG 12, ADM 1, 2737:142.

41. Drummond to Prevost, 16 Aug. 1814, NAC, RG 8, I, 685:101. Return of Killed, Wounded and Missing …, by Harvey, 15 Aug. 1814, NAC, MG 11, CO 42, 157:155.

42. Drummond to Prevost, 18 Aug. 1814, NAC, RG 8, I, 118:141. Drummond to Prevost, 16 Aug. 1814, *ibid.*, 685:101.

43. Drummond to Yeo, 18 Aug. 1814, *DHC*, 1:182.

44. Drummond to Prevost, 21 Aug. 1814, *ibid.*:183. Drummond to Prevost, 2 and 8 Sept. 1814, *ibid.*:190 and 195.

45. Prevost to Bathurst, 27 Aug. 1814, NAC, MG 11, CO 42, 160:349.

46. Yeo to Prevost, 23 Aug. 1814, NAC, RG 8, I, 733:47.

47. Chauncey to Jones, 20 June 1814, USNA, M125, 37:82. Drummond to Prevost, 21 and 23 June 1814, NAC, RG 8, I, 683:300 and 303.

48. Chauncey to Jones, 7 July 1814, USNA, M125, 37:137. Gregory's commission as lieutenant was finally received at Sackets on 7 July, Chauncey to Jones, 7 July 1814, *ibid.*:138. Gregory and his party applied for prize money for these actions and received some for the captured gunboat: No. 576, Prize-Money for Capturing a British Gunboat, and Burning a Vessel of War on the Stocks in 1814, *ASP:Claims*, 1:823.

49. Wingfield, NAC, MG 24, F 18:40.

50. *Ibid.*, 42.

51. Wingfield dates this escapade as happening on 12 August 1814 , but as with other dates in his memoir, it is very likely incorrect. The Americans sailed on 1 August and Hickey logbook, HMS *Prince Regent* noted: "cutter returned with 1 schooner and 1 sloop," 2 Aug. 1814, NAC, MG 12, ADM 51, 4488.

52. Wingfield, NAC, MG 24, F 18:20. Gregory's capture described on 42-3. Chauncey to Gregory, Yeo and Mix, 28 Aug. 1814, CL. Chauncey to A. Hart and D. Gregory, 29 Aug. 1814, *ibid.* Gregory to Chauncey, 27 Aug. 1814, enclosed in Chauncey to Jones, 29 Aug. 1814, USNA, M125, 38:144.

53. Yeo to Croker, 10 Sept. 1814, NAC, MG 12, Adm. 1, vol. 2737, p. 193. Yeo to Prevost, 10 Sept. 1814, NAC, RG 8, I, vol. 733, p. 65. For a description of the *St. Lawrence's* dimensions and ordnance, see Appendices A and H.

54. Chauncey to Jones, 17 Sept. 1814, USNA, M125, 39:64.

55. This description of the Plattsburgh campaign based on: Hitsman, *The Incredible War of 1812*, 215-231; Everest, *The War of 1812 in the Champlain Valley*, 179-92; Roosevelt, *The Naval War of 1812*, 337-54.

56. Bathurst to Prevost, 3 June 1814, Hitsman, *The Incredible War of 1812*, 249.

57. Prevost to Downie, 10 Sept. 1814, enclosed in Yeo to Croker, 24 Sept. 1814, NAC, MG 12, ADM 1, 2737:195. Other enclosed documents include: Prevost to Downie, 8 and 9 Sept. 1814; and Downie to Prevost, 7, 8 and 9 Sept. 1814.

58. Cited in Coore to Yeo, 26 Feb. 1815, Wood, *Select British Documents*, 3:394.

59. Prevost to Bathurst, 11 Sept. 1814, NAC, MG 11, CO 42, 157:187.

60. Pring to Yeo, 17 Sept. 1814, enclosed in Yeo to Croker, 24 Sept. 1814, NAC, MG 12, ADM 1, 2737:195.

61. Yeo to Croker, 29 Sept. 1814, *ibid.*:206.

62. Changes in command were noted in the following logbooks: 2 Oct. 1814, Harris Logbook, HMS *Niagara*, NAC, MG 12, ADM 52, 3928 (Harris had been transferred to this ship at the end of August); and 30 Sept. and 3 Oct. 1814, Collier–O'Conor Logbook, HMS *Princess Charlotte*, *ibid.*, ADM 51, 2700.

63. Fisher to Croker, 15 Sept. 1814, enclosed in Yeo to Croker, 17 Sept. 1814, NAC, MG 12, ADM 1, 2737:179. Also enclosed: Fisher to Yeo, 30 Aug., 1 Sept. and 14 Sept. 1814; Yeo to Fisher, 29 July, 8 and 15 Sept. 1814.

64. Yeo to Croker, 17 Sept. 1814, *ibid.*

65. Griffith to Yeo, 26 July 1814, NAC, RG 8, I, 733: 49. Yeo to Prevost, 23 Aug. 1814, *ibid.*: 47. Kempt to Freer, 22 and 23 Aug. 1814, *ibid.*:44 and 51. Yeo to Freer, 27 Aug. 1814, *ibid.*:59. Upton to Prevost, 24 and 29 Aug. 1814, *ibid.*:58 and 61. Muster for the gunboat flotilla, PRO, ADM 37, 5000. Illustration of Prevost (p. 304), comment from *DCB*, 5:696.

66. Commander Charles Owen requested a leave from the gunboat flotilla so that he could join the squadron and participate in any action that developed: Owen to Coore, n.d. (probably 6 Oct. 1814), NAC, RG 8, I, 733:60.

67. Drummond to Prevost, 6 Oct. 1814, *ibid.*, 686: 5. Drummond to Prevost, 2 Oct. 1814, *ibid.*:1.

68. Drummond to Prevost, 15 Oct. 1814, NAC, RG 8, I, 686:31. Drummond to Prevost, 10 and 11 Oct. 1814, *ibid.*:9 and 19.

69. Yeo had refused such a proposal as far back as August, Prevost to Bathurst, 27 Aug. 1814, NAC, MG 11, CO 42, 157:27.

70. Chauncey to Brown, 10 Aug. 1814, CL.

71. Prevost to Bathurst, 18 Oct. 1814, NAC, MG 11, CO 42, 157:260.

72. Prevost to Bathurst, 19 Nov. 1814, *ibid.*:360.

73. Of the attack on Baltimore, Cochrane wrote to Melville on 17 September 1814 that it had been undertaken: "contrary to my opinion, but extremely urged by the General, to which I reluctantly consented but to preserve unanimity between the two services;" cited in Lord, *The Dawn's Early Light*, 299. Friction between Cochrane and Cockburn is detailed in Pack, *The Man Who Burned the White House*, 199-200. Problems between the services are discussed in Dudley, "Chauncey and U.S. Joint Operations" and Drake, "Yeo and Prevost: A Study in Command Relations."

74. Wingfield, NAC, MG 24, F 18:43-4.

75. Yeo to Harvey, 19 Oct. 1814, NAC, RG 8, I, 686:84. Drummond to Prevost, 18 Oct. 1814, *ibid.*:34.

76. Drummond to Prevost, 20 Oct. 1814, *ibid.*:77.

77. Drummond to Prevost, 23 and 30 Oct. 1814, *ibid.*:85 and 114.

78. Chauncey to Jones, 17 Sept. 1814, USNA, M125, 39:64. Ridgely to Chauncey, 18 Sept. 1814, enclosed in Chauncey to Jones, 20 Sept. 1814, *ibid.*:71.

79. Izard to Chauncey, 26 Aug. 1814, and Chauncey to Izard, 11 Sept. 1814, enclosed in Chauncey to Jones, 11 Sept. 1814, USNA, M125, 39:39. Izard to Chauncey 15 and 16 Sept. 1814 and Chauncey to Izard, 15 and 16 Sept. 1814, enclosed in Chauncey to Jones, 17a Sept. 1814, *ibid.*:64. Chauncey to Jones, 18, 19a and 24 Sept. 1814, *ibid.*:66, 68 and 95. See also "The Journal of Barzallai Pease," Malcomson, *Sailors of 1812*, 91-5. Pease was the commander of the army transport flotilla.

80. Chauncey to Jones, 1 Oct. 1814, USNA, M125, 39:114.

81. Chauncey to Eckford, 29 Sept. 1814, CL.

82. Chauncey to Jones, 8b Oct. 1814, USNA, M125, 40:15.

83. Chauncey to Jones, 8b, 11a, 12c, 17b and 31b Oct. 1814, *ibid.*:15, 24 28 46 and 82.

84. Drummond to Prevost, 5 Nov. 1814, NAC, RG 8, I, 686:121.

85. 12 Nov. 1814, *Kingston Gazette*. Drummond to Prevost, 9 Nov. 1814, NAC, RG 8, I, 686:144. Drummond to Yeo, 4 Nov. 1814, *ibid.*:130. Drummond to Prevost, 23 Oct. and 5 Nov. 1814, *ibid.*:96 and 134.

Chapter 18: "Returning Peace at Length is Heard": Winter Arrives and the War Ends

1. From *Returning Peace*, a song by M.S. Bidwell, 25 March 1815, *Kingston Gazette*.

2. Drummond to Prevost, 13 Nov. 1814, NAC, RG 8, I, 686:170. Yeo to Drummond, 14 Nov. 1814, *ibid.*:173. Drummond to Freer, 14 Nov. 1814, *ibid.* Re: the American raid, see McArthur to Armstrong, 18 Nov. 1814, *DHC*, 2:308.

3. Shipbuilding plans are discussed in: Drummond to Prevost, 9 Nov. 1814, NAC, RG 8, I, 686:144; Drummond to Prevost, 22 Nov. 1814, *ibid.*, 733:123; Poyntz to Yeo, 19 Nov. 1814, *ibid.*:129; Yeo to Prevost, 26 Nov. 1814, *ibid.*:131. The needs for a vessel on Lake Huron are enclosed with Yeo to Croker, 14 Oct. 1814, NAC, MG 12, ADM 1, 2737:221.

4. Board of Officers Report, 29 Oct. 1814, NAC, MG 12, ADM 106, 1997. Strickland to Navy Board, 29 Oct. 1814, *ibid.*

5. The arrival dates of Hall and Stickland are uncertain. Bell complained to Prevost in July 1814 about being superseded (Bell to Prevost, 7 July 1814, NAC, MG 24, A9, 1:359). Hall was mentioned in letters during the fall and sailed with the squadron during its second voyage (Drummond to Prevost, 5 Nov. 1814, *DHC*, 2:288). O'Conor's mission was mentioned in Yeo to Croker, 26 Oct. 1814, NAC, MG 12, ADM 1, 2737:237. For more on Hall, see Spurr, "Sir Robert Hall (1778-1818)."

6. *Ibid.*, 9. See also Thomas Malcomson, "HMS *Psyche.*"

7. Yeo to Croker, no date (mid-Dec. 1814?), NAC, MG 12, ADM 1, 2738: 20. Yeo also praised Collier (Yeo to Croker, 1 Jan. 1814, *ibid.*:22). Yeo to Croker, 26 Oct. 1814, *ibid.*, 2737:237.

8. Yeo to Croker, 1a Jan. 1815, NAC, MG 12, ADM 1, 2738:24. This was in response to a letter from the Admiralty that Yeo noted was dated 29 Oct. 1814. In response, he submitted various lists and correspondence copies: Yeo to Croker, 1b and 1c Jan. 1815, *ibid.*:33 and 41. Regarding two 74s, see Yeo to Croker, 29 Jan. 1815, *ibid.*:46.

9. Chauncey to Jones, 5 Nov. 1814, USNA, M125, 40:104. See also: Chauncey to Jones, 8 Nov. and 20 Nov. 1814, *ibid.*, 40:114 and 41:21. The indent of materials is enclosed with Chauncey to Jones, 8 Nov. 1814, CL.

10. Chauncey to Jones, 28 Nov. and 10 Dec. 1814, USNA, M125, 41:51 and 99. Chauncey to J. Jones, 30a and 30b Nov. 1814, CL.

11. Lake Erie Court Martial Papers, 9 and 16 Sept. 1814, Wood, *Select British Documents*, 2:306.

12. *Ibid.*:308.

13. Notes of the discussion in the Admiralty Board room were made on the reverse side of Yeo's cover letter for the package of correspondence between Fisher and him (Yeo to Croker, 17 Sept. 1814, NAC, MG 12, ADM 1, 2737:179).

14. Prevost to Bathurst, 21 Sept. 1814, NAC, MG 11, CO 42, 157:207. Yeo to Croker, 29 Sept. 1814, NAC, MG 12, ADM 1, 2737:206.

15. See the Prevost biography in *DCB*, 5:696. Prevost had had conflicts with members of the legislative branch in Lower Canada.

16. Croker to Yeo, 12 Dec. 1814, NAC, MG 12, ADM 2, 1381:74.

17. Admiralty to Owen, 12 Dec. 1814, *ibid.*:67.

18. Hickey, *The War of 1812*, 281-99.

19. See Eckert, "William Jones."

20. Jones to Madison, 26 Oct. 1814, Jones Papers, Historical Society of Pennsylvania.

21. Chauncey responded to Jones, 3 Jan. 1815, CL.

22. J. Jones to Homans, 20 Jan. 1815, USNA, M125, 42:57. Chauncey to Crowinshield, 25a, 31 Jan. and 1b Feb. 1815, *ibid.*:72, 94 and 98.

23. Chauncey to Yeo, 23 Feb. 1815, CL.

24. Prevost to Hickey, 3 Feb. 1815, NAC, RG 8, I, 734:38. Yeo to Croker, 25 Feb. 1815, NAC, MG 12, ADM 1, 2738:78.

25. For dimensions of the *Wolfe* and *Canada*, see Appendix A, Table 1. In Admiralty Records, the warships were identified as No. 1 and No. 2 until the mid-1820s when *Wolfe* and *Canada* appeared, Stacey, "The Ships of the British Squadron," 323.

26. 23 Feb. 1815, *Montreal Gazette.*

27. Coore to Yeo, 26 Feb. 1815, *Montreal Gazette.*

28. Yeo to Croker, 23 March 1815, NAC, MG 12, ADM 1, 2738:81.

29. 19-24 March 1815, Captain's Logbook, HMS *Princess Charlotte*, NAC, MG 12, ADM 51, 2700. Owen to Prevost, 22 March 1815, NAC, RG 8, I, 734:56. Yeto to Croker, 23 March 1815, NAC, MG 12, ADM 1, 2738: 81. Owen to Croker, 25 March 1814, *ibid.*:110. Chauncey to Yeo, 3 March 1815, CL.

30. This incident, extracted from *The Baltimore Telegraph* was reported in *Naval Chronicle*, 33 (1815), 469, ending with "Owen waited upon the aggrieved officer with an apology, this was rejected as insufficient, and Sir James agreed to submit to such terms as Commodore Decatur should approve; the terms were complied with, and of course were satisfactory."

31. This incident is recounted in the Hickey biography in *RNB*, supp.3, 234-5.

32. Yeo to Croker, 19 Aug. 1815, NAC, MG 12, ADM1, 2738:135.

33. Yeo to Croker, 15 and 23 May 1815, *ibid.*:82 and 87. Yeo to Melville, 30 May 1815, *ibid.*:83. Yeo to Hope, no date (Aug. 1815?), *ibid.*:137. Yeo to Croker, 20 Sept. and 1 Oct. 1815, *ibid.*:162 and 168. Yeo might also have been helped by the "interest," or patronage, of Lord Melville, the First Lord of the Admiralty.

34. The Plattsburgh Court Martial, 18-21 Aug. 1815, Wood, *Select British Documents*, 3:400- 98.

35. For the Prevost biography, see *DCB*, 5:696.

36. *Naval Chronicle*, 36 (1816), 346. *Ibid.*, 40 (1818), 244. George Yeo was promoted to commander in 1818 (*ibid.*:500) but died the next year after a fall aboard HMS *Newcastle* (*DNB*, 21:1235).

37. See Chauncey biography, *DAB*, 2:40.

38. Biographies of the following: Woolsey, *DAB*,10:517; Perry, *ibid.*, 7:490; Eckford, *ibid.*, 3:4; Crane, *ibid.*, 2:510. For Myers's biography, see Cooper, *Ned Myers*, Introduction by Dudley (1989 reprint), vii-xix. For Gregory's biography, see *Dictionary of American Naval Fighting Ships*, 3:154. For Sinclair's biography, see Malcomson, *Sailors of 1812*, 14.

39. Biographies of the following: Wingfield, *NBD*, 1310; Pring, *ibid.*, 931; Collier, *ibid.* 215; O'Conor, *ibid.*, 829; Barclay, *DCB*, 7:45; Mulcaster, *ibid.*, 6:730; Spilsbury, *ibid.*, 6:730; Richardson, *ibid.*, 10:615.

40. The later careers of the warships are described in: Palmer, "Sackets Harbor and the 'New Orleans;'" Preston, "The Fate of Kingston's Warships;" and Stacey, "The Ships of the British Squadron on Lake Ontario, 1812-1814."

41. Scott, *Memoirs of Lieutenant-General Scott*, 1:113.

42. Dudley, "Chauncey and U. S. Joint Actions on Lake Ontario," 152.

Appendix A: Overview of the British and American Squadrons on Lake Ontario, 1812-1814

1. Statements of the Naval Force on Lake Ontario, Oct. 1814; Jan. 1815; (June?) 1815; NAC, MG 12, ADM, 106, 1997. Cartwright to Hamilton, 2 Nov. 1793 and Mackay to Beckwith, 25 April 1794, Preston, *Kingston Before the War*, 202-3. Board of Survey on *Simcoe*, 24 Feb. 1813, NAC, RG 8, I, 729:104. Stacey, "The Ships of the British Squadron."

2. A Return of Vessels of War . . . by Chauncey, 18 July 1813, Chauncey Letter Book. Sinclair to Cocke, 25 Aug. 1813, Malcomson, *Sailors of 1812*, 51.

3. Palmer, "James Fenimore Cooper and the Navy Brig *Oneida*."

4. Chauncey to Hamilton, 26 Nov. 1812, USNA, M125, 3:192.

5. These dimensions based upon Sinclair to Cocke, 4 July 1813, Malcomson, *Sailors of 1812*, 45 and the dimensions of the US Frigate *Essex* to which the *Pike* was compared, Chapelle, *American Sailing Navy*, 165, 183.

6. Crisman, *The Jefferson: The History and Archeology of an American Brig from the War of 1812*, 307-10. The brigs were modelled after the sloop *Peacock*, Chapelle, *American Sailing Navy*, 260-1.

7. In Chauncey to Jones, 11 June 1814, USNA, M125, 37:54, the commodore mentioned that the *Mohawk* was larger than the frigate *New York*, which measured 1130 tons, 144' 2" between perpendiculars, 37' abeam and 11' 9" in depth of hold, Chapelle, *American Sailing Navy*, 164.

8. Palmer, "Sackets Harbor and the "*New Orleans*."

9. Chauncey to Hamilton, 19 Nov. 1812, USNA, M125, 33:31a; List of Vessels Purchased Prior to March 3, 1813 by Chauncey, 15 June 1813, USNA, M625, 76.

Appendix B: The Opposing Squadrons, Autumn 1812

1. Report upon the Provincial Marine Establishment ..., by Gray, 24 Feb. 1812, NAC, RG 8 I, 728: 86. Gray to Vincent, 16 Jan. 1813, *ibid.*, 729:28. Gray to Prevost, 12 March 1813, *ibid*:120.

2. Chauncey to Hamilton, 6 Nov. 1812, USNA, M125, 25:167. Woolsey to Hamilton, 23 July 1811, USNA, *M148*, 9:17:144. Board of Survey on the *Simcoe*, 24 Feb. 1813, NAC, RG 8, I, 729:104. Regarding the *Toronto*, Gray to Prevost, 29 Jan. 1812, *ibid.*, 728:77. Stacey, "The Ships of the British Squadron."

3. Chauncey to Hamilton, 6 Nov. 1812, USNA, M125, 25:167. Chauncey to Dearborn, 8 Nov. 1812, CL. Elliott to Porter, 3 Nov. 1812, *DHC*, 4:177. Woolsey to Hamilton, 3 Aug. 1812, USNA, M148, 10: 21:138. A Return of Vessels of War, by Chauncey, 18 July 1813, CL.

Appendix C: British Gunboat Flotillas During and After 1813

1. Scheme of a Squadron of Gunboats …, by Yeo, 21 July 1813, NAC, RG 8, I, 730:52.
2. A List of His Majesty's Gun Boats …, by O'Conor, 26 Jan. 1814, NAC, MG 11, CO 42, 160:320. Statement of the Force …, by Yeo, April 1814, NAC, MG 12, ADM 1, 2737:78.
3. Proceedings of Lieutenant Daniel Salter …, NAC, MG 12, ADM 51, 4096. Regarding dimensions, see June 1817, NAC, MG 12 , ADM 106, 1998. See also Beattie, *Gunboats on the St. Lawrence River* and Amer, *The Construction of the Browns Bay Vessel.*

Appendix D: The Opposing Squadrons in May and June 1813

1. Yeo to Croker, 26 May 1813, NAC, MG 12, ADM 1, 2736: 70. Myers to Freer, 2 April 1813, NAC, RG 8, I, 729:53. Harvey to Baynes, 11 June 1813, *ibid.*, 679:76. Comparative Statement of the Force …, 24 July 1813, NAC, MG 11, CO 42, 151:100. Daniel Pring's appointment in command of the *Wolfe* is mentioned in Prevost to Bathurst, 18 July 1813, *ibid.*:69. Stacey, "The Ships of the British Squadron."
2. A Return of Vessels of War, by Chauncey, 18 July 1813, CL. The commanders are based upon a circular issued by Chauncey around 12 June 1813, *ibid.* Chauncey to Jones, 4 June 1813, USNA, M125, 29:14. Cooper, *Ned Myers*, 75.

Appendix E: The Opposing Squadrons During the Engagements of 8–11 August 1813

1. Comparative Statement of the Force …, 24 July 1813, NAC, MG 11, CO 42, 151:100. General Order by Baynes, 26 July 1813, *DHC*, 6:281. Stacey, "The Ships of the British Squadron."
2. A Return of Vessels of War …, by Chauncey, 18 July 1813, CL. See also A View of the Force of the Squadron by Chauncey, 15 July 1814, *ibid.*
3. No consistent method appears to have been used by the commodores when they portrayed "weight of metal." In a report completed on 8 Oct 1813, Yeo stated, without explanation, that the weight in metal for his squadron, having 91 guns at that time, was 1967 tons (NAC, MG 12, ADM 1, 2736:138). Similarly, without explanation, a report by Chauncey on 15 July 1814 seems to have calculated broadside weight of metal by adding one or two side-mounted guns to the total on the other side of the vessel (An Exhibit of the Nature of Force …, by Chauncey, 15 July 1814, CL).

Appendix F: The Opposing Squadrons at the Engagement near the Genesee River, 11 September 1813

1. Record of 18-30 Aug. 1813, Logbook, US Sloop *Sylph*, Burton Historical Collection. Chauncey to Jones, 19 and 28 Aug. 1813, USNA, M125, 30:119 and 162. General Order by Chauncey, 26 Sept. 1813, CL.

Appendix G: The Opposing Squadrons at the "Burlington Races," 28 September 1813

1. Yeo to Croker, 8 Oct. 1813, NAC, MG 12, Adm. 1, vol. 2736, p. 138. Also Yeo to Warren, 29 Sept. 1813, *ibid.*, p. 127. Stacey, "The Ships of the British Squadron."

Appendix H: The Opposing Squadrons in 1814

1. Statement of the Naval Force on Lake Ontario, April 1814, by Yeo, NAC, MG 12, ADM 1, 2737:78. Other notable summaries, which present conflicting views of the squadron's armament, were prepared in October 1814 by Richard O'Conor, in January 1815 by Robert Hall and in June(?) 1815 by Thomas Strickland. These summaries appear in NAC, MG 12, ADM 106, 1997. Stacey, "The Ships of the British Squadron."
2. A View of the Force on Lake Ontario …, by Chauncey, 15 July 1814, CL.

Bibliography

PRIMARY SOURCES – ARCHIVAL

Alderman Library, University of Virginia, Charlotteville, Virginia
Arthur Sinclair Papers, John Hartwell Cocke Papers (#642)
Buffalo and Erie County Historical Society, Buffalo, New York
Jacob Brown Manuscripts, Box 2, Microfilm 65.
Burton Historical Collection, Detroit Public Library, Detroit, Michigan
Woolsey Family Papers, including logbooks of the *Sylph* and *Jefferson*
County Record Office, Hertford, Hertfordshire, UK
Halsey Papers, Johnston Family Papers (16221-16356)
National Archives of Canada, Ottawa

> Manuscript Group 11, Colonial Office 42, Original Correspondence, Secretary of State, Lower Canada, Vols. 143-165, Microfilm Reels B125-B133.

> Manuscript Group 12

>> Admiralty 1, Secretary's Department, In Letters from Captains. Yeo: Vols. 2736-8, Microfilm Reels B2941-2. Mulcaster: Vols. 2177, 2181-5, Microfilm Reel B2632. O'Conor, Cunliffe Owen & Owen: Vols. 2261-68, Microfilm Reels B2634-5, B2686-7. Popham: Vols. 2345, 2347-51, 2354, Microfilm Reels B2790-1. Spilsbury: Vols. 2539, 2542-43, 2546, 2551, Microfilm Reels B2800-1.

>> Admiralty 1, Admiralty and Secretariat, Papers, In Letters, Reports of Courts Martial, 1814, Sept. (Barclay court martial), Vol. 5445, Microfilm C-12856.

>> Admiralty 2, Secretary's Department, Secret Orders and Letters, Vols. 1375-81, Microfilm Reels 3932-4.

>> Admiralty 51, Captain's Log, *Princess Charlotte*, Vol. 2700; Captain's Log, *Prince Regent*, Vol. 4488; Daniel Salter's Log, Gunboat squadron, etc., Vol. 4096, Microfilm Reel C12892.

>> Admiralty 52, Master's Log, *Princess Charlotte, Star, Niagara* and *Prince Regent*, Vol. 3928, Microfilm Reel C12890.

>> Admiralty 106, Admiralty Navy Board In Letters From Yards, Canada, 1814-1832, Vols. 1997-2002, Microfilm Reels B1001-B1005.

> Manuscript Group 13, War Office 57, Commissariat Dept., In Letters, Canada, 1811-15, Vol. 14, Microfilm Reel C10867.

> Manuscript Group 24, 19th Century Pre-Confederation Papers

>> A9 Select Papers Relating to Major General Augustin and Sir George Prevost and Family. The Records of the Prevost Papers by W. A. J. Prevost, May 1949. Microfilm Reel A1926 Sir George Prevost's Memorial Book

>> F14, Melville Letters

>> F18, Four Years on the lakes of Canada in 1813, 1814, 1815, 1816; by a Naval Officer under the command of the late Sir James Lucas Yeo Kt., Commodore and Commander in Chief of H. M. Ships and vessels of War employed on the Lakes. Also nine months as Prisoner of War in the United States of America, by David Wingfield.

F24, Jonas Simonds, 1813-1814

F25, Great Britain, Admiralty Lake Service

F58, Sir John Chambers White

F95, A biography in manuscript form of William Howe Mulcaster

G59, John Macdonell, 1813

L8, Jacques Viger, Ma Sabredache

Manuscript Group 40, E 1, House of Lords, Accounts and Papers, "Report #9: Copies of all Correspondence and Orders …," *Papers Relating to the War with America*, 1815, vol. 75, Microfilm Reel B-359.

Record Group 5, A1, Upper Canada Sundries, Civil Secretary's Correspondence, 1808-1814, vols. 7-21, Microfilm Reels C4505-08, C4543-44.

Record Group 8, I, "C" Series, British Military and Naval Records

Transports, 1790-1896, Vols. 373-380, Microfilm Reels C2932-34.

Royal Navy and Provincial Marine, 1779-1845, Vols. 722-742, Microfilm Reels C3242-46.

United States, War of 1812, 1806-1834, Vol. 673-76, Microfilm Reels C3171-74, C3231-36.

The Freer Papers 1811-1815, Vols. 1706-1710, Microfilm Reels C3839-40.

National Archives of the United States, Washington, D.C.

Record Group 45, Naval Records Collection of the Office of Naval Records and Library.

Area File of the Naval Records Collection, 1775-1910, Area Seven, No volumes Noted, Microcopy 625, Reels 76, 77.

Letters Received by the Secretary of the Navy from Captains, 1805-1861, Vol. 25-42, Microcopy 125, Reels 25-42.

Letters Received by the Secretary of the Navy from Commanders, 1804-1886, Vol. 1-3, 1813, Vol. 1-3 1814, Microcopy 147, Reels 4, 5.

Letters Received by the Secretary of the Navy from Commissioned Officers Below the Rank of Commander and from Warrant Officers, 1802-1884, Vols. 9-21, Microcopy 148, Reels 9-11.

Letters Sent by the Secretary of the Navy to Officers, 1798-1868, Vols. 10-11, Microcopy 149, Rolls 10-11.

Records of General Courts Martial and Courts of Inquiry of the Navy Department, 1799-1867. Vols. 4, 5. Microcopy 273, Reels 6, 7.

Entry 92, Muster and Pay Rolls of Shore Establishments 1800-1835: Sackets Harbour, 1813-1826.

Journal of H.M.S. *Wolfe*, later named *Montreal*, Flagship of Sir James Yeo on Lake Ontario, 8 June-20 December 1813.

British P. O. W.s, Rolls and Lists, RB 1812-15, Boxes 579 & 580. Record Group 107: Registered Letters Received, (Main Series) 1801-1839, B-118

New-York Historical Society, New York.

Chauncey Letterbooks: April 1809-September 1812; August 1813-July 1814

Pennsylvania Historical Society, Philadelphia, Pennsylvania

Uselma Clarke Smith Collection, William Jones Papers, Box 4, 1814

Brown Letters, Gratz Papers, Case 4, Box 32

Public Record Office, London, England

Admiralty 37, Musters of the Establishments on the Canadian Lakes, Vols. 5000, 5002, 5128, 5245, 5377, 5636, 5629, 5642.

McCord Museum, McGill University, Montreal

R. H. Barclay Papers

Syracuse University Library, Department of Special Collections, Syracuse, New York

Pease Papers, Journal 15

William Clements Library, University of Michigan, Ann Arbor

Jacob Jennings Brown Papers

Chauncey Letter Books September 1812-August 1813; July 1814-1817

The Melville Papers

PRIMARY SOURCES – PUBLISHED

Newspapers and Periodicals

Kingston Gazette, 1812-14
Naval Chronicle, 1805-18 (London)
Quebec Gazette, 1808-15
The Quebec Mercury, 1808-15
Upper Canada Gazette, 1811-12
The War, 1812-13 (New York)
War Journal, 1813 (Portsmouth, New Hampshire)
York Gazette, 1811-12

Published Documents

Cruikshank, E. A. ed., *The Documentary History of the Campaign upon the Niagara Frontier 1812-1814.* 9 vols. Welland: Lundy's Lane Historical Society, 1896-1908. 9 vols.

——, *Records of Niagara in the Days of Commodore Grant and Lieutenant-Governor Gore: 1805-1811.* Niagara-on-the-Lake: Niagara Historical Society, 1931.

Dudley, William S. ed., *The Naval War of 1812: A Documentary History.* Washington: Historical Center Department of the Navy, 1985, 1992. 2 vols.

Firth, E. G. ed., *The Town of York 1793-1815.* Toronto: Champlain Society, 1962.

Preston, Richard A. ed., *Kingston Before the War of 1812.* Toronto: Champlain Society, 1959.

U.S. Congress, *American State Papers: Claims.* Washington, D. C.: Gales and Seaton, Volume 1.

U.S. Congress, *American State Papers: Military Affairs.* Washington, D. C.: Gales and Seaton, 1832. Volume 1.

U.S. Congress, *American State Papers: Naval Affairs.* Washington D. C.: Gales and Seaton, 1834. Volume 1.

Wood, William C. H. ed. *Select British Documents of the Canadian War of 1812.* Vols. 13-15, 17. Toronto: The Champlain Society, 1920-28.

PUBLISHED MEMOIRS, DIARIES, JOURNALS, CORRESPONDENCE

American

Adams, Henry. ed., *The Writings of Albert Gallatin. New* York: Antiquarian Press, 1960. 3 vols.

Armstrong, John. ed., *Notices of the War of 1812.* New York: General Dearborn & Wiley and Putnam, 1840. 2 vols.

Beard, James Franklin. ed., *The Letters and Journals of James Fenimore Cooper.* Cambridge: Harvard University Press, 1960. — vols.

Campbell, William W. ed., *The Life and Writings of De Witt Clinton.* New York: Baker and Scribner, 1849.

Cooper, James Fenimore. *Ned Myers; or A Life Before the Mast.* Reprint. Annapolis: Naval Institute Press, 1989.

"The First Campaign of an A.D.C.," *Military and Navy Magazine of the United States* 1-4 (1833-35).

Ford, Paul Leicestor. ed., *The Works of Thomas Jefferson.* New York: G.P. Putnam's Sons, 1905. 12 vols.

Fredericksen, John C. "The War of 1812 in Northern New York: The Observations of Captain Rufus McIntire," *New York History* 68 (1987), 297-322.

Hastings, Hugh. ed., *Public Papers of Daniel D. Tompkins, Governor of New York 1807-1817.* Albany: J. B. Lyon, 1902. 3 vols.

Hopkins, James F. ed., *The Papers of Henry Clay.* Lexington: University of Kentucky Press, 1959. 5 vols.

Hull, William. *Memoirs of the Campaign of the Northwest Army of the United States, A. D. 1812.* Boston: True and Greene, 1824.

Hunt, Gaillard. ed., *The Writings of James Madison.* New York: G. P. Putnam's Sons, 1908. 9 vols.

"Kennon Letters," *The Virginia Magazine of History and Biography*, 30-40 (1922-32).

Meriwether, Robert L. ed., *The Papers of John C. Calhoun.* Columbia: University of South Carolina, 1959, 19 vols.

Wilkinson, James. *Memoirs of My Own Times.* Philadelphia: Smail, 1816. 3 vols.

British and Canadian

Barrow, John. ed., *The Life and Correspondence of Admiral Sir William Sidney Smith.* London: Bentley, 1848. 2 vols.

Graves, Donald E. ed., *Merry Hearts Make Light Days: The War of 1812 Journal of Lieutenant John Le Couteur, 104th Foot.* Ottawa: Carleton University Press, 1993.

Malcomson, Robert. ed., *Sailors of 1812: Memoirs and Letters of Naval Officers on Lake Ontario.* Youngstown, N.Y.: Old Fort Niagara Association, 1997.

Merritt, William Hamilton, "Journal of Events Principally on the Detroit and Niagara Frontiers," William Wood, ed., *Select British Documents of the Canadian War of 1812.* 3 vols. Toronto: The Champlain Society, 1920, 1923, 1928, 3:544-648.

Neilson, J. L. "Diary of an Officer in the War of 1812-14," *Queen's Quarterly* 2 (1894-5), 318-28; 3 (1895-6), 23-30.

Spragge, George. ed., *The John Strachan Letter Book: 1812-34.* Toronto: The Ontario Historical Society, 1946.

Stacey, C. P. "Upper Canada at War, 1814: Captain Armstrong Reports," *Ontario History* 48 (1956), 37-42.

Tupper, F. B. ed., *The Life and Correspondence of Major-General Sir Isaac Brock, K. B.* London: Simpkin, Marshall and Co., 1845.

SECONDARY SOURCES – BOOKS

Adams, Henry. *History of the United States of America During the Administration of Thomas Jefferson and James Madison.* New York: Albert and Charles Boni, 1930. 4 vols.

Amer, Christopher F. *The Construction of the Browns Bay Vessel.* Microfiche Report Series 266, Environment Canada – Parks, 1986.

Baillie, Laureen. ed., *American Biographical Index.* London: K. G. Saur, 1993.

Beattie, Judith. *Gunboats on the St. Lawrence River (1763-1839).* Manuscript Report Number 15, National and Historic Parks Branch, Department of Indian Affairs and Northern Development, 1967.

Benn, Carl. *The Battle of York.* Belleville: Mika, 1984.

——. *Historic Fort York: 1793-1993.* Toronto: Natural Heritage/Natural History Inc., 1993.

Berton, Pierre. *The Invasion of Canada 1812-13.* Toronto: McClelland and Stewart, 1980.

——. *Flames Across the Border 1813-1814.* Toronto: McClelland and Stewart, 1981.

Bouchette, Joseph. *A Topographical Description of the Province of Lower Canada with Remarks upon Upper Canada.* London: W. Faden, 1815.

Bowler, R. Arthur. ed. *War Along the Niagara: Essays on the War of 1812 and Its Legacy.* Youngstown, New York: Old Fort Niagara Association, 1991.

Brant, Irving. *James Madison: The President, 1809-12.* New York: Bobbs-Merrill, 1956.

—— *James Madison: Commander-in-Chief, 1812-1836.* New York: Bobbs-Merrill, 1961.

Cain, Emily. *Ghost Ships.* Toronto: Musson, 1983.

Callahan, Edward. ed. *List of Officers of the Navy of the United States and of the Marine Corps from 1775 to 1900.* Registrar, Bureau of Navigation, Navy Department, 1901, reprinted New York: Haskell House, 1969.

The Canadian Encyclopedia. Edmonton: Hurtig, 1985, 3 vols.

Chapelle, Howard I. *The History of the American Sailing Navy: Their Ships and Their Development.* New York: Bonanza, 1949.

Chartrand, René. *Uniforms and Equipment of the United States Forces in the War of 1812.* Youngstown, New York: Old Fort Niagara Association, 1992.

Clowes, William L. *The Royal Navy: A History From the Earliest Times to 1900.* 7 vols., Reprint. London: Chatham Publishing, 1997. Vols. 4 and 5.

Cooper, James Fenimore. *History of The Navy of the United States of America.* 2 vols., Cooperstown: H. & E. Phinney, 1848.

Crisman, Kevin. *The Eagle: An American Brig on Lake Champlain during the War of 1812.* Annapolis: Naval Institute Press, 1987.

——. *The Jefferson: The History and Archaeology of an American Brig from the War of 1812.* Ann Arbor: UMI (University Microfilms International), 1989.

Cruikshank, E. A. ed. *Drummond's Winter Campaign.* Niagara Falls: Lundy's Lane Historical Society, n. d.

——. *The Battle of Fort George.* Reprint. Niagara-on-the-Lake: Niagara Historical Society, 1990.

Cuttridge, Leonard and J. D. Smith. *The Commodores: The Drama of a Navy Under Sail.* London: Peter Davies, 1970.

Dictionary of American Biography. New York: Scribner, 1958-64. 22 vols.

Dictionary of American Fighting Ships. Washington: Navy Department, 1968, — vols.

Dictionary of Canadian Biography. Volumes V-IX. Toronto: University of Toronto, 1976-88.

Dictionary of National Biography. London: Smith, Elder, 1885, 65 vols.

Dunnigan, Brian L. *The British Army at Mackinac, 1812-1815.* Mackinac: Mackinac State Historic Parks, 1980.

Elting, John R. *Amateurs, To Arms! A Military History of the War of 1812.* Chapel Hill: Algonquin Books of Chapel Hill, 1991.

Everest, Allan S. *The Military Career of Alexander Macomb and Alexander Macomb at Plattsburgh.* Plattsburgh: Clinton County Historical Association, 1989.

Fowler, William M. *Jack Tars and Commodores: The American Navy 1783-1815.* Boston: Houghton Mifflin, 1984.

Goodwin, Peter. *The Construction and Fitting of the English Man of War, 1650-1850.* Annapolis: Naval Institute Press, 1987.

Gourlay, Robert. *Statistical Account of Upper Canada.* 2 vols. London: Simpkin and Marshall, 1822.

Graves, Donald E. *Sir William Congreve and the Rocket's Red Glare.* Bloomfield, Ontario: Museum Restoration Service, 1989.

——. *Red Coats and Grey Jackets: The Battle of Chippawa, 5 July 1814.* Toronto: Dundurn Press, 1994.

——. *"Brilliant Little Affair," Battle at Crysler's Farm, 1813.* Ottawa: Canadian War Museum, 1995.

——. *Where Right and Glory Lead! The Battle of Lundy's Lane, 1814.* Toronto: Robin Brass, 1997.

Gray, William. *Soldiers of the King: The Upper Canadian Militia, 1812-1815.* Erin, Ontario: Boston Mills, 1995.

Haeger, John Dennis. *John Jacob Astor: Business and Finance in the Early Republic.* Detroit: Wayne State University, 1991.

Harland, John. *Seamanship in the Age of Sail.* Annapolis: Naval Institute Press, 1984.

Harris, Robin S. And Terry G. Harris, ed., *The Eldon House Diaries: Five Women's Views of the 19th Century.* Toronto: The Champlain Society, 1994.

Haythornwaite, Philip and William Younghusband. *Nelson's Navy.* London: Osprey Publishing, 1993.

Hickey, Donald R. *The War of 1812: A Forgotten Conflict.* Chicago: University of Chicago Press, 1990.

Hitsman, J. Mackay. *The Incredible War of 1812: A Military History.* Toronto: University of Toronto Press, 1965.

Hutcheon, Wallace S. Jr. *Robert Fulton: Pioneer of Undersea Warfare.* Annapolis: Naval Institute Press, 1981.

Katcher, Philip. *The American War, 1812-1814.* London: Osprey Publishing, 1990.

King, Dean. *A Sea of Words: A Lexicon and Companion for Patrick O'Brian's Seafaring Tales.* New York: Henry Holt and Company, 1995.

Lavery, Brian. *The Arming and Fitting of English Ships of War, 1600-1815.* Annapolis: Naval Institute Press, 1987.

——. *Nelson's Navy: The Ships, Men and Organization, 1793-1815.* London: Conway Maritime Press Ltd., 1989.

Lees, James. *The Masting and Rigging of English Ships of War, 1625-1860.* London: Conway Maritime Press, 1984.

Lord, Walter. *The Dawn's Early Light.* New York: W.W. Norton & Company, Inc., 1972.

Lossing, Benson. *The Pictorial Field-book of the War of 1812.* New York: Harper and Brothers, 1868.

Lovett, Leland P. *Naval Customs: Traditions and Usage.* Annapolis: Naval Institute Press, 1939.

Mahan, A. T. *Sea Power in Its Relations to the War of 1812.* 2 vols. London: Sampson, Low, Marston & Co., 1905.

Malcomson, Robert and Thomas Malcomson. *HMS Detroit: The Battle for Lake Erie.* St. Catharines, Ontario: Vanwell Publishing, 1990.

Marshall, John. ed., *Royal Navy Biography. London:* Longman, 1823-1835. 4 vols. and 4 supplements.

Martin, Tyrone G. *A Most Fortunate Ship: A Narrative History of "Old Ironsides."* Chester: Connecticut, Globe Pequot Press, 1980.

McKee, Christopher. *A Gentlemanly and Honorable Profession: The Creation of the U.S. Naval Officers Corps, 1794-1815.* Annapolis: Naval Institute Press, 1991.

Mika, Nick and Helma. *Kingston, Historic City.* Belleville, Ontario: Mika Publishing, 1987.

Moore, Jonathan. *Preservce Our Wrecks: Photo Project Final Report.* Kingston: Preserve Our Wrecks, Kingston, 1998.

Morgan, Henry J. *Sketches of Celebrated Canadians.* Quebec: Hunter, Rose, 1862.

O'Brien, Brendan. *Speedy Justice: The Tragic Last Voyage of His Majesty's Vessel* Speedy. Toronto: University of Toronto Press, 1992.

O'Byrne, William R. *A Naval Biographical Dictionary.* London: Murray, 1849.

North, Douglass C. *The Economic Growth of the United States: 1790-1860.* Englewood Cliffs: Prentice-Hall, 1961.

Pack, Jame. *The Man Who Burned the White House: Admiral Sir George Cockburn, 1772-1853.* Annapolis: Naval Institute Press, 1987.

Pratt, Fletcher. *Preble's boys: Commodore Preble and the Birth of American Sea Power.* New York: William Sloane Associates, 1950.

Reilly, Robin. *The British at the Gate: The New Orleans Campaign in the War of 1812.* New York: G.P. Putnam's Sons, 1974.

Roosevelt, Theodore. *The Naval War of 1812.* Reprint. Annapolis: Naval Institute Press, 1987.

Skeen, C. Edward. *John Armstrong, Jr., 1758-1843: A Biography.* Syracuse: Syracuse University Press, 1981.

Stacey, C. P. *The Battle of Little York.* Toronto: The Toronto Historical Board, 1971.

Stagg, J. C. A. *Mr. Madison's War: Politics, Diplomacy and Warfare, in Early American Republic, 1783-1830.* Princeton: Princeton University Press, 1983.

Steppler, Glenn A. *A Duty Troublesome Beyond Measure: Logistical Considerations in the Canadian War of 1812.* Masters of Arts Thesis, McGill Unversity, 1974.

Summers, Jack L. and René Chartrand. *Military Uniforms in Canada, 1665-1970.* Ottawa: National Museums of Canada, 1981.

Tucker, Spencer. *Arming the Fleet: U. S. Naval Ordnance in the Muzzle-Loading Era.* Annapolis: Naval Institute Press, 1989.

Way, Ronald. *The Day at Crysler's Farm: November 11, 1813.* Morrisburg: The St. Lawrence Parks Commission, n. d.

Welsh, Jeffrey William and David Curtis Skaggs. ed. *War on the Great Lakes: Essays Commemorating the 175th Anniversary of the Battle of Lake Erie.* Kent: Kent University Press, 1991.

Wilder, Patrick. *The Battle of Sackett's Harbour.* Baltimore: The Nautical and Aviation Company of America, Inc., 1994.

SECONDARY SOURCES – ARTICLES

Brock, T. L. "H.M. Dock Yard, Kingston Under Commissioner Robert Barrie, 1819-1834," *Historic Kingston* 16 (1967), 3-23.

Brown, Kenneth. "The William Jones Papers," *The Pennsylvania Magazine of History and Biography* 66 (1942), 479-82.

Cain, Emily. "Building the Lord Nelson," *Inland Seas* 41 (1985), 121-129.

——. "Provisioning Lake Ontario Merchant Schooners, 1809-1812: *Lord Nelson (Scourge), Diana (Hamilton), Ontario* and *Niagara,*" *Freshwater* 3 (1988), 21-6.

Casey, Richard F. "North County Nemesis: The Potash Rebellion and the Embargo of 1807-09," *The New-York Historical Society Quarterly* 64 (1980), 31-49.

Claxton, Patrick. "The Live Fire Shoot," *Niagara League News* 7 (1997), 1-2.

Cruikshank, E.A. "The Royal Newfoundland Regiment – Part One," *Selected Papers from the Transactions of the Canadian Military Institute.* no. 5 (1893-94), 5-15.

——. "The Contest for the Command of Lake Ontario in 1812 and 1813," *Transactions of The Royal Society of Canada* 10 (1916), 161-223.

——. "The Contest for the Command of Lake Ontario in 1814," *Ontario History* 21 (1924), 99-159.

Dawson, Henry B. "Attack on Oswego, 5-7 May 1814," *Inland Seas* 36 (1970), 61-2.

Douglas, W. A. B. "The Anatomy of Naval Incompetence: The Provincial Marine in Defence of Upper Canada Before 1813," *Ontario History* 71 (1979), 3-25.

Drake, Frederick." Commodore Sir James Lucas Yeo and Governor General George Prevost: A Study in Command Relations, 1813-14," in *New Interpretations in Naval History: Selected Papers from the Eighth Naval History Symposium*, ed. William B. Cogar (Annapolis: Naval Institute Press, 1989), 156-171.

Dudley, William S. "Commodore Isaac Chauncey and U.S. Joint Operations on Lake Ontario, 1813-14," in *New Interpretations in Naval History: Selected Papers from the Eighth Naval History Symposium*, ed. William B. Cogar (Annapolis: Naval Institute Press, 1989), 139-155

Eckert, Edward K. "William Jones: Mr. Madison's Secretary of the Navy," *The Pennsylvania Magazine of History and Biography* 96 (1972), 167-82.

Ellison, David. "David Wingfield and Sacketts Harbour," *Dalhousie Review* 52 (1972), 407-13.

Hollon, E. W. "Zebulon Montgomery Pike and the York Campaign, 1813," *New York History* 30 (1949), 259-75.

Humphries, C. W. "The Capture of York," *Ontario History* 51 (1959), 1-21.

Graves, Donald E. "The Second Regiment of United States Light Dragoons, 1812-1814," *Military Collector and Historian* (1982), 101-8.

——. "Field Artillery of the War of 1812: Equipment, Organization, Tactics and Effectiveness," *Arms Collecting* 30 (1992), 39-48.

——. "William Drummond and the Battle of Fort Erie," *Canadian Military History* 1 (1992), 25-44.

——. "American Ordnance of the War of 1812: A Preliminary Investigation," *Arms Collecting* 31 (1993), 111-120.

Langley, Harold D. "Respect for Civilian Authority: The Tragic Career of Captain Angus," *The American Neptune* 40 (1980), 23-37.

Malcomson, Robert. "Controversial Relationships among the British before and after the Battle of Lake Erie," *Inland Seas* 46 (1990), 187-97.

——. "The Barclay Correspondence: More from the Man Who Lost the Battle of Lake Erie," *The Journal of Erie Studies* 20 (1991), 18-35.

——. "The Captures of the Schooner *Julia/Confiance*," *American Neptune* 51 (1991),83-90.

——. "Upper Canada Preserved: Isaac Brock's Farewell to Arms, Queenston Heights 1812," *The Beaver* 73 (1993), 4-15.

——. "War on Lake Ontario: A Costly Victory at Oswego, 1814," *The Beaver* 75 (1995), 4-13.

——. "George Inglis: Insights About the Man Who Hauled Down the British Flag at Put-In-Bay," *The Journal of Erie Studies* 24 (1995), 71-80.

——. "Gunboats on Lake Ontario in the 1812 War," *Seaways' Ship in Scale* 7 (1996), 1:31-38; 2:27-31; 3:40-44.

——. "Xebecs for the Great Lakes War," *Model Ship Builder* no. 101 (1996), 51-4

——. "HMS *St. Lawrence*: The Freshwater First-Rate," *The Mariner's Mirror* 83 (1997), 419-33.

Malcomson, Thomas. "September 1813: The Decidedly Indecisive Engagements Between Chauncey and Yeo," *Inland Seas* 47 (1991), 299-313.

——. "HMS *Psyche*: A Frigate in Frame," *Seaways' Ships in Scale* 4 (1993), 16-21.

Mecredy, Stephen D. "Crisis Confronting Construction: The History of Point Henry During the War of 1812," *Historic Kingston* 33 (1984), 3-14.

Nelson, Daniel. "Ghost Ships of the War of 1812," *National Geographic* 163 (1983), 288-313.

——. "The Sinking of the *Hamilton* and *Scourge* – How Many Men Were Lost?" *Freshwater* 2 (1987), 4-7.

Palmer, Richard F. "James Fenimore Cooper and the Navy Brig *Oneida*," *Inland Seas* 40 (1984), 90-99.

——. "Sackets Harbour and the '*New Orleans*'," *Bulletin of the Jefferson County Historical Society* 8 (1984) 3-16.

Paullin, Charles O. "Naval Administration Under Secretaries of the Navy Smith, Hamilton, and Jones 1801-1814," *Proceedings of the United States Naval Institute* 32 (1906), 1289-1328.

Preston, Richard A. "The First Battle of Sackets Harbour," *Historic Kingston* 11 (1961-2), 3-7.

———. "The Fate of Kingston's Warships," *Ontario History* 44, (1952), 85-100.

———. "Broad Pennants at Point Frederick," *Ontario History* 50 (1958), 81-90.

Ritchie, M. K. & C. "A Laker's Log," *The American Neptune* 17 (1957), 203-211.

Scammel, E. H. "The Rush-Bagot Agreement of 1817," *Ontario History* 13 (1915), 58-66.

Skeen. C. Edward. "Monroe and Armstrong: A Study in Political Rivalry," *The New York Historical Society Quarterly* 57 (1973), 121-147.

———. "Mr. Madison's Secretary of War," *The Pennsylvania Magazine of History and Biography* 100 (1976), 336-55.

Spurr, John W. "Sir James Lucas Yeo, A Hero on the Lakes," *Historic Kingston* 30 (1981), 30-45.

———. "Sir Robert Hall (1776-1818). *Historic Kingston* 29 (1980), 3-15.

Stagg, J. C. A. "Enlisted Men in the United States Army, 1812-1815: A Preliminary Study," *The William and Mary Quarterly* 43 (1986), 615-45.

Stacey, C. P. "Commodore Chauncey's Attack on the Kingston Harbour, November 10, 1812," *Canadian Historical Review* 32 (1951), 126-138.

———. "The Ships of the British Squadron on Lake Ontario, 1812-1814," *The Canadian Historical Review* 35 (1935), 311-323.

Strum, Harvey. "A Gross and Unprovoked Outrage: Niagara Incident," *Inland Seas* 48 (1992), 284-290.

Index